PRAISE FOR M

"An inside look at the Montreal Mafia's power, influence and dysfunction." *Mirror* (Montreal)

"Much like the mob itself, *Mafia Inc.*'s narrative tendrils are long and widespread. . . . The genius of *Mafia Inc.* is its all-important connections between organized crime, legitimate business and government. The chapter on the alleged cozy relationship between former Liberal minister Alfonso Gagliano and the Rizzuto clan (Gagliano denies any Mafia ties) is alone worth the price of admission." *Maclean's*

"[Cédilot and Noël] have aggressively exposed corruption, putting withering pressure on see-no-evil politicians." *Edmonton Journal*

"If you read only one book this year, it must be *Mafia Inc.* It reads like a thriller because it is one. You'll find out about all of the scamming and scheming in the circles where organized crime contracts the very work that makes the most money for its bosses, whose money laundering can no longer keep up with the sheer amount of cash brought to them every day and who are investing the rest in legitimate business, where they become even richer. . . . You'll understand why certain politicians are dancing to their tune, why some Mafia members target the highest of public offices, not just in municipal government but at the provincial and federal levels too. . . . To understand how this powder keg came to be, you must read *Mafia Inc.*" *Le Devoir*

ANDRÉ CÉDILOT & ANDRÉ NOËL

translated by MICHAEL GILSON

MAFIA

INC.

THE LONG, BLOODY REIGN OF CANADA'S SICILIAN CLAN

VINTAGE CANADA

VINTAGE CANADA EDITION, 2012

Published in Canada by Vintage Canada, a division of Random House of Canada
Limited, Toronto, in 2012. Originally published in hardcover in Canada by Random
House Canada, a division of Random House of Canada Limited, in 2011. Previously
published in Canada in French by Les Éditions de l'Homme. Distributed by Random
House of Canada Limited.

Vintage Canada with colophon is a registered trademark.

www.randomhouse.ca

Page 517 is a continuation of this copyright page.

Library and Archives Canada Cataloguing in Publication

Cédilot, André
      Mafia Inc. : the long, bloody reign of Canada's Sicilian clan / André Cédilot and
André Noël ; translated by Michael Gilson.

Includes index.
Translation of: *Mafia inc.*

ISBN 978-0-307-36041-0

      1. Mafia—Québec (Province)—History. I. Noël, André, 1953–
II. Gilson, Michael III. Title.

HV6453.C3213Q8 2011   364.10609714   C2011–902237–0

The translation of this book was assisted by a grant from the Government of
Québec (SODEC).

Where the authors had access to English-language documents only through versions
already translated into the French, those documents appear in this book having been
translated back into English

Cover and text design by Andrew Roberts
Cover images: (Nicolò Rizzuto) The Canadian Press / Montreal La Presse—Alain
Roberge, (bullet hole) Don Farrall / Photodisc

Printed and bound in the United States of America

10 9 8 7 6 5 4 3 2 1

CONTENTS

vi Rizzuto, Manno, Caruana and Cuntrera
    Family Trees
1 Foreword

5 Chapter 1: Corpses
27 Chapter 2: Vendetta
51 Chapter 3: From Cattolica Eraclea
    to Montreal
77 Chapter 4: Sicilians and Calabrians
101 Chapter 5: Assassinations
127 Chapter 6: The Narcobourgeoisie
153 Chapter 7: Hash and Coke
177 Chapter 8: From Venezuela to Italy
201 Chapter 9: Operation Compote
225 Chapter 10: The Money Trail
249 Chapter 11: Project Omertà
277 Chapter 12: Conquering Ontario
301 Chapter 13: Mafia Inc.
327 Chapter 14: Jailed
347 Chapter 15: Illustrious Relations
371 Chapter 16: Operation Colisée
407 Chapter 17: Tentacles
437 Chapter 18: Collapse

479 Epilogue
495 Chronology
501 Glossary
503 Bibliography
513 Acknowledgements
517 Photo Permissions
519 Index

RIZZUTO FAMILY

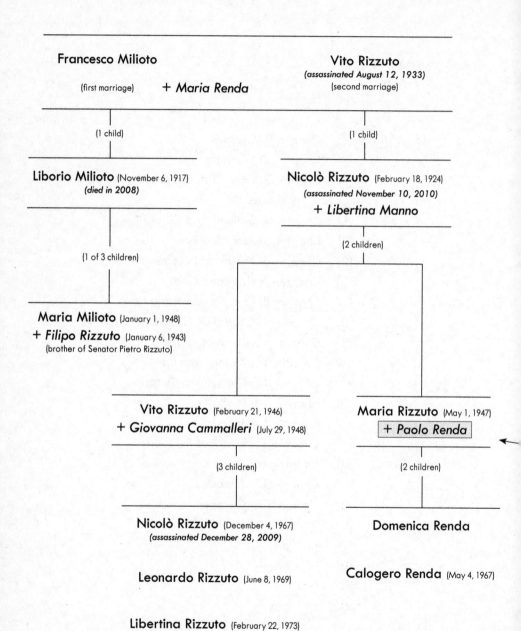

Francesco Milioto

(first marriage) **+ Maria Renda**

Vito Rizzuto
(*assassinated August 12, 1933*)
(second marriage)

(1 child)

(1 child)

Liborio Milioto (November 6, 1917)
(*died in 2008*)

Nicolò Rizzuto (February 18, 1924)
(*assassinated November 10, 2010*)
+ Libertina Manno

(1 of 3 children)

(2 children)

Maria Milioto (January 1, 1948)
+ Filipo Rizzuto (January 6, 1943)
(brother of Senator Pietro Rizzuto)

Vito Rizzuto (February 21, 1946)
+ Giovanna Cammalleri (July 29, 1948)

Maria Rizzuto (May 1, 1947)
+ Paolo Renda

(3 children)

(2 children)

Nicolò Rizzuto (December 4, 1967)
(*assassinated December 28, 2009*)

Domenica Renda

Leonardo Rizzuto (June 8, 1969)

Calogero Renda (May 4, 1967)

Libertina Rizzuto (February 22, 1973)

MANNO FAMILY

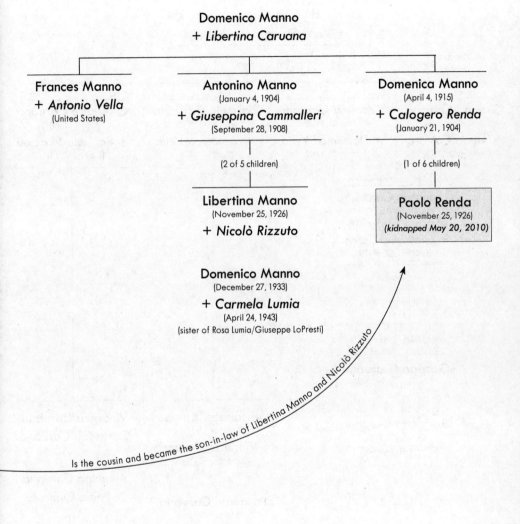

Domenico Manno
+ *Libertina Caruana*

Frances Manno
+ *Antonio Vella*
(United States)

Antonino Manno
(January 4, 1904)
+ *Giuseppina Cammalleri*
(September 28, 1908)

Domenica Manno
(April 4, 1915)
+ *Calogero Renda*
(January 21, 1904)

(2 of 5 children)

(1 of 6 children)

Libertina Manno
(November 25, 1926)
+ *Nicolò Rizzuto*

Paolo Renda
(November 25, 1926)
(kidnapped May 20, 2010)

Domenico Manno
(December 27, 1933)
+ *Carmela Lumia*
(April 24, 1943)
(sister of Rosa Lumia/Giuseppe LoPresti)

Is the cousin and became the son-in-law of Libertina Manno and Nicolò Rizzuto

CARUANA FAMILY

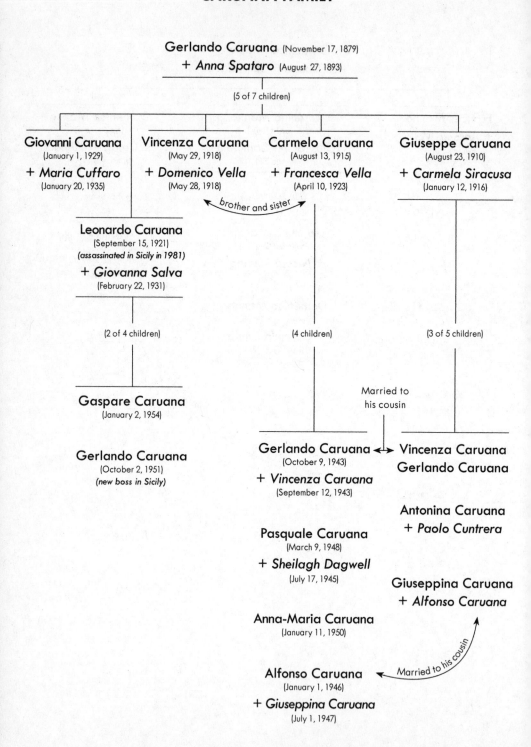

Gerlando Caruana (November 17, 1879)
+ Anna Spataro (August 27, 1893)

(5 of 7 children)

Giovanni Caruana
(January 1, 1929)
+ Maria Cuffaro
(January 20, 1935)

Vincenza Caruana
(May 29, 1918)
+ Domenico Vella
(May 28, 1918)

Carmelo Caruana
(August 13, 1915)
+ Francesca Vella
(April 10, 1923)

Giuseppe Caruana
(August 23, 1910)
+ Carmela Siracusa
(January 12, 1916)

brother and sister

Leonardo Caruana
(September 15, 1921)
(assassinated in Sicily in 1981)
+ Giovanna Salva
(February 22, 1931)

(2 of 4 children)

(4 children)

(3 of 5 children)

Gaspare Caruana
(January 2, 1954)

Married to
his cousin

Gerlando Caruana
(October 2, 1951)
(new boss in Sicily)

Gerlando Caruana
(October 9, 1943)
+ Vincenza Caruana
(September 12, 1943)

Vincenza Caruana
Gerlando Caruana

Pasquale Caruana
(March 9, 1948)
+ Sheilagh Dagwell
(July 17, 1945)

Antonina Caruana
+ Paolo Cuntrera

Anna-Maria Caruana
(January 11, 1950)

Giuseppina Caruana
+ Alfonso Caruana

Alfonso Caruana
(January 1, 1946)
+ Giuseppina Caruana
(July 1, 1947)

Married to his cousin

CUNTRERA FAMILY

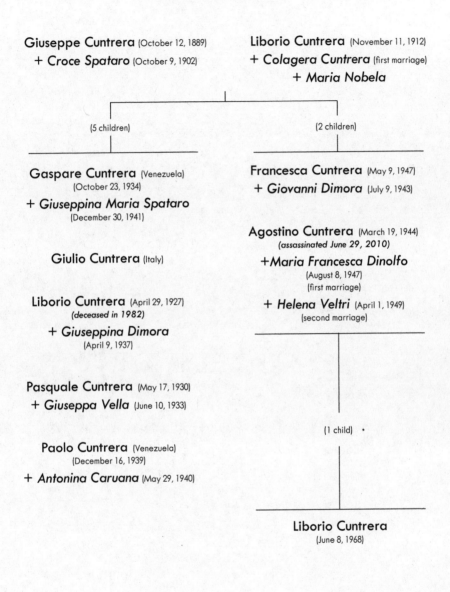

Giuseppe Cuntrera (October 12, 1889)
+ *Croce Spataro* (October 9, 1902)

Liborio Cuntrera (November 11, 1912)
+ *Colagera Cuntrera* (first marriage)
+ *Maria Nobela*

(5 children)

(2 children)

Gaspare Cuntrera (Venezuela)
(October 23, 1934)
+ *Giuseppina Maria Spataro*
(December 30, 1941)

Giulio Cuntrera (Italy)

Liborio Cuntrera (April 29, 1927)
(deceased in 1982)
+ *Giuseppina Dimora*
(April 9, 1937)

Pasquale Cuntrera (May 17, 1930)
+ *Giuseppa Vella* (June 10, 1933)

Paolo Cuntrera (Venezuela)
(December 16, 1939)
+ *Antonina Caruana* (May 29, 1940)

Francesca Cuntrera (May 9, 1947)
+ *Giovanni Dimora* (July 9, 1943)

Agostino Cuntrera (March 19, 1944)
(assassinated June 29, 2010)
+*Maria Francesca Dinolfo*
(August 8, 1947)
(first marriage)
+ *Helena Veltri* (April 1, 1949)
(second marriage)

(1 child) •

Liborio Cuntrera
(June 8, 1968)

FOREWORD

"YOU HAVE NO IDEA what 'Mafia' means?" the president of the Commission d'enquête sur le crime organisé (CECO, the Quebec Police Commission hearings into organized crime) asked Pietro Sciara in November 1975, as part of the commission's investigation into the criminal activities of Montreal's Cotroni organization. "No," Sciara replied matter-of-factly.

The Sicilian mobster made that denial despite incontrovertible evidence, provided by electronic surveillance, that he had played a crucial role some years earlier in the conflict between Paolo Violi, then the number two man in the Montreal Mafia, and one Nicolò Rizzuto. Well aware that he had incriminated himself on tape, Sciara preferred to seek the refuge of *omertà*, the famous code of silence. Three months later, in February 1976, he was coldly gunned down as he left a movie theatre. The Mafioso had paid with his life for failing to support his Sicilian compatriots.

It was thanks to the televised CECO hearings that people in Quebec and the rest of Canada first learned about Sicilian Mafiosi—men like Nicolò Rizzuto, Domenico Manno, Giuseppe LoPresti and Leonardo Caruana. Quebecers knew, of course, how the Cotroni brothers, Vincenzo and

1

Frank, had ruled the Montreal underworld for decades; their deeds often made the front pages. Testimonies at the CECO, however, revealed that the Montreal "family" in fact comprised not one but two distinct clans: the Calabrians, led by Vincenzo "Vic" Cotroni, who were from Italy's mainland, and the Sicilians, who had emigrated from the towns of Siculiana and Cattolica Eraclea, in the province of Agrigento. They had come to Canada between the mid-1950s and mid-1960s, and their organization had branches in South America and the United States.

No criminal charges were laid as a result of the CECO investigation. But its explosive revelations were devastating for the Calabrian clan; the police wiretaps and bugs had brought to light the serious rifts between Montreal's Calabrian and Sicilian Mafiosi. The resulting strife would lead to a bloody denouement, with a series of settlings of accounts that culminated in January 1978 with the dramatic execution of Paolo Violi. A changing of the guard had taken place within the Montreal Mafia, heralding a new era: the reign of the Rizzuto family.

The structure and operations of organized criminal activity in Montreal have changed a great deal since the 1940s, a time when the city teemed with brothels, gambling houses and dives, under the complacent eyes of the municipal authorities. Beginning in the 1950s, American mobsters moved in and took over the action. With Carmine Galante, an influential member of the infamous Bonanno family of New York, at its helm, the Montreal Mafia truly began to organize. They stepped up their "supervision" of the gambling joints and institutionalized that protection racket in every nightclub and restaurant. When the American gangsters began to focus specifically on heroin trafficking, Galante seized the strategic importance of Montreal: it was close to New York, with extensive port facilities that made it a perfect hub linking Europe with the major cities of the Eastern Seaboard. The Cotroni clan, already well entrenched, would serve as the bridgehead between the drug producers of Corsica and Marseilles and the huge market of users in New York, making Montreal one of the world's most important waypoints for narcotics at the time. But the Sicilians in the shadow of the Cotroni clan, including Nicolò Rizzuto and the members of the Cuntrera-Caruana family, also grasped the magnitude of this lucrative racket—and they were not about to sit by and let the Calabrians keep the biggest piece of the action to themselves.

After the turmoil of the 1970s and a period of forced exile in Venezuela, the Rizzutos, father Nicolò and son Vito, returned to Montreal in the early 1980s. From then on, under their command, the Montreal Mafia began a radical, unforeseen expansion. Under the aegis of Vito Rizzuto, with the benefit of his father's experience and advice, criminal activity in the city was organized like a business. Before long, large-scale drug trafficking would propel the Sicilian organization to the top of the underworld pyramid and a leading role on the mob scene in Canada and around the world. Wielding charisma and possessed of considerable skills as a mediator, Vito Rizzuto quickly won the unanimous backing of those around him and the respect of the bosses of other local criminal organizations. He surrounded himself with informed advisers and criminals, and the organization achieved complete control over its territory.

Men come and go, but institutions and their structures abide. This has been the key to the strength and renown of Cosa Nostra for more than a century—and it is doubtless true of the Rizzuto organization. Deploying its organizational model inspired by the Sicilian crime families, over the years the family implemented a system of alliances among the dozen or so clans making up the Montreal Mafia, and in so doing has consolidated its authority and made police infiltration difficult.

The Rizzuto organization comprises three tiers of authority. At the top is what might be termed the senior executive: the Mannos, Rendas and Rizzutos, linked by blood ties as well as marriage. The family's broad criminal strategies are mapped out at this level. Marital connections also extend to the second level of the organization: the lieutenants, some of whose children are married to those of the top-level bosses. From this level, all criminal operations are coordinated and carried out. The third level comprises a wide array of associates, not necessarily all of Italian origin, but who have expertise in a particular sphere of activity, either criminal or legal. Lawyers, financiers and front men of all stripes place their know-how in the service of the organization, helping it launder the staggering amounts of money generated by criminal activities.

It is the story of Vito Rizzuto and members of his family that journalists André Cédilot and André Noël recount in these pages. They chronicle the family's beginnings as country wardens in the Sicilian town of their birth, through to their arrival in Canada and their rise within the ranks of the Canadian Mafia. And finally they chronicle the family's decline, beginning in 2004 with the arrest of Vito Rizzuto, and continuing through the historic police roundup of November 22, 2006, which heralded the end of the Rizzuto family's dynastic rule over the Montreal underworld.

Pierre de Champlain,
author of *Mobsters, Gangsters and Men of Honour:*
Cracking the Mafia Code

CHAPTER 1

CORPSES

Vacant lots have always attracted kids and always will. Those of Ozone Park are no exception. The children of this neighbourhood in Queens, one of New York's five storied boroughs, are no different from those anywhere else in the world: they love to explore these plots of land abandoned by grown-ups, where wild grasses grow freely in disorderly thatches that stir the imagination. Where heaps of rubble may hide treasures. Or dead bodies.

Until the nineteenth century, vegetable farmers still grew crops on this part of Long Island. One entrepreneur raised goats—not so much for their milk or meat but for their hides, which he fashioned into gloves. New York City's tentacular sprawl had yet to extend much beyond Manhattan; but once the Long Island Rail Road pushed through the fields that lay between Brooklyn and Howard Beach, real estate developers did what they do best: they built. They put up cottages on the farmland and gave the new subdivision a name with a suitably bucolic ring to it: "Ozone Park" evoked the pleasant maritime aromas brought by cool Atlantic breezes. Manhattan urbanites had to be quick to sign their purchase offers if they hoped to move in and have their families enjoy the healthy sea air—which they did, en masse. The area eventually attracted its share of well-known figures, including folk-music legend Woody Guthrie. Franco-American author Jack Kerouac penned his famed beat opus *On the Road* here. Thousands of Italian Americans would also settle in Ozone Park, among them the infamous Mafioso John Gotti.

But on this particular afternoon of May 24, 1981, a bracing salty breeze wasn't the only thing that greeted some neighbourhood kids as they scoped out a vacant lot on Ruby Street, part of a warren of arteries in the centre of Ozone Park. They were intrigued by the sight—and smell—of "something strange" coming out of the ground. So they started digging. Accounts of what the boys discovered next diverge. One journalist wrote that they initially spotted the heel of a cowboy boot protruding from the dirt. Another version claims they stumbled upon a hand covered in fabric. As a rule, young boys are a gutsy lot—especially in a gang. Such youthful intestinal fortitude has its limits, though, and these boys turned tail and fled the scene. One ran straight home to his parents, who called the police.

Officer Andrew Cilienti oversaw the exhumation. The corpse had been wrapped in a blood-soaked drop cloth. Around the left wrist was a Cartier watch, worth at least $1,500; its hands were frozen at 5:58 A.M. and the day/date indicator read May 7. A tattoo adorned the fore-arm: two hearts and a dagger, symbolizing a failed romance. Elsewhere, the body bore obvious gunshot wounds: the man's life had been ended by three .38 calibre slugs. Just as obvious was the fact that the remains could not have been lying there more than a few days. Forensics tech-nicians had no difficulty taking the victim's fingerprints, and a match soon came back: the dead man was Alphonse "Sonny Red" Indelicato. Four days later, his son-in-law, Salvatore Valenti, formally identified the body.

Sonny Red's family hailed from a town called Siculiana, in the prov-ince of Agrigento, Sicily. One of his murderers, Vito Rizzuto, was born in Cattolica Eraclea, a mere twenty kilometres away. In May 1981, Vito was thirty-five years old. Soon after the killing, he quietly made his way home to his wife and three children in Saint-Léonard, in east-end Montreal. There, he continued attending to his business at the heart of a formidable and flourishing criminal empire—an underworld network based in Montreal, with sturdy branches spread throughout Canada and ramifying into Italy, the United States, Venezuela and Colombia. By the time of Sonny Red's death, money had begun flowing in huge amounts into the coffers of that empire: the fruits of loansharking, illegal gambling, fraud, corruption and public works contracts, protection money from shopkeepers and entrepreneurs—and, especially, the proceeds from the importing and distribution of tonne after tonne of heroin, cocaine and hashish.

The name Rizzuto was known to police—but at this juncture, that was mostly thanks to Vito's father. In 1975 in Montreal, a police witness had testified before Quebec's public commission on organized crime (Commission d'enquête sur le crime organisé, or CECO) that Nicolò (Nick) Rizzuto intended to take control of the Italian Mafia in Quebec. It would be a decade before the name of his son, Vito, first appeared in the files of the Royal Canadian Mounted Police's (RCMP's) drug squad.

In 1981, the police knew nothing about Vito's involvement in the slaying of Sonny Red and two other mob captains in a building in Brooklyn, not far from Ozone Park. The order for the triple hit had come from high up in the Bonanno clan, one of the Five Families of the New York Mafia (and the massacre would later be depicted in the film *Donnie Brasco*, starring Al Pacino and Johnny Depp). A year later, Vito left Saint-Léonard and moved to the northwest part of the Island of Montreal, into a sprawling mansion on Antoine-Berthelet Avenue, which backs onto a narrow strip of woodland, part of the Bois-de-Saraguay nature park, not far from the Rivière des Prairies, Montreal's "back river."

Standing over six feet tall, slim and well built, with an easy, flowing gait and dark, almost black hair carefully combed backward, Vito Rizzuto never left his home unless impeccably dressed. He controlled his empire for more than two decades with his father, Nicolò—who, on his return from a Venezuelan prison in 1983, had his own mansion built next door to Vito's. More than once during those years, the RCMP, the Sûreté du Québec (the provincial police, or SQ) and the Montreal police tried in vain to put both father and son behind bars. The younger Rizzuto kept on playing golf on the best courses, dining in the finest restaurants, hobnobbing with lawyers, businessmen above suspicion, city councillors and members of Parliament. He became a legend in Quebec and a man respected by a sizable proportion of Montreal's Italian community. Criminal biker gang bosses like Maurice "Mom" Boucher, leader of the Hells Angels in Quebec, and Salvatore Cazzetta, head of the rival Rock Machine, waged ruthless, all-out war against each other but shared a deference toward the all-powerful godfather.

Prosecutors were seemingly powerless in their efforts to thwart him. In 1986, Vito was acquitted of drunk driving charges. In 1989, in Sept-Îles, Quebec, accusations that he had masterminded the importing of thirty-two tonnes of hashish were dropped. In 1990, the Newfoundland Supreme Court failed to find him guilty of importing another sixteen tonnes of hash. In 1994, the RCMP arrested several of his cohorts as part of Operation Compote, set up to investigate drug trafficking and money laundering, but once again the godfather walked. In 1998, the Caruana brothers—Alfonso, Gerlando and Pasquale, all close associates of the Rizzuto clan—were arrested and convicted in Toronto of cocaine trafficking. But no charges were laid against Vito.

As the years went by, Vito Rizzuto doubtless consigned the memory of the triple slaying in Brooklyn to some dark corner of his mind. After all, who could possibly connect a body uncovered in a vacant lot in a dilapidated neighbourhood in Queens to the man who had become the great prince of the Montreal mob? A halo of impunity had grown around him; now it contaminated him to the point that he felt invincible. When he was finally arrested in January 2004, Rizzuto displayed amazing aplomb as he let police officers cuff him at his front door. Twenty-three years after the murder of the three Bonanno captains, a U.S. federal grand jury had indicted him on racketeering conspiracy charges and was demanding his extradition. Vito had always beaten the rap. He was born under a lucky star. Why would it abandon him now?

He was incarcerated at the Rivière-des-Prairies Detention Centre, a facility crowded with accused prisoners awaiting trial. An habitué of upscale restaurants, Rizzuto couldn't bear the facility's cafeteria food. He tried sandwiches and soft drinks, but eventually got fed up with them as well and asked his wife, Giovanna, to bring him fruit juice and protein shakes—the kind bodybuilders drink. Before long, his appetite waned. He lost weight and grew morose. His lawyers demanded, and secured, a transfer. They hoped he would be sent to the maximum-security penitentiary at Donnacona, near Quebec City, or a medium-security facility like the Leclerc Institution, in Laval, where he would be in the company of several criminal bikers and Mafiosi with whom he was well acquainted.

For security reasons, Rizzuto was instead transferred to the Regional Reception Centre in Sainte-Anne-des-Plaines, north of Montreal, which briefly houses inmates serving terms of two years or more while they are assessed for transfer to the correctional facility best suited to their criminal profile. Its name is one that could only have been devised by federal bureaucrats intent on hiding the truth: "Regional Reception Centre" sounds better suited to a fruit and vegetable wholesaler. But it is in fact a maximum security penitentiary, adjacent to another prison for offenders with mental health problems, and to the Special Handling Unit, a super-maximum security facility housing criminals deemed extremely dangerous—who, at the time, included Mom Boucher.

The food there is better than at the Rivière-des-Prairies Detention Centre, but prisoners must eat in their cells—meals are served through a slot in the door—and at specific times. When he arrived, Rizzuto learned he would have to use a communal shower and, because of overcrowding, share a cell with another inmate. Occasionally, he would make himself a coffee in a small common room containing twenty or so chairs, a few tables, a counter and a sink, but he seldom mingled with other prisoners. Donald Matticks, a convicted drug trafficker and former employee of the Port of Montreal who was being held at Sainte-Anne-des-Plaines pending transfer to another facility, was one of the few he saw fit to associate with. The pair would spend hours together talking and playing cards. An ex–dock worker, Donald was the son of Gerald Matticks, an influential member of Montreal's West End Gang, Irish mobsters whose specialty was importing hashish and cocaine through the city's port.

Vito's relations with the prison guards were cordial, nothing more. He spent most of his time reading, which included poring over the U.S. government's indictment against him. Like other detainees, he was forbidden to have any so-called contact visits. He had to speak to visitors through a mouthpiece in a glass partition. His wife or children came every day, between 4 and 6 P.M. His lawyers weren't subjected to such precise restrictions and could meet him at other times of day. Vito also spent a lot of time on the phone.

He made regular calls to his wife as well as to a very close friend, Vincenzo Spagnolo, to keep tabs on how things were going in his absence. Spagnolo, the owner of Buffet Le Mirage, a banquet hall in Saint-Léonard, would answer with a hearty "Hey, Mr. V., how are you?" During one of these conversations, the restaurateur mentioned how truly honoured he felt to have Rizzuto call him at work. "You know you've always been one of my favourites," Vito replied. "When I get permission to make a phone call, I take fifteen minutes for my wife, and fifteen minutes for you."

The two men made typical small talk in English and the Sicilian dialect, chatting about their moods, their families and their businesses. "There's a lot of competition," Spagnolo griped. "The other halls are starting to cut prices and it's hurting me." These were complaints as trivial as any that might be exchanged between ordinary businessmen. Spagnolo blamed the "damn governments" for the pervading economic gloom. He and Vito commented on the ups and downs of the restaurant business: so-and-so had just opened a bar, someone else had closed his restaurant, a particular stretch of Saint-Laurent Boulevard was "dead," the outlook for hotel-industry development was more attractive in Laval than in Montreal. . .

Vito had a lot of questions about the construction industry. He asked for news about the latest real estate projects: who the developers were, whether the contractors entrusted with the work were "people we know." He was especially interested in goings-on in Montreal's Little Italy, a neighbourhood that straddles Saint-Laurent Boulevard just south of Jean-Talon Street.

Every now and then, the godfather would ask his friends if there were any problems with the *picciotti*—a term derived from the Sicilian dialect that, in Mafia jargon, refers to street-level soldiers. Sometimes, Spagnolo would hand the telephone to one acquaintance or another who was eager to hear news of Vito. On one occasion, the godfather joked that his fellow inmates were mostly in their late thirties, but none of them referred to him as an "old guy," which to him meant he still had the bearing of a younger man. He did complain, however, that his waistline had expanded somewhat since he had been incarcerated, and blamed it on the poor prison food.

Though confined to a high-security penitentiary, Rizzuto kept on doing business, like a magician slipping through the bars and walls of the prison. According to Italian police, it was from this correctional complex rising in the middle of a field in Canada, surrounded by towering fences topped with barbed wire, that he issued instructions for the securing of a massive contract worth $7.3 billion Cdn to build a 3,690-metre-long bridge spanning the Strait of Messina between Italy and Sicily. Police in Rome issued a warrant for his arrest while he was imprisoned at Sainte-Anne-des-Plaines.

Thousands of newspaper and magazine articles have been written about Rizzuto. Few people in Canada, however, have any inkling of the extraordinary power wielded by the Italian Mafia in their own country. It is not simply an association of killers, smugglers and swindlers, but a secret organization that exerts influence in social, economic and political spheres to an unsuspected degree. The late Gilbert Côté, former director of the Montreal police force's intelligence division, was one of the few analysts who fully grasped the threats to democracy posed by the Mafia. He tried for years to alert public opinion to the danger before his untimely death from cancer in 2006. Canadians, especially in Quebec, he unceasingly warned, "need to wake up and spur their governments to action before the situation gets out of control, the way it is in Italy." Unfortunately, no one seemed to listen.

Côté saw a direct link between governments' elevated levels of debt and the corrupting power of the Mafia. The more pervasive the criminal influence, the more money—billions of dollars—is misappropriated via dubious public works contracts, and the less there is to pay for things like schools, hospitals, elder care or environmental protection. In charting the life and deeds of Vito Rizzuto, this book records, as comprehensively as possible, the innumerable marks that his far-reaching criminal enterprise has left on society.

In 2004, a few months after Vito Rizzuto was jailed at the Sainte-Anne-des-Plaines penitentiary complex, FBI agents made another grisly discovery in Ozone Park, right beside the vacant lot where, twenty-three years earlier, the schoolboys had stumbled upon the still-fresh corpse of Sonny Red Indelicato. The neighbourhood hadn't changed much. The few scattered houses along Ruby Street had continued to deteriorate, surrounded by semi-trailer parking lots, abandoned buses and dumpsters sniffed at by stray dogs.

Wearing knee-high, lime-green rubber boots, the federal agents waded around the bottom of a muddy pit, guided by forensic experts. Three earthmovers dug slowly into the soil, shunting aside cement debris, while the blue-gloved agents picked up clumps of muddy earth and dropped them onto sieves. After a week, the search had turned up a tibia and fibula, a hip bone and another bone from either a hand or foot. Encouraged, the investigators kept digging. Their bounty grew and soon included several skull and jaw fragments.

It would take weeks before DNA from the bones could be matched to specific individuals. But the agents had a fairly good idea who the dead men were. It was no accident that this particular makeshift graveyard had turned up such secrets. And before the results of DNA testing came back, they found two items that were very interesting indeed: an old Citibank credit card bearing the name Dominick Trinchera, and a Piaget wristwatch. When the FBI men described the watch to the wife of one Philip Giaccone, she confirmed that it matched the one he'd been wearing at the time of his disappearance, in 1981.

The murders had been ordered by Joseph Massino, a hulking mobster with a double chin who let himself be called "Big Joey." The moniker did not merely describe the man's physical bulk; it also referred to the position of power that he constantly sought to occupy. At the time, Massino was the interim boss of the powerful Bonanno crime family while its nominal head, Philip "Rusty" Rastelli, was behind bars.

In Rastelli's absence, three *caporegimes* (captains, or *capos*), Sonny Red Indelicato, Dominick "Big Trin" Trinchera and Philip "Philly Lucky" Giaccone, had been plotting to take control of the Bonanno organization. At least, that was what Big Joey Massino suspected—and his opinion was shared by Salvatore Vitale, another Bonanno family capo, whose comparatively trim physique had earned him the nickname "Good-Looking Sal."

Massino visited Rastelli in prison, warning his boss that there was every chance he would be assassinated upon his release. Then he went before the Commission, the Mafia "oversight board" comprising representatives of New York's Five Families, to secure authorization to eliminate the three rebel captains. The Commission members were hesitant at first but relented when Massino informed them that Sonny Red and his two colleagues had recently been stocking up on automatic weapons and were ready to go on the offensive. The three presumed conspirators were summoned to a meeting with other Bonanno capos at a social club on Thirteenth Avenue in the Dyker Heights neighbourhood of Brooklyn. It was a trap. Indelicato, Trinchera and Giaccone were gunned down as soon as they walked into the club. Some of the triggermen had been summoned from Canada to do the job; one of them was Vito Rizzuto.

In the broader scheme of things, the exhumation of Trinchera's and Giaccone's remains did little more than stir an old, unpleasant memory for Vito Rizzuto. More worrisome to him was the damning testimony provided by Good-Looking Sal Vitale, who had broken *omertà* after his arrest in 2003. It was his testimony that gave the U.S. authorities what they needed to demand the Canadian godfather's extradition. Then, in January 2005, Rizzuto was stunned to learn that Big Joey Massino himself had turned rat as well. Vito hired the best legal experts he could find to fight his extradition. They included six seasoned lawyers from Montreal, as well as John W. Mitchell, a renowned New York City–based criminal defence attorney who had been one of John Gotti's lawyers before his death in prison in 2002. Rounding out the team was Alan Dershowitz, the Harvard law professor, criminal law specialist, prolific author and "attorney to the stars" whose past clients included Claus von Bülow, O.J. Simpson and Jim Bakker. Rizzuto had assembled a seemingly invincible dream team—which then lost the case.

Had the U.S. authorities brought murder charges against Vito Rizzuto, the Canadian government might never have agreed to his extradition, for the simple reason that he would have faced the death penalty; Canada generally does not hand over its citizens to countries that practise capital punishment. Instead, they indicted him on racketeering conspiracy charges under the Racketeer Influenced and Corrupt Organizations (RICO) Act. Charges under that legislation carry a five-year statute of limitations. The indictment alleged that the conspiracy Rizzuto was accused of committing on behalf of the Bonanno clan—which included the three murders—extended from February 1981 to December 2003.

Rizzuto's defence hinged on whether the statute of limitations began in 1981 (the time of the murders) or applied to the five years leading up to 2003, the year charges were laid under the RICO Act, more specifically its "continuing criminal enterprise" statute. His lawyers were on thin ice with this argument, and it failed. They next attempted to convince the courts that in Canada the rules of evidence in matters of extradition have been so whittled down as to be incompatible with Canadian law. This, too, failed to sway the judge. As a last resort, the defence team argued that extraditing a Canadian citizen merely on documentary evidence was a violation of the Canadian Charter of Rights and Freedoms. The U.S. grand jury had, of course, backed its extradition request with evidence on paper, but in the defence lawyers' opinion, it was just that: a pile of paper. They insisted that the validity of the evidence had to be established by questioning the witnesses who had provided it. The request was clearly unreasonable, but after thirty-one months of legal wrangling, Vito Rizzuto was ready to hang on to any lifeline he could.

The prisoner who awoke in his cell at the Regional Reception Centre in Sainte-Anne-des-Plaines on Thursday, August 17, 2006, was still a hopeful man. He knew that the Supreme Court of Canada was due to rule on his appeal request within hours. Would it strike down the rulings of the lower-court judges, all of whom had dismissed his defence team's arguments? Would his final appeal be granted? He could only hope. Rizzuto put on his prison-issue white T-shirt and jeans, ate breakfast and went to meet his wife, Giovanna, in the visiting room. At age sixty, he still looked good, despite having spent two years in detention.

Meanwhile, four unmarked cars belonging to the City of Montreal Police Force parked discreetly on a shooting range in a field near the penitentiary complex. In one of them sat Detective Nicodemo Milano, a veteran of the force's organized-crime squad. Fluent in Italian, he had tracked Rizzuto for three weeks before arresting him in January 2004. Beside him was Patrick Franc Guimond, another experienced officer who had amassed a mountain of information on the Mafia since being assigned to the police's intelligence division. Both were impatiently awaiting the Supreme Court ruling.

At that moment, an FBI jet touched down on a runway at Montréal–Trudeau Airport, some sixty kilometres from the prison, and taxied to a secondary strip. Agent Brian Tupper and his colleagues from the Bureau's New Jersey office were ready to collect their prisoner.

The Montreal police had planned the transfer operation down to the last detail with their FBI counterparts and a project manager with Correctional Service of Canada, Luciano Bentenuto. If Rizzuto's final appeal bid was denied, he was to be sent to the United States as quickly as possible and under heavy escort—but discreetly, to reduce the risk of an escape attempt or the presence of journalists. The transfer also had to happen without the knowledge of other penitentiary inmates.

The police probably remembered all too well the escape of Richard Vallée, a member of the Hells Angels, in June 1997. Awaiting extradition for the murder of a police witness in the United States, Vallée gave his guards the slip while receiving medical care in Montreal's Saint-Luc

Hospital. He then hid out for six years in Costa Rica. The Canadian police who lost him probably wanted to go into hiding as well.

It was shaping up to be a fine August day. The Sainte-Anne-des-Plaines prison complex was bathed in early-morning sunshine. Clouds had given way to clear skies the day before. The temperature was a pleasant twenty-two degrees Celsius, which meant Milano and Franc Guimond could roll down the car windows and turn off the ignition; there was no need for air conditioning. At 10:45 A.M., word came. The Supreme Court refused to hear the appeal. The way was cleared for Vito Rizzuto's extradition.

The police convoy got underway and headed for the penitentiary. When Milano and Franc Guimond arrived inside the building, Rizzuto appeared surprised. This self-described "jack of all trades"—a da Vinci of organized crime, a Teflon don after the fashion of John Gotti, a gentleman who commanded respect from one and all—was about to be shackled like a common criminal and trundled off to the United States, a country he feared and had always avoided. "In a country which condemns individuals to 125 years of prison, it is easy to find informers which are ready to say anything to save their skin," he had once said, unaware he was being recorded by police microphones. The godfather had lost his arrogant panache. The swagger was gone. Vito was a beaten man. His lucky star had indeed forsaken him.

As Milano and Franc Guimond prepared to cuff him, he turned to a guard and asked why he hadn't been told of the impending extradition. His voice had gone from the mellow baritone of a man accustomed to wielding charm to the faint whisper of one who knows he is condemned. Despite it all, he remained a good sport: before leaving the prison, he asked that his TV set and some food he'd bought from the canteen be given to the inmates committee.

Milano and Franc Guimond escorted Rizzuto to a van, where a member of the Montreal police tactical unit was waiting. The driver gunned the engine and they headed for the airport, escorted by the three other unmarked cars, each carrying heavily armed officers. The don normally spoke calmly and coolly, but on this morning railed against the

RCMP and the SQ, claiming that the way they'd shadowed him for nearly thirty years was tantamount to harassment.

Rizzuto had a long memory. He blasted the police for Project Jaggy, an operation conducted thirteen years earlier that had netted Raynald Desjardins, Vito's right-hand man and neighbour (he owned a home worth more than $400,000 in the same Saraguay development). Desjardins had been arrested, along with sixteen other individuals linked to the Hells Angels and the Mafia, for plotting to import 740 kilos of cocaine by ship from Venezuela. The Coast Guard had been keeping a discreet eye on the vessel, the *Fortune Endeavor,* and when she ran into trouble off the coast of Nova Scotia and had to be towed to Halifax, the smugglers had dumped their precious cargo, hidden in sewer pipes, into the waters of the Atlantic. Desjardins had been handed a fifteen-year prison term and fined $150,000.

A seething Rizzuto kept on venting, next about Project Choke. This was another police investigation in the 1990s, which had led to the arrest and conviction of Calabrian Mafiosi, including Frank Cotroni and his son Francesco, also on cocaine smuggling charges. Sitting with Vito in the van, officers Milano and Franc Guimond were all ears. As they listened to the don sounding off, they knew full well that those investigations had also targeted—and almost caught—Rizzuto himself. This sudden interest in other people's business indicated to them that perhaps it was Vito's business too.

Switching from Italian to English as if he were speaking one and the same language, Rizzuto insisted to the two investigators that he was the only one who could keep a relative peace among Montreal's various criminal organizations—as if seeking to persuade them that they were making a serious mistake in shipping him off to the United States. Without him, he said, the delicate underworld balance would be shattered. When he was done spitting venom at the Mounties and the SQ, he began dispensing advice. The police, he said, would be better off going after Montreal's street gangs, who in his opinion were the emergent force in organized crime in the city.

Then, weary of his tirade, he waxed sentimental. He was sure the RCMP was readying a killing blow against his Sicilian clan. He hoped they would spare his father, Nicolò, "an old and sick man" who, he claimed, was involved in no crime and should be left to enjoy one of the few pleasures he had left in life: sipping espressos with other patrons of the Consenza Social Club on Jarry Street in Saint-Léonard. What Vito didn't know was that the club—the Montreal Mafia's de facto head office—was crammed with hidden police microphones and cameras. Some customers, of course, didn't go there just to drink coffee. They came to deliver wads of cash to the elder Rizzuto, who would slip them into his socks.

When he exited the vehicle and saw the FBI plane on the tarmac, Vito blanched, as if the reality of his extradition was just setting in. The doors of the jet were open. Agent Tupper asked the Montreal cops to shackle the prisoner's feet. His back bent, Vito hobbled up the ladder. The doors slid shut.

An hour later, the plane touched down in New Jersey. Vito Rizzuto stood on U.S. soil for the first time in twenty-five years. He was briefly interrogated by agents, who then transported him to the United States District Court in Brooklyn, just a few blocks from Thirteenth Avenue, where he and his accomplices had gunned down Sonny Red Indelicato, Dominick "Big Trin" Trinchera and Philip "Philly Lucky" Giaccone.

At 4:30 P.M., he went before Nicholas G. Garaufis, a judge with piercing eyes and the thin-framed glasses of an intellectual. Garaufis was known among other things for handing down an eight-year prison sentence to Joseph Caridi, a Mafioso nicknamed the "Tony Soprano of Long Island," who had extorted the owners of a seafood restaurant for between seven and ten thousand dollars a night.

At the time, the district court in Brooklyn was one of the battlefields on which an epic war between the U.S. government and the New York Mafia was unfolding. Judge Garaufis was a key player. He was presiding over the trials of several members of New York's Five Families, notably the Bonanno family, the one most inclined to internecine settlings of accounts. One of its captains, Louis "Louie HaHa" Attanasio, had just appeared before Garaufis when Rizzuto was escorted into the courtroom. The crimes of which each was accused had taken place around the same time and were not dissimilar.

Louie HaHa, a well-known Bonanno capo, was accused of conspiracy in the 1984 murder of Cesare Bonventre. Considered a big wheel in the Bonanno family, Bonventre had fallen out of favour with the boss, Joe Massino, who had ordered his execution. Louie HaHa and Good-Looking Sal Vitale had lured an unsuspecting Bonventre into a car. As Vitale pulled into a warehouse garage, Louie HaHa put two bullets into Bonventre's head. Still very much alive, Bonventre fought on, forcing Vitale to stop the car. As Bonventre tried to crawl away on the concrete floor, Louie HaHa fired two more shots through his skull, finishing the job.

They sliced Bonventre's corpse in two and dumped the halves into a pair of two-hundred-litre glue barrels, which they hid in a warehouse in Garfield, New Jersey. Forensic experts toiled for three months before identifying the remains. Twenty-two years later, Louie HaHa was standing before Judge Garaufis. Aware that the evidence was overwhelming, he pleaded guilty.

Vito Rizzuto, who had taken part in the triple slaying of the Bonanno men with Salvatore Vitale at the behest of Joe Massino, knew that the evidence against him was just as damning as the evidence against Attanasio. But, true to form, combative and resolved to test his luck as long as possible, Rizzuto pleaded not guilty.

He was led away to the Metropolitan Detention Center, where Massino had previously been held before turning informant. The place had a sordid reputation. Human rights activists called it "Brooklyn's Abu Ghraib," a reference to the infamous prison in suburban Baghdad where U.S. soldiers had tortured and humiliated Iraqi insurgents. The comparison was doubtless exaggerated, but several Middle Eastern immigrants arrested after 9/11 had been transferred to the Brooklyn jail, and many later claimed to have suffered sleep deprivation, humiliating acts, violence and sexual abuse.

The facility had also housed many Mafia turncoats. "The same methods that were being used in Iraq are being used at the Metropolitan

Detention Center," Massino's lawyer David Breitbart said in May 2004 before Judge Garaufis. Breitbart was denouncing police officers, prosecutors and prison guards who, he pleaded, were guilty of putting undue pressure on mobsters and coercing them into testifying against his client. "They seduce men. They bribe them. They torture them into becoming a witness," he added when Massino himself turned informer to avoid facing the death penalty for one of the murders he had ordered.

The heads of New York's five infamous crime families were all dead or jailed for life, or had decided to "sing." But Vito Rizzuto swore to remain very much alive, to tough it out a few years in prison and never to betray any member of Cosa Nostra. Sicilian to the core, he was and would remain a "man of honour."

In the eight long months he spent in the Metropolitan Detention Center in New York, Vito kept his word. He did eventually decide, however, to plead guilty. In the end, he got what he wanted: a shorter prison term. His lawyers had little choice but to negotiate a plea deal with the U.S. prosecutors. Joe Massino's and Salvatore Vitale's testimonies were irrefutable. All of the information they had provided to the prosecution had proved accurate, including the resting places of Trinchera, Giaccone and Indelicato in Ozone Park. Not only that, but Vitale had described in painstaking detail for Judge Garaufis the execution of the three renegade Bonanno captains. Worst of all, he had repeatedly told the court that the lead triggerman that night had been Vito Rizzuto.

Sal Vitale testified that Massino had called a meeting of all the Bonanno family capos for Tuesday, May 5, 1981, at a social club on Thirteenth Avenue in Dyker Heights, a mostly Italian neighbourhood in Brooklyn. The two-storey brick building served as a mob headquarters. Ugly and windowless, it was fronted by a wrought-iron fence that kept undesirable visitors out—not that any would dare go near the place; it was the sort of establishment where Mafiosi felt at ease, but which passersby gave a wide berth. The club belonged to a member of the Gambino crime family, of which John Gotti was a part.

Since it was ostensibly an "administrative meeting," no one was supposed to show up armed. This was the directive that the three rebel captains had received. Trinchera, Giaccone and Indelicato may well have suspected that Massino was drawing them into a trap. They would have found it hard to believe that brokering peace within the family was really on the agenda. But they had no choice: a call to a "sit-down" is an order, and to disobey such an order is to sign one's own death warrant.

Big Joey Massino had summoned his three executioners from Montreal, themselves Bonanno family members: Rizutto, one named Emanuele and another man whom Vitale knew only as "the old-timer." When, during questioning, the prosecuting attorney asked him "why some of the shooters were from Canada," Vitale explained it was "because of a security issue. It would never leak out. And after the murders, they [the three Canadians] would go back to Montreal."

Next, Massino demanded that a fourth man join the shooting party: Vitale. Since he had served in the army, Vitale was given a Tommy gun or "grease gun"—the storied Thompson submachine gun much loved by gangsters during Prohibition and widely used by U.S. troops in the Second World War. In automatic mode, it could fire up to seven- hundred rounds per minute. Vito and Emanuele were handed pistols; "the old-timer" was armed with a sawed-off shotgun. The four men were told to put on ski masks and hide in a closet in the adjoining coatroom. Other capos present were assigned to watch over the premises and guard the door. The operation could have gone awry: as he was preparing his Tommy gun, Vitale accidentally pulled the trigger, spraying five bullets into the wall. Massino chewed him out for it—all the more so since he had warned the ambushers to be careful: "Don't shoot unless you have to, because I don't want bullets flying all over the place."

The four assassins crammed themselves into the closet, with the door slightly ajar, and lay in wait for the three capos to arrive. Rizzuto kept a wary eye on his old friend Gerlando Sciascia, posted at the other end of the room. Sciascia, like Vito, was from Cattolica Eraclea in Sicily. His American acolytes called him "George from Canada," because he regularly represented the Bonanno family's Canadian crew on visits to

New York. Sciascia had a heavy shock of silver-grey hair, brushed backward to uncover his forehead. It was his job to give the order to shoot: as soon as the trio of rebel captains arrived at the social club, he would signal the gunmen by running his hand through his hair.

When the three capos came down the two steps from the front door into the foyer, Sciascia gave that signal. Rizzuto was the first to burst out of the closet. "Vito led the way," said Salvatore Vitale at Joe Massino's trial. "I was last. I heard Vito say, 'Don't anybody move. This is a holdup.' . . . I seen Vito shoot. I don't know who he hit. I see Massino punch Philly Lucky [Giaccone]. All hell broke loose."

Dominick Trinchera rushed the assailants and was immediately felled by gunfire. Vitale knelt near the exit door, Emanuele and the "old-timer" at his sides. "I froze for five seconds on one knee," he recalled. "The shotgun went off. [Sonny Red] fell between me and the old-timer. He fell to my left, laying in the foyer. I seen [Sciascia] reach in the back, pull out a gun and shoot him on the left side of the head. By that time, it was all over."

Vitale pulled off his mask, grabbed his walkie-talkie and called Goldie Leisenheimer, who was standing guard outside: "Goldie, where are you?" he asked. Once he knew Leisenheimer had come around the corner, outside, Vitale was supposed to let a few men out of the club. But he noticed to his amazement that almost everybody had already left, out a door that he didn't know existed. Santo "Tony" Giordano, a captain of the "Zips"—an exclusively Sicilian faction of the Bonanno clan—was lying on the floor, hit in the back by "friendly fire." A licensed pilot, he was crippled by the shot but did fly again with the aid of another pilot. In July 1983 Giordano's plane crashed near Edwards Airport in Bayport, New York, killing him and his co-pilot.

A cleanup crew, including Benjamin "Lefty Guns" Ruggiero (played by Al Pacino in the film *Donnie Brasco*) took care of wrapping the bodies in drop cloths and carting them away. According to Vitale, Ruggiero had trouble lifting Trinchera's three-hundred-pound bulk and was impressed at how his sidekick, a mobster nicknamed "Boobie," managed to load Trinchera's and the two other bodies into a van. The corpses were handed over to members of the Gambino family, including John Gotti's brother Gene, who had agreed to "make them disappear." John Gotti was doing his old friend Joe Massino a favour.

In the wake of the carnage, the social club on Thirteenth Avenue was "a mess," Vitale told Judge Garaufis: "There was too much blood. We couldn't clean it up." Big Joey Massino decided the only option was to set fire to the building, which they did. As the social club burned, Massino and Gerlando Sciascia went to report to Vincent "The Chin" Gigante, who was the Genovese family boss. The tabloids had nicknamed him the "Odd-father," noting that he could often be seen wandering, unshaven, muttering to himself near Sullivan Street in Greenwich Village, where he lived with his mother. He sometimes went on these excursions clad in pyjamas, slippers and a moth-eaten bathrobe. Big Joey Massino and everyone who was anyone in mobland knew this crazy-old-man behaviour was nothing but a ruse to fool the police. Vincent "The Chin" was perfectly lucid—and obsessively circumspect, forbidding his captains and soldiers from even uttering his name. If they spoke about him, they were supposed to rub their chins instead, hence the nickname.

When mobsters looked at Vincent "The Chin," they could see that his gaze was far from empty, and he was nowhere near senile. That day, out of respect for the boss's position, Massino and Sciascia went to tell Gigante that he was henceforth the most powerful captain in the Bonanno family. In the Mafia underworld, more than in any other milieu, power comes from the mouth of a gun.

The day after the murders, a police surveillance team photographed Vito Rizzuto and Gerlando Sciascia, accompanied by Big Joey Massino, leaving the Capri Motor Lodge in the Bronx and walking to the dark blue Buick sedan that would take the two men back to Montreal. From that moment on, Rizzuto's standing in the Bonanno family was assured. But his relations with the Cuntrera-Caruana family of Sicilian Mafiosi would remain just as important to him. Years later, Salvatore Vitale would travel to Montreal to meet Rizzuto and ask him to become the official head of the Bonannos in Canada, only to hear Vito politely decline. He refused to be made a captain. Vitale described the encounter to Judge Garaufis: "I meet with Vito. I asked him, 'Who do the men respect? Who could be a good captain?' He said: 'My father,' and that isn't the way to go. We wanted him to take the position and he avoided the question and I felt it best to leave it alone." At any rate, Vito explained, in Montreal there was no boss; there were twenty "men of honour," and they were all equal.

Another Bonanno family capo, Dominick "Sonny Black" Napolitano, had tried to convince Joe Massino to let his new recruit, a man named Donnie Brasco, take part in the execution of the three rebel capos in the social club on Thirteenth Avenue. Brasco, who looked the part of a real tough, especially in the way he swaggered like a prizefighter, claimed to be an accomplished burglar, jewel thief and fence. He had been a Bonanno hanger-on for six years. Sonny Black vouched for Brasco and hoped he would be invited to be part of the proceedings on the night of May 5, 1981. "He wanted Donnie to play a significant role in the murders," Vitale recalled, adding that Sonny Black wanted "to make him an official member in the Bonanno family." Massino refused; he trusted his Canadian recruits more than this upstart who'd come out of nowhere. His instinct would prove right.

After the massacre, fearing that Sonny Red Indelicato's son, Anthony "Bruno" Indelicato, would try to avenge his father's death, Sonny Black Napolitano thought it wise to move first and execute him. He asked Donnie Brasco to go with him. "Asked," of course, was a euphemism for "ordered." Brasco was in a bind. He had two options: obey or be forced to disclose his true identity. Option number two was the only possible solution. Brasco could be involved in all manner of plotting— and indeed, it was his job to do just that—but he obviously couldn't be a party to murder. Just as he was about to take action, Sonny Black was visited by two FBI agents at his own social club, who mockingly informed him that Donnie Brasco was in fact an undercover agent (his real name was Joe Pistone) who had managed to infiltrate the family for years. "Brasco" had had a front-row seat from which to spy on the Bonannos and the other families they dealt with.

Things turned out pretty well for Joe Pistone. Under the protective umbrella of a new identity, he wrote a best-selling book about his experiences, which was made into an equally successful movie. The fallout was less than pleasant for Sonny Black Napolitano. He had messed up in a way that anybody might have, but in his case the error was fatal. In mobland, saying you're sorry just doesn't cut it. Sonny Black would have to pay. For Big Joey not to make him pay would show weakness to his troops and to the other families. Testifying before Judge Garaufis, Salvatore Vitale recalled how Sonny Black's payment was planned in August 1981: "I went on a walk-talk with Joe Massino in Howard Beach, and he said: 'I have to give him [Sonny Black] a receipt for the Donnie Brasco situation.' I understood that to mean he wanted him dead."

Frank "Curly" Lino, a Bonanno capo who had fled the scene of the May 5 slayings, was to pick up Sonny Black at a restaurant in Brooklyn and tell him they were going to a meeting at a house on Staten Island. Sonny Black probably knew what he was in for and resigned himself to his fate. Some claim that he had already bequeathed a number of possessions to family and friends, including a gold watch and other items he was very fond of.

When they arrived at the house, Curly Lino pushed the victim down the basement stairs. At the bottom step, ready to die, Napolitano fell to his knees and didn't get up. A waiting gunman named Bobby shot Sonny Black once, but as he pulled the trigger again, his weapon jammed, emitting a barely audible click. "Hit me one more time. Make it good," Sonny Black mumbled painfully—a fitting gangster epitaph. An instant later, the smell of powder filled the air; his last wish had been granted.

Joe Massino sat outside in a van, ready to step out and finish the job in case Sonny Black tried to escape. When Lino emerged, the deed done, he walked straight to the van and handed Massino the keys to Sonny Black's car, which was still parked in Brooklyn.

"Was everything all right?" Big Joey asked.

CHAPTER 2

VENDETTA

THE NEW MISS MONT-ROYAL was an unpretentious eatery, with a sign out front displaying a selection of its specialties: pizza, spaghetti, shish kebab, charcoal barbecued steak. The establishment had air conditioning and the required permit to sell beer, wine and liquor. It stood at 707 Mont-Royal Avenue East, across from the Church of Notre-Dame-du-Très-Saint-Sacrement, in Montreal's Plateau Mont-Royal district. In time, a used book and record store would replace the restaurant. But in the 1960s and '70s, it served simple food to this working-class neighbourhood, decades before a gentrifying influx of arty types and young professionals changed it forever. The restaurant's co-owner, forty-two-year-old Rosario Gurreri, hailed from the same Sicilian town as Vito Rizzuto: Cattolica Eraclea.

As they filed out of church on Sunday, March 5, 1972, surprised parishioners were greeted by the sight of several police cruisers and a morgue van parked across the street in front of the New Miss Mont-Royal, where many of them liked to go for coffee after mass. Early that morning, Gurreri had left his home on Bouldaque Street in Saint-Léonard, a smallish but booming town in east-end Montreal that was home to most of the city's Italian community. At seven-fifteen or so in the morning, he unlocked the doors to his restaurant and proceeded to the kitchen to light the stoves for the day. A man, or more likely two, quietly followed him inside and attacked him with a butcher's cleaver, hacking at his neck and head a dozen times. Before fleeing, the killer or killers sank a hunting knife into Gurreri's chest.

Half an hour later, a waitress arrived for work. When she got to the kitchen, she found the lifeless body of her boss, sprawled on his stomach, blood pooled around him. She called Gurreri's brother, who called the police. When the morgue employees turned the body over to lift it onto a stretcher, they saw a gaping gash in the victim's face. The police found the knife. After a cursory search, nothing appeared to have been stolen from the establishment. The cash register hadn't even been opened. Police ruled out theft as a possible motive for the murder.

At first, investigators thought it might have been a crime of passion, judging by the way the killer had gone at the victim. But they didn't rule out the possibility that the restaurant owner had refused to pay his *pizzo*, or "protection money," to the Italian mob—though such a breach could hardly have been reason enough for such savage retribution.

A week later, Lieutenant-Detective Guy Gaudreau of the homicide squad informed the press that police were seeking two men, Leonardo Salvo, alias Pollari, age forty, and Leonardo Cammalleri, fifty-two. The suspects were already wanted by authorities in Italy for another murder, that of union organizer and politician Giuseppe Spagnolo, killed sixteen years earlier in Cattolica Eraclea. Back in Italy, Gurreri had incriminated Spagnolo's killers, and that was the reason why the co-owner of the New Miss Mont-Royal had been so brutally eliminated.

The assassination of Giuseppe Spagnolo speaks volumes about the true nature of the Sicilian Mafia, its history, the way it operates and its ramifications in Canada—beginning first and foremost with the Rizzuto family—as well as Canadian judicial authorities' incomprehensible indolence toward it. Virtually no one on this side of the Atlantic has ever heard of the slain political leader, but in Sicily, his memory endures. Journalist Calogero Giuffrida wrote a book about his life, with a preface by historian Francesco Renda, which was published in 2005 under the title *Delitto di Prestigio* (*Crime of Prestige*).

A bronze bust of the farm worker turned activist adorns a building on the Via Enna in Cattolica Eraclea. A wreath is laid there every year. Commemorations are held at regular intervals to remember the man who became the town's first elected mayor since the founding of the Italian Republic, a man who spent his entire life fighting for the rights of the peasant poor.

The son of a farmer, Spagnolo was born in 1900 in Cattolica Eraclea, located in Agrigento Province in southwestern Sicily and considered a Mafia stronghold. He left school after only two years to work the fields with his father. In the evenings, he taught himself to read and write. The teenage Spagnolo was too young to take part in the First World War. Peasants who had fought in the trenches, though, returned to Sicily imbued with socialist ideas. They began to demand, with mixed success, that the farmlands belonging to powerful barons and other nobles be shared among the workers. Spagnolo joined the fight. He was married and the father of three children, and personally suffered the same injustice as thousands of other farm workers. He barely managed to feed his family, growing wheat, corn and cotton, and picking almonds, pistachios, olives and carob beans in leased orchards.

His embrace of social causes led him to defy the regime of Benito Mussolini, which was protecting the interests of the industrial and agrarian bourgeoisie. In 1935, authorities arrested Spagnolo for anti-Fascist activity and sent him with other peasants to the penitentiary on the island of Pantelleria, halfway between Sicily and Tunisia, where he was interned for four years. There, the company of political prisoners helped radicalize him. After the Second World War and the death of Mussolini, he sought the mayoralty of Cattolica Eraclea under the banner of the Zappia leftist front, against the Christian Democrats, a party supported both by the Mafia and the landowning nobility, including Baron Francesco Agnelli, who owned most of the territory in and around Cattolica Eraclea.

Spagnolo won the election. He implemented several initiatives in favour of land redistribution and adopted measures benefiting the poorest citizens—for example, taxing water based on household income, not number of occupants. He would lose the next election, but that didn't keep him from his activism; he founded a farm co-operative that urged peasants to defy the landowners and the Mafia, and plant crops in fallow fields. His reward was a savage beating at the hands of eight men, with his twenty-six-year-old son Liborio looking on. Later, his home was set on fire in a bid to kill him; the arsonists were never caught.

To protect his family, Spagnolo took to sleeping in the fields on the outskirts of the town, refusing to go home. During the night of Saturday to Sunday, August 13 to 14, 1955, as he lay in a field in the Contrada Bissana between Cattolica Eraclea and Ciancina, a group of men that he knew well approached him and shot him repeatedly at close range.

Carabinieri were patrolling along the Platani River, which flows west of Cattolica Eraclea. In spite of the dim light, they saw three masked men riding horses, or perhaps mules, on the opposite shore, near the spot where Spagnolo had been killed. They also saw that one of them was thrown by his mount, which had a black coat, but he did not try to hold the animal back; it fled.

Spagnolo's wife and son worried the next morning when they didn't hear from him. They searched for most of the day. They finally found his body in a blood-soaked haystack. Though shocked and saddened, they were not surprised: more than forty-five unionists and leftist politicians had been assassinated by the Mafia between 1945 and 1955, along with countless peasants. Spagnolo's wife and son lifted his body into a cart and took him back to town. Dr. Salvatore Marino performed the autopsy and found that Giuseppe Spagnolo had been killed by seven bullets fired from shotguns made in Palermo by the Vincenzo Bernardelli company. The barrels had been sawn off.

Later, during Mass at Sant'Antonio Abate Church, Father Don Dinaro informed the faithful that a black donkey branded with the letters ox had been found wandering in the countryside. One Rosario Gurreri announced that it belonged to him. The *carabinieri* arrested him and accused him of being one of the three men they had seen on the banks of the Platani, near the scene of the crime. Gurreri initially denied any involvement, but three days later he made a confession.

A month earlier, the prisoner told the police, he had been approached by Leonardo Cammalleri, Leonardo Salvo and Giacinto Arcuri. To hear Gurreri tell it, the three men asked him to take part in Spagnolo's murder "for reasons of honour": they claimed Spagnolo had offended Cammalleri's mother-in-law. The exact nature of the affront remained unclear, but Gurreri intimated that it was a sexual impropriety.

He told the police that he had refused to be a party to the crime, but that he had agreed to lend Arcuri his mule on the evening of August 13. Gurreri had saddled the animal and led it to the shore of the Platani. He also admitted having seen Cammalleri that evening; the man had been wearing a long black cape but carried no weapon. Gurreri then said that he had run into Arcuri on the Via Monsignor Amato, a street in Cattolica Eraclea, the day after the murder. He concluded his testimony by stating that Arcuri told him that he and his accomplices had killed Spagnolo but had lost the donkey as they fled the approaching *carabinieri*.

The police began to search for the three suspects. They had information suggesting that the men had initially been hidden in the home of Antonino Manno, the unchallenged head of the Mafia over a broad territory bound by the towns of Cattolica Eraclea, Siculiana and Montallegro. Those who knew Manno were convinced that he had orchestrated Spagnolo's assassination, and that the gunmen were merely doing his bidding. Manno was the father-in-law of Nicolò Rizzuto—who by the time of the murder had already emigrated to Montreal—and lived near the Chiesa Madre (the Mother Church) in Cattolica Eraclea.

A rumour spread rapidly: the fugitives, disguised as women, had taken refuge in the Chiesa Madre, where Father Giuseppe Cuffaro was hiding them in the sacristy. When confronted, the priest claimed that Spagnolo had committed suicide—which would have been a miracle given the fact that his body had seven bullet wounds. Spagnolo's daughter urged residents to assemble in the piazza in town and demand that the priest deliver her father's murderers into the hands of justice. The three suspects managed to escape the church, still in women's clothing. With the help of Antonino Manno and his extensive network of Mafia contacts in North America, they were able to book passage across the Atlantic, fleeing to Canada and the United States.

Father Cuffaro refused to say a funeral Mass for Spagnolo on the pretense that the dead man had been a Communist and thus a non-believer. The ceremony was therefore organized by Spagnolo's family and friends. Hundreds of people came to pay their respects. The men wore white shirts and the women, black scarves. Francesco Renda, an intellectual who many years later would write the preface to *Delitto di Prestigio,* the book in memory of Spagnolo, gave the eulogy. The citizens of Cattolica Eraclea had gathered, and several political parties throughout Sicily had sent delegations. A long cortège followed Spagnolo's coffin to the cemetery.

Gurreri, Cammalleri, Salvo and Arcuri stood trial in the Assizes Court of Agrigento, the capital of the province of the same name. When called to testify, Antonino Manno made no secret of his contempt for the institution and refused to answer the prosecution's questions. Leonardo Cammalleri and Leonardo Salvo were sentenced, *in absentia,* to life in prison. But during the trial, a letter from a priest in Montreal had reached the court. The clergyman wrote that Giacinto Arcuri had just been killed in a traffic accident in Canada. What the letter didn't make clear was that the dead Giacinto Arcuri was not the same man as the Giacinto Arcuri on trial for murder. The Sicilian authorities asked no questions, however, and closed the case, thus confirming the wisdom of the Sicilian proverb "a friend with influence is more precious than a hundred pieces of gold."

The accused Giacinto Arcuri had not been killed in any road accident. He was alive and well in Montreal and would eventually move to Toronto. (Thirty years later, after his conviction for the murder of Giuseppe Spagnolo had been rendered moot because of his presumed death, he would be among those posting $2.5 million bail for mobster Gerlando Sciascia as he awaited trial on heroin trafficking charges.)

Cammalleri, too, managed to live free as a bird in Canada. He was cautious, however. He posed as a Venezuelan national by the name of Giuseppe Antonio Nardo. In 1966, his daughter Giovanna married the young Vito Rizzuto in Toronto. Cammalleri did not enter the church;

he stayed outside in his car for the entire ceremony. No police officers disturbed him as he sat there, despite the fact that he was the subject of an official wanted notice issued by the Italian authorities—and that Maria Spagnolo, Giuseppe's daughter, who had also immigrated to Canada, had notified the police that her father's murderer would be among the wedding guests.

Salvo, named in the same wanted notice, hid out in Buffalo, New York. As for Gurreri, he spent four years in a Sicilian prison. He was not convicted of murder, merely of being an accessory to it. Several questions remained unanswered, however. Peasants swore they had seen four men, not three, leaving the scene of the crime on the night of Spagnolo's murder. Seven shots had been fired. The *lupara*, the sawed-off shotgun that was the Mafia's weapon of choice, is a hunting gun with two smooth-bore, side-by-side barrels; it can fire only two cartridges.* Why would one of the three killers have reloaded and fired a third shot? Was it not more likely that there had been four killers? And was Rosario Gurreri the fourth man?

At any rate, on his release from prison, Gurreri emigrated as well and arrived in Canada on July 9, 1962. He opened his restaurant on Mont-Royal Avenue under the name Michel Gurreri, but in the end, he couldn't hide behind a French-sounding name. Once the Montreal police learned who he was, they had no doubt as to the motive for this man's murder: he had been the victim of a blood feud—a *vendetta,* which in Italian means "vengeance."

The word "Mediterranean" comes from the Latin *mediterraneus,* meaning "in the middle of the earth." Sicily, the largest island in the Mediterranean Sea, was thus in the centre of the world as the Greeks and Romans understood it. It was a location that conferred a strategic advantage, as the

---

* The word *lupara* is derived from *lupo,* Italian for "wolf," the animal traditionally hunted with this weapon. The shotguns' barrels were sawn off to make them easier to use in vegetation—as well as harder to spot under a coat in an urban setting. The *lupara* is one of the oldest firearms in existence in Sicily.

Allied forces would find in 1943. To control Sicily was to control the Mediterranean. The island's original inhabitants were invaded by the Phoenicians, formidable seafarers from what is now Lebanon, who perfected naval construction techniques. They were supplanted by the Greeks, Carthaginians, Romans, Vandals, Ostrogoths, Byzantines, Arabs, Normans, Aragonese, Spanish and Bourbons, not to mention the French, the Germans and even, for a short time, the English and their allies: Americans and Canadians.

That history of unceasing conquests profoundly marked the character of Sicilians, causing them to mistrust strangers and turn always to their families, as the godfather himself, Joseph Bonanno, explained in his autobiography, *A Man of Honor:*

> Sicily has been buffeted by foreign influences for well over two thousand years . . . Greek genius built the temple at Segesta, but Sicilian genius made it possible to endure subjugation and to survive long after the Greek town fell to ruin. Out of necessity, Sicilians put all their talents and energy into creating a life-style of survival, a peculiar and distinctive way of life that over the years became Tradition. Prevented from participating in the rule of their own land, Sicilians withdrew all the more into their own families. Everyone inside the family was a friend, all outsiders were suspect.

Exploited by colonial laws and cheated by the civil servants of foreign states, Sicilians developed their own laws and codes, and their own ways of doing business, Bonanno continues: "In an unjust world, it was necessary to create one's own justice. A Sicilian of the old Tradition gives his highest allegiance to his family. Outside of that, however, he's proudly independent."

Of course, such a description of the Sicilian character by one of history's most infamous Mafiosi is an attempt—and a particularly unsubtle one at that—to justify contempt for the law. It is a contempt that has nothing to do with the chivalrous rebellion mythologized by the likes of a Robin Hood, and everything to do with the lure of money and the thirst for power; the "family" was nothing more than a means to indulge one and slake the other. Despite this, the psychological profile of Sicilians that Bonanno draws is not entirely unfounded.

In his autobiography, Bonanno recalls a fable on the origin of the Mafia—which, once again, cast an organization of killers in the choice role. Like many legends, the story of the Sicilian Vespers is partly rooted in historical fact, specifically a popular uprising against their domination at the hands of the French king, Charles of Anjou. The rebellion began in Palermo and Corleone on March 31, 1282—the Tuesday after Easter. Tax collectors were posted outside the doors to churches, accosting the faithful who had come for vespers. Bonanno takes up the story:

> As it happened, a young lady of rare beauty, who was soon to be married, was going to church with her mother when a French soldier by the name Droetto, under the pretext of helping the tax agents, manhandled the young lady. Then he dragged her behind the church and raped her. The terrified mother ran through the streets, crying, *Ma fia, ma fia!* This means "My daughter, my daughter" in Sicilian. The boyfriend of the young lady found Droetto and killed him with a knife. The mother's cry, repeated by others, rang through the streets, throughout Palermo and throughout Sicily. *Ma fia* soon became the rallying cry of the resistance movement, which adopted the phrase as an acronym for *Morte Alla Francia, Italia Anela*—"Death to France, Italy cries out."

In fact, etymologists are lost in conjecture when it comes to the origins of the word "Mafia." The *Dictionnaire historique de la langue française* claims it was borrowed from the Sicilian and originally meant "grace, allure, audacity." That remains to be seen. The word first entered the popular imagination around 1863, when the play *I mafiusi di la Vicaria*, by the Sicilian writers Giuseppe Rizzoto and Gaetano Mosca, was first performed.

As early as 1828, the chief prosecutor of Agrigento reported to the courts about a group of a hundred or so people bound by an oath of allegiance who were active in various illicit pursuits: theft of cattle, intimidation, extortion of funds both public and private, and murder. The fraternity comprised citizens of all social strata, including property owners, priests, storekeepers and known criminals. They were active in Cattolica Eraclea, Cianciana, Santo Stefano di Quisquina, Palazzo Adriano and many more small towns in the region. The prosecutor never employed the word "Mafia" in his report, however.

Historical conditions were ripe in Sicily for the emergence of such covert brotherhoods. For centuries, the feudal landlords and popes who ruled the island had imposed an arbitrary brand of justice. Little by little, the idea spread that private justice was preferable. Going before the official courts was seen as a sign of cowardice. The nobler method of redressing a perceived slight was to invoke the clan code of honour. Vendettas were encouraged.

Central to this value system is *omertà,* the code of silence. Foreigners who travel in Sicily will often notice that the shutters on houses are closed. "Whoever is blind, deaf and mute will live a hundred years in peace," goes a Sicilian proverb. *Omertà* means much more than merely being able to shut up. It is the first precept of a strict code of honour. Some etymologists believe the word derives from *omu,* which means "man" in Sicilian. A man who violates this rule is no longer a man; he is a coward. In this system of honour, one's dignity matters more than one's life. *Omertà* is virility taken to the extreme: you are better off dying than forfeiting your true nature as a man.

Under the code of silence it is categorically forbidden to co-operate with the forces of law and order or even to address them, even if one is the victim of a crime. If someone is convicted of a murder he never committed, he must serve his time and never tell the police the identity of the true culprit. *Omertà* embodies the values of loyalty and solidarity in the face of authority. You can kill your worst enemy, but to betray him is shameful. The Mafia made that rule their own and enforced it not only among their kind, the so-called men of honour, but among the entire population.

In the stasis of a feudal system, however, where the all-powerful landowners held the monopoly on economic resources as well as on the use of violence, it was difficult for a parallel criminal organization to flourish.

The situation would change with the birth and unification of modern Italy. In 1860, Giuseppe Garibaldi and his Redshirts landed at Marsala, on Sicily's west coast, chased the last remnants of Bourbon rule from the island and reunited it with the rest of Italy. A notorious anticleric, Garibaldi famously likened Pope Pius IX to "a cubic metre of manure," professed ideals of social justice and promised agrarian reforms as well as the abolition of a tax on the grinding of wheat. He drew popular support. Two thousand *picciotti* (rebellious young peasants, often criminals) had joined his troops in routing the French from Sicily.

Once Garibaldi left, his promises revealed themselves for what they really were: so many words. The anticipated redistribution of lands amounted essentially to an exchange of deeds between the wealthiest landowners. Food prices soared. Riots became commonplace and criminality grew to epidemic proportions. Thugs acted as middlemen, demanding commissions on the sale and leasing of land. Rural leaseholders, called *gabelloti,* managed the estates for the barons, who typically lived in Palermo or Naples. They were assisted by *campieri,* armed guards. Together these men formed the structure of the Mafia, which became indispensable to the rich and powerful. The biggest landowners, including the Catholic Church, relied on them to maintain order.

Gabelloti and *campieri* determined the relations between the landowners and peasants. The peasants paid the *campieri* for the right to farm, and the owners paid the *gabelloti* to protect their assets. The *campieri* would march through the centre of cities and towns and, with the flick of a hand or a nod of the head, identify the men who were allowed to work the land that day, simultaneously snubbing those they wanted nothing to do with. Obviously, the odds of known socialists, trade unionists or indocile workers being chosen were quite slim. During tense periods of social conflict, the *campieri* trained private armies to enforce the landowners' will.

The abundance of cheap labour in Sicily deterred mechanization, and the island went on providing agricultural resources while the north of Italy industrialized. Improvements in communications between the island and the peninsula—notably a daily ferry between Palermo and

Naples—enabled the Mafia to extend its political influence all the way to Rome. Political parties needed its services to win elections. The right to vote was reserved for landowners and citizens who could read or write—barely 10 percent of the population. In practice, the members of honourable society decided who could vote. Not surprisingly, the winning candidates systematically included Mafiosi or their allies, especially in the western part of Sicily.

The same system was implemented at the local level. Mayors associated with the Mafia were empowered to distribute permits for the sale of tobacco, salt and stamps. The police, prosecutors and judges of Palermo and Agrigento had to show complacency when Mafiosi were suspected of crimes, lest these officials be isolated, threatened or eliminated. The *capomafia* of each district was an important person, who commanded a kiss on the hand and to whom payment had to be made should one desire employment in the public service. The Sicilian press remained mum about the rampant corruption, claiming that the Mafia didn't exist.

In the years between 1860 and the First World War, poverty and the crushing of the peasant unions drove 1.5 million Sicilians to emigrate. Most of them went to the Americas, both North and South, and in particular the United States. Among them were highly ranked personages of the Sicilian Mafia, like Giuseppe Balsamo. After arriving in New York in 1895, he built an organization known as the Black Hand, which specialized in extortion, targeting even the poorest of their compatriots.

Up to 90 percent of Italian Americans were threatened with reprisals if they dared disobey the requirements of the Black Hand. Ignazio Saietta, a Sicilian gangster who lived in New York City's Little Italy, strangled his victims and burned their bodies in East Harlem. A lieutenant in the New York City Police Department (NYPD) and pioneer in the investigation of organized crime in the United States, Joseph Petrosino, took on the Black Handers and was eventually sent to Italy to gather intelligence and evidence. Within days, he was assassinated—he is still the only member of the NYPD ever to be murdered overseas. Balsamo was suspected of having ordered the killing.

Italians arriving in Montreal were exploited by immigration agents called *padroni,* who exhibited typical Mafia behaviour. Cases of abuse became so flagrant that in 1905 the federal government established a royal commission to look into the immigration of Italian workers to Montreal and alleged fraudulent practices by employment agencies.

During the First World War, the *campieri* of Sicily grew rich on the black market. They supplied the army with horses and mules. Meanwhile, peasants called up to fight died by the thousands in the trenches, or broke their backs working dawn to dusk in the fields. When peace was finally declared, the Mafia's arrogance knew no bounds. No longer content to function merely as a state within the state, it began demanding exorbitant tariffs from the biggest landowners in exchange for the safekeeping of their property. Woe to those who refused to pay. All this proved too much for the fascist dictator Benito Mussolini, who dispatched a prefect named Cesare Mori to Palermo to clean up the island's affairs.

Given carte blanche, vested with virtually limitless powers, Mori had thousands of people, many of them innocent, thrown in prison. His men kidnapped women and children to force their Mafia husbands and fathers to surrender. If that tactic proved unsuccessful, he laid siege to towns, going so far as to have the water supply cut off. His nickname, *il prefetto de fero* (the iron prefect), suited him like a glove. The Ucciardone in Palermo, a prison since medieval times, acquired the nickname "Casa Mori." Many members of the Mafia were forced to flee Italy. One of them, who had an arrest warrant issued against him, was Giuseppe (Joseph) Bonanno. He and his cousin Peter Magaddino went to Cuba and, from there, entered the United States illegally.

The landowners naturally applauded the measures implemented by Mussolini and the Fascists, because they meant they no longer had to pay off the *campieri.* But in fact, the government had merely replaced the Mafia, seizing their monopoly on violent intimidation and wielding it to their advantage.

Il Duce declared victory in the war against the Mafia. In 1929, Mori was appointed a senator and recalled to Rome. His term came to an end just as he was beginning to uncover the relations between the Mafia's leaders and powerful political figures. Those well acquainted with the underworld organization knew that Mussolini's thunderous speeches hid an insidious truth: he may have cut off the beast's tentacles, but the heart and head remained. The "third tier" of the Mafia, made up of seemingly respectable people in high places, went on plotting in the comfort of the shadows—and kept the organization very much alive.

In the meantime, in the United States, the Mafia was experiencing boom years thanks to Prohibition. The Volstead Act had become law on January 16, 1920, and it marked the beginning of a beautiful decade for American organized crime. At first, the Mafia clans ran their own clandestine distilleries, but too many of them were shut down and destroyed by the police. It was far easier, and far more lucrative, to buy the forbidden liquor in a foreign country and smuggle it in as contraband.

That foreign, and friendly, country lay just to the north. The bootleggers imported massive amounts of alcohol from Canada. Their largest supplier was the Bronfman brothers' dynasty. Driven out of Saskatchewan by public opinion and a provincial government outraged by his family business dealings with mobsters south of the border, Samuel Bronfman settled in Montreal, where he built one of the largest distilleries in the world and eventually bought out another, Joseph E. Seagram's and Sons. Production was overwhelmingly destined for the United States; only 20 percent of the liquor distilled in Canada was consumed domestically. Around 1930, when the Canadian government began cracking down on exports southward, the Bronfmans set up shop in the French-controlled islands of Saint-Pierre and Miquelon, in the Gulf of St. Lawrence.

Their agents negotiated with the most infamous of American mobsters, including Frank Costello and Meyer Lansky of New York. Some claim that Sam Bronfman travelled to New York to meet with Lansky, who would eventually become principal counsellor, or *consigliere*, to Salvatore "Charlie Lucky" Luciano, the founder of the modern Mafia. Near the end of his life, an embittered Lansky asked: "Why is Lansky a 'gangster' and not the Bronfman and Rosenstiel families? I was involved with all of them in the 1920s, although they do not like to talk about it today and change the subject when my name is mentioned."

Be that as it may, the rain of dollars that poured into the Mafia's coffers during the "dry years" exacerbated inner tensions. The Castellammarese War, which erupted around 1930 in New York, would result in a body count in the dozens and culminate with the implementation of power structures that remain operational to this day, not only in the United States but in Canada as well. The name given to this power struggle between clans referred to Castellammare del Golfo, a small town that sits halfway between Palermo and Marsala, on the western coast of Sicily, and is renowned as the birthplace of many an influential member of the Mafia in America, among them Joseph Bonanno, Salvatore Maranzano and Joseph Barbara.

By 1930 the boss of Cosa Nostra in New York, the Marsala-born Giuseppe Masseria, was sufficiently alarmed at the growing threat posed by the Castellammarese faction, led by Salvatore Maranzano, that he ordered his hit men to take out its soldiers one by one. Maranzano struck back. A year later, the bloody turf war had claimed eighty-five victims in both camps. Maranzano briefly became *capo di tutti i capi*, "boss of all bosses." On the advice of Lansky and Costello, Lucky Luciano—who had made a fortune with bootlegging rackets and had been Masseria's lieutenant since 1925—soon manoeuvred deftly to settle the conflict on his own terms. The Castellammarese War had attracted plenty of police response, and that was bad for business. He had Masseria rubbed out, and before long it was Maranzano's turn.

Born Salvatore Lucunia in Sicily in 1897, Lucky Luciano arrived in New York City at age nine. By the time he was a teenager, he was already a gang leader. He was once severely wounded when his throat was slashed by rivals who left him for dead. He survived but bore long scars of the attack across his neck, leading his men to bestow the "Lucky" sobriquet.

With Masseria and Maranzano out of the way, Luciano took control of the New York Mafia. It was on his suggestion that the "Commission" was created—a sort of board of directors on which the heads of the city's Five Families sat and were tasked with settling mobland disputes.

They were joined by Al Capone, from Chicago, and Stefano Magaddino, from Buffalo.

Some Mafia historians and analysts, however, attribute paternity of the Commission to Maranzano. "Salvatore Maranzano arrived in New York in 1927, saying he had been given a mission by the Palermitan boss to unite the American families under a single chief," states an analysis document by the RCMP intelligence service. "After a bloody war, in the spring of 1931, in the Bronx, he organized the first official meeting of Cosa Nostra, the name chosen for the American Mafia. At that meeting, Maranzano divided Cosa Nostra into new families, including five in New York. In the fall of that year, Luciano had Maranzano killed, because he was planning to become the boss of bosses in the United States."

The Five Families survive to this day. In decreasing order of stature, they are the Gambinos, Genoveses, Bonannos, Luccheses and Colombos. There is no longer any "boss of all bosses" per se in the U.S. Mafia, but the head of the Gambino family asserts dominance over the others, in particular the Bonanno family. The latter is not the biggest outfit in terms of membership, but it stands out from the others in more than one respect: it is the most violent and the most intrinsically Sicilian. The Bonanno organization accepts few members who are not from Sicilian families, unlike the Genovese family, for instance, whose longtime head was Vincent "The Chin" Gigante, born in Manhattan of Neapolitan parents.

With the founding of the Commission, the Bonannos inherited control of the largest Mafia branch outside New York: the Montreal crew (Chicago and Buffalo are not branches, as they are headed by independent families). The Montreal Mafia was never considered a "sixth family" on a par with the original five, however. Vito Rizzuto himself, when he pleaded guilty for his role in the three captains murder plot in 2005, told the court he was a soldier in the Bonanno family. This does not mean the Montreal Mafia has never displayed any degree of desire for autonomy from the New York parent, but these vague ambitions have never amounted to any real independence. Ultimately, Montreal remains under the heel of the Commission. Whenever the Bonanno family is in disarray—and it often has been—it is generally the members of the Commission's ruling Gambino family who are charged with settling disputes, and that includes those in Montreal.

In 1936, Luciano was convicted and received a sentence of thirty to fifty years in prison for running the largest prostitution ring in American history. He was eventually sent to the maximum-security prison at Dannemora, in Upstate New York, twenty-five or so kilometres west of Plattsburgh.

In February 1942, the *Normandie,* a luxury liner being refitted to carry U.S. troops to Europe, caught fire and sank in the Hudson River. Was it an accident or sabotage? The Office of Naval Intelligence took no chances; New York City's waterfront had to be protected, so its officers sought the help of the Mafia members who controlled the docks. At their suggestion, the navy later contacted Luciano.

Lucky agreed to help the navy but in return insisted on a transfer to more comfortable digs: the Great Meadows Penitentiary, halfway between Lake Champlain and Albany, the state capital. Though he was now Inmate No. 15684, he still wielded considerable influence among his troops. The extent of his co-operation with the U.S. military remains open to much debate, but the fact remains that there was not a single labour action or act of sabotage in the ports of the Eastern Seaboard for the remainder of the Second World War. Luciano apparently provided the government with invaluable information and, through intermediaries, convinced the Mafia in Sicily not to offer any resistance once the Allies landed on the Mediterranean island.

In fact, the prospect of the Allied invasion quite enthused Luciano, much to the amusement of his friend Meyer Lansky. Years later, Lansky would tell his biographers that Luciano was prepared to take skydiving lessons so that he could join the paratroopers who would drop from the skies over Sicily. "I had to laugh at the thought of Charlie landing in a tree or on top of a court," his *consigliere* recalled. "Poor old Lucky—playboy to prisoner to paratrooper in his dreams." At any rate, Luciano certainly pushed the right anti-fascist buttons with the intelligence officers who interrogated him: "I told 'em somethin' hadda be done with this guy Hitler. I said that if somebody could knock off this son of a bitch, the war would be over in five minutes."

Within months of the war's end, New York State governor Thomas E. Dewey commuted Luciano's sentence, on the condition that he return to Italy. In his years as a prosecutor and district attorney before being elected, Dewey had built a reputation as a man of integrity, known for his fierce opposition to the Mafia. He'd sent Lucky to prison ten years earlier; now he sang his praises for having served the nation. "Upon the entry of the United States into the war, Luciano's aid was sought by the Armed Services in inducing others to provide information concerning possible enemy attack," he explained. "It appears he co-operated in such effort, although the actual value of the information procured is not clear. His record in prison is wholly satisfactory."

The first Allied landings in Europe, code-named Operation Husky, took place on July 10, 1943, on the south coast of Sicily. Axis troops had just bitten the dust in North Africa. U.S. president Franklin D. Roosevelt and British prime minister Winston Churchill had met six months earlier in Casablanca to map out their strategy. As the Phoenicians and Romans had centuries earlier, they saw that control of Sicily was the key to dominion over the Mediterranean. The island was poorly defended. Still, British and Canadian troops fought bloody battles in the eastern part of Sicily against well-trained German battalions. The Americans had an easier time in the west, the Mafia's stronghold: Lieutenant General George S. Patton would boast of having achieved "the fastest blitzkrieg in history" in marching some three hundred kilometres in four days to reach Palermo, on the north coast.

The U.S. forces were crushingly superior to the unmotivated and ill-equipped Italians. Besides, having experienced bloody repression under Prefect Mori, the Mafiosi had no need of Luciano's urgings to help drive out the *Fascisti*. Plenty of things have been said and written about these aspects of the Sicilian campaign, including claims by some authors that the Mafia protected Allied troops from enemy sniper fire along major roads and provided guides on mountain routes.

There are also stories of Mafia bosses, including Calogero Vizzini, playing a major role in the rapid advance of the U.S. troops, but serious historians discount them as pure legend. Regardless, Don Vizzini was named an honorary U.S. Army colonel and appointed mayor of the town of Villalba by occupation forces. The leftist writer Michele Pantaleone, later a prominent anti-Mafia journalist and politician, was a native of the same town, and one of the first to criticize the policies of the Allied Military Government of Occupied Territories (AMGOT). In his opinion, "the Allied occupation and the subsequent slow restoration of democracy reinstated the Mafia with its full powers, put it once more on the way to becoming a political force, and returned to the Onorata Societa [the Honoured Society] the weapons which Fascism had snatched from it."

The Americans preferred to see Mafia members rather than communists heading the town councils and other government organizations of Sicily. After an initial flirtation with separatist ideas, Don Calò Vizzini and the majority of the Mafia bosses sided with the Christian Democrats—as did the U.S. Office of Strategic Services (OSS), the forerunner of the Central Intelligence Agency (CIA).

The Christian Democrat Party won the elections of 1948 and would rule Italy for the next forty-five years as part of innumerable coalitions. One of the party's main objectives, which both the Mafia and the U.S. government backed enthusiastically, was to keep the communists as far from the seats of power as possible; the Italian Communist Party was the largest among the member countries of the newly formed North Atlantic Treaty Organization (NATO). This strategic alliance with the Mafia would, however, contribute to making Italy one of the most corrupt and indebted of the world's developed countries.

Don Calò Vizzini's stature within the Mafia is also disputed. One fact is known: he founded a candy factory in Palermo with Lucky Luciano, who had settled in Naples after his deportation from the United States. The candies were exported throughout Europe as well as to the United States and Canada. In 1954, the Rome daily *Avanti!* ran a photo of the factory under the headline: "Textiles and Sweets on the Drug Route." Though they were never able to amass proof to substantiate their suspicions, the police were convinced that the candy trade was a cover for a far more lucrative one: heroin.

Don Calò died that same year of natural causes. The *New York Times* story on his passing was titled "Sicilian Mafia 'King' Dies." Indeed, many did view him as the *capo di tutti i capi;* others countered that the title did not exist in the Sicilian Mafia, and they are probably right. At any rate, he received a grandiose funeral in Villalba, the town over which he had reigned supreme. Thousands of black-clad peasants were joined by politicians, priests and Mafia dons including Giuseppe Genco Russo and Don Francesco Paolo Bontade in silent march behind the hearse bearing the man who, when he was alive, had ordered people murdered by the dozens.

"When I die, the Mafia dies," Don Calò had once said. But his death no more signalled the demise of the Mafia than the eventual closing down of the Palermo candy factory spelled an end to the manufacture of heroin in Italy. On the contrary.

On October 10, 1957, Lucky Luciano stood surveying the lobby of the Grande Albergo e delle Palme, the most exclusive hotel in the history of Palermo. Today swallowed up by the Hilton chain, the Grande Albergo was originally built as a sumptuous private home, north of the lively neighbourhood around the Vucciria market where goldsmiths, scrap metal dealers, shoemakers and pasta merchants had proliferated. Converted into a luxury hotel in the nineteenth century, the establishment had seen its share of famous and distinguished guests within its walls, including Richard Wagner, who stayed there in the 1880s, in a grand suite with a blue ceiling and walls bedecked with huge mirrors, eventually completing his final opera, *Parsifal.* It was also there that the composer sat for a famous portrait by Renoir.

Over the next four days, Lucky would hold court in this lavish palace, welcoming some two and a half dozen visitors who, though arguably just as famous as Wagner, were rather less distinguished. And indeed it was in the *Sala Wagner* that this summit meeting of U.S. and Sicilian Mafia bosses was held. The American delegation was headed by Joseph Bonanno. Almost all his men hailed, like him, from Castellammare del Golfo. They included his *caporegime* Carmine Galante, who had lived in

Montreal from 1952 to 1955, and John Bonventre, his vice-capo. His cousins Antonio, Giuseppe and Gaspare Magaddino, whose family controlled Buffalo, were in attendance, as was Detroit boss John Priziola.

The Sicilians were led by the head of the ruling *famiglia* in Castellammare del Golfo, another man named Magaddino, a relative of the Buffalo family. Others included Don Giuseppe Genco Russo, a unanimously reviled mobster who styled himself the new boss of bosses and successor to Don Calò Vizzini, and men whose importance would become apparent years later: Salvatore "Ciaschiteddu" (Little Bird) Greco, Gaetano Badalamenti and Tommaso Buscetta, who would also spend time in Montreal and, much later, become a high-profile *pentito*—a "penitent."

The emissaries of the Sicilian and U.S. Mafias spent those four days mapping out co-operative strategies for rendering the business of heroin trafficking as efficient as possible, taking advantage of existing cigarette smuggling routes. In the post-war years, Luciano had made Havana a profitable hub for moving the drug into the United States. But revolution had come to Cuba's shores, and new connections were needed.

Luciano and Bonanno suggested that their Sicilian counterparts adopt the model of the Commission, established twenty-six years earlier in New York, and create a structure to regulate the 150 or so clans engaged in bloody infighting on the island. Provincial committees were set up to settle disputes, along with a central, interprovincial commission that was to be called the "Cupola." The new Mafia would be more urbanized, more aggressive, more business-oriented. Salvatore Greco was appointed *segretario*, or leader, of the Cupola.

This structural change meant American Mafiosi could deal directly with the Cupola to facilitate the importing of massive quantities of heroin. At the time, the trade in the drug was dominated by the famous French Connection: the main suppliers were Corsicans, and the opium was produced in Turkey—farmers there held permits to grow poppy plants and legally supply pharmaceutical companies, but many sold their excess crops to drug traffickers.

The Turkish opium was transformed into morphine base, then sent to Syria or Lebanon for transfer to the clandestine laboratories of Marseilles and Paris, operated by the Corsicans. Enter highly trained French chemists who knew the techniques for refining morphine base into heroin of exceptional quality. From there, the white powder was bagged and eventually exported to the United States, often passing through Montreal.

On November 10, 1955, the RCMP had found fourteen sacks of heroin weighing a kilogram each in a search of the *Saint-Malo,* a cargo ship out of Le Havre that had just docked in the Port of Montreal. The street value of the dope was more than fourteen million dollars. It was the biggest haul of its kind ever in North America. "In the early 1950s, the clandestine processing of heroin from morphine base had shifted to the hands of the French Corsican traffickers, along with a substantial share of the import trade into the United States," a U.S. Senate subcommittee investigating organized crime reported in 1963. "The advent of the Corsicans as major traffickers brought changes in the smuggling operations; for years, the main port of entry had been New York, but now the French Corsicans supplied the drugs to their French-speaking Canadian confederates for smuggling into the United States."

During his years in Montreal, Carmine Galante, Joe Bonanno's right-hand man, had mingled with the Canadian accomplices of the French Connection. He was well positioned to judge the sheer magnitude of the profits to be made in the dope trade. The Mafia leaders agreed to do business with the Corsican syndicates; if they could become their sole client, so much the better. Indeed, illicit labs in Sicily had already begun morphine refining operations before the meeting at the Grande Albergo. These operations would be pressed into greater service.

A follow-up conference was scheduled for a few weeks later, in November, this time in the United States. That month, a routine investigation triggered by a complaint about a bounced cheque led a New York State trooper, Sergeant Edgar D. Croswell, to a hotel in Binghamton, an upstate town halfway between New York and Buffalo, not far from the border with Pennsylvania. Croswell was intrigued by the behaviour of a young man at the hotel reception desk who booked three rooms and informed the clerk that his father would be settling the bill. The young man was the son of Joseph Barbara, an area resident of some repute—not so much as the local distributor of Canada Dry soft drinks but for shadier dealings. Every police officer in the area knew Joe "The Barber" Barbara was a close associate of Buffalo Mafia boss Stefano Magaddino. And it was public knowledge that Barbara handed out generous bribes to local law enforcement. Croswell's palms, however, were not among those being greased.

On the afternoon of November 13, the eager sergeant, accompanied by state-police investigator Vincent Vasisko travelled to the Parkway Motel. There they saw two expensive cars, one of which had out-of-state plates. Croswell began noting the licence numbers and checking the owners' identities. One belonged to Buffalo capo James LaDuca. The other was registered to Buckeye Vending of Cleveland, with the tag MN373—the company was run by John Scalish, the boss of Cleveland. The same two cars were seen by Troopers on the parkway later that night.

The next day, November 14, accompanied by two Treasury agents, Croswell and Vasisko drove to the home of Joseph Barbara, an imposing stone manor fronting a twenty-hectare estate that extended to the top of a hill in the small town of Apalachin, just west of Binghamton. Some thirty cars and limousines were parked in front of the stone house. They set up a roadblock at the foot of McFall Road, leading to the estate. The guests panicked. Some, including Vito Genovese, attempted to flee by car but were stopped. Others ran through mud, with only shiny leather shoes on their feet, and tried to flee through the woods, at the risk of tearing their expensive silk suits and losing their gold cufflinks. Many escaped in the confusion. Reinforcements were sent and, in the end, the police nabbed a total of fifty-eight mobsters.

Among the guests at the "convention" that day were Joe Bonanno and possibly Carmine Galante. Police still believe that there is good reason to believe Stefano Magaddino, Detroit boss Joe Zerilli and Chicago boss Sam Giancanna were among those who escaped. In all, anywhere from sixty to a hundred Mafia leaders (accounts vary) from all across the United States as well as Canada and Italy had come to Apalachin. When police sorted through the list, they found that half of the captured men had been born in the United States and the other half in Sicily. None of the gangsters was armed. Almost to a man, they assured the arresting officers that they had come simply to visit their friend Joe Barbara, having heard that he had fallen ill. Investigators eventually learned that the guests had been summoned by Vito Genovese, who planned to assert his authority as boss of bosses. But a crucial item on the agenda at Apalachin was the sealing of the deal that would see the Sicilian and American Mafia work together in the narcotics trade, as had been decided at the earlier summit at the Grande Albergo.

As planned, Montreal would get a piece of the action. A choice piece.

CHAPTER 3

FROM CATTOLICA ERACLEA TO MONTREAL

DECADES AGO, the *comune* of Cattolica Eraclea bustled with activity. More than ten thousand men, women and children—peasants, artisans, shopkeepers—worked the fields, took sheep out to pasture, pressed olives, sold tools or bought fruit and transported it to the provincial capital, Agrigento, to be loaded onto ships and exported. Since the Second World War, the town's population has shrunk by half, but a few kilometres to the south, the seaside remains animated. In the summer months, Sicilians like to kick back on the beach at Bovo Marina, near the splendid Greek ruins of Eraclea Minoa. They escape the stifling sun by strolling in the shadow of white chalk cliffs or relaxing under the soft green pines. Nearby, the *Valle dei templi*, the Valley of Temples, site of the Ancient Greek city of Agrakas, attracts archaeology buffs by the thousands.

Tourists are a rare sight in the town proper, however, and it doesn't rate a mention in travel guides. A visitor will be hard pressed to find a hotel. Perched on its hill, Cattolica Eraclea is dying a slow death. There is no danger of the cars that roll through its quiet, narrow streets striking any children. On the benches in the piazza, dignified, severe old-timers exchange only terse greetings. They refrain from speaking with strangers, whose comings and goings they follow with suspicious eyes.

It all seems frozen in time: the houses with their decaying walls, the monuments, the empty churches and, beyond the fields, the Platani river, whose bed runs dry on the hottest days of summer. The town is not completely out of step with modernity, however; the municipal council has its own Web site—on which it decries the mass exodus of its sons and daughters to Canada and the United States, "a sad phenomenon whereby the number of inhabitants has sharply declined." Indeed, there are far more entrepreneurs and professionals on the membership list of the Associazione Cattolica Eraclea di Montreal, in Saint-Léonard, than in the town that gave it its name.

A few *palazzi* built toward the end of the eighteenth century, notably by Prince Giuseppe Bonanno, the Marquis Borsellino and a physician also named Borsellino, stand in testimony to the wealth of the town's erstwhile masters. The neo-classical Palazzo Municipale, dating from the Fascist period, is not without appeal. An imposing marble plaque on the wall of the clock tower memorializes the young men of the town lost during the two World Wars. The names of Cattolica Eraclea's great families are engraved on countless headstones and mausolea that stand in rows along the cemetery's flower-gilded laneways.

Canadians, should they ever visit, would have a vague feeling that they know these names: Manno, Renda, Arcuri, Cammalleri, Salvo, Sciascia, LoPresti, Ragusa, Sciortino, Milioto and so on. They have seen them in the newspaper, heard them on the radio or television—sometimes in connection with remarkable deeds and destinies, sometimes with darker enterprises. The recollections are not stirred by chance: most of the people resting in the Cattolica Eraclea cemetery have descendants in Quebec and Ontario.

The most notable of these surnames is Rizzuto, shared not only by Mafia "men of honour" such as Nicolò and his son, Vito, but also by a distant relative of theirs with an illustrious career, Pietro Rizzuto. Born into a poor family, he became a successful businessman and politician in his adopted country, and was named to Canada's Senate at age forty-two.

His reputation spread across the Atlantic and is a source of pride for the inhabitants of Cattolica Eraclea, the cemetery warden explains enthusiastically. "A great man," he says, escorting his visitors to the entrance of the cemetery and carefully pulling shut the heavy cast-iron gates.

Close by, the single bell tower of the Chiesa Madre (Mother Church), dedicated to the Holy Spirit, dominates the piazza. Built in the seventeenth century in the relatively sober Sicilian baroque style, it has stood in silent witness to bloody wars, riots and demonstrations. Within its stone walls, Nicolò Rizzuto's forebears celebrated christenings, weddings and funerals.

Parents in Sicily traditionally gave their children the names of their own parents and continue to do so: Vito Rizzuto's grandfather, born in 1901, had also been christened Vito. In 1923, he wed Maria Renda, a widow. Her first husband, Francesco Milioto, had been shot and killed as he tried to rob another farmer in San Giorgio, a rural area in the *comune* of Cattolica Eraclea. Before his death, the couple had had a son, Liborio Milioto.* Maria was the sister of a Mafia boss, Calogero Renda, a *campiere* in the neighbouring town of Siculiana. Thus a new branch was added to the family tree, at once simple and complicated, of the extended Mafia clans of Agrigento Province, in whose towns and villages Cosa Nostra has held sway for decades. Simple, because the same surnames are entered in marriage contracts from generation to generation; complicated, because identical given names are as well.

Moreover, cousin marriages were common in the region—the potential for acceptable unions being limited given the deep mistrust of strangers and anyone not part of the clan. Large numbers of Cattolica Eraclea inhabitants, therefore, appear to be related not just by blood but by marriage. Unravelling this skein of family ties demands much concentration and is an exercise that borders on the dizzying.

---

* The story of Cattolica Eraclea's families is epic. Years later, Liborio Milioto, Nicolò Rizzuto's half-brother, had a daughter, named Maria in keeping with the tradition. She in turn married Filippo Rizzuto, a brother of future Senator Pietro Rizzuto. Liborio Milioto died in Montreal a few years ago.

Vito Rizzuto, Sr., and Maria Renda had a son, named Nicolò. Vito then emigrated illegally to the United States with his brother-in-law Calogero Renda. He was murdered on August 12, 1933, in a quarry in Patterson, New York. It was retribution for his having set fire to a building. Calogero Renda returned to Sicily and went to work for Baron Francesco Agnello, who owned large tracts of land in the Contrata di San Giorgio, a district near Siculiana.

Orphaned of his father at age nine, Nicolò Rizzuto from an early age earned a reputation as a *malandrino*—a fairly pejorative term that, in the Sicilian culture of the time, was not to be confused with "Mafioso." Small-time brigands, these men were outlaws, unlike the Mafiosi, who held proper jobs and had often symbiotic relationships with townspeople and landowners as *gabelloti* or *campieri*. Rumour had it that the young Nicolò had become enraged when he learned of the deaths of two of his friends at the hands of local authorities during the Fascist years. It was said that he had sworn to avenge their deaths.

Nicolò's first arrest came in 1945, as he was preparing to sell 350 kilograms of contraband wheat on the black market. The same year, his mother, Maria Renda, was also arrested for selling illicit wheat, a crime of which her own father had been convicted as well.

As it had during the war years, the Italian government exercised a monopoly over the wheat trade. In theory, the reason was to ensure fair distribution, but in practice, the policy only worsened shortages of the commodity. To feed their families, Sicilians had no choice but to break the law. The people had the painful impression that, unlike the poor peasantry, rich landowners faced little or no trouble from the law if they failed to hand over the expected quantities of wheat to the state. What wheat was available on the market cost a fortune. To put the people's misery in perspective: a loaf of bread cost the equivalent of fifty cents, and a *carabiniere* earned about $1.75 a week.

Nicolò Rizzuto married Libertina Manno the same year he was arrested for the first time. He was barely twenty-one years old; she, eighteen. The Mannos lived near the Chiesa Madre, and the wedding took place there. Nicolò's family lived behind the town's second church, the Chiesa Madonna della Mercede. The pair were at once neighbours and distant cousins.

In taking Libertina Manno as his bride, the young Nicolò also married into the Mafia. Years later, Libertina's uncles Pasquale Manno and Leonardo Cammalleri would be convicted of murder. Libertina's father, Don Antonino, was the head of the *Famiglia Manno,* Cattolica Eraclea's ruling Mafia clan. They occupied the land once owned by the Marchese Borsellino, in the *contrata* of Monte di Sara. Looking at photographs of Don Antonino Manno, one notes the piercing gaze of a man who appears mistrustful of most everything and everyone. Discreet, not to say secret, he refrained from ostentatious displays of his wealth and power. There was nothing to distinguish his two-storey home from those of his neighbours. In spring and summer, the front balcony overlooking the street would be covered in flowers, compensating for the lack of a back garden. The powerful don preferred to cultivate modesty. Electrical and telephone cables were not strung on the rough-plastered facade of his home until many years after its construction.

"The Mafia in the time of Don Nino were discreet," the Sicilian Mafia historian Francesco Renda recalled of Antonino Manno. "Don Nino was very seldom seen on the street or anywhere in public. He lived like a ghost. His power was known to the people, but they never saw him."

Men like Don Nino were mediators. They owed their public stature not to their heritage but to the power they wielded. They were masters at settling disputes without recourse to outside authority. Circumstances sometimes dictated that assassination be the solution, but they would have that dirty work done by others, such that they were only rarely accused of any crimes. When they were, acquittal was usually the outcome, and with each such reprieve they gained even more prestige and power.

Having allowed Nicolò to win his daughter's hand, Don Nino gifted the young couple with a pretty house in a Cattolica Eraclea neighbourhood, Pero di Giulio, known informally as Puligiù. He helped his son-in-law get a job with the Sciortino family, which ran a flour mill in the town of Siculiana, twenty kilometres to the south.

It was while working at the mill with his elder half-brother, Liborio Milioto, that Nicolò Rizzuto got to know one Pasquale Cuntrera. Himself an aspiring Mafioso, Cuntrera looked after Baron Agnello's land. Other members of the Cuntrera and Caruana families worked for Don Nino Manno, whose mother was a Caruana. They too owned a flour mill in the Siculiana region. Years later, in Venezuela, Nicolò Rizzuto would become godfather to a daughter of Pasquale Cuntrera, who by then was a boss of this important Mafia family.

Nicolò's reputation as a bandit notwithstanding, one elderly woman in Cattolica Eraclea recalled him with fond nostalgia. "Zio Colà (Uncle Nick) should forever wear the cassock for the parishioners who come to church every year to celebrate the Feast of the Virgin Mary," she said. Then, tears welling in her eyes, she added: "They say he is as generous in Canada as he was here. He was always good to the people."

At four in the morning on February 21, 1946, Nicolò's son, Victor "Vito" Rizzuto, was born in the family home. Libertina was assisted in childbirth by a sixty-nine-year-old midwife. The baby was baptized in the Chiesa Madre. A sister, Maria, was born a year later. In 1952, after the family flour mill closed down, Nicolò, following in his father's footsteps, booked a transatlantic passage and entered the United States illegally. There, Nicolò Buttafuoco, an associate of the Bonanno crime family, took him under his wing. Likely he planned to settle there permanently and bring his wife and children over, but U.S. authorities wasted little time tracking him down and sent him back to Palermo. Nicolò eventually crossed the Atlantic again, this time winding up in Venezuela, where he lived in secret. He then returned to Sicily and began making arrangements—legally this time—to emigrate to North America.

Father Giuseppe Cuffaro of the Chiesa Madre backed his efforts. This was the same priest who would later provide sanctuary for the killers of the trade unionist Giuseppe Spagnolo. Padre Cuffaro vouched for Rizzuto, despite the fact that he was identified with the Mafia, asserting that Nicolò was a man with a sterling reputation who would surely make a valuable contribution to his new country, Canada. By western Sicilian standards, Rizzuto was not a poor man. His children would never have gone hungry had he remained in Agrigento Province, where his father-in-law, Antonino Manno, continued to reign as the Mafia chieftain. But Nicolò was young, ambitious and enterprising, and Canada looked to him, as it did to thousands of Sicilians, to be a land full of possibilities.

Nicolò was twenty-nine years old when he boarded the MS *Vulcania* with his wife, Libertina, and their children, Vito and Maria. On February 21, 1954, they stepped off the ship onto Halifax's storied Pier 21. It was young Vito's eighth birthday. The family headed immediately for Montreal, which had a well-established and fast-growing Italian community. Canada's largest city at the time, Montreal was a magnet for Sicilian immigrants, whereas the Calabrians from the south of Italy's boot preferred to settle in Ontario, where there were plenty of jobs to be found in the building trades as well as on the huge St. Lawrence Seaway project.

On the family's immigration forms, Nicolò is identified as a farmer, and Libertina as a housewife. The young couple arrived in Canada with barely thirty dollars between them. Nicolò told the immigration officers that he planned to live with relatives of the family on De Lorimier Avenue, near the right-of-way for the future Metropolitan Autoroute.

The family then moved to the Villeray district. Known for the spiral staircases fronting its two- and three-storey row houses, it also encompasses Montreal's Little Italy neighbourhood. Many of the homes had small fenced-in gardens at the back, good for growing grapes. On Sundays, the neighbourhood's Italian parishioners worship at the Church of the Madonna della Difesa, or Église de Notre-Dame-de-la-Défense, at the corner of Henri-Julien Avenue and Dante Street. The red-brick church, built in Romanesque style, features a pre-war fresco depicting Mussolini on a white horse. Villeray was not exactly a poor neighbourhood, but the Rizzutos felt hemmed in there, even though the children could play in Jarry Park, just blocks away, where in a decade's time, baseball's Montreal Expos would begin playing home games against their National League rivals. The family soon moved farther east on the Island of Montreal, to Saint-Léonard, nicknamed *La Città Italiana* for its sizable population of Italian origin.

Nicolò Rizzuto founded a company with his brother-in-law Domenico Manno, Grand Royal Paving. He joined the Sicilian Association of Montreal, an organization whose members included heroin traffickers like Nicolò Morello and Carlo Campo. To anyone but their closest friends, Rizzuto and his two fellow Mafiosi corresponded to the traditional image of hard-working, honest Italian immigrants. (Morello, a father of seven, would later be killed in a bar in Saint-Léonard.)

Young Vito, who spoke not a word of English or French when he arrived in Montreal, was schooled in English, the language of business, at St. Pius X Secondary School on Papineau Avenue. One of his classmates, Tony Volpato, was active on the student council, which aimed to instill values of co-operation, initiative, leadership and loyalty. As an adult, Volpato would instead gain fame as a member of the Cotroni clan. Vito dropped out in Grade Nine. On August 18, 1965, he was fined twenty-five dollars and jailed eight days for disturbing the peace.

On November 26, 1966, Vito married Giovanna Cammalleri in Toronto. He was twenty years old and had just obtained his Canadian citizenship. Giovanna was two years his junior, and they were first cousins once removed. Born, like Vito, in Cattolica Eraclea, Giovanna was just seven years old when her father, Leonardo, took part in the murder of Giuseppe Spagnolo, the union activist and the *comune*'s first mayor. After the murder, he fled to Canada with his wife and children.

Giovanna Cammalleri Rizzuto gave birth to her first child on December 4, 1967, the year of the World's Fair in Montreal. Following the Sicilian tradition, the *bambino* was named for his grandfather Nicolò, while the couple's first daughter, who arrived on February 22, 1973, would be named for her paternal grandmother, Libertina. In the meantime, a second son, Leonardo, had been born on June 8, 1969.

Vito worked at the Cheetah Club, a bar housed in a building that belonged to his father, at the corner of Beaubien Street and Saint-Laurent Boulevard. Before his second son was born, he found himself in trouble with the police for having started a fire in a small shopping mall in Boucherville, on Montreal's South Shore. Around one in the morning on May 16, 1968, he and Paolo Renda, his brother-in-law, were busy pouring gasoline on the floor of the latter's business premises, the Renda Barber Shop, intending to burn it down. A wayward spark ignited the accelerant too soon, the flames leaping so fast that they set the two arsonists ablaze. When firefighters and police arrived, they found Renda outside, his clothes still smouldering, and took him to hospital.

A few hours later, the police learned that a man matching the description of Renda's accomplice had made his own way to another hospital to be treated for burns. The motive for the arson was simple: Renda wanted to collect the insurance he had taken out on his barbershop. Other businesses in the mall suffered heavy losses. The two men were charged with arson. On Vito Rizzuto's police photo, his face appears thin, nearly emaciated. His hair is long, in a Beatles cut, and he stares sullenly into the lens. He was tall, too, in stark contrast to many famous gang leaders of the time, many of whom, despite differing cultural origins, stood barely over five feet tall—Vincenzo Cotroni, Paolo Violi, Armand Courville and the American Meyer Lansky come to mind.

Four years later, in 1972, while his wife was pregnant with Libertina, Vito was convicted of fraud and arson and sentenced to two years in prison. He was released after eighteen months. Renda, meanwhile, served two years and nine months of a four-year sentence.

A year before his sentencing, Vito was still working at the Cheetah Club, a bar that police were keeping a close eye on, attempting to glean information about his father. Forty years later, Alain Brunelle, who in the early 1970s was part of Montreal police vice squad, recalled how, at the time, informers repeatedly told him and fellow investigators that Nicolò Rizzuto covertly controlled several construction sites in Montreal.

"People told us he was the one calling the shots in construction," Brunelle recounted in an interview with the authors. "At one point in the summer of 1971 I went to Saint-Léonard with a colleague, hoping to talk to him. We questioned some employees of Grand Royal Paving who were laying asphalt in a driveway. The foreman wouldn't talk to us, but one of the workers told us, hush-hush, that Nick was in Venezuela."

The following autumn, Rizzuto bought a ranch in that South American country, three hours' drive from its border with Colombia. In all likelihood, he was following orders. The Sicilian clans in Agrigento Province had sent him and other emissaries to Canada for a very specific purpose: use Montreal as a base to set up outposts in Venezuela, where they could make deals with the Colombian cocaine cartels.

Nicolò Rizzuto probably missed the almond orchards and cotton fields of his native province when he arrived in Montreal, but luckily for him, something else was growing there: crime. Montreal had won a reputation as an "open city." And open to all manner of illicit activities it was "Canada's Sin City," headlines in U.S. newspapers blared. It was home to some two hundred nightclubs, an incalculable number of illegal gambling houses, and brothels aplenty. Things were so out of control that the U.S. Army and Navy, fearing rampant venereal disease, recommended that men on leave not stay in the city.

The most celebrated object of those soldiers' and sailors' lust was Willis Marie Van Schaack, better known by her stage name, Lili St-Cyr. Born into a showbiz family in Minneapolis, she performed nude for the first time in Montreal in 1944 at the Gayety Burlesque Theatre. It was the beginning of a beautiful friendship, as she became the cabaret's star attraction for the next seven years. In overwhelmingly Catholic Quebec, at a time when an omnipotent clergy moulded minds with the threat that impure souls were headed straight to hell, locals enjoying this brand of entertainment were committing a grave sin. Lili would remain a popular icon even after she retired from dancing, thanks to a mail-order lingerie business, The Undie World of Lili St. Cyr.

One man would make his mark on The Main—Saint-Laurent Boulevard, the traditional dividing line between east and west Montreal and its francophone- and anglophone-majority neighbourhoods respectively—and throughout the city: Vincenzo Cotroni, born in 1911 in a small town in Calabria, the southern tip of Italy's mainland. He had immigrated to Quebec in 1924 and left school so early that he never really learned to read or write. The later ascendancy of the Rizzuto family is closely tied to the story of the Cotronis and the context of organized crime in 1950s Montreal.

After apprenticing as a carpenter, Cotroni switched career ambitions and tried his hand at professional wrestling, under the name "Vic Vincent." He trained under Armand Courville, who came from a family of sixteen children and taught the rudiments of the sport to aspiring youngsters. Proudly mustachioed, with a head planted between two massive shoulders, Courville was also a man who literally took the law into his own hands, keeping bothersome individuals at bay with his fists and buying off the politicians, city councillors and policemen who threatened to close down his many gambling dens and speakeasies. He also provided no small measure of assistance to candidates who retained his services during election campaigns.

Courville taught his Sicilian protegé the rudiments of his game. Hired indiscriminately by both the Liberal Party and the Union Nationale, the two goons drove voters out of polling stations with baseball bats. "I was the Liberal Party's chief of police," Courville once told a reporter from *La Patrie*. Cotroni, meanwhile, was convicted of assaulting an electoral officer. It wasn't his first arrest: at eighteen, he had been charged with the rape of a teenager named Maria Bresciano, who had spurned his marriage proposal. While Cotroni was free on bail awaiting his trial, the young woman withdrew the charge and agreed to become his fiancée. They would remain husband and wife until her death—but Maria's loyalty didn't stop Cotroni from keeping a mistress for many years (he even had a son with her and insisted that the boy be raised in Florida, far from the Montreal underworld).

Courville and Cotroni became business partners—in legal pursuits but also, and especially, illicit ones. They would remain close associates for some fifty years. The two partnered with the Marseilles-born brothers Edmond and Marius Martin to open the Cabaret Au Faisan Doré, at the corner of Saint-Laurent Boulevard and Sainte-Catherine Street. The nightspot became hugely successful thanks to its star emcee, Jacques Normand, and performances by such famous names as Charles Aznavour, Luis

Mariano, Tino Rossi and Charles Trenet. The six-hundred-seat venue— frequented by office workers and taxi drivers, judges and lawyers, university professors and doctors—also launched the careers of French-Canadian entertainers like Fernand Gignac, Roger Baulu, Raymond Lévesque, Monique Leyrac and Denise Filiatrault.

Vic "The Egg" Cotroni didn't get rich promoting *la chanson française,* however. His fortune would be earned through vice rackets: prostitution and, especially, gambling and bookmaking. As a hot spot for the latter, Montreal rivalled Havana and Las Vegas. The proximity of New York, the emergence of new telecommunications technology, regular visits by thousands of military men headed to or returning from Europe, the sudden crackdown on illegal gambling south of the border—all these factors attracted U.S. criminal organizations to "the Paris of North America." Cotroni became their man in Montreal.

A professional gambler and crack mathematician by the name of Harry Ship repurposed several apartments on Sainte-Catherine Street into bookmakers' offices, equipping them with telegraph machines. The tickers relayed the results of horse races and other sporting events all over the United States and Canada, as they happened. Each bookie manned five telephones. The premises were raided thirty-four times in just six years. Ship would pay the fines without complaining, and operations would pick up right where they left off. That the police were so accommodating is not surprising: the fines represented a sizable revenue stream for the city.

The manager of another bookie joint explained the workings of the system to Justice François Caron, who was presiding a commission of inquiry into gambling and commercialized vice (Commission d'enquête sur le jeu et le vice commercialisé), and was seconded by two crusading lawyers, Pacifique "Pax" Plante and Jean Drapeau. The police officer heading a raid on a gambling house would typically be offered "a twenty- or a fifty-dollar bill by management." Of course, this had nothing to do with corruption. "It was simply to thank the officers for being gentlemen and doing their duty," the witness explained. In all, the Caron Commission heard 374 witnesses, who explained in detail how the police and politicians were complicit in allowing Montreal's illicit gambling dens and brothels to prosper.

Harry Ship was eventually arrested. A compulsive gambler, he had lost a great deal of money and now had to pay more fines—hefty ones. He invoked a poverty defence before Justice Caron: "The horses forgot to win," he sighed. Ship was thousands of dollars in debt to Meyer Lansky, Frank Costello and a bookie partner of Lucky Luciano's. In other words, he owed the New York Cosa Nostra, and that was the sort of reckoning likely to get you into serious trouble.

The American bosses asked two émigré mobsters in Montreal, Luigi Greco, a Sicilian, and Frank Petrula, a Ukrainian, to "take care" of Ship. The threat wasn't as ominous as all that—in this case, it meant sharing the profits of his rackets with the Lansky-Luciano outfit. With Vic Cotroni's help, Greco and Petrula helped themselves to a share of the profits of a bookmaker even more prominent than Ship: Harry Davis, who was also an opium, morphine and heroin peddler, cabaret and brothel owner, and had a lengthy list of prior convictions for such offences as bribing civil servants.

In short order, Montreal would become a bona fide gold mine for the New York Mafia. The city was already a base of operations for several Corsican criminals, among them Antoine D'Agostino, who also went by the names Michel Sisco, Albert Blain, Alberto Dujardin and Carlos Alberto Ferrara. D'Agostino had concocted quite the sob story to dupe Canadian immigration authorities: he claimed to have been born in British Columbia and sent to live in Italy after his mother died. He added that he had been captured and imprisoned by the Nazis, but managed to escape and flee to Casablanca. From there, he said, he had sailed to Canada on a British ship and claimed refugee status upon arrival.

D'Agostino's real story was even more outlandish. A leading underworld figure in Paris's Montmartre, he had been recruited into the Gestapo by the Nazis to hunt down Resistance fighters, Jews and Communists. After liberation, fearing capture and execution, he dropped out of sight and assumed a new identity, which was easier than it might have been given the fact that he spoke five languages. When the dust settled, he resurfaced in Paris, running several brothels and nightclubs—and, more important, acting as a pivotal player in the international heroin trafficking ring set up by Lucky Luciano.

The dope was typically hidden in secret compartments built into automobiles crossing the Atlantic in the cargo holds of luxury liners bound for the Port of Montreal, where security was far more lax than on the East Coast of the United States. One of D'Agostino's key partners was Lucien Rivard, a colourful Montreal gangster whose spectacular Bordeaux prison break would earn him the title of Canadian Press Newsmaker of the Year in 1965.

D'Agostino's mailing address in Montreal was the Au Faisan Doré nightclub. He could also be found at the Café de la Paix (which was on the ground floor of a building owned by Vic Cotroni) or the Contact Club. Officers with the RCMP narcotics division, digging for information on D'Agostino's acquaintances, checked the Contact Club's telephone records and realized that several calls had been made to New York, more specifically to Sebastiano Bellanca (a.k.a "Benny the Sicilian" or "Benny Blanka"), a Gambino family soldier and notorious drug trafficker.

D'Agostino was wanted by police in Mexico and France. He had an impressive network of contacts that ran the gamut from Montmartre whores to a Montreal priest. Arrested and convicted of drug smuggling, he was imprisoned in the Saint-Vincent-de-Paul Penitentiary in Laval, where he was gripped by a sudden religious fervour and began leading Bible readings for his fellow inmates.

His arrest didn't exactly bring the French Connection to its knees. Heroin bound for New York continued to transit through Montreal, shepherded by an alliance of Québécois, Corsican, Sicilian and American smugglers. The drugs were moved across the U.S. border hidden in cars, often lower-end Chevrolets—traffickers including Frank Cotroni liked them because it was easy to hide the dope in the armrests. Nicolò Rizzuto had got it right when he surmised that Canada's biggest metropolis had potential.

Another Mafioso, Carmine Galante, had also grasped that potential. Of all the mobsters who arrived in post-war Montreal, none was more influential. Nicknamed "Lilo" or "Mr. Cigar" because he had a cigar clenched between his teeth almost permanently, he gave the local Mafia a second wind after D'Agostino's incarceration.

Born in 1910 in a Harlem slum, Galante was the son of a fisherman who had immigrated to the United States from Castellammare del Golfo. Before he was ten years old, he had been deemed an incorrigible delinquent. At seventeen, he was convicted of armed robbery and jailed in New York's storied Sing Sing prison. By age twenty, he was charged with the murder of a police officer but was acquitted for lack of evidence. Later, he served time after a botched truck hijacking led to a gunfight in which Galante wounded his arresting officer and a seven-year-old girl.

A declassified FBI report on Galante, which runs to 1213 pages, quotes a psychiatric assessment conducted on him while he was in prison: "It was noted that the subject was neat in appearance but dull emotionally. He had a mental age of 14½ and an IQ of 90. He was diagnosed as an aneuropathic, psychopathic personality; emotionally dull and indifferent with prognosis as being poor."

The tiny Galante—he stood barely more than five feet tall—liked to boast that he was a patriot and a good Catholic. He took pains to ensure that the children he had with his mistress, who was twenty years his junior, would not be stigmatized as illegitimate. He devised a solution to this thorny problem of ethics: he ordered one of his henchmen to marry her.

In January 1943, "Lilo" made a spectacular entrance on the mobland scene when Vito Genovese, the boss of one of New York's Five Families, assigned him the mission of assassinating Carlo Tresca, a labour organizer and publisher of an anti-Fascist weekly in the city. Genovese, a close associate of Lucky Luciano, had taken refuge in Italy after a murder. There, he had befriended no less a personage than Benito Mussolini, who was outraged by Tresca's anti-Fascist stance. Witnesses to the murder on Fifth Avenue saw a short, stocky man raise a handgun, shoot the journalist at point-blank range and step into a black Ford, which then sped away. Tresca died instantly. Carmine Galante was arrested not long afterward, having been spotted the night before in a black Ford with the same plates as those spotted on the car at the hit, but was simply charged with breaking his parole conditions. The successful hit considerably raised his profile in mob circles.

He changed bosses and was promoted to a prestigious position: driver for Joe Bonanno. After the end of the Second World War, he began a series of return trips to and from Montreal. At the time, the city had become a refuge for U.S.-based bookmakers who feared they would be called to testify before the U.S. Senate Committee inquiry into organized crime headed by Estes Kefauver. Galante was tasked with ensuring that the relocated bookies kept on paying their share to the New York Mafia families. In 1953, by which time he was working for Bonanno, Galante moved to Montreal to run illegal betting and gambling houses. Jointly with Luigi Greco and Harry Ship, he bought the Bonfire, a restaurant on Décarie Boulevard, near the Blue Bonnets Raceway.

With the help of hired goons, he shook down the city's bar and night-club owners, pimps and prostitutes, bookmakers and abortionists. The amounts extorted for the privilege of his "protection" funnelled up to fifty million dollars per year into the Bonanno family's coffers. He placed his men in the syndicates and moved into the drug trade. Though poorly educated, he spoke English and Italian and also had a smattering of French.

The declassified FBI report notes that "the subject [Galante] was reported to dictate policy, set rates and tariffs for the American gambling syndicate in Montreal, Canada." The document goes on to list offices on Sherbrooke Street, Mountain Street and Mansfield Avenue in downtown Montreal.

Galante formally established a Bonanno family *decina,* or "cell," in Montreal, swearing in several members, chief among them Luigi Greco and Vic Cotroni. The latter had a flaw, being Calabrian and not Sicilian, but he sufficiently impressed "Lilo" that the two befriended each other and, later, became godfathers to their respective children.

In 1954, Galante sent Greco and Frank Petrula to Italy to meet Lucky Luciano. RCMP investigators already suspected Galante of having forced Lucien Rivard to work with Cotroni's brother, Giuseppe "Pep" Cotroni, in heroin trafficking operations. After Petrula returned to Montreal, the Mounties searched his luxury home. They found no drugs but did make an interesting discovery. Hidden behind tiles in the bathroom was a safe containing a list of journalists and politicians who had been paid off by the Mafia during the just-completed municipal election campaign. According to Petrula's notes, organized crime interests had spent more than $100,000 in a bid to discredit the Civic Action League and its mayoralty candidate, Jean Drapeau, who was fresh off four years assisting "Pax" Plante on the Caron Commission. The money had also been used to pay thugs who terrorized voters at polling stations.

Drapeau still won the election, but the affair shed cold light on the corrupting power of the Mafia. Petrula's gaffe was unforgivable, and his associates feared he might start talking to the police. He disappeared. Rumour had it that Luigi Greco, whose legitimate public face was as a small-time pizzeria owner, had run Petrula's body through a meat grinder.

Carmine Galante was deported back to the United States. He was made a *caporegime*, then a *sottocapo* (underboss) to Joe Bonanno, and accompanied the latter to the Mafia summits at the Grande Albergo in Palermo and at Joseph Barbara's estate in Apalachin, New York. After those strategic meetings, which sealed the heroin trafficking agreement between the Sicilian Mafia and the New York Cosa Nostra, Galante brought increasing numbers of young Sicilians into his crew. They would be nicknamed "Zips" by their U.S. mob counterparts because of their rapid-fire Sicilian dialects. The Zips arrived in New York in large numbers, working in pizzerias as a front for the dope-importing operations: the French Connection would eventually be supplanted by the "Pizza Connection."

Galante himself would be edged out of business: he was arrested in 1960 for his involvement in a vast plot to import heroin with the younger Cotroni brother, "Pep," and two years later was sentenced to twenty years in prison, after two trials punctuated by various incidents and one unusual accident: the head juror of one of the trials broke his spine falling down a flight of stairs in an abandoned building.

Lucky Luciano's establishment of the Commission in 1931 had put an end to the bloody turf wars among New York's major Mafia clans. One member of the clan that emerged from those wars victorious, Joseph Bonanno, then aged twenty-six, had managed to extend his operations not only throughout the United States' largest city—which, he said, the families called "The Volcano"—but also to Canada, California and the American Southwest. Narcotics trafficking, illegal gambling, prostitution, loansharking and protection rackets had propelled him into the select millionaires club. He was at the very heart of the alliance between the Sicilian Mafia and the American Cosa Nostra.

Driven by the desire to win on all fronts, including that of respectability, Bonanno had invested a considerable share of his ill-gotten gains in companies that were entirely above board: cheese factories and clothing manufacturers, moving and storage companies, pizzerias, cafés and funeral homes. "For nearly a thirty-year period after the Castellammarese War no internal squabbles marred the unity of our Family and no outside interference threatened the Family or me," he proudly asserted in his autobiography.

Bonanno's own arrogance and hubris would contribute to the collapse of the long truce between the Five Families and force him to seek sanctuary in Montreal. The Volcano was spitting fire anew, and its plume of smoke drifted northward. The eruption would have serious implications, reinforcing the Montreal Mafia's position as subordinate to its New York counterpart. Years later, it was within this well-delineated framework that Nicolò Rizzuto and his son, Vito, would come to power.

Born in Castellammare del Golfo in 1905, Giuseppe "Joseph Charles" Bonanno had immigrated to the United States at a very young age but was later forced to return with his parents to Sicily. Later, with an arrest warrant issued by the anti-Mafia prefect Cesare Mori hanging over his head, he fled to Cuba, then re-entered the United States illegally, on board a fishing boat. He wasted little time climbing the rungs of the Mafia.

Conceited, reluctantly saddled with the unflattering sobriquet "Joe Bananas," he saw himself as special and did nothing to hide his contempt for the heads of the other families, which didn't exactly earn him many friends among them. He told anyone who would listen that he was descended from a long line of Sicilian princes, that his grandfather had been a major ally of Garibaldi at the time of Italian unification, and that his father, Salvatore, might well have been ordained a priest had he not sacrificed himself for his family. In fact, Bonanno *père* had preferred theft and murder to worship and prayer.

In 1964, at the height of his powers, Bonanno tried to become the head of the Commission, pre-emptively eliminate his rivals and be anointed *capo di tutti i capi* of the American Cosa Nostra. The other families began to worry. Their concern grew to alarm when they learned that Bonanno had taken out contracts on New York City bosses Carlo Gambino and Tommy Lucchese, and even on his cousin Stefano Magaddino, the boss of the Buffalo crime family, which had a branch in Hamilton, Ontario, and had designs on Toronto. Bonanno plotted the murders with his close associate Joseph Magliocco. Magliocco hired one of his main hit men, Joseph Colombo, to do the jobs, but Colombo betrayed Magliocco and warned Gambino and Lucchese.

Sensing all-out war was near, Bonanno decided to drop out of sight for a while and travel. In his autobiography, he tells of how a businessman, John DiBella, persuaded him to partner in the Grande Cheese Company of Fond du Lac, Wisconsin. "The cheese plant had been the source of contention between rival groups in Chicago," he wrote. "These people played rough, and fighting broke out." DiBella had sought and obtained Bonanno's protection. Bonanno continues:

> When my business associate John DiBella of the Grande Cheese Co. found out about my upcoming travels, he asked me to make Montreal my first stop. Mr. DiBella had a close friend from his hometown in Sicily, Joseph Saputo, who was also in the cheese business. Because of immigration quotas, Mr. Saputo and his family hadn't been able to enter the United States. As the next best thing, Mr. Saputo immigrated to Montreal, Canada, where he established the Saputo Cheese Co. He was now looking for investors to expand operations.
>
> Fay [Bonanno's wife] and I went to Canada, expecting to be there but a short time.

> At the cheese plant, Mr. Saputo and I agreed to a deal. Mr. Saputo
> signed a letter of intent, stating that once I made payment, I would
> own twenty percent of the business.

Bonanno opened an account with the Canadian Imperial Bank of Commerce. The branch manager recommended that he apply for permanent resident status in Canada, as this would make it easier for Bonanno to secure funding, and he would have no problem staying in the country.

Joe Bonanno was by this time a celebrity in the United States. The previous year, Joseph Valachi, a soldier with the Genovese family, had broken the Mafia code of silence—*omertà*—to become the first and one of the most famous mob informants, explaining the innermost workings of the American Mafia before a U.S. Senate subcommittee. Valachi had described Bonanno as one of the heads of the Five Families of Cosa Nostra.

The Senate hearings—headed by Senator John L. McClellan of Arkansas and backed by Robert F. Kennedy, then the attorney general in his brother John F. Kennedy's administration—were televised and had a huge impact. It was no longer possible to deny the existence of the Mafia, as FBI Director J. Edgar Hoover had done up to then. The name Bonanno had gained notoriety—suddenly and undesirably, at least as far as the man himself was concerned. Canadian immigration officers, understandably curious as to what he was doing in the country and what business he had in Montreal, decided to ask him a few questions. Bonanno went to meet them at the appointed hour and place:

> I repeated my intentions of investing in a Canadian business for the
> purpose of expanding a cheese plant and hiring more people. I was
> helping Canada reduce its unemployment. To back up my state-
> ment, I had brought the letter of intent signed by Joseph Saputo.

Instead of being granted the permanent resident status he had applied for, the Genovese family boss was arrested on the spot. Canadian immigration argued that in his application, he had neglected to mention that he had a criminal record in the United States: a Brooklyn garment factory that he co-owned had been charged with violating minimum-wage statutes. Bonanno continues:

> I didn't want to be deported. If Canada deported me as a persona non grata, I would lose my rights to invest in the Saputo Cheese Co. Also, now that it was obvious the United States was behind my predicament, I knew that once I was deported back to the United States, the FBI would be waiting for me.

Bonanno was immediately incarcerated at Bordeaux Prison in Montreal. It was his first time behind bars, and it was to leave a profound impression. Upon his arrival, the guards removed his wristwatch, ring, cigars and the two thousand dollars in cash he had on him, then locked him in a minuscule, cold and dusty cell, with dank condensation on the walls and cockroaches roaming the floor. In the evening, a plate containing a bit of meat, some barely cooked beans and a dry heel of bread was slipped under the door: "The meat tasted as if it had come off a sick caribou," he wrote. "I spat it out."

In short order, however, the incredible news that "le boss" had graced Bordeaux with his presence spread throughout the facility. A guard brought the prisoner a blanket and, at his request, agreed to go and reassure his wife, Fay, who was staying in the Saint-Michel neighbourhood where the Saputo factory was located. Bonanno was transferred to a more comfortable wing; the chief of guards made sure he was assigned the best cell in the prison. He then invited Bonanno to his office and proffered cognac and a cigar.

"This is your cognac and these are your cigars," he announced. "A friend of yours is now a friend of mine. This friend of yours told me you can't live without your cognac and cigars . . . so here we are." Bonanno had little choice other than to broker a compromise:

> I had to promise to abandon my investment in the cheese plant.
> I could not return to Canada unless I first notified the authorities.

For its part, Canada would release me from prison and wouldn't deport me. However, once released from prison, I had to leave Canada voluntarily and return to the United States.

News of Bonanno's impending departure caused near-bedlam among the inmates: "They yelled and rattled things. They told the guards they wanted to see me before I left the prison. They clamored to see me . . . as if I were a movie star." At the chief of guards' suggestion, he marched down the hall of the main prison block. Inmates whooped, cheered and flashed the victory sign; some shouted out their names and offered to go to work for him. *"Le boss!"* they called out. *"Le grand boss!"*

Joseph Bonanno was somewhat less cordially welcomed upon his return to the United States. As soon as he arrived, FBI agents handed him a subpoena. Stefano Magaddino, the Buffalo boss, openly railed against his cousin's venture north of the border: "He's planting flags all over the world!" he allegedly said. Bonanno's version, in *A Man of Honor,* was that:

> Stefano chose to interpret my Montreal trip as an imperialistic venture. Let me explain. It had long been acknowledged in my world that certain Families and their Fathers had spheres of influence outside their own resident cities. For example, Toronto had long been recognized as being within Magaddino's sphere of influence. Montreal, on the other hand, was considered within the domain of the Bonanno Family.

No doubt fearing that those words would be construed as an avowal of his desire to proceed with a division of territories among Mafia clans, Bonanno hastened to add:

> If Toronto was considered within Stefano's province, all that meant was that Stefano, as opposed to another Father, had the right to establish contacts within the Sicilian community in Toronto.
>
> What bothered Stefano about my Canadian trip was not that I went to Montreal but that I might use Montreal as a jumping-off point

to encroach on his cherished Toronto. There was no truth to this. I was looking to extricate myself from my world, not to entangle myself in territorial disputes. I wouldn't even have gone to Montreal in 1964 if the Saputo investment opportunity hadn't come up.

Giuseppe (Joseph) Saputo was born in 1905 in Montelepre, a town some thirty kilometres from Castellammare del Golfo, birthplace of Joe Bonanno. The Saputo family has always maintained that they were unaware of Bonanno's Mafia involvement and were only acquainted with his business partner John DiBella of the Grande Cheese Company. Their denials continue to this day.

The Mafia's highest authority in New York, the Commission, summoned Bonanno to explain himself, but he smelled a trap and declined the invitation. Perhaps fearing a return to bloody infighting like that which had characterized the Castellammarese War at the turn of the 1930s, bosses Carlo Gambino, Tommy Lucchese and Stefano Magaddino opted for a relatively non-invasive method: rather than have Bonanno rubbed out, they would divest him of his authority and install his lieutenant, Gaspare DiGregorio, as head of the family.

"Joe Bananas" rejected the deal. On October 21, 1964, the day before he was scheduled to go before a grand jury, he was kidnapped in Manhattan. The abductors' car drove all night before finally stopping at an upstate country house.

Stefano Magaddino greeted his guest with an acerbic "Hello," adding: "Excellent country, isn't it?"

"A little cold for me," Bonanno said.

"Oh, it gets much colder in Montreal," Magaddino retorted.

Bonanno was held for six weeks. He eventually convinced his cousin Stefano to let him go, pledging to give up the family throne. Once free, he failed to keep that promise. His son Salvatore (Bill) Bonanno took up the fight against DiGregorio in a bid to ensure that the family would continue to be ruled by a Bonanno; this rift between the rival clans came to be dubbed the "Banana Split." The younger Bonanno travelled regularly to Montreal to ensure the city did not fall under the control of

DiGregorio and Magaddino, in the process contacting Vic Cotroni on several occasions. The latter described one of those meetings in court, when he sued *Maclean's* for libel, after the magazine had described him as Montreal's Mafia kingpin. The Montreal daily *Le Devoir* reported:

> During his lengthy testimony, Mr. Cotroni admitted that he knew, in some cases intimately, several individuals publicly named by various commissions of inquiry and police forces, including the FBI and the RCMP, as members of La Cosa Nostra. He explained that in 1966, at the home of a friend, Mr. Giuseppe Saputo—owner of the Saputo & Figli Ltd. cheese plant in Saint-Michel—he had met with a group of New Yorkers.

That group comprised Salvatore (Bill) Bonanno and his associates: Vito De Filippo and his son Patrick, Peter Magaddino, Peter Notaro and Carlo Simari. Their visit to Montreal took place under direct police surveillance. On the evening of November 28, 1966, the six American tourists were riding in two cars when officers stopped the first one, then the second, at the corner of Jean-Talon and Hutchison Streets. Luigi Greco, Vic Cotroni's number-two man, was with them. The police seized four loaded handguns in the cars and arrested the entire party.

That morning, Bernard Couture, a young SQ officer, had been assigned to shadow Vic Cotroni. The latter was at the wheel of a grey Cadillac, accompanied by his protegé Paolo Violi. When the two men stopped in front of a shopping centre at the corner of Jean-Talon Street and Pie-IX Boulevard, according to Officer Couture, they were joined by Salvatore Bonanno and two unknown men. The quintet headed for a pay phone. Couture saw Cotroni, Violi, Giuseppe Saputo and Joe Bonanno speak on the phone in turn. The officer asked for backup; there were now too many cars to follow. He was told to stick with Saputo, who then drove to his company's head office in Saint-Michel. "In the parking lot, there were two vehicles, whose licence plates indicated they were registered to Magaddino and Notaro," Couture later recalled in an interview.

That evening, after they arrested Salvatore Bonanno and his six companions, the police questioned them intensively. They asked what Bonanno was doing in Montreal. He replied that he was there to look after his father's interests in the Saputo cheese company.* Bonanno and his party, except for Luigi Greco, were detained for two days before being taken to the airport and deported to the United States.

Joe Bonanno sent a message to his enemies: should any of his loyal subjects be murdered, he would avenge that death by having a capo of the offending rival clan killed. Two years went by, punctuated by a number of fatalities. Gaspare DiGregorio, the Commission's appointed successor to Joe Bonanno, suggested to Bill Bonanno that a sit-down be arranged to talk peace. It was a set-up. When the Bonanno delegation arrived, DiGregorio's men greeted them with shotgun and automatic weapons fire. Bill Bonanno and his crew defended themselves with their handguns. Hundreds of shots were exchanged. Miraculously, there were no injuries, but the incident proved to the Commission that the hotheaded DiGregorio might be a problem.

Just as Joe Bonanno appeared to be gaining the upper hand, he suffered a serious heart attack. He decided to retire to Arizona with his son Bill and cede the family throne to Paul Sciacca, who had succeeded DiGregorio. Bonanno continued to helm operations in the U.S. Southwest but gave up control of New York and Montreal.

The Bonanno family would go on to see a succession of bosses: Natale Evola, Philip Rastelli, Joseph Massino, Vincent Basciano. Whenever one of them was imprisoned, someone would take his place— Carmine Galante, for example, or more recently, Salvatore "Sal the Iron Worker" Montagna, born in Montreal and the founder of a metalworking company in Brooklyn. None of these chiefs would achieve the

---

* The car driven by Salvatore Bonanno on November 28, 1966, belonged to Giuseppe Monticiollo, Giuseppe Saputo's son-in-law. Around the same time, Monticiollo was sponsoring his brother's immigration to Canada. Later, when a Canadian immigration officer asked him why he had lent his car to Bonanno, he answered, "Because he has a stake in the Saputo company."

stature of Joseph Bonanno, the last surviving founding member of the Commission. But the "family" survived him.

Vic Cotroni had made sure to remain neutral during the "Banana Split" years. After Galante's forced return to the United States a decade earlier, Cotroni had risen through the mob ranks, becoming the sole leader of the Bonanno family's *decina* in Montreal and relegating the Sicilian Luigi Greco to the rank of lieutenant. But a fire was smouldering, and like New York, Montreal would soon be ablaze.

Nicolò Rizzuto lay low in the shadows, tending the coals.

CHAPTER 4

SICILIANS AND CALABRIANS

T HE INTELLIGENCE OFFICERS discreetly "attending" Vito Rizzuto's wedding in Toronto on November 26, 1966, failed to arrest the father of the bride, who sat in his car and waited for the end of the ceremony— this in spite of the fact that Leonardo Cammalleri was wanted by Italian authorities for his role in the murder of Giuseppe Spagnolo. They did, however, note the presence of some very special guests, who included Frank D'Asti and, more important, Paolo Violi.

D'Asti, aged fifty-two, was second-in-command to Nicola Di Iorio, who in turn was one of Vic Cotroni's lieutenants. Di Iorio managed the Victoria Sporting Club, the Mafia's biggest gaming house in Greater Montreal. He was also a particularly active drug trafficker and had an extensive network of contacts among politicians. Both D'Asti and Di Iorio were under intense police scrutiny as they slowly but surely went about forging solid ties with the provincial Liberal Party. In 1969, they made financial contributions to Pierre Laporte's run for the party leadership. Laporte lost to Robert Bourassa, but D'Asti and Di Iorio continued to support him in the hopes that he would be appointed minister of justice in a Bourassa government and would thus be well positioned to put a stop to the police's incessant raids on their nightclubs and gambling houses. Bourassa instead named Laporte minister of labour and immigration. But he also made him vice-premier, the second most important position in the provincial government. When Laporte was kidnapped by members of the separatist Front de libération du Québec (FLQ), sparking the October Crisis of 1970, his abductors wrote a manifesto, which was read on Télévision de Radio-Canada, the CBC's French-language network. In it, the separatists alleged that the Liberals' election win was "a victory for Vic Cotroni." D'Asti offered his services to Laporte's secretary to help find him, but it was in vain: within a week, the minister had been killed by his captors.

In hindsight, the most surprising name on the guest list at Vito Rizzuto's wedding was that of Paolo Violi, a man who would soon be openly at war with the father of the groom, Nicolò Rizzuto. That conflict would culminate with Violi's assassination. Years before Violi's demise, the Quebec Police Commission hearings into organized crime (CECO) had described strife within the Montreal Mafia. "The Commission has heard repeatedly about the Rizzuto incident," a CECO report reads. "This is a serious dispute that has pitted the leaders of the 'family,' Vincent Cotroni and Paolo Violi, against one of their subordinates, the Sicilian Nicholas [sic] Rizzuto." "Serious dispute" is perhaps an understatement. Forty years later, the Mafia in Canada is still very much feeling its effects.

Two days after Vito Rizzuto's wedding, police officers observed Paolo Violi and Vic Cotroni again, in Montreal. The police still did not know the exact position Violi occupied within the criminal organization, but they knew what kind of guy he was.

Like Cotroni, Violi hailed from Calabria. He was born on February 6, 1931, in the town of Sinopoli. His father, Domenico, was ostensibly a simple shepherd. In fact, he was considered by Italian police to be the local boss of the 'Ndrangheta, the Calabrian criminal organization. Paolo was classified delinquent by his teen years. A 1947 Italian police report described the then sixteen-year-old as "a dangerous person with an impulsive nature, capable of anything because of his propensity for violence."

Violi immigrated to Canada in 1951, at age twenty, and settled in Toronto. Nearly penniless, he shared a room with a heroin trafficker, an active member of the French Connection. On May 24, 1955, he had a parking-lot encounter with another Calabrian immigrant by the name of Natale Brigante. An altercation ensued, allegedly over a woman. It escalated into a vicious fight. Brigante brandished a knife and stabbed his opponent. Wounded in the chest, just below the heart, Violi had no choice but to draw a .32 calibre pistol and shoot Brigante four times—at least, that was the version he recounted to police. Brigante collapsed to the ground, mortally wounded. Violi was arrested and charged with manslaughter. Showing the scar from the stab wound as proof, he pleaded self-defence and was acquitted. Nonetheless, the police contended that Violi was acting on orders, settling a vendetta launched in the old country.

The deed enhanced the young Violi's underworld profile. Giacomo Luppino, the leader of the 'Ndrangheta in Hamilton, took him under his wing. Luppino was an old friend of Violi's father, Domenico, who had immigrated to the United States and settled in Parma, near Cleveland. Luppino reported to Stefano Magaddino, the Buffalo Mafia boss. The stars were aligning in favour of a rapid rise to the top of the criminal heap for Violi. That ascension included courting Grazia Luppino, his boss's daughter. The relationship was by all accounts strongly encouraged by Giacomo Luppino, and Violi succeeded in winning Grazia's hand. They would marry in 1965.

After he moved to Montreal in 1963, Violi changed bosses: he was soon reporting to Vic Cotroni. The boss of the *decina* liked the young man so much that he agreed to be best man at his wedding and, later, godfather to one of his children. Cotroni needed a Calabrian deputy as counterweight to the Sicilians in the organization like Luigi Greco and Nicolò Rizzuto. Violi became one of Cotroni's four lieutenants, on equal footing with Greco, Nicola Di Iorio and Frank Cotroni, Vic's younger brother.

It is difficult to ascertain what Stefano Magaddino thought of Violi's taking up with a group that answered to his New York rival Joe Bonanno. He may have chalked Violi's departure into the loss column, but at the same time, he may have seen it as a chance to extend his influence as far as Montreal. At any rate, he was not well pleased when he learned that Violi and Vic Cotroni had met with Joe Bonanno's son in Montreal. His Hamilton associate, Giacomo Luppino, reassured Magaddino as to their neutrality, however.

When he arrived in Montreal, Violi opened a café on Jean-Talon Street, in Saint-Léonard. The Reggio Bar, and the adjacent Gelateria Violi, provided a good front: "customers" would come in for an espresso or some ice cream, then leave. Sensitive discussions could take place in a small office in the back, while more critical operations were mapped out in the basement.

One day in December 1970, a stranger opened the door to the Reggio. He said his name was Bob Wilson and introduced the blonde who was with him as his wife. They were interested in the apartment above the café; Violi had put up a For Rent sign in the front window.

The café fell silent. A short, stocky man stood behind the counter. Adjusting his glasses, Wilson recognized Paolo Violi, although he had never seen him in person. The café owner surveyed the visitor warily, his beady black eyes staring him up and down. One of his associates began the interrogation. Wilson wasn't Italian and could provide no references. He said he was an electrician from Ontario. Still, he and Violi came to an agreement; the rent would be $125 per month. Violi, whose earnings were derived from all manner of enterprises, rackets and fraudulent schemes, was not one to look askance at any sum of money. In this instance, though, he was making what was probably the worst mistake of his life. Bob Wilson's real name was Robert Ménard, and he was working undercover for the Montreal police.

Soon after he moved in, Ménard and a team of technicians fitted the apartment with hidden microphones that would record every word uttered in the café downstairs for the next several years. Violi's phone was already tapped. From his balcony or his window, Ménard took down the licence numbers of cars that pulled up in front of the café. One day, his cover was very nearly blown when Violi asked him to fix a light bulb that wouldn't switch on. Ménard knew precious little about electrical work; he had merely taken a crash course from his brother, a master electrician. He pretended to inspect the wiring and connections. "You've got a real problem here," he said to the owner while flipping the switch up and down. "Just one thing left to check." He climbed up a ladder and examined the bulb. It was simply burnt out.

"Ya shoulda checked the fuckin' light first, eh, Wilson?" Violi joked.

"Well, I like to complicate things, okay?" Ménard acknowledged. "Hey, I'm fuckin' tired. Come and have a coffee with me."

"I hope you're not gonna charge me for that!" Violi said.

"Well, I hope you're not gonna raise my rent," Ménard shot back.

"No, no, no, I won't," the owner promised. "You're a good boy. You're a good boy, Bob, I like you!"

In time, Ménard and Violi struck up a friendship—a false friendship in the policeman's case. They would sometimes sit on the steps of the café and make small talk. An angry Violi would rail against the "goddamn separatists" who, in his eyes, were ruining the province. Like many residents of Saint-Léonard, he was unhappy that his children were forced to attend French school. He wanted them to be brought up in English, "the language of business."

The police had gone so far as to put together a fake criminal record for "Bob Wilson," garnishing it with convictions for various petty offences. The artifice was designed to dispel any doubts on Violi's part, should he decide to look into his new tenant's past. The "wife" who had accompanied the undercover officer to the Reggio Bar soon "broke up" with him. Poor "Wilson" then pretended to be heartbroken. In short, Violi was duped for years. The Reggio recordings were provided to several police forces, not only in Canada but in the United States and Italy as well. When the CECO began disclosing choice excerpts from the tapes, they had a devastating impact. They confirmed what witnesses testifying before the commissioners had already hinted at: Paolo Violi was a vicious, ignoble human being.

Violi ran Saint-Léonard. He systematically extorted every Italian merchant in the neighbourhood, including a small-time window-washer: "At one point, he received a telephone call asking him to prepare a bid for a window-washing contract at the Reggio Bar, owned by Paolo Violi," states one of the CECO reports. "When he arrived on the premises, two individuals made him descend to the basement of the establishment; one of them identified himself as Jos Macri. There, he was intimidated in Paolo Violi's name. He was ordered to make out three five-hundred-dollar cheques to ensure the 'protection' of his business. Jos Macri pointed a revolver at the window-washer. Paolo Violi then came down to the basement 'to wrap up the deal.' The witness begged Violi to intervene on his behalf. Violi let him go after making him sign two cheques." When the window-washer refused to take Violi on as a partner in his company, he lost the majority of his customers and was forced to go out of business.

Another businessman, Mauro Marchettini, told the CECO what happened after he opened a pool hall at the corner of Lacordaire and Jean-Talon Streets, not far from the Reggio. The problem was Violi already ran a poolroom in the area. Suppliers at first stopped making deliveries to Marchettini, and then the threats became more direct. When Marchettini stubbornly refused to close up shop and go elsewhere, Violi dispatched his brother Francesco, who beat Marchettini with a long paddle normally used for churning ice cream. "I was told I could open that kind of business, but not on Lacordaire Street, and not on Jean-Talon east of Lacordaire," the unfortunate entrepreneur told the CECO.

Using violence and intimidation, Violi monopolized the sale of Italian ice cream in Montreal's north and east ends. A CECO witness explained that there was only one other manufacturer of Italian ice cream in the city, but Violi forbade him from selling any outside his own *gelateria*. "Violi is not one man, he's a thousand men," the witness said. The boss also offered his services as a mediator. He told the brothers Lino and Quintino Simaglia, who owned a small business, that he could assist them in settling a dispute with a Toronto-based company. These mediation services, of course, were not provided gratis: Violi ordered that the two brothers pay him one thousand dollars every year, at Christmas. Lino Simaglia told the CECO that they hadn't dared say no. Neither brother was a rich man, and the "present" they had to give to Violi meant that they couldn't afford to give their own children any gifts at Christmas.

Italian entrepreneurs in east-end Montreal weren't the only victims of the godfather of Saint-Léonard. In his testimony before the CECO, one Tony Mucci reluctantly admitted that Violi had suggested that he demand five thousand dollars in tribute money from the owner of a bar called Tre Colori in Chambly, a town on Montreal's South Shore. When he testified, Mucci was serving an eight-year prison term for the shooting of crime reporter Jean-Pierre Charbonneau in the *Le Devoir* newsroom. Charbonneau, who escaped serious injury but was wounded in the arm, had been exposing the activities of the Mafia, and particularly the Cotroni-Violi clan, writing column after column about rampant corruption in Saint-Léonard. Had Violi ordered the hit on Charbonneau? Mucci swore that he had not acted at the urging of higher-ups, but the commissioners remained skeptical.

One Saint-Léonard citizen, Frank Tutino, decided to run for a seat at city hall—without asking Violi's permission. The godfather sent his *consigliere,* Pietro Sciara, to warn Tutino that his enterprise would be a risky one. Tutino thought about it and paid a quick visit to Violi at the Reggio Bar. The boss began by "asking" Tutino to withdraw his candidacy and went on to threaten his family. Then, somewhat magnanimously, he offered to refund what money he had already spent on his campaign. Tutino stood firm—and hired bodyguards. He lost the election.

Many Mafia historians assert that, unlike Nicolò Rizzuto, who took a broad vision, Violi was narrow-minded. They claim that his ambitions were limited to relatively petty skulduggery and that his turf barely extended beyond the Montreal area. That view is unfounded. The godfather of Saint-Léonard travelled and cultivated contacts abroad. On February 16, 1970, he arrived in Acapulco with twenty or so Mafia bosses and lawyers from Quebec, Ontario and the United States. They met at the Las Brisas Hilton and at a villa owned by former Montrealer Louis Bercowitz, who had been convicted in October 1946 for the murder of gambling czar Harry Davis. Those present included Hamilton, Ontario, capo John "Johnny Pops" Papalia and Meyer Lansky.

Born Majer Suchowlinski into a Jewish family in Grodno (part of Russian-controlled Poland-Lithuania, now Belarus), Meyer Lansky was never a "made" member of Cosa Nostra, which has always been the exclusive preserve of Italians or Italian Americans. He nevertheless provided valuable advice to the organization throughout his life. He guided Lucky Luciano as he deftly manoeuvred his way to the pinnacle of the American Mafia, and deserved credit in part for the creation of the Commission, the Five Families' regulatory body. He helped his friend Bugsy Siegel muscle in on Las Vegas and contributed to the founding of its celebrated Flamingo Hotel, in which he held a stake. He opened casinos, hotels and nightclubs in Cuba and derived huge profits from them before being forced out by Fidel Castro. Considered a genius of the gambling industry and a master money launderer, Lansky had secret accounts in Switzerland to which he funnelled colossal sums via a complex network of shell and holding companies.

Thanks to electronic surveillance, the RCMP knew about the Acapulco meetings before they even began. They tipped off the FBI, which in turn conveyed the information to Mexican law enforcement. After monitoring their comings and goings, the police in Acapulco interrogated the mob bosses, but they were evasive. The Canadian, American and Mexican police believed the goal of the meetings was to find a way to profit from the advent of casinos in Quebec; the provincial government was planning legislation to allow them. News of the gathering, reported in Montreal by *La Presse* three weeks after it happened, sparked controversy, since the paper claimed that a prominent criminal lawyer, Raymond Daoust, had been in attendance, along with well-known U.S. Mafia lawyers like Moses Polakoff, who had defended Lucky Luciano.

Gradually, Paolo Violi eclipsed Vic Cotroni's other lieutenants, starting with the Sicilian Luigi Greco. Violi was leery of getting too deep into the narcotics trade, however, not wishing to attract police attention. He knew that the courts were especially severe when it came to drug dealers and traffickers. "Stick with stealing; it's less risky," was his advice to one *picciotto*—a low-level Mafia soldier—who asked him to finance a narcotics transaction.

Violi was a keen observer of developments within the U.S. and Sicilian Mafias. The diminutive Calabrian craved the respect of the Sicilians. He constantly complained that Nicolò Rizzuto failed to show him the proper deference, accusing Rizzuto of "[going] from one place to another, here and there," without reporting to Violi, as mob protocol dictated. For Paolo Violi, nothing was more important than respect (*il rispetto*). He would berate his underlings for swearing in front of the children playing outside the Reggio Bar and the Gelateria Violi. And out of respect for his wife, Grazia, he did not pursue other women.

Violi's attitude greatly displeased Nicolò Rizzuto, who believed the Montreal *decina* should be run by Sicilians, especially given the fact that the Bonannos were the most Sicilian of New York's Five Families. He did not impugn Vic Cotroni's leadership but having to answer to two Calabrians at once was hard to take. Rizzuto viewed Violi as a man of little importance and had precious little time for imprecations of respect from a man whom he held in such contempt.

Nicolò Rizzuto had been a member of the *decina* led by the Calabrian Vic Cotroni since the late 1950s or early 1960s but quite naturally gravitated toward his fellow Sicilians, in particular Luigi Greco and other compatriots from his home province of Agrigento. Many had settled in Montreal at the same time as Rizzuto, including his most loyal allies, the members of the Caruana and Cuntrera families, most of whom came from the Siciliana region and whom he had known in his youth.

Immigration Canada reports state that Pasquale and Liborio Cuntrera arrived in Canada in 1951, before Rizzuto, and became Canadian citizens in 1957. The Cuntreras gave the impression of being typical hard-working immigrants, getting jobs as barbers or snowplow drivers, gradually earning enough to open stores or pizzerias. Behind this facade of honesty, they were in fact formidable narcotics traffickers. Along with the Caruanas, they would eventually be known in the Italian press by such names as "the Rothschilds of the Mafia" or "the bankers of Cosa Nostra," by reason of their considerable expertise in laundering money and investing drug profits in legal economic avenues.

Events in Italy that might be termed historic resulted in a massive influx of Sicilian Mafiosi to various parts of North America, notably

New York and Montreal. In 1957, when Lucky Luciano created the Cupola along with Joe Bonanno, Carmine Galante and Tommaso Buscetta during the conclave at the Grande Albergo in Palermo, a *segretario,* or leader, was chosen, in the person of Salvatore "Ciaschiteddu" Greco. For six years, Sicily was free of Mafia strife. Years later, when Buscetta became an informant, he said he could recall not a single murder of a "man of honour" during this *pax mafiosa.* There was no reason for squabbling: the Sicilian families were rolling in money and had ousted all of their competitors. They dealt almost exclusively with the Corsicans, who refined four-fifths of the world's heroin in their Marseilles labs. Through its agreements with the heads of the New York Families such as the Bonannos, the Sicilian Mafia had unfettered access to a vast market. It flooded the United States with heroin.

At the beginning of the 1950s, approximately fifty thousand Americans were addicted to the drug. Their numbers swelled exponentially; twenty years later, there were half a million. These hundreds of thousands of junkies stole and even killed to get their fixes. No criminal activity in history had ever generated such a particular brand of misery. Entire neighbourhoods—Harlem, for example—were ravaged. Life became unbearable for residents, who regularly fell victim to armed robbery and burglaries. No trade had ever generated such staggering profits, either.

Depending on the size of the order, a kilogram of morphine base was worth anywhere from six to nine thousand dollars. Once refined into 90 percent pure heroin, it sold for between forty and fifty thousand dollars a kilo. By the time it reached New York City, the wholesale price was $200,000, and the street value, two million dollars. Traffickers tended to move the drug in shipments of twenty to a hundred kilos at a time. The rapacious Sicilian syndicates clawing at the entrails of North American cities would eventually see their wings clipped, however—victims of their immoderate greed.

Their misfortunes began in December 1962 with the transatlantic shipment of a major consignment of heroin financed by the various Palermo criminal factions. One clan boss was foolish enough to keep the profits to himself, and the leader of another family, the La Barbera clan, took the initiative and had him executed. Ciaschiteddu Greco expelled the La Barbera boss from the Cupola for the unauthorized hit. Settlings of accounts then ensued, at the alarming rate of one homicide per day, in what became known as the First Mafia War.

On June 30, 1963, men stole an Alfa Romeo Giuletta, stuffed the trunk with a hundred kilograms of explosives and parked the car on a street in Ciaculli, the Greco clan's stronghold in suburban Palermo. After a citizen phoned in a tip about the suspicious vehicle, seven *carabinieri* were sent to inspect it. One of them opened the trunk. The blast that tore into the afternoon sky pulverized the nearest villa and gouged a deep crater into the street, into which fell what was left of the seven officers and three bystanders.

The carnage had powerful political and social repercussions. Outraged Sicilians demonstrated en masse, forcing the Italian government into action. Ten thousand soldiers were deployed to Palermo and the surrounding area, where they conducted house-to-house searches—no fewer than 1,200 in ten weeks. They seized hundreds of weapons along with millions of rounds of ammunition and arrested nearly two thousand people. An initial anti-Mafia law, "Dispositions against the Mafia," was eventually enacted, and implemented by a new anti-Mafia commission.

A core group of Cupola leaders, including Salvatore Greco, met and decided to curtail criminal activities until the storm passed. Hundreds of Mafiosi who had not been arrested left Sicily and mainland Italy, scattering throughout the world, notably in Montreal, São Paulo, Caracas, Mexico City and New York. The Cuntrera-Caruana family, also referred to as "the Siculiana clan," received authorization to continue operations outside Sicily. What appeared at first to be a disastrous blow in fact provided the necessary impetus for the Sicilian Mafia to expand across the globe. The aftermath of the Ciaculli massacre had repercussions as far as Montreal, where Nicolò Rizzuto's clan would gain strength, to the detriment of Paolo Violi's organization.

Years later, investigating judge and "Mafia hunter" Giovanni Falcone would deliver a negative assessment of these events: "From this terrifying bloodbath . . . Cosa Nostra has emerged . . . stronger than ever, more compact, monolithic, rigidly hierarchical and more clandestine than ever." The *piovra*, the "octopus," now had tentacles stretching almost everywhere in Europe and the Americas.

Ciaschiteddu Greco landed in Caracas and assumed a new identity: Rento Martino Caruso. The Venezuelan capital offered many advantages, not least the heat and sun, which were not especially disorienting for a man from southern Italy. The social and political climate, relatively stable and unaffected by the unrest of the Cuban revolution, was reassuring for investors. The economic environment seemed custom-made for those involved in less-than-legal business dealings: there were no banking laws, no niggling regulations, no extradition treaties with other countries. Moreover, the police corps tended to be poorly educated and underpaid, and therefore easily corruptible. Roads were in good condition throughout the country. Its coastline, which extends for 2,550 kilometres along the Caribbean Sea, made it attractive for exporters of all stripes. More important still, Venezuela has a little-patrolled border with Colombia, where the coca plant blossoms over thousands of hectares. In short, the country was a paradise for men like Greco.

The members of the Siculiana clan also emigrated to Venezuela, and to Brazil and Canada as well. In 1964, its head, Pasquale Caruana, was granted permission by the Cupola to institute a "head office" in Venezuela. The Cuntrera-Caruana family tree, with ties to those of the Vella, Cuffaro and other families, is incredibly complex. As in many Sicilian families, every first-born son and daughter takes the name of his or her grandfather or grandmother, and there is much intermarriage. Alfonso Caruana, for example, was married to Giuseppina Caruana, whose sister was the wife of Gerlando Caruana, Alfonso's brother. In other words, the two brothers married two sisters, who also happened to be their cousins.

The brothers Alfonso, Gerlando and Pasquale Caruana initially settled in Brazil but moved to Montreal in 1967 and 1968. There they were reacquainted with two dozen or so kin related to them by blood or by marriage, including two sons, a son-in-law and a constellation of cousins. All gravitated toward Nicolò Rizzuto.

Nicolò's father-in-law, Antonino Manno, eventually managed to immigrate to Canada. He had made repeated entreaties to immigration authorities since 1954, but all were in vain: his reputation as Cattolica Eraclea's Mafia boss had crossed the Atlantic. He arrived in Montreal on September 11, 1964, armed with special authorization from the Canadian minister of immigration, secured thanks to the intercession of a member of Parliament.

Tommaso Buscetta came to Montreal in 1969, when he was forty-one. Buscetta was a key figure of the Sicilian Cosa Nostra, as evidenced by his attendance at the 1957 Grande Albergo conclave in Palermo. Years later, he would gain fame as the most notorious *pentito* in the history of the Mafia: it was he who revealed the existence of the Cupola to Judge Falcone. Buscetta was a narcissist, supremely confident in his ability to charm. A handsome womanizer, he once boasted of having lost his virginity to a prostitute at age eight, in exchange for a bottle of olive oil. He claimed to have stayed in Quebec under the alias Roberto Cavallero while being treated for a venereal disease. He was also said to be one of the most prolific and efficient hit men in the employ of the Palermo-based La Barbera brothers. In 1968, an Italian court convicted him *in absentia* for his role in a double murder; but, long since departed for Montreal, he would never be arrested on the charge.

Buscetta's friend Salvatore "Totò" Catalano, who lived in Queens, New York, introduced him to the Cuntrera-Caruanas in Montreal. He presented Buscetta to Pasquale Cuntrera as a man of honour from the Porta Nuova family. In the same vein, Catalano introduced Cuntrera to Buscetta as a man of honour from the Siciliana family. These quintessential greetings among Mafiosi aimed at building mutual trust. Buscetta moved in with Pasquale Cuntrera for a while, then stayed in a hotel. Alfonso Caruana was his driver. During his stay in Montreal, Buscetta was seen on several occasions with Frank Cotroni; police were convinced that they were discussing the coordination of heroin shipments to North America. The two men also planned the illegal immigration of Sicilian citizens. An intelligence document compiled by the Canadian Ministry of Immigration accused the Cotroni brothers of having helped more than a thousand

Sicilians gain illegal entry to the United States through Canada, mostly across the Quebec border. Most of these clandestine immigrants were attended to by New York's Mafia families and put to work for companies that they controlled: essentially, restaurants, pizzerias and construction companies. Some of them played significant roles in the so-called Pizza Connection, in which dozens of pizza parlours were used as fronts for heroin distribution. Other illegals settled in Quebec, swelling the ranks of the Sicilian faction within the Montreal *decina*.

Buscetta also met with Nicolò and Vito Rizzuto. He had a serious discussion with the elder Rizzuto about the status of Sicilians in the Montreal Mafia. He concluded that the Rizzutos were not full-fledged members of the Siciliana clan, as the Cuntrera-Caruanas were, but Bonanno family members. He encouraged them to assert themselves: he too felt that it was abnormal for Sicilians to be under the thumb of Calabrians like Vic Cotroni and Paolo Violi. Buscetta travelled to Toronto as well, where he stayed with Leonardo Cammalleri, Vito Rizzuto's father-in-law.

Pasquale Cuntrera, Buscetta's host during his sojourn in Montreal, filled him in on the particulars of heroin routes: the drug, he said, "comes by ship to Canada, and from there it gets sent to New York by road." By that time, the Cuntrera-Caruanas had "become the leading importers of heroin from Canada to the United States," RCMP investigators noted. Their middleman was Giuseppe Bono, the *capomafia* of Bolognetta, a municipality not far from Palermo; he would buy the dope in Marseilles.

Pasquale Cuntrera later left Montreal and moved to a suburb of Caracas. He purchased a lavish home protected from prying eyes by majestic pine stands and concrete walls nearly five metres high, with strategically placed surveillance cameras that swept the grounds night and day. Cuntrera invested in narcotics trafficking as well as apparently legal enterprises in the tourism, farming and real estate industries. He also cultivated contacts among the leaders of the major political parties. In 1970, his new base of operations in Venezuela expanded with the arrival of his brothers Paolo, Gaspare and Liborio along with his cousins Pasquale and Giuseppe Caruana.

Nicolò Rizzuto, too, succumbed to the lure of the south. He had previously invested in a residential building on Diane Street in Longueuil, on Montreal's South Shore, with Pasquale Cuntrera. In November 1971, he joined a consortium that bought a ranch in Barinas, a Venezuelan state well known for rampant political corruption. The other members of the consortium were big wheels indeed: Salvatore "Ciaschiteddu" Greco, the former head of the Sicilian Cupola; Carlo Gambino, a member of New York's largest crime family; Antonio Napoli, one of North America's most industrious heroin suppliers; and Gaspare Cuntrera, Pasquale's brother. The Ganaderia Rio Zappa, as the land and company were known, was officially a cattle company and came with its own airstrip. It was just 160 kilometres from the Colombian border, which facilitated contacts with cocaine wholesalers. In employing this strategy, Rizzuto was hardly a pioneer: operating ranches near Colombia was a popular strategy in his line of business, among other reasons because the smell of manure tended to confuse sniffer dogs. With Tommaso Buscetta, Rizzuto also mapped out the routes and methods for transporting coke from Venezuela to Canada. He recycled an old trick of Joe Bonanno's, which involved camouflaging the drug in shipments of packaged food items—powdered milk being ideal. Pasquale Cuntrera thought this was a great idea and followed Nick's example. Rizzuto's acquaintances and numerous travels to and from Montreal, Palermo, New York and Caracas attracted the attention of investigators. As early as 1970, when he went to Sicily with his wife and mother-in-law, U.S. authorities asked Canadian and Italian police to monitor his comings and goings. By then, Rizzuto had a robust network of contacts in those four cities.

Nicolò Rizzuto and Pasquale Cuntrera travelled regularly back and forth between Italy and Venezuela. Cuntrera went to see Meyer Lansky in Rome. The two men had already met in Toronto. This time, Cuntrera solicited Lansky's counsel on laundering the profits from the drug connection he had set up in South America. Lansky proffered one extremely valuable piece of advice: invest as often as possible in legitimate enterprises. Cuntrera went about founding and acquiring numerous companies, including an automobile dealership and a grocery store in Italy.

He also invested in another building in Montreal with Nicolò Rizzuto, this time on Fleury Street.

When in Italy, Rizzuto stayed at 255 Via Marittima in Frosinone, a suburb of Rome, not far from Ostia, where members of the Cuntrera-Caruana clan held sway. He invested one million dollars in state-sponsored projects with three of them: Paolo Cuntrera, Alfonso Caruana and Salvatore Vella. Tipped off by Interpol, Italian authorities learned that the men were suspected of crimes in Venezuela, including arson and drug trafficking. Except for Vella, who was the only one of the trio who had retained his Italian citizenship, they were deported.

Officially, Nicolò Rizzuto was a simple soldier in the Montreal *decina* led by Vic Cotroni and Paolo Violi. The rules dictated that he keep them informed of his activities and his travels, but he regularly flouted those directives. When Cotroni and Violi badgered him, wanting to know the reasons for his latest trip to Venezuela or Italy, he didn't even bother to answer. The CECO correctly grasped the nature of the rift between the heads of the Montreal family and their Sicilian "subordinate": "This affair, which has resulted in special mediation by foreigners from Sicily and New York, had its roots in behaviour deemed unacceptable by Cotroni and his entourage," the commission noted in one of its reports:

> The main reproaches aimed at Rizzuto were that he was a lone wolf, that he stayed away from occasions where members of the "family" could meet and discuss together, that he showed respect neither to his superiors nor to those placed under his charge, that he lied about his real intentions, that he bypassed the line of command and acted on his own initiatives in important matters, and finally that he would come and go without letting anyone know what he was doing . . . On numerous occasions, Vincent Cotroni and Paolo Violi have spoken of their intention and their power to expel Rizzuto from the family ranks.

In the Mafia, "expulsion" sounds an awful lot like "execution." Rizzuto was well aware that his life was in danger, and he admitted to Tommaso Buscetta that this was one of the reasons he had left Montreal.

Far from placating the situation, Rizzuto's extended absences only kindled Violi's and Cotroni's mistrust. On December 14, 1971, the SQ got wind of a meeting in the town of L'Épiphanie, northeast of Montreal, organized by Paolo Violi and his brothers Rocco and Francesco. Vic Cotroni was to be in attendance. The gathering was in a home on Imperia Street. A sumptuous lakeside residence, it belonged to Leonardo Caruana but was listed in his son Gerlando's name. (On the day of the latter's wedding in Sicily in 1981, Leonardo Caruana was shot dead in front of his home in Palermo. In 2007, Italy's *Direzione Investigativa Antimafia* described Gerlando Caruana as the head of the Siculiana clan.) Among the twenty-six invited guests was Giuseppe "Pino" Cuffaro, who had emigrated to Montreal in 1953 from his hometown, Montallego, in Agrigento Province. He was related by marriage to the Cuntrera-Caruanas. Pietro "Zio Petrino (Uncle Pete)" Sciara, a Sicilian fugitive who was *consigliere* to both Cotroni and Violi, was also there. But one man was conspicuously absent: Vic Cotroni. He had turned back while on his way to L'Épiphanie. Police wondered whether he had been tipped off that they were watching.

The central item on the agenda was the role of Nicolò Rizzuto. Relations with him were worsening by the week. "Violi said that Rizzuto had been jealous of him since Luigi Greco had given him control of operations on Montreal's West Island, which prevented Rizzuto from wielding greater influence within the Cotroni *decina,*" an RCMP intelligence brief reads. Violi had reason to feel threatened. Even when spoken hundreds of kilometres away, the seditious words of his rebel soldier had reached his ears. Rizzuto had had the gall to travel to New York, where he'd met the head of a Sicilian faction, Nicolino Alfano, and bad-mouthed Violi. Back in Montreal, he had reiterated his complaints to his uncle Calogero Renda.

It was obvious that, among his lieutenants, Vic Cotroni favoured Paolo Violi. That meant Violi could hope to succeed him one day, while Rizzuto would continue to play second fiddle. Violi sought to persuade his troops that his rival should be banished. "How could discipline be ensured, when one of their members refused to follow orders?" he grumbled. The meeting was a bust; no consensus could be reached. Rizzuto had far too many allies among the guests, including those who, like him, hailed from Agrigento Province. The tensions remained. Over the next five years, five of the men in attendance that night would be killed.

An incensed Violi travelled to Calabria and Sicily seeking support. Judging from the opinion of Antonino Calderone, a Mafia boss in the Sicilian province of Catania, he was greeted there with contempt. Don Calderone, who later became a famous informant, wrote of the disgust he felt toward Calabrians like Violi: "There are no Cosa Nostra families or men of honor in Calabria," he said in his memoirs, *Men of Dishonor: Inside the Sicilian Mafia,* written with Pino Arlacchi. He went on:

> Paolo Violi didn't make a great impression on me. He was a brag-gart, a big, fat man who didn't seem to have much upstairs. In any case, he was going to Calabria because he thought there were "men of honor" there. Things are different, in fact, in America. American "men of honor" aren't just Sicilians, but even Calabrians and Neapolitans. It doesn't matter. At this point one could ask: if Violi was Calabrian and an important Mafioso, how is it possible that he didn't have a direct channel, that he didn't personally know 'ndran-ghestiti [members of the 'Ndrangheta] of Calabria? . . . We Sicilians, however, did not make Calabrians men of honor . . . And then the Calabrians would talk, talk, talk. They talked all the time. Not to others, of course, but among themselves. They would have endless arguments about their rules, especially in the presence of us men of honor. They felt uneasy because they knew that in reality they were inferior to the Cosa Nostra, and they would try to confuse men of honor with all those quibbles and verbal snares.

During the same trip, Violi secured an audience with Giuseppe Settecasi, the *capomafia* of Agrigento Province. Settecasi listened patiently as his guest rattled off his grievances about Nicolò Rizzuto. Then he decided to go to Canada to investigate for himself. He also took the opportunity to attend the May 16, 1972, wedding of Don

Giacomo Luppino's son Domenico in Hamilton, Ontario. The ceremony gave the impression that relations between Sicilian and Calabrian
criminal factions were amicable, since the guest list included well-
known Calabrians such as Vic Cotroni (not to mention Luppino's
father and son) as well as Montreal-based Sicilian émigrés Giuseppe
Cuffaro, Antonio Caruana and Emanuele Ragusa. Settecasi refused to
take sides. On the one hand, he felt a far greater kinship with Nicolò
Rizzuto, a *paesano* from his home province of Agrigento. On the other,
he didn't want to risk offending the Americans and touching off hostilities by taking a stand against Violi.

Violi therefore turned to New York, where he sought the support of
Natale "Joe Diamond" Evola, the Bonanno family boss. The man had
been saddled with the "Diamond" moniker ever since the wedding of
Joe Bonanno's son Salvatore (Bill): the bride's ring had gone missing and
turned up in Evola's pant cuff. Evola in turn sent emissaries to Montreal:
Nicolino Alfano, Nicolò Buttafuoco and Michael Zaffarano were welcomed there by Domenico Arcuri, a Sicilian cab driver who was a
member of the Montreal *decina* and a close associate of Pietro Sciara.

Like Arcuri, the visitors were far more sympathetic to Rizzuto than
to Violi. Twenty years earlier, Buttafuoco had taken Rizzuto under his
wing when the latter slipped into the United States illegally. Not surprisingly, the Bonanno delegation concluded that the Cotroni-Violi group
should keep Rizzuto in its orbit. Violi was informed of the decision in
his home on Comtois Street, in Saint-Léonard. The envoys also met with
Nicolò Rizzuto, who happened to be in Montreal on one of his infre-
quent visits. They urged him to keep his superiors better informed about
his activities and his contacts, especially with foreigners. A week later,
still grousing, Violi filled his boss Vic Cotroni in on the Americans' visit:
"I told them that [Nicolò Rizzuto] goes from one place to another, here
and there, and he says nothing to nobody. He does his business and
nobody knows anything . . . He doesn't want to change . . . He has
nothing more to do with you, and is going to New York." The New York
Mafia Commission ratified the decision made by the Bonanno family
intermediaries. Violi had tried in vain to persuade its members to

authorize Rizzuto's elimination. Now it was Violi who had lost face, placing him in a dangerous and potentially fatal situation.

One evening in late fall 1972, Vic Cotroni's lieutenant Luigi Greco was renovating his restaurant, Pizzeria Gina, on Jarry Street in Saint-Léonard. First mopping the floor with kerosene, he then began to clean off accumulated dirt and grease with a metal scraper. There was a spark and an explosion. Seriously burned, he was taken to hospital, where he succumbed to his injuries. Greco was Sicilian but had played a peace-keeping role within the organization. He got along well with the Calabrians and had been magnanimous enough to attend Paolo Violi's wedding in Hamilton in 1965. His death shook the fragile foundations of the Montreal Mafia. From then on, it was clear that the city wasn't big enough for both Paolo Violi and Nicolò Rizzuto.

Accompanied by his son, Vito, then aged twenty-six, Nicolò Rizzuto returned to Venezuela. Rumour had it that Violi had put a contract out on him, despite the fact that the Commission in New York wouldn't back it.

Two of Vic Cotroni's four lieutenants were out of the picture. Greco was dead, while Vic's brother Frank had been busted for drug trafficking and would soon receive a lengthy sentence in the United States. A third, Nicola Di Iorio, wasn't interested in becoming boss of the *decina*. That left the power-hungry Paolo Violi. In the fall of 1973, events convinced him that he was destined to ascend in the Mafia hierarchy. Natale "Joe Diamond" Evola died of cancer, and an election was scheduled to choose the new head of the Bonanno family. The captains of the clan were sum-moned to the Hotel Americana in New York; the Montreal *decina* had a vote. Since Vic Cotroni was barred from entering the United States, Violi was invited to represent Montreal along with Joe Di Maulo. To Violi's delight, the main candidate (and interim boss) Philip "Rusty" Rastelli wanted his vote. Rastelli knew Montreal well: while on the lam, he had taken refuge there in the early 1960s and had benefited from the Cotroni organization's hospitality. Violi backed Rastelli, who became the official head of the Bonanno family in February 1974. "One good turn deserves another," Violi would waste little time in reminding Rastelli.

Two months later, on April 22, the police microphones that Robert Ménard and his crew had installed captured an interesting conversation in the *gelateria* on Jean-Talon Street. Violi was talking with Pietro Sciara and Giuseppe "Pino" Cuffaro. The latter asked whether he could be inducted into the Montreal outfit, and Violi refused: "No, 'cause you see, Pino, things here—I know all about how it is in America. Someone who comes here from Italy—it's orders, and you better believe it—he has to stay here for five years under us. After the five years are up, then everyone can see what he's like. Before we let a *picciotto* near us, he has to deserve to stay. We'll know if he is good or not."

On May 10, Cuffaro and an Italian Mafioso named Carmelo Salemi pressed the issue. Salemi, who lived in Agrigento, was visiting Montreal. He wanted Giovanni Caruana, the former boss of a *cantone* in Agrigento Province who had emigrated to Venezuela, to have the status of Mafioso when in Montreal. Violi gave up all pretense of diplomacy and took an abrupt tone to show the other men who was boss: "You come here, but you can't talk about affairs of the family," he insisted.

"And the business that has gone on for several years, the business of your family?" Cuffaro asked.

"But none of that," Violi went on. "That's wrong . . . They [Italians] come here, change their residence—they come here close to us, they have to wait five years with us and after that they can join. If there is an opening and if we want to give it to them. That's the way it's done."

The snub was particularly insulting to men who felt they had proven their worth. Paolo Violi was out-and-out telling them they would have to submit to a lengthy trial period before their candidacy would even be considered. Salemi, a high-ranking member of the Agrigento Mafia, insisted that Violi recognize Cuffaro, but the self-styled *padrone* of Saint-Léonard would not capitulate.

"You aren't part of us," he explained. "If you belong over there, you can't just come over here. You can't talk about your family here. You can't talk about anything . . ."

He added that his crew could not vouch for Sicilians who might find themselves in difficulty in Montreal: "Let's say you take it into your head to do something on your own—something heavy—and you don't say anything to anybody and something happens to you . . . Tell me, how do you get out of it then? Do you see how things stand, Carmelo?"

Salemi insisted that Giovanni Caruana be admitted into the organization. "You people in Italy have bad habits," Violi answered. "He was made in Siculiana, now he's in Venezuela, suppose he wasn't to go back to Siculiana, then he wants to come here . . . You people want your own law here, but it's different here."

On May 13, Violi met with the Sicilians again. He repeated that there was unity in Montreal among the representatives of the American Cosa Nostra families: he himself answered to the Bonannos but kept good relations with the Magaddino family in Buffalo, who controlled Ontario. Newly arrived Sicilians, however, were *persona non grata:* "We here have contacts with all of the families in the United States. We are all friends."

On May 17, Cuffaro reiterated his plea. He asked Violi to set up a meeting with Vic Cotroni, who had the last word when it came to inducting new members in Montreal. "I would like to meet him," he said.

"Yes, one day," Violi replied.

"I am at your disposition."

"I thank you, and expect that with time, we will be able to arrange it."

"Consider me like one of you," Cuffaro went on. "To carry out your orders, and that's my desire."

Violi didn't bend, and the Sicilians remained excluded.

That summer, the CECO cited Vic Cotroni for contempt and ordered him jailed: he was evasive on the stand, giving answers that were clearly intended to be of no use to the court whatsoever. Violi hoped he would be officially named to replace him as head of the Montreal family, but Cotroni had given no clear instructions in that regard. In January 1975, Violi shared his bewilderment with two of his confidants, Salvatore Sorrentino and Pietro Sciara. As with every exchange that took place in the Gelateria Violi, their conversation was recorded. "When Vic was put in prison, he didn't see anyone about putting someone in charge," Violi said. "He got out after two days, at Christmastime; he met with me, but he didn't tell me: 'Look, while I'm inside, you take charge here and handle the *picciotti*.' Since Vic's inside, now, somebody's got to take responsibility." He dispatched Sorrentino and Sciara—the adviser he trusted most—to New York City to ask for instructions from Philip Rastelli, the new boss of the Bonanno family. The initiative bore fruit: Rastelli assented to Violi's assuming the duties of interim boss. Violi ecstatically shared the news with associate Joe Di Maulo, on January 18, 1975: "He [Rastelli] told me: 'When Vic gets out, tell him to call me, and if a change needs to be made, I'll talk to Vic, but for now, you're taking over.'" Cotroni would soon be out of jail, but for the moment, Violi could boast of being his equal, or almost. His satisfaction would be short-lived: he was soon charged with rigging securities on the Montreal Stock Exchange and then with attempted extortion. Worse, the CECO exposed the Expo 67 tainted meat scandal. Vic Cotroni, Paolo Violi, Salvatore Sorrentino and Armand Courville, the wrestler who had given Violi his start in the Montreal criminal world, were co-owners of Reggio Foods, a meat wholesaler that sourced its wares from companies in the business of recovering livestock that had died of disease or natural causes. Though the meat was unfit even for dog food, the carcasses were cut up and processed into sausages and pepperoni.

The public learned that a significant amount of tainted meat had been used to make hamburgers sold on the site of the 1967 World's Fair. Then, in 1973, Reggio Foods had won the contract to supply the Quebec Summer Games, in Rouyn-Noranda: more than forty athletes fell ill and several events were disrupted. Quebecers were already glued to their TV screens for the CECO hearings when the commissioners began disclosing lengthy excerpts from the ice cream parlour tapes. Paolo Violi's reputation as a model citizen who donated to charities and gave out free ice cream to neighbourhood kids was reduced to less than zero. Like Cotroni, Violi refused to violate *omertà* in front of the crime commission. In fact he refused to testify at all, which earned him a jail sentence for contempt, like Cotroni before him. He may have respected the vow of silence, but the Mafia would never forgive him for being so stupidly careless as to let a cop bug his place of business. The recordings, which revealed the full scope of his criminal activities, would eventually prove extremely useful to law enforcement in Canada, the United States and Italy—not to mention fatal to Violi.

Meanwhile, in New York, "Rusty" Rastelli soon found himself in prison as well, just as Carmine "Lilo" Galante was paroled. The latter moved quickly to supplant Rastelli as Bonanno family boss. Galante, too, knew Montreal well; he had lived there. Sicilian-born, he was in favour of inducting his compatriots into the outfit and, unlike Violi, would impose no five-year probationary period. Nicolò Rizzuto paid Galante a visit and asked him to push Violi, whom he felt had become a dead weight and an embarrassment to the family, out of the leadership structure. It is reasonable to assume Galante wasn't averse to the idea: over the next few years, Violi and his associates would be knocked off one by one. While he waited to be rid of them, Nicolò returned to Venezuela with the brothers Liborio, Pasquale and Gaspare Cuntrera. He opened a restaurant in Caracas and, obviously not above a little dark humour, named it El Padrino ("The Godfather"). He would use this latest South American layover to bide his time and bolster ties to the Cuntrera-Caruanas and the Colombian cocaine cartels. His son, Vito, and family soon made the trip south as well.

CHAPTER 5

ASSASSINATIONS

O N VALENTINE'S DAY, 1976, Pietro Sciara took his wife out to the movies—to see the Italian-dubbed version of *The Godfather: Part II*, directed by Francis Ford Coppola and starring Al Pacino and Robert De Niro. It was screening at the Riviera, a depressing brick structure in an equally depressing industrial no man's land in north-end Montreal. The movie house belonged to Palmina Puliafito, Vic Cotroni's sister.

Three months earlier, Sciara had testified before the CECO. Sporting a polka-dotted tie under a pinstripe suit, he tried to appear laid-back, but tensed up once the commissioners asked him if he was familiar with the word "Mafia." "'The Mafia?' I don't know," he answered aggressively. "What's that, 'the Mafia'?" (Indeed, the words "Mafia" and "Cosa Nostra" were never spoken in the original *Godfather* film: Paramount Pictures, bowing to cries of racism from the head of one of the Five Families, Joe Colombo, had deemed it more prudent to have the characters refer to their organization by the less inflammatory terms "family" and "syndicate.") Sciara answered the CECO commissioners' questions solely in Italian and would only admit that he was acquainted with Paolo Violi and had met with him often at the Reggio Bar.

Born in Siculiana, Sciara had spent a good part of his life in Cattolica Eraclea, where he had come into the orbit of Don Nino Manno, Nicolò Rizzuto's father-in-law. During the Second World War, Sciara had been recruited into the Italian Air Force. Later, he had served as a *campiere*, guarding land for the Marquis Borsellino, the owner of the *palazzo* of the same name on the Piazza Roma. Italian authorities declared him to be a Mafioso under the anti-Mafia legislation enacted in 1963, following the Ciaculli massacre. Found guilty of *delinquenza per associazione* (crime by association) and placed under house arrest in the Piedmontese *comune* of Balzola, in northern Italy, Sciara had preferred to flee to Canada. He lived on De Bellefeuille Street in Saint-Léonard, where his neighbours included Leonardo Caruana. Sciara's right-hand man was Domenico Arcuri, a Sicilian-born taxi driver. The CECO hearings revealed that Sciara had worked as a night watchman for Inter-State Paving, the company owned by Senator Pietro Rizzuto. "I do not know everyone in the employ of my company," the influential senator would later insist during a lengthy interview with a *La Presse* reporter.

Given his origins, it might have seemed natural for Pietro Sciara to side with Montreal's Sicilian mobsters in their fight with the Calabrian faction. But loyalty was a factor: Sciara had become *consigliere* to both Vic Cotroni and Paolo Violi, and he took the duty to heart. Violi even addressed him using the term of endearment "Zio Petrino" (Uncle Pete). Sciara had backed Violi's efforts to have Nicolò Rizzuto expelled from the *decina*. He was also pleased with the election of Phil Rastelli as Bonanno family boss, a process from which Montreal's Sicilian faction had been excluded. And he had successfully pleaded on behalf of Violi in his bid to win Rastelli's approval as acting head of the Montreal clan. All these were reasons for the Sicilians to view Sciara as a traitor.

On the way out of the Riviera cinema, Sciara affectionately took his wife's arm. As they walked toward their car, three armed men appeared out of the shadows. The sixty-year-old *consigliere* was felled by a blast to the head from a .12 gauge shotgun. His wife was wounded in the arm. Nearby, a fourth man waited at the wheel of a van with its engine running, in which the murdering trio rapidly made their escape. The police found the van, but not the killers.

Payback was not long in coming. Less than a month later, on March 10, 1976, a high-ranking adviser to the Rizzuto clan, Sebastiano Messina, was shot dead by an unknown assailant as he sat in his café-bar on Tillemont Street. Violi suspected that Messina was one of Pietro Sciara's killers.

The opening salvoes had been fired in what would prove to be a war of attrition between the clans.

Paolo Violi was serving out the one-year jail term imposed by the CECO for his refusal to testify. As the time went by, he was probably safer in his cell at the Bordeaux Prison than behind the counter at the Reggio Bar. In his absence, he asked his brother Francesco, nine years his junior, to look after the family interests.

On the evening of February 8, 1977, Francesco was at work at his restaurant-supply firm, Violi Importing & Distributing, in Rivière-des-Prairies, on the eastern tip of the Island of Montreal. One or more men, armed—as at least one of Sciara's killers had been—with .12 gauge shotguns, burst in and fatally shot him.

Paolo Violi was no fool: he knew he had fallen out of favour with the other forces vying for control of the Montreal Mafia. At night, he asked the prison guards to make sure the door to his cell was locked. He wasn't the only one convinced that his days were numbered; the prison authorities reckoned they were as well, and as a result he was not granted permission to attend his brother's funeral.

After his release, Violi sold the Reggio Bar to the brothers Vincenzo and Giuseppe Randisi, Sicilian mobsters allied with the Cotroni clan. Despite the heightened danger, Paolo continued to frequent his former head office, which had changed names: the Reggio was now known as the Bar Jean-Talon. Violi continued to attend meetings and card games there. The tension was palpable, and activity feverish, but if Violi was afraid, he didn't show it. He was overconfident by nature.

Eventually, Violi agreed to a sit-down with Nicolò Rizzuto. Some of their close associates evidently felt a peaceful resolution of the conflict was still possible, but the two clan bosses held firm. No microphones captured this particular conversation, but it is reasonable to assume that Rizzuto asked Violi to step aside, and the latter rejected the entreaty outright. His hubris and sense of Mafia honour apparently trumped his will to live.

Police got wind of other planned hits. A tip from a resident of Saint-Léonard led police to a van stuffed with weapons, ski masks and white coveralls in the parking lot of the Langelier shopping centre, not far from the Bar Jean-Talon. After several days of further investigation, they decided to tail two suspects, Domenico Manno and Agostino Cuntrera. They were frequently seen meeting with other Sicilian Mafiosi in local eateries. One evening, officers watched the pair head to the Bar Jean-Talon "as if they were reconnoitring the place," as one investigator wrote in his report. On Thursday, January 19, 1978, after listening in on a conversation between Violi and Vincenzo Randisi, the bar's new co-owner, the police were sure they were close to nabbing Manno and Cuntrera in the act. They watched as the two stepped out of a white Cadillac near the Bar Jean-Talon and entered through a door leading to the basement. But Violi wasn't there: he hadn't shown up for his meeting with Randisi. He had been held up at home, the supervising investigator on the case wrote, by an "electrical problem."

On another occasion, officers stationed on the second floor of a duplex on Druillettes Street watched through a window as two masked men got out of a van and headed quickly toward the Reggio Bar. They gave up, however, when they realized that so much snow had piled up in the alleyway behind the establishment, it would likely hamper their escape.

The police had now been shadowing Manno and Cuntrera for about three weeks, and it was proving expensive. Top brass and the investigating team agreed to call off the surveillance for the weekend. On the Sunday, around suppertime, Violi answered his telephone at home: it was Randisi, inviting him to come to another card game at his old establishment. Violi finished eating, kissed his wife, Grazia, and their children, put on a coat and went out. Snow was falling in large, fluffy flakes. After he arrived at the Bar Jean-Talon, he called home to tell Grazia that he wouldn't be home too late. The bugs had been removed from the establishment for some time by then, but the phone line had been tapped anew. Not long after, a man was heard picking up the receiver. He announced to the person on the other end of the line, in a low voice: "*Il porco è qui*"—the pig is here.

Violi sat down at a table in the bar, accompanied by several card players. Shortly after 7:30 P.M., a masked man who had been hiding in the basement ascended the stairs at the rear of the ice-cream bar and strode purposefully through the room. He carried a *lupara,* the double-barrelled, sawed-off shotgun favoured by Sicilian mobsters for permanent settlings of accounts. This particular weapon was a Zardini, a rare model manufactured in an Italian village. The shells were uncommon too, containing pellets larger and more destructive than those normally available in North America. From where he was sitting, Violi could not see the assassin approach, and if his tablemates did, none of them so much as batted an eyelash. The killer pressed the barrel of the *lupara* to Violi's skull, behind his ear, and pulled the trigger. The forty-six-year-old godfather of Saint-Léonard collapsed to the floor. A police photograph taken in the aftermath of the hit shows him lying flat on his back, blood pooled around his head, arms and legs outstretched as if crucified. Minutes later, Domenico Manno phoned his brother-in-law, Nicolò Rizzuto, in Venezuela and laconically shared the news: "*Il porco è morto*"—the pig is dead. Grazia Violi also got a telephone call, from a man saying there was "trouble at the ice-cream bar" on Jean-Talon.

Violi surely had known that his death warrant had been signed. The Montreal police had offered protection in exchange for his collaboration, but he declined; the idea of becoming an informant disgusted him. He also refused to run or hide. This came as no surprise to Robert Ménard, the undercover cop who had gotten to know him well while posing as his tenant for six years. "Paolo was not a runner," he said years later. "Paolo was not the type who would run away from anything . . . He was going to weasel to the cops? Not when your balls turn to brick. Not Paolo. Never! He's just not the type. To him, honour, that was it. I'm not glorifying the son of a bitch. I'm just saying that was the way he was."

Vic Cotroni, too, must have known Violi would be eliminated sooner or later, but he lacked the clout to step up and prevent it from happening. Vic had cancer and was steadily weakening; as he did, new forces were asserting themselves in Montreal's mobland. The Mafia was bringing in fresh blood, and the Sicilians were taking over. More important, in New York, the Commission had given its assent for Violi's execution. Had Vic Cotroni interceded or voiced his disapproval too insistently, he would have been next on the hit list.

Cotroni nonetheless showed up for Violi's lavish funeral at the Church of the Madonna della Difesa in Montreal's Little Italy. Several Calabrian Mafiosi from Ontario, chief among them Giacomo Luppino, Violi's father-in-law, made the trip. Domenico Violi, Paolo's father, travelled from Parma, in suburban Cleveland, once again obtaining special authorization from the Canadian department of immigration. It had been less than a year since he had buried his son Francesco. There were no emissaries from the American Cosa Nostra: the families sent floral wreaths only. Flowers also arrived from Italy. The church was filled to capacity, and a sizable crowd of curious onlookers massed outside as snow fell.

The police suspected six men of being mixed up in the murder, all of them with connections to Nicolò Rizzuto. An arrest warrant was issued for Nicolò's son-in-law, Paolo Renda, who in 1968, ten years earlier, had, along with Vito Rizzuto, set fire to his Boucherville barbershop. Renda managed to flee to Venezuela before the warrant was signed, and would return to Montreal only after it was lifted. Investigators have always believed that the hit was planned by Paolo Renda's father, Calogero, but he was never charged. Suspicions were also directed at Giuseppe LoPresti.

Charges initially laid against Vincenzo Randisi, one of the brothers who had bought the Reggio Bar from Violi, were withdrawn. Randisi stated he had simply seen a stranger enter the café and shoot Violi. Three other suspects pleaded guilty to charges of conspiracy to commit murder. The first, Domenico Manno, was Nicolò Rizzuto's brother-in-law. The second, Agostino Cuntrera, who had arrived in Canada in 1965, was the cousin of the brothers Liborio, Gaspare and Pasquale Cuntrera, and the owner of a Mikes restaurant franchise at the corner of Jean-Talon Street and Pie-IX Boulevard, where several basement meetings had been held. The third man, Giovanni DiMora, was Agostino Cuntrera's brother-in-law and his partner in managing the restaurant.

Manno had a prior conviction for running a gambling house, but the conspiracy charges were Cuntrera's and DiMora's first brushes with the law. Quebec Superior Court Justice Claire Barrette-Joncas took the time to praise the pair as hard-working citizens. In her opinion—if one were to set aside their involvement in painstakingly planning a cold-blooded murder—they were good guys: "They were model immigrants," she declared, "who performed the most modest tasks in an effort to earn a living and to slowly and laboriously build themselves a trade." There was insufficient evidence to accuse them of first-degree murder. Thanks to the surveillance operation and electronic eavesdropping, however, the police had enough to indict them on conspiracy. Cuntrera, Manno and DiMora had little choice but to plead guilty, and they both did time.

Two and a half years after Paolo Violi was slain, his brother Rocco, then aged forty, was the target of a botched hit. Rocco was known to police but less so than his brother Francesco, who had always been ready to defend Paolo's interests. Rocco had been deported from the United States after attending the funeral of Carlo Gambino, the powerful head of the family of the same name. He also had arrests and convictions for running gambling houses, but that was about it. Still, the Rizzuto clan viewed Rocco as a potential threat. As long as he was alive, he might want to exact revenge on his brothers' killers.

On July 28, 1980, Rocco Violi was at the wheel of an Oldsmobile, stopped at a red light on Pascal-Gagnon Street in Saint-Léonard, when two bikers rode up alongside. One raised a sawed-off shotgun and fired, but failed to hit his target. Rocco stamped on the accelerator and pulled away but was soon caught. A second shotgun blast did not miss. Wounded in the head, Rocco underwent surgery at Maisonneuve-Rosemont Hospital and survived—but not for long.

On October 17 of the same year, in his home on Houel Street in Saint-Léonard, Rocco sat down at the kitchen table with his family. It would be the last time he did so. The table was beside the window. In a building behind the house, a sniper had been perched for some time, waiting for this precise moment. He raised his rifle, his target in the telescopic sight, and squeezed the trigger once. The bullet pierced the window glass and thudded into Rocco's body, killing him instantly. The murder weapon, a .308 calibre Remington, was later found at the Le Baron Complex, an office building on Jean-Talon Street East.

Domenico Violi once again made the trip from Cleveland, to bury a son for the fourth time (Rocco's twin, Giuseppe, had been killed ten years earlier in a road accident). The Violi brothers' widows decided to pack up and move with their children to Ontario, under the protective umbrella of Don Giacomo Luppino and his Hamilton Mafia coterie.

Nicolò Rizzuto would remain in Venezuela for a while yet, but his son, Vito, returned to Montreal later that year to pave the way for the family's definitive conquest of the city. Although the way was now clear, the Rizzutos would have to wait for the demise of Vic Cotroni before their ascension to power could be complete. Cotroni was a pioneer of the Montreal underworld and had played no small role in establishing the Bonanno family's bridgehead in Canada. He was too prestigious to be removed.

The late 1970s and early 1980s were a time especially rife with mob assassinations, not only in Montreal but in New York and Sicily as well. The motives were not always interconnected, but it was clear that the underworld was in serious upheaval. The most spectacular hit was on Carmine "Lilo" Galante, who had presided over the modernization of Montreal's Mafia in the 1950s.

When he was paroled in 1974 after serving twelve years, Galante had challenged Phil Rastelli's recent appointment as Bonanno family boss. As Joe Bonanno's one-time *consigliere*, Lilo felt the throne was his by right. Since Rastelli happened to be headed to prison just as Galante was getting out, the way was clear for him to manoeuvre as he pleased.

It was Galante who had earlier green-lighted Nicolò Rizzuto's order to eliminate Paolo Violi and bring in new members, even though authority to liquidate made members of the Mafia and induct new ones was reserved for the boss. Galante took the liberty of including Sicilians, such as

Baldassare Amato and Cesare Bonventre, in his crew. The "Zips" had the reputation of being as loyal as they were vicious: Galante was sure they would bolster his ranks. A participant in both of the 1957 "summits," at the Grande Albergo in Palermo and in Apalachin, New York, Galante had been one of the principal architects of the Mafia's international narcotics franchise. Now, he demanded nothing less than a monopoly on heroin trafficking with the Sicilians.

Carlo Gambino, head of the eponymous crime family in New York, was felled by a heart attack in 1976. His body was barely cold in the ground when Galante began making open pronouncements that he should be crowned head of the Commission. It was not long before this self-aggrandizing offended the heads of the Five Families, not least Phil Rastelli. When his loyal lieutenant Big Joey Massino visited him in prison, Rastelli asked him to go before the Commission and seek authorization to eliminate the would-be usurper. The request was well received, in particular by Paul Castellano, the new head of the Gambino family. The Commission sanctioned the killing of Lilo Galante.

An insidious plot was concocted, and the contract was given to Amato and Bonventre, the Zips that Galante had enthusiastically inducted into the clan and who had become his bodyguards. They would have no choice but to betray their new boss. The pair were well acquainted with Galante's routine: he often did business and took meals on Knickerbocker Avenue, in a rundown area of Bushwick, in the heart of Brooklyn. The neighbourhood (originally Boswijck, a seventeenth-century Dutch word, one translation of which is "refuge") had once teemed with bars and beer halls, making it a favourite haunt of night owls. Joe Bonanno had set up his headquarters there. But Knickerbocker Avenue had lately fallen on hard times. The value of homes and stores, many of them abandoned, had plummeted. Most of Bushwick's traditional Italian population had moved out, soon to be replaced by African Americans and Puerto Rican immigrants. Those in the most impoverished strata of society have nowhere to escape to—save, perhaps, artificial paradises. The most desperate among them were the ideal customers for purveyors of heroin. They were a destitute but sizable clientele.

Some old-time eateries on Knickerbocker were extant, like Joe and Mary's Italian-American Restaurant, which belonged to Giuseppe "Joe" Turano, a cousin of Carmine Galante. The Zips liked to hang out at the few remaining pizza parlours, where the Sicilian dialect was spoken. The avenue had become their turf. The Knickerbocker Avenue neighbourhood had been one of the few spared during the riots that followed the New York City blackout in July 1977: the troublemakers, greeted by the sight of gun-toting property owners, had wisely decided to continue their pillaging elsewhere.

On July 12, 1979, Carmine Galante was dropped off at Joe and Mary's. It was a sweltering summer afternoon, too hot to eat inside, so his cousin set a table on the patio. The meal had barely begun when three Bonanno family members arrived: Galante's bodyguards, Baldassare "Baldo" Amato and Cesare "The Tall Guy" Bonventre, were accompanied by Leonardo "Nardo" Coppola, a drug trafficker renowned for his loyalty to Galante. The quartet polished off their dishes of fish and salad and emptied their wine glasses. Lilo lit up one of his famous stogies and sat back, waiting for dessert and coffee. Around 2:45 P.M., three ski-masked men ran into the patio area.

One of the killers stood squarely in front of Galante and opened fire, yelling: "This is for you, Galante." The Mafioso was struck three times by shotgun fire: in the neck, the right shoulder and the head. The force of the blasts knocked him backward over his chair. An overhead photo shows him sprawled on his back, his ubiquitous cigar still clamped between his teeth. None of the assailants bothered to filch the wad of bills, $860 in total, in his pocket. Galante died as he had lived: police believe he had ordered or perpetrated upwards of a hundred murders during his long career. He was sixty-nine years old.

Nardo Coppola, Galante's loyal associate, and Giuseppe Turano, his cousin and the owner of Joe and Mary's, also lay dead on the patio: killed to either keep them from giving testimony about the crime or from seeking retribution for it. Witnesses out front on Knickerbocker Avenue saw the three masked men leaving the restaurant in obvious haste. Galante bodyguards Amato and Bonventre followed; they could easily have shot at the fleeing killers but did nothing. They were obviously part of the plot but couldn't be charged, for lack of evidence. It took police several years to arrest somebody for the murder of Carmine Galante: Anthony "Bruno" Indelicato, the son of Alphonse "Sonny Red" Indelicato, one of the three renegade Bonanno captains who would be executed two years later on Long Island by Vito Rizzuto and his accomplices. Anthony was sentenced to twelve years in prison.

On November 16, 1980, sixteen months after the hit on Galante, Anthony Indelicato and Cesare Bonventre were among the hundreds of guests gathered at the Pierre Hotel in New York City for a lavish reception following the wedding of Giuseppe Bono, the senior member of the ruling Mafia clan in Ciaculli, the suburb of Palermo forever marked by the car bomb that killed seven *carabinieri* in 1963. With them were other influential Zips, like Salvatore "Totò" Catalano and his associate Giuseppe Ganci. When Canadian police investigators got a look at the photos, though, it was another face in the crowd of mobsters and drug traffickers that most piqued their interest: Vito Rizzuto's. The fact that he had been invited to such an important gathering, barely a month after the last Violi brother had been wiped off the map, was evidence of his unconditional acceptance within U.S. Mafia circles.

Some three hundred Mafiosi and their wives had been invited to the ceremony at Saint Patrick's Cathedral in Midtown Manhattan and to the reception at the Pierre, a five-star hotel ten blocks farther north on Fifth Avenue, facing Central Park. Not all of them had the chance to pose for pictures with Bono and his bride, Antonina Albino, but Vito Rizzuto and his wife, Giovanna, were among those granted the privilege. Standing in front of a trellis adorned with white flowers, Antonina, the daughter of a Queens pizzeria owner, was resplendent in white. The groom, in a dark suit with a carnation boutonniere, wasn't exactly the fashion-model type. The diminutive Bono wore rimless glasses and could do little to hide the fact that his hair was rapidly thinning. It was his second marriage. Next to his Snow White, he looked more like a spiffed-up version of one of the seven dwarfs.

What Bono lacked in looks, he made up for in wealth and power. He had hired two bands to play the reception, and paid $64,000 to rent the space at the Pierre, a Manhattan landmark celebrated for its Euro-chic elegance and elaborate frescoes. Bono claimed to have earned his fortune in the hotel industry, but police forces in North and South America as well as Europe suspected him of being a high-level international narcotrafficker. He maintained close connections to such varied criminal elements as the head of the Neapolitan Camorra, Michele Zaza; the Zips who had whacked Lilo Galante; and the South American confederates of Nicolò and Vito Rizzuto. Bono was among the masterminds of the Pizza Connection, and one of the main suppliers of heroin to the Cuntrera-Caruana clan. Two years previously, alerted to the fact that Italian authorities were closing in on him, he had left Sicily and moved most of his operations to Venezuela. Bono was a "man of honour" and demanded to be treated as such: even his brothers were required to kiss his knuckles in a show of respect.

U.S. authorities ordered the wedding photographer to hand over his work. The photos showed the hundreds of "distinguished" guests parading past the main entrance of the Pierre, including most of the leaders of the Gambino, DeCavalcante and Bonanno families. Montreal was well represented, not only by Vito Rizzuto and his lawyer, Jean Salois, but by Vito's lieutenant Giuseppe LoPresti, who like his boss was born in Cattolica Eraclea. A suspect in the murder of Paolo Violi, LoPresti fraternized with Cesare Bonventre whenever he visited New York City. Investigators also recognized Gerlando "George from Canada" Sciascia, yet another native of Cattolica Eraclea, along with Domenico Arcuri, Sylvestro Polifroni and Michel Pozza, the Montreal mob's key financial adviser.

In the Mafia, happy events like weddings succeed and precede bloodier episodes with metronomic regularity. Today's killers are tomorrow's targets. In the time it takes to guzzle a glass of champagne, allies become adversaries. Life seems bereft of meaning unless it is juxtaposed with death. And so while the capos and soldiers were hitting the dance floor with their belles at the Pierre ballroom, more murders were being plotted on both sides of the Atlantic.

Giuseppe Settecasi, who had made half-hearted efforts to placate the conflict between Paolo Violi and Nicolò Rizzuto, lived in an Agrigento apartment building surrounded by a tall wrought-iron fence and equipped with a sophisticated surveillance system. Its residents—judges, lawyers and businessmen—imagined themselves safe from the gunfire that rang out day after day in this turbulent part of Sicily. Settecasi was involved in a dangerous business: financing heroin labs. On March 23, 1981, after his usual card-game appointment in a small café at the train station, he arrived home. One of his neighbours heard a detonation and called police. When investigators arrived and examined Settecasi's lifeless body, they made a curious discovery. His skull was coated in a thick layer of paraffin. Underneath was a bullet hole.

The same year, Leonardo Caruana, a close associate of Settecasi, was shot in front of his Palermo home as he returned from his son's wedding. The old man had lived for a time in Montreal, where he had known Rizzuto *consigliere* Pietro Sciara, the first victim in the war that led to the annihilation of the Violi clan. In the early 1970s, Caruana had had a falling out with Nicolò Rizzuto; their differences of opinion included the fact that Caruana saw no point to the infighting between the Sicilian and Calabrian factions of the Montreal mob. There was no clear motive for his murder. It is possible that he was taken out because he had voiced disagreement within his clan, but the more likely reason for his killing is that he was a close associate of Settecasi.

In such circles, the slightest transgressions were punishable by death. The heroin trade had by now reached its zenith. Those who supplied the pipeline but flouted the established rules were eliminated. An RCMP investigation revealed that, during this time, Pasquale Cuntrera had withdrawn U.S.$500,000 from a Swiss account to pay one of the Palermo bosses, who was in league with one Salvatore "Totuccio" Inzerillo. The latter ran clandestine narcotics labs near the Sicilian capital, supplying the New York market via Montreal. He was also a careless man. He took the initiative of having Gaetano Costa, the chief prosecutor of Palermo, killed. The act, understandably, drew greater attention from authorities. Worse, Inzerillo decided to ship a consignment of heroin to his brother in New York—without the consent of the Cupola. Such unauthorized deliveries tended to be frowned upon by Sicilian, American and Canadian traffickers.

Inzerillo's life ended in a hail of AK-47 fire as he left the home of his mistress. "The gunmen fired through the sealed window of a new bullet-proof Alfa Romeo; they had tested out the weapon on a jeweler's bullet-proof showcase beforehand and found that a concentrated spray of fire on a small patch of glass worked very well," the late journalist Claire Sterling recounted in *Octopus: The Long Reach of the International Sicilian Mafia*. Inzerillo's was only one death in what became known as the Second Mafia War, a systematic killing spree that would extend throughout Sicily, to the rest of Europe, to the United States and into South America. Officially, the Cupola was now headed by Michele "The Pope" Greco—a distant relative of Salvatore "Ciaschiteddu" Greco, the Ciaculli Mafia boss who had fled to Venezuela and ran a "cocaine ranch" there with Nicolò Rizzuto. But in practice, the highest authority of the Sicilian Mafia was under the control of Don Luciano Leggio (then in prison) and Salvatore "Totò" Riina, who came from the town of Corleone, sixty kilometres south of Palermo. The Second Mafia War would see twenty-one members of Salvatore Inzerillo's clan slain.

Inzerillo's fifteen-year-old son, Giuseppe, was abducted and killed. Before shooting him in the head, however, his captors cut off his arm: the very limb with which, the boy had vowed, he would shoot Totò Riina and avenge his father's death. Then one of his brothers, Pietro, turned up in the trunk of a Cadillac in Mount Laurel Township, New Jersey: his lifeless body, hands bound behind his back, was wrapped in a plastic bag. Five one-dollar bills were stuffed into his mouth; another between his testicles.

The Corleonesi under Riina rubbed out another rival, Stefano Bontade, along with the 120 "men of honour" in his clan. "Gaetano Badalamenti lost eleven relatives. A nephew was tortured, shot and cut into pieces in West Germany," Claire Sterling wrote. "An entire buried car cemetery was dug up later in Agrigento province, with the charred skeletons of other bosses shot and burned before burial." The Second Mafia War lasted three years and saw upwards of a thousand Mafiosi killed. The Corleonesi lost very few soldiers.

The assassination in Brooklyn of the three rebel Bonanno capos, perpetrated by Vito Rizzuto and his accomplices, was to have far more decisive repercussions on the Montreal Mafia than any of the killings in Sicily. The episode put Nicolò's son's criminal career into overdrive.

Meanwhile, in New York City, the execution of Carmine Galante had done little to ease the tensions within the Bonanno ranks. The head of the family, Rusty Rastelli, was serving a long sentence at the Lewisburg Federal Prison in Pennsylvania and was thus indisposed to discipline his troops. Captains Alphonse "Sonny Red" Indelicato, Philip "Philly Lucky" Giaccone and Dominick "Big Trin" Trinchera had come to believe they were now viewed as dispensable by Rastelli's faction. Desperate to hold on to power, they discreetly secured support from the Genovese family. Captains loyal to Rastelli had the blessing of the Gambino and Colombo families.

Joe Massino remained unfailingly loyal to Philip Rastelli, visiting him in prison and passing on his instructions. When Carmine Galante asked him to abandon this go-between role, Massino refused, telling Lilo: "He [Rastelli] is like my uncle. He raised me, baptized me [into the Bonanno family]. I can't abandon him." It was Massino who then conveyed Rastelli's entreaty to the Commission seeking authorization to eliminate Galante.

In spring 1981, a Colombo family soldier warned Massino that the three capos were readying a power grab that would involve the permanent removal of their opponents, including Massino. He sought counsel from his allies on the Commission, Paul Castellano and Carmine Persico, respectively heads of the Gambino and Colombo families. Their suggestion: he should defend himself. Massino construed that advice as authorization to take out the three dissident captains.

The rest is described elsewhere in these pages: Massino and his brother-in-law, Salvatore Vitale, asked the Sicilians in the family to give them a hand; the Zips called in the cavalry in the form of their trusted Montreal allies, who sent a hit squad consisting of Vito Rizzuto, another shooter referred to as "the old-timer," and a third man named Emanuele; the signal to shoot was given by Gerlando "George from Canada" Sciascia.

Vito and his accomplices had acted as good soldiers, getting in up to their necks for the Bonanno family and, by extension, the Commission. They'd signed their oaths of allegiance in the blood of the murdered capos, in the process bumping their profile within the family circle up several notches. Neither Vito nor his father, Nicolò, however, could lay claim to absolute rule over Montreal. Vic Cotroni's brother, Frank, had recently been freed from prison and had resumed his duties. He was decidedly not pleased at the Rizzutos' bid to oust the Calabrians from the organization by knocking off the brothers Violi one after another. He considered resuming the vendetta but was dissuaded by Vic. Frank's grumbling turned to exasperation when he learned that Michel Pozza, the Calabrian outfit's main money man, was now hiring out his services to the Sicilians. Cotroni decided to have him eliminated. It was a move that would have unexpected consequences.

The fifty-seven-year-old Pozza was neither Calabrian nor Sicilian. He had been born in Trento, in northern Italy. Soon after immigrating to Montreal, he enrolled in university, studying finance. He paid his tuition by working as a doorman at the Casa Loma, a popular club on Sainte-Catherine Street East run by the Cotronis. It was there that he met Cotroni lieutenant Luigi Greco. Pozza regularly supplied Greco with financial advice until the latter's fatal floor-cleaning accident, when he made the mistake of using kerosene as a solvent. Seemingly eager to collaborate with any faction, Pozza had also become an associate of Paolo Violi and attended his wedding in Hamilton in the company of Vic Cotroni and Joe Di Maulo. His advice to all and sundry among the Mafia was to reinvest their profits in the licit economy and get involved in labour unions. He himself became active in the International Ladies' Garment Workers' Union. The CECO described him as "one of the important figures in the Montreal Mafia."

Pozza was no fool. After the Violi brothers were assassinated, he had sensed the winds were shifting. He abandoned the Calabrians and took up with the Sicilians: they were the ones doing the most business and therefore had the most money in need of laundering. Every transaction meant a tidy commission for him. In 1979, Salvatore Catalano, a prominent Zip in the Bonanno family, introduced Pozza to Vito Ciancimino, the former mayor of Palermo. The meeting took place in the resort town of Mondello, a suburb of the Sicilian capital. Police believe the agenda included narcotics trafficking and investments to be made in Canada.

The following year, narcotrafficker Pasquale Cuntrera, on his way from Venezuela, stopped off in Montreal, where he met with Pozza. The latter had been among the minority of non-Sicilians invited to the Giuseppe Bono wedding at the Pierre, in New York City. Police observed him several times in the company of Gerlando Sciascia and Giuseppe LoPresti, including on September 24, 1982, at Vito Rizzuto's home. Four days after that meeting, he was dead.

Pozza was well aware that his fraternization with the Sicilians irked his former partners like Frank Cotroni. When he returned home to Mont-Rolland (a village in the Laurentian Mountains since merged with a neighbouring municipality, Sainte-Adèle), before parking his Audi in the driveway he would drive back and forth a few times, past the front of his house on Desjardins Street, making sure no sniper was hidden in the bushes.

Pozza was invited by Frank and Vic Cotroni to meet them at the home of their sister, Palmina, who looked after the family's financial interests. Pozza sat down in the kitchen and began conversing with Vic. Frank arrived later, accompanied by Réal Simard, who held two jobs for him: driver and hit man. The young Simard, the nephew of the wrestler-turned-mobster Armand Courville, had already murdered two of Frank Cotroni's enemies and would go on to kill five more. Vic would shortly have a new assignment for him. "When we got there, Vic was in the kitchen with Pozza, and the conversation was heated," Simard recalled years later, after he became an informant. Frank Cotroni joined his brother in the kitchen with Pozza, while Simard waited in the living room with Palmina. Suddenly he heard Vic raise his voice and swear at Pozza. "I want you to report to Frank," he warned.

Frank Cotroni ordered Pozza to ditch the Rizuttos and come back to work for him exclusively. Pozza left without promising anything. Frank, on his way out to his car with Simard, whispered: "Something has to be done about him." Simard got the message. On September 28, he made his way to Mont-Rolland. Under cover of darkness, he lay in wait in the bushes across from Pozza's house. Around two in the morning, Pozza drove up in his Audi, and Simard sprang from his hiding place. He pulled out a .22 calibre pistol and shot Pozza once in the body and a second time to the head, following his mentor's admonition: "You never leave a body without giving it a bullet in the head," Frank Cotroni had once told him.

Police went through Pozza's papers at his office on Papineau Avenue and at his home in Mont-Rolland. They found a copy of a confidential government of Quebec report that recommended legalization of slot machines and casinos in the province. There was also a trove of bank records linking Vito Ciancimino, the ex-mayor of Palermo whom Pozza had met in 1979, to real estate deals in Canada. Ciancimino's sons, Giovanni and Sergio, had travelled to Quebec and invested some $2.6 million there. This included the purchase of a building in Greenfield Park, on Montreal's South Shore, and another on Saint-Joseph Boulevard in Drummondville, halfway between Montreal and Quebec City. Serving as front men for their father, the two brothers had been making similar investments since around 1976. Police eventually determined that the money came from drug deals orchestrated by Vito Rizzuto's associates, the brothers Cuntrera.

Vito Ciancimino, who had grown up as the son of a barber in Corleone, became an influential member of the Christian Democratic Party and was in charge of public works in the Palermo city administration at a time when Mafia-controlled developers began tearing down heritage buildings in the city centre and putting up shoddily built apartment blocks in their place. The boom came to be known as the "Sack of Palermo." In one four-year period, city council awarded 80 percent of 4,250 building permits to five shell companies allied with the Mafia. The mob-controlled entrepreneurs pocketed grant money destined for restoration projects and demolished several art deco *palazzi*. One building, a masterwork by the great Sicilian art nouveau architect Ernesto Basile, came down overnight. It was due to be declared a historic building, which would have saved it, but the

Mafia-linked developers saw to its demolition before the paperwork could go through. Numerous parks were paved over. As a result, the heart of one of Europe's finest cities was transformed into a collection of soulless concrete bunkers, each more unattractive than the last. Fortunately, some parts of old Palermo were spared the wrecking ball.

When sacker-in-chief Vito Ciancimino was later elected mayor of Palermo, it provoked outrage. He was soon investigated by the anti-Mafia commission and forced to resign. He remained beyond the reach of the law for years, however. The discovery in Michel Pozza's Mont-Rolland home of documents implicating Ciancimino helped change all that, and he became infamous as the first Italian politician to be convicted for membership in the Mafia. When he was arrested and hand-cuffed in front of television cameras in November 1984, he fainted.

Besides the bank records found in Pozza's home, the evidence against the former mayor of Palermo came from testimony given by Tommaso Buscetta, perhaps the most famous *pentito* in the history of the Mafia. He had fled Sicily after the Ciaculli car bombing and had been convicted for murder *in absentia*. In 1960, a witness had seen Buscetta and an accomplice abduct two men at gunpoint; the victims were never found. The clan to which Buscetta belonged was attempting to muscle in on the Palermo construction industry at the time.

One of his first arrests came in 1969, at the Saint-Bernard-de-Lacolle–Champlain border crossing between Quebec and New York State. Buscetta was travelling with two New York Cosa Nostra members in a car belonging to a known Montreal Mafioso and was in possession of four Canadian passports. He managed to elude U.S. customs agents and return to Quebec. The following year, he crossed into the United States again and was arrested. When Italian authorities did not press for his extradition, he was released. Buscetta went to live in Brazil; he was eventually arrested and extradited to Italy, where he served eight years in prison.

In 1980, he gave police the slip while on day parole. He hid out in Palermo but, sensing the imminent outbreak of the Second Mafia War and the probable defeat of his allies Stefano Bontade, Salvatore Inzerillo and Gaetano Badalamenti, he headed for Paris. Armed with another fake passport, Buscetta flew by Concorde to Brazil and bought a swank apartment in Copacabana, the storied chic neighbourhood of Rio de Janeiro. He was soon back into narcotics trafficking, big time.

As Buscetta had predicted, war erupted within the Sicilian Mafia. When the dust settled, several of his allies lined up with the victors: the Corleonesi under Don Luciano Leggio and Salvatore "Totò" Riina. Gaetano Badalamenti went to see Buscetta in Rio and pleaded with him to return to Sicily and direct a counterattack against the Corleonesi. Buscetta refused, but Don Leggio and Totò Riina's men, when they learned of the meeting, construed it as a plot against them. Buscetta's Brazilian brother-in-law disappeared. A fortnight later, his two sons, Antonio and Benedetto, vanished in turn. His son-in-law was killed in his pizzeria in Palermo, a fate that soon befell his elder brother Vincenzo as well, murdered along with his son in their glassworks in the same city.

Buscetta decided to take refuge north of the Brazilian port city of Belém, near the mouth of the Amazon, and wait for the Corleonesi to come for him. In 1983, he flew to São Paulo. His wife travelled there to meet him, unaware that she was being followed by the police. Buscetta was arrested, along with eleven traffickers. Brazilian authorities seized cases of documents, including records of long-distance phone calls and invoices for travel from Rio de Janeiro and São Paulo to Caracas, New York, Montreal and several European cities. When Buscetta learned that he would be extradited to Italy, he tried to commit suicide by swallowing strychnine. He was saved at the last minute.

Incarcerated at the Rebibbia high-security prison near Rome, Tommaso Buscetta decided to become an informant. "The new Mafia no longer has any values, nor respect for anyone," he complained—conveniently ignoring his involvement in several murders and the fact that he had flooded poor neighbourhoods in the metropolises of America with hundreds of kilos of heroin. In truth, there was no "new Mafia": the Mafia had always been an organization of wanton killers. The only difference was that it was now led by Buscetta's enemies. Despite the many voluntary omissions in his testimony, the famous turncoat proved to be an invaluable source of information.

Buscetta had the privilege of being debriefed by a brilliant man who, unlike him, possessed true values: the investigating magistrate Giovanni Falcone. The very first time Buscetta met Falcone, in a São Paolo prison, the Mafioso proffered this admonition:

> I don't believe the Italian State really intends to fight the Mafia. I warn you, Judge. After these interviews with me you will become a celebrity. But they will seek to destroy you, physically and professionally. And they'll do the same to me. Don't forget, an account opened with Cosa Nostra can never be closed. Do you still wish to interview me?

Judge Falcone, then aged forty-four, was, like Buscetta, a native of Palermo. For the past four years he had been investigating the network led by Salvatore Inzerillo, the Palermitan trafficker responsible for sending massive quantities of heroin to New York. State authorities had learned a lesson with the murder of another magistrate, Gaetano Costa, which had been ordered by Inzerillo. They had created a pool of anti-Mafia judges, sending a clear message: the killing of a judge would not impede any inquiry, because information would now be shared among multiple investigators.

For three months, from morning to evening, Buscetta detailed to Falcone the rules, philosophy, structure and operation of Cosa Nostra, emphasizing the importance of family and blood ties. Once the *pentito's* testimony was complete, Judge Falcone and three of his assistants compiled an 8,600-page dossier on the history of the Mafia, its members and its practices. At the famous *Maxiprocesso* (Maxi Trial) that ensued, the anti-Mafia judges issued more than 450 arrest warrants in Italy. "[Buscetta] handed me the key to the Mafia's structure, its organization, its methods," Falcone wrote. "From then on, I was able to decipher the Mafia's languages and moves." The informant explained that a Mafia family was the basic cell of the organization in Sicily. It comprised soldiers, who reported to a *capodecina*—literally, "head of ten," the approximate number of men under his command. Each *capodecina* was supported by a *consigliere,* or adviser. Three or four families together made up a *mandamento,* or district. The district heads met in each province of Sicily and had representatives on the interprovincial Commission, or Cupola.

"I am often asked if a man of honour can choose not to kill. My answer is no," Falcone explained in *Men of Honour: The Truth about the Mafia.* He went on:

> No one can choose to turn down an order from the Commission or from the head of their family . . . Participation in an act of violence is usually rigorously logical, and it is this logic which makes Cosa Nostra the feared organization it is. I often emphasize this concept because it is only by recognizing the Mafia for what it is—a serious and supremely organized criminal organization—that we will be in a position to fight it . . . [T]he man of honour cannot allow himself the luxury of expressing doubts about the circumstances of a murder. Either he is capable of eliminating the victim with complete efficiency and professionalism or he is not. End of story.

While Falcone was conducting his interrogations, the chief of police in Agrigento, Filippo Nicastro, happened to read the Montreal police summary of the numerous telephone conversations recorded in the Reggio Bar thanks to the undercover work of Sergeant-Detective Robert Ménard, alias Bob Wilson. The reports had languished on a shelf in the Sicilian police station for eight years. Nicastro handed them over to Judge Falcone. The anecdote is recounted in *Men of Honour,* and Falcone quotes excerpts from the conversation during which Giuseppe Cuffaro tried to persuade Paolo Violi to accept Sicilians into the Montreal Mafia:

> [T]his interesting conversation in Sicilian dialect, translated into English, was transmitted to Italy in 1976. It passed through various offices of the Ministry of the Interior before reaching the tribunal of Agrigento, which was dealing with the Cuffaro case, where it is filed away. Fortunately, one fine day in 1984, just after an interview with Buscetta, a painstaking magistrate from Agrigento calls me:

"I have here a few translations of recordings made in Canada in 1972 that seem to confirm what Buscetta is saying . . ."

Falcone realized the importance of the Cuntrera-Caruana clan. "The Cuntrera and Caruana families for their part founded genuine industrial empires, in Canada and Venezuela, working hard from the beginning of the Sixties up until today," he wrote. "We know that in the Eighties the Sicilian Mafia, led by the Cuntrera and Caruana families . . . took over a large part of the heroin traffic destined for the United States."

The judge also summed up his probe into the activities of former Palermo mayor Vito Ciancimino:

. . . I discovered that three Swiss bank accounts, in the name of an Italian suspect—let us call him Mr. X—had been used for sudden and significant movements of capital in 1981–82 . . . I asked the Swiss authorities' permission to examine the relevant documentation. The permission was granted. But the accounts suddenly dried up. I continued the investigation and discovered that the sums—five million dollars—had been transferred to a Panamian company. There they were divided into two parts: two and a half million transferred again to a bank in New York, the remaining two and a half million moved to a bank in Montreal. But its peregrinations did not stop here. They continued up until 1991.

Falcone condemned Mafia infiltration of the licit economy and the perversion of the public calls for tenders process. He was also distressed about the political influence of the Sicilian Mafia: "I believe that Cosa Nostra has been involved in all the important events in Sicily, beginning with the Allied landing . . . during the Second World War and the election of Mafia mayors after the liberation," he concluded.

Judge Falcone travelled to Canada on a number of occasions, specifically to Quebec, meeting with investigators, poring over documents and interviewing witnesses. In 1985, he spent three days on the fifth floor of the Palais de Justice in Old Montreal, gathering information to complement his investigation of Vito Ciancimino and his money laundering methods. He heard a dozen witnesses behind closed doors in the courthouse: they included bankers, notaries and the widow of Michel Pozza, Franca. Those fortunate enough to have met Falcone in Montreal recall a man with a good sense of humour. This was doubtless an effective antidote to ennui: the magistrate often took up investigations that had been stalled by the murders of colleagues, which the Mafia called *cadaveri eccellenti:* "excellent cadavers," or "illustrious corpses." Falcone was a chain-smoker, seemingly unconcerned by the long-term health effects of tobacco. Perhaps he sensed that he would meet his death at the hands of something other than heart disease or cancer. He was not overly concerned about his own comfort; he was a crusader on behalf of his people and had faith in ultimate victory. "The Mafia is not a curse from God," he famously said. "The Mafia is a human phenomenon and thus, like all human phenomena, it has had a beginning and an evolution, and will also have an end."

Falcone vacationed in Western Canada, crossing the Prairies by car and visiting the Rocky Mountains. He enjoyed the chance to travel alone with his wife, Francesca, escorted by a single RCMP officer. It was a far cry from what he had become accustomed to in Italy, where he rode in sedans with reinforced body panels and bulletproof windows, accompanied by marksmen and, occasionally, under helicopter escort. Between seventeen and sixty bodyguards were permanently assigned to him and his wife.

Falcone was the main instigator of the Maxi Trial, which took place in 1986 and 1987. Tommaso Buscetta was a principal witness. More than 350 of the 474 Mafiosi charged were convicted of serious crimes. In the meantime, Buscetta had already testified at the so-called Pizza Connection Trial in New York, against his former ally Gaetano Badalamenti, among others. No members of the Rizzuto and Cuntrera-Caruana clans were called to testify during that trial, although some of their names had popped up during the investigation. Judicial authorities were just beginning to gain some understanding of their importance.

———

On September 16, 1984, the godfather of the Montreal Mafia, Vic Cotroni, succumbed to cancer. He was seventy-three years old. In his book on the history of organized crime in Quebec, former RCMP Criminal Intelligence Directorate analyst Pierre de Champlain wrote that the lead hearse was trailed by twenty-two others and practically sagging under the weight of floral arrangements. A brass band blew endless iterations of Chopin's Funeral March. Vito Rizzuto, Giuseppe LoPresti and several other mobsters attended the ceremony at the Church of the Madonna della Difesa. Well-known personalities paying their last respects to the old don included vaudeville and TV entertainer Claude Blanchard and the publisher of *Corriere Italiano,* Alfredo Gagliardi.

With Cotroni gone, the way was now clear for Nicolò and Vito Rizzuto.

CHAPTER 6

THE NARCOBOURGEOISIE

Every spring, as it has for centuries, an expansive carpet of white trilliums covers the floor of the Bois-de-Saraguay. The woodland, which extends southward into the borough of Cartierville from the Rivière des Prairies, is notable for being the best-preserved on the Island of Montreal. Rare species—at least for Quebec—that botanists have identified there include the American hornbeam, black maple, shagbark hickory and butternut. Many of the trees are centuries old. The woodland's stewards have included the Sulpicians, the island's first seigneurs, or landowners, and others who succeeded them. Rich families like the MacDougalls and Ogilvies built stately homes nearby, but in doing so took care to preserve the natural surroundings.

By the late 1970s, however, developers had bought up a large swath of the woods and subdivided it for new residential construction. Citizens protested vehemently, joined by well-known personalities, including Pierre Dansereau, the renowned ecologist who had helped found the Montreal Botanical Garden in the 1930s. The grassroots campaign compelled the provincial government to proclaim the Bois-de-Saraguay a natural district, the first ever in an urban setting in Quebec.

The woodland was saved, but one developer managed to have his subdivision excluded from the governmental decree. It built imposing, modern homes in the Bois-de-Saraguay and sold them to rich families. Vito Rizzuto moved into the neighbourhood in 1982, a year after taking part in the slaughter of the three captains in Brooklyn. "Behind every great fortune there is a great crime": the aphorism, often attributed to Honoré de Balzac, could have been written about Vito and his partners. With drug money and other income from their various rackets pouring in, the Mafiosi were intent on joining the bourgeoisie and showing off their material wealth. Vito left middle-class Saint-Léonard and settled into his wooded bastion, away from prying eyes. Since Rizzuto knew almost all his neighbours, it wasn't exactly practical for police to stake out his home from some nearby bushes. Many of the homes on Antoine-Berthelet Avenue belonged to family members or close acquaintances, and it wasn't long before the media dubbed it *la rue de la mafia*—"Mafia row."

Vito's expansive residence, officially owned by his wife, Giovanna, was built on a 1,300-square-metre lot. The house was not a bad investment: the 2010 municipal valuation roll listed its worth as $917,500. In May 2011, it was put up for sale at an asking price of $1,995,000. The Canadian wing of Sotheby's International Realty, specializing in luxury properties, attempted to wax poetic in its online listing:

> Beautiful stone residence . . . custom built to the highest quality standards . . . [L]ocated on a beautiful lot adj. to an immense wooded area . . .
>
> Elegant granite floors grace the large entrance and cross-hall . . . A family room with wood-burning fireplace and marble mantle imported from Italy overlooks and provides the covered patio that spans the width of the house . . .
>
> A curved staircase leads the way upstairs to find a large landing with built-ins, creating a grand home office. The second floor also gives way to a luxurious and large master suite replete with a separate living area, a large dressing room and closet and a well-appointed

bathroom finished with fixtures and tiles are from Italy. The three additional bedrooms all have their own on-suite bathrooms and large closets . . .

The photos showed the home's ample garage with three wide doors extending off the main building, which is itself wider than a bowling alley is long; the facade, an awkward mix of grey stone and faux half-timbers set into stucco; and leaded glass windows in the same mock Tudor style.

Vito's sister, Maria, moved in next door with her husband, Paolo Renda (who had been arrested and convicted along with Vito after the bungled arson in his Boucherville barbershop and subsequently fled to Venezuela when under investigation for the murder of Paolo Violi). He had returned to Canada after three other members of the clan pleaded guilty to charges of conspiring to commit murder. Back in Montreal, he was running gambling houses again. A confidential police document states that the developer who sold the lots on Antoine-Berthelet Avenue was in fact Paolo Renda: "It is interesting to note that these properties [on Antoine-Berthelet Avenue] are part of a real estate development created and managed by Paolo Renda and that the majority of lots and homes have been sold to persons suspected of criminal activity."

Nicolò Rizzuto had a huge, half-million-dollar home built on the same street, next to that of his daughter, Maria. He sold it to his wife, Libertina, for the same price. Nick had been spending most of his time in Venezuela during these years, but after the rub-out of Paolo Violi, he was no longer hesitant to make the trip to Montreal. The visits, however, were always brief. He was constantly on the move between Caracas, Milan, New York and Montreal. The summer of 1982 found him in Italy, where police shadowed him, intrigued by his links to one Vito Palazzolo, a funds-transfer specialist who later went into seclusion in South Africa. Thousands of U.S. banknotes were being deposited at the Chemical Bank in New York, with the money later funnelled to Swiss accounts, namely at the Handelsbank in Zurich and the Credit Suisse in Bellinzona, an Alpine town not far from the border with Italy.

Nicolò Rizzuto was in regular contact with Giuseppe Bono and Michelangelo LaScala, both major suppliers of heroin. Police intercepted one conversation in which large sums of money were discussed, using code words. The terms, vague and mysterious, gave the impression that Nick wanted to recover a debt. He told the man on the phone to pick up a suitcase in Milan and deliver it to Venezuela. The wiretaps enabled police to conclude that Nick had, intriguingly, arranged for some luxury furniture to be shipped to his home on des Vannes Street in Saint-Léonard, where he was still living while his new house on Antoine-Berthelet was being built. The furniture came from Tuscany and was to be delivered to Montreal via Halifax. The shipping costs alone amounted to nearly $100,000.

The fourth Rizzuto clan member to move to Antoine-Berthelet Avenue was Giuseppe LoPresti. Through his wife, Rosa Lumia, born in Cattolica Eraclea like he was, LoPresti was related to the Mannos and, in turn, to the Rizzutos—no small detail in the Sicilian Mafia's use of blood ties as a defence against betrayal. LoPresti, variously nicknamed "Poor Joe" and "Sad-Eye Joe," had immigrated to Canada in 1969. He was an important link in the chain between the Sicilians and the American Cosa Nostra in moving narcotics from South America to New York via Montreal. According to Yvon Thibault, a sergeant with the RCMP's intelligence unit, LoPresti was, after a fashion, the Rizzutos' ambassador.

Lastly, Gerlando "George from Canada" Sciascia, acting through his proxyholder, Vincenzo Cammisano—a restaurant owner and yet another Antoine-Berthelet Avenue resident—purchased the lot next to LoPresti's. Born on February 15, 1934, in Cattolica Eraclea, Sciascia had come to Canada in 1955. Three years later, he slipped into the United States illegally, only to be arrested. Despite this, he managed to obtain a visa and settled in New York, where he lived in a small house in the Bronx and ran a pizza parlour on Long Island. He would later apply for permanent residency in Canada only to see his request denied.

Sciascia worked closely with LoPresti in coordinating heroin imports into the United States through Canada and was involved in laundering the profits of the trade all over the world. He oversaw the activities of the Montreal *decina* for the Bonanno family.

A 1982 report by the Montreal police force entitled *L'état de la situation du crime organisé* ("Status Report on Organized Crime") described the Mafia as public enemy number one. Like the CECO commissioners in 1976, however, the analysts' prime focus was the Calabrian clan and the Québécois gangsters affiliated with the Cotroni organization. They still had not grasped the importance of the Sicilian factor and only mentioned the names of Nicolò and Vito Rizzuto in passing.

In the meantime, Vito Rizzuto was living the good life in Montreal, refining his *grand bourgeois* taste for fine wines and whiskies. In the evening, he made the rounds of the city's upscale bars and restaurants. He tended to combine the practical and the pleasurable on such occasions, using them to broaden his network of contacts and do business both licit and illicit. He went to bed in the wee hours and slept in: there was always plenty of time to get in a round of golf later in the afternoon. A huge boxing fan, he attended almost every major bout in Montreal and the surrounding area. One day he took in a match in Cornwall, Ontario, not far from the border with Quebec, with Johnny Pops Papalia. The Calabrian-born Papalia had cut his teeth on the Montreal organized crime scene, alongside Luigi Greco and Carmine Galante. Rizzuto was ringside at the Montreal Forum for another fight, accompanied by the three men convicted for conspiring to murder Paolo Violi: Domenico Manno, Agostino Cuntrera and Giovanni DiMora. It was also another occasion for him to meet up with Claude Faber, one of Frank Cotroni's lieutenants. Later, he made another appearance at the Forum with Agostino Cuntrera and other Mafiosi for an eagerly awaited match between Mario Cusson and Dave Hilton.

Vito travelled to Toronto often, to meet Pietro Scarcella, a mobster born in the same town as Joe Bonanno, Castellammare del Golfo. After he arrived in Ontario, Scarcella became a carpenters' union organizer and a driver for another mobster, Paul Volpe, who was working in casinos in Port-au-Prince, Haiti. In November 1983, Volpe's lifeless body was found in the trunk of his wife's BMW, parked at Toronto's Pearson International Airport; police believe Scarcella led his boss to the killers. Vito Rizzuto openly consorted with traffickers and murderers. Some of them would go to see him at his home on Antoine-Berthelet Avenue. On at least three occasions between July and October 1982, he played host to Sabatino "Sammy" Nicolucci, whose prior convictions included drug possession and forgery. In February 1984, the two flew to Venezuela on the same plane.

In the wake of the three capos murder in 1981, Vito no longer travelled to the United States. When flying out of Canada, he avoided routes with stopovers in U.S. cities. He was clearly afraid of being arrested. He was even "afraid that a mechanical problem might force a pilot to land in U.S. territory," according to one Montreal police investigator. American police forces and prosecutors had insufficient evidence to bring charges against him, but they were convinced of his guilt. The FBI clearly set out its suspicions in an internal report prepared in 1985 and entitled "La Cosa Nostra in Canada." In it the Bureau considers the possible motive for the massacre of the renegade Bonanno captains: "It is not completely clear whether they were killed for their involvement in the [murder of Carmine Galante] or for their attempt to obtain a larger amount of proceeds from narcotics trafficking. The significant factor surrounding these murders is that Vito Rizzuto, Nick Rizzuto's son, is suspected of being involved in these murders. This gives further support to the theory that the Sicilian factions from the Bonanno and Montreal families are criminally aligned."

Vito Rizzuto had nothing of the psychopathic nature of Carmine Galante—suspected of more than a hundred murders—but getting on his wrong side was nonetheless inadvisable. According to police, he had his say in a succession of attacks that rocked Montreal's ice cream industry.

On May 12, 1983, a bomb exploded behind a Dunkin' Donuts restaurant on Henri-Bourassa Boulevard in east-end Montreal, right beside a franchise of Baskin-Robbins. The owner got the message: he stopped selling his ice cream to Italian banquet halls and buffets, and from then on he received no threats.

The next target was Crémerie Roberto, a dairy bar on Bélanger Street, also in east-end Montreal. The owner first received threats by phone, which he failed to take seriously. Then, in September 1983, his car was set on fire. In March 1984, his ice cream–making equipment was mysteriously sabotaged. Then he was savagely beaten by masked men who burst into the dairy bar. Finally, a perfectly respectable man—whose wife, as it happened, would later be elected a Liberal member of Parliament—paid him a visit and politely convinced the dairy bar manager that it was time he showed a little understanding. He got the message. Once he ceased delivering his delicious Italian gelati to hotels and major restaurants in the Greater Montreal Area, his problems went away.

Attacks on others continued. A small explosive device was left at the door of a candy manufacturer. A few days later, a homemade bomb caused serious damage inside the San Marco pastry shop on Jean-Talon Street East. Then in December 1984, several sticks of dynamite exploded in the Rachelli ice cream factory in Saint-Laurent, causing damage estimated at $750,000. The company, owned by two Milanese businessmen, had set up shop in Montreal at the invitation of the Quebec Ministry of Food and Agriculture. The previous summer, Roberto and Sergio Rachelli had invested two million dollars to build the factory, with the provincial and federal governments pledging to grant subsidies of $210,000 and $260,000 respectively. The investors, who owned the Societa Gelateria Rachelli, founded in Milan in 1935, hoped to corner a significant share of the Canadian market for Italian ice cream. Representatives of the governments as well as of the city of Montreal, along with a Catholic bishop, were on hand for the factory's inauguration. The bomb blast rocked the building just two weeks later. Terrorized, aghast at the apathy of the Canadian authorities and disconcerted by the powerlessness of the police, the two brothers closed up shop in Saint-Laurent and went back to Milan. They began to fear attacks on their ice cream facilities in Italy. "I didn't know the Mafia was so influential in Canada," one of them said.

The Montreal ice cream war was far from over. Réjean Chaput, age forty-eight, was killed by an assailant wielding a nine-millimetre pistol as he crossed Chabanel Street, in the north end. In his car, police found several documents pertaining to ice cream sales. One Frederic Ellmenrich died after being shot three times on the same street, in front of his place of business, Fufu Industries Inc., a maker and distributor of Italian ice cream. A few years later, his partner Vincenzo Miraglia was also killed.

Oddly, there was never so much as an inkling of trouble at Crémerie Ital Gelati, located at 5884 Jean-Talon Street East. The ice cream parlour belonged to Domenico Arcuri, who had purchased its assets from the estate of the late Paolo Violi. This was the same Domenico Arcuri who had gone to Montreal's Dorval Airport in 1972 to pick up the two Bonanno family envoys dispatched in a bid to broker peace between Violi and Nicolò Rizzuto. Arcuri, a Sicilian, was sufficiently well regarded within the Mafia hierarchy to have been invited to the Bono wedding at the Pierre in New York. He had become part of Vito Rizzuto's inner circle. The police suspected that Ital Gelati represented Arcuri's share of the booty after the Sicilian clan's victory over the Calabrians. Additionally, the Rachelli brothers of Milan had most unwisely tried to prevent this company from securing a permit to operate a dairy factory. Thirty years later, Ital Gelati still controls the Italian ice cream market in Montreal.

To his credit, however, Vito Rizzuto had not attempted to take advantage of his clan's triumph by further humiliating the Calabrians. Instead, he won them over—or at least quelled their rancour. No reprisal was decreed against Frank Cotroni for the murder of Michel Pozza, Rizzuto's "laundryman." Focusing all his energies on growing his profit margins, Vito was not about to let sentiments be a distraction. Since Cotroni benefited from a formidable network of drug-trafficking contacts, Vito reasoned that he might as well turn that fact to his advantage. He won the support, if not the sympathy, of Giuseppe "Joe" Di Maulo, a Calabrian and a pillar of the Montreal Mafia.

Di Maulo had none of the bluster of a Frank Cotroni, but people familiar with the Mafia at the time believed he played a vital role in the Calabrian faction—or what was left of it—and was a key to its future. Cotroni's criminal dossier was growing ever thicker, so much so that he would soon be spending most of his time in prison. He had received hefty sentences for drug trafficking, and police suspected he was behind several murders. Di Maulo's rap sheet, on the other hand, was fairly slim: he had served a thirteen-month term for weapons possession in 1961 and been acquitted on murder charges stemming from a triple slaying at the Casa Loma club on Sainte-Catherine Street in 1971.

Blessed with an undeniable talent for diplomacy, Di Maulo had the necessary ambition to smooth the friction between Sicilians and Calabrians and develop good relations with Vito Rizzuto, the new boss. That did not, however, keep him from remaining loyal toward Frank Cotroni. Indeed, his eldest daughter, Mylena, married Cotroni's son, Frank Jr. Di Maulo would act as a sort of mediator between the factions, meeting with representatives of one in a downtown restaurant, and delegates of the other in the long-established Italian district of Saint-Léonard. His contacts were not limited to Mafia members; his years spent managing and renovating nightclubs had allowed him to widen his network of business contacts and cultivate friendly relations with politicians, lawyers, notaries, artists, entrepreneurs, even judges.

Like Vito Rizzuto, Joe Di Maulo knew how to earn money other than by pointing a gun at everything and everyone in sight. By running gambling dens and massage parlours, for instance. And like Vito, Joe knew when it was time to fight and when it was better to run. When he felt the police closing in, he had gone into exile in Florida for two years.

Di Maulo was married to the sister of Raynald Desjardins, one of the few "old-stock" francophone Quebecers to gain the trust of the Italian Mafia's inner circle. A former nightclub waiter, Desjardins had reoriented his career to become a heroin and hashish trafficker. In the spring of 1984, he travelled with Vito Rizzuto to Milan. The Italian city is famed as a fashion capital, of course, but the two partners weren't there to shop for designer suits. Two months after that trip, Milanese police seized a 3.5-tonne consignment of cannabis from Lebanon, bound by ship for the United States, where it was to be sent on to Montreal by truck. The suspect picked up in Milan was carrying a pager registered to Desjardins.

Vito Rizzuto had retooled himself into a modern, efficient Mafioso. Without disavowing blood ties and the dominance of his Sicilian family, he was now working not only with Calabrians in Quebec and Ontario, but also with non-Italians like Raynald Desjardins and the Dubois brothers. He joined forces indiscriminately with the South American drug cartels and the Irish mobsters of Montreal's West End Gang and, eventually, the Hells Angels. Rizzuto planted himself steadfastly at the centre of operations. He exercised a unique brand of authority thanks to his ability to draw together disparate groups and individuals, who set aside their natural rivalries and worked toward one goal: wealth. He rose to become the godfather of Canadian organized crime, although that title was officially reserved for his father, Nicolò.

Besides drug trafficking, Vito and the various Sicilian and Calabrian crime families were involved in all the classic underworld activities: loan-sharking, theft, fraud, gambling, bookmaking (including video lottery terminals), counterfeit currency, prostitution, pornography, contraband alcohol and tobacco, the sale of alcoholic beverages after hours, and so on.

"They were believed to be disorganized following the work of the CECO," noted RCMP Sergeant Yvon Thibault in a report presented at an international conference on organized crime held in the fall of 1991 in Fort Lauderdale, Florida. "On the contrary, they expanded. It was the beginning of the internationalization of the Montreal mafia."

"In implementing a branch in Montreal, the Sicilian Cosa Nostra had to show superior adaptability in order to grow," the RCMP noted in another report. "It therefore recruited non-Sicilians into its ranks, who proved to be useful because of their contacts in other local and national organizations, in Toronto for example, but also internationally."

On February 7, 1983, Nick Rizzuto's name was entered in an investigative dossier filed with an investigating magistrate in Rome by the Criminalpol branch of the Italian State Police. The charge, titled "Bono Giuseppe + 159," identified the 159 accomplices of Bono, the drug kingpin whose wedding at the Pierre in Manhattan had been attended by hundreds of Mafiosi. The Criminalpol investigators in Milan described Nicolò Rizzuto as a trafficker on the same level as Bono himself. His name appeared next to heavyweights like Salvatore Catalano, the boss of the Bonanno Zips; Tommaso Buscetta (who was still in Brazilian exile at the time but would soon spill his secrets to Judge Giovanni Falcone);

Michele Zaza, of the Camorra (the Neapolitan Mafia); Sicilian boss Bernardo Brusca; Gerlando "George from Canada" Sciascia; and many others. Criminalpol noted that, since the dismantling of the French Connection, Bono's network had branched out across the planet. The investigators suspected them of having distributed three tonnes of heroin refined in Italy from morphine base.

In 1984, the RCMP thought they had Vito Rizzuto on their hook, but he slipped through their fingers. It was only the first in a series of failures and frustrations for Canadian federal law enforcement. This particular probe began with the discovery of twelve kilos of cocaine at Vancouver International Airport. The drugs had been hidden in false-bottomed suitcases. Four suspects were nabbed, including a South American doctor who decided to talk. Police learned that the intended recipient of the shipment was an Italian Montrealer named William Papier; he was supposed to pick up the suitcases in a Vancouver hotel. Papier's name was already in the RCMP's files in Montreal. Police suspected he worked for Sabatino "Sammy" Nicolucci, the man who had visited Vito Rizzuto in his new home on Antoine-Berthelet Avenue on at least three occasions in the summer and fall of 1982. The RCMP believed Nicolucci and his crew were moving a dozen or so kilos of coke every three months. When Papier called Nicolucci from Vancouver in the middle of the night, police were listening in.

"I just had a close call," Papier said. "There's cops all over the hotel."

"Shut up!" Nicolucci hissed.

"It was so close, Sammy!" a panicked Papier yelped.

"Shut the fuck up," Nicolucci warned. "We'll see each other when you get back to Montreal," he added, then hung up.

Sergeant John Norris left RCMP Quebec headquarters in Westmount and flew to Vancouver. He thought he had sufficient evidence to charge Nicolucci and Papier, even though the latter, aware he was being tailed, hadn't taken possession of the cocaine shipment. His enthusiasm was curbed by the local prosecutor, Emily Reid, who explained that a brief telephone conversation would not constitute sufficient proof. Back in Montreal, Norris and his fellow officers kept up surveillance on Nicolucci and Papier. A month later, they heard the two suspects discussing vacation plans but were sure their conversation was actually a coded reference to another cocaine shipment. The Mounties only had one concrete piece of information to go on, however: Nicolucci was supposed to catch a plane to Venezuela on February 4, 1984. That morning, the RCMP officers used a light plane to track his movements in Montreal. They watched as he got into a taxicab, got out in front of a public building, went in one door and then exited from another, suitcases in hand, hailed another cab and headed for Dorval Airport.

Other officers continued trailing him on the ground. Nicolucci was greeted at the airport by thirty-seven-year-old Sylvestro Polifroni, alias Sylvio Marro, who had prior convictions for his involvement in gambling houses and counterfeiting. Three and a half years earlier, Polifroni had been among the guests at the Bono wedding in Manhattan. Yet more interesting was the fact that Nicolucci and Polifroni boarded the same plane out of Dorval as Vito Rizzuto and his wife, Giovanna. Vito was recognized by an officer who had already shadowed him at the behest of RCMP intelligence. The four passengers transited through Toronto and Barbados before deplaning in Caracas.

Sergeant Norris and a Vancouver colleague, Larry Sizler, immediately boarded a flight to Venezuela. As soon as they arrived, they went straight to the U.S. Embassy in downtown Caracas. Jim Lockaby, an agent with the Drug Enforcement Administration (DEA), was waiting for them. He led his Canadian colleagues on a ten-minute car ride to an unobtrusive building where he introduced them to a Venezuelan secret-service agent. "Señor D" was in his sixties and a bona fide walking encyclopedia, familiar with the movements of several prominent politicians and businessmen in the country and their links to local and international narcotraffickers. After making small talk, he locked the door to his office, then walked over to some shelves against one wall and gave them a gentle shove with his shoulder. The shelves pivoted inward to reveal a room whose walls were covered with organizational charts and photographs.

"Señor D" proceeded to expound upon Venezuela's pivotal role in the worldwide drug trade. The faces in the photos included those of the

Cuntrera and Caruana families, already labelled as major-league traffickers and money launderers, and those of members of other Siciliana
Mafia families: the Cuffaros, the Vellas . . . and the Rizzutos. After this
session worthy of a clichéd spy film, Norris and Sizler were introduced
to Commissioner Ivan Israël Waizer, head of counter-espionage for the
Venezuelan State Police. Wiazer informed the RCMP officers that
Nicolucci and Polifroni first stopped in to see Nicolò Rizzuto in his home
and had then booked rooms at the Hilton Caracas, one of the finest
hotels in the capital. Nicolucci's room had been registered in the name of
Pasquale Cuntrera, the senior member of the Siciliana clan in Venezuela.
Wiazer's men had bugged both rooms and were set up in a room one
floor above, listening in.

A few days after his arrival in Caracas, Vito Rizzuto knocked on the door
to Polifroni's room, stepped inside and started talking to him and Nicolucci.

"They've got a new president," he told them in English, referring to
Jaime Lusinchi, who had been sworn in on February 2. "We've lost our contacts, but it'll only be a few weeks and everything will be back to normal."

"Shhh!" a voice was heard saying.

The police heard footsteps in the room below, then someone turning
on the sink and shower faucets to muffle the sound of their conversations. Ten days later, Nicolucci left Venezuela for Santa Cruz, in Bolivia,
which by this time was producing 80 percent of the world's cocaine
supply. (In 1980, DEA agents had landed in the Bolivian jungle, posing as
smugglers, and had succeeded in taking delivery of four hundred kilos
of the white powder.) The Bolivian interior minister, nominally in
charge of narcotics repression, was himself a trafficker. Canada had no
co-operation agreement with Bolivia, so the RCMP officers were unable
to follow Nicolucci to his next destination; the DEA therefore picked up
the trail. Meanwhile, in Montreal, the Mounties continued monitoring
wiretapped conversations in Canada. They learned that Nicolucci was
due back in Caracas on February 23, where his girlfriend, Diane
Blanchette, was to meet up with him. From there, the couple went to
Aruba, the island close to Venezuela and Colombia that was then still
part of the Netherlands Antilles.

At the same time, a woman named Gloria Mercado de Ballivian flew from Miami to Aruba. Police were sure that her task was to collect payment from Nicolucci for the twelve kilos of coke that had been seized in Vancouver and perhaps arrange a further transaction. Sergeant John Norris headed for Aruba as well. He would later learn that the suspects had been alerted to his presence.

The probe, conducted simultaneously in five countries—Canada, Venezuela, Bolivia, Aruba and the United States—had soon amassed sufficient evidence to link Sammy Nicolucci and William Papier to the Vancouver haul. The two men were arraigned in Montreal Superior Court, and subsequently tried and found guilty by a jury. Each was sentenced to fourteen years. They appealed, but the verdict was upheld.

At the conclusion of that investigation, RCMP officers arrived at Vito Rizzuto's residence on Antoine-Berthelet Avenue, armed with a search warrant. The new godfather politely ushered the policemen in, his face and manner showing no nervousness whatsoever. Obviously, the search wasn't going to turn up a thing. When the officers had finished going through drawers, cupboards and closets, Rizzuto escorted them to the front door, a wry smile on his lips. From that moment on, he was logged in police files as the leader of the Mafia in Montreal.

In July 1984, the Mounties had barely closed their file on Sabatino Nicolucci when Vito Rizzuto's name popped up again, this time as part of a heroin investigation. Posing as a trafficker eager to expand his dealings in Western Canada, an undercover officer from Calgary had bought heroin from members of the Sicilian outfit in Montreal, hoping to move all the way up the chain to Vito. Staking out a small Italian café on Bélanger Street from a building across the street, investigators observed Vito and Raynald Desjardins conversing on the sidewalk on multiple occasions.

The undercover man succeeded in baiting known traffickers, including Giuseppe Armeni, who had already done time for murder, and his nephew Domenico, along with members of the Morello family. But the cop eventually gave up under the pressure of his assignment. After eighteen months of intensive efforts, he still had nothing that would incriminate Vito Rizzuto. Once, when he insisted on meeting the boss, his contact warned him that he would have to be patient: "We've known him for twenty years; you're gonna have to wait. He'll talk to you when he's ready to talk to you." The RCMP's frustration was just beginning. They knew what Vito was up to, but they had nothing on him. The investigation was called off. Police eventually launched another. The investigators were again convinced that the plumber-in-chief was Vito Rizzuto, but netting him was something else entirely. In this case, the man who turned on the taps to pump in the drugs was a former doorman at a strip bar on Montreal's South Shore by the name of Denis Lemieux.

A doorman could hope to earn about a thousand dollars a week in tips. It was clear that Lemieux was pulling in far more than that. His uncommon financial prowess had enabled him to purchase two bars, including Le Privé, on Bishop Street in downtown Montreal. He moved out of his modest bungalow on Westley Boulevard in Saint-Hubert, and into a spacious mansion in Saint-Denis-sur-Richelieu, farther east on the South Shore. Depending on his mood, he drove either a Mercedes 300 or a Mazda RX-7. The very exemplar of a 1980s narcobourgeois, he travelled extensively and cultivated extremely profitable contacts.

Lemieux's original source was Nicolucci, but it was his meeting with Luis Cantieri, a multilingual Brazilian in league with the Rizzuto clan, that put him on the road to big money. Cantieri knew Quebec well: he had once played for the Castors de Montréal, a semi-professional soccer team. He had connections in Argentina, Peru, Haiti, Venezuela and India, and especially in Caribbean countries, where Lemieux would travel to meet the suppliers. Cantieri's role was to orchestrate the shipments. The cargo followed an elaborate path. From São Paulo, it left by ship bound for New York or Baltimore. From there, it was trucked to Saratoga, in upstate New York and, 250 kilometres to the north, crossed the border into Quebec in a concealed compartment in a tractor-trailer. Lemieux took delivery of about fifty kilos per year by this route, a considerable amount for the time, and dealt most of the merchandise out of his Bishop Street bar.

Lemieux was eventually busted in 1985 and sentenced to fourteen years in prison. (Freed after serving one-third of his term, he soon resumed his drug operations but was killed in November 1992 along with three other people, including two innocent women in their twenties, by machine-gun-wielding assailants in a residential building in Brossard, on the banks of the St. Lawrence Seaway on the South Shore of Montreal.) Luis Cantieri was also arrested and convicted along with two co-conspirators: travel agent Jean Lamarche and a globe-trotting businessman-cum–drug runner named Norman Rosenblum. That investigation showed police that cocaine imports to Montreal had reached unprecedented proportions. Coke was the drug of choice for many. Rather than being wafted into a soporific state, users experienced an intense "rush" and felt alert, quick-witted, confident and brilliant. It was relished by everyone from stockbrokers to lawyers, politicians and musicians.

This burgeoning market stoked the greed of suppliers, importers and resellers alike. But in the criminal realm as elsewhere, the aphorism "too much of a good thing" is an apt one. The excessive supply of cocaine drove prices down sharply. Before long, enterprising dealers were converting the powder into the more crystalline form known popularly as "crack" or "freebase." Crack cocaine could be sold in smaller quantities and, therefore, to more customers. It was inexpensive to produce and easy to ingest: much like hashish, users could simply smoke it, rolled into cigarettes or using glass pipes. Cocaine had never been so accessible: a "rock" could be had for as little as three dollars. But the dealers weren't losing out. Crack's rush was immediate and intense but fleeting, so users got hooked quickly and needed more and more. The social impact of the drug was devastating. Cocaine was no longer reserved to the rarefied realms of stock exchanges and professional firms; it was now ravaging inner-city streets. Its victims began showing up in hospital emergency rooms at an alarming rate. In the United States, the first "crack babies," characterized by abnormally low birth weights, were born to addicted mothers in late 1984. The epidemic did not attain such severe proportions in Canada, but it caused extensive harm nonetheless.

The misfortune of so many brought joy to a rapacious few. The profits from trafficking in the cocaine boom complemented those of the Rizzuto and Cuntrera-Caruana clans' long-established heroin trade. The skyrocketing revenue presented a daunting problem for the Montreal Mafia, however: thousands of banknotes were piling up and were in danger of rotting—literally—unless they could be funnelled back into the licit economy.

When an Italian prosecuting judge named Gioacchino Natoli came to Montreal as part of his investigation of Pasquale Caruana and Giuseppe Cuffaro, one of the many witnesses he heard from was a clerk at a branch of the Montreal City and District Savings Bank (now Laurentian Bank of Canada). The woman told him how a large quantity of two-, five- and ten-dollar notes that she had been asked to count "didn't smell right."

"Do you mean the money physically smelled bad?" the prosecutor asked.

"That's right," she said. "It smelled musty."

From 1978 to 1981, Sicilian mobsters paid weekly visits to the City and District branch in Dollard-des-Ormeaux, on Montreal's West Island, carrying up to $500,000 at a time in hockey-equipment bags. Alfonso Caruana and his cronies would pull up in front of the bank in a van and drag the heavy sacks inside. Clerks would spend half a day counting the small-denomination bills in the basement, after which they would hand over nice, clean bank drafts to these most unconventional clients.

RCMP Sergeant Mark Bourque was able to trace U.S.$36 million worth of that money funnelled into Swiss accounts. Interrogated by Judge Natoli at the Montreal courthouse, the manager of the bank, Aldo Tucci, candidly explained: "They were entrepreneurs who had a company in Venezuela. But I was simply following the instructions I was given." He said he had notified Raymond Garneau, the chairman and CEO of the bank (and a former Liberal minister of finance in the provincial government of Robert Bourassa), and that Garneau had approved the deposits. Garneau denied this, stating that he had signed no such authorization, but he admitted that he had wondered whether the bank could refuse the money without being exposed to legal proceedings.

Giuseppe Cuffaro deposited more than seventeen million dollars in small bills at a branch of the Hellenic Canadian Trust on Parc Avenue and at a branch of the National Bank of Canada on Saint-Michel Boulevard. Sergeant Bourque was revolted by the behaviour of the Canadian banks. In his opinion, there was a very good reason why the Cuntrera-Caruana clan had made Canada their home: the country was a heaven-sent pool for them to wash their dirty money in.

But Canada wasn't the only such paradise. On November 27, 1978, Alfonso Caruana and Giuseppe Cuffaro were searched when they arrived in Zurich on a flight from Mirabel International Airport, just north of Montreal. Customs officers found $600,000 stashed in the false bottoms of their suitcases. The two passengers claimed the cash was from the sale of a boat. They paid a fine and were sent on their way. Alfonso Caruana had been dirt-poor when he arrived in Canada in 1968: he had only one hundred dollars in his pocket. It was obvious the two men were in the business of laundering money, but they were breaking no laws.

Caruana and Cuffaro travelled constantly. In 1981 and 1982, Cuffaro left Montreal at least ten times. A probe of his American Express account revealed that he had made business trips to Zurich, Caracas, Miami, Aruba, Rome, Bologna, Palermo, Nassau, London, Hollywood (in Florida), New Delhi and New York, often more than once. He also found time to visit Singapore, Rio de Janeiro and Bangkok. The Sicilian Mafiosi were decidedly in the vanguard of the globalization of capital flow.

In the space of a few years, tens of millions of dollars coursed through accounts controlled by Alfonso. With Giuseppe Bono, among others, as a partner, Caruana set up front companies in Milan. At one point he spent a month in Thailand with Cuffaro. He already owned homes in Canada and Venezuela when he bought a luxe villa in Melide, on the outskirts of the banking district of Lugano, a city in the Italian-speaking Swiss canton of Ticino, just two hours' drive north from Milan. Police observed him there conducting an exchange of money with Mafia boss

Antonio Salamone, part of the Greco clan, who had come especially from Brazil to meet him.

Lugano is a study in both natural beauty and financial expediency. Straddling the border, Lake Lugano reflects the Italian Alps in the southernmost third of its waters, and the Swiss Alps in the northern two-thirds. The canton of Ticino is the third-largest financial centre in Switzerland, after Zurich and Geneva. The banking industry alone employs nearly ten thousand people in the city of Lugano. Historical connections with Italy are multitudinous. Most important of all to men like Alfonso Caruana was the Swiss authorities' legendary, maniacal reverence for bank secrecy.

In 1982, Alfonso moved to England to take over the business of his cousin, Liborio Cuntrera, who had died of cirrhosis of the liver. Vito Rizzuto's Tudor revival home on Antoine-Berthelet Avenue may have been a posh pad, but it paled in comparison with Broomfield Manor in Godalming, Surrey. Caruana bought it for £450,000, almost a million Canadian dollars at the time. He paid cash. Built in the Georgian style, it boasted six ample bedrooms as well as a heated, lighted swimming pool. Elegant flower beds surrounded a basin with a waterfall. The three-hectare grounds, enclosed in a 2.5-metre-high wall, included kennels and tracks for dog racing. Pasquale Caruana lived not far from his brother Alfonso, in a residence only slightly less sumptuous. The Hook was located in the upscale London suburb of Woking, which like Godalming is part of the so-called stockbroker belt. It too had an indoor pool and a dog track, but featured a sauna instead of a water garden. It had cost Pasquale almost as much as what Alfonso had paid for Broomfield Manor. The luxury real estate agent's listing had described it as "ideal for the busy businessman who needs easy access to Heathrow and London [airports]."

Liborio Cuntrera's body was repatriated to Italy for burial. He had been living in England for seven years, during which time his brothers Pasquale, Gaspare and Paolo called Venezuela home. Liborio had emigrated from Sicily to Canada in 1951, when he was twenty-two, and became a naturalized Canadian citizen. He had never been arrested—quite the feat considering his pivotal role in the Cuntrera-Caruanas' narco-empire and money-laundering network. He had been a close associate of Francesco Di Carlo, a gangster of no small note in Mafia history.

Di Carlo also lived in Woking, in a mansion called Brankdene; it too was encircled by a lofty fence. Two huge Alsatians guarded the property. At night, the gates would occasionally swing open to admit limousines; area residents mistakenly believed that the lord of the manor was in the hotel business. After Liborio Cuntrera's death, Di Carlo began to visit his neighbours Alfonso and Pasquale Caruana frequently.

The peace and quiet of Surrey's nouveaux riches seemed not particularly troubled by the discovery, early in the morning of June 18, 1982, of the body of Roberto Calvi. He was found hanging beneath Blackfriars Bridge in London's financial district, with bricks stuffed into his clothing to weigh it down, and the equivalent of fifteen thousand dollars in various currencies in his pockets. Calvi was the chairman of the Banco Ambrosiano, which had just gone bankrupt. His nickname in the press was "God's banker."

He had earned that sobriquet because the private bank's principal shareholder was the Institute for Works of Religion, otherwise known as the Vatican Bank, headed at the time by Archbishop Paul Marcinkus, an American. Calvi was also a member of a Masonic lodge called Propaganda Due (or P2), whose grand master was Licio Gelli. The motives for the Calvi murder remain nebulous, but it appears some influential members of the Mafia were extremely displeased at having lost the colossal sums they had deposited at the Banco Ambrosiano. Roberto Calvi's son Carlo, a banker living in Montreal, remains convinced his father was killed because he was privy to the secret financial dealings of the Mafia and the Vatican. In 1997, a prosecutor in Rome laid charges against several suspects. One was Giuseppe "Pippo" Calò, known as the "Mafia's cashier," who sat on the Cupola and was on the side of the victorious Corleonesi during the Second Mafia War.

Francesco Di Carlo was implicated too. When he decided to co-operate with authorities in 1996, Di Carlo denied having been the murderer of "God's banker" but did acknowledge that Pippo Calò had asked him to do the deed. According to Di Carlo, the killing had been ordered by both Calò and Licio Gelli, the P2 grand master.

Di Carlo was also alleged to have been part of the plot to assassinate Carlo Alberto Dalla Chiesa, who was a friend of the Canadian Senator Pietro Rizzuto. In 1982, Dalla Chiesa, a general of the *carabinieri,* was named a prefect for Palermo to combat the Mafia. The appointment provoked an outpouring of joy. Sicilians placed great trust in the general, who had a well-founded reputation as a true servant of the state. He dared to call things as he saw them: the Sicilian Mafia could not prosper without collusion by politicians, specifically members of the Christian Democratic Party—and he unhesitatingly identified the most corrupt among them. The Mafia feared him. One hundred days after his arrival in Sicily, he was assassinated along with his wife, Emanuela, and their driver/bodyguard. The killing had been ordered by the Corleonese boss Totò Riina.

Another "illustrious corpse," as the Mafia was fond of saying.

Di Carlo's name was on the lengthy list of the accused at the Maxi Trial in Palermo. Italian authorities maintain that they notified British law enforcement as early as 1976 of Di Carlo's presence in suburban London. They even provided his address, apparently, but for reasons unknown he was never arrested.

Di Carlo regarded his wealthy neighbour Alfonso Caruana as a brother. After he became a *pentito,* Di Carlo told prosecutors that the Corleonesi had wanted him to eliminate Caruana, but he had refused. Had he really received that order? Perhaps Di Carlo, known in English mob circles as "Frankie the Strangler," sought to cultivate an image of a good guy to whom the idea of killing a close friend was abhorrent. One thing is certain, however: he collaborated actively with the Cuntrera-Caruana clan, among other things, on a major operation to transport heroin to Montreal. The dope was hidden in furniture.

On August 21, 1984, a few days after a consignment of teak furniture cleared customs in the Port of Felixstowe, in England, a cheque in the amount of thirteen thousand dollars was deposited in a Montreal bank branch. Nine days later, the cargo was en route to Canada, and the money was in a bank in Bangkok, Thailand. The transaction was unremarkable and attracted no attention. But by December 2 of that year, it no longer appeared insignificant at all. That day, a routine search by British customs officers turned up 250 kilograms of hashish hidden in another shipment of furniture. The shipper was Shalimar Enterprise, based in Kashmir; the consignee was London-based Elongate Ltd. Once off-loaded at Felixstowe, the furniture was supposed to transit through a London warehouse before being sent on to Montreal. New manifests were to be created for the shipment to fool Canadian authorities into believing the goods' country of origin was England, and not Kashmir. In this way, the traffickers hoped to reduce the suspicions of HM Customs and Excise investigators—who nonetheless seized the drugs and arrested two Montreal-based envoys of Pasquale Caruana and Antonio Zambito.

In early 1985, British customs learned that Elongate Ltd. was expecting another consignment of furniture, this time from Thailand-based Chiangmai Treasure Co., Ltd. As soon as the ship docked at the Port of Southampton, officers rushed to open the container. They found nothing but furniture. In May, Chiangmai sent another containerized shipment. An unsuspecting Francesco Di Carlo told customs that it was to be transshipped to Montreal, freight paid, to an import-export company that was headed by Antonio Zambito and had been founded by Pasquale Caruana and his brothers. Drug-sniffing dogs helped customs agents find several packets of almost pure heroin carefully hidden inside compartments in luxury teak tables. They kept part of the dope and allowed the rest to proceed to Montreal, counting on the RCMP to nab whoever showed up to collect it.

A month later, on the Felixstowe docks, a dog handler had to strain with all his might to keep his sniffer dog, Ben, from tearing the leash from his hands. His colleagues had just opened another container of furniture. Ben was barking furiously with good reason: among the wares were two tables identical to those that had been examined in May in Southampton, and each contained thirty-five kilos of brown heroin. Once again, the container had been shipped from Thailand, destination Montreal.

RCMP drug squad investigators were on the alert and placed the Montreal suspects under surveillance. A report states that they were especially intrigued "by almost daily meetings held by individuals of Italian nationality" at a small convenience store on des Galeries d'Anjou Boulevard in east-end Montreal. The store's owner, Salvatore Vella, was seen speaking with Pasquale and Gerlando Caruana, Giuseppe Cuffaro, Luciano Zambito and Filippo Vaccarello. Some of these same individuals occasionally went to a warehouse that they had rented in Saint-Laurent, in the western part of the Island of Montreal.

During the surveillance operation, officers observed Filippo Vaccarello and an individual unknown to them enter the office of the accounting firm of Alfonso Gagliano, who the previous year had been elected as the Liberal member of Parliament for the riding of Saint-Léonard. The reason for that visit has never been made clear. The RCMP noted this fact in a report, which it subsequently sent to the office of the future prime minister, Jean Chrétien. *La Presse* reporters looked into the MP's unusual relations. Another individual, Dima Messina, a financial representative of Vito Rizzuto who specialized in money laundering, had also been seen in Gagliano's office in the late 1980s. When asked about the matter, the MP replied that he knew neither Vaccarello nor Messina. "Italian names ring a bell . . . but no," he said. "They are not clients. I checked with my wife. Vaccarello? That means nothing to me. There has been information to the effect that Messina was in my accounting office . . . I really don't know. It's a mystery. My office is a public place: if a client sends someone to pick up an envelope or a document, we give it to them; we don't ask questions."

Pasquale Caruana was one of the principal suspects in the case of the furniture smuggling scheme. He lived in a lavish home on Belleville Street, in South Shore Longueuil, which had taken two years to build and cost $1.5 million. Vincenza, the wife of his brother Gerlando, owned mountains of jewellery. RCMP Sergeant Mark Bourque noted that just about every day, she would invite neighbouring housewives, with much ceremony, for an afternoon snack.

Another shipment of teak furniture arrived in the Port of Montreal on June 19, 1985. The next day, the RCMP intercepted a conversation between Pasquale and Gerlando Caruana. They were discussing the purchase of a plastic bag sealer to aid in the repackaging of the heroin.

"I need this thing and I'm going to buy it tonight," Gerlando said.

"Yeah, okay. Everything's okay," was Pasquale's reply.

The Mounties seized fifty-eight kilos of heroin in the Saint-Laurent warehouse. On June 21, four members of the network were arrested in Great Britain, and four more in Montreal. Canadian police lacked sufficient proof to bring in Pasquale Caruana, but their British counterparts nabbed Francesco Di Carlo; an English court later sentenced him to twenty-five years. Antonino Cassarà, assistant to the chief of police of Palermo and one of the main authors of the "Bono Giuseppe + 159" report, went to interrogate Di Carlo in prison. Three days after he returned to Sicily, he was gunned down by at least a dozen assailants as his horrified wife looked on. The hit had been ordered by the Corleonesi clan under Totò Riina. Cassarà's name was added to the increasingly long list of illustrious corpses.

The RCMP arrested Gerlando Caruana, Luciano Zambito, Filippo Vaccarello and Lucio Bedia (the latter was eventually acquitted). Gerlando's brother Alfonso realized that staying in Great Britain was a risky proposition. He put his mansion in the stockbroker belt up for sale and fled to Venezuela. His wife and children returned to Montreal, and he eventually joined them there. They moved into a house in Laval worth some $200,000. Compared to Broomfield Manor, it was a modest home indeed. But the time for playing at bourgeois gentleman of the manor had passed. Alfonso Caruana now had to assume the role of an honest, hard-working everyman. He opened Pizzeria Toscana, on Jean-Talon Street in Saint-Léonard, where he kneaded and flipped dough while his wife, Giuseppina, worked the cash register.

Revenue Canada nevertheless took an interest in him. In 1986, the federal agency seized $827,624 in his bank account, having noted that millions of dollars had transited through it. Caruana contested the seizure in writing. In a sworn affidavit, he stated that he had not been a resident of Canada during the period in question and therefore did not owe any income tax on the money. Revenue Canada officials responded that he had laundered some nine million dollars through Canadian banks and that Italian authorities were seeking to indict him on drug trafficking charges. They invited him to meet with them and explain his actions. Alfonso declined, telling the taxman he could keep the money, and then fled once more to Venezuela.

"According to the public prosecutor of Palermo, the Cuntrera-Caruana clan controls a very large heroin trafficking network," notes a 1990 strategy report by Quebec's organized-crime research office (Bureau de recherche du Québec sur le crime organisé). "Italian police believe it sold more than five hundred kilos of heroin around the world between 1980 and 1988. This represents proceeds of $4 billion."

While continuing to deal in heroin, Vito Rizzuto decided to diversify and boost his network's revenues by importing several dozen tonnes of hashish. That sideline would very nearly force him to trade the comfort of his lavish home on Antoine-Berthelet Avenue for a jail cell. But, as usual, fortune was on his side, and he escaped the clutches of the police and the legal system with relative ease.

CHAPTER 7

HASH AND COKE

THIS WAS THE GENIUS OF Vito Rizzuto: if a transaction was likely to involve any risk, he subcontracted it; he would put up the money for his partners, offer them guidance and put them in contact with suppliers, but he never—or very seldom—got his own feet wet. On the phone, he spoke in code; in person, he often limited himself to a nod or shake of the head. But anybody who needed to know, knew exactly what he meant. And it galled the police to no end. The baron of Antoine-Berthelet Avenue was never going to repeat the errors of Paolo Violi, the hapless Calabrian who had braided his own noose by yammering on like a magpie in his bugged ice cream parlour.

No shortage of young wannabes were clamouring to go to the front lines for Vito Rizzuto, galvanized by considerable sums of money. And Vito encouraged them. One such aspirant was Christian Deschênes. Intelligent and ambitious, he had studied administration at Université du Québec à Trois-Rivières. He was strong and agile and had fared well on campus hockey and football squads. After leaving school, he went to Lebanon, telling friends that he'd joined up with the Christian Phalangists, the far-right militia who would sadly become famous for

having perpetrated the September 1982 massacre of between 700 and
3,500 (estimates are contested) men, women, children and elders in the
Palestinian refugee camps of Sabra and Shatila, in Beirut, while members of the Israeli military had the sites surrounded.

On his return from Lebanon, Deschênes went to work at the Castel
Tina, a strip club in Saint-Léonard that belonged to Paolo Gervasi, an
associate of the Sicilian clan. Unlike those at Chez Parée downtown, the
fanciest such establishment in Montreal, the doormen at Castel Tina
weren't the tuxedo-clad type. Back in the 1970s, the charred bodies of
two repeat offenders suspected of a triple murder had been found, one
lying on top of the other, in the trunk of a car abandoned at the rear of
the establishment. In 1980, Mafioso Nicolò Morello had been gunned
down in a stairwell. "It wasn't a dive, but it wasn't exactly high-class neither," recalls one gangster-turned-informant.

The Castel Tina's seedy reputation wasn't about to keep Vito
Rizzuto from hanging out there. He would regularly be seen at the bar
raising a glass with friends, but socializing wasn't his only reason for
visiting. He often retreated to an upstairs office to make phone calls.
Whenever he did, the doormen—Deschênes among them—were
under orders to screen arriving patrons. Deschênes also did other jobs
for Vito. One of them began on September 22, 1986, when Deschênes
and an accomplice, James Morgan, flew to Larnaca, Cyprus, with a
stopover in London. In Cyprus, they travelled to the port city of
Limassol and boarded the *Petros Z,* a cargo vessel with Pakistani registry. The skipper was an Ontarian named Thomas Malcolm Johnson.
The freighter sailed to Lebanon, where the party was met by Christian
Phalangist generals. Among them was Samir Geagea, a key leader of
the Christian militia, which had fought a bloody war in the country's
mountainous central region against forces loyal to the Progressive
Socialist Party of Walid Jumblatt.

Deschênes oversaw the loading of twenty-four tonnes of hashish
onto the *Petros Z,* and the smugglers settled in for a long, uncomfortable
voyage, first through the Mediterranean and then across the Atlantic
Ocean. During the trip, Deschênes boasted to the captain, Johnson, that

he had got into the hashish importing business using money he'd earned as a Phalangist mercenary. The real story was that he'd borrowed $400,000 from the owner of a gas station in Laval, north of Montreal, to buy the hash that now sat, tightly packed in bales, in the hold of the *Petros Z.* Others had invested the rest of the money, chief among them Vito Rizzuto. On October 19, as an ocean storm raged, the cargo was transferred from the mother ship to the *Sandra & Diane II,* a small fishing vessel registered in the Magdalen Islands, a tiny archipelago in the middle of the Gulf of St. Lawrence that is part of Quebec.

The hash was off-loaded at Dock Number 3 in the Acadian village of Chéticamp, on the western coast of Cape Breton Island, Nova Scotia, then divided up and put onto three rented Ryder trucks. At around five-thirty in the morning on October 20, one of the trucks swerved off the road eighty kilometres farther south, near Baddeck, and got stuck on the shoulder. Police arrived at the scene and got a look at the cargo. Poorly hidden amongst freshly caught perch and sacks of other fish were eight tonnes of hashish.

The alert went out, and a second truck was stopped on the Trans-Canada Highway near Florenceville, New Brunswick. A search revealed another eight-tonne load of hash, as well as weapons. Deschênes was following close behind in a Toyota Cressida with his girlfriend, a barmaid from the Castel Tina, and two other men. All were arrested.

Nine days later, Montreal police located the third white Ryder truck. It had been abandoned in the Rivière-des-Prairies neighbourhood, on the eastern tip of the Island of Montreal. The keys were still inside, but the licence plates had been removed. There was no sign of the hash. All that was left in the truck box were sixty-nine crates emptied of the fish they had contained. Investigators painstakingly went over the truck and lifted fingerprints from a single individual. Police later estimated that the remaining eight tonnes of hash had earned the traffickers a cool $22 million, while the cost to purchase the drugs plus travel and other expenses would have been in the neighbourhood of $7.5 million. In other words, even though police had seized two-thirds of the goods, the estimated profit was still fourteen million dollars.

A thorough search of Deschênes's Toyota and his personal effects turned up a bonus for investigators: the number of a Swiss bank account and a slip of paper on which was scrawled the name "Vito" and a telephone number. A second note said, *"Crédit à Vito: 280 000 $"* ("Credit to Vito: $280,000"). The RCMP asked Swiss authorities to run the bank account number. They found that millions of dollars had been transferred to that account from the Caisse Populaire Notre-Dame-de-la-Merci, a Desjardins Credit Union branch in northeastern Montreal. Police ramped up their investigation.

The money was often conveyed to the credit union branch in small-denomination notes, stuffed into attaché cases or hockey bags. Dima Messina, one of Vito Rizzuto's laundrymen, had persuaded the assistant manager to issue bank drafts payable to the bearer. The drafts were then sent to Switzerland, Dubai, New York, Hawaii, Italy and Spain. Those arriving in Spain were cashed by an Egyptian named Samir George Rabbat, reputedly one of the top ten hashish brokers in the world.

Rabbat had been arrested in Montreal in 1982, just as he was about to move into a newly built home only blocks away from Vito Rizzuto's residence on Antoine-Berthelet Avenue. He had excellent connections with hemp producers in Lebanon's Bekaa Valley. After leaving Montreal, he had settled in Marbella, the resort town on the Costa del Sol in southern Spain. Besides running drugs, he was heavily involved in weapons smuggling, not only in the Middle East, but also in Colombia, where the FARC rebels were his clients.

The captain of the *Petros Z* decided to talk to police, and his testimony was damning. Among other things, he indicated that the Phalangist chieftains had demanded large sums of money before allowing the ship to leave Lebanon. In the fall of 1988, Christian Deschênes was sentenced to ten years in prison. He avoided a further five-year term by paying a $500,000 fine. Part of that sum came from the $266,636 in cash that he had in his possession at the time of his arrest in New Brunswick. He was then paroled barely two years later, on January 9, 1991. In the eyes of the RCMP, the premature release was suspicious. "The unusual parole process followed in this case resulted in two subsequent investigations," a confidential report states. "Those investigations revealed that influential persons were in favour of Christian Deschênes's early release." The report does not name any of those "influential persons."

Slips of paper appearing to incriminate Vito Rizzuto—especially the note mentioning $280,000 in credit—had been found, but this was not enough to bring charges against him; indeed, he was never even questioned in the case. The partial botching of the hashish importing operation led by Deschênes didn't trouble Vito, either. He had plenty of other partners with whom he could embark on similar ventures. The Christian Phalangist militia leaders in Lebanon were all too keen to supply him with hashish, tonnes of it at a time, in exchange for weapons and money. In truth, the Montreal Mafia had a long history of dealing with Lebanese contacts. A decade earlier, in 1975 and 1976, police had listened in as Frank Cotroni telephoned Suleiman Franjieh, then president of Lebanon and part of the country's Christian minority, at his home. Cotroni had gone to Cyprus to negotiate a shipment of 550 kilos of hashish. The RCMP estimated that at the time, 90 percent of the hash imported to Canada was being transited through the wartorn island nation.

In 1980, the FBI learned of the theft from a Boston armoury of a huge quantity of firearms and ammunition, including M16 automatic rifles. They were smuggled to Montreal and then sent on to Lebanon, where they were traded for hashish. Police informants told of an "incident" during which Mafia members, eager to demonstrate the efficiency of the weapons they were preparing to hand over to their Lebanese clients, shot at occupants of a Palestinian refugee camp.

Not long after the arrest of Christian Deschênes, RCMP officers intercepted a conversation between Vito Rizzuto and his right-hand man, Raynald Desjardins, who by now had bought a home on Gouin Boulevard in the same upscale neighbourhood as Antoine-Berthelet Avenue. Although they spoke in code, the police understood this much: the two men had recently sunk quite a large amount of money into a huge

hashish buy in Lebanon, but the remainder of the operation was dragging on needlessly.

Sometime in the fall of 1987, the *Charlotte Louise* dropped anchor
in Trinity Bay, on the northeast coast of Newfoundland. The vessel, a
thirty-metre fishing trawler, was laden with sixteen tonnes of Lebanese
hashish. Three moonlighting fishermen hired by a man named Gerald
Harvey Hiscock hefted the bales onto a speedboat, which then ferried
the precious cargo to an abandoned island in the bay called Ireland's Eye.
Barely three square kilometres in size, the island contains a natural harbour well protected from North Atlantic storms. Fishermen first settled
on the island in 1675, but by the time Newfoundland joined Confederation
in 1949, the community was disappearing. In the late 1960s, a government
plan sent the island's remaining inhabitants—sixteen of them—to be re-
settled in larger communities. Several houses and sheds remained standing, in the shadow of the picturesque St. George's Anglican Church,
offering an enterprising smuggler a perfect place to stash his booty.

Gerald Hiscock had family ties to the area and knew the island well.
He also had a certain amount of criminal experience. In May 1980, he'd
been busted for importing seventy kilos of hashish. He was aided and
abetted in that particular enterprise by none other than the man then in
charge of the RCMP drug squad, Staff Sergeant Paul Sauvé; the two were
arrested when police raided Sauvé's downtown Montreal apartment.
The Mountie was fired and sentenced to five years in prison. Hiscock
collaborated with the police and was rewarded with a mere two-year
term. Once released, he'd returned to his reprobate ways: when he
supervised the transfer of the hashish from the *Charlotte Louise* to
Ireland's Eye, he was out on bail following charges in another massive
cannabis importing scheme.

The captain of the trawler, Brian Erb, was also on police files for
involvement in drug smuggling. But he was especially renowned as a
colourful latter-day adventurer. A dozen years earlier, he had made headlines by purchasing and salvaging a hundred-metre freighter that had
been stranded in the St. Lawrence River. He refitted the old tub and
renamed it *Atlantean No. 1*. Before long, though, it was impounded by

creditors for nonpayment of debts and auctioned off. Convinced he had been swindled, Erb rounded up a crew of twenty-or-so teenagers, boys and girls, boarded the ship on a guarded dock in Quebec City and set out down the icy St. Lawrence, hoping to reach international waters, where they would be safe from capture. The RCMP and the Coast Guard pursued the ship for eleven days before the modern-day freebooter and his ragtag crew, slowed by the ice floes, finally gave up.

In late October 1987, RCMP officers boarded the *Charlotte Louise* at Blanc-Sablon, a small Quebec fishing community just across the Strait of Belle-Isle from Newfoundland. After an extensive search, they hit pay dirt: five hundred kilos of hashish sealed in waterproof sacks and stashed in the ship's water tanks. They arrested three men and a woman from the Montreal area, but Captain Erb escaped and dropped out of sight. The police were convinced, however, that a far larger amount of hashish had recently landed in the region.

In the fishing communities around Trinity Bay, people had been noticing some odd comings and goings on the water. Hiscock and his three labourers were busy moving the bales of hash out of the ruined buildings of Ireland's Eye to an isolated location on the mainland and reloading them onto a truck with Quebec licence plates. The RCMP descended on the tiny island, while other officers caught up with the truck on the Trans-Canada Highway, some fifty kilometres to the west, near Gander International Airport. The drugs were hidden under a layer of onions.

Investigators returned to their transcripts of the wiretapped conversations between Vito Rizzuto and Raynald Desjardins. Some time before the seizure, Desjardins had called Rizzuto from Newfoundland, saying he would soon be back in Montreal, and when he was, he would fill him in on some details. He added that "something [would be] happening next week." The men were again choosing their words carefully, but the police would later insist to crown prosecutors that "something" obviously meant the transfer of the hashish.

The hash had indeed arrived at Ireland's Eye one week after that conversation. Desjardins had been spotted in Newfoundland with one Michel Routhier, owner of a restaurant in Belœil, Quebec, and Routhier had been seen with Hiscock before the bales were transferred from Ireland's Eye to the truck ostensibly carrying onions.

Rizzuto was arrested and charged along with Desjardins, Routhier, Hiscock and the latter's three hired hands. Rizzuto spent the Christmas holidays behind bars. In March 1988, after he was freed on bail, he was seen with Dima Messina, his main money mover. Vito didn't appear to be especially bothered by the fact that he was facing serious charges for hashish smuggling. He rode around town in his current vehicle of choice, a $250,000 Ferrari Testarossa registered to Messina, and kept on doing business, seemingly unfazed. The police did learn, however, that he was furious—not with them, but with one of his front men, Antonio Calabrò. The careless underling had siphoned money from the till of a South Shore bar to fund a deal that had gone sour. In his world, such an indiscretion was grounds for immediate termination. Before long, nobody could find Calabrò anywhere. His body was never located, and his family refused to assist police in their investigation of his disappearance.

The trial of Rizzuto, Desjardins and their accomplices for the importing of sixteen tonnes of hashish to Newfoundland began in October 1990 at the courthouse in St. John's, the provincial capital. It turned out to be an unmitigated disaster for the government, thanks to a monumental blunder committed by the RCMP.

During the trial, Rizzuto had taken to eating at Newman's, a restaurant on the ground floor of the Radisson Plaza Hotel in St. John's. RCMP officers, having heard that Vito had another hash smuggling operation in the works, had secured authorization to conduct electronic surveillance on him, whatever the location. They knew that he took his meals in the company of his lawyer, Jean Salois, and the lawyer defending his co-accused, Pierre Morneau. The Mounties should have known the eavesdropping was a risky option: such conversations are protected by lawyer-client privilege, and obtaining a warrant to listen in on them requires a special procedure. Apparently, they weren't too worried about the potential breach of protocol. Officers decided to hide a bug in the base of a table lamp at Newman's. Corporal Terry Scott of the RCMP detachment in St. John's discreetly asked the restaurant manager to seat Rizzuto and the lawyers at table six, on which sat the bugged lamp.

One evening, a New Brunswicker came to the restaurant for supper. His name was Guy Moreau—a name that, to an English-speaking Newfoundlander, is easily confused with that of Pierre Morneau, so Moreau was seated at table six. When Morneau and his guests arrived a few minutes later, the manager realized the error and asked a waiter to take the lamp from table six and switch it with the one at the table where the Morneau party was sitting. When he picked up the lamp, the waiter found it strangely heavy. He examined it more closely and found it had some suspicious dents in it. He spoke about it to a co-worker, who wrote a note for the lawyers that read, "Be careful, you might be bugged." Then he slipped the note onto the table. Two days later, the lawyers were back at table six and so was the doctored lamp. The lawyers inspected it and found the hidden microphone.

Back in court, they were incensed—all the more so because they had learned that two of their hotel rooms had been subject to electronic surveillance as well. The RCMP countered that they were not interested in recording their conversations, but in gathering information on another suspected plot. The protest fell on deaf ears. Their handling of the operation had been so abysmal that it irreparably discredited the case against the suspected smugglers. Judge Leo Barry of the Newfoundland Supreme Court ruled that the police had stepped outside the bounds of their warrant. On November 8, 1990, he told Rizzuto and his three suspected accomplices, Desjardins, Hiscock and Routhier, that they were free to go. The only men found guilty in the case were two of the three labourers, Robert Trépanier and his son Robert Jr., of Laval, Quebec. They were handed nine- and seven-year sentences respectively.

The young waiter who had tipped off the lawyers about the bugged lamp, meanwhile, lost his job.

It wasn't the only botched police investigation involving Rizzuto. In October 1988, a year after the boarding of the *Charlotte Louise* at Blanc-Sablon and the Ireland's Eye bust, Sûreté du Québec officers arrested drug dealer Normand Dupuis at the airport in Sept-Îles, on the north shore of the St. Lawrence. Dupuis had just taken delivery of 587 grams of cocaine. He was not only a dealer but a heavy user with a serious addiction problem, and a father of three. He decided to co-operate with the police, confessing to the investigating officers that he was involved in something bigger: a scheme to import thirty-two tonnes of Lebanese hashish. The mastermind of the operation, he revealed in a thirteen-page affidavit, was none other than Vito Rizzuto.

Dupuis had worked as a fisherman on the North Shore, and he knew the waters of the Gulf of St. Lawrence like the back of his hand. The previous summer, he said, he had met the owner of a boating store in Montreal, who introduced him to Vito Rizzuto. "He was a tall, slim guy who drove a BMW or a Porsche," Dupuis told police. "He was introduced to me as *Monsieur Vito Rizzuto, le boss.*" He said Rizzuto had fronted him $80,000 through a middleman to buy an old thirty-five-tonne boat, the *Jeanne-D'Arc,* and outfit it for high-seas navigation. Dupuis was to rendezvous in international waters with another ship that had sailed from Lebanon, take delivery of several tonnes of hash and bring it in to port at Longue-Pointe-de-Mingan, Quebec, a village between Sept-Îles and Blanc-Sablon. The cargo ship had run into mechanical trouble off the Azores, and the huge consignment, with a street value of $280 million, had never made it to Quebec.

Dupuis named his price for co-operating and agreeing to testify against Rizzuto: he told his handlers he wanted $10,000 to move away from the North Shore; a new identity and a passport; $120 a month during his jail time; and the money necessary for him and his girlfriend to complete a drug rehab program in Oka, west of Montreal. He pleaded guilty to the charges of cocaine possession and conspiracy to import hashish, and received a reduced sentence, serving his time in a wing reserved for informants at the Parthenais Detention Centre in Montreal, where he easily obtained day passes. The following summer, he telephoned Jean Salois, Vito Rizzuto's lawyer, and asked for an appointment with him. Salois was leery, fearing some sort of trap. He agreed to meet with Dupuis but had the man photographed upon entering and exiting his office. He also arranged to have their conversation recorded.

Dupuis made Salois an offer that, to the informant's mind at least, was attractive: he would agree not to testify against Salois's client in exchange for a "lifetime pension" worth $1 million. Salois said nothing in response to the offer. But the interview had provided him with the means to discredit the star witness at his client's upcoming trial, and it wasn't going to cost him a cent. He handed the photos and the recording over to the prosecution.

Dupuis was sentenced to a further thirty-two months in prison for obstruction of justice. The key witness for the prosecution had been exposed as an opportunistic clown. Without his testimony, the government suddenly didn't have much of a case. It went ahead regardless, and in December 1989, a practically insouciant Vito Rizzuto showed up for the trial at the courthouse in Sept-Îles. Two witnesses, one of whom was among his co-accused, swore that Vito had nothing to do with the planned hashish deal. "Every time Dupuis met the boss, it wasn't Vito; it was Val," claimed Pierre-Louis Lepage, of Magog, Quebec, referring to Valentino Morielli. Quebec Court Judge Louis-Charles Fournier ruled that, while there had undoubtedly been a plot to smuggle drugs, there was "not an iota of evidence with regard to the participation of Vito Rizzuto," adding that not only had it been impossible to corroborate Dupuis's testimony at the preliminary inquiry, but it was also contradicted by witnesses called to trial.

With the verdict pronounced, Rizzuto rose, politely thanked the judge, shook his lawyers' hands and walked from the courtroom, free as a bird. A year later, he would be let off just as easily in the Ireland's Eye hashish case and, in a rare display of receptivity to a reporter's question, observed laconically: "One word can mean so much, especially when that word is 'acquittal.'"

Vito, it seemed, was as untouchable as the halo around the moon, and after these initial acquittals, that aura would envelop him for years to come. It also seemed to protect a number of his most trusted associates. In July 1990, police seized twenty-seven tonnes of Lebanese hash at Baleine, on the eastern tip of Cape Breton Island. The drugs had a street value of around $280 million. Long-time Rizzuto crony Antonio Volpato was the Sicilian clan's investor this time, in partnership with Montreal's West End Gang. Leaders of the latter group were arrested and charged, but not Volpato. The series of busts convinced Rizzuto that it was time to tread carefully. "I need to make myself scarce for a while," he told a close associate. He had another good reason to ease up on the hashish-importing component of his business portfolio: his Middle Eastern sources were drying up because of war. In October 1990, Syria invaded Lebanon, crushing the Christian forces. It wasn't a serious blow to the Sicilian clan, however: a temporary dip in the supply of one drug could easily be offset by ramping up their traffic in another. One with a far more attractive cost-benefit ratio: cocaine.

At 11:30 P.M. on November 17, 1992, North American Aerospace Defence Command (NORAD) operators based in Florida picked up a suspicious aircraft movement on their radar screens. A Convair 580 had taken off from somewhere on the Guajira Peninsula in northern Colombia, some 1,850 kilometres from Miami, with no flight plan filed. This was no light plane ferrying a handful of tourists; a Convair 580 had passenger seating for up to forty. Two U.S. Coast Guard surveillance aircraft, a Falcon and a Piper Cheyenne, were dispatched to intercept it. The pilots observed that the Convair's navigation lights were turned off, further proof that this was no regularly scheduled flight. The sophisticated radar tracking on-board the Falcon and the Piper enabled the Coast Guard to shadow their quarry effectively regardless of weather conditions.

At the controls of the Convair was a forty-four-year-old Quebecer named Raymond Boulanger. He had previously managed a hotel in Bonaventure, on Quebec's Gaspé Peninsula, before relocating to Colombia, where he now worked for a cocaine transporter named Luis Carlos Herrera-Lizcano, who dealt indiscriminately with the rival Cali and Medellín cartels.

Boulanger flew over the Dominican Republic on a heading that would take him across Bermuda. Units of the U.S. military base at Guantánamo Bay, Cuba, went on alert. A third surveillance plane took over for the

Falcon and the Piper, and settled in to shadow the Convair at a distance of fifteen kilometres. The Americans notified Canadian authorities that the Convair was due to penetrate their air space south of Halifax. Two CF-18 fighters took off from Canadian Forces Base (CFB) Goose Bay, in Labrador, and closed in on the turboprop at Mach 1.8.

The pilots made their first contact with the Convair above Saint John, New Brunswick. They performed several manoeuvres, signalling the pilot to stand down, then eased up alongside, so close that they were able to repeat the order to Boulanger using hand signs. Boulanger refused and flew on westward, over Quebec. Their fuel running low, the CF-18s were forced to land in Fredericton, New Brunswick. It was 7:15 A.M. Nine Bell OH-58 Kiowa helicopters left CFB Valcartier, near Quebec City, and CFB Saint-Hubert, just east of Montreal, to give chase, but they could only do so at low altitude and at their maximum speed, which was less than 225 kilometres per hour.

Around nine in the cold November morning, Boulanger put the Convair down on a strip at an abandoned Canadian Forces base at Casey, in the heart of Quebec's boreal forest, about 350 kilometres north of Montreal. At the height of the Cold War, the base had been part of the Distant Early Warning (DEW) Line, which ringed Canada's Far North as a defence against incursions by Soviet bombers. Not much was left of the facility, save the frayed wires and decaying walls of its former radar stations. A tracery of bumpy forest roads linked Casey to the small town of La Tuque, 150 kilometres to the east.

The daring pilot taxied away from the runway in a vain attempt to camouflage his snow-white aircraft. His three Colombian companions fled into the forest, clad only in jeans and T-shirts. The outside temperature was minus twenty-seven degrees Celsius. Boulanger holed up in a cabin that belonged to a mining company and attempted to reach his partners by telephone, without success. Three hours later, the army located the Convair. A helicopter landed in front of the cabin, and Boulanger was arrested on the spot.

After a lengthy search, Canadian Forces soldiers and RCMP officers found the three Colombians, by now suffering from hypothermia and only hours from death. In the evening, around nine o'clock, officers stopped a van on a forest road some eighty kilometres to the south. The two occupants claimed they were on a hunting trip. One was carrying a driver's licence in the name of Denis Lévesque, but police quickly confirmed his true identity: he was none other than Christian Deschênes, the most adventuresome of Vito Rizzuto's point men. The other man was named Antonio Sforza. They had made it as far north as Casey but were now attempting to escape in the opposite direction.

In 1986, Deschênes had been sentenced to ten years in prison for his part in unloading a twenty-four-tonne shipment of Lebanese hashish on the coast of Cape Breton Island, but had resumed his smuggling ways after being granted a curiously early release.

The van was registered to a numbered company in Laval. Inside, police found containers of aircraft fuel, a .12 gauge rifle, a .38 calibre revolver and fifteen thousand dollars in cash. When investigators examined the Convair, they found the forty or so seats had been removed and replaced with forty-five fuel drums and two containers. The Convair 580 has a standard range of 1,800 kilometres, but the flying distance from Colombia to Quebec was more than 4,500 kilometres, requiring the crew to replenish the aircraft's fuel tanks while in flight. It was an extremely risky method that could have meant a premature end to the trip, in the form of a mid-air explosion. A bigger surprise, however, awaited police when they opened the containers: 3,919 kilos of cocaine divided into 152 packets, each wrapped in a large aluminum pouch. Being the good businessmen they were, the suppliers had affixed a note in English on each one: "Perfect Quality for Our Best Customers."

At the time, it was by far the biggest single cocaine seizure in Canadian history. Police estimated the street value of the drugs to be a staggering $2.7 billion and pegged the cost of the smuggling expedition alone at between $15 and $20 million. At least nine criminal organizations, with Montreal's Sicilian clan at the top of the pyramid, had financed the operation. Raymond Boulanger stood to earn $1.2 million, and Christian Deschênes $1 million, had the job been successful. The cocaine was to have been distributed throughout Canada and into the eastern United States. The mega-bust caused a temporary shortage of the drug on the streets of Montreal, and its wholesale price spiked from $32,000 to $38,000 per kilo. Deliveries soon resumed, however, and the market returned to normal.

At his court appearance in La Tuque, Boulanger winked slyly at reporters, who had dubbed him *"le pilote de Casey."* He pleaded guilty, as did his Colombian accomplices. The conspirators were handed sentences ranging from twenty to twenty-three years in prison. Christian Deschênes was headed back behind bars as well. In late April 1993, he was sentenced to twenty-three years, with no possibility of parole before serving ten years. Oddly, he would be released in November 2001, after only eight and a half years.

In May 1992, police became aware of regular meetings between Vito Rizzuto's right-hand man, Raynald Desjardins, and Maurice "Mom" Boucher, along with other members of the Hells Angels Motorcycle Club. Historically, the Mafia brain-trust had looked down on biker gangs. They did, however, appreciate their tattooed brawn, efficient intimidation tactics and propensity to pull triggers first and ask questions later, and they were not above retaining bikers' services ad hoc. But brawn doesn't always equal brains, and the bikers seemed prone to regular demonstrations of their limited intelligence. Their abusive shows of force goaded the Quebec government and police forces into striking back, with uncommon vigour.

In March 1985, members of the Hells Angels' breakaway North Chapter had slaughtered five of their Laval "brothers" in a clubhouse in Lennoxville, near Sherbrooke, for "interfering with the smooth running of the club." They had also gotten rid of a "hang-around" whom they suspected of being on the police's payroll, in Saint-Basile-le-Grand, a South Shore suburb of Montreal. Their preferred mode of corpse disposal was to weigh down the victims with barbell plates and dump them off a dock into the St. Lawrence River. The method lacked finesse, to put it crudely, and no one was surprised when the axe of justice eventually fell. Three bikers decided to turn state's evidence, including Yves "Apache" Trudeau, a founding member of both the original Montreal Hells Angels and the breakaway North Chapter. Trudeau ratted out forty-two cronies and pleaded guilty to forty-three counts of manslaughter. As a result, some two dozen club members and sympathizers went to jail.

By the early 1990s, however, the Hells Angels were on the rebound.

Mom Boucher was a key architect of the biker gang's renaissance. Born in 1953 in the small Gaspé town of Causapscal, he had two things in common with Vito Rizzuto: he was charismatic and he wielded a natural authority over his men. But the resemblance ended there. Boucher had clashed with his abusive father, a construction worker, from a young age; Rizzuto respected his father and had invited him to build a house next to his. Boucher's son, Francis, grew up a white supremacist, eventually organizing a neo-Nazi gathering called Aryan Fest 1992; two of Rizzuto's children became lawyers.

Maurice Boucher attacked his enemies with his head down and thought nothing of having prison guards killed. Vito Rizzuto, as his father had done during his ascension to power in Montreal, preferred tactics more suited to a chess player. Settling disputes over a round of golf or a few drinks was more his style. That didn't keep him from committing or sanctioning murders, but when he did so it was always in a calculated fashion, never impulsively. Boucher had barely finished eighth grade, and by his late teens was a hard-core substance abuser, ingesting everything from hashish to Valium, speed, coke, heroin and LSD. The drug cocktails rendered him paranoid, to the point that he slept with a .303 calibre rifle. He eventually fell in with what, to him, passed for a family: the ss, a feared street gang that dealt drugs in their home base, Pointe-aux-Trembles, and elsewhere in east-end Montreal. By the time he was thirty years old, Boucher had served lengthy prison terms for armed robbery and sexual assault.

Like many smaller clubs, the ss folded under pressure from the Hells Angels. Some members were assassinated; others turned their lives around. Others went solo. The rest were amalgamated ("patched over," in biker parlance) into the Hells Angels. Boucher was part of the latter contingent. He decided to quit using drugs: no more destroying his brain cells. And in turn, he followed the credo "healthy mind, healthy body":

he replaced his addiction to substances with workout sessions, spending several hours a day sculpting his physique in the gym. Mom Boucher soon rose to become the leader of the Hells Angels in Montreal.

The leaders of Quebec's two most powerful criminal organizations were in agreement on one principle: they stood to make far more money by working together than by sparking a war to control the rapidly growing drug trade. Demand for drugs seemed endless. The two kingpins inaugurated their partnership with, among other things, an ambitious venture to bring in massive amounts of cocaine from South America. The bikers would be in charge of transportation, with the Mafia as the principal venture capitalists. Working together, the two outfits plotted to import no less than five thousand kilos of coke in a single operation involving multiple loads. To set it up, Raynald Desjardins—who by then had reached the ten-year mark of his tenure as Rizzuto's closest criminal associate outside of his family circle—teamed with several outlaw bikers, including Richard Hudon and André Imbeault, two full-patch members of the Hells Angels' Quebec City chapter.

The RCMP had a mole in place from the beginning, however, and followed every step of the unfolding conspiracy. They learned that Richard Hudon was leaving for South America to negotiate the deal with the suppliers. They also saw Boucher hand over a suitcase, which they suspected held one million dollars—the biker consortium's share of the purchase price—to Desjardins in an east-end Montreal park. The cocaine left Venezuela by sea early in the summer of 1993. On July 9, Desjardins picked up his cellphone and called Rizzuto, telling him he needed to see him right away. One of the few people who could raise his voice to the boss and get away with it, Desjardins was heard screaming into the phone. Circumspect as usual and aware that the conversation was almost certainly being recorded, Rizzuto answered simply: "Okay, we'll meet."

On July 14, four Hells Angels left Marystown, Nova Scotia, on board the *Fortune Endeavor,* which rendezvoused with a ship in international waters, where 740 kilos of cocaine were transferred. Unbeknownst to them, the skipper was working with the RCMP. The dope was stowed in the *Fortune Endeavor*'s hold, in waterproof packets hidden inside nine cast-iron sewer pipes, each three metres in length and twenty-five centi-metres wide. The lengths of pipe were in turn wrapped in fishing nets. The initial plan was to dump them overboard off the shores of Anticosti, an island at the entrance to the St. Lawrence River. A trawler, the *Annick C II,* would then locate them using sonar, haul them up and bring them in to port. A crew of divers was ready to assist.

But the *Fortune Endeavor* ran into mechanical trouble, and the bikers on board had a bad feeling that they were being followed. Their intuition was correct. On August 6, with no choice but to accept a tow from a Coast Guard vessel, they resigned themselves to jettisoning their cargo early, off Sheet Harbour, Nova Scotia. RCMP officers were watching from shore.

Luc Bordeleau, a Hells Angels "prospect" who was also an experi-enced deep-sea diver, had got his hands on a camera system that would survey the ocean floor, a hundred metres down, and transmit live pic-tures to a screen on board a boat at the surface. The smugglers never got a chance to put the high-tech gear to use.

Police swooped in at 5 A.M. on August 25, raiding thirty-nine separate addresses in Quebec, Nova Scotia, New Brunswick and Newfoundland and Labrador, and arresting nineteen people. Their targets included the Hells Angels' clubhouses on Taschereau Boulevard in Longueuil, on the South Shore of Montreal, and in a town then known as Saint-Nicolas, across the St. Lawrence from Quebec City. The ground floor of the Saint-Nicolas bunker was so well fortified that members of the RCMP tactical unit had to break a window on the floor above to enter the building.

The police seized four trawlers and a speedboat, as well as an extrava-gant yacht, the *Matthew D.,* docked at the marina next to the Château Montebello, the "luxury log cabin hotel" near Ottawa where Winston Churchill had once met with Allied leaders during the Second World War. The yacht belonged to Raynald Desjardins. Then aged forty-three, Desjardins was nabbed in his luxury home not far from the "Mafia Row" of Antoine-Berthelet Avenue.

The police weren't the only ones employing an infiltrator. Just prior to the August 25 arrests, Officer Jean Lord, assigned to the RCMP's VIP protection section, telephoned Desjardins to tell him he had first-hand information for him, in exchange for a substantial cash payment. Desjardins was convinced it was a trap and, once he was arrested, told the Mounties they had a mole in their midst.

He had hoped that exposing Lord would help him reach a plea deal, but his gambit failed. The officers who interrogated him were eager to get him to spill details on Vito Rizzuto's involvement in the scheme. But Desjardins wasn't about to rat out his boss.

"Vito's my buddy; I'm going to do my time," he told them coldly. "And when I get out, I'll go shake his hand."

The RCMP, incidentally, mounted a sting against the corrupt cop, which involved a double agent baiting him with a kilo of cocaine. Lord was found guilty and received a fourteen-year sentence. "I was fed up with being poor," he said to the colleagues who collared him. He was a twenty-three-year veteran of the Mounted Police.

After months of searching, the Canadian Navy submersible *Pisces IV* detected the cocaine-stuffed sewer pipes off Sheet Harbour, perched at the lip of an underwater cliff, fifty-five metres down. On November 14, 1994, the pipes were hauled up onto the deck of the dive support vessel HMCS *Cormorant*. The 740 kilos of coke would have fetched between $500 and $700 million on the street.

"The removal of Raynald Desjardins, loyal right-hand man to Montreal Mafia chieftain Vito Rizzuto, deals a particularly costly blow to the Italian clan," commented Staff Sergeant Denis Dumas of the RCMP drug section in Montreal. "He is the key man in the Sicilians' drug importing and distribution network, both wholesale and retail."

Desjardins pleaded guilty and was sentenced to a fifteen-year prison term as well as ordered to pay a $150,000 fine. In his ruling, Quebec Court Judge Jean-Pierre Bonin emphasized the severity of the punishment, noting that Desjardins was a high-ranking member of an organized crime network and the orchestrator of the smuggling plot. Luc Bordeleau and several other outlaw bikers were also sent to prison. Neither Mom Boucher nor Vito Rizzuto faced any charges, however.

The start of his long incarceration was apparently rather trying for Desjardins, a man used to celebrating, giving orders and appreciating fine wines in upscale restaurants. Weeks after he began serving his time at the Leclerc Institution, a medium-security facility in Laval, north of Montreal, he was already pegged as a rabble-rouser. An internal inquiry by Correctional Service of Canada found him responsible for violent clashes that broke out between two groups of prisoners. The inquiry determined that Desjardins was at the head of one clan vying for control over the inmate population. Then, he was apparently at the centre of a plot to drug the institution's employees. His accomplice, Antonio Morello, whose father had been killed at the Castel Tina strip bar, allegedly asked an inmate assigned to kitchen duty to lace the prison staff's food with phencyclidine (PCP)—a powerful hallucinogenic also known as "crystal" and "angel dust," among other street names. The inmate refused. The next day, he was found in his cell whacked out on an excessive dose of the drug, too much of which can lead to cardiac arrest. After doctors saved him, he said that another inmate had tried to force him to drug the employees. "This threat resulted in a great deal of concern among personnel," noted a Correctional Service of Canada officer, clearly a virtuoso when it came to understatement.

In spite of these escapades, Desjardins was treated like a king in prison. He had a computer in his cell, set into a shelving unit custom-built by a cabinetmaker and lit by an attractive lamp "borrowed" from the prison gym. One day, he decided that the running track in the prison courtyard needed refurbishing. He telephoned a building contractor friend of his, then allegedly announced to the prison administrators, "It's on me." The next day, the workers showed up with all their gear. While they worked, Desjardins and several Hells Angels chatted with the boss as he sat in his truck.

Some time later, another truck arrived, carrying seafood. A small party was in progress in the prison. "We heard what was going on," an investigator with the Montreal police told *La Presse*. "We contacted the prison administration and told them to turn the truck around. Things can only go so far, after all."

A committee looked into the matter and concluded: "The balance of power has been broken. Influential prisoners with links to organized crime, and their entourage, enjoy conditions of detention exceeding established standards." The investigation revealed that Hells Angels, members of their affiliated biker gangs and Mafia members easily secured permission to be housed together in the same cell blocks of the prison. They were allowed many more visits than the average inmate, and far more conjugal visits with wives or mistresses, in cabins specially fitted out for privacy. Most of them didn't eat in the cafeteria and forced other inmates to give up their allotments of food from the prison canteen. The bikers and Mafiosi were given the most interesting jobs—salaried positions in the gym, with the social work department, at the canteen or in the radio room—while other prisoners were stuck with less gratifying tasks in laundry, kitchen and housekeeping services. The committee's report cited the example of one block at Leclerc where access to the telephone was "controlled by inmates identified with the Hells Angels, to the point that some inmates were unable to make calls." Members of organized crime groups possessed furniture, clothing and luxury items that were normally forbidden to inmates.

The affair grew into a scandal. Despite denying all the accusations against him, Desjardins was transferred to the high-security Donnacona Institution near Quebec City. He expected to be paroled after serving one-third of his fifteen-year sentence. Unusually, he ended up having to serve two-thirds of the term and was not released until 2004.

Another man fairly high up in the Rizzuto organization, Pierino Divito, had assisted Desjardins in the failed *Fortune Endeavor* operation, but the police wouldn't learn of his involvement until they completed another sting a year later. The fifty-six-year-old Divito was a long-standing member of the Montreal mob. He had gone before the CECO inquiry in 1976 and sworn that he did not know Paolo Violi (no one believed him). After the Sicilians sidelined the Calabrians, Divito had joined Emanuele Ragusa's family. While helping Desjardins bring the 740-kilo load of cocaine into Canada on the *Fortune Endeavor,* he was simultaneously preparing a scheme of his own to import another load seven times as large.

Divito knew that once he'd persuaded the Colombian sellers that his was a serious offer, buying and moving that much coke would take a small army. He enlisted the services of a middleman with the requisite clout. Pasquale Claudio Locatelli was an Italian crime boss famed at the time for a daring prison escape in France tailor-made for a newspaper headline: "Sprung by helicopter from roof as stunned guards looked on." He had a fleet of nine sea-going vessels, including a twenty-seven-metre yacht, which he used to run drugs, weapons and all manner of illicit merchandise. One of his ships, the *Jadran Express*, had been seized in the Adriatic, loaded to the gunnels with Russian arms destined for the Bosnian Serb militias. Locatelli, then aged forty-two, was a key middleman between the Italian Mafia and the Cali drug cartel.

The *Pacifico*, a ninety-metre freighter registered in Cyprus, was purchased and rechristened *Eve Pacific*, and it set out for the northernmost point of Venezuela. At a predetermined rendezvous point, Colombian planes flew low and dropped more than five tonnes of cocaine into the water. The cocaine was recovered by some of the fifteen members of *Eve Pacific*'s multinational crew (which included two women) and stowed in the hold. Jurgen Kirchhoff, the German skipper, then set course for Canada. Once the ship reached the North Atlantic, it was followed by five Lockheed CP-140 Aurora long-distance patrol aircraft from CFB Greenwood, Nova Scotia. Two hundred and fifty kilometres from the Canadian coast, the cargo was transferred onto the *Lady Teri-Anne*, a thirteen-metre fishing trawler, while some two hundred police officers and Canadian Forces and Coast Guard personnel kept a close eye on the proceedings from shore. As the *Eve Pacific* came within one hundred kilometres of the coast, the Canadian Navy destroyer HMCS *Terra Nova* took over for the planes. Kirchhoff and his co-conspirator Raymond Leblanc, an Acadian from Bouctouche, New Brunswick, had no idea they were being tracked.

When the *Lady Teri-Anne* reached Shelburne, Nova Scotia, on February 22, 1994, they found the roads leading from the docks blocked by five RCMP vehicles. Armed officers rushed the boat and started arresting the smugglers. The coke seized from the hold tipped the scales at

5,419 kilos, a tonne and a half more than the 3,919 kilos found in the Convair at Casey. A new record.

At the same time, HMCS *Terra Nova* intercepted the *Eve Pacific* and, with military helicopter support, escorted her to CFB Shearwater, in Halifax. The fifteen crew members, including an unfortunate African passenger who had nothing to do with the smuggling operations, were arrested. Police also collared Pierino Divito, in an unusual location: a hospital bed in Halifax. He'd been admitted the night before, suffering from chest pains. Also caught in the dragnet were Divito's son Mike, aged twenty-eight, and Raymond Leblanc.

Pasquale Locatelli and his right-hand man, Marc Fiévet—a one-time informer for the customs service of France, who owned a number of shipping companies—were picked up in Spain. Pierino and Mike Divito received lengthy prison sentences. They were also wanted by U.S. authorities on charges of importing cocaine. The Divitos' lawyer fought the subsequent extradition request in vain.

Some of his troops had fallen on the battlefield, and several thousand tonnes of hashish and cocaine had been lost, but the commander-in-chief, Vito Rizzuto, could still muster plenty of resources. "If sold on the street, the cocaine, hashish, marijuana and heroin seized in Canada in 1993 alone would have earned criminals between $1.5 and $4 billion," a 1995 Montreal police force document stated. "Amounts seized correspond to about 10 percent of imports," Pierre Sangollo, director of special investigations, elaborated, "which means drug sales generate earnings of approximately $30 billion a year for organized crime, mostly in Quebec: money that leaves the country, or disrupts economic structures here at home."

Data compiled by the Montreal police pointed to Quebec criminal networks as the primary customers for around 90 percent of the cocaine and hashish seized in Canada since 1988. "The leaders of the Sicilian Mafia in Canada are in Montreal," Sangollo added. "The Mafia has built alliances with other groups, such as the Hells Angels, and is behind massive importations of narcotics for the entire country . . . Quebecers should be aware of the power and impact of organized crime. The underground economy is one reason why governments are in debt."

CHAPTER 8

FROM VENEZUELA TO ITALY

W HILE THE CUNTRERA-CARUANA-RIZZUTO clan had a destructive influence in Canada, it was nothing compared to what they
had wrought in Venezuela. The criminal organization had deeply infiltrated the country's economic and political structures. Nicolò Rizzuto and
his associates' investment was no ordinary ranch operation. Entire con-
voys of cocaine were arriving there from Colombia; one analyst believed
the drugs crossed the border in trucks carrying livestock, perhaps even
hidden in cows' stomachs. The clan ran a gigantic holding company called
Aceros Prensados, which encompassed factories, hotels, real estate agencies, as well as shipping companies, service providers and building contractors. In Venezuela alone, its assets were in the neighbourhood of
$500 million. Italy's anti-Mafia crusader, Judge Giovanni Falcone, was
attempting to extradite brothers Pasquale, Gaspare and Paolo Cuntrera,
but the Venezuelan government refused to co-operate.

The clan backed one of the country's two main political parties,
which shared power alternately: the Comité de Organización Política
Electoral Independiente (COPEI), which was part of the larger family of
Christian Democratic parties. Its leader, Luis Herrera Campíns, who had

won the presidential election in 1979, attended the wedding of Paolo Cuntrera's daughter Maria to Antonino Mongiovì. In 1984, Venezuela's other dominant party, Acción Democrática (AD), retook power. In the next election campaign, the Cuntrera-Caruana clan actively supported the new COPEI leader, Eduardo Fernández, who styled himself as "El Tigre." In November 1987, when Fernández's wife and daughter spent two weeks in Montreal, they stayed at the home of Gennaro Scaletta, an associate of Nicolò Rizzuto and Agostino Cuntrera.

The clan's patronage of COPEI was public knowledge. Such brazen support for the country's main opposition party, however, was probably not the wisest of decisions. Three months after Señora Fernández and her daughter's trip to Montreal, local police arrested Gennaro Scaletta in Venezuela, along with three other men: Antonino Mongiovì, Paolo Cuntrera's son-in-law; Federico del Peschio (who would be killed in 2009 behind La Cantina, his restaurant on Saint-Laurent Boulevard in Montreal); and Nicolò Rizzuto.

Investigators went over Rizzuto's residence with the proverbial fine-toothed comb. They found a belt that was unusually heavy. Inside were five packets of cocaine, weighing seven hundred grams in all. The quality of the powder varied from one packet to the other, suggesting that they were samples for prospective customers. Rizzuto was sentenced to eight years in prison—a stiff penalty compared to those handed out for similar offences up to that time in Venezuela. He was sent, along with his co-accused, to a penitentiary near Caracas, where he was housed in a far more comfortable cell than other inmates. But he still wanted out, and fast. Vito would later claim that half a million dollars had been paid to a lawyer who had promised an acquittal for the elder Rizzuto, but whatever he'd paid had been a complete loss.

A month after Nick's arrest, the Venezuelan justice minister, José Manzo González, was forced to resign. A former police officer had accused him, with evidence to support his charge, of selling confiscated weapons and drugs. The Attorney General, Alfredo Gutierrez Marquez, had to step down the same day: according to the allegations, an airstrip on land owned by his brother was being used by Colombia's Medellín cartel to transport cocaine. The finance minister, Héctor Hurtado Navarro, admitted that corruption in his country had reached stratospheric heights: "If there is a problem, people tend to pay a bribe," he told *The Wall Street Journal*. Montrealer Domenico Tozzi, a laundryman for Rizzuto clan members, knew how things worked. He left for Venezuela with U.S.$800,000. He later boasted that he had delivered the money to the right person, bringing about Nicolò Rizzuto's release from prison. The family patriarch was sixty-nine years old.

Nick's lawyers have steadfastly maintained that his release, four years after his arrest and imprisonment, had nothing to do with a bribe and everything to do with health problems. His parole conditions stipulated that he had to report to the police every two weeks. After four months, he informed them that he had a prostate condition, and that this should persuade the Venezuelan authorities to let him go home to Canada. The authorities relented, and Rizzuto's wife, Libertina, accompanied by two friends, flew to Venezuela to pick him up. Their return flight stopped first at Pearson International Airport in Toronto, where Rizzuto told Canadian customs officials that he wished to receive medical care at the Royal Victoria Hospital in Montreal. Nick, Libertina and the rest of the escorting party landed at Montreal's Dorval Airport at four in the afternoon on May 23, 1993. Vito was there to welcome them, along with some thirty friends and relatives.

If the elder Rizzuto really did have a prostate problem, it would seem that it wasn't properly treated, because he was to invoke the same medical condition fifteen years later as an excuse for release from another prison. It is not known whether he saw a urologist at the Royal Victoria Hospital, but he was certainly seen at the Consenza, the social club located at 4891 Jarry Street East in Saint-Léonard that served as the Sicilian clan's headquarters until 2006. He also went often to the Castel Tina strip club, which belonged to his good friend Paolo Gervasi.

Normand Brisebois, a criminal turned informant, knew both Nick and Vito Rizzuto at the time. Years later, he remembered them as unflappable: "At first glance, they seemed cold, but they were both really okay guys. They were also very calm and completely in control." Both father and son favoured unpretentious clothes, Vito preferring casual wear, while Nick always wore a custom-tailored suit, with a fedora permanently topping his head—"just like in 1930s gangster movies," Brisebois recalled. Neither wore any jewellery other than their wedding rings.

The Venezuelan authorities hadn't needed much coaxing to allow Nicolò Rizzuto to leave the country, even though his parole wasn't up. One year to the day before his return to Canada, tragic events on the other side of the Atlantic had taken place, and they had international repercussions—including the fact that the Siculiana clan was no longer welcome in Venezuela.

In the spring of 1992, rumours were rampant that Judge Giovanni Falcone, the figurehead of the struggle against Italian organized crime, would soon be named to helm a new judicial body, making him the first anti-Mafia magistrate with the power to prosecute criminals throughout Italy. Since the Mafia organizations worked together, it was only logical that the country's various police forces should be coordinated under a single command structure. Falcone had now been based in Rome for a year, as the director of the Justice Ministry's Criminal Affairs Bureau. He was in the habit of travelling back home to Palermo whenever he could. It was a dangerous habit, but he took precautions, flying in unmarked jets with unannounced flight plans. Up to seventy carefully selected men, most of them sharpshooters, were officially tasked with ensuring his safety and that of his family. To curb the risk of any conspiracy within their ranks, each day Falcone designated eight bodyguards at the last minute to escort him. The slightest leak could prove fatal.

On Saturday, May 23, 1992, the judge decided to take the wheel of his armoured Fiat Croma at Palermo's Punta Raisi Airport for the last leg of the journey home. His wife, Francesca, who was also a magistrate, was beside him, and one of their bodyguards was in the rear seat. Falcone sped toward the city centre at 160 kilometres per hour along Autostrada A29, behind a lead vehicle, a second bulletproof Croma occupied by three other men from his security detail, and followed by yet another armoured Croma carrying the other four bodyguards.

A road crew had been working on the highway that week and had put down a new layer of asphalt near the exit for Capaci, a village between the airport and Palermo. From behind a boulder on a hill overlooking the scene, a Mafia assassin watched the motorcade approach. At the moment Falcone's white Fiat reached the repaved section of roadway, the assassin pressed a detonator, setting off a 550-kilogram bomb containing TNT and nitroglycerine, hidden in a culvert. Seismographs at Italy's National Institute of Geophysics and Volcanology recorded the massive shock wave at precisely 17:56:48. The lead car and Falcone's were catapulted into the air by the force of the blast; television pictures showed the magistrate's white Fiat half buried in rubble, debris strewn over a radius of several hundred metres. Firefighters had to cut into the wreckage of the lead car to extract the mangled bodies of the three guards. Although the follow car had been somewhat shielded from the explosion by the two others, its four occupants were seriously injured. More than a dozen other people, who were in four other vehicles caught in the blast, were also injured. The roadway was torn up over a distance of five hundred metres.

The magistrate and his wife were not killed outright. Giovanni Falcone succumbed to his injuries a few minutes after arriving at the hospital in Palermo. He was fifty-three years old. Francesca, aged forty-six, died during the night. The next day, thousands of shirt-sleeved Palermitans clapped rhythmically for ten minutes as the victims' colleagues bore the caskets into the courthouse for the wake. But when the Italian president and two cabinet ministers arrived, the applause from the crowd turned to shouts of "Shame!" "Out!" and "Justice!"

State dignitaries were again jeered at the funeral for the victims, at the Basilica of San Domenico in Palermo. The crowd gathered on the forecourt shouted, "Assassins!" Inside, the strains of Mozart's *Requiem*—he was Falcone's favourite composer—filled the nave. Partway through the service, the young widow of one of the bodyguards, Rosaria Schifani, interrupted a prayer reading to point an accusing finger at the leaders who had made the trip from Rome. "I appeal to the men of the Mafia . . . because they *are* in here . . . but are certainly not Christian . . . For you too there is the possibility of forgiveness . . . I forgive you . . . but you must get on your knees, if you have the courage to change." She paused and cried, "But they don't want to change—they won't change!" before breaking into tears.

"Who knew? Who notified the authors of this deed and allowed them to act with such precision?" asked an outraged Cardinal Salvatore Pappalardo, the archbishop of Palermo, while the Italian interior minister buried his head in his hands. Sicily's trade unions organized a one-day general strike, which was accompanied by a massive demonstration in the streets of the capital. Unions elsewhere in Italy responded by ordering a one-hour work stoppage throughout the country.

Perhaps the most surprising testimonial was that of the informant Tommaso Buscetta: "I trusted Falcone," he confessed years later to sociologist and author Pino Arlacchi, recalling his long debriefing sessions with the investigating magistrate. "Not because of any sort of magnetism in his personality; he was a timid man, with a gentle gaze, who did not try to come across as a superior being blessed with extraordinary qualities. And yet, he conveyed to me something indefinable, like a beneficial, restorative impulse." Buscetta said he was stunned by the news of Falcone's death: "That day, I saw a great tree fall to the ground. The tallest, strongest tree in the forest. But I had anticipated such a misfortune. On several occasions I had advised Falcone to be very careful of falling into habits."

Falcone had already been the target of an assassination attempt in June 1989. A booby-trapped sports bag, left among some rocks on the beach below his house outside Palermo, was noticed by his bodyguards before the explosives it contained could be detonated. "One usually dies because one is alone, or because one has got into something over one's head," the courageous magistrate once wrote. "In Sicily the Mafia kills the servants of the State that the State has not been able to protect."

Less than two months after Falcone's assassination, his friend and fellow anti-Mafia magistrate Paolo Borsellino was also killed. He had made the mistake of telling his mother that he was coming over for a visit—unaware his phone line had been tapped by men working for the Corleonesi boss Salvatore "Totò" Riina. As he rang the doorbell at his mother's home on the Via D'Amelio in Palermo, a bomb in a car parked at the edge of the sidewalk exploded, killing him and five members of his bodyguard detail instantly. At Borsellino's funeral, Archbishop Pappalardo called the faithful to revolt. "Rise up, Palermo!" he cried. The Italian government no longer had any choice but to act. Seven thousand soldiers were deployed to Sicily.

The man who had detonated the blast that killed Giovanni Falcone was identified: he was Giovanni Brusca, a member of Totò Riina's hit squad known as U' Verru (the swine) in the Sicilian dialect. His father, Bernardo Brusca, was a notorious Mafioso who had attended the wedding of Giuseppe Bono, along with Vito Rizzuto, among many others, at the Pierre Hotel in New York. When Giovanni Brusca learned he had been informed upon, he kidnapped the eleven-year-old son of the man who had exposed him. After torturing the boy and sending gruesome photos to his father in an attempt to force him to recant, "the swine" ordered an accomplice to strangle the boy and dissolve his body in a vat of acid. Brusca was eventually arrested in 1996 at a country house near Agrigento. As the prisoner arrived at the Palermo police station, one carabiniere could not keep himself from breaking the rules: he pulled off his ski mask, as if to say he was no longer afraid to show his face to the Mafia. Then he pushed his way through the phalanx of guards escorting Brusca and punched him in the face.

In the fall of 1992, the Italian government asked for the co-operation of all the countries known to be harbouring exiled Mafia bosses. Authorities in Caracas received a list of fifty-seven Mafiosi to be extradited from Venezuela at the earliest possible date. Prominent on the list were the names of Pasquale, Paolo and Gaspare Cuntrera. Falcone and Borsellino had long suspected them of having laundered some seventy million dollars via Canada, Venezuela and Italy, and considered Pasquale Cuntrera the capo of the Siciliana mob family. The Venezuelans procrastinated. Washington waded into the fray with typically American strong-arm tactics, sweeping aside the most basic of diplomatic conventions. The DEA threatened to send in a commando team to apprehend the Cuntrera brothers itself. The challenge was taken seriously. In June, U.S. authorities had arrested Brigadier-General Ramon Alexis Sánchez-Paz, the former chief of Venezuelan army intelligence, in Miami, after he bought twenty kilos of cocaine from undercover DEA men. And the spectacular arrest of Panamanian general Manuel Noriega and his subsequent conviction in Miami for drug trafficking, racketeering and money laundering was still fresh in people's memories.

Washington stepped up the pressure, threatening economic sanctions against Venezuela. In September 1992, the Venezuelan government gave in, and the Cuntrera brothers were flown to Italy. Their multi-million-dollar fortune would be of no use to them: authorities seized the family's assets, which included funds in sixty-five bank accounts as well as hotel and casino investments. Mafia members who had not been arrested and charged moved quickly to sell a sixty-five-hectare ranch on the border with Colombia. The DEA did not celebrate too loudly, however: it suspected the buyers were front men for the Gambino family of New York.

After their plane landed in Rome on September 12, 1992, the Cuntrera brothers were whisked to the prison on Pianosa, a microscopic island in the Tuscan Archipelago. The ten-square-kilometre islet in the Mediterranean had been used to incarcerate prisoners since the time of Emperor Augustus. Two thousand years later, security rules barred any vessel from approaching to within 1.6 kilometres of its coast. The story of the three brothers might have ended there, but it didn't. Pasquale, the boss of the clan, was sentenced to a twenty-one-year term and transferred to Parma prison, in the north of Italy—whence he managed to escape in 1998 because of a "bureaucratic error" surrounding his sentence appeal procedure. Apparently, he succeeded in convincing the prison authorities that he was entitled to parole pending the court's ruling on his appeal request. He promised to report to police and offered assurances that he could be easily reached. Suffering from diabetes, he left the prison in a wheelchair. His appeal was rejected, but in the meantime he had vanished into thin air. The minister of justice offered her resignation; Prime Minister Romano Prodi refused to accept it.

Italian police searching for Pasquale Cuntrera got an unexpected lead from the RCMP. By 1996, the Mounties had already been investigating Alfonso Caruana and his brothers, Pasquale's nephews. Alfonso had left Canada to hide out in Venezuela in 1986 but had returned in 1993, resuming large-scale drug trafficking operations from a new base: Toronto. The RCMP had placed taps on several telephone lines, including pay phones that Alfonso tended to use when conversations were most sensitive. One day in May 1998, he was heard speaking with his uncle Pasquale from one such phone booth. He told Pasquale that arrangements could be made to get him into Canada with a forged passport, and from there . . . well, those Canadians were so very accommodating!

There was an international warrant out for the arrest of Alfonso Caruana. He had been convicted *in absentia* by a Palermo court for being the leader of a ring that had imported some eleven tonnes of cocaine to Italy between 1991 and 1994. At the time of his phone conversation with his uncle Pasquale, Alfonso was living in Woodbridge, a neighbourhood in Vaughan, north of Toronto. Officially, he earned five hundred dollars a week as a car jockey and washer for a used-vehicle dealership.

Uncle and nephew were heard consoling each other over a sad event: the death during the previous week of Frank Sinatra. Then the phone call ended. The RCMP's goal was to accumulate sufficient evidence to prosecute Alfonso Caruana in Canada rather than arrest him and turn him over to Italian authorities, as suspects' appeals of extradition procedures tended to drag on endlessly.

Thanks to electronic surveillance, police were able to locate Pasquale Cuntrera: he was hiding out with his wife near the small resort town of Fuengirola, on Spain's Costa del Sol, a spot favoured by celebrities including Antonio Banderas and Sean Connery. Italian and Spanish police went after the fugitive and found him strolling arm in arm with his wife along a palm-lined boulevard. He no longer needed his wheelchair but walked with a cane. He offered no resistance to the arresting officers and was sent back to prison in Italy.

Alfonso Caruana took over as the head of the clan. The sentence handed down by the Palermo court stated that his involvement in the importing of eleven tonnes of coke was "further indication of the extremely high capacity for criminal action" displayed by the Canadian citizen. Caruana, the court added, "had evaded all judicial actions in recent decades and succeeded in reaching the summit of the international drug trade, making use of his network of criminal contacts and demonstrating such a degree of expertise that he is considered one of the leading organizers of this activity."

Changings of the guard were also taking place in New York. There, as well as in Montreal, bosses were dying, whether of natural or ballistic causes, or being sent to prison to serve lengthy terms. Others took their place.

The Bonanno family's star had already been paling for several years when its head, Philip "Rusty" Rastelli, succumbed to liver cancer in 1991. Convicted on racketeering charges, Rastelli had spent a good part of the 1980s behind bars and had died at seventy-three, just days after being released on humanitarian grounds. He was buried in St. John Cemetery, in Middle Village, Queens—in the company of several congressmen but also two dozen infamous leaders of New York Mafia families. They include Carlo Gambino, who gave his name to the largest of the Five Families; Vito Genovese, one of the rare mobsters to lay claim to the title "boss of all bosses"; and Charles "Lucky" Luciano, who founded the Commission in 1931. At a suitable distance from Rastelli's grave is that of Carmine "Lilo" Galante, the cigar-chomping boss who had been executed under Rastelli's orders.

By the early 1990s, however, those members of the Bonanno family who were still above ground weren't that much more animated than those resting six feet under it. They were now looked down upon by the four other families. The successful infiltration by FBI agent Joe Pistone, alias Donnie Brasco, had heaped scorn upon them. Such unforgivable stupidity had led to the Bonannos being stripped of their vote on the Commission.

The new boss, Joe Massino, had not abandoned all hope. Big Joey favoured a strategy grounded in caution: think before acting, advance slowly but surely. He too had been imprisoned several years on racketeering charges. The long sabbatical behind bars had given him time to imagine ways to breathe new life into the Bonanno family. He also discovered the virtues of silence and circumlocution. He refused to emulate the new boss of the Gambino family, John "The Dapper Don" Gotti, whose assassination of the former boss, Paul Castellano, as a means of usurping power was a violation of protocol: Gotti had not obtained the prior consent of the Commission. Massino liked Gotti personally, which was sensible insofar as the two lived just a block from each other in the Southwest Queens neighbourhood of Howard Beach. (After he ordered Vito Rizzuto and other hit men to take out the three rebel Bonanno capos in 1981, it was to Gotti that Massino turned to dispose of the bodies.)

Joe Massino was more discreet than his friend. While Gotti paraded in front of photographers and TV camera operators, and revelled in his tabloid celebrity status, Massino was notoriously camera-shy and, despite his capacious girth, had a knack for disappearing whenever police photographers tried to train their lenses on him. Despite deploying ultra-sophisticated surveillance technology, investigators were never able to record even the slightest incriminating remark. "Joe wanted to do it [become Bonanno family boss] the right way. He wanted to wait for his boss to die, to assume the power," Salvatore "Good-Looking Sal" Vitale, his friend and brother-in-law, later said. The Bonanno family soldiers were looking for stability in the wake of the Donnie Brasco fiasco, and that was exactly what Massino brought.

Massino advised his men to keep a low profile, steer clear of seedy bars and put an end to meetings in their Brooklyn social clubs. He ordered them to never say his name out loud, and if they absolutely had to talk about him, to simply point to or tug on their ear (he got the idea from another wily New York boss, Vincent "The Chin" Gigante.

This way, the police would never be able to catch a Bonanno soldier on tape saying anything like "Big Joey told me to whack So-and-So."

For example, police were never able to accuse Massino of having sanctioned the murder of Joe LoPresti, a key Bonanno soldier in Montreal and a good friend and neighbour of Vito and Nick Rizzuto. After Good-Looking Sal Vitale, Massino's lieutenant, became an inform-ant, he let it be understood that Massino had taken the liberty of agree-ing to LoPresti's elimination despite the fact that such executions are supposed to be decided at the highest level.

Like Vito Rizzuto, who was two years older, and Gerlando Sciascia, fourteen years his senior, Giuseppe "Joe" LoPresti, born on January 24, 1948, came from Cattolica Eraclea. He was married to Rosa Lumia, a native of the same town; the couple had two children. LoPresti arrived in Halifax in 1969 and was quickly inducted into the Montreal Mafia. Proudly Sicilian, he naturally sided with the Rizzutos in their war against the Calabrian Paolo Violi, and was a suspect in the latter's 1978 murder. Two years later, he was among the guests at the extravagant Bono wed-ding at the Hotel Pierre.

With an athlete's build, standing six-foot-two, his black hair always impeccably combed, LoPresti was an elegant man, but he avoided the limelight. He owned the Casablanca, a Montreal nightclub, and had stakes in several companies, but was not given to ostentatious displays of his wealth. He wore subdued grey suits that suggested he was an ordinary businessman looking to get ahead in life without a fuss. And get ahead he clearly did: at the age of forty-four, he was a millionaire.

LoPresti often spoke in a neutral, emotionless tone so he wouldn't attract attention. Seemingly innocuous words, depending on his inflec-tion, could mean something altogether different. Occasionally, however, he broke his own rules. His voice was unmistakably among those heard in police recordings made in New York in the early 1980s.

The electronic surveillance had taken place in the home of Angelo Ruggiero, a close associate of John Gotti and his brother Gene, of the Gambino Family. Ruggiero, a corpulent and crude figure, had earned the moniker "Quack Quack." He suffered from plantar fasciitis, a painful heel inflammation, in one foot, which caused him to waddle like a duck. Moreover, he simply could not stop talking. Gotti once berated him on the phone, telling him to "keep [his] fucking mouth shut." Quack Quack's loquacious nature was a godsend to police, who had extensively bugged his home in Cedarhurst, Long Island.

In May 1982, police keeping an eye on the funeral of Salvatore Ruggiero, Angelo's brother, were intrigued by the fact that Joe LoPresti was in attendance, and decided to tail him. The Montrealer seemed to be everywhere, meeting everyone—in short, he was clearly an emissary of some kind. Officers watched as he went to pick up Gerlando Sciascia, alias "George from Canada," at Quack Quack Ruggiero's home. Joe and George were then seen meeting with Cesare "The Tall Guy" Bonventre at a Dunkin' Donuts in Queens. Bonventre, a fellow "Zip," worked for Bonanno boss Carmine Galante. Police then observed LoPresti with Salvatore "Totò" Catalano, another notorious Bonanno Zip. It was Catalano who had introduced Tommaso Buscetta to Pasquale Cuntrera years earlier in Montreal.

On May 16 a hidden microphone in the basement of Ruggiero's home captured a most interesting conversation: Joe LoPresti told Quack Quack that he had been speaking with his heroin supplier, a member of the Cuntrera–Caruana clan in Caracas. "He said he was 100 percent certain that our load is coming. It's in Canada say a week and a half before it's here," he said.

Around the same time, George from Canada—who obviously was no more gifted at the art of code-talking than was LoPresti—told Ruggiero: "I got thirty things . . . that's why I'm here." Even a police cadet could have guessed that "thirty things" meant thirty kilograms of heroin.

The investigation concluded with charges being laid against Joe LoPresti, Gerlando Sciascia, Angelo Ruggiero, Eddie Lino and several other members of the Bonanno and Gambino families for importing thirty kilos of heroin. They were in up to their necks in the so-called Pizza Connection, the heroin importing network that relied on Sicilians on either side of the Atlantic. Soldiers in the Gambino family were by now very nervous. Their boss, Paul "Big Paul" Castellano, had threatened to kill those among his troops who dared get mixed up in drug trafficking—a racket that he felt was far too dangerous. Indeed, police had stepped up efforts and often succeeded in persuading drug dealers to turn state's evidence. Castellano wanted his men to focus on less risky enterprises like stock market fraud, which brought in a lot of money but resulted in lighter prison sentences should the perpetrators be caught.

Lawyers for the accused obtained transcripts of the police surveillance tapes. Castellano demanded a copy. If he didn't get one, he warned, he would depose John Gotti and reassign his soldiers to other captains. Gotti was well aware that if his boss read the transcripts, he would uncover the truth. Not only had Gotti created a narcotics smuggling faction within the family, but the recordings proved that he and his associates discussed it with people outside the family, another off-limits practice. On December 16, 1985, Castellano and his new underboss, Thomas Bilotti, were gunned down in front of the Sparks Steak House, on Forty-sixth Street in Midtown Manhattan. The killers disappeared into the crowd of Christmas shoppers. One of them was Eddie Lino, who faced heroin trafficking charges along with Quack Quack Ruggiero and the others. With Castellano out of the way, John Gotti ascended to the Gambino family throne.

On the day the prattling Quack Quack and his Pizza Connection cronies were arrested, Joe LoPresti was in New York, and the FBI easily collared him. Gerlando Sciascia managed to escape back to Montreal, where he lived for a time under an assumed name before authorities tracked him down. The U.S. government wanted him extradited. Sciascia was arrested on a Montreal street by Sergeant Yvon Thibault, of the city's RCMP detachment, on November 7, 1986. Sciascia was imprisoned for the next two years, during which he fought to have the extradition order overturned. The struggle was in vain, and in late 1988 he was back in New York to answer the heroin trafficking charges.

John Gotti's brother Gene was among the accused. He asked a friend to buy off a member of the jury. The friend promised the juror a BMW if he would support Gotti's acquittal. What Gotti had failed to realize was that the juror had been excused by the judge two days earlier because he was not a U.S. citizen. The FBI found out about the attempted bribe, and a mistrial was eventually declared.

The group of co-defendants disintegrated: Angelo "Quack Quack" Ruggiero died of cancer; Gene Gotti and John Carneglia, a Gambino soldier, were tried separately and sentenced to fifty-year prison terms. A new trial, with Gerlando Sciascia, Joe LoPresti and Eddie Lino facing narcotics trafficking charges, began early in January 1990. John Gotti's underboss, Salvatore "Sammy the Bull" Gravano, put up ten thousand dollars to bribe a juror. (This time, the police only learned of the corruption a year later, when Gravano became an informant.) Sciascia, LoPresti and Lino were acquitted after four weeks.

The three co-accused would then be murdered one after another, but for different reasons. Eddie Lino was the first to be rubbed out, on the order of Vincent "The Chin" Gigante, boss of the Genovese family. Lino was killed in November 1990 by two corrupt NYPD detectives. The cops, driving an unmarked patrol car with a warning beacon activated, ordered Lino to pull his Mercedes-Benz to the side of a freeway service road in Brooklyn, then shot him to death. Gigante's intent was to weaken his hated rival, John Gotti; taking out one of his captains did the job.

As for Joe LoPresti, he returned to Montreal after his acquittal and resumed his business. He managed a building company, Construction LoPresti, along with several other businesses, including a video poker machine company that he ran with his son Enzo. In late April of 1992, Joseph Mark Sciascia, son of Gerlando Sciascia, called LoPresti at home. The younger Sciascia owned a Mikes restaurant franchise in east-end Rivière-des-Prairies with Agostino Cuntrera, who had been part of the conspiracy to murder Paolo Violi. Joseph also claimed to be a co-owner of Quelli Della Notte, a swanky Italian restaurant on Saint-Laurent Boulevard. He told LoPresti he needed to see him immediately. LoPresti asked if it could wait a few days. "I need to see you right away," Joseph Sciascia repeated curtly. Police never found out the reason for the call; they knew only that LoPresti had to follow orders from George from Canada, Joseph Sciascia's father.

On April 29, three days after the call from Joseph Sciascia, LoPresti left his neo-Tudor-style home on Antoine-Berthelet Avenue, got into his cherry-red 1988 Porsche and drove to a restaurant on Décarie Boulevard, in western Montreal. He was unsuspecting, despite the fact that life had taught him to be constantly on his guard and that several of his associates had been killed in recent years. In all likelihood, when LoPresti entered the restaurant he met with a man he trusted, because he parked his Porsche in a lot nearby and left with the man.

Somehow, LoPresti soon found himself in a car wash, where an unknown assailant shot him in the back of the neck with a small-calibre weapon. He was forty-four years old. It is not clear whether he knew that his life was in danger, but one thing is certain: he did not defend himself. It was a clean, careful hit: a sign of respect. The body was wrapped in a plastic bag, tied with cord, transported in a vehicle and abandoned, covered in a painter's drop cloth, next to a gravel road leading to the railway tracks in Rivière-des-Prairies. Around eight-thirty in the evening, a railway worker who had spotted bloodstains on the ground called CN police, who alerted Montreal police. Investigators found approximately four thousand dollars on the body—proof that theft was not the motive for the murder. The victim's ID, however, was missing.

The next day, police found the red Porsche, licence plate number KMK 558, in the Décarie Boulevard parking lot where its owner had left it. Inside, a pager was beeping repeatedly. Officers called the requester's number: Enzo LoPresti, the victim's twenty-three-year-old son, answered. Enzo identified his father's body at the police morgue on Parthenais Street. The visitation was held in a funeral home on Beaubien Street in Montreal. Several friends and relatives came to pay tribute. Vito Rizzuto arrived in a white Jaguar and offered his condolences. A number of Mafiosi from New York and Toronto also turned up at the funeral home. Well-known business people, including Lino Saputo, owner of the Saputo cheese company, attended the funeral. "Joe LoPresti was an important person in the Italian community," Saputo explained simply, several years later.

An important person, indeed. Investigators racked their brains for many months trying to understand the motive for the murder. To them, the slaying had all the hallmarks of a Mafia hit authorized at the highest level, very probably by Gambino family boss, John Gotti. At least, that was what Gotti underboss–turned-informant Salvatore Gravano claimed. Perhaps there had been a disagreement over the sharing of profits from drug deals.

More illuminating testimony came years later from Salvatore Vitale, the underboss to Bonanno family head Joe Massino. When Vitale testified at the trial of several Bonanno family members, he recalled a conversation with Gerlando Sciascia. "George from Canada" was LoPresti's boss and was furious at him for using drugs. "It didn't make sense to him that a capo could be getting high," Vitale explained. "He thought it harmed our prestige in the eyes of the other families." Vitale added that Sciascia had asked him for permission to eliminate LoPresti. Vitale had green-lighted the hit, on behalf of his boss, Massino. "If that is what you want to do, do it," he said. "Take care of business."

It would be surprising if Sciascia had in fact decided to take out LoPresti for the simple reason that he was using drugs. There was surely a more useful motive for the murder, which had been carried out in the purest mobland style. It certainly appears, however, to have been sanctioned by high-ranking persons in the New York Mafia, not only Sal Vitale.

Gerlando Sciascia was the last of the accused trio to die. After his 1990 acquittal, he resumed efforts to obtain permanent resident status in Canada for himself and his Scottish-born wife, Mary. In his application, made to the Canadian Consulate in New York, he said he wished to enter Canada under the country's investor immigrant program, explaining that he owned two restaurants and a car wash, and that he was prepared to invest U.S.$200,000 in Canada. He added that he spoke both English and French, and that his son, Joseph Mark, was already a resident of Montreal. Susan Burrows, a visa officer at the Consulate, rejected the application. In a less-than-encouraging letter, she wrote: "reasonable grounds exist to believe that you are a member of an organized crime group; namely, the American Cosa Nostra."

Joseph Mark Sciascia appealed Burrows's decision. A senior official in the immigration department not only agreed with Burrows; he went one better, branding Gerlando Sciascia "a danger to the public in Canada." The official wrote in a report, "I am concerned that Mr. Sciascia's close relationship to figures of the Mafia in New York, Sicily and Montreal would strengthen the Mafia situation in Montreal. Mr. Sciascia is a danger to the Canadian public because of his involvement with the Mafia and the nature of the activities carried out by these organizations."

In 1988, a U.S. Senate subcommittee report on organized crime had named Sciascia as a member of the Bonanno crime family. Under amendments to Canada's Immigration Act made in 1993, anyone belonging to an organized crime group was barred from entering Canada.

Sciascia challenged the "public danger" label before the Federal Court of Canada. Justice Marshall Rothstein found in his favour and ordered that the declaration be set aside. This cleared the way for Sciascia's son Joseph Mark to appeal to the Immigration and Refugee Board to overturn the visa officer's decision barring his father from entering Canada. Despite that victory, the younger Sciascia withdrew his appeal request, and his father gave up his attempts to become a permanent resident of Canada. The Canadian immigration department continued to refer to Sciascia as a "subject linked to the Mafia." "George from Canada" earned the distinction of being the only person ever barred from immigrating to Canada by reason of association with the Mafia. He was notified that, should he attempt to set foot in the country, he would be detained.

He moved into an upscale home on Stadium Road, in the Bronx, a fair distance from the spot where, in 1981, he had run his hand through his hair, signalling the hit squad to wipe out the three renegade Bonanno captains. He was now sixty-three, his hair greyer but still thick. Incorrigibly fashion-conscious, he still combed that hair into a pompadour style and was a sharp dresser. He looked more like a rich jeweller than a crook. And in fact he did open a jewellery store, on East Tremont Avenue in the Bronx.

Nineteen ninety-seven, the year Sciascia was deemed *persona non grata* by Canadian authorities, also saw the release in theatres of a film that surely piqued his interest—as well as that of Vito Rizzuto, Salvatore Vitale and Joe Massino. Entitled *Donnie Brasco*, it starred Al Pacino as

Mafioso Benjamin "Lefty Guns" Ruggiero (no relation to the brothers Salvatore and Angelo Ruggiero) and Johnny Depp as Special Agent Joe Pistone, FBI, alias Donnie Brasco, who infiltrated the Bonanno family. The film helped popularize an expression dear to American Mafiosi: "Fuggedaboutit." Another memorable line, spoken by Pacino's character, was "A wise guy's always right. Even when he's wrong, he's right." The movie's reconstitution of the three capos murder contained no allusions to George from Canada's and Vito Rizzuto's roles. But no doubt Sciascia felt a degree of discomfort when he realized that this unsavoury slice of his life had been immortalized on the silver screen.

Sciascia had taken part in the massacre of the three captains at the request of Joe Massino, but by 1999, the latter seemed to have forgotten about that gesture of loyalty. Massino was at the height of his power. He was now "The Last Don," as New York's other godfathers were all in prison: John Gotti, of the Gambino family; Vincent Gigante, of the Genoveses; Vittorio Amuso and Anthony Casso, of the Luccheses; and Carmine Persico and Victor Orena, of the Colombos. The Bonannos were the exception. After the Donnie Brasco affair, their numbers had dwindled to below one hundred. Massino, however, had managed to rebuild their ranks, and he was now the head of a crew of 150, divided into fifteen efficient teams, including the Montreal *decina*. As the only boss not behind bars, Massino exercised his power like a monarch, brooking no digressions. He had promoted his friend Anthony Graziano to the rank of captain. Graziano, nicknamed "T.G.," was renowned for his sadistic ways: he occasionally tortured his victims with the flame from a cigarette lighter. But he brought in a lot of money.

Sciascia, who was supposed to "work" with Graziano, started complaining about his erratic behaviour. He thought the new captain was unreliable and bemoaned his tendency to dip into the cocaine he was dealing. "Every time I see this guy, he's stoned," Sciascia told Sal Vitale, and he asked him to mention it to Massino. Swearing "on [his] children's eyes," T.G. assured Massino that he wasn't doing coke. Massino settled the rift between his two captains his way: during a wedding anniversary party, he took Sal Vitale aside and told him, "George has got to go." The boss obviously construed George from Canada's remonstrations as a challenge to his leadership. Massino was leaving for a holiday in Cancún, Mexico, the next morning, and he wanted the job done before he returned.

On Thursday, March 18, 1999, Sciascia got a note at his jewellery store, which read simply, "Pat D 79." It meant that he was to go and meet a captain named Patrick DeFilippo in a diner on Seventy-ninth Street in Manhattan. At the diner, DeFilippo told him he was taking him to another location for a sit-down with someone who could help settle the dispute with Graziano. The two left the diner and got into a burgundy-coloured Ford van, driven by John "Johnny Joe" Spirito, a Bonanno associate. As they drove, DeFilippo pumped four bullets into Sciascia: one in the left side of the chest, a second in his left eye, and two others in his head. Spirito headed down Boller Avenue, a dead-end street in the Bronx, where DeFilippo dumped the lifeless body of George from Canada onto the road, across from a small church.

A man visiting his girlfriend on Boller Avenue told the police he had seen a van pull a 180-degree turn at the end of the street. At first, he thought the driver must have turned down the wrong street. Then he saw the bloodied body of a man lying on the road. No one had heard any gunshots. A woman said the man's silver-grey hair was well combed and he was wearing expensive-looking clothing. "He looked like somebody's grandpa lying there," she told a reporter from *Newsday*.

Sciascia was sixty-five years old. Unlike the execution of Joe LoPresti, the killing of George from Canada showed none of the consideration due a "man of honour." The New York Mafia usually showed their corpses more respect—more, at least, than unceremoniously dumping them in the street. Yet Gerlando Sciascia had been slain by members of the Bonanno family, with the collusion of old friends even, like Sal Vitale. Vitale had nothing against Sciascia, but he had obeyed orders, knowing that if he protested he would sign his own death warrant.

The hit squad had a good reason for throwing Sciascia's body from the van. Massino wanted the killing to look like a drug deal that had gone wrong, not a "sanctioned hit," and he wanted to avoid reprisals from Montreal. He put the word out on the street that he was looking for Sciascia's killers and ordered forty Bonanno soldiers to attend the funeral. Even Pat DeFilippo, the triggerman, pretended to mourn George from Canada. Massino, though, stuck with his policy of avoiding locations where he might be filmed or photographed. In his book *Five Families: The Rise, Decline, and Resurgence of America's Most Powerful Mafia Empires*, *The New York Times* journalist Selwyn Raab wrote that Massino told two of his captains that Sciascia's punishment was appropriate. "It served him right for telling me how to run the family," he explained to one. "That'll teach him to talk about my capos," he said to the other.

At a meeting at a diner in Howard Beach, Sal Vitale told Massino that he and his associates had been forced to get rid of the burgundy Ford van in which Sciascia had been killed. They hadn't been able to get the bloodstains out of the seats. "Poor George must have bled to death," Massino sighed, adding that he would dip into the family funds to make sure Johnny Joe Spirito, the van's owner, would be reimbursed. The boss then congratulated Vitale on a job well done.

In 2007, Vitale was interrogated at length about the grisly episode during the trial of Patrick DeFilippo, accused of the murder of Gerlando Sciascia. Massino's orders were clear, Vitale recalled: the Bonanno boss asked him to meet with each of the family's fifteen captains individually and explain to them that no one knew why George had been whacked. Vitale told them, "If you find anything out, bring it to our attention. We want to know who killed George."

"What was the purpose of telling the captains that?" federal prosecutor Greg Andres asked him in court.

"To put up a smokescreen, a diversion," Vitale answered.

"At some point after the murder of George, did you go to Canada?"

"Yes."

"Why did you go to Canada?"

"Joe Massino wanted me to go up there to speak to Vito [Rizzuto], to get what was going on, to familiarize ourselves [with] what was going on in Canada now that George was dead."

"Did you go alone?" Andres asked.

"No, I went with Anthony Urso," Vitale replied. Urso had just been named acting *consigliere* for the Bonanno family.

"When you were up there, did you attempt to put somebody in George's place with respect to his position in the Bonanno family [that of captain responsible for the Montreal crew]?"

"I probed the area; who did they respect up there. Who is the man up there. Vito said: 'We are all brothers. We are all equals.' First, he was very annoyed that no one told him about George. I don't think he believed that it was a drug deal gone astray."

"What else did you discuss with Vito when you were in Canada?"

"How many individuals—how many made men are in Canada. He told me nineteen."

"Do you know who paid for the trip to Canada?" the prosecutor asked.

"The Bonanno family paid for it . . . I laid out the money for the hotel, for the food, for me and Tony [Urso], and when I got back, Joe [Massino] said, 'How much did you lay out?' and I said, 'Nine hundred.' He gave me the nine hundred."

The Bonanno family wanted to make Vito Rizzuto captain in Gerlando Sciascia's stead. Vitale insisted, but Vito refused the promotion and suggested his father. There was no doubt that the murder of George from Canada had upset him: they were both from Cattolica Eraclea originally, they got along well, and they had worked together to build a new heroin pipeline; furthermore, no one had consulted Vito before executing his friend. And Vito saw no benefit in taking Gerlando Sciascia's place. For one thing, the position would have required regular travel to New York, which would have been difficult, since he knew he could not cross the U.S. border without risking arrest.

Several members of the Montreal Mafia attended the meeting with the two New York envoys, Vitale and Urso. Vito purposely left an empty chair at the table—the one that should have been occupied by Gerlando Sciascia. He asked the Bonanno captain and *consigliere* many questions about the circumstances of Sciascia's murder. He was clearly furious and didn't believe for one moment that his friend had been killed because of a botched drug transaction. After the meeting broke up, Urso accompanied

Vito Rizzuto to some choice Montreal bars and restaurants. Another participant in the meeting, Joe Di Maulo, left with Vitale. Good-Looking Sal thought his number was up: he was sure he was being led into a trap and would be taken out. Instead, Di Maulo took him to meet some other members of the Montreal crew.

The assassination of George from Canada would cast a permanent pall over relations between the Bonanno family and the Rizzuto clan. But business continued.

And Vito remained a good soldier.

CHAPTER 9

OPERATION COMPOTE

From the offices of their law firm on the seventh floor of the
Yale Building, at the corner of Peel Street and De Maisonneuve Boulevard in downtown Montreal, Giuseppe (Joe) Lagana and his partners
had a bird's-eye view of a neat, modern facility on the other side of the
street that specialized in exchanging currency. The agency, registered
to a numbered company, 2841–6923 Québec, and operating under the
corporate name Centre International Monétaire de Montréal (CIMM, or
Montreal International Currency Centre), had opened its doors on
September 29, 1990, right beside an entrance to the Peel metro station.
It was located on the ground floor, in the same space as a money-
changing counter that had closed after a series of holdups and burglaries. Behind the bulletproof front window, passersby could admire
tasteful prints on the walls, varnished hardwood accents, and orange-
tinted marble flooring. Bill-counting machines sat on tables and, in the
rear, a door led to a secure room away from prying eyes. The CIMM's
staff of three men and one woman answered customers' questions
with consummate diligence and conducted more than three hundred
transactions per week.

Lagana, aged thirty-eight, was a lawyer above suspicion. He lived north of downtown, in the upscale Town of Mount-Royal. His wife was also a lawyer, with a reputable firm, and one of his partners was the mayor of Montreal West, another suburb. Few people were aware, however, that Joe Lagana's biggest client was Vito Rizzuto. The mob was always looking for ways to solve a perpetual problem: it had too much money. With thousands of ten-, twenty- and one-hundred-dollar notes piling up left, right and centre, the Mafiosi had reasoned that entrusting these huge loads of cash to lawyers might be a good idea. Since members of the bar are bound by professional confidentiality, police usually struggle to persuade a judge to authorize electronic surveillance or searches of law offices.

Narcotics traffickers were finding it increasingly difficult to make large cash deposits at banks, where they were likely to face awkward questions. For the past two years, financial institutions had been urged to report any suspicious transactions to the RCMP. In Montreal alone, the street dealers working for the mob could rake in a million dollars every two days. The wads of bills would be stored in apartments, to which Lagana regularly sent couriers to pick up the money.

Being a lawyer for organized crime is not a job for the faint-hearted. On October 15, 1985, Frank Shoofey, a criminal defence lawyer whose clients included the Hilton family of boxers, was shot three times in the head and twice in the chest as he stood in the corridor outside his office on Cherrier Street, near Montreal's La Fontaine Park. On May 13, 1991, Sydney Leithman, who was representing a Cali drug baron by the name of Jairo Garcia, was killed at the wheel of his Saab convertible shortly after leaving his Town of Mount-Royal home. The hit man, wielding a .45 calibre weapon, shot him four times in the head. On September 10 of the same year, Paul Beaudry, another defence attorney whose clients included Colombian *narcotraficantes*, was shot in his Old Montreal office. Fatally wounded in the stomach, he managed to pursue his two assailants a short distance before collapsing in the building's lobby. Other lawyers had been taken to court or penalized by the bar association, often for conspiring with their clients.

From his vantage point above Peel Street, Lagana kept a close eye on the Centre International Monétaire for a year before setting foot on the premises. He had envoys put out feelers: one of them inquired about the possibility of exchanging amounts in the neighbourhood of $100,000. In June 1991, a man walked into the CIMM and asked if he could wire $500,000 to a foreign country. His name was Kazimir Sypniewski, age sixty-seven, and he worked as a security guard in the Yale Building, where Lagana's law firm was located. The currency exchange counter employees would be no fools: it was highly unlikely that a man on a security guard's salary would have half a million dollars to transfer to an offshore account. But they allowed the transaction regardless.

Dollar after dollar, deposit after deposit, Joe Lagana grew increasingly confident in the new exchange counter across the street. Before long, his partners, Richard Judd, forty, and Vincenzo Vecchio, thirty-six, were dropping in to the posh facility with suitcases, hockey equipment bags, shoeboxes and plastic grocery bags filled with low-denomination banknotes. The small bills were exchanged for bank drafts, U.S. currency or "pinkies," thousand-dollar Canadian bills that the Bank of Canada had recently stopped printing, precisely for the purpose of making money laundering more difficult. The funds were then transferred to any of about two hundred bank accounts in Europe, the United States and South America.

What the mob lawyers didn't know was that the Centre International Monétaire de Montréal had been set up by the RCMP to lure money launderers of all stripes. The polite and friendly staff were all undercover police officers and had been trained at the National Bank of Canada to convincingly perform their tasks as cashiers. Video cameras hidden in the walls of the facility filmed customers' transactions, and microphones picked up their every word.

The Mounties had also set up another covert operation: a courier company called Courtex. From its offices on the other side of De Maisonneuve Boulevard, investigators photographed customers as they entered and exited the CIMM. Those who seemed suspicious were then tailed.

The reverse sting operation was identified by several code names beginning with the letter *c* (which designated the RCMP's Quebec section), the most well known of which were "Operation Compote" and "Operation Contract." It was overseen by Staff Sergeant Yvon Gagnon, who was an imaginative man. He had concocted a slew of stratagems to attract the CIMM's desired (i.e., criminal) clientele, while dissuading unwanted (i.e., honest) customers. This included posting police officers easily identifiable as such outside other foreign exchange counters nearby, who openly filmed suspicious clients as they approached, in hopes of steering them to the only facility that didn't seem to be under surveillance: their covert one. The CIMM bought advertising space in daily newspapers promising easy fund transfers overseas and distributed flyers in neighbourhoods where targets were known to live, mostly in the South Shore city of Brossard. "All suspicious customers will be billed 1% extra," a weekly internal RCMP report says. "This will allow us to distinguish legitimate customers from illicit ones. The latter, trusting in our discretion, prefer to continue doing business with us in spite of the surcharge." Two months later, investigators were already patting themselves on the back: "With the help of the advertising, we concluded 274 financial transactions, an increase of more than 30% over the previous week," Corporal Pierre Bolduc enthusiastically noted in his weekly report dated October 19, 1990. Only a month since the CIMM began operations, he added, "two major investigations" had been turned over to the drug squad.

Operation Compote, the largest undercover operation in the history of the RCMP, owed its existence in part to pressure from the DEA. The American agency had long been aware of South American expatriates flying from Montreal to Cartagena, Colombia, their suitcases bulging with narcodollars. And as part of its investigations of criminal networks in Houston, Cincinnati and Denver, it had also noted the existence of a suspicious currency exchange business at the corner of McGill College Avenue and De Maisonneuve Boulevard, the National Foreign Exchange Office, which was a paradise for money launderers. The U.S. ambassador in Ottawa had brought up the matter with Canadian authorities.

On September 20, 1991, Kazimir Sypniewski, the Yale Building security guard, walked across the street to the CIMM and hefted $470,000 in twenty-dollar bills onto the counter. When he left, officers discreetly followed as he went back into the Yale Building and upstairs to Joe Lagana's law firm. Looking back through its files, the RCMP noticed the lawyer's name had popped up in a number of drug squad investigations: specifically, Lagana was linked to Vito Rizzuto and his well-known laundryman, Dima Messina. The following month, the CIMM staffers made an intentional mistake: after counting the stacks of notes deposited by Sypniewski, they handed him two cheques instead of the usual four. Later, Lagana telephoned the CIMM to report the slip-up: there were two cheques missing, he said. "So sorry, our mistake," the staffer replied. "We'll issue the two others right away." The Mounties' suspicions were confirmed: Sypniewski was simply a messenger, and Lagana was his paymaster. Some time later, an RCMP team drilled a tiny hole into the wall of the corridor outside Lagana's office and carefully placed a bug inside, making sure to remove all traces of the job. They had to work fast; even at night, there were frequent comings and goings on the seventh floor of the Yale Building, which the law firm shared with a telemarketing call centre.

In the months that followed, Sypniewski continued hauling banknotes, several hundred thousand dollars at a time, across the street to be exchanged into bank drafts. And Lagana wasn't the only client taking advantage of the currency exchange counter's friendly and courteous service. At the end of its first year of operation, the CIMM had made a profit of $23,297; Canadian taxpayers wouldn't have to put up any money for the investigation, and the money launderers were covering the cost of the operation that would eventually pinch them. On a plastic bag that had been used to carry banknotes deposited at the fake currency exchange counter, investigators found fingerprints matching, among other people, Francesco Cotroni Jr., son of the Calabrian clan chieftain. Frank Jr. was also observed across the street from the CIMM, talking to Joe Lagana and Giovanni Marra; the latter was a high-level narcotics dealer and long-time Cotroni family associate.

Confident now that the currency exchange was willing to accept large sums of cash without asking questions or alerting the police, Lagana met with the man he knew as its manager. His alias was Pierre Morais, and Lagana told him he would soon have more money to exchange, in the millions of dollars. Not a problem, the undercover officer replied.

Early in 1992, a man named Domenico Tozzi introduced himself to CIMM staffers as an associate of Lagana's. He said he was president of a company called Toscani Import, and that he had fifteen million dollars that he wanted to transfer to the United States: "It's for one of my customers; he's had the money for eight years and he's fed up of hanging on to it," he explained to the CIMM cashiers at a meeting in Lagana's offices.

The fifty-year-old Tozzi acted the part of a big shot who threw big money around and knew wheelers and dealers. Tozzi's every word was being recorded, and RCMP officers listened with glee: the man was boasting to them about how he'd laundered money for the past twenty or so years.

"Oh yeah?" one officer asked ingenuously. "Do you know . . . what's his name already . . . Vito Rizzuto?"

"Sure," Tozzi said. "He's the big boss. He's the one who decides everything, but he doesn't touch anything. He's very well known to police. He can't be too visible, otherwise he'll end up in prison . . ." Then, in a hushed tone, he added, "Vito is a Sicilian. He's dangerous and he isn't afraid of anyone."

Tozzi himself never met directly with Vito, he explained. If he did see him, it was in Lagana's offices. According to Tozzi, Rizzuto wasn't content to oversee the financial dealings of the Sicilian Mafia; he also helped other criminal gangs out. For instance, he was handling a transaction for Robert Steve Johnston, "one of the big bosses of the West End Gang," Tozzi said, referring to Montreal's Irish mob. "The Italian big boss in Montreal is in charge of transferring the first ten to twenty million from Johnston," he continued. "He makes the decisions. He really doesn't want to lose this customer." Johnston was looking to repatriate a sum of between thirty and forty million dollars lying dormant in a Liechtenstein account, Tozzi explained.

Tozzi bragged of having contacts all over the world—the United

States, France, Colombia, Mexico—and dropped several names. "I know the Mexico City chief of police very well; I've done business with him in the past," he let slip to a CIMM staffer one day, with a knowing wink. Tozzi had a solid network in Africa, doing business in Senegal, among other countries, where he exported everything from tobacco to wine coolers to military material. He claimed to have applied to become an honorary consul of Nigeria. Officers carefully noted this last admission: they knew that a diplomatic passport offered several perks, not least of which was permission to cross borders carrying diplomatic pouches— which were almost never subjected to searches by customs officers.

It was during this series of meetings that Tozzi claimed he was the one who paid the $800,000 bribe to secure the release of Nicolò Rizzuto from prison in Venezuela. He made the boast while having dinner with the undercover officer posing as the manager of the currency exchange on April 1, 1993. In a report dated April 30, Sergeant Marc Lavoie referred to the conversation between Tozzi and "Pierre Morais": "As for Tozzi, he himself brought $800,000 to Venezuela to get out of jail Nick Rizzuto, the father of Vito," he wrote.

The Mounties widened their surveillance. They observed Jorge Luis Cantieri in a vehicle owned by Tozzi's company. Cantieri, a Brazilian then aged forty-one, described himself as a businessman involved in the import-export trade. He owned the company Mercanti Holdings and several businesses controlled by the numbered company 2697203 Canada. Along with accomplices like the globe-trotting businessman Norman Rosenblum, Cantieri had been found guilty of smuggling cocaine and hashish in the mid-1980s.

Out on parole since March 1990, Cantieri was officially barred from leaving Canada. Yet he was travelling frequently to Europe, Colombia, Ecuador, Panama and Costa Rica, and getting richer by the day. Besides owning a luxury home in Dollard-des-Ormeaux, in northwest Montreal, he had land in Vaudreuil, just off the western tip of the Island of Montreal, and an apartment on Nuns' Island, an upscale suburban area just south of downtown, and was about to make an offer on an apartment in Nice, on the French Riviera.

Dirty money was flowing into the CIMM. The trap was working like a charm. It was an interesting break from routine. The police didn't have to chase the criminals; the criminals were dropping in to see them—and with smiles on their faces, to boot. But the millions they were unloading at the currency exchange weren't enough to constitute proof beyond a reasonable doubt, as demanded in a court of law. The police would have to show that the money represented the proceeds of the narcotics trade. Once they were sure they had Lagana's confidence, the undercover officers at the CIMM led him to understand that they had partners who were ready to do business of another kind. That is, they were prepared to help them transport drugs. The CIMM, they explained, was the Montreal branch office of an investment consultancy in Amsterdam—in reality, another fake company that the RCMP had created, this time jointly with police in the Netherlands.

The offer came at just the right time. The Mafia and the Hells Angels had joined forces in a plot to import 558 kilos of cocaine from Colombia. The Colombians were equipped with power yachts and prepared to hand over the drugs at a location in the Caribbean Sea, north of Santa Marta. From there, the cargo needed to be delivered to Great Britain, where it would be picked up by members of the Sherbrooke, Quebec, chapter of the Hells Angels and sold to British members of the gang. All that was missing was a vessel equipped for transatlantic travel, and an adventurous captain. The RCMP created a bogus London-based shipping company and secretly chartered a boat in Miami, in collaboration with U.S. customs and the DEA, telling Lagana and co. that it was normally used to ferry supplies to oil rigs off Venezuela.

Lagana fell for it. He met with undercover police in the Netherlands, who were posing as smugglers, to work out the details of how the drugs would be transported. Norman Rosenblum, who already had two prior convictions for international drug trafficking, flew to Colombia. The RCMP undercover agents feigned impatience. The transaction was dragging on; what was the problem? they asked. Calls were made. Rosenblum was chomping at the bit: the cargo was ready, he told Lagana. The Colombians wanted to make the drop immediately; they had to act fast because an ocean storm was brewing. Lagana made several calls to Europe. According to the deal that had been arranged, only Cantieri—as the man with the connection to the Colombian suppliers—could green-light the shipment. But Lagana couldn't reach Cantieri; he was busy with his apartment deal in Nice.

Lagana went ahead and authorized the shipment without Cantieri's sanction. When the Brazilian found out, he was not pleased. He called Lagana and said there were still clauses to be worked out in the contract with the Colombians. They hadn't reached agreement on the "insurance"; in other words, how to share the losses in case the deal was compromised—for example, if the drugs were seized.

It was too late: the delivery order had been given.

On August 17, 1994, the RCMP's chartered supply ship approached the Colombian coast near Santa Marta, a port city and tourism hub with a population of about 500,000. Rosenblum met up with the suppliers as planned, aboard the power yacht. He enthusiastically helped out in transferring the fourteen bales of cocaine, weighing a total of 558 kilos, trading jokes with crew members. They included Sergeant Pierre Jeannotte and Corporal Claude Bellemare of the RCMP, though Rosenblum believed them to be simple seamen; he was also ignorant of the fact that the ship's captain was an undercover U.S. customs agent. To his mind, everything was going according to plan. Rosenblum was ecstatic. The transfer complete, he headed back to shore with his suppliers, then flew to Vancouver. The supply ship sailed to Miami, where the drugs were removed from the hold and sent by air to Montreal, to be retained as evidence.

The putative co-conspirators at the CIMM told the traffickers that the ship was headed to England, where the Hells Angels were to take delivery. Then they went on the offensive, demanding to be paid for the transportation end of the deal, otherwise they wouldn't make the delivery. Their fee: one million dollars. On Monday, August 29, Lagana's lawyer partners, Richard Judd and Vincenzo Vecchio, went to pick up the money from Shimon Ben-David, an associate of well-known Montreal drug trafficker Morris Mayers, and then delivered it to the fake currency exchange. Judd was carrying a burgundy suitcase; Vecchio, a black one.

Each contained $250,000 in one-hundred-dollar bills. Later that day, they made the same return trip, delivering the balance of the fee. The lawyers counted up the bills and pocketed $70,000 as commission.

At six in the morning on Tuesday, August 30, about five hundred federal, provincial and municipal police officers made some sixty arrests in Montreal, Quebec City, Trois-Rivières, Vancouver and Toronto. At the request of RCMP officers who had travelled to London, British police also arrested Pierre Rodrigue, age thirty-two, and David Rouleau, age thirty, the two members of the Sherbrooke Hells Angels whose job was to pick up the cocaine. They were imprisoned pending extradition to Canada. London police also picked up Morris Mayers but released him later the same day.

The Mounties had 558 kilos of coke sitting in their evidence room, and proof that Lagana and his Mafia associates had washed $97 million in drug money over a four-year period. The indictment ran to 1,500 pages, was based on 3,500 recorded conversations, and listed evidence amassed to support charges against 57 people.

Lagana, Judd and Vecchio were among those charged. They pleaded guilty and were sentenced to prison terms of varying length. Kazimir Sypniewski, the Yale Building security guard who had deposited millions of dollars at the RCMP's fake currency exchange at Lagana's request, died aged seventy on January 17, 1995, before his case could come to trial. Emanuele Ragusa, fifty-four, a well-known member of Montreal's Sicilian Mafia, faced twenty-eight separate counts on various charges. Jorge Luis Cantieri was handed a fifteen-year prison sentence. Domenico Tozzi, Norman Rosenblum, Pierre Rodrigue, David Rouleau, Jean-Pierre Renault and several others also went to jail. Renault, originally from the Beauce region south of Quebec City and a former lawyer, had previously been arrested in 1985 for having set up the first cocaine lab ever discovered in Canada, in Rosemere, a suburb north of Montreal.

One name, however, was conspicuously absent from the list of accused: Vito Rizzuto. "We have evidence suggesting that he is part of the conspiracy [to launder profits from the sale of cocaine]. But because of certain legal principles, we cannot file this evidence against Mr. Rizzuto,"

prosecutor Danielle Côté said at an August 31 news conference announcing the wrap-up of Operation Compote and the dismantling of the CIMM.

As the sting operation wound down, investigators had been virtually
certain they would finally be able to nail the big boss. They had recorded
several conversations between Rizzuto and Lagana and photographed
them together. On January 18, 1994, they had watched as Vito parked
his Jeep Cherokee on Peel Street; a few minutes later, Lagana exited a
building and got in. Two and a half weeks later, on February 4, they had
seen Rizzuto and Lagana in the same building with Jorge Luis Cantieri.
And the year before, on September 23, they had observed Rizzuto and
Cantieri dining together at Le Latini restaurant, on Jeanne-Mance Street
in downtown Montreal.

One meeting in particular had fired investigators' hopes. After
taking possession of the 558 kilos of cocaine off the Colombian coast,
the RCMP asked Swiss authorities to freeze certain bank accounts in
their country. The Mounties wanted to prevent the accounts from
being emptied once they filed their charges against the conspirators.
Lagana was notified of the request by a Swiss banker. Large sums had
been deposited in those accounts, for which he was responsible. Lagana
immediately picked up the phone and called Vito Rizzuto at home. It
was five in the morning. He asked Vito to come to his office as soon
as possible to attend to an urgent matter.

The RCMP had proof that the Swiss accounts were key cogs in Lagana's
money-laundering machine. The covert cashiers at the CIMM had transferred funds to those accounts at the lawyer's behest. Now they had a
chance to gather evidence of Vito Rizzuto giving instructions on the
management of those accounts. It would be enough to lay charges
against him. With the bug hidden in the wall of Lagana's law office, they
hoped to catch Rizzuto in the act.

Their hopes soon faded. In Lagana's office, Rizzuto adhered to the
same strict rule he had followed for years in such situations: he said
almost nothing. When he did speak, it was in cavernous tones, and he
slurred his speech. Worse, the bug had inadvertently been concealed
next to the building's main waste-water evacuation line, causing the

conversations to be muffled by the sound of toilets flushing. The RCMP sent the tape to an FBI sound lab in Washington, but their experts were able to eliminate only part of the unwanted sounds. The lead prosecutor in the case, Claude Bélanger, determined that what was left of the recording would be inadmissible in court.

After the official conclusion of Operation Compote, a small celebration was held at RCMP Quebec headquarters in Westmount. A hundred or so police officers, lawyers, Canada Customs agents and tax inspectors toasted their triumph in the third-floor mess hall. It was a time to rejoice. Over the past four years, the covert operation had seen $160 million moved through the CIMM. Of that amount, nearly $140 million had been brought in by criminals. The police happily informed Revenue Canada about the thousands of transactions involving clandestine cash. The operation hadn't cost taxpayers a cent—better still, the RCMP had earned a net profit of $2 million.

Several investigators, however, remained frustrated that Rizzuto was beating the rap—again. Was there really no way he could be charged? they asked Claude Bélanger. None, the lead prosecutor replied. Rizzuto could only be named an "unindicted co-conspirator" in the plot to import 558 kilograms of cocaine.

"Had we laid charges against Rizzuto, we could have exposed everything we had on him to the courts and the entire population," Sergeant Yvon Gagnon, the man who had overseen Operation Compote, said years later. "Our revelations would certainly have weakened his leadership. We sincerely believed we had a good chance of convicting him."

The operation had allowed police to net an impressive number of criminals. The most notorious of the bunch was fifty-six-year-old Vincenzo "Jimmy" Di Maulo, Joe Di Maulo's older brother and a close friend of Frank Cotroni. He was charged with forty-six counts of money laundering and drug trafficking. He eventually admitted to washing more than $10.5 million in dirty cash between 1990 and 1994 via the CIMM and was convicted for his role in a plan to import 2,500 kilos of cocaine from

Colombia. Unfortunately for him and his associates, the drugs were now at the bottom of the Caribbean Sea: the *Tromso,* a ferry purchased in Florida and repurposed for smuggling, had sunk off the coast of Jamaica.

Di Maulo was a repeat offender and well known to police. Twenty years earlier, he had taken part in the murder of Robert "Ti-Cul" Allard, the right-hand man of infamous Québécois gangster and multiple murderer Richard Blass. In the 1960s, Blass and his gang had challenged the Italian Mafia's hegemony over Montreal organized crime, unhesitatingly taking out Mafiosi. Found guilty of killing Allard in 1970, Di Maulo had been sentenced to a life term, but won parole in 1981. Since that time, he had amassed a fortune estimated at fifteen million dollars. He was a true success story, personifying the integration of organized crime into the licit economy.

Operation Compote proved that Di Maulo had relied on the services of Domenico Tozzi to launder his profits from the drug trade. As part of his unwitting confessions to undercover RCMP officers, the loose-lipped Tozzi had often sung the praises of his good friend Di Maulo, whom he had known for more than thirty years. "He's done time in the past, but now he's a respected businessman," he told "Pierre Morais," the covert currency exchange manager, as the two dined (and downed copious amounts of alcohol) at Restaurant Carpaccio on Montreal's University Street, on April 28, 1992.

Di Maulo had parked a considerable portion of his ill-gotten gains in his Swiss accounts. He had also recycled some of his narcodollars through real estate ventures in Montreal and the surrounding area. This allowed him to project an image of a leading, respectable property developer—and that of a good corporate citizen: every year, he helped organize a charity golf tournament to benefit Santa Cabrini Hospital, in east-end Montreal.

Di Maulo's property development company had its head office in a building called Place Cardinal, at 5365 Jean-Talon Street East, also home to Saint-Léonard's municipal courtroom. The office shared its reception and secretarial services with the law firm of Francischiello, Tibshirani and Associates. Nicknamed Capo Bianco because of his white hair, the rich Mafioso was also the head of an international conglomerate that had been incorporated in Panama and was connected to Swiss bank accounts. The conglomerate provided funding to eighteen companies that had made major investments in Quebec and elsewhere. Di Maulo managed funds not only for the Italian Mafia, but for other criminal organizations including the Dubois clan and the West End Gang.

Di Maulo owned residential buildings and land in Saint-Sauveur, a ski resort town at the foot of the mountain of the same name, in the Laurentians. The year he asked Domenico Tozzi to help launder his drug money, he launched the second phase of an extensive residential development in the picturesque community. The project, poetically named "Au Tournant du Boisé" (The Bend in the Woods), was evaluated at $18 million and planned for 119 apartments to be built. Officially, two businessmen owned the 58,000-square-metre development. One of them, Jean Corneau, spoke to *La Presse* not long after the Mafioso was sent back behind bars. "Mr. Di Maulo was a gentleman with me," he said. "I didn't have to spend a penny to acquire the first lot. I pay him a piece rate, as each unit is sold."

Other lots in the same neighbourhood were in the name of the wife of Adrien Dubois, the youngest of the Dubois brothers from Saint-Henri, and Paul Fontaine, a Hells Angels member. At the time of his arrest on August 30, 1994, Di Maulo was planning a new venture in partnership with Corneau, a residential development adjacent to the Mirage golf course in Terrebonne, northeast of Montreal. Corneau was killed some years later in a road accident.

Year in, year out, Di Maulo played at least a dozen rounds of golf with Vito Rizzuto. Domenico Tozzi had called him "the king of the drug importers." Not all of his transactions were profitable, though: Di Maulo lost a million dollars when the *Tromso* went down off the coast of Jamaica, and had to bid adieu to the 2,500 kilos of coke the ship was supposed to have been carrying; Tozzi said he felt sorry for him.

When he was arrested, Di Maulo knew he was likely to be handed a lengthy prison sentence. Two of his friends, Fernando De Francesco and

The seventeenth-century Chiesa Madre (Mother Church) with its single bell tower overlooking Cattolica Eraclea.

Perched on a low hill, Cattolica Eraclea was once a prosperous farming community.

Nicolò Rizzuto lived in this house before he immigrated to Montreal in 1954 with his wife and two children.

The home of Antonino Manno, grandfather of Nicolò Rizzuto.

Few vehicles travel the quiet, narrow streets of Cattolica Eraclea.

Nicolò Rizzuto and Libertina Manno married in 1945. He was twenty-one years old; she was eighteen.

The couple's marriage certificate, found in the archives of Cattolica Eraclea.

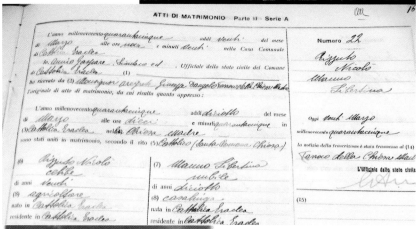

Nicolò Rizzuto had just turned thirty when he arrived in Montreal.

November 26, 1966: The wedding of Vito Rizzuto and Giovanna Cammalleri in Toronto. Nicolò and Libertina stand with their son and his bride.

The wedding of Maria Rizzuto and Paolo Renda (at right) in Montreal. Left, Giovanna and Vito Rizzuto; middle, Libertina and Nicolò Rizzuto.

NYPD mugshots of Carmine "Lilo" Galante.

November 28, 1966: Salvatore "Bill" Bonanno (far right) and five other U.S. Mafiosi are arrested in Montreal; police seize four handguns from their cars. At far left is Luigi Greco, the Sicilian clan's representative in the Cotroni crime family.

Paolo Violi at the time of the CECO hearings, at which he refused to testify.

Giuseppe "Joe" LoPresti.

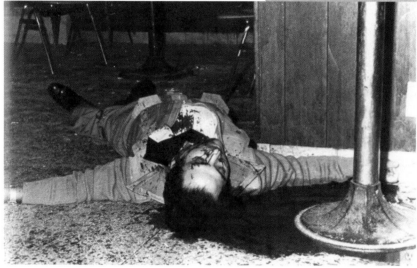

February 22, 1978: Paolo Violi lies slain on the floor of the Bar Jean-Talon (formerly the Reggio Bar).

Agostino Cuntrera (left) and Domenico Manno, two of the three men who pleaded guilty to conspiracy to murder Paolo Violi.

November 16, 1980: Vito Rizzuto and his wife, Giovanna, attend the lavish reception after the wedding of Mafia kingpin Giuseppe Bono in Manhattan.

Also attending the Bono wedding reception, mere months before they would be murdered, were renegade Bonanno family capos Philip "Philly Lucky" Giaccone, Dominick "Big Trin" Trinchera and Anthony "Sonny Red" Indelicato.

May 6, 1981: The day after the murder of the three capos, Vito Rizzuto and Gerlando Sciascia are photographed by police as they leave the Capri Motor Lodge in the Bronx. With them are Bonanno family associates Joseph Massino and Giovanni Ligammari.

Italian judge Giovanni Falcone, whose investigations brought him on occasion to Canada. The 1992 assassination of the anti-Mafia crusader caused a public outcry in Italy.

Falcone died in the white car seen at right, shattered by a bomb hidden in a highway culvert outside Palermo, on May 23, 1992. His wife and three of their bodyguards were also killed in the attack, blamed on the Mafia.

Outraged citizens unfurl banners following the murder of Giovanni Falcone.

Vincenzo "Vic" Cotroni.

Luigi Greco.

Frank Cotroni.

Frank Cotroni, seen here with Paolo (Paul), the second of his five sons, who would be murdered in 1998 in the driveway of his Repentigny, Quebec, home.

Lawyers Vincenzo Vecchio, Richard Judd and Joseph Lagana were frequent custom-ers at the currency exchange covertly operated by the RCMP in downtown Montreal from 1990 to 1994.

Christian Deschênes, a close associate of the Sicilian clan, was arrested while attempting to recover a huge shipment of Colombian cocaine flown into a remote airstrip in Quebec.

Pasquale Cuntrera.

Pasquale Caruana.   Gerlando Caruana.

April 29, 1995: Alfonso Caruana, his hair dyed black, is seen in stills from police surveillance video of the wedding of his daughter in Toronto.

Two views of Salvatore Cazzetta, former head of the Rock Machine biker gang and one of the most influential figures in Montreal organized crime.

Normand Marvin "Casper" Ouimet and Mario Brouillette, two members of the latter-day "business-oriented" incarnation of Quebec's Hells Angels.

October 8, 2000: The Hells Angels and the Rock Machine cement their truce at Bleu Marin restaurant in downtown Montreal.

Normand Robitaille (foreground), of the Hells Angels Nomads, negotiated the wholesale price of cocaine with the Montreal Mafia in the summer of 2000.

Outlaw bikers André Chouinard, Jean-Guy Bourgouin and Normand Robitaille were all arrested and convicted in the wake of Operation Springtime 2001.

Happier times before the fall: Vito Rizzuto with his elder son, Nicolò (Nick) Jr., and his younger, Leonardo. Nick would be murdered in December 2009.

The remains of Philip Giaccone and Dominick Trinchera, two of the three murdered Bonanno capos, were found in 2004 in Ozone Park, New York, not far from the spot where, twenty-three years earlier, a group of children had stumbled upon the still-fresh corpse of Anthony Indelicato. The discovery would prove a key step in the extradition of Vito Rizzuto to the US and his later incarceration in a Colorado prison.

The men who betrayed Vito Rizzuto: Joseph "Big Joey" Massino (left), head of the Bonanno family, and his right-hand man (and brother-in-law), Salvatore "Good-Looking Sal" Vitale.

August 17, 2006: after the final appeal to block his extradition to the United States is denied, Vito Rizzuto is led under heavy police escort to Montréal–Trudeau Airport, where he will board an FBI jet.

Domenico Macri, a rising star in the Sicilian clan ranks, was shot to death in August 2005.

One Sicilian clan associate particularly upset by the murder of Macri, whom he viewed as a brother, was Francesco Del Balso.

The killing of Nick Rizzuto Jr. (left) and the kidnapping of Paolo Renda (right) were severe blows against the Rizzuto family. The two are seen here at the funeral of Domenico Macri.

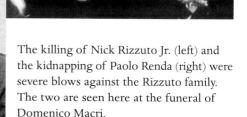

Calogero "Charlie" Renda (bottom left), his father, Paolo (middle right), and Rocco Sollecito (middle, with dark glasses) at the Macri funeral.

Four frames from police video surveillance of the Consenza Social Club on Montreal's Jarry Street. Between February 2, 2004, and August 31, 2006, carefully concealed cameras recorded 192 separate transactions in the backroom of the club. Men brought in bundles of cash in plastics bags or boxes; the bills were then counted on a round table and divided into stacks, destined for the Sicilian clan's top five leaders: Nicolò Rizzuto and his son, Vito, Paolo Renda, Rocco Sollecito and Francesco Arcadi..

Nicolò Rizzuto in his final years.

Vito Rizzuto.

Rocco Sollecito.

Lorenzo "Skunk" Giordano.   Francesco Arcadi.

The final blow: a single bullet hole in the kitchen window of Nicolò Rizzuto's home on Antoine Berthelet Avenue in Montreal, from the shot that killed the clan's patriarch on November 10, 2010.

Ricardo Di Massimo, spoke to one of their neighbours, Corporal Jocelyn Chagnon, who worked for the RCMP Proceeds of Crime unit. They promised to pay him $100,000 if he persuaded the prosecution to offer a lighter sentence: eight years' imprisonment instead of twelve. Chagnon pretended to accept the bribe. He met with De Francesco and Di Massimo on several occasions, each of which was filmed by police. Di Maulo's wife, Micheline Kemp, paid Chagnon an initial instalment of $15,000. She was arrested and convicted, as were De Francesco and Di Massimo. Di Maulo received a twelve-year sentence as planned, and assets from his $4.5 million in personal wealth were seized—for the most part, the buildings and land in Saint-Sauveur.

In the space of less than three years—between December 2, 1991, and July 28, 1994—Domenico Tozzi had moved more than $27 million in small-denomination notes through the RCMP's covert currency exchange. Police stated that the cash came entirely from narcotics smuggling operations run by organized criminal groups. Several of the CIMM's customers, including Jimmy Di Maulo, did indeed belong to the Mafia, while others were from different communities.

On November 23, 1993, an excited Di Maulo strode into the CIMM. "There's a whole pile of money to exchange!" he announced frantically, explaining that "The Jews just got a 25-tonne shipment of hashish in the Port of Montreal." More than once during the investigation he was overheard saying that he planned to bring in thirty million dollars for "the Jewish mob." "The money was to be transferred to Switzerland, then to Israel, to finance both legal and illegal activities," an RCMP report stated.

The shadow of Morris Mayers hung over the plot to transfer the 558 kilos of cocaine to the Sherbrooke Hells Angels in London. Mayers, arrested in England along with two Angels, was released for lack of evidence. Only later did police succeed in taking down his network. Mayers owned a ranch and a stake in a gold mine in Suriname (part of the former Dutch Guiana, in South America) and had extensive contacts in Israel.

"Domenico Tozzi's specialty is moving money around the world," lead prosecutor Claude Bélanger said at the end of the trial. Tozzi was convicted, sentenced to ten years in prison and fined $150,000. When he refused to pay the fine, he had two more years tacked on to his jail term. Polite and affable, he said, "*Gros merci* (thanks a bunch)," to Judge Jean-Pierre Bonin after the latter read out his sentence. Tozzi was released two years later, after serving one-sixth of his sentence.

While Vito Rizzuto was not indicted, he certainly felt the impact of Operation Compote. One of the fifty-seven accused was a man by the name of Valentino Morielli. He was charged, along with Jimmy Di Maulo, of attempting to import 2,500 kilograms of cocaine on board the *Tromso*. On November 21, 1996, at the request of the prosecution, Vito was called to testify at their trial. Rizzuto and Morielli were both aged fifty at the time. Rizzuto said in court that he had first met the accused and his family when he was around ten years old; they grew up together in the Villeray neighbourhood. "He's a friend, but we don't do business together," he explained, adding that the last he had heard, Morielli was serving beer in a tavern, but that he didn't know anything more.

The police, however, knew that Morielli was Rizzuto's right-hand man, having replaced Joe LoPresti, who had been the Montreal Mafia's "ambassador" to the Bonanno family until his murder in 1992. Morielli had three prior convictions for theft and drug trafficking. He'd also had a brush with death during a near-disastrous smuggling attempt in 1985. He had been with a team of drug runners on board two small fishing vessels, *Gaspésienne VI* and *Gaspésienne VII*, on the way to pick up a shipment of hashish from Beirut, when they were caught in a squall some three hundred kilometres south of Newfoundland. Both boats sank, leaving Morielli and his accomplices to drift for several days in lifeboats. The episode obviously failed to quell his taste for adventure, as he would subsequently be brought up on more trafficking charges.

The presumed head of the Montreal Mafia on the witness stand was a rare sight indeed. Prosecutor Claude Bélanger, not about to pass up such a golden opportunity, questioned Rizzuto as aggressively as he could but couldn't come up with much. Bélanger sought to prove that

Rizzuto had met with Morielli on multiple occasions while the latter planned the operation to transfer the 2,500-kilo cocaine shipment to the *Tromso*. The ferry refitted as a freighter was now lying on the ocean floor, but the proof of the smuggling plot—cash and cocaine—was safe in the covert currency exchange and the RCMP's evidence room.

Under intense questioning, Rizzuto finally admitted that Morielli, like Jimmy Di Maulo, was one of his favourite golfing partners. The baron of Antoine-Berthelet Avenue, it seemed, took his golf seriously and had played on so many courses in and around Montreal as well as on various Caribbean islands that he couldn't remember their names. He said he played about a hundred times a year.

"For the last seven years, am I to understand that you play around one hundred games—more than a hundred games a year?" Bélanger asked.

"Yes," Vito answered.

If, as could logically be assumed, he had played several of those rounds in the company of Morielli, it seemed impossible that they never would have discussed the cocaine importing scheme. At any rate, Morielli was found guilty and sentenced to ten years in prison.

Operation Compote also exposed the activities of narcotrafficker Jean-Pierre Leblanc. The Hells Angels chapter in Trois-Rivières, halfway between Montreal and Quebec City, relied on him to import massive quantities of Jamaican hashish. Leblanc was nicknamed the Rancher of Bécancour because he ran a huge beef farm in the municipality of that name, across the St. Lawrence River from Trois-Rivières. His livestock included at least 365 head of purebred steers and cows. He was just one of many drug traffickers who, oddly, seemed to have an immoderate interest in cattle raising.

Leblanc, however, made a lot more money with his network of mules than his cattle. Young people were hired to travel to Kingston, Jamaica, where they were given up to seven hundred grams of hashish each. Before boarding the plane for the return flight, they would swallow the "gum," pressed into pellets and carefully wrapped in Cellophane. Then they would go through customs at the airport in Montreal hoping the Cellophane wouldn't rupture while in their stomachs.

Some couriers also hid hash on their person before boarding cruise ships sailing between the Bahamas and Miami. The drugs were then transported by road into Quebec, to be dealt on the street in Montreal as well as in the Mauricie and Beauce regions, around Trois Rivières and south of Quebec City, respectively. Leblanc personally negotiated his purchases with his Jamaican contacts. Investigators with Customs and Excise believed that between two and three hundred mules had worked for him. Between April 14, 1991, and September 24, 1993, Leblanc had deposited $3.4 million at the RCMP's fake currency exchange. He was sentenced to eight years in prison, but released after serving one-sixth of his term, or sixteen months. His ranch, farm equipment and livestock were confiscated, along with apartment buildings that he had bought in a new development in Cap-de-la-Madeleine, a suburb of Trois-Rivières.

One of the CIMM's biggest customers was nowhere to be found, however, when police made their early-morning bust on August 30, 1994. Police had tailed Sabatino "Sammy" Nicolucci, aged forty-seven, ten years earlier when he and Vito Rizzuto had boarded a plane to Venezuela, where a drug transaction was concluded (see Chapter 6), and then arrested him after the investigation stemming from the seizure of a dozen kilos of cocaine at Vancouver International Airport. The following year, 1985, he was sentenced to fourteen years in prison. But upon his parole in 1991, he had energetically resumed his narcotics trafficking career. The RCMP calculated that he had laundered $31 million through the Peel Street currency exchange in a span of less than three years. He had also abetted Jorge Luis Cantieri and Norman Rosenblum in the plot to ship the 558 kilos of coke to England.

An arrest warrant was issued, but it couldn't be executed: Nicolucci had been kidnapped by Colombian drug smugglers early in August. In July, he'd gone on a twenty-thousand-dollar Alaskan cruise, for a romantic cause: his honeymoon. After his return, he went to the Castel Tina, the infamous strip club in east-end Montreal. On August 2, 1994, a group of local representatives of the Cali cartel stopped by the club to see him.

After heated words were exchanged in Spanish, Nicolucci agreed to accompany his captors away from the club.

That evening, at 7:58 P.M., police officers listening in on the tapped telephone line of Emanuele Ragusa, a senior member of the Sicilian clan, heard an alarming conversation. A distraught Nicolucci said to Ragusa: "They want the bill to be paid, otherwise they're holding on to me." Another man grabbed the phone and repeated the warning in French: "You'd better move; your friend is going to stay with us until the bill is paid, to the last peso." He told Ragusa to warn Nicolucci's wife, Lina Carpinelli, not to alert the police.

The kidnappers then allowed Nicolucci to call his new bride. He spoke to her in Spanish but used code words so that she would understand that he wanted her to contact Joe Lagana and tell him Sammy had a pressing need for banknotes. Lina Carpinelli called the lawyer immediately: "My husband's been kidnapped. He needs money," she said. Lagana tried to reassure her, told her not to say any more over the phone and suggested that she call Emanuele Ragusa.

The Cali emissaries wanted $1.7 million—the amount Nicolucci owed them for 280 kilos of cocaine that had been delivered but that he had refused to pay for because he had deemed its quality to be substandard. The soured deal had been dragging on for several months and had been the subject of harsh discussions among the leaders of the cartel, in Florida and in Cali. The Colombians were threatening to cut off the supply lines to the Montreal Mafia.

There was frantic activity in the Rizzuto camp. Nicolucci's life was in danger. Ragusa was eager to find the money, but obviously, putting such a huge sum together on such short notice posed a problem, even for the Mafia. Domenico Tozzi's assistance was sought, but efforts failed. Ragusa then called someone named Vincenzo; police reckoned this was Vincenzo "Jimmy" Di Maulo. Ragusa asked him if he had any loose cash and whether others could contribute. "I'm going to try and hold them off by sending them a bit of money," he said, fearing Nicolucci's captors might do away with him. Envoys for the Rizzuttos and the Colombians negotiated almost daily during the month of August, usually by phone, occasionally in person.

Investigators, just as eager to find Nicolucci but for different reasons, visited the abductee's wife, but she refused to co-operate. "He's gone on holiday," she told Sergeant Detective Jean-Michel Lussier of the Montreal police. Using the numbers in the call registry of Nicolucci's cellphone, officers determined that he was being held in a chalet in the Laurentians. When the kidnappers saw that the police were patrolling the neighbour-hood, they whisked their prisoner to New York, then moved him to Miami, close to the senior representative of the Cali cartel in Florida, a man referred to as "Fernando" and known as their "lawyer." Fernando stubbornly insisted on payment for the coke delivery, reiterating over the phone the demand that the debt be settled "to the last peso."

On August 29, the Rizzuto clan agreed to pay $900,000 and sent repre-sentatives with part of the amount to the RCMP's currency exchange for transfer to the Cali cartel members. By that time, however, the police believed Nicolucci's life was no longer in danger, and seized the money. The next morning, they made their massive arrests and shut down the CIMM.

The kidnappers took Nicolucci to Colombia, where he was placed under a sort of house arrest, to serve as surety: the Colombians were going to hold on to him until their coffers were filled anew thanks to fur-ther drug sales to the Montreal Mafia. In February 1995, local police found him in a house in Cali. As there was an international warrant out for his arrest, he was taken to court. Nicolucci fought his extradition to Canada, but in vain. He remained in prison. Three days after his court appearance, an unknown individual telephoned the Canadian Embassy in Bogotá and threatened reprisals against its staff if Canada continued to press its extra-dition request. Sergeant Varoug Pogharian was the RCMP liaison officer posted to Bogotá at the time. On March 10, in a confidential report to RCMP headquarters in Ottawa, he explained that the embassy was on alert.

"The mission in Bogotá has always taken threats against the Embassy and its staff very seriously," the sergeant wrote, adding:

> Criminals in Colombia often follow through on such threats, with-
> out warning and without restraint. In Colombia, the odds of captur-
> ing the perpetrator of a crime, whether major or minor, are very

slim. The odds of that crime then being punished are even slimmer. The result is a climate of impunity within the population, and often the most outlandish ideas turn into real acts of violence.

It was the first time Canada had made an extradition request to Colombia, Pogharian continued. It was based on an 1888 treaty between the United Kingdom and Colombia. The sergeant was not particularly optimistic, believing the process could drag on for a year. He worried that, in the meantime, the criminals would set off a car bomb outside the embassy.

It was obvious to Pogharian that if Nicolucci were extradited, the Cali cartel members would never see the money that he owed them. "Before his arrest, Nicolucci had been named in an investigation into a Colombian cartel," he wrote. "If the allegations are true, there is every reason to believe he is setting up a major drug shipment to Canada as a means of paying off his debt. This is clearly the reason why the Colombian traffickers do not want to see him extradited to Canada."

Nicolucci was close to some Colombian drug barons being held in the same prison, the RCMP liaison officer continued, explaining that Nicolucci prepared meals for them, and the atmosphere was very friendly. "Consular staff state that he gained a good deal of prestige in a short time among the other detainees," Pogharian reported:

> No doubt he owes that status to the influential people who are visiting him in prison. During the interview [with Canadian Embassy representatives], Nicolucci entered a room where other prisoners were playing cards. At a simple hand signal from him, everyone left without saying a word. . . . During the meeting with the consular officers, Nicolucci was polite and courteous. He did not seem surprised that threats had been directed at the embassy. To his mind, they are proof of how badly his hosts want him to remain in Colombia.

Pogharian raised the possibility that Nicolucci's "hosts" might try to get him out of the prison before the Colombian court ruled on the extradition request. This would be most easily done, he emphasized, by bribing the guards. The liaison officer recommended that the RCMP ask the Colombian authorities to "move Nicolucci to another prison to minimize the risk of an escape." Colombia finally agreed to extradite Nicolucci in early 1996; he was brought back to Montreal under heavy escort on May 30. Following a lengthy trial during which he acted in his own defence, Nicolucci was found guilty on more than 150 counts and sentenced to nineteen years in prison.

On June 27, 1995, Joe Lagana, the Peel Street lawyer with close ties to Vito Rizzuto, was given a thirteen-year jail sentence for importing 558 kilos of cocaine and laundering $47.4 million. His partners, Richard Judd and Vincenzo Vecchio, each received a seven-and-a-half-year term. The court ordered the seizure of Lagana's bank accounts and assets—worth a combined $2.5 million and amassed during the four years that the RCMP investigation was active. Prosecuting attorneys complained that the sentence was too lenient. But in the eyes of some, it wasn't lenient enough. The federal Liberal government of the time enacted legislation requiring the National Parole Board to automatically release non-violent offenders serving their first term in a federal penitentiary after serving one-sixth of their time rather than one-third. As a result, Lagana went free on August 27, 1997, having served two years and two months instead of the thirteen-year sentence pronounced by the judge.

The majority of the Rizzuto clan's money launderers benefited from this same legislative godsend. It was perhaps not for nothing that Domenico Tozzi had thanked Justice Jean-Pierre Bonin after his sentence was read out. Handed a ten-year prison term (plus the additional two years for refusing to pay the fine), he got out after just two years. He may well have realized that he would only be out of commission for a relatively short time. At any rate, a good number of police officers and prosecuting lawyers had the distinct impression that the legislative change was tailor-made for swindlers, drug traffickers and, especially, Mafia honchos. Some wondered flat out whether the Mafia might have a powerful lobbyist working for them in Ottawa.

The new statutory provision was skilfully camouflaged amid a welter of amendments. At the time of its enactment, then justice minister Allan Rock announced—with copious amounts of advertising to accompany the move—a strengthening of laws with regard to sex offenders and other dangerous criminals. The amendment to the "accelerated parole review," meanwhile, was buried twenty pages into a huge omnibus bill containing several measures that had little to do with one another. The amendment was so well hidden that it escaped the attention of Parliament and even lawyers specialized in prison law.

Journalists at Montreal's *La Presse,* upon learning that Lagana and his accomplices were to be released after serving one-sixth of their sentences, sought an explanation. No one was able to tell them what had prompted the government to display such generosity. "I am not aware of who made the proposal, but we agreed because early release after serving one-third has been working well since 1992," said National Parole Board chairman Willie Gibbs. "We thought it would work well at one-sixth."

As observers wryly noted, with that kind of reasoning, Gibbs might as well have attempted to justify early release after one-twelfth of time served. Even before this new legislation came into force on August 1, 1997, the Quebec Bar along with parole officers had decried the harmful effects of automatic release after one-third of time served, warning parliamentarians that the measure would result in prisons being emptied of defrauders and heavyweight drug traffickers. According to the Bar, automatically freeing non-violent offenders after a third of time served would likely prompt "small and medium-sized criminal organizations" to recruit people fitting that profile and capable of committing bloodless crimes. In a 1994 report, the Bar suggested doing away with automatic parole in such cases. The Liberal government of Prime Minister Jean Chrétien threw the report in the shredder . . . and instituted automatic release after one-sixth of time served.

Still, the premature release of Joe Lagana, Domenico Tozzi and several other money launderers and narcotics traffickers sparked outrage. In 1999, the federal government announced that members of organized criminal groups would no longer benefit from the measure and would henceforth have to serve one-third of their sentences before being released.

That "tightening" of legislation, as it turned out, was little more than window dressing. It applied only to inmates who had been convicted under new anti-gang legislation—as it turned out, a single person in all of Canada. (Most absurd of all, the man was a down-and-out heroin addict who had in fact helped Montreal police arrest members of the city's Mafia.)

CHAPTER 10

THE MONEY TRAIL

J OE LAGANA WASN'T THE only one thrown into a panic upon learning that the RCMP had asked authorities in Switzerland to freeze the Rizzuto family's accounts. He had immediately notified Vito, whose mother, Libertina, then aged sixty-eight, was on a plane to Switzerland within hours. The family had to act fast before other accounts were frozen. Libertina arrived in Lugano, in the canton of Ticino, on August 31, 1994. That evening, she met with Luca Giammarella, aged forty-seven, an acquaintance of her husband who lived across the street from the Rizzutos on Antoine-Berthelet Avenue. He too had rushed to Lugano. The next morning, Mrs. Rizzuto and Giammarella paid a visit to the local branch of Credit Suisse Trust, part of Credit Suisse Group and specializing in wealth-management services. There, they controlled an account with a balance of more than 800,000 Swiss francs (roughly the same amount in Canadian dollars at the time) since 1988. Elsewhere in Switzerland, the Rizzuto clan had parked millions of dollars away from the eyes of Canada's taxman in accounts with financial institutions in Lugano, Geneva, Zurich and other Swiss cities.

Switzerland occupied a special square on the Rizzuto clan's international chessboard, alongside Italy, the United States, Colombia, Venezuela and, as will be seen later, countries as distant from each other as Panama and the Philippines.

As clients of Credit Suisse, Libertina Rizzuto and Luca Giammarella were in lofty company. Swiss authorities had previously uncovered a slush fund in a branch of that financial institution in Chiasso, a small city twenty-five kilometres to the south of Lugano, right on the border with Italy. The fund contained the proceeds of Italian tax evasion schemes. Credit Suisse had also been home to part of the hidden assets of the former Philippine dictator Ferdinand Marcos and his wife, Imelda. In March 1986, the Swiss Federal Council had moved to freeze the Marcos's assets in all of the country's financial institutions but, as if by chance, the family's deposits with Credit Suisse had been transferred just a day earlier to neighbouring Liechtenstein, another tax haven.

Credit Suisse Trust advertised a wide array of services to clients, including help with setting up companies in countries like Panama and Liechtenstein. In the eyes of many a critic, the Swiss banking system had a particular "behaviour failure." *Swiss Whitewash* (*La Suisse lave plus blanc*) was the title of a book by writer, sociologist and politician Jean Ziegler that received a less-than-stellar welcome in his native country when it was published in 1990. The Alpine paradise, outwardly so clean and neat, was a haven not only for dirty money deposited by dictators and criminals of all stripes, but also assets that were confiscated by the Nazis from thousands of the Jews they persecuted during the Second World War.

The many advantages offered by Switzerland to the wealthiest of the wealthy are not recent inventions. More than two centuries ago, the Calvinists of Geneva provided a haven for French aristocrats fleeing the revolution, where they could bank their *louis d'or*. In 1934, the Swiss Parliament passed the Banking Law, which made it a crime for any individual or group to violate banking secrecy; offenders could be imprisoned or fined. Sixty years later, when Libertina Rizzuto travelled to Lugano, fully one-quarter of the world's private asset portfolios, some $2.3 trillion, was held in Swiss banks.

Meyer Lansky, the American Cosa Nostra's financial consultant par excellence, was just one of many gangsters to grasp the usefulness of banking secrecy. In 1931, Al Capone had famously been convicted of tax evasion. Swiss banks provided a way for the Mafia to avoid this type of predicament. Lansky opened an account and transferred the profits of his illicit activities to it, after first ensuring that they transited through a series of holdings and shell companies. Once that was done, it was child's play to use the banked funds as collateral for securing loans as immaculate as the white snow of the Alps. When the Lanskys of the world wanted to withdraw or transfer money, the doors of the respectable institutions of Zurich, Geneva and Lugano opened wide before them.

Libertina Rizzuto and Luca Giammarella were no doubt expecting just that sort of royal treatment on September 1, 1994, when they stepped into the Credit Suisse Trust branch in Lugano. Things didn't quite happen the way they hoped. When Giammarella explained that he wished to close his account and leave with the balance in cash—hundreds of thousands of Swiss francs that he planned to stuff into the handbag he held—the Credit Suisse employees asked him to wait in an adjoining room while they held a brief confab.

A few years earlier, Credit Suisse had been embroiled in a major scandal that ended up costing Swiss justice minister Elisabeth Kopp her job. Credit Suisse had been a favoured depository institution for two Lebanese brothers, Jean and Barkev Magharian, who had laundered hundreds of millions of dollars in profits from the Pizza Connection's heroin trade. The Swiss Federal Banking Commission had published a twenty-eight-page report severely criticizing Credit Suisse for turning a blind eye to the transactions.

Libertina's and Luca's patience was not to be rewarded: instead of smiling bank employees returning to tell them they could proceed with the transaction, they found themselves face to face with the police. The officers asked them to accompany them to the local station, where they were questioned separately. Mrs. Rizzuto indicated that the funds in the account under Giammarella's name actually belonged to her and her husband, Nicolò. She added that the hundreds of thousands of Swiss francs represented income from family businesses in Venezuela—among them a chicken farm—and that she wished to transfer the money to another bank, to be eventually withdrawn to pay income taxes owed by her husband in Canada. She explained that Nicolò had stayed behind in Montreal, unable to travel because of illness.

The Credit Suisse Trust staff's call to the police was not motivated by ethical considerations. Swiss authorities had ordered the country's banking institutions to freeze accounts belonging to the Rizzuto clan, and the Credit Suisse Lugano branch had been informed of an imminent investigation. Libertina Rizzuto's convoluted explanation about a reserve fund to pay Canada's taxman fooled no one. Both she and Luca Giammarella were taken into custody.

In addition to Joe Lagana, others in the Rizzutos' orbit had been reaping the benefits of Swiss bank accounts: Sabatino "Sammy" Nicolucci, the cocaine trafficker who had been kidnapped by the Colombians; Beniamino Zappia of Milan; and Giuseppe LoPresti, murdered two years previously. In Lugano alone, fourteen accounts had been opened in the Rizzutos' name, at branches of the Banca Privata Edmond de Rothschild, the Société de Banque Suisse, the Union Bank of Switzerland and Credit Suisse.

But suspicion did not constitute proof, and Fabrizio Eggenschwiler, the public prosecutor of the canton of Ticino, wanted to take his investigation as far as possible. Eggenschwiler was certain that the Rizzutos' millions, which had been routed from one account to another over several years, represented the proceeds of criminal activity. He asked Canadian authorities to provide any and all information that might help him convict Libertina Rizzuto and Luca Giammarella for money laundering, Mafia associations and violation of the Swiss Narcotics Act. In his request, he specified that the pair could not be held in preventive custody for more than six months.

"I have asked Canadian police to send me the results of their investigation into the origin of the money that Mrs. Rizzuto had in her possession, as well as information about the Rizzuto family and how their money-laundering operations function," Eggenschwiler told La Presse. The newspaper then broke the story of Vito's mother's Swiss adventures. "Without these documents from Canada, we will probably be forced to release [Libertina Rizzuto and Luca Giammarella], unless we invoke a special procedure to extend their preventive detention," the public prosecutor added.

A public accountant with the Justice Ministry office in Lugano had compiled a list of the many transactions employed by the Rizzuto clan in laundering considerable sums of money. According to Eggenschwiler, tens of millions of dollars had been moved through their accounts.

The RCMP sent the information requested, but it was clearly insufficient in the eyes of Swiss authorities. Jean Salois, the Rizzutos' lawyer, flew to Switzerland, where he attended two hearings and examined the dossier provided to the Swiss by Canadian authorities, whereupon he declared that it contained no information that could be used to justify his clients' incarceration. The Lugano public prosecutor had no choice but to release Libertina Rizzuto and Luca Giammarella. They were freed after having paid bail amounts of 200,000 and 50,000 Swiss francs respectively.

The affair soon reached the floor of the Canadian Parliament. Michel Bellehumeur, a member of Parliament for the Bloc Québécois, the official opposition party at the time, stood in the House of Commons on March 2, 1995, and asked an embarrassing question for the governing Liberals: "Mr. Speaker, my question is directed to the prime minister," he said. "This morning, La Presse reported that Libertina Rizzuto and Luca Giammarella, suspected by the Swiss authorities of trying to launder three million dollars through Swiss banks, were released, although the investigation continues. It seems their release came as a result of the half-hearted assistance the RCMP gave Swiss police authorities. Could the prime minister explain why the RCMP failed to give the Swiss authorities their full co-operation when they refused to provide information crucial to legal proceedings in Switzerland?"

Prime Minister Jean Chrétien let Patrick Gagnon, the parliamentary secretary to the Solicitor General, answer in his stead: "Mr. Speaker, I have just been advised of this case, and I will make a note of the opposition critic's question," he said. But Bellehumeur did not relent: "What explanation does the prime minister have for the fact that the only officer familiar with the case involving Mrs. Rizzuto and Mr. Giammarella was on holiday when the Swiss authorities had to release these two individuals, failing the co-operation of the RCMP?" The parliamentary secretary to the Solicitor General promised that a response would be forthcoming "in due time."

The next day, March 3, Bellehumeur pressed his case: "Yesterday, we learned that the RCMP's lack of co-operation with Swiss authorities had resulted in the release of two Canadian nationals who had been charged with money laundering and detained for six months in Switzerland," he said. "Today, for the second time in a year, the U.S. State Department indicated that Canada is one of the countries where money laundering is most prevalent and easiest to do. Since Canada is truly a sieve when it comes to money laundering, what is the government waiting for to legislate and put an end to that illegal activity?"

Though the prime minister remained silent, his senior staff did not. "Mr. Speaker, with the ease of international money transfers, money laundering by the underworld is a concern for all industrialized nations," replied Allan Rock, minister of justice and Attorney General of Canada. "Through the inference of the Solicitor General, Canada is collaborating with other nations around the world to form a united front against this insidious threat to our economic security and, frankly, to our laws against crime. The Solicitor General, through his collaboration with the United States of America and European nations, is working closely with authorities abroad to take effective steps to deal with money laundering in Canada," he said.

"The Canadian government is certainly not co-operating with Swiss authorities," Bellehumeur retorted. "I also urge the minister to read the U.S. State Department's report. It has plenty to say about this issue. Does the minister realize that, because of the lack of legislation, each year ten billion dollars are being laundered in Canada, and does he realize that his failure to act only encourages such illegal activity?"

Rock closed the debate by reiterating that Canada was "collaborating with authorities abroad" and assured Parliament that current money-laundering legislation was "sufficient to meet the challenge." The U.S. State Department report to which the Bloc Québécois member referred stated that Canada was not only a hub for narcotics trafficking, but a paradise for money launderers. Its authors listed Canada among the sixteen major money-laundering countries, alongside Switzerland, Italy, Venezuela, Panama and several small Caribbean states. The Canadian government had amended the Proceeds of Crime Act in 1995; it urged financial institutions to keep records of transactions in excess of $10,000 for five years.

The authors of one U.S. State Department *International Narcotics Control Strategy Report*, however, lamented the fact that the Canadian requirements did not extend to criminal prosecutions, as was possible under U.S. law. In its subsequent edition of the same report, the State Department remarked that there was no Canadian law *requiring* banks to report suspicious financial transactions to police; reporting was voluntary. Canadian banks were attractive to drug money launderers "because of branches located in traditional tax haven countries in the Caribbean," the report added.

In that same month, March 1995, a group of Montreal police force, SQ and RCMP analysts stated in a report that the amount of money laundered in Canada each year was not ten billion dollars, as some sources had reported, but twenty billion. "For the Mafia, maintenance of banking secrecy is the key to the future of their money laundering," the analysts wrote. "Governments in certain tax havens offer their clients banking secrecy in addition to tax shields. In Canada, the Mafia is currently working to infiltrate and control certain banking institutions. . . . There is indeed a serious money-laundering problem in Canada, and it is getting worse."

In their report, "Is Canada Safe from Organized Crime?", the police analysts expressed alarm at the colossal sums invested by the Mafia in the licit economy, as well as the organization's potential political influence:

> Our observations show that the Mafia is investing in real estate, the restaurant business, the automobile market, construction, the hotel trade, the food industry and several other areas of activity. . . . We are especially apprehensive about the possible duplication in Canada of

the Italian model, whereby the Mafia has taken complete control of the Christian Democratic Party through such means as investing in its election fund. In Canada, certain decisions made by the various levels of government clearly demonstrate that those who contribute to parties' electoral funds receive preferential treatment.

Whether for the awarding of public contracts, changes to zoning by-laws, the regulation of construction workers or the management of horse racing, numerous government decisions favour interests with links to organized crime. As the Italian experience has shown—and once again, this model has been observed here—the Mafia intercedes both upstream and downstream in the public-works contracting process. Upstream, it corrupts and bribes civil servants and politicians to win public contracts; downstream, it employs fraud and black-market labour to lower subcontracting costs. Though incontrovertible evidence is lacking, we believe that several billion dollars in proceeds from organized crime is invested each year in licit activities in Canada. We are also convinced that certain businessmen responsible for managing these activities are exerting undue influence on our governments, and in the process threatening the democratic underpinnings of our society.

The Quebec-based police analysts hoped to mobilize law enforcement agencies across Canada in an effort to persuade the federal government to amend the Criminal Code and make organized crime . . . a crime. They pointed out that several countries, including the United States, France and Italy, had moved to make criminal syndicates illegal. Their efforts were rewarded, up to a point: anti-gang legislation was eventually enacted in June 1997, but it didn't have particularly sharp teeth.

After her release from custody in Switzerland in March 1995, Libertina Manno Rizzuto returned to Canada and her beloved Nicolò. The couple celebrated their fiftieth wedding anniversary in grand style at the Sheraton Montreal Centre-Ville, making their entrance into the hotel ballroom to the strains of the theme from *The Godfather*. More than three hundred guests attended, including the upper crust of the city's

Sicilian Mafia. Video recordings were made of the event—to the delight of investigators years later when they were seized during searches of the family's sumptuous homes on Antoine-Berthelet Avenue.

Libertina Rizzuto and Luca Giammarella reached an out-of-court settlement with the Swiss authorities. The government of Switzerland agreed to withdraw its accusations in exchange for a payment of just over two million dollars. It remitted half the amount to the government of Canada.

The RCMP rejected accusations that the assistance it provided to the Swiss investigation was "half-hearted." Insofar as they had no evidence to justify the arrest of Vito Rizzuto's mother, the Mounties said they were surprised at the Swiss authorities' behaviour. "Everyone was surprised by that," said Sergeant-Major Yves Roy, the officer in charge of the RCMP's Integrated Anti-Drug Profiteering Section. "We didn't ask the Swiss authorities to proceed with that arrest; they did so of their own accord. We provided information to Switzerland, but they didn't appear to be satisfied," he concluded.

The results of the CIMM sting operation, however, gave Swiss investigators a boost. They began probing suspicious bank accounts that had been opened by Canadians in their country. Two bank managers were suspected of having helped Montreal mobster Vincenzo "Jimmy" Di Maulo and his associates wash six million dollars in drug money; one of them was arrested on May 19, 1995, and charged with laundering three million dollars through the RCMP's fake currency exchange.

The story of the Swiss accounts came back to haunt the Rizzuto family fifteen years later. In February 2010, Nicolò Rizzuto was charged with tax evasion and summoned to appear at the Court of Québec in Montreal. The eighty-five-year-old patriarch was accused of hiding $5.2 million in Swiss banks and failing to report $728,000 in interest income. Pending the outcome of the case, the Canada Revenue Agency ordered that a mortgage be instituted against Rizzuto's home on Antoine-Berthelet Avenue as well as two of his cars, a Jaguar and a Mercedes.

Old Nick pleaded guilty to two counts of tax evasion and agreed to pay a $209,000 fine. Crown prosecutor Yvan Poulin explained that the fine was in addition to taxes and interest that Rizzuto was also being forced to pay under an out-of-court settlement. Those amounts, however, remained confidential. Before the hearing began, the old man stood in the courtroom, his trademark fedora on his head, and insisted he had acted in good faith. "The money was from my business in Venezuela," he said with a shrug. "I didn't think I had to declare it."

The RCMP had succeeded in convincing authorities in several countries to freeze most of the accounts into which it had transferred traffickers' funds via its covert currency exchange. Panama proved the most difficult sell. Three days before making their August 30 swoop, RCMP officers travelled to the tiny Central American nation, which harboured a significant portion of the dodgy accounts. The Mounties presented a raft of documents proving that the deposits represented the profits of criminal activity. The Panamanian bank branch managers listened politely to their entreaties—and said no. The officers took their request higher up the bureaucratic chain, to no avail. One month later, the Panamanian government still refused to intercede with the banks.

The RCMP was undaunted. Four investigators took turns pressing the investigation in Panama, living in an apartment they rented specifically for this purpose. In all, they spent four months painstakingly reproducing the drug money trail. Eventually, they persuaded the Panama Solicitor General's Office to support them in their efforts. They were joined by agents of the U.S. DEA.

Essentially, the system worked as follows. The Montreal Mafia would place an order for cocaine with the Cali cartel in Colombia. Vito Rizzuto's reputation was such that, unlike the Hells Angels or other criminal outfits, he was not always required to pay for the cargo upon delivery. The cartel extended the payment deadline for its most loyal clients. After it arrived at its destination, the merchandise was sold on the Montreal market—or elsewhere—by street dealers. The banknotes piled up, and a middleman—for example, lawyer Joe Lagana—handled their pickup. An obliging currency exchange accepted the cash and wired cheques or bank drafts to secret accounts in an offshore bank.

That bank would then transfer part of the money to one of its branches in Panama, which in turn would issue cheques payable to companies incorporated in the Colón Free Zone (CFZ), located at the eastern end of the Panama Canal, in the Caribbean Sea. In some cases, cheques might be sent directly to the companies. Those companies then issued fake invoices to businesses in the small city of Maicao, Colombia—all of which were in fact front companies for the leaders of the Cali cartel. A business located in Colón might, for example, pretend to sell one million dollars' worth of clothing to an import company in Maicao, when in fact no goods ever changed hands. In other cases, importers bought actual merchandise in the CFZ at extremely competitive prices, then resold them in exchange for Colombian pesos in Maicao. There were other, even more complex, schemes.

Investigators with the RCMP, the DEA and Panamanian police uncovered evidence that at least eighty companies, most of them operating out of the CFZ, were recycling the Cali cartel's drug trade profits through some 140 wholesale businesses in Maicao. Several of the companies were headed by Lebanese nationals. Panamanian authorities arrested three of them and temporarily froze the assets of three companies: Chaher International, Shadj and Dalila Fashion.

The CFZ, the world's second-largest free-trade zone after Hong Kong, and the largest in the Americas, was first envisioned by bankers in the United States as early as 1929. The Panamanian government has made it one of its principal economic levers. Containerized goods on board the thousands of ships that pass through the canal each year can be imported and re-exported free of customs duty fees, tariffs, taxes and quotas. More than 1,700 companies have opened business counters in the tiny, 2.4-square-kilometre zone, through which commodities worth in excess of seven billion dollars—and more than 250,000 visitors—pass every year. Sellers accept payment by cheque, money order, wire transfer or cash. Their main customers are Colombian merchants.

Most of those 250,000 visitors are honest, bargain-hunting business people—but not all. "Colombian traffickers . . . will exploit any means possible to safely launder their drug proceeds," a DEA report states. "One such form of money laundering is known as the Black Market Peso Exchange (BMPE). The BMPE is a complex system currently used by drug trafficking organizations to launder billions of dollars of drug money each year utilizing the advantages of Panama's Colón Free Zone (CFZ), which serves as an integral link in the Colombian money laundering chain." Exchanging foreign currencies into pesos was a further hurdle for Colombian traffickers, hence the black-market route.

Maicao is a city in Guajira, on the northern tip of Colombia, close to the Venezuelan border, approximately 750 kilometres east-northeast of Colón. In 1991, as part of a government job growth incentive, Colón was granted special status as a free-trade zone, allowing goods to be imported tax-free. Officially this status aimed to create employment for workers turning raw materials into finished goods for re-export. In practice, it proved a gold mine for the drug cartels and their money launderers. Incidentally, the modest town of 100,000 includes a sizable population of Middle Eastern origin, including many Lebanese.

The RCMP's covert currency exchange operation exposed the central role of the CFZ in their suspects' money-laundering operations, and they sought to expand their investigation to Maicao. They asked Sergeant Varoug Pogharian, their liaison at the Canadian Embassy in Bogotá, to mount an operation jointly with Colombian authorities.

Pogharian sent the information that the RCMP had compiled to the Dirección de Impuestos y Aduanas Nacionales de Colombia (DIAN), the country's tax and customs agency. He then met with DIAN officials, who strongly cautioned the Canadians against precipitating any action. The liaison officer briefed RCMP headquarters in Ottawa on the meetings and the Colombians' concerns: the Maicao region, he noted, is a contraband zone in which "immigrants of Syrian and Lebanese origin who are known criminals" were active. Sergeant Pogharian added:

> For the first time, the Colombian authorities have formal proof of the Maicao merchants' links to the Cali cartel. Because of our investigation, huge amounts of money will likely be seized from the cartel. We believe that for our safety as well as theirs, the Colombian government

should remain cautious. It is possible that they will not follow up on our request; after all, it is their men who would be put in harm's way.

The Colombians will be less keen than the Panamanians on having investigators from another country do a job that is in their purview. . . . If we decide to go ahead, it would be best to keep as low a profile as possible, otherwise we could be endangering the safety of the Embassy and its staff.

Still fresh in Pogharian's mind, clearly, were the bomb threats against the Canadian Embassy following the arrest of Sammy Nicolucci, the Montreal trafficker with ties to the Rizzutos, as part of the August 30, 1994, police swoop. Colombian criminals are only too willing to turn words into deeds, he explained, recalling the numerous killings and attempted killings that had surrounded the arrest, escape and execution of Medellín cartel kingpin Pablo Escobar the year before. "Colombian drug traffickers are inclined to respond with violence when they sense an imminent threat to their freedom or their money." The Canadian Embassy in Bogotá was not an especially well-secured building, he warned: "The U.S. Embassy is a virtual fortress. Its staff members constantly travel in armoured vehicles. They cannot (again, for security reasons) go to public places in their leisure time, nor venture outside Bogotá. Staff at the Canadian Embassy have no such constraints, and do not want them."

Despite these concerns, DIAN investigators decided to proceed with a large-scale operation in Maicao and planned multiple raids on city businesses to take place on March 20, 1995. But they were nervous. On March 15, Pogharian met with Officer Juan Gabriel Ronderos, in charge of special investigations. The next day, Pogharian reported to Ottawa headquarters:

Ronderos is now convinced that he will face threats as soon as they make a move in Maicao. For this reason, he has decided to resign a few weeks from now, and keep out of sight overseas for a few years. His superior is going to do the same. The rumour is that someone from the old guard will step in as the new director of the DIAN. The

new DIAN head will probably be an ally of the traffickers and smugglers. This sort of two steps forward, two steps back situation is
common here. . . .

The Guajira region is known for its merciless settlings of
accounts. I have asked Ronderos not to mention any Canadian
involvement if he does decide to go ahead with a raid in Maicao
before resigning. If we are excessively intrusive, we could be seen as
white knights who decided to attack the Colombian cartels. In which
case we must understand that this would result in very unpleasant
consequences for the Embassy and its staff.

The Maicao operation was called off. On March 22, Pogharian
informed his RCMP superiors that Juan Gabriel Ronderos had resigned—
and so had the director of the DIAN. "As you know, Ronderos was the key
man," the liaison officer wrote. A few days later, the newly appointed
DIAN director quit as well. "Apparently, he started receiving death
threats," Pogharian wrote. "I have heard that these threats came from
inside the DIAN, from corrupt former customs officers recently re-hired
by the DIAN." The Mounties' man in Bogotá recovered all of the RCMP
and DIAN documentation pertaining to the aborted mission in Maicao.

Another thread picked up by police during surveillance as part of
Operation Compote led to one of the most improbable tales ever to
involve the Montreal Mafia: the Rizzutos had, apparently, been tasked
with the mission of recovering a fortune in gold bullion stashed in Swiss
bank safes by the deposed—and by then deceased—Philippine dictator,
Ferdinand Marcos.

Marcos and his wife, Imelda, were driven out of Manila's Malacañang
Palace in 1986, their regime brought down by a popular revolt, and sought
refuge in Hawaii. Imelda was famously forced to leave behind some 2,500
pairs of shoes, 1,000 handbags, 500 gowns and 15 mink coats. The new
government set about trying to recover part of the estimated five billion
dollars that the couple had plundered from the country's citizens during

their two-decades-long dictatorial reign. After her husband's death in 1989, Imelda Marcos was allowed to return from exile in 1991, and she ran in the presidential election a year later. At that time she was forced to answer the question on every Filipino's lips: How had she amassed her fortune?

She announced at a news conference that her husband had found part of a fabled treasure, "Yamashita's Gold," in the Philippine jungle when he was a guerrilla fighting invading Japanese forces during the Second World War. A long-standing legend has it that General Tomoyuki Yamashita, who governed the Philippines after his forces captured the country in late 1941 and early 1942, had hidden tonnes of gold looted during his Southeast Asian campaign in various jungle caches all over the archipelago. Imelda explained that her valiant husband had given some gold ingots to his men but had kept some for himself, eventually socking it away in Switzerland. "It's become something like an urban legend–type story," Rico José, a professor at the University of the Philippines and an authority on the Japanese occupation, said in 2005, when asked to comment on this story straight out of an Indiana Jones movie. Former Philippine Solicitor General Francisco Chavez has been even more trenchant, saying, "The myth of the Yamashita treasure is only being utilized to explain away a clear case of graft and corruption." True, there has never been any credible proof that Yamashita's Gold ever existed. There is, however, ample evidence that the strongman ruler and his footwear-addicted wife helped themselves to billions of dollars during their twenty years in power, siphoning funds from the state coffers, pocketing gargantuan bribes and misappropriating subsidies from the World Bank and the International Monetary Fund. It was thus entirely plausible that the Marcoses could have stolen gold bars from the Central Bank of the Philippines and stored them in offshore banks.

At 4:35 P.M. on August 6, 1993, the RCMP intercepted a three-page fax demonstrating that Vito Rizzuto and his associates, Joe Lagana and a certain Hummy Shumai, had been asked to recover the gold bullion. The letter of authorization had been notarized in the city of Cabanatuan, in the Philippines, and faxed from there. The document indicated that the three authorized legal representatives were being hired "to negotiate a claim from Fiordeliza T., special curator given responsibility for the estate of her father, Severino G. Sta. Romana."

Severino G. Santa Romana, it seemed, was a former Philippine general who had been close to the Marcoses throughout his military career. Before his death, he had managed to convince his daughter that he was entitled to the Marcoses' gold, because he had been by the former dictator's side on the day they discovered part of the Yamashita treasure.

The hard copy of the letter of authorization was seized a year later during a search of Lagana's Peel Street law office in Montreal. It specified that part of the booty lay dormant in a vault at a Zurich branch of the Union Bank of Switzerland. Half of "the money, bonds and metals" was to be distributed to the general's heir, and the other half to the hired treasure hunters.

An RCMP report stated that thousands of gold bars bearing the seal of the Central Bank of the Philippines reserve were said to be stored in secret vaults in Zurich and Hong Kong. The most imaginative estimates put the value of the fortune at five thousand tonnes of gold. The investigation revealed that Vito Rizzuto and his partners expected to be paid $4.2 billion if they succeeded in their quest. Vito was to split this tidy commission with Joe Di Maulo and several other associates. Around forty people in Canada, the United States, Europe and Asia were mixed up in the treasure hunt. Three European bankers supposedly stood to pocket $200 million each if they managed to turn the spoils over to the putative heiress.

Police documents show that a retired French lawyer and a criminal with a specialty in international fraud met with the presumed head of the Montreal Mafia early in March 1994. An RCMP report notes that the lawyer felt ill at ease "because of the people involved." The three men met at Vito Rizzuto's home on Antoine-Berthelet Avenue and at Bongusto, a restaurant in Montreal's Little Italy neighbourhood.

The following month, "Pierre Morais," the RCMP officer posing as manager of the CIMM, reported that Joe Lagana had told him that Vito Rizzuto had already spent $1.5 million trying to track down the Marcoses' gold, travelling first class and staying in upscale hotels. Lagana said he was about to fly to Switzerland to help out, and he invited Morais to come along, saying he would pay for his trip; this was more than the Mounties could have asked for. They subsequently intercepted a telephone conversation during which the lawyer emphasized that discretion was the watchword in the operation: Rizzuto feared that things might unravel if his name were directly linked to the treasure hunt.

Montreal police had in fact known about the venture for two years, long before the daughter of the dead Filipino general faxed her notarized letter. According to Sergeant-Detective Michel Amyot, now retired, the force's anti-gang squad "had heard about tonnes of gold supposedly for sale on the Montreal market." It had all started with a loansharking case. A group of Montreal businessmen, including a notary and an accountant, had decided to go looking for part of the Marcoses' gold. But it was an expensive proposition, and the less-than-scrupulous prospectors had borrowed large sums from Giovanni Bertolo, a drug trafficker on the Rizzuto clan payroll, who demanded an exorbitant interest rate. When the treasure seekers hit a brick wall, they had no money to pay back the loan.

Bertolo brought Vito Rizzuto up to speed. The don set out after the treasure himself, his appetite whetted by the prospect of colossal profits. The first step was to secure letters of authorization from the owners of the gold, in the names of a dozen or so front companies. Based on what Rizzuto had been able to find out, the letters were in safety deposit boxes in a variety of banks in Zurich, Hong Kong and New York. Vito travelled extensively—except, of course, to the United States, where he didn't dare set foot. He went to Manila, via Vancouver and Hong Kong. The RCMP urged authorities in the Philippines to follow him as soon as he arrived at the airport, but they weren't too enthusiastic about doing the Canadian police a favour: they had other fish to fry, they replied—or the equivalent in diplomatic language. And yet, their own interests were at stake: the country was certainly entitled to recover the despot's gold.

Vito's gold-digging also took him to Switzerland. He was spotted in Zurich in the company of Roberto Papalia, one of his British Columbia associates, who had been banned by the Vancouver Stock Exchange because of suspicious transactions. With his brother Antonio, Papalia owned a small gold mine on Texada Island, in the Strait of Georgia, north of Vancouver. Police were never able to establish whether there was any link between potential exploitation of the mine and Rizzuto's search for the Marcoses' gold. Had the ingots been located, might Vito and the Papalia brothers have claimed the gold came from the mine? In the end, police never did ascertain whether Vito found the pot of gold at the end of that particular rainbow.

His business with the Papalia brothers wasn't the first time the don had tested the waters of high finance. A civil trial in Ontario that ended in 1993 revealed that Vito had played a pivotal role in a stock-market scam. The artifice had begun back in the 1980s and eventually blew up in his face.

Penway Explorers was an obscure mining exploration company that owned several claims in Northern Ontario. Penway was essentially an empty shell; its revenues were practically nil. Nevertheless, shares in the company were traded on the Alberta Stock Exchange. In the space of thirteen months, from July 1986 to August 1987, their value increased tenfold, from sixty cents to more than six dollars per share. The following year, they crashed, far more suddenly than they had risen, to thirty cents a share.

The yo-yoing share prices were the result of a classic ploy called "pump and dump": the value of a stock is artificially jacked up through purchases of large amounts of shares. Often spurred on by a broker who is in on the scam, innocent and inexperienced investors smell a bargain and start buying up shares themselves. The share price soars, then the swindlers all sell their shares at a profit at the same time, leaving the cheated investors empty-handed. Their only recourse is through the courts. A pump-and-dump scheme was precisely the reason for the steady rise and swift fall of the Penway stock: crooked brokers had blown up the balloon, having agreed to burst it at an opportune time. A forty-year-old trader named Arthur F. Sherman, who sold large amounts of Penway stock, was part of this particular ruse. He worked for a Toronto-based brokerage house called McDermid St. Lawrence Securities, whose senior executive knew nothing of the plot.

In May 1988, the charlatans were fooled at their own game. Penway share prices plummeted back to penny-stock levels before they had time to dump their stocks as agreed. Their suspicions were directed at Sherman. Everything pointed to him having run off with the money. Trying to con the Mafia is an inadvisable move, to say the least, and about to emerge from the background was Vito Rizzuto, not at all pleased to find himself in the role of the plucked pigeon.

Lise Ledesma, a receptionist at McDermid St. Lawrence Securities, received intimidating phone calls from people claiming their name was Rizzuto, demanding to speak to Arthur Sherman. One of the callers had been put through by an operator who spoke Spanish, suggesting that the call originated in Venezuela, where Nicolò Rizzuto spent a lot of time. Then Vito showed up at the brokerage offices in person, accompanied by two sinister-looking goons. They insisted on seeing Sherman.

According to Ledesma, Sherman grew nervous. On May 9, he disappeared after telling people he was going to play golf. Two weeks later, he called his boss, John Shemilt, and informed him he was on the island of Aruba, just off the coast of Venezuela. He said he planned to return to work at the end of the month. When he didn't come back by the agreed-upon date, he was fired. Someone later claimed to have spotted him in Barcelona. The spooked broker, no doubt several million dollars richer, was never heard from again. He was officially pronounced dead in 1995, enabling members of his family to collect his life insurance.

What followed was one of the more surreal court cases in Canadian legal history. The crooks who had been involved with Sherman filed suit in the Ontario Court of Justice to claim their due. They said they were former clients of Sherman; the suit named the broker, but since he had vanished, it also sought damages from his former employer, McDermid St. Lawrence Securities. The plaintiffs demanded $3.5 million, which, they alleged, was the value of their 530,400 shares in Penway at their peak worth of $6 per share.

The accusers included R.R. (Bob) Campbell, a lawyer who had been disbarred in Ontario, and Costa Papadakis, a small-time speculator. The two claimed to represent investors who had entrusted large sums to them to purchase Penway stock and wished to remain unidentified. The brokerage house, McDermid, reacted vigorously. Hearings took place intermittently over forty-five days between April 1992 and April 1993. The more he heard, the more Mr. Justice George Adams was convinced that the actual owner of the shares, hidden behind a host of front men, was Vito Rizzuto.

The judge learned that Campbell had received hefty sums of money from Vito and his loyal laundryman Dima Messina. He learned even more thanks to Papadakis. Michel Gagné, an investigator with the Montreal police who specialized in organized crime, testified how Papadakis had confided to him that Vito was a personal friend, and that he had attended the birthday party of one of Rizzuto's children.

Papadakis admitted to having personally borrowed $100,000 from Messina, which he had then lent to Campbell. He also admitted that he had driven Vito Rizzuto from Montreal to Toronto so that he could "meet with someone about a mining property," the judge wrote.

The money invested by Bob Campbell and Costa Papadakis came entirely from people close to Vito, including Dima Messina, Rocco Sollecito, Gennaro Scaletta—and his own mother, Libertina. Sollecito ran the Consenza Social Club in Saint-Léonard, which served as a head-quarters for the Rizzuto clan. Scaletta had been arrested in Venezuela at the same time as Vito's father, Nicolò. Large parts of their "investments" had initially been paid in small cash denominations: ten- and twenty-dollar bills.

Justice Adams clearly understood the true nature of the Penway stock transactions. There was no legitimate reason for the sudden sharp rise in share prices; the company's operations were embryonic and there were no plans for expansion. He concluded that the transactions were rigged and the sales bogus. Nearly 90 percent of the transactions had originated with the small group of schemers—who, at one point, owned slightly more than half of the shares in circulation.

"On the evidence, I find the only person acting as a true owner [of the shares] was Vito Rizzuto," the judge concluded. The lawsuit was dismissed, and the judge ruled that Papadakis's claims had no credibility whatsoever: "[Mr. Papadakis] would be in his late fifties and testified that he has not had a full-time job since his early twenties," he said. "That job had been in the stock market industry but [he] admitted it had been lost as a result of him having stolen securities and that he had been convicted for this offence." The role of broker Arthur Sherman, who had disappeared and was probably deceased, appeared ambiguous to the judge. "My finding entails that, if anything, Sherman was up to 'no good' with the plaintiffs and with Mr. Rizzuto," he wrote. "While the plaintiffs urge that Sherman's disappearance amounted to an admission he had stolen their shares . . . other problems might equally explain his absence, as, indeed, might the wrath of Mr. Rizzuto."

The lawsuit provided ammunition for Revenue Canada tax inspectors. They were being handed, on a silver platter, evidence that Vito Rizzuto was hiding taxable income. On October 6, 1995, a notice of assessment on an amount of $1.5 million was delivered to his home on Antoine-Berthelet Avenue. The amount corresponded to the sum that Vito had personally invested in Penway stock between 1986 and 1988. The taxman was also seeking payment of a fine in the amount of $127,690 for "gross negligence."

Vito contested both the notice of assessment and the fine and took his appeal to the Tax Court of Canada in Montreal. In documents filed with the Court's Registry, Revenue Canada reiterated the decision by the Ontario judge and repeated that Rizzuto "controlled all of the Penway stock transactions carried out by nominee shareholders." It was he, the tax agency added, who had provided the money to purchase the Penway shares—a significant quantity of which had been paid in cash.

The Penway investments came around the same time as Rizzuto's arrest following the seizure of thirteen tonnes of hashish in Newfoundland on November 30, 1987, the investigators added. Of course, that undelivered cargo represented a dead loss for the Mafioso, but it was public knowledge that authorities never managed to lay their hands on more than a fraction of the drugs imported into the country— probably 10 percent at the most. Though there was no explicit accusation, the tax inspectors were insinuating that the ten- and twenty-dollar bills that had been used to purchase so much of the Penway stock were drug money. One statement entered into the court record by Revenue Canada, however, could not have been more clear-cut: "The applicant is known as 'the Godfather' of the Italian Mafia in Montreal."

In his brief to the court, Rizzuto's tax lawyer, Paul Ryan, countered that Rizzuto "never made the advances to the individual shareholders and therefore did not earn the [$1.5 million] in income that Revenue Canada claims he did." Vito was willing to admit only that he and his wife, Giovanna, had lent Rocco Sollecito $100,000 to purchase shares in Penway.

Revenue Canada officials and the federal government attorneys wanted to go for Vito's jugular, and they didn't hide it. They informed the Tax Court of Canada that the trial would last two weeks and announced that they would call some fifty witnesses, including Vito's mother, Libertina. They were prepared to summon Raynald Desjardins, a narcotics trafficker and one of Vito's closest associates, from his current residence—a cell in a federal penitentiary—and force him to answer their questions. Judge Pierre Archambault, who was to preside at the trial, requested that the services of Italian and Sicilian interpreters be retained. Courtroom security was beefed up to ensure the trial went smoothly. Court reporters awaited the signal that would draw them to the trial like hummingbirds to nectar.

The hearings were to begin on Monday, August 19, 2001. On Thursday 16, reporters learned that an out-of-court settlement had been reached. Their disappointment was palpable. "We felt like we had a strong case, but we wanted to avoid the media circus that was sure to happen," Ryan told them. In Rizzuto's lawyer's opinion, there was another reason for the sudden turnaround: interest had continued to accrue on the unpaid taxes on the $1.5 million in earnings and had already inflated the original amount demanded by 400 percent. One thing was for certain: Vito Rizzuto hated publicity—and problems. Discretion was his hallmark.

The federal government refused to reveal the amount of the settlement. La Presse, which had broken the story, learned from a reliable source that it amounted to $360,000. A number of civil servants confided in private that they were outraged. But they didn't dare criticize their employer in public. The chairman of the government's Standing Committee on Public Accounts, an opposition MP, filed a motion in Parliament asking "[t]hat a humble Address be presented to Her Excellency [the Governor General] praying that she will cause to be laid before this House a copy of all agreements and related documents and/ or correspondence, reports, minutes of meetings, notes, e-mail, memos and correspondence, entered into between the government and Mr. Vito Rizzuto, as it relates to the tax case brought before the Tax Court of Canada in 2001." On the grounds that tax matters are private, the government rejected the "humble address."

Canadians never learned why their government agreed to abandon the case in exchange for a payment as low as $360,000, nor whether agreement had been reached on a lower fine.

CHAPTER 11

PROJECT OMERTÀ

ANOTHER MAN BEING HOUNDED by Canadian tax authorities was Alfonso Caruana, the new head of the Cuntrera-Caruana clan. Try as he might to ignore them, the assessment notices were piling up. In 1986, Revenue Canada had seized $827,624 in his bank accounts as payment for back taxes. After initially contesting the decision, Caruana had given up and flown the coop to Venezuela, hooking up with Nicolò Rizzuto and the Cuntrera brothers.

When he returned to Canada in November 1993, the tenacious revenue inspectors were quick to remind him of Benjamin Franklin's timeless adage about the only certainties in life. The inspectors knew beyond all doubt that Caruana had amassed a colossal fortune in the narcotics trade. The Cuntrera-Caruanas were anathema to Italian judge Giovanni Falcone, who often said of them: "If we wish to destroy the drug trade, we must apprehend them." Indeed, just three days before his assassination, the anti-Mafia crusader had met with the Venezuelan justice minister to request that the leaders of the clan be extradited to Italy.

René Gagnière, who worked for a special Revenue Canada unit in Montreal, devoted a four-year slice of his career to investigating Alfonso

Caruana, which included poring over invaluable data gathered by RCMP Sergeant Mark Bourque. One piece of information in particular caught his attention: in 1981, during a span of just eight months, no less than $21.6 million had transited through one of Caruana's accounts. The money had been deposited in small bills, withdrawn soon after in the form of bank drafts, then routed to Swiss accounts.

Immediately after Caruana's return to Canada, Revenue Canada inspectors sent him a new notice of assessment. The amount due was nearly $30 million: $8.6 million in unpaid income taxes, plus accrued interest and various penalties representing a further $21.2 million.

Caruana's response to the taxman's request came on March 6, 1995: he filed for bankruptcy, declaring assets of $250. At the time, the self-described pauper was living at his sister-in-law's house on Grosvenor Avenue, in Westmount, Montreal's richest neighbourhood. He soon quietly moved with his wife to an elegant home in Woodbridge, just north of Toronto.

On April 29, as he entered the upscale Sutton Place Hotel on Bay Street in Toronto's downtown core, an unsuspecting Caruana was caught on videotape by Detective-Constable Bill Sciammarella and his unit based in the town of Newmarket, also north of the city. Using a camera hidden behind a window in a government building across the street, the police were conducting a favoured and almost always productive brand of surveillance: they were filming a Mafia wedding.

Among the tuxedoed guests, police recognized Vito Rizzuto and several of his henchmen: Agostino Cuntrera, who had been convicted for his role in the murder of Paolo Violi; Francesco Arcadi, a nearly illiterate hard case who served as Vito's lieutenant (despite the fact that he was Calabrian) and specialized in bookmaking and drug dealing; Rocco Sollecito, formerly the owner of the Consenza Social Club; and other equally distinguished gentlemen. As police watched, another guest, a fiftyish man wearing glasses, pulled up to the hotel in a Mercedes. His well-coiffed hair was black—unnaturally so for a man his age. Sciammarella and his crew videotaped his entrance. He turned out to be Alfonso Caruana, father of the bride, Francesca Caruana, who was getting hitched to one Anthony Catalanotto.

In June 1996, Inspector Paolo Palazzo of Turin, Italy's *Raggruppamento Operativo Speciale Carabinieri, Sezione Anticrimine* (Special Operational Group, Organized Crime Unit) requested Canadian assistance in tracking down Alfonso Caruana and his brothers, whom they suspected of running a vast transnational narcotics trafficking and money-laundering network from their base in Canada. Working with the American DEA, the Italians had amassed information proving that the clan's operations had continued unabated following the September 1992 expulsion from Venezuela of the Cuntrera brothers, Pasquale, Paolo and Gaspare, and their subsequent arrest in Italy.

Sciammarella's unit, working with the RCMP, launched its own investigation. They began keeping tabs on various suspects, identified from their video recording of the wedding of Alfonso's daughter the year before. The Caruanas were doing business in the United States, Italy, South America, Switzerland, France, Germany and Great Britain, but they didn't travel much themselves. The probe proceeded at a snail's pace until the Mounties caught a break: a U.S. undercover agent who had infiltrated the underworld in Atlanta, Georgia, told them that a South American broker had approached him about taking delivery of a million dollars in Canada. Finally, the investigators had uncovered money flowing between the Caruanas and their international drug business.

Fifty-year-old Alfonso Caruana was living in a spacious white house rented from his nephew Giuseppe Cuntrera in a newly developed subdivision of Woodbridge. The twenty-five tightly spaced luxury homes stood near an expansive country club, a creek and a protected woodland. Caruana's two-storey residence at 38 Goldpark Court was far more modest than the posh manor house he had occupied in London's stockbroker belt during his time in Great Britain, but its well-manicured front lawn and elegantly patterned driveway nonetheless suggested that the tenant had considerable income at his disposal. Alfonso and his wife, Giuseppina Caruana, owned a late-model Volkswagen Golf GTI and a 1994 Toyota Previa, and he soon bought a Cadillac. Alfonso's younger brother Pasquale, then aged forty-eight, lived in Maple, a twenty-minute drive northeast. Their older brother Gerlando, fifty-three, resided in

Rivière-des-Prairies, in east-end Montreal. He had been released from prison in March 1993 after serving one-third of a twenty-year sentence for his role in the plot to smuggle heroin concealed in exotic teak furniture shipped from Thailand via England (*see Chapter 6*).

In early 1997, Revenue Canada took Alfonso Caruana to Quebec Superior Court in Montreal, challenging his claims of bankruptcy and seeking to convict him for delinquency in paying the thirty million dollars in back taxes, interest and penalties that he owed. The lawyer for the federal tax agency, Chantal Comtois, noted that Caruana was a Canadian citizen but for years had not paid a penny in income tax. She alleged that when he had fled to Venezuela eleven years earlier, it was to evade Revenue Canada's grasp.

At the bankruptcy hearing, Caruana, represented by defence attorney Vincent Chiara, cast himself in the role of a struggling ordinary working man forced to ask family members for help in making ends meet. He claimed to earn a net salary of about four hundred dollars a week working at a used-car dealership. "I wash cars, I move them around," he sighed. He said he spent one hundred dollars a month on gas and public transit fares. His wife, Giuseppina, the court was told, worked in a disco. Their combined monthly income was around $3,500, but their rent alone cost them $1,500. The tax collection department was being asked to swallow a real sob story.

Revenue Canada lawyer Comtois was unmoved, and Superior Court Justice Derek Guthrie wasn't about to fall for the accused's tale of woe either. Comtois wondered how it was possible that, in a mere eight months, $21 million had passed through the bank account of a family of such modest means.

"The money wasn't all mine," Caruana said through an interpreter.

"But $21 million in your name . . . that's an awful lot of money, don't you think?" Comtois asked.

"I did it that way to provide services to others," was Caruana's reply. He testified that most of the money belonged to his uncle Pasquale Cuntrera and his brother-in-law, Giuseppe Cuffaro, and that he had personally deposited only $800,000 in the account—money that he claimed he eventually lost in a failed bid to restart a pig farm in Valencia, Venezuela.

The judge wanted to know how the money had wound up in Caruana's account. "You went back and forth—Venezuela, Montreal, Switzerland?" he asked.

"No, I had it brought to me," Caruana answered.

"By whom?" a visibly annoyed Justice Guthrie wanted to know.

"By travellers," Caruana said.

By then frustrated herself, Comtois asked, point-blank: "Are you not the godfather of the Italian Mafia?" The judge ordered the question withdrawn. The Revenue Canada lawyer then brandished a magazine article claiming that the Cuntrera-Caruana clan owned 60 percent of the island of Aruba, just north of Venezuela and Colombia. Holding the magazine out to Caruana, she asked what he thought of the allegation. "If only it were true," he said.

It was perhaps no longer true as of 1997: under international pressure, the government of the former Dutch colony had expelled members of the family. Prior to that, however, many observers had remarked that the clan wielded considerable economic and political influence in the island nation. In the opening sentences of *Thieves' World: The Threat of the New Global Network of Organized Crime*, Claire Sterling wrote:

> The world's first independent mafia state emerged in 1993. The sovereign Caribbean island of Aruba, sixty-nine square miles of emerald hills and golden sand, proved to belong to the Sicilian Mafia in fact if not in name . . . Aruba was bought and paid for by the most powerful mafia family abroad: the Cuntrera brothers—Paolo and Pasquale—of Siculiana, Sicily, and Caracas, Venezuela, who had amassed a billion dollars of their own in their twenty-five years as kingpins of the mafia's North American heroin trade.

Comtois asked Caruana if it was true that he once owned 160 square kilometres of land in Venezuela, near the Colombian border. "Everything is false," he replied. (He wasn't lying: the federal lawyer had seriously

underestimated the area of the land in question. Through front companies, Caruana and his associates had in fact owned some 400,000 hectares in Venezuela, or 4,000 square kilometres.)

Just prior to leaving Montreal for Venezuela in the late 1980s, Caruana
and his wife had sold two buildings they owned on Jean-Talon Street, a
plot of land in the Pointe-aux-Trembles neighbourhood, and a house in
Laval, all for approximately $1.2 million. But where had the money they
used to buy those properties come from in the first place? Comtois
wanted to know. When she took the stand, a callow Giuseppina Caruana
replied that she couldn't recall.

"Still, the money didn't just fall from the sky!" the judge exclaimed.

"These were amounts that I brought back a little at a time from
Venezuela," she said.

At the conclusion of the hearing, Justice Guthrie was a hair's breadth
from branding Alfonso and Giuseppina Caruana liars. "I don't believe a
word he said," he told the court, saying that Caruana "had almost no
memory of extraordinarily large sums of money and what he did with
[them] . . . I don't believe the bankrupt [Caruana] and his wife, whose
testimonies were full of holes, hesitations and incomplete explanations,
but I must render my judgment based on proof, not suspicions."

Revenue Canada was therefore unsuccessful in recovering the
amounts due. The Caruanas were officially bankrupt. The judge had to
be content with ordering the couple to pay $90,000 of the tax bill to the
federal government in monthly instalments of $2,500 over a three-year
period. Caruana and his wife returned to Toronto. As they exited the
courtroom in Montreal, Alfonso could not suppress a smile, while his
lawyer, Chiara, answered journalists with a wink when they asked if he
was happy with the court's decision.

If Alfonso Caruana thought his troubles were over, he was sorely mistaken. The RCMP had launched a secret probe, Project Omertà, specifically targeting him and his clan. A key accomplice of the family, a man
named Oreste Pagano, had been operating as a Mexico-based middleman

between Colombian cocaine sellers and the Cuntrera-Caruanas. Near the conclusion of Project Omertà in 1998, Pagano became an informant and went on to provide very illuminating testimony about the power of the clan and the role played in it by Vito Rizzuto.

A month after he gave his evasive replies to Chantal Comtois and Justice Derek Guthrie at Quebec Superior Court in Montreal, Alfonso Caruana was at Pearson Airport in Toronto, picking up a visitor: Oreste Pagano. Travelling under the alias Cesare Petruzziello, Pagano had boarded a plane in Port of Spain, Trinidad. Caruana drove his guest to his home on Goldpark Court.

Round-the-clock RCMP surveillance teams took turns listening to their headsets, working to decipher the coded language their suspects used on the phone. They were soon convinced that Pagano had a very specific task to perform while in Canada: he would arrange for the delivery of thousands of dollars to the clan's Colombian cocaine suppliers. He was also heard making several calls to South America to set up cocaine shipments totalling nearly two thousand kilos to Canada and Italy. Police listened as talk revealed plans for a second consignment of five thousand kilos, destination unknown.

One supplier, Juan Carlos Pavo, told Pagano that he had sent two couriers to Canada to pick up the money; they were staying in a Toronto hotel. Giuseppe Caruana entrusted Pagano with two gym bags containing $750,000 in twenty-dollar bills. Pagano headed for a meeting with the couriers to deliver the bags but gave up when he realized he was being tailed by police. He made one more attempt but again noticed he was being followed. He paid the couriers for their trouble, told them to go back to South America and then got back on a plane himself. The aborted exchange was just one minor episode in the long association of Alfonso Caruana and Oreste Pagano.

Pagano was born on July 15, 1938, in Naples. The fact that he was from the mainland normally would not have ingratiated him with the Sicilian Mafia. But he had extensive criminal experience and an outstanding network of contacts that made him indispensable. No doubt he would have found Caruana's poverty defence at his bankruptcy hearing hilarious: if anyone knew that Caruana was obscenely rich, it was Pagano. And if there was anyone who knew the true meaning of poverty, that person too was Oreste Pagano.

Growing up during the Second World War, he had often gone hungry. His father, an out-of-work electrician, struggled to feed his wife and their children, two daughters and two sons. And with the family's house near the port of Naples repeatedly suffering damage from Allied bombs, simply surviving was a daily challenge. Pagano's father tried to earn some money for his family by fashioning cosmetics bags from tortoise shells, but to little avail. "What I remember the most is a very miserable childhood," Pagano recalled decades later after he eventually decided to confess to police.

At an age when Canadian children normally begin elementary school, the young Oreste was begging for change on the mean streets of Naples. One day he decided he would be better off trying to make a living outside the family home. "I always tried to get away from this poverty," he said. "And so at the age of eight, nine years old, I started running away from home." Every time Oreste disappeared, his mother begged the police to go and find him. By age fourteen, he was deemed incorrigible and sent to reform school, where he lived for two years. When he got out, he hightailed it to Rome. One evening, he and a friend were out walking in the capital when a transvestite approached them, offering cash in exchange for sexual favours. The two young ruffians threw the unfortunate man to the ground, beat him up and stole his money. They were eventually arrested, charged with theft and convicted. Pagano was sentenced to four months in prison. During his testimony, he called the episode "the first real disaster of [his] life"—for his criminal record later kept him from getting a legitimate job.

Once freed, he settled in Brescia, a city of about 150,000 halfway between Milan and Venice. There, he married his first wife and got a job selling linens in the street. Finding the earnings from that line of work inadequate, he supplemented his income through activities that tended to be more profitable, though they were hardly commendable: fraud, theft, forgery. Before long he was back behind bars on a weapons charge.

That second trip to jail would mark a turning point in his life. "I met a certain Raffaele Cutolo," he recalled. Cutolo, who had earned the nickname *o' Professòre* thanks to his academic way of speaking and passion for teaching up-and-comers the workings of various con games and criminal schemes, was serving a life term for first-degree murder. From his cell, he was working to revive the Camorra, the Neapolitan equivalent of the Mafia. He recruited prospects from among the prison population and had them swear allegiance to his *Nuova Camorra Organizzata* (NCO), during a ritual that involved extracting a drop of blood from the initiate's wrist.

Cutolo provided financial assistance to Pagano and his family. The apprentice showed his eternal gratitude by giving his protector a stray spaniel that had been found and cared for by a kind soul. Then, after his release from prison, Pagano sent clothing, food and money to Cutolo's older sister and loyal accomplice, Rosetta. Nicknamed *Occh'egghiaccio* (Eyes of Ice), Rosetta was a hardened criminal who once nearly succeeded in blowing up the police headquarters in Naples. She regularly visited her jailed brother, bringing donations from followers on the outside. In 1978, Raffaele escaped from prison. "He calls me to . . . go to Naples because he wants to talk to me," Pagano recalled. The fugitive asked if he could hide out at Pagano's house in Brescia. Pagano enthusiastically obliged. One evening, he told his house guest that he was going out for a while, and went to a gambling den in Milan. Among the players that night were several highly placed men of honour in the Sicilian Mafia, including Alfredo Bono. "That night, it was my unlucky and lucky night," Pagano said. By early morning, he had soundly beaten Bono at cards. The latter settled the large debt with promissory notes, which Pagano then gave to Cutolo, who was headed back to Naples in secret.

The head of the NCO was discovered and arrested, however. The police also laid their hands on the money drafts, and when they saw that they bore Pagano's signature, they had proof of his complicity in Cutolo's escape. Pagano spent another two years behind bars. As soon as he was freed, he resumed his drug dealing—which earned him another ticket to jail. His life became a not-so-merry-go-round of incarceration and freedom. After five years of one jail term had elapsed, just before Christmas 1988, prison authorities granted him a temporary release pass. When he returned home, he was so appalled at the sight of his children's poverty that he decided against returning to prison. He was going to make big money and get his family out of the poorhouse. They fled overseas. "This is where I really started drug trafficking," he told his Canadian handlers. "I had never abandoned my family."

He started slow, shipping a few kilos of cocaine to Italy, first from Spain and eventually from a new home base: Venezuela. In 1991, a Sicilian trafficker, also on the run, introduced Pagano to Alfonso Caruana. Over dinner on Margarita Island, a popular resort destination in Venezuela, Caruana asked him if he had contacts who could help him purchase very large quantities of cocaine. Pagano had the contacts; Caruana had the money—lots of it. It was the beginning of a fruitful friendship. "Finally I could see something good," Pagano said. "At least now I could get out of poverty." He knew the Cuntreras and the Caruanas by reputation and correctly described them as one extended family: "They are descendants of the Mafia," he said in one of his debriefing sessions. "The grandfather [of Alfonso Caruana] was a Mafioso. His father was a Mafioso. The uncles are Mafiosi."

Pagano retained a measure of nostalgia about his life. During his lengthy sessions with RCMP investigators, he repeatedly said he had been born into an honest family, blaming his criminal existence on an accumulation of unfortunate circumstances. "My father was an honest and humble working man . . . My mother is a housewife, very honest . . . No member of my family has ever been in prison . . . If I were born in Canada, I would never have a charge in my life . . . The Canadian legislation is very permissive . . . because before you arrest a person and . . . put them in prison, you need concrete evidence. That is why I am saying that if I had been born in Canada, I would never have been convicted," he said.

Pagano achieved his goal: he escaped from poverty. After a few years in the narcotics trade, he was able to display some of the ostentatious symbols of wealth: sparkling gold Rolexes, other very expensive jewellery, million-dollar homes in Latin America, Italy and Florida. He liked gambling, specifically baccarat. (His love for that game, incidentally, led police to crack the code he and his accomplices used when exchanging telephone numbers. It was inspired by the scoring in baccarat, in which the point values of cards in a hand are added up, with the best possible score being nine. Each digit in the coded telephone number had to be subtracted from nine to arrive at the correct digit: two meant seven, six meant three, etc.)

The RCMP kept Pagano on their radar all through Project Omertà. By the spring of 1998, he was working out of the office of a real estate agency that he owned in Cancún, Mexico. He set up a delivery of two hundred kilos of cocaine, to be delivered to his contact in Houston, Texas, while Alfonso Caruana assigned members of his crew in Montreal the task of finding couriers to pick up the powder. At 12:48 P.M. on April 21, the RCMP intercepted a conversation between the two men. Pagano referred to "stuff" that was stashed and couldn't be moved right away. "We will wait a week and then do it," he advised Caruana, then asked him how much he had sent. Answer: "1.4 and 250." Meaning: Can$1.4 million and U.S.$250,000.

Alfonso's brother Gerlando had the right man for the Houston pickup: Nunzio LaRosa, age fifty. LaRosa hired two young truckers who had experience moving dope across the border: twenty-nine-year-old John Curtis Hill, of Sault Ste. Marie, Ontario, and thirty-one-year-old Richard Court, from Saint-Laurent, Quebec. The pair travelled by pickup truck to meet him in Houston. LaRosa was given instructions to hide the two hundred keys of blow under a false floor in the truck. But he was nervous and stupid, and anxious for the load to get to Montreal: the operation was running behind schedule. He divvied up the bricks of powder, packed them in eleven large black plastic garbage bags, tossed them pell-mell behind the driver and passenger seats, and threw a sleeping bag over it all. U.S. officers, tipped off by their RCMP co-investigators, were observing the entire scene as it unfolded at a Shamrock service station.

On Saturday, May 16, Hill and Court hopped into the van and set off, while LaRosa and an accomplice, a fifty-one-year-old Montrealer named Marcel Bureau, followed in a second vehicle. An hour out of Houston, northbound on U.S. Route 59, Hill forgot to signal a lane change. It was the moment Texas Department of Public Safety Troopers C.E. Kibble and John Hart were waiting for. They signalled for Hill to pull over. More intelligent men might have seen through the ruse, but the two couriers fell for it. The state troopers searched the vehicle, immediately found the coke and took Hill and Court into custody. But they let LaRosa and Bureau continue on their way: they wanted them to think the bust was simply rotten luck for Hill and Court, not part of a carefully mounted international narcotics investigation. The RCMP tightened its net. Alfonso Caruana knew he was under surveillance; even his neighbours had noticed the unmarked police cars cruising the area over the past few months. The Project Omertà team had finally amassed the evidence they needed to take down the Caruana clan: a seized cargo of cocaine and several hundred hours of electronic surveillance, during which the suspects discussed exchanges of money and narcotics. They planned mass arrests, to take place at dawn on July 15.

Some eighty police officers were marshalled in Montreal; another fifty in Toronto. Two RCMP officers flew to Mexico City. The Canadian investigators asked their Mexican counterparts to arrest Oreste Pagano on July 15, which happened to be his birthday. For some reason, they didn't wait until the appointed hour—7 A.M. EDT—to move in: dozens of armed officers broke down the door to Oreste's house around two in the morning.

"Oreste, Oreste, how are you? Happy birthday!" was one officer's greeting, just after a bleary-eyed Pagano awoke to the sight of police cars surrounding his house and the sound of helicopter blades thwacking the night air overhead. Along with his son-in-law, Alberto Minelli, whose job was to launder the profits of their drug trafficking, he was handcuffed, whisked to a military prison, photographed and then taken to a small airport. There the two were put on a small plane bound for Mexico City, and transferred to Toronto on board a Gulfstream jet crammed with soldiers.

The Mexican pilot decided to fly over the United States without making a refuelling stop, and the Gulfstream penetrated Canadian airspace much sooner than expected. Having received no flight plan, air traffic controllers were surprised when the pilot radioed for authorization to land. Official recordings captured the confusion in the control tower: "Where the hell did this Mexican military plane come from?" one air traffic controller is heard saying to a colleague. He then asks the pilot: "What are you doing in this airspace? Please identify yourself."

Apparently, this was the spicy Mexican recipe for getting rid of undesirables. The Canadian style was, as usual, bland by comparison. Officers rang doorbells, held up arrest warrants and ushered the offenders into the rear seats of patrol cars. Nine were pinched in Montreal and Toronto, including Alfonso Caruana, his brothers, Gerlando and Pasquale, and a nephew, Giovanni.

"These arrests were the culmination of a two-year investigation which has effectively dismantled an alleged Mafia family, the Cuntrera-Caruana group," RCMP Inspector Ben Soave, head of the CFSEU, said emphatically. Press conference descriptions of the scope of police operations are often embellished, but in this case, Soave's words were not hyperbole. Italy's *carabinieri* had put the Cuntreras behind bars; now the Mounties and other Canadian police had netted the Caruanas.

Officers searched Alfonso Caruana's house and found $40,000 in cash along with jewellery worth $304,229 hidden in a secret compartment. They also inspected the office of Giuseppe Cuntrera (son of the late Liborio Cuntrera) in Toronto and discovered a suitcase hidden in the drop ceiling. It contained $200,000 in twenty-dollar bills. Oreste Pagano would later confirm that this money was partial payment for a further shipment of coke, yet to be delivered. The police next paid a visit to the office of a second Giuseppe Cuntrera, son of Paolo. The keys to two safes attracted their attention. When they opened the strongboxes, they found more than Can$390,000 and more than U.S.$11,000, along with jewellery and collectible coins worth in excess of $310,000.

Three months later, in October 1998, Venezuelan authorities seized some 400,000 hectares of land in the state of Bolívar, six apartments, a dozen luxury automobiles, two yachts, and the contents of several bank accounts, totalling U.S.$14 million. In the Greater Toronto Area, the RCMP identified eleven buildings and eighteen businesses linked to the Cuntrera-Caruana clan. They included a gym, a nightclub, a restaurant, a supermarket, a tanning salon, a car wash, a pool hall, a travel agency, a meat-packing plant, a hotel management company and an import-export firm, along with several shell companies—holdings and numbered companies with no actual operations, used exclusively for money laundering. Millions of dollars per year had transited through the account of one company that officially reported annual sales of less than ten thousand dollars.

At the time of their arrests, Alfonso Caruana was preparing to return to Venezuela, while his brother Gerlando was setting up a holding company to muddy the traces of money earned legally and illegally in Montreal. He hoped one day to settle quietly with his girlfriend in Belize, in Central America. While awaiting their trial on drug trafficking and money-laundering charges, Oreste Pagano, Alfonso Caruana and the members of their organization swelled the ranks of the boarders at the Toronto East Detention Centre. Pagano may have been a high-ranking member of the Neapolitan Camorra, but that didn't equate to credentials in the eyes of the higher-ups in the Sicilian Mafia. He was not one of them. He had served the Caruanas well, but now he was of no further use. The Caruanas owed him a lot of money—some of it for a five-hundred-kilo cocaine shipment that had made it to its destination in Montreal—but refused to pay him. Pagano didn't even have enough money to hire a lawyer: his assets, though scattered throughout several countries, had all been seized.

One day, as inmates stretched their legs in the prison's exercise yard, Pagano walked up to Alfonso Caruana, who proceeded to act as though his former associate didn't even exist. It was this humiliating snub that sparked Pagano's decision to turn state's evidence. He sent a message to prison authorities that he wanted to talk to the police. The first debriefing took place at the detention centre. Pagano dangled a carrot: he was ready to spill information that would not only furnish investigators with extra evidence against the Caruanas but also provide proof of the involvement of other ringleaders, including the Rizzutos. In return, he wanted a lot: a new identity, secure relocation for him and his family, return of the money and property that had been confiscated by the Mexican police, freedom for his girlfriend, who was currently imprisoned in Venezuela, and an escort to help her get out of the country, among other things. Pagano was transferred to another correctional facility. Negotiations dragged on for months, and lawyers for the Canadian government eventually made some concessions. They attempted to recover two million dollars that Pagano had kept in a safe at his home in Cancún, but the money had "disappeared" on the night of his arrest. In the end, the turncoat was given money so that he could hire a lawyer.

Once a satisfactory deal was reached, Pagano made a lengthy confession, documented in twenty-six hours of videotaped declarations. An initial session took place in July 1998 at a Travelodge hotel in Sudbury, Ontario, far from the eyes and ears of underworld acquaintances. Pagano confirmed that in 1991, after meeting Alfonso Caruana on the Venezuelan island of Margarita, he had set up eight cocaine shipments. Asking his handlers for a pen and paper, he jotted down several figures and added them up—the total amount of coke had been 3,500 kilos, he informed the police. Shipments to Canada always went through Montreal, often by sea but sometimes by truck. The street value of the cocaine was between thirty thousand and fifty thousand dollars per kilo. Some deliveries failed. Shipments were sometimes seized by police; this had happened in Puerto Cabello, Venezuela, and Houston, Texas. Such were the risks of the trade, Pagano said. But, he added, the profits were far greater than the losses.

Pagano told his police handlers that Alfonso Caruana paid him $28,000 per kilo of coke at the time. Picking up the pen again, he calculated that Caruana must have earned around $36 million thanks to him. He arrived at that total by subtracting his commission and the amount paid to the Colombian wholesalers. Caruana, he explained, had never revealed to him how much he made from trafficking: "He never told me exactly . . . Nor would I ever ask him, because I think that these questions are a bit intrusive between people."

Pagano explained that cocaine deliveries picked up again, and even increased in frequency, after the two hundred kilos were seized near Houston in May 1998. A few weeks later—on June 3, to be precise—a boat loaded with five hundred kilos of the white powder left Venezuela bound for Montreal. A man Pagano identified only as Yvon, who claimed to be a legitimate businessman running a trout farm, was to take delivery of the shipment on his sailboat. From Cancún, Pagano had to make calls to make sure the cargo had arrived safely in Montreal.

By July 14, Pagano still had no news. "I called the lawyer, Chiara, to know whether something had happened to Alfonso," he told investigators. "Chiara [said] that nothing had happened. Therefore, I asked for the telephone number of Gerlando [Caruana] and I called him. I asked him if everything was fine, if Alfonso was fine and if the goods had arrived. He told me that the goods had arrived . . . Then, the same night, I was arrested."

Montreal was only the North American drop-off point for the coke that the Caruanas bought; they also made regular deliveries to Europe. The head of Project Omertà, RCMP Inspector Ben Soave, estimated that the clan moved between two and three hundred kilos to various locations every three weeks. In Italy, the group had previously been linked to shipments totalling eleven tonnes. Members of the clan were not particularly upset if the odd shipment fell into police hands; in one conversation overheard by investigators, they described the loss of the two hundred kilos that had left Houston as "the price of doing business," Soave explained. "That loss of six million dollars [the estimated value of the cocaine] took part of maybe a couple of minutes in the conversation and then they went on to the other shipments they had lined up. Well, six million dollars would break a lot of businesses in Canada, and for them it was the subject of a few minutes' discussion. I'm sure they had concerns about what went wrong, but, you know, life went on."

"If organized crime were a hockey game, Mr. Caruana would be [Wayne] Gretzky," Soave concluded.

Pagano next met with police, accompanied this time by a federal government prosecutor, on September 21, 1999. The location was Room 925 of the Embassy Suites Hotel in Markham, near Toronto. Pagano explained how he had spent time with the Cuntrera brothers in Venezuela, before their arrest and extradition to Italy, as well as with

Alfonso Caruana, before his return to Canada. Back then, the clan often hid cocaine shipments in barrels of tar, and frequent deliveries were made to Genoa, Italy.

Finding sources of the drug was never a problem; big-time Colombian exporters numbered in the hundreds. Most had ties to revolutionaries and guerrilla groups, Pagano said, adding: "I wanted to explain to you . . . the trafficking of drugs will never end." He ridiculed the U.S. "war on drugs" and similar efforts by Western countries, saying that the millions sent to the governments of Colombia and Peru to stem the northward flow of narcotics were regularly siphoned off, and that cocaine production in those countries had doubled in recent years despite the increased aid. "All the money that is sent to these governments is only used to buy arms," he said.

It would be only a matter of time before everyone learned that he was talking to the police, Pagano nervously predicted. Former business contacts would then be lining up to murder him. "I have many enemies that want to kill me," he said. "They would like to cut me up to little pieces . . . I need security for me and my children."

With Alfonso Caruana now in prison, a successor would surely be named to head the Cuntrera-Caruana clan. Who would be the one to make that decision? Pagano's handlers wanted to know. He reminded them that, as a Neapolitan, he was seen as an outcast. "That [decision] would be made in Sicily," he surmised. "I wouldn't know. They are Sicilian; I am not Sicilian."

"You have to be Sicilian to know these secrets?" one of the interrogators asked.

"Exactly," Pagano replied.

On November 18, 1999, Pagano was questioned again at the Embassy Suites Hotel. During this session he revealed how Alfonso Caruana and Vito Rizzuto had felt betrayed by senior Venezuelan government officials whom they had bribed but who had failed to help them.

Alfonso Caruana had become infuriated, Pagano said, after Venezuelan authorities arrested the three Cuntrera brothers, seizing hotels they owned and opening their safety deposit boxes. Clan members believed they had been the victims of a plot: Alfonso was convinced the Americans were behind it all and had paid off the Venezuelans to bust the Cuntreras. He quoted a Sicilian proverb: "Whoever has money and friendship can screw justice."

Alfonso Caruana had gone so far as to contemplate assassinating the Venezuelan interior minister, the informant revealed. But he decided the best strategy was to save his own skin. "Not long after that, Alfonso left the city [Caracas] and came here to Canada . . . He feels very safe in Canada . . . He knows that being a Canadian citizen, after his release, he will be free in every aspect," Pagano explained. Caruana had told him that in the worst-case scenario, he would spend no more than five years in prison. "He says, 'Even if [I] get twenty-five years of jail, which is the maximum imprisonment . . . I only serve five years.'"

Caruana was half right. In February 2000, trapped by Pagano's duplicity and thousands of pages of transcribed phone conversations, he pleaded guilty in Ontario Superior Court to charges of importing and trafficking in narcotics. He was sentenced to eighteen years—a term that was commuted to three years, to end in April 2003. But he was never able to enjoy so much as a second of freedom. Ontario police kept Alfonso in custody, citing an international arrest warrant that called for his extradition to Italy, where he had been convicted *in absentia* by a Palermo court. The sentence was severe: twenty-two years' imprisonment for his role in importing massive amounts of cocaine.

Caruana fought the extradition order as long as he could. In November 2004, a lower court ruled that he should be deported to Italy. The Mafioso took his case to the Ontario Court of Appeal, which upheld the ruling. The Supreme Court of Canada then refused to allow a final appeal request, and Caruana was extradited on January 29, 2008. His brothers, Gerlando and Pasquale, were sentenced in Canada to jail terms of eighteen and ten years respectively. Oreste Pagano pleaded guilty to several charges on December 7, 1999, and was immediately sent to Italy—where, in return for his collaboration with authorities, he received a payment of $100,000, protection for his family, and assurances that he would be taken into the national witness protection program. On

November 17, 2004, interrogated by Italian investigators, he described his relations with Vito Rizzuto in detail.

"I know Vito Rizzuto, and I had the chance to work with him in the 1990s," he said. "In particular I can tell you that I heard about him in Venezuela, while I was staying at the Hotel Royal, owned by Pasquale Cuntrera. Umberto Naviglia pointed to Vito and told me that he was the boss of the Mafia in Canada, linked with the Sicilian Mafia . . . In 1993, Alfonso Caruana introduced me to [him]. The meeting took place in a hotel in Montreal where Caruana and I were staying. Rizzuto joined us in the afternoon after a golf game. At the time, I had a Venezuelan passport with a fake identity; my name was Cesare Petruzziello. I learned at that time that Vito was an avid golf player."

Pagano went on, explaining how he subsequently met Vito at the wedding of Alfonso Caruana's daughter, in Toronto: "At that time, Vito proposed the first deal in relation to the importation of cocaine into Canada, from Venezuela, through a man that he trusted. This guy was a Canadian and he owned a mine in Venezuela. I practically had to deliver the cocaine to him . . . That importation was successful, and I knew because I was involved in that deal. I knew that the deal was coordinated by Vito Rizzuto."

Every month, the owner of the Venezuelan mine, which was located in the state of Bolívar, shipped minerals to Canada for processing. Pagano used this connection to send an initial one-hundred-kilogram load of cocaine. Other shipments followed.

"Also in the 1990s, Vito Rizzuto asked me the favour to arrange the murder of a Venezuelan lawyer," Pagano revealed. "The lawyer defended his father [after the 1988 cocaine possession charge] and asked for $500,000 in legal fees, with the promise that he would be acquitted, and released right away, but he failed and his father was convicted . . . At that time, I was living in Venezuela, but I didn't feel I could carry that out. I tried to find a reason to postpone it, but I could not do that without compromising my relationship with Vito Rizzuto, because not to comply could create serious and dangerous consequences for me. I tried to postpone, tried to find excuses.

"Then at the end of 1994, we organized another importation for five hundred kilos, using the same channels. That importation didn't go well. The drugs were seized in Venezuela. Many people were arrested, including the son of the owner of the gold mine . . . After the seizure I expressed my disappointment to Vito, but he told me he would find out if anyone had made a mistake. Not only would he pay, but he would also bring me the head of the person responsible on a plate. Then he paid part of my investment.

"So I met him again a few months later, when his son Nicolò Jr. got married [on June 3, 1995]," Pagano continued. "I attended the wedding with Alfonso Caruana and his wife. At the wedding, I saw someone that I recognized. I asked Alfonso, 'Who is that guy?' He told me that it was Salvatore Scotto,* the representative of the Bono family in Italy. He was wanted for the murder of a police officer and his pregnant wife, but he came to Canada to pay the respect of [that] major Sicilian Mafia family to Rizzuto . . . The wedding was attended by almost six hundred people. There were representatives of New York and Sicilian families, but I didn't ask for their names."

Pagano took advantage of the wedding to huddle with Vito Rizzuto and map out a massive cocaine importing scheme. The Montreal godfather said he wanted to bring in up to ten thousand kilos. Pagano's job would be to get the drugs onto a Canadian ship departing from Venezuela. Once in international waters, the cargo would be transferred from the mother ship to a second vessel. "In that case, the second boat avoided customs," Pagano explained to the Italian investigators.

As part of his earlier videotaped statements in Canada, Pagano had told RCMP officers about the symbiotic relationship between the Rizzuto and Caruana clans: "When I met Vito, I realized that he trusted the two [Caruana] brothers. I had the impression that they were all part of the same organization . . . They are neither rivals nor competitors because

---

* Scotto was arrested by Italian police in 2001, after eight years on the run, and received a life sentence for his role in the 1992 Palermo car bombing that killed anti-Mafia judge Paolo Borsellino and his five-man bodyguard detail.

many times they would work together . . . I know that Vito Rizzuto was the boss of the Mafia in Canada . . . [He] is a kind of manager . . . He utilizes people who don't belong to his family to do the dirty work. In Italy, everything is done within the organization. They don't use outside people."

One month prior to the arrest of Oreste Pagano, an event occurred that may have seemed relatively trivial but in fact spoke volumes about Vito Rizzuto's "manager" role as well as his ascendancy over a significant swath of the Montreal underworld, not just members of the Mafia. In a manner befitting his godfather role, Vito was a keen arbitrator of conflicts.

Monday, June 15, 1998, was shaping up to be a slow news day in Montreal's Palais de Justice: the courthouse corridors were practically deserted, and none of the trials in progress seemed worthy of attention. Journalists were chatting about what they'd done on the weekend and sharing jokes with lawyers. On a whim, a reporter for *La Presse* went up to Room 3.08, where a preliminary hearing was being held for an Ontario drug trafficker named Glen Cameron. The odds of the writer getting enough material for a story seemed slim: the case had been subjected to a publication ban. He took a few notes, then slipped his notebook into his back pocket and stepped back out into the hallway. A ripple of commotion spread around the third floor: there was Vito Rizzuto, exiting a small conference room used by lawyers and clients. He leaned against the wall, speaking in hushed tones with his lawyer, Jean Salois.

The reporter called a photographer, who rushed over. The don gracing the courthouse with his presence was a rare sight indeed. The photographer clicked away, shooting one picture after another, his camera's motor drive whirring. Rizzuto ducked behind his lawyer in a vain attempt to evade the lens. Then, growing annoyed, he buttonholed the two men from *La Presse*. "Seems to me you've taken enough pictures," he said in English, his tone firm but polite.

It turned out Rizzuto had been called by the prosecution to testify at Cameron's preliminary hearing. His testimony was postponed, however. Eleven days later, on June 26, Vito stood in the witness box in Room 3.08.

Cameron was accused of having laundered three million dollars in drug money. He was an independent trafficker who supplied hashish oil to the Rock Machine biker gang in Montreal, as well as to criminal bikers in Kingston, Sudbury and Toronto—territories coveted by the Hells Angels.

At the start of the so-called Biker War in 1994, the Hells Angels had warned Cameron to stop dealing with their rivals, the Rock Machine. He basically told them to take a hike. This was, obviously, an unwise tactic. Their second warning came in the form of a machine-gun attack. Cameron was hit in the leg, an injury that would leave him with a permanent limp. The assailant then pointed the barrel of his weapon at Cameron's temple. "Why are you doing this to me?" Cameron croaked, sweating from every pore. Nine months later, he had resumed supplying hash oil to customers on both sides of the Biker War. A few years later, a Montreal police officer told him that the Hells Angels were still out to get him.

Cameron went to Vito Rizzuto, asking him to intercede with Maurice "Mom" Boucher, leader of the Nomads, the Hells Angels' elite club in Quebec. He offered the Mafia chieftain at least fifty thousand dollars in exchange for his arbitration services. Rizzuto acknowledged in court that he had met with Cameron on two occasions at a seafood restaurant in the Marché de La Tour shopping centre, in Saint-Léonard. He said he had agreed to get involved as a favour to a friend, Juan Ramón Fernández.

Fernández, a loyal Rizzuto soldier, had first met Cameron in prison, when the latter approached him in the company of another trafficker from his organization, Luis Lopes. Subsequently, relying on contacts outside, Fernández had helped Cameron and Lopes import hash oil from Jamaica.

At their first meeting, Rizzuto conversed with Cameron and two acquaintances in the rear of the seafood restaurant, then huddled alone with Cameron for ten minutes or so. "Cameron, he told me . . . that he would do anything . . . if I could fix things," Vito told the judge. As the meeting wrapped up, the godfather said, "Let me see what I can do for you." At a second meeting, Vito explained that he had met with the Hells Angels and that Cameron had nothing more to fear from them.

A police search of Cameron's house in the small town of Glenroy, Ontario, had turned up a datebook for 1997. Cameron had written, on two pages, the number "50,000" and the word "Vito." Under questioning by the lawyer for the prosecution, Rizzuto admitted that Cameron had wanted to pay him for his mediation services, but he had refused to accept any money. His version of the story was that he told Cameron he "didn't want anything," but urged Cameron to do a favour for Fernández if ever the opportunity came up.

By 2000, there were clear signs that the Nomads had gained the upper hand in their bloody conflict with the Rock Machine. Vito Rizzuto, naturally, had aligned with the side that looked set to emerge victorious. In the past, he had been content to work with Mom Boucher on an ad hoc basis; now, he moved to make their partnership a formal one. In April, he delegated his son Nicolò to hold a series of exploratory meetings with Normand Robitaille, a member of the Nomads and a trusted associate of Mom Boucher. The goal was to mark out cocaine distribution territories and set a wholesale price for the drug on the Montreal market.

The negotiations took place in secret; rank-and-file members of both the Nomads and the Sicilian Mafia knew nothing about them. Some Mafia drug dealers eventually learned of the meetings, but kept on doing business with the Rock Machine anyway. One of them was Salvatore Gervasi, a hulking thirty-one-year-old. His father, Paolo Gervasi, was an old-school Mafioso who had consorted with the Rizzutos for years and owned the Castel Tina strip club in Saint-Léonard, where Vito kept an upstairs office. The doormen allowed Rock Machine members into the club, despite the patches they overtly displayed on their leather jackets and vests. The bikers even had a permanently reserved table.

Salvatore Gervasi's main contacts in the Rock Machine were the paunchy Tony Plescio—held in high esteem by the elder Gervasi as well—and members of the Dark Circle, considered the biker club's elite death squad. Vito and his lieutenant Francesco Arcadi repeatedly asked Paolo Gervasi to tell his son to stop dealing with Rock Machine members.

If Paolo did, the warnings went unheeded.

On April 20, 2000, Salvatore Gervasi was shot in the neck and killed. The assassins wrapped a plastic bag around his head, then loosely rolled his body up in a tarp and stuffed it into the trunk of his Porsche, which they left near the corner of Couture and Belmont Streets in Saint-Léonard—not far from the victim's parents' home, his last known address. Passersby found it odd that the expensive sports car was sitting there with its sunroof open, and alerted police. Investigators called it a "clean hit"; in other words, it bore the hallmarks of a Mafia murder.

A grieving Paolo Gervasi, obsessed with finding his son's killers, met with Vito Rizzuto on a number of occasions, hired a private detective, and travelled to Italy looking for clues. He reportedly offered $400,000 to whoever could finger the killers, and compiled a blacklist of twelve likely suspects. Then, in a rage, he ordered his own club, the Castel Tina, bulldozed.

Gervasi and Francesco Arcadi met in a restaurant, but police were unable to ascertain what was said. Days later, on August 14, 2000, a man approached Gervasi as he left a bank on Jean-Talon Street. He spoke to him briefly, then pulled out a gun and shot him. Seriously wounded, Gervasi was taken to hospital.

Two days later, Arcadi conferred with Vito Rizzuto in the alleyway behind the Consenza club in Saint-Léonard. Police found a way to eavesdrop but were only able to capture snatches of the conversation. "There's only one way, a bullet to the head," one of the Mafiosi said. Had they decided it was time to liquidate Gervasi? No one can say for certain.

At any rate, a bomb was rigged to explode under Gervasi's Jeep Cherokee on February 25, 2002. Police got an anonymous tip about a suspicious package beneath the vehicle, which was parked in front of the Consenza. The charge consisted of a dozen sticks of explosives—Magnafrac, to be precise—connected to a remote-control receiver. Had the device gone off, it could have left a very messy scene indeed: the Consenza was in the middle of a small strip mall. Police immediately evacuated businesses and residences within a wide perimeter. Staff at a nearby daycare centre hustled children onto a hastily requisitioned school bus: as soon as the door shut, the driver sped the kids away.

There would be no further warnings or failed attempts on the life of Paolo Gervasi. On January 19, 2004, he had just walked out of a Jean-Talon Street pastry shop and got behind the wheel of his Jeep when a man approached the vehicle and opened fire. The bullets shattered the side window and tore into Gervasi, killing him instantly. He was sixty-two years old and had spent the last four years of his life searching for the men who had murdered his son.

In June 2000, the preparatory negotiations between Nick Rizzuto Jr. and Normand Robitaille were deemed successful, and a meeting was scheduled to finalize a deal with the Hells Angels. Vito decided to attend in person. He was accompanied by three other Mafiosi, including Tony Mucci (infamous as the man who had walked into the newsroom of the daily newspaper *Le Devoir* on May 1, 1973, and shot three times at journalist Jean-Pierre Charbonneau, wounding him in the arm). The summit was held at the Tops Resto-bar, owned by real-estate magnate Antonio (Tony) Accurso. Normand Robitaille headed the biker delegation, seconded by Michel Rose and André Chouinard. Mom Boucher called Chouinard to say he was on his way but, for reasons unknown, he never showed up.

The Sicilians and the Hells Angels agreed to fix the wholesale price of cocaine at fifty thousand dollars a kilo, the highest in Canada—and anywhere in the Americas, for that matter. They also decided how to split up distribution on the Island of Montreal: the Mafia could sell the drug in the city's north and northeast ends: in Saint-Léonard, Anjou and Rivière-des-Prairies, as well as the Little Italy district. They also retained their distribution monopoly in the bars and clubs on lower Saint-Laurent Boulevard, Crescent Street and other tony downtown spots. All the rest was decreed to be Hells Angels turf. At first glance, it looked like a significant concession by the Mafia. In reality, they gave up very little, since their specialty was bulk sales and not street-level retail distribution. It was a savvy move on Vito's part: he was assured of the Hells Angels' support in enforcing the outrageous hike in the price of cocaine, which would only swell the profits from traffic in the drug.

There were other meetings. On July 17 and 31, 2000, thirty-three-year-old Nick Jr. and an associate, Miguel Torres, discussed cocaine deals with Robitaille in an Italian restaurant on Saint-Laurent Boulevard. That summer, an average of 250 kilos of coke was being dealt in Montreal every week. Investigators, though, had a front-row seat from which to track the traffickers' moves: Robitaille's bodyguard, Dany Kane, was an informant. Kane was very active and privy to all manner of conversations, which he regularly recorded for the benefit of police. At the end of one exchange, Robitaille told Kane that the Italians were very powerful, "and that if they were at war with them, the Hells Angels would have more trouble with them than they had with the Rock Machine." Robitaille was also impressed by Vito Rizzuto's sense of fair play, telling Kane, "He's an okay guy."

Not surprisingly, the new arrangement worsened tensions between the rival biker gangs. The leaders of the Rock Machine, founded fifteen years earlier by Salvatore Cazzetta, were not pleased that they'd been frozen out of the deal. Their violent conflict with the Hells Angels had flared up in July 1994 and would last until June 2002, resulting in more than 160 deaths in Quebec, including several innocent bystanders. In 1995, an eleven-year-old boy, Daniel Desrochers, was killed by a shard of metal from a vehicle that exploded outside a biker hangout on Adam Street in Hochelaga-Maisonneuve, a working-class neighbourhood in east Montreal. The tragedy sparked public fury and led to the creation by the RCMP, the SQ and Montreal police of a crack anti-biker unit dubbed *Carcajou* (Wolverine). Two prison guards, Diane Lavigne and Pierre Rondeau, were shot and killed in 1997. On August 26, 1999, Serge Hervieux, a father of two, was shot to death at his place of work, a garage in Saint-Léonard, by an assailant wielding a .357 Magnum. The killer had mistaken Hervieux for a co-worker with the same first name: Serge Bruneau, a major cocaine supplier for the Rock Machine.

On July 7, 2000, Hélène Brunet, a thirty-one-year-old waitress, was gravely wounded in a shooting at a café in Montreal's north end. She was serving breakfast to two Hells Angels members when a pair of masked men burst in and opened fire. One of the Angels used Brunet as a human shield; the other was shot dead. Then on September 13, 2000, veteran crime reporter Michel Auger was shot several times in the parking lot of his newspaper, *Le Journal de Montréal*. He survived, but the attempt on his life spurred a further wave of public anger. Police forces in Quebec ramped up efforts to put the bikers out of commission.

On the one hand, the situation was to the Sicilian Mafia's advantage. Police lacked the resources to fight crime on all fronts and, as long as their energies were channelled into hunting down the biker gangs, they couldn't clamp down as firmly on Italian organized crime. On the other hand, public pressure in reaction to the Biker War eventually prompted the federal government to toughen up its anti-gang legislation, putting criminal groups of all stripes at greater risk of prosecution. Police were given broader powers and, whenever convicted individuals could be linked to organized crime, they faced stiffer jail sentences. Vito Rizzuto and other influential members of the Montreal mob decided it was time to put a stop to the violence.

Analysts including Guy Ouellette, of the sq, and Jean-Pierre Lévesque, with Criminal Intelligence Service Canada (CISC), are fairly sure the Mafia played a role in peace talks between the Hells Angels and Rock Machine. On September 26, 2000, three weeks after the attempted murder of *Journal* reporter Auger, Mom Boucher met up with the leader of the Rock Machine, Fred Faucher, in a room at the Quebec City courthouse. A peace deal was cemented on October 8 at Bleu Marin, an Italian restaurant on Crescent Street in downtown Montreal. A photographer for crime tabloid *Allô Police* got a message on his pager: Would he come down to the restaurant and capture the moment for posterity? It was a good marketing coup: the photos of the rival biker "brothers" formalizing their truce, surrounded by assorted henchmen, caused a sensation.

"Rather than suffer the consequences, the representatives of the various organized crime families exerted pressure to ensure they would reach an understanding," CISC's Lévesque commented. "The first to speak up were the heads of the Italian Mafia . . . The bikers up against the Italian Mafia; that's a bit like comparing Marty McSorley to Mario Lemieux," he said. (McSorley, a tough-guy defenceman then with the

Boston Bruins, was being tried in criminal court and would eventually be convicted of assault with a weapon for striking an opponent with his stick, while the Pittsburgh Penguins' Lemieux, a gentleman player and superstar, had by then been inducted into the Hockey Hall of Fame.)

If the bikers were consciously rolling out a public-relations campaign, it soon fizzled. On October 10, Mom Boucher was arrested: the Quebec Court of Appeal had ordered a new trial in the case of murdered prison guards Lavigne and Rondeau. Then on December 6, Fred Faucher and fourteen members of the Rock Machine, who had just "patched over" to the Bandidos—a powerful bike gang with clubs in the United States and Europe—were packed off to prison as well. And police were readying even bigger arrests. But in the meantime, blood continued to be spilled. The truce was clearly a sham.

Three members of the Rowdy Crew, a gang affiliated with the Hells Angels, attacked one Francis Laforest in front of his home in broad daylight, beating the twenty-nine-year-old man to death with baseball bats. Three weeks earlier, Laforest had refused to let the bikers sell drugs in his bar in Terrebonne, an off-island suburb northeast of Montreal.

The December 2000 amalgamation of the Rock Machine into the Bandidos gave the latter group a beachhead in Ontario. The Hells Angels responded by absorbing the members of most other clubs in the province—Satan's Choice, Last Chance, the Lobos and the Para-Dice Riders—as well as a handful of dissident Rock Machine and Outlaws members. At a ceremony held on December 29 in Sorel, Quebec, 179 Ontario bikers became full-patch Hells Angels, and eleven others were accepted as prospects.

Ontario had emerged as a new battleground. Canada's richest and most populous province represented a huge market for narcotics sales and all manner of other rackets.

It was a prize toward which Montreal's Sicilian Mafia, ruled by the iron hand of Vito Rizzuto, next turned its attention.

CHAPTER 12

CONQUERING ONTARIO

O N THE DAY MOM BOUCHER was arrested, October 10, 2000, Vito Rizzuto was visiting a funeral parlour in Toronto. He had come to pay his respects to the grieving family of one of his key associates in Ontario, Gaetano "Guy" Panepinto, who had been murdered the week before at age forty-one. Vito was accompanied by three of his top men: Paolo Renda, his brother-in-law and the family's *consigliere;* Rocco Sollecito, the former manager of the Consenza Social Club; and Francesco Arcadi, his Calabrian lieutenant.

A bright red Harley-Davidson, which the deceased had painstakingly assembled out of parts from two used bikes, was proudly displayed in front of the building. As the pallbearers bore the casket from the funeral home, about fifty bikers in attendance, club colours emblazoned on their jackets, straddled their own mounts. At the time, they were still members of the Para-Dice Riders, the Last Chance and other independent clubs, but they were soon to be absorbed into the Hells Angels. Engines snorting, they rode in formation with Panepinto's hearse to the funeral at St. Clare Catholic Church. Their presence was a sign of respect to a man who had been a trusted business associate.

That Vito and his associates would travel to Toronto for this particular funeral spoke to the importance that the Montreal Mafia ascribed to Ontario—and, to a lesser degree, to their apparent tolerance of the criminal biker gangs, who tended to be loud, impulsive and occasionally troublesome.

As it happened, the man in the coffin had been in the death business himself. Guy Panepinto was the co-owner of the Canadian subsidiary of Casket Royale, a U.S. company that sold deeply discounted coffins, funerary urns and sympathy cards. The company was, ostensibly, driven by a compassionate motive: in charging low prices, they were not exploiting the vulnerability of bereaved families. Their motto was "Do not make an emotional loss a financial loss." Panepinto's store, on St. Clair Avenue West in Toronto's Corso Italia, offered very reasonable prices indeed. Most of his caskets retailed for between $1,800 and $2,000, about half what they would cost at a traditional funeral home. A bargain at $295, the bottom-line model, the "George," was made of pressboard and lined with faux buckskin. Casket Royale even had a macabre loss leader in its inventory: children's coffins cost nothing.

Like many Mafiosi who tried to atone for their sins by donating to hospital foundations and other charities, Panepinto had a split personality—good Dr. Jekyll by day, unsavoury Mr. Hyde by night. One of his partners in Casket Royale, Frank Natale Roda, was a man who'd had half his arm blown off when a bomb he was carrying exploded early. The bomb had been destined for a rival drug dealer whom Panepinto and his associate suspected in the murder of Eddie Melo, the former light-heavyweight boxing champ who had been chauffeur and bodyguard to mob boss Frank Cotroni on his visits to Ontario. The courts had ruled that Panepinto was involved in the botched bombing.

Panepinto's daytime gig may have been selling cheap coffins, but evenings found him running a gambling house, and later at night he was given to stealing stereo systems from electronics warehouses. He was a Sicilian, and he was Vito Rizzuto's right-hand man in Ontario. On the night of October 22 to 23, 1997, he was seen by police in the company of the Montreal godfather and a notorious member of the Ontario

Mafia, Pat Anthony Musitano, at an Italian restaurant in Hamilton, Ontario's "Steeltown." To any but a well-informed observer, the meeting might have seemed unremarkable. After all, Vito wasn't a hermit: it was normal that he should share a meal with friends every once in a while. But that October 1997 dinner took on new significance once police learned that Pat Musitano had ordered hits on two Ontario Mafia leaders—and the more police looked, the more they saw the sombre shadow of the Montreal godfather floating over those killings as well.

The Rizzutos, father and son, had reigned unchallenged over Quebec for years. But their hold on the underworld in the province to the west was anything but firm. Mobland, Ontario, was fragmented country with divided rule. Many observers believed Vito wanted to move in and clean up, as his father had done twenty years earlier in Quebec by eliminating Paolo Violi and his brothers.

Comparing files, investigators were able to place Vito Rizzuto in Ontario shortly before and after each of the murders orchestrated by Musitano.

When it had created the Commission back in 1931, the American Cosa Nostra had decreed that their interests in Quebec would be controlled by the Bonanno crime family of New York City, while Ontario belonged to the Magaddinos of Buffalo. Joe Bonanno and Stefano Magaddino were cousins from the same Sicilian town, Castellammare del Golfo. The two godfathers had their share of conflicts over the years; when Magaddino suspected his cousin of widening his territorial ambitions, he had his men kidnap Bonanno (*see Chapter 3*). In the end, though, each family had respected the other's turf. Southern Ontario remained the preserve of the Buffalo family until Magaddino's death in 1974, but in the years since, his successors had had trouble keeping a lid on things.

Giacomo Luppino was the Buffalo crew's long-time representative in Ontario. He never marshalled the power necessary to strike back after the murder of his son-in-law, Paolo Violi, by the Rizzuto clan. He died in 1987, having reached the venerable age of eighty-eight, and was replaced by John "Johnny Pops" Papalia, who despite his other nickname, The Enforcer, was no more successful in imposing hegemony over his entire territory, which nominally encompassed the cities of Toronto and Hamilton as well as the Niagara Peninsula. In Hamilton, despite the fact that it was his home base, Johnny Pops had to share power with the Luppinos and, especially, the Musitanos.

The Papalia, Luppino and Musitano families were all from Calabria, but that didn't prevent conflict within their ranks.

Back in Italy in 1929, patriarch Angelo Musitano had murdered his own sister when he found out she was pregnant out of wedlock. He then dragged the poor girl's body by the hair all the way to her boyfriend's house, where he shot the young man twice. The boy survived and went to the police. Musitano fled, first to France and then to Canada, where he lived under an assumed name. Police tracked him down thirty-six years later and deported him to Italy, where he served out his prison term. His nephew Domenic sided with Johnny Pops Papalia, but his great-nephew Pasquale (Pat) fell in with Vito Rizzuto.

Vito had other allies in Ontario, starting with the Caruana and Cammalleri families, who came from his home province of Agrigento, Sicily. Leonardo Cammalleri, father of Vito's wife, Giovanna, had never been charged by Canadian authorities for the 1955 murder of trade unionist and politician Giuseppe Spagnolo in Cattolica Eraclea; nor had he been questioned after the slaying of Rosario Gurreri in Montreal in 1972, although he was a suspect. Leonardo's brother Antonio Cammalleri headed the family's criminal operations in Ontario. Vito could also count on the support of another Cattolica Eraclea native, Giacinto Arcuri. Rizzuto's strategy was to start by getting rid of the clan headed by Johnny Pops Papalia, who in the 1990s was the senior Mafia chieftain in Ontario. Papalia had two lieutenants: Enio "Pegleg" Mora, in Hamilton, and Carmen Barillaro, in Niagara Falls.

Mora was the first to die. Weighing in at a hulking 260 pounds, he had lost his left leg below the knee several years earlier in a shootout with burglars who had come to rob a gambling house that he was "protecting." He was able to identify one of the assailants, and after a prosthesis was fitted and he was able to walk again, he hunted the man down and fatally shot him. Legend also had it that he had once accompanied

Johnny Pops to shake down a man who had taken too long to repay the boss. Mora poured gasoline over the unfortunate debtor and then pushed him toward Papalia, who stuck a cigarette between the man's teeth and began sparking his lighter. The debtor got the hint.

In the 1990s, Mora borrowed $7.2 million from Vito Rizzuto and gave the bulk of the money to Papalia and Carmen Barillaro. Johnny Pops used the funds to open an upscale restaurant on Avenue Road in Toronto and a similarly posh nightclub in the city's west end. The rest of the money disappeared. The Rizzuto clan demanded to be repaid but got nowhere. "They can't touch us," Barillaro boasted. That was a mistake.

On September 11, 1996, as Pegleg Mora pulled his gold-coloured Cadillac into the driveway of a farm in Vaughan, north of Toronto, someone shot him four times in the head at point-blank range. He then hoisted Mora's lifeless, massive frame into the trunk of the Cadillac, drove several kilometres and abandoned the car at a crossroads. Mora was fifty-two. Giacinto Arcuri was arrested and charged with Mora's murder, but he was acquitted for lack of evidence.

Next on the hit list was Papalia. His father, Antonio, had been famed as a bootlegger in Ontario. Johnny Pops spoke with pride about him: "I grew up in the '30s, and you'd see a guy who couldn't read or write but who had a car and was putting food on the table. He was a bootlegger, and you looked up to him," he said during the only full newspaper interview he ever gave, to Peter Moon of *The Globe and Mail*. Johnny Pops cut his mob teeth in Montreal, alongside Sicilian bosses Luigi Greco and Carmine Galante. A made member of Cosa Nostra, Johnny Pops helped set up the French Connection, which eventually earned him a five-year stay in a U.S. federal prison in Lewisburg, Pennsylvania. After his release, he returned to Hamilton and went to work for Giacomo Luppino, who was then the Magaddino family's man in Ontario.

Papalia and his brothers made a fortune in gambling and drugs. They rented more than two thousand vending machines and were among the leading beer distributors in Ontario. Johnny Pops certainly had a sense of humour. When Moon asked him about his sources of income, he answered: "I go into a bar and I tell them my name and I intimidate people into taking our equipment. That's what the police tell you, isn't it? Listen, I'm lucky to have a couple of good brothers who look after me." And when Moon intimated that Papalia was attempting to take control of organized crime in Ontario in the wake of Luppino's death, he exclaimed, "What's organized crime? Listen, I'm sixty-two and I'm tired and I have to crawl out of bed every morning."

But none of those good brothers were around at one-thirty in the afternoon on Saturday, May 31, 1997, when a young man named Kenneth James Murdock went to Papalia's place of business, Galaxy Vending, on Railway Street in downtown Hamilton. "Could I have a minute of your time . . . outside?" he asked the godfather. Papalia, who knew Murdock, accepted the invitation, followed him outside and offered him a cigarette. The two men strolled slowly out to the parking lot. Murdock told Papalia he had known his father in prison, then complained that the Musitanos owed him money, and asked if Papalia could help him get his money back. The entire story was a fabrication. After twenty minutes, Papalia told Murdock, "Do what you want to do. I'm not going to involve myself," and turned away. Two witnesses then saw Murdock draw a small-calibre weapon, shoot Papalia in the head and flee in a green pickup truck. The bystanders then ran to the fallen mobster's side. He was taken to Hamilton General Hospital, where he was pronounced dead an hour later. He was seventy-three years old.

Later that afternoon, Murdock met with Pat Musitano at his restaurant, The Gathering Spot, on James Street North, just a five-minute drive from Galaxy Vending.

Normally, the Ontario godfather's funeral should have attracted top bosses from Toronto, Buffalo and Montreal. Few of them went, however. Given the particular context, the most notable attendee was Pat Musitano, the man who had paid Murdock to eliminate Papalia. Hiding behind dark sunglasses, his black vest open to reveal his ample midriff, Musitano was greeted with the regard due his rank. On police surveillance photos, he has the air of a conquering hero as his *compari* kiss him on each cheek.

The shock waves in Buffalo from Johnny Pops's murder led to a summit meeting. Papalia's Niagara Falls lieutenant Carmen Barillaro attended and vowed to others present that he would avenge his boss's death. "I'm gonna take care of that fat tub of lard myself," he said, referring to Pat Musitano, according to witnesses' reports. A high-ranking member of the Buffalo family informed Musitano, who decided a pre-emptive strike was in order.

Pat's brother, Angelo Musitano, and Ken Murdock drove to Niagara Falls, Ontario, on July 23, 1997. Barillaro was alone in his house on Corwin Avenue. His wife and daughters had gone out to shop for party favours; the next day was to be Barillaro's fifty-third birthday. Musitano parked his car not far from the house; Murdock got out and went to knock on the door. When Barillaro answered, Murdock asked if the shiny red Corvette parked in the driveway was for sale. It sounded like a bad joke. Barillaro tried to slam the door, but Murdock stopped him, pointed a nine-millimetre hand-gun at him and said he had a message for him from Pat. Barillaro dashed into another room, then spun around and lunged at Murdock. He was a big man who had worked out with weights for years. Murdock shot twice. Barillaro dropped dead. His body was found by his wife and daughters.

Three days later, Pat Musitano was celebrating at The Gathering Spot. Mob acquaintances brought him gifts. Another telephoned to say, with a laugh: "I'll be there in ten. Uncork a good bottle of wine and let it breathe."

It took police more than a year to solve the murders of Papalia and Barillaro. The following year, they arrested Ken Murdock on charges of extortion. Once they had him in custody, officers played a tape recording for him of the Musitanos threatening to do him in. Murdock signed an agreement to collaborate with the police. In exchange for his protection, he revealed that the slayings of Papalia and Barillaro had been ordered by the Musitano brothers, against whom he then agreed to testify. "I killed Papalia for two thousand dollars and forty grams of cocaine, then I killed Barillaro," he told a judge in 1999.

Eventually, intelligence units with various police forces were convinced that the Musitanos had not acted alone in getting rid of Johnny Pops Papalia and his lieutenants Enio Mora and Carmen Barillaro.

According to Murdock's version of events, Niagara Falls mobsters were fed up with being a mere satellite of the Buffalo outfit, which they felt now lacked organization and scope. "They preferred dealing with the guys in Toronto and Montreal," he explained to his handlers. "They were fed up of paying tribute money to the Americans." Murdock told the police that he had been waiting for an order from Pat Musitano to take out Natale and Vincenzo Luppino, the sons of the late Giacomo Luppino. Murdock also said that a hit on Paolo Violi's sons, Domenic and Giuseppe, was in the cards.

Pat Musitano had met with Vito Rizzuto's Toronto associate Gaetano "Guy" Panepinto in April 1997—a month before Papalia's murder and three months before Barillaro was slain—at a swanky Mediterranean restaurant at Casino Niagara in Niagara Falls. The two men had discussed investments that Vito was planning in Ontario. On the night of October 22 to 23, 1997, after the murders, Musitano met Rizzuto and Panepinto at a restaurant in Hamilton. Two days later, Musitano called Panepinto to ask whether Rizzuto was happy with how the meeting had gone. "It was good," Panepinto said. "He's very happy . . . He gave us some advice before heading back to Montreal."

Delegating management of his Ontario dealings to a man as unpredictable as Guy Panepinto may not have been among Vito's wiser business decisions. The "Discount Coffin Guy" was built like a linebacker but had scarcely more judgment than a teenager, and working closely with the powerful Montreal godfather gave him a sense of impunity. He would not tolerate the slightest competition—as in the case of Domenic Napoli and Antonio Oppedisano, two upstart crooks who had fled Italy and settled in the Toronto area. The pair, who were reportedly cousins, had started installing video lottery machines in bars on Panepinto's territory without his consent. Their terminals paid out cash to winners, whereas Panepinto's merely offered free game credits.

Panepinto lodged a formal complaint, but no one in the Mafia seemed willing to put the new arrivals on notice. Napoli and Oppedisano were members of the 'Ndrangheta, the Calabrian equivalent of the Mafia. In Ontario, they were under the umbrella of the local 'Ndrangheta boss,

Antonio Commisso, who lived on Hollywood Hills Circle in Woodbridge (the same northern Toronto suburb where Alfonso Caruana resided).

In March 2000, after a dispute with Panepinto, the two cousins went missing. Before long, there were rumblings that they would never be found alive. Rumour had it that Panepinto had killed them, dismembered the bodies in the basement of his casket shop and then burned them piece by piece.

News that Napoli and Oppedisano had vanished travelled all the way to Calabria. Suspicious Commisso family members, aware of Panepinto's close ties to Vito Rizzuto, decided to go to Montreal and investigate further. Did Vito know something about the two men's disappearance? Was he the one who had ordered them killed? The don replied that he had nothing to do with any of it—and everything pointed to him telling the truth. Vito was annoyed at the thought that his man in Ontario would have ordered hits without first clearing it through him, as protocol dictated. Jettisoned by his protector, Panepinto knew his life was hanging by a thread. He went to Montreal and kept a low profile. A few months later, a close associate told him that the danger had passed, and he could head back to Toronto.

That associate had been misinformed.

On October 3, 2000, Panepinto was sitting comfortably in the leather driver's seat of his maroon Cadillac, waiting for traffic to pass at an intersection on Bloor Street just east of Highway 427 in the Toronto suburb of Etobicoke, when a silver minivan pulled even with him on his left. From the rolled-down passenger-side window, six shots spat out, striking Panepinto in the shoulder, chest and abdomen. The Cadillac rolled slowly through the intersection before coming to a rest against the porch of a vacant house. Tires screeching, the killers' van sped away.

Alerted by the noise, neighbours ran to the Cadillac and saw the forty-one-year-old driver lying dead with his head against the steering wheel. "That's what we see on TV, and you think it's not real, but real sometimes," one neighbour later told a reporter, saying she was glad her children had finished playing outside only an hour before the shooting. Vito Rizzuto's Ontario henchman had met his death just minutes away from his $500,000 home on quiet, tree-lined Laurel Avenue, where he lived behind a high iron fence with his wife of seventeen years, Anita, and their three sons.

On the seat of the Cadillac beside the victim, police found architect's plans for Jam Billiards & Lounge. The owner of this nightclub in Barrie, a city north of Toronto, attended Panepinto's funeral. Investigators noted that the owner had secured a loan of $200,000 from a numbered company belonging to the Cuntrera brothers. Despite police protests, the Alcohol and Gaming Commission of Ontario granted the club an alcohol permit.

Two years later, after thoroughly searching the Casket Royale outlet on St. Clair Avenue for three hours, detectives emerged with two bags, one plastic and one paper. Whatever was in them, apparently the police never found the remains of the two 'Ndranghetisti that Panepinto was rumoured to have killed there. But the police seemed to think that the Calabrians themselves had enough proof to finger Panepinto as the killer, because in a report dated June 23, 2009, the RCMP stated that Vincenzo "Jimmy" DeMaria, a higher-up in the Calabrian mob in Toronto then serving time for another murder, was an accomplice in Panepinto's slaying. The National Parole Board ruled that the allegation was unsubstantiated, however, and ordered the prisoner released.

The Panepinto episode warned Vito Rizzuto that expanding into Ontario was no easy task; the Calabrians had a strong presence there. When the 'Ndrangheta decided to take out his senior associate in the province, Vito had no choice but to accept it. He was decidedly not lord and master of Ontario.

More bad news was headed his way. In April 2001, an investigation by the Ontario Provincial Police (OPP), backed by the RCMP and the SQ, culminated with the arrest of fifty-four individuals who had been running a vast illegal betting ring overseen by Vito Rizzuto and active mostly in Ontario. Among them were Giuseppe "Joe" Renda, age forty-two, who was close to the Rizzuto family and had recently moved to Toronto from Montreal, and Stefano Sollecito, son of Rocco Sollecito, a long-standing associate and close friend of the Rizzutos.

The network extended from Montreal to Ottawa, Toronto, Hamilton and other Ontario cities. Bookmakers and debt collectors used the

Internet, mobile phones, BlackBerry hand-held devices and various kinds of wireless technology to take bets on all manner of major North American sports events: pro football, basketball and hockey games, as well as horse races and U.S. college games. The amount of the bets was in the neighbourhood of $200 million per year. One man had wagered $100,000 on a single football game.

The coordinated raids on thirty-one homes and seven businesses netted guns, ammunition, drugs and bulletproof armour stolen from police, as well as ski masks and $245,000 in cash. "It was a drug trafficking investigation that put the OPP on their trail," SQ Sergeant Robert Thibault said at a news conference in Montreal. "Gambling networks like this one make money not only by taking a cut on the wagers, but through loansharking and by forcing bettors who don't pay to carry drugs.

"Potential customers have to be referred by a known customer," Thibault went on. "This is to prevent infiltrations by police. The bookies set the odds by studying sports teams' results. For example, they might establish that the Toronto Maple Leafs are twice as likely to win a game than the Montreal Canadiens. So the odds are two to one. But the bookie takes a cut, so that might reduce the odds to one-and-a-half to one. A bettor who puts down $100 on a Canadiens victory therefore collects $150 if his team wins, and the bookie gets $50. The loser, meanwhile, has to pay up quickly. If he can't, he'll be extended credit, but at an exorbitant rate, often 2 percent per week, which is 104 percent a year. If that bettor can't pay back the capital and interest, he can expect a visit from an enforcer, who will intimidate, injure or potentially kill him. Often, however, the network will require that person to pay his debt by carrying drugs. The idea is to make money by every possible means."

The arrested bookies pleaded guilty, in the process avoiding trials at which they would have made public their oddsmaking strategies. Authorities seized Joe Renda's fifty-thousand-dollar Lincoln Navigator. Its downcast owner decided to return to Montreal, a city that he knew well and where he would be more at ease now that he had been unmasked.

Vito refused to throw in the towel. He replaced Panepinto with a new emissary for the Greater Toronto Area: a man who was as brilliant as he was bloodthirsty. Juan Ramón Fernández was a Spanish national who had never been made a member of the Sicilian Mafia but whose tough-guy reputation had won him the godfather's esteem. During his career, which included long stints in prison, he had built up contacts with Colombian drug suppliers, Calabrian mobsters, the Hells Angels, Montreal's West End Gang and other criminal groups. They were the sorts of relations that could be assets in multicultural Ontario.

A handsome, muscle-bound specimen with dark hair and a brooding gaze, Fernández turned heads wherever he went. He was unfailingly loyal to Rizzuto, and he terrorized those around him. One night in January 2002, as he was driving near Toronto's Kensington Market with a Hells Angels leader, he spotted a Sri Lankan immigrant who had owed him money: "Fuckin' piece o' shit Tamil," he told his companion, unaware that a hidden microphone in his car was picking up his every word. "Shoulda seen when I slapped 'im last time—the blood coming out." On another occasion, police watched as a mobster—despite the fact he was himself a tough customer—trembled in Fernández's presence, to the point that his coffee cup rattled against the saucer.

Fernández was born in Spain on December 23, 1956, and immigrated to Montreal with his parents when he was five. He never applied to become a naturalized citizen of Canada, which would eventually earn him the right to be deported from the country—twice. He started working out at the gym as a teenager and learned martial arts. Soon he was putting his physical abilities to use breaking into homes and stealing money, jewellery and credit cards. Years later, he confessed to having been a "somewhat rebellious and hotheaded young man"—but refused to admit that he had maintained the same character traits into adulthood. Several crimes and misdemeanours later, he came into contact with the Montreal Mafia and was hired as a driver and bodyguard by Frank Cotroni.

When he was twenty-two, Fernández told his seventeen-year-old girl-friend, an exotic dancer, to have sex with an associate of his. She refused, so he hit her—so hard that she later died in hospital. He pleaded guilty to involuntary manslaughter and was sentenced to twelve years' imprisonment. Prison authorities were soon informed that he readily threatened inmates who got on his wrong side. As soon as he was released, he was threatened with deportation to Spain but succeeded in appealing the order for twelve years. His day job was as a salesman for a car dealership on Metropolitan Boulevard in Saint-Léonard; at night he worked in a club controlled by the Rizzuto clan.

In the early hours of February 12, 1991, a bomb exploded behind a Pizza Hut franchise on Jean-Talon Street in Saint-Léonard. At the time, Pizza Hut was owned by PepsiCo. For the first of its planned chain of restaurants in Montreal, the U.S.-based multinational had selected a neighbourhood with a sizable Italian community likely to appreciate its pizzas. Had the PepsiCo brain trust done its market research properly, they might have twigged to the fact that in that neighbourhood, opening a business aimed at a client base of mostly Italian origin was a risky undertaking: the territory was already controlled by businessmen who didn't take kindly to competitors. In this case, Agostino Cuntrera—notorious for, among other things, his role in the rub-out of Paolo Violi in 1978—had the local monopoly on pizza: he owned a Mikes franchise just metres away from the Pizza Hut site.

Before the bombing, persons unknown had already set fire to the Coming Soon sign heralding construction of the Pizza Hut, then tried to burn down the building itself. After that attack, the stubborn owner rebuilt the restaurant, and Montreal police investigated. They bugged the phone at Mikes and, on February 26, heard Cuntrera's daughter telling her mother that the Pizza Hut owner obviously didn't want to understand and perhaps had a death wish. Police eventually surmised that Juan Ramón Fernández had played a role in the Pizza Hut explosion, as well as in another bomb attack against a metal plating plant that had dared to compete with a Mafia-controlled company. According to police, Fernández paid a Halifax Hells Angels member, Patrick "Frenchy" Guernier, to place both bombs.

As a mobland "supervisor," Fernández was "the classic example of an enforcer used by La Cosa Nostra," one police report stated. He was "a mobile-type drug supplier; i.e., he operates from his vehicle and is constantly on the move, using cellphones and pagers to stay in contact with his customers," according to another. Analysts believed he reported directly to Raynald Desjardins (who, as previously mentioned, was one of the rare French Canadians granted admittance to Vito Rizzuto's inner circle). Fernández was also caught on camera with Vito by a hidden police photographer: the Spaniard was shorter but stockier than the Montreal godfather and walked slightly behind him, showing the respect due his boss.

Police seized three kilos of cocaine, along with $32,000 in cash, in the trunk of a Jaguar that Fernández had borrowed from the car dealership where he worked. Sent back behind bars for a forty-two-month term, he won election to the inmates' committee at Archambault Penitentiary in Sainte-Anne-des-Plaines, north of Montreal. On April 10, 1992, he got married in the prison chapel. He was granted permission to invite brothers Raynald and Jacques Desjardins and their wives, along with a few fellow inmates. Prison authorities, however, refused his request to have Vito Rizzuto attend.

Inside the penitentiary, Fernández hung out with William McAllister, of the West End Gang, and Frenchy Guernier, the Hells Angel identified by police as having set the explosives at the Saint-Léonard Pizza Hut franchise and metal plating plant. Fernández had little trouble securing temporary parole from prison authorities. On one such release, when he was supposedly visiting his mother, he went to Mafia meetings or dropped in to see Raynald Desjardins at his luxury home on Gouin Boulevard West, in the same Saraguay neighbourhood where Vito Rizzuto lived. The police were furious: "We had to bang our fists and put a stop to the day paroles," one officer recalls. Furious, Fernández flew into a rage and smashed some computer hardware in the prison.

The authorities decided a transfer was in order. The medium-security Leclerc Institution, in Laval, refused to accept him as an inmate after a union representative told management of employees' fears that Fernández would instill a climate of violence. He was sent instead to the Donnacona Institution, a maximum-security facility located in a suburb of Quebec

City, where he wasted little time in having some nude dancers brought in, at his expense, for a show. Raynald Desjardins's wife regularly made the 220-kilometre trip by road from her home in Montreal to go and see him. Another frequent visitor was her cousin, Carole Jacques, a lawyer who had been a Progressive Conservative member of Parliament for the riding of Mercier from 1984 to 1993. (A few years later, Jacques and her former riding organizer, Jean-Yves Pantaloni, were convicted on influence peddling charges for soliciting kickbacks from two businessmen seeking federal government subsidies for industrial projects in Jacques's riding. As part of a subsequent RCMP investigation, Jacques was suspected of having given a copy of the police file on Raynald Desjardins—then in jail for his role in the 1987 plot to import 740 kilos of cocaine via Ireland's Eye, off Newfoundland—to a corrupt federal parole officer. Only the parole officer was charged and convicted in the case.)

From his cell, Fernández set up a scheme to import Jamaican hashish with Glen Cameron, one of Rock Machine's key suppliers. He recruited inmates and convinced them to become drug mules after their release. Fernández himself was paroled in 1999 and was immediately deported to Spain, the country of his birth. But he soon found his way back across the Atlantic, settling in Florida, in an apartment that belonged to his lawyer, Carmine Iacono (a member of the Progressive Conservative Party rank and file who would later run under that banner in the 2003 Ontario provincial election, in the riding of Vaughan–King–Aurora, north of Toronto). Finally, Fernández moved to Ontario, under the aliases "Joey Bravo" and "Johnny Bravio," and began reporting to Gaetano "The Discount Casket Guy" Panepinto.

After Panepinto was gunned down at the wheel of his Cadillac in early October of 2000, Fernández discreetly took his place. Panepinto's murder prompted police in York Region, north of Toronto, to launch Project R.I.P.—a sly nod to Panepinto's former line of work. Their investigation into his former associates soon led them to Juan Fernández. He was picked up in March 2001 in a café in Woodbridge.

On April 3, 2001, Fernández was deported to Spain for the second time—and again returned to Canada, this time stealing the identity of

James Gordon Shaddock, who had been born on May 26, 1956, at Women's College Hospital in Toronto, and died aged twelve. Police were soon on to him, but decided to place him under surveillance rather than arrest him and deport him a third time. They tapped his phone line and before long were aghast at his lust for consumer goods. Fernández had moved in with his girlfriend, Lori Ploianu, in a seventeenth-floor condo at 4450 Tucana Court in Mississauga, a city west of Toronto.

Using credit and debit cards in the name of Shaddock, he bought three giant-screen projection TVs from The Brick furniture and electronics outlet in Rexdale, a north Toronto suburb: two fifty-one-inch Panasonic models at $2,898 and $3,198, and a fifty-three-inch Sony for $2,488. Police listened in as he told a friend of his named Danny about his new toys.

"Can I grab some stuff too?" Danny asked excitedly.

"Who?" Fernández replied.

"Me!" Danny said.

"Of course you could get some stuff."

"Oh yeah?"

"Yeah, you get what you want—televisions, whatever you want," Fernández promised.

"Okay."

"Get for your father, get for Frank, uh, get, uh, sure."

"That's beautiful, man," Danny exclaimed.

Fernández had orchestrated the fraud so well that he had a credit margin of $3.8 million, all in the name of a boy who had died thirty-three years earlier. He "spent" $19,000 on a white gold engagement ring studded with five diamonds for Ploianu and treated himself to a gold necklace for $3,187, along with a leather jacket, mobile phones, top-of-the-line running shoes, leather sofas and computer equipment. Some of these purchases were resold. Police eavesdropped on another conversation: Ploianu was asking Fernández how much she should charge a friend of hers, Andrea, for some of the items.

"Andrea might buy my couches, eh," she told him. "No point giving them away for free."

"No, if she's going to buy them and the tables, perfect," Fernández agreed.

"Yeah. What do you think? A thousand bucks, it's okay?"

"Yeah, but yeah."

"I asked her if she wants to buy them and she said . . . I go, 'Listen, you don't have to pay me right away. You can pay me slowly if you like.'"

"Yeah."

"Like three hundred a week, four hundred, you know."

Such tidbits from the domestic life of an unscrupulous gangster no doubt provided some entertainment to the police officers listening in, but they were only appetizers. The police would soon be sinking their teeth into much more valuable information: Fernández and his cronies were getting set to import large quantities of narcotics.

York police shared the results of the probe with the RCMP in Montreal, who launched Operation Calamus. Thus began another effort to pinch Vito Rizzuto. Having rounded up virtually the entire membership of the Hells Angels Nomads and the Rockers, their puppet club, as part of Operation Springtime in 2001, police in Quebec could finally focus their energies on the Mafia.

A truck driver of Portuguese origin, who was a former narcotics courier, agreed to work with the Mounties in exchange for $300,000 and a promise that pending charges against him would be dropped. He had previously moved drugs for Abraham "The Turk" Nasser, a Colombian cocaine supplier. The Turk's main connection in Montreal was a man named Rodolfo Rojas.

The truck driver told police that Fernández had been introduced to Rojas by a lawyer named José Guede, who, in vouching for Fernández, cited the latter's prior experience as a narcotrafficker and loyalty toward Vito Rizzuto. Guede worked for the criminal defence firm of Loris Cavaliere, one of the Rizzuto family's lawyers. (Two of Vito's children, Libertina and Leonardo, practised in the same firm.)

In mid-December 2001, Fernández went to a meeting at the Centre Callego, a Spanish social club on Saint-Laurent Boulevard in Montreal. Around the table were Abraham "The Turk" Nasser, his contact Rodolfo

Rojas, lawyer José Guede and the Portuguese truck driver, who was wearing a wire. On the agenda: an operation to bring in one thousand kilos of cocaine for distribution in Toronto.

If the deal went down as the group hoped, they planned to import more shipments and flip them to Montrealer Antonio Pietrantonio, nicknamed Tony Suzuki because he held a stake in a Suzuki car dealership in the Hochelaga-Maisonneuve neighbourhood. Pietrantonio was never charged in connection with this particular plot, but he had prior drug trafficking convictions.

Fernández and The Turk met in person and conferred by phone almost daily for the rest of the month. Nasser couldn't decide how to move the coke, deliberating over using fish, textile and fruit importing outfits. Since the September 11 terror attacks, customs agents had been watching all cross-border shipments with particular zeal, so to conceal their wares, traffickers were taking extra care to choose consignments of merchandise that were least likely to arouse suspicion. On December 30, the truck-driver-turned-RCMP-informant told Fernández that The Turk had finally made up his mind.

"Okay, man, good news," he reported. "Our friend says it's a fruit store . . . Yeah, he has mangoes to sell and everything."

"Beautiful," a satisfied Fernández replied.

The traffickers refined their strategy, deciding to use a fruit company in Toronto and another in Venezuela or Paraguay. All that remained was to choose a name for the company, fill out the paperwork, and design a logo. That was the fun side of the job.

Coming to a profit-sharing agreement was the hard part. Back from Colombia, The Turk informed his partners that he wanted a 20 percent cut. Problem was, he'd calculated that percentage based on the revised wholesale price for cocaine in Montreal, which Vito Rizzuto and the Hells Angels had set the previous year at fifty thousand dollars a kilo. Thanks to his close connections with the Mafia and the bikers, Fernández had intimate knowledge of that agreement and had never since called it into question. Now, suddenly, he had reservations. He argued that it was more of a guideline than a directive, adding that the high price that the drug commanded in Montreal wouldn't fly in Toronto, where there were market fluctuations.

Early in the new year, the dispute over pricing still hadn't been settled. The informant's cover hadn't been blown either, but The Turk sensed something wasn't right. He told the double agent he was going to lay low for a while, because a police officer he knew in Bogotá had told him the RCMP were on to him.

Fernández, meanwhile, was in a funk. He missed his biker friends. During a phone conversation with an associate named Jay, he explained how he was used to doing deals with members of the Nomads and Rockers. But now they were all in jail. "I was with one of the main guys in Montreal," he said. "They're fucked. They're all inside. All of the Nomads are inside, the Rockers are inside." On the evening of January 29, a bug concealed in his car recorded his conversation with Steven "Tiger" Lindsay, a member of the Hells Angels chapter based in Woodbridge. He complained that Vito Rizzuto hadn't had enough time to broker a truce between the Hells Angels and the Rock Machine. "My partner told them all, eh. Told the fuckin' Rock Machine and told the Angels to try to . . . a thing, and told Mom. And then when Mom started fixing up everything it was too late. He [Vito] told 'em. He told 'em a long time: 'Mom. Mom . . . they're [the police] gonna come with this, they're gonna come with that. You're gonna see, they're gonna really ruin you, Mom.' Then Mom said, 'Yeah, you're right, let's fix it.' Then it was too late . . . They opened the doors for the fuckin' pigs. They opened the door. They gave them the power."

Lindsay then told Fernández the story of Toronto mayor Mel Lastman's involvement with a weekend convention of more than two hundred Hells Angels, two weeks previously, at a hotel in Toronto's entertainment district. The *Toronto Sun* had run a front-page photo of the mayor shaking a biker's hand. Lastman had also accepted the gift of a T-shirt emblazoned with the club's "Death Head" logo. The tabloid quoted Lastman's impressions of the brief encounter: "It was great. I walked in and they were yelling, 'Hey Mel! Hey Mel!'" In his opinion, the Angels were simply in town to have a good time and spend money. The photo upset plenty of people, including many in Quebec. "I ask the politicians in Toronto to ask the bikers how they got that money," the province's public security minister, Serge Ménard said. "If the Hells Angels visit their city to spend money, they're probably there to make some. And if the people of Toronto want to know how the bikers make their money, we'll be willing to explain." Police in Toronto were outraged as well, and the furor eventually prompted the mayor to throw the souvenir T-shirt in the garbage, also in front of newspaper cameras.

"Piece o' shit asshole," Lindsay commented as Fernández rounded a corner. "We're voters, right? [Lastman should] have told fuckin' top cop there . . . 'Fuck yourself; I'm the fuckin' mayor . . . ' Fuckin' made two hundred votes."

"Yeah, but what a fuckin' idiot," Fernández agreed. "These people laughed at him."

Lindsay then rambled on about how he'd assaulted a man who'd owed him money, but that the beat-down hadn't brought him any satisfaction. Fernández replied that he was having a similar problem with a man named Constantin "Big Gus" Alevizos, a former associate of the late Gaetano Panepinto. Big Gus wore his sobriquet well, standing six-foot-six and weighing over 450 pounds. Fernández suspected him of having bilked Vito Rizzuto to the tune of $600,000; there were rumours that he'd given part of the money to a female acquaintance of Panepinto's, who of late had been seen tooling around town in a Maserati. Fernández told Lindsay he was thinking about killing Alevizos or asking one of his partners, Pietro "Peter" Scarcella, to do it.

On February 13, 2002, police were privy to a conversation between Fernández and their informant. Fernández was describing a large cocaine shipment that he and Vito Rizzuto had organized. They'd hidden the drug in shipments of food, working with a Toronto-based food importer called Jimmy. But Rizzuto—to whom Fernández referred variously as "The Old Man," "V" or "my partner"—was nervous. "The guy we have, with the grocery, the Old Man don't wanna deal no more . . . He's paranoid because of the [September] eleventh thing . . . I went to see Jimmy; everything is passed in big machine with the X-ray, with the dogs . . .

See, my partner, the Colombian, in Cali . . . They're ready to give us as much as we want in Portugal, but to bring it over here, this is almost impossible. Everything is X-rayed, everything. They're saying it's for terrorist acts. Toronto, they're going crazy now with the States. They're busting the Arabs, the Iranians, everything. It's fuckin' bad." Fernández told the informant how he and Rizzuto had had plenty of success bringing in drugs aboard east coast lobster boats.

On March 20, Fernández was speaking to Frank Campoli when the latter put Rizzuto on the line. As usual, the godfather spoke in guarded tones.

"Hey," Vito said. "You . . . What happened, you got lost? You couldn't find your way?"

"Yeah," Fernández said with a laugh, adding: "Listen . . . I'm gonna go down because I have to see you . . ."

"So take care," Vito advised. "Next week . . . But just—uh, be careful."

Three days later, on March 23, Fernández met up with the RCMP informant in a restaurant on Steeles Avenue in Toronto. He again complained about Big Gus Alevizos, saying that the "big bastard gym owner" still owed him $600,000. "I want him—" he began, but trailed off and finished his sentence, the informant later said, by putting his index finger to his temple and mimicking a gun going off. Fernández then told the RCMP agent that he was going to give him a Ruger .357 Magnum revolver and a twelve-millimetre rifle to do the job.

Two months later, in May, Fernández gave the double agent a dirty sock containing a revolver and ammunition, and ordered him to take out Big Gus. The assignment placed the police in an untenable situation: they couldn't allow the murder to go ahead, but pulling their informant out would unmask him, and Fernández might well give the contract to another hit man. The Spaniard had to be brought in as soon as possible, even if it meant jeopardizing the investigation into the cocaine smuggling plot. Police set up a roadblock on Highway 417, north of Toronto, and stopped Fernández's SUV, which was still bugged. The microphone picked up the voice of one of the arresting officers: "Put your hands up! Put 'em up! Put 'em up high!" In the passenger seat, Fernández's girlfriend was a nervous wreck. With his characteristic cool, he reassured her:

"They're just cops, babe; just relax." He was arrested and charged with counselling to commit murder.

The rest of the conspirators, thirty-one of them in all, were arrested on September 18, 2002, during coordinated raids in Ontario, Quebec, New Brunswick and New Jersey. Among those caught in the dragnet was the RCMP informant's intended target, Constantin "Big Gus" Alevizos, a major Canadian dealer in MDMA, more popularly known as ecstasy. The "designer amphetamine" was then at the peak of its popularity among nightclubbers and ravers.

Operation R.I.P., which had lasted two years, brought the police plenty of prizes, including a large-scale pill press in Sainte-Agathe-des-Monts, in the Laurentian Mountains north of Montreal, that was churning out coloured ecstasy tablets by the shovelful. They also confiscated ten litres of gamma-hydroxybutyrate (GHB), a psychotropic substance often called the "date-rape drug"; anabolic steroids; psilocybin ("magic") mushrooms; painkillers that had been stolen from a pharmacy; marijuana hidden in the spare tire of a vehicle crossing the border into the United States; counterfeit credit cards manufactured using machines that decrypted the data in the magnetic strips of the original cards; several sticks of dynamite; Uzi submachine guns equipped with silencers; counterfeit passports; and last but not least, more than ten million dollars in cash.

Big Gus was charged with conspiracy to traffic in drugs. Gaetano Panepinto, had he still been alive, would also have been arrested, according to Detective Inspector Paul Sorel, the officer in charge of York Regional Police Investigative Services. Panepinto's successor as the gang leader, Juan Ramón Fernández, now faced further counts, including trafficking, on top of the original counselling to commit murder charge. The police knew he had orchestrated the importing of at least a hundred kilos of cocaine, but they had never found out whether the drugs had made it to Canada after they'd been forced to arrest the Spanish national early. That precaution eventually proved pointless: Alevizos was slain in 2008, outside a halfway house in Brampton, Ontario, a Toronto suburb.

Thirty-five-year-old José Guede, the Rizzutos' lawyer, was arrested a week later, on September 25, 2002. The formal charges filed at the

Montreal courthouse named Vito Rizzuto as a co-conspirator, but—not for the first time—police lacked sufficient evidence to arrest him. The court documents alleged that Guede had set up a drug importing scheme with Colombian traffickers, Juan Ramón Fernández and Steven "Bull" Bertrand, a big-time cocaine importer who supplied the Hells Angels. The smuggling plot, police alleged, was part of the Montreal Mafia's plans to branch out into Ontario and simultaneously cement its alliance with the Angels.

Prosecutors felt they had an excellent case against Guede. On the witness stand, the double agent gave a bona fide treatise on drug trafficking when he took the stand. He explained how the wholesale price of cocaine could fluctuate while dealers awaited delivery of shipments, and how losses were soaked up. The closer the coke got to North America, the higher its wholesale price rose: in the port of Colombia, it might sell for as little as two thousand dollars a kilo. In Mexico, it was worth seven thousand; in Texas, fourteen thousand. By the time the powder reached Montreal, a kilo sold for fifty thousand dollars. As for setting up a fruit import-export company as a cover to move the drugs—in this case, a company in the business of transporting mangoes—that was an old idea often employed by South American traffickers.

The prosecution's case began to come undone, however, when the trial reached the cross-examination stage. The trucker-turned-snitch testified that the cocaine shipment was destined for Tony Pietrantonio, who had been recommended by José Guede. At the preliminary inquiry, however, he hadn't named Vito Rizzuto's lawyer but Hells Angels' associate Steven Bertrand. Under cross-examination, the double agent's RCMP handler tried to salvage the proceedings, but Quebec Court Judge Jean-Pierre Dumais ruled that the informant had contradicted himself. "It is clear in my mind that [the RCMP officer] attempted to prop up the credibility of the source agent by tampering with the playing field," the judge told the court. "His misconduct is severe enough to be a detriment to the superior interest of justice. For the worst breaches, the court must apply the most serious sanction . . . and hereby orders a stay of proceedings." The Quebec Court of Appeal later upheld the decision.

The prosecution had it easier in the case of Juan Ramón Fernández. The muscular pretty-boy gangster looked in a foul mood as he was escorted into a courtroom for sentencing in Newmarket, twenty-five kilometres north of Toronto, on June 29, 2004. The reason may have been a bad night's sleep: a sympathetic prison guard had brought him a particularly comfortable pillow, but another less charitable guard had later confiscated it. Justice Joseph Kenkel sentenced Fernández to a twelve-year jail term on a variety of criminal organization charges.

Justice Kenkel emphasized that the accused had demonstrated "a level of market sophistication in his criminal activity." Fernández appeared impassive upon hearing his sentence, and the fact that he would once again face deportation to Spain upon his release—but he was distressed when told that he wouldn't be able to recover all of his jewellery, including watches, bracelets and a gold chain with a cross pendant. "It's not just a bracelet," he griped into the microphone installed in the Plexiglas-enclosed prisoner's dock. The hearing was adjourned and the convicted Fernández was returned to his prison cell, hands cuffed and feet shackled, pending a subsequent hearing to determine the fate of the jewellery.

Fernández was sent to the maximum-security Millhaven Institution in Bath, Ontario, where he continued to exasperate prison authorities, among other things orchestrating a savage assault on a fellow inmate. In 2009, the National Parole Board ruled that he should remain incarcerated. He was now considered a "person of interest" in the investigation into the murder of Big Gus Alevizos the year before. The Parole Board also cited the prisoner's "egocentricity, narcissism, grandiosity" and "psychopathic tendencies."

From Gaetano "Guy" Panepinto to Juan Ramón Fernández to Constantin "Big Gus" Alevizos, Vito Rizzuto had enlisted some odd fellows indeed in his quest to muscle in on Canada's richest province. All was not lost, but the Ontario underworld had so far proven as difficult to govern as a rudderless sailboat.

CHAPTER 13

MAFIA INC.

D ESPITE HIS ORGANIZATION'S setbacks in Ontario, as the clock ticked over into a new century Vito Rizzuto remained a picture of easygoing confidence. Whatever troubles he was facing, they seemed not to affect him. He stood head and shoulders above most underworld figures in Montreal, literally and figuratively, his svelte frame contrasting favourably with the corpulent form of many a Mafioso and plenty of criminal bikers. Though generally diffident, he clearly enjoyed conversation—provided, of course, that he trusted the person to whom he was speaking. When annoyed, however, he might easily adopt a gaze as glacially hostile as the steel barrel of a revolver and speak in a sepulchral tone such that one had to listen carefully to catch everything he said. All in all, though, the image he projected was one of calm and efficiency.

The days following his fifty-fifth birthday, in February 2001, found him in a rare talkative mood. Then at the height of his power, holding court at La Cantina, the Saint-Laurent Boulevard restaurant owned by his friend Federico del Peschio, Vito spoke with pride about the wealth his family had accumulated since arriving in Montreal in 1954. He told his dozen or so tablemates how he had come to Canada the same year as Senator

Pietro Rizzuto, who like him was a native of Cattolica Eraclea, Sicily. They belonged to two very different branches of the Rizzuto family tree and were thus only distantly related. However, Vito clearly viewed himself as being on the same level as the Liberal Senator, who had died three years earlier. In fact, he said, among the residents of their hometown, his family had an even more prestigious reputation than did Pietro Rizzuto's. Ever the night owl, Vito followed up that meal, which had been washed down with plenty of wine, with more drinks at a bar downtown.

He adhered to his morning routine, rarely rising before ten or eleven. His wife, Giovanna, would check stock prices on the computer, while Vito began his day with a scan of the latest items posted to ganglandnews.com, a site devoted to the U.S. Mafia run by veteran crime reporter Jerry Capeci, author of the best-selling *Complete Idiot's Guide to the Mafia*. Vito was hardly an Internet whiz, but he was curious to see what Capeci had to say about the Bonannos of New York.

Since taking over as boss, Joe Massino had stopped the crime family's downward slide and disciplined its troops. Only a few years before, his outfit had been seen as the ugly duckling among New York's criminal organizations, but by the 2000s, it had become the most dynamic of the Five Families. The Bonannos had even regained their seat on the Commission. FBI investigations were starting to take their toll, however, with arrests and indictments constantly making the news. On November 8, 1999, Montreal's *La Presse* had reported that the FBI suspected Vito Rizzuto of involvement in the three capos massacre, perpetrated eighteen years earlier on Massino's orders. Rizzuto had believed that the Americans would never amass sufficient evidence to bring formal charges against him. He was wrong.

Vito usually spent Thursdays at the Consenza Social Club, a café wedged between a cheese shop and a tanning salon in a small strip mall on Saint-Léonard's Jarry Street. Officially, the place was open to anyone, but an unfamiliar customer could expect to be greeted with an icy silence from the regulars, their dark stares immediately sending the message that the stranger would be best to sample the espresso at another establishment. Cosenza is one of the provinces of Calabria, on the toe of the Italian boot. Even with the spelling mistake, it was an odd name for the headquarters of Montreal's Sicilian Mafia. Regardless, Vito and his father, Nicolò, felt comfortable there. If they felt nostalgic, they could cast a glance at the picture of Cattolica Eraclea pinned to one wall. "The Cos," as regulars referred to it, was where Vito would go to meet his lieutenants, like Francesco Arcadi, and seek advice from his father or from Paolo Renda, considered the family's *consigliere*.

Every business manager has to learn to live with stress. The postulate is all the more imperative when the business is crime. At any time, the head office of Mafia Inc. could become the target of adversaries looking to pick a fight. Vito could ill afford to ignore such risks that came with the territory. He was to be reminded of this on Friday, July 13, 2001.

That day, officers with the SQ arrested two gangsters who were headed for the Consenza, intent on kidnapping Francesco Arcadi and another customer, forty-two-year-old Frank Martorana, whose specialty was rolling back vehicle odometers. Such abductions, of course, were not especially atypical in criminal circles, but there was an unusual aspect to this case: the man who had ordered the kidnapping of the Rizzuto associates was none other than Christian Deschênes, who had been a close collaborator of Vito's for many years. In friendlier days, the Montreal godfather had attended the baptism of one of Deschênes's sons. He had also helped him import tonnes of hashish.

Deschênes, aged forty-four and a resident of Lorraine, a suburb north of Montreal, was eager to recover $800,000 that Arcadi and Martorana had owed him for a decade. His partner in the kidnapping plot was a cousin of his spouse: Denis-Rolland Girouard, aged fifty, from the ski resort town of Saint-Sauveur, in the Laurentians.

Deschênes had served a lengthy prison term following the 1992 seizure of almost four thousand kilos of Colombian cocaine on an abandoned runway deep in Quebec's boreal forest north of Montreal (*see Chapter 7*). By all accounts, he had behaved well during his years in jail. A psychologist who assessed him noted that he was of above-average intelligence and displayed advanced capacity for introspection. The National Parole Board, meanwhile, opined that Deschênes seemed to have "turned a corner in his criminal life" and took him at his word when he said he planned to walk the straight and narrow.

As soon as he was transferred to a halfway house in October 2000, Deschênes began thinking about putting together enough money to buy, import and resell another cargo of drugs. Four months later, on a sunny February afternoon, he orchestrated a spectacular heist at the Marché Central de Montréal, a huge shopping centre located just north of the Metropolitan Autoroute. He and four accomplices studied the movements of an armoured truck belonging to the Secur company. When the two Secur guards entered a Costco store by the rear door, on their way to pick up the weekend cash receipts, the robbers blocked the door with a stolen pickup truck, then proceeded to force the armoured truck open by running it with a tractor-trailer cab. They helped themselves to $1.1 million, then set fire to the pickup and the transport truck, and fled in a Dodge Caravan minivan, abandoning it after a few minutes and setting that vehicle ablaze too. Deschênes deposited his share of the spoils, $200,000, in a bank in the Bahamas.

That amount was apparently insufficient, however, because he planned a second venture, this time to recover the $800,000 that Francesco Arcadi and Frank Martorana owed him. Unbeknownst to Deschênes, his accomplice Girouard was relaying his every move to Montreal police, who in turn were passing the information on to the SQ. Deschênes and Girouard planned to stroll into the Consenza, waving guns, and force Arcadi and Martorana to get into their car. Then they were going to lock them in a steel cage in the basement of a house in Saint-Liguori, near Joliette, seventy kilometres northeast of Montreal. Deschênes was determined to shoot any Consenza customers who might stand in their way, including Vito Rizzuto: "If Rizzuto's there and he steps in, I'm gonna take him down too," he warned.

When the SQ officers realized that Deschênes and Girouard were headed for the tiny café on Jarry Street, they feared that the kidnap attempt might go awry and end in violence. They stopped the men and searched their vehicle but found nothing. Subsequent searches were more rewarding. At Deschênes's girlfriend's house in Lorraine, they seized an AK-47 automatic rifle, two nine-millimetre pistols, a .357 Magnum, two bullet-proof vests, ammunition and walkie-talkies. Shortly thereafter, in the rear of a garage in Saint-Léonard, they found another cache of weapons, including nine sticks of dynamite and five machine guns.

Vito found out about the plot, but he had better things to worry about. Summers are brief in Quebec, and his priority was to get in as many games of golf as he could. He would hit the links of the most prestigious clubs, including Le Mirage, a thirty-six-hole complex some thirty kilometres north of Montreal owned by singer Céline Dion and her impresario husband, René Angélil.

Evenings were a time to dine in the finest restaurants. Most ordinary patrons would suffer heart palpitations upon seeing the bill in these establishments, but Vito was no ordinary patron. More often than not, the meals, accompanied of course by plenty of good wines, were offered gratis. The restaurant management knew that, like a baron in feudal times, Vito Rizzuto had the power to confer wealth on persons who won his favour—and, conversely, condemn those unlucky enough to lose it. Thus the gift of an especially fine bottling was a negligible price to pay for habitués of the baron's court who sought to climb the ladder of Mafia Inc. or take out insurance against some untoward, unforeseen event. Furthermore, Vito covertly owned, in whole or in part, many of the establishments where he ate and drank—and in such cases, of course, he never saw a bill.

In the spring of the following year, one such evening of wining and dining ended rather badly for Vito. Early in the morning of May 30, 2002, after emptying several glasses with friends, he settled in for the drive home, behind the wheel of the blue Jeep Grand Cherokee that he had been driving for the past two years. At around a quarter to four, he headed west on De Maisonneuve Boulevard, where he apparently began zigzagging within his lane. At least, that was how the police officer who pulled him over described it. When Rizzuto rolled the window down, his breath smelled strongly of alcohol. The officer took him in to the station. His speech slurred, Vito stated that he was "a businessman" and refused to submit to a Breathalyzer test. He was released on a promise to appear in Montreal Municipal Court to answer charges of impaired driving.

The police noted that the Jeep was registered in Ontario—more precisely, a database search revealed, to a company called OMG Media Group, based in Vaughan.

The municipal court hearing was delayed twice and finally went ahead on February 12, 2003. Journalists with *La Presse* learned of the charge well before Rizzuto was due to appear, did some digging on OMG and reported their findings in the newspaper. The affair had suddenly taken a curious turn and soon erupted into a scandal. Vito being charged with impaired driving was a relatively trivial story; however, his links with OMG were anything but. The firm had signed contracts with several cities, including Montreal, sometimes through the sorts of circuitous routes that smacked of a Mafia effort to infiltrate the licit economy and curry favour with municipal bodies.

OMG Media Group's pitch to city administrations promised a win-win solution: municipalities could recycle newspapers and beverage containers that too often wound up as sidewalk litter, and gain a new revenue stream in the process. The idea was to install combination garbage and recycling bins along busy arteries. The receptacles, made of plastic in Quebec and stainless steel in Ontario, had three compartments: one for garbage, one for recyclable bottles and cans, and one for newspapers. OMG offered a turnkey solution that included the sale, installation and maintenance of the bins, as well as pickup of their contents and transportation to sorting centres. These operations were to be financed by the sale of advertising space on the sides of the bins. The municipalities stood to gain in several ways: their employees would no longer have to pick up discarded newspapers from streets; part of the advertising space would be made available to them to display public service messages; and OMG would pay them a monthly royalty fee out of the ad revenues.

OMG, which was initially named Olifas Marketing Group, was founded in 1996 by Salvatore Oliveti, who lived in Woodbridge. He was a familiar sight in the Toronto suburb, where he had once hosted an Italian-language community television show. Giancarlo Serpe, who had been closely linked to Mafia associate Enio "Pegleg" Mora until the latter's murder in Vaughan in 1996, sat on the company's board of directors with Oliveti and his wife. According to police, Serpe was the last person to have seen Mora alive. Another OMG employee was Frank Campoli. He was a cousin to Vito Rizzuto's wife and had attended the 1995 wedding of their son Nick Jr. During the trial following the Penway affair—the stock swindle involving the mining company—Campoli had been described as Vito's man in Ontario. The two men had been photographed in the company of Juan Ramón Fernández, who had been heard on wiretaps telling anyone who would listen that he also had a stake in OMG.

In 1997, OMG signed its first contract, with the city of Etobicoke (later amalgamated with Toronto). It soon had others with Ontario cities includ-ing Ottawa, Hamilton, London, Markham, Windsor and St. Catharines, as well as with universities and school boards. OMG also made plans to expand into Italy, Eastern Europe and the Caribbean. The New York City Department of Education awarded it a contract to install 2,700 bins on its property.

In 1999, Salvatore Oliveti opened a branch of the company in Montreal with Michael Strizzi, a friend of Vito Rizzuto. The firm initially set up shop in Saint-Léonard before moving to LaSalle, a suburb in southwest Montreal. Strizzi also ran another company called Techno-Select, which specialized in hydrocarbon recycling. According to a statement by one of OMG's Montreal executives, the company approached "relations" at Montreal's city hall.

The City of Montreal issued a call for tenders; seven firms responded. OMG was not the lowest bidder, but for reasons unknown, the winning firm was unable to honour the terms of the contract. The municipal adminis-tration then began using language suggesting a public-sanitation disaster was imminent: apparently, there was a sudden, critical need to place bins emblazoned with advertising on city sidewalks. An official municipal docu-ment described "the urgent need to purchase bins to improve the cleanli-ness of Montreal's business districts and its thoroughfares."

The police department warned the city administration of the possible links between OMG and the Mafia. When asked about this later, Mayor Pierre Bourque said he could not recall having heard that caution. For his part, Jean Fortier, president of the city's executive committee and, in that capacity, the most important figure in the administration after the mayor, got wind of the same allegations, but from another source—more precisely, the winning bidder that had decided to withdraw.

Fortier asked for a closed-door meeting of the executive committee. Bureaucrats left the room, and Fortier announced, "I think we're about to award a contract to a firm with Mafia links." Laughter erupted in the room. Fortier had no proof to support his claim; his colleagues gently accused him of placing too much faith in idle gossip. The contract was signed, and the bins began to appear on city streets. Guzzo Cinemas, a movie theatre chain belonging to the family of the same name, was one of the few private-sector customers in the Montreal area to use the new advertising medium. Meanwhile, *La Presse* journalists had left messages at the home of Vito Rizzuto and the office of his lawyer Loris Cavaliere, but the godfather did not return their calls. The reporters wanted to know more about his links with OMG. A frustrated Rizzuto let his irritation show during a dinner at La Cantina. "They should leave me alone!" he said to Federico del Peschio, the restaurant's owner. *La Presse* sports columnist Réjean Tremblay happened to be dining there with friends, and del Peschio introduced him to Vito.

"Why are the reporters making such a big deal out of this?" Rizzuto complained to Tremblay. "I mean, I have the right to eat three meals a day just like anyone else!"

OMG president Salvatore Oliveti protested vehemently when *La Presse* published an article about his company's ties to Rizzuto. He swore that he was not acquainted with Vito. He said he had met him at a function organized by his former community TV employer. But what about the fact that Rizzuto had been driving a Jeep registered to the company? he was asked. Oliveti explained that the vehicle had been loaned to Michael Strizzi, director of OMG's Quebec wing. He reckoned that Strizzi had in turn lent the Jeep to Vito. "I really think this is all about me being Italian and speaking with a big accent," he told a Toronto reporter.

The chairman of Toronto's public works committee, Brad Duguid, retorted that the ethnic background of OMG's executives was no concern of his. He was worried about links to the Mafia and called for a police investigation. "If presented with facts that suggest any company we're doing business with has connections to organized crime, we are going to do all that we can to sever our relationships with those companies," he said.

Salvatore Oliveti took that threat seriously. As a preventive measure, he fired Strizzi, the company's Quebec director, for having lent Vito Rizzuto the Jeep. The ostentatious gesture was clearly aimed at dispelling allegations of the company's links to the Mafia boss. Several people at Montreal City Hall seemed to buy it. No senior municipal bureaucrat was willing to comment. Pierre Bourque's successor as mayor, Gérald Tremblay, was similarly tight-lipped, calling for the city's legal affairs department to conduct verifications. The contract remained in effect.

In the end, reality always trumps illusion. OMG, it turned out, was blatantly unconcerned with cleanliness and had little intention of paying the promised royalties to the City of Montreal. City councillors remarked that the company was not placing new bins in the authorized locations and was neglecting to maintain the existing ones; moreover, collection of recyclables from the bins was a slapdash operation. Four years after the contract was signed, the borough of Ville-Marie, which encompasses downtown Montreal, had been paid a mere $5,000 in royalties, rather than the expected $170,000. The city was forced to face facts and ask its partner to remove the bins. OMG, or what was left of it, was sold to a Mexican company and changed its name.

In the meantime, police continued their investigation, and tax inspectors soon joined the fray. Thanks to electronic surveillance that picked up Juan Ramón Fernández telling people he held shares in OMG, the claim came back to haunt him in court. During Fernández's 2004 trial for trafficking and conspiring to murder Big Gus Alevizos, the federal prosecutor told the court that Fernández was an OMG shareholder.

During another wiretapped conversation, Frank Campoli was heard telling Fernández that he could borrow one of OMG's trucks to transport a large cargo of tiles. One day, when Fernández's girlfriend complained that they were running short of money, he told her, "Don't worry, we won't starve. Don't worry about it. There's the OMG coming through." Then, two months later, Fernández was overheard telling a mob associate: "We're just working on other things. We had Spanish people from me, from Spain, for the OMG thing and if it goes through there, well, there's a lotta, lotta, lotta money there for me in there."

In February 2010, the Canada Revenue Agency filed documents in the Tax Court of Canada alleging that Vito Rizzuto's wife and their three children had owned shares in OMG in the amount of $1.6 million. Within three weeks of *La Presse*'s revelations of the company's links to the Mafia godfather, the Rizzutos had sold their 10,500 shares to Salvatore Oliveti— the same Salvatore Oliveti who had sworn that he didn't know Vito and had indignantly accused observers of racism when they had cast doubt on that claim.

The documents filed in tax court stated that four members of the Rizzuto family had each claimed $419,000 in proceeds from that sale, and the Canada Revenue Agency wanted its share. The four members of the family were Vito's wife, Giovanna, and their three children: Nick Jr., the eldest, as well as Leonardo and Libertina, both lawyers.

On July 13, 2002, a month and a half after his impaired-driving arrest, Vito Rizzuto strode through the imposing front doors of the Notre-Dame Basilica in Old Montreal, joining a throng of some three hundred people for a wedding. The city's most famous church faces Place d'Armes, a pretty square surrounded by tall office buildings. It provides an open space from which camera lenses can be trained on the forecourt of the church with no obstructions. Conscientious attendance at religious ceremonies seems to be hard-wired into Mafia members' DNA. Perhaps such scrupulous observance is undertaken in hopes of winning some redemption for their transgressions. Be that as it may, this fervour is joyfully welcomed by members of law enforcement, not to mention by priests, to whom the Mafiosi tend to pay generous tithes. On this day, well-camouflaged police photographers clicked away both in front of the church and, later, near the Sheraton Hotel in Laval, where the reception was held. Besides photos of Vito and his father, Nicolò, the police got some good shots of Paolo Renda, the family *consigliere,* and Agostino Cuntrera, who had served time for his part in the murder of Paolo Violi. The esteemed guests had gathered to celebrate the marriage of Emanuele Ragusa's son, Pat, to Elena Tortorici, whose family hailed from Cattolica Eraclea, Sicily.

Emanuele Ragusa was in attendance but took pains to avoid the photographers he knew would be there, remaining outside in his limousine. Why should the father of the groom not want to be seen and admired at his son's side on this auspicious occasion? The problem was that Ragusa was not allowed to be anywhere near the church, much less in a banquet hall with known members of an organized crime group. He was serving a prison term for drug trafficking and had obtained temporary parole, but under the terms of that release, he was supposed to remain in his home. His truancy would mean serious trouble for him—and would also lead him to make some ingenuous statements about the Mafia.

Then aged sixty-two, Ragusa was a pillar of Montreal's Sicilian Mafia. Born on October 20, 1939, in Cattolica Eraclea, he crossed the Atlantic at age nineteen and lived in New York before settling in Montreal. As a young man, he often vacationed in his native Sicily. "It's so beautiful," he said years later, emotionally, during one of his National Parole Board hearings. "But most of all, my father and mother were over there." That filial affection would soon be accompanied by romantic love for a young girl. Like Vito Rizzuto's wife, the object of Emanuele's affections was a Cammalleri. She was named Angela and was just sixteen when he married her. Emanuele's sister, meanwhile, married a man named Sciascia, from the same family as Gerlando "George from Canada" Sciascia, who was murdered in 1999.

The name Emanuele Ragusa first surfaced in criminal investigations in the early 1970s, long before that of Vito Rizzuto became widely known. Although he officially reported to Calabrians Vic Cotroni and

Paolo Violi, Ragusa was very much a part of the Montreal Mafia's Sicilian faction. He played a pivotal role in the French Connection in the city. Later, when that famous heroin trafficking ring was dismantled and the Sicilian labs took over the refining of morphine base, Ragusa became one of their favoured clients. One of his partners, a major-league heroin smuggler, was investigated by the *carabinieri* in Sicily and eventually arrested. Subsequent to that man's trial, Ragusa was convicted *in absentia* by an Italian court.

By the 1980s, Ragusa was popping up on Italian authorities' radar with increasing frequency. He visited Giuseppe Cuffaro, a money launderer for the Cuntrera-Caruanas, and lent his cellphone to Alfonso Caruana, who for a number of years was the head of that clan. Ragusa was also on the long list of Mafiosi targeted by Judge Giovanni Falcone at the Palermo Maxi Trial. Italian authorities requested his extradition from the Canadian government. The charge was Mafia associations, but this was not a crime in Canada, and the request was denied.

In August 1994, Ragusa was arrested and charged for drug trafficking as part of Operation Compote, the "reverse sting" that revolved around the RCMP's undercover currency exchange counter in downtown Montreal. He was released on bail pending his trial, which meant he could attend the June 30, 1995, wedding of his daughter Eleonora to Vito Rizzuto's eldest son, Nicolò Rizzuto Jr. Guests at the ceremony at Le Centre Sheraton in Montreal included Vito, of course, and Agostino Cuntrera, but also Domenico Manno, one of the three men who served time for the murder of Paolo Violi; Francesco Arcadi, Vito's Calabrian lieutenant; Frank Campoli, who would later be involved in the OMG recycling bin advertising affair and who was a cousin, by marriage, of Vito's wife; and Oreste Pagano, the unfortunate accomplice of Alfonso Caruana and eventual police informant. In short, a fair number of the "usual suspects." Another of Ragusa's daughters, Antonia, had married Luigi Vella, a drug trafficker and cousin of Alfonso Caruana. In the Ragusa family, sons and daughters exclusively married daughters and sons of Sicilian families, all from the province of Agrigento, and preferably from Cattolica Eraclea: Cammalleris, Sciascias, Vellas, Rizzutos, Tortoricis . . .

With his trial following his arrest in the RCMP currency exchange sting still pending, Ragusa, along with eleven others, was arrested as the result of a further narcotics investigation. The probe, conducted by the SQ, New York State Police and the U.S. DEA, led to the seizure of seventy-five kilos of cocaine in New York. Ragusa's accomplice this time was Stephan (Steve) Zbikowski, a Quebec mining engineer who ran a company that did business—not all of it above board—in Venezuela.

Ragusa's involvement in the first drug trafficking case (brought to light by the currency exchange sting) led to him being convicted and sentenced to a twelve-year jail term in 1996. While he was imprisoned, the U.S. government demanded his extradition in relation to another trafficking case. But someone in the Canadian government decided that the U.S. evidence was unfounded, and the Americans' extradition request was rejected—just as the Italians' had been. Clearly, Canada was a great place to live if you were an international criminal. Taking advantage of the recently legislated policy of early release after one-sixth of time served for non-violent offenders, he left prison just two years after his incarceration.

Ragusa was transferred to a halfway house and did odd jobs a few hours a day at the Mission Bon Accueil, a homeless shelter in Saint-Henri, a working-class neighbourhood in southwest Montreal. The idea was for him to gain an awareness of how tough things were for some less fortunate members of society. This "therapy" failed miserably. One day, supervisors searched his bag and found that he had stolen two steaks from the shelter's kitchen. They asked Ragusa not to return to the shelter and reported him. He was immediately called before the National Parole Board. "When I saw the steaks in the kitchen, I couldn't resist," he pathetically explained to the commissioners. "It had been so long since I'd eaten steak." He admitted that he had "taken advantage of the situation." "It wasn't a good idea," he mumbled, like a child being scolded by his parents. He was barely more loquacious when asked to describe his values. "I love my wife, my son and my two daughters," he answered. "And I've always worked, my whole life!" He said he had managed a construction company, but it had gone bankrupt. And what values have you instilled in your children, given that your two daughters are married to Mafiosi? one of the commissioners wanted to know. "It's their decision," Ragusa answered. "They go well together. Listen, I've been here since 1958 and I've always lived with Italians." His release was annulled; the parole board commissioners ordered that he remain in prison.

In 2000, Ragusa made a request for day parole so that he could attend the baptism of his grandson, born to his daughter Eleonora and Nick Rizzuto Jr. The request was denied, precisely because Vito was expected to attend the ceremony. Two years later, Ragusa made a similar request but conveniently neglected to mention that he was planning to attend his son's, Pat's, wedding at the Notre-Dame Basilica, as well as the sumptuous reception to follow at the Sheraton in Laval. He assured the prison authorities that he simply wished to visit with family members and would remain in his home.

Of course, police noticed Ragusa in front of the church, sitting in a limousine with tinted windows, and realized he had violated the terms of his parole. But, they wondered, had he simply decided to put in a quick appearance before quietly returning home? They went to his house later that night and knocked on the door, but no one answered. Back at the prison, Ragusa admitted that he had lied when he had requested his weekend pass.

A repentant Ragusa said he had feared that officials would refuse to let him see his son on his wedding day, just as they had prevented him from attending his grandson's baptism. "I was afraid they'd say no again. I acted improperly. It was poor judgment, and I won't do it again." He insisted that he had not been to the church or the reception, which seemed unlikely since police had evidence to the contrary. "I stayed at my place. All I wanted was to get a picture with my son on his wedding day. Because I was at home alone, my wife even left the reception to come and bring me some food." The old Mafioso swore he hadn't fraternized with any criminals that night. It was a blatant lie, and he remained incarcerated.

Ragusa was granted a new hearing before National Parole Board commissioners in February 2003. The panel had taken the time to consult a thick file on him. The word "Mafia" appeared at least once on every page.

Italy had requested his extradition for Mafia associations, in vain. The RCMP described him as an influential figure in Montreal's Sicilian clan. But what is the Mafia? one of the commissioners wanted to know. Usually, whether they are in Sicily, the United States or Canada, Mafiosi insist that no such organization exists, that it is a whimsical construct of journalists starved for copy—or police who, starved for evidence, arrest unfortunate upstanding citizens. Even amongst themselves, Mafiosi never employ the term. At most, they will refer to "Cosa Nostra" (this thing of ours).

"I don't believe there's any such thing as the Mafia," Bonanno boss Joe Massino once told a curious reporter. "A bunch of Italian guys go out to eat together, and they call it the Mafia." Parole board commissioners Renaud Dutil and Pierre Cadieux probably expected a similar answer from Ragusa. To their surprise, he did not deny the existence of the Mafia. His candour stunned everyone, including his lawyer, Ginette Gravel. "In Italy, I think, the Mafia is an organization . . . a good organization," Ragusa explained. "Anyone can be called a Mafioso. It comes from Sicily. Here, it's *paesani* all from the same village, maybe fifteen or twenty people."

In the end, a man who was candid enough to admit he had stolen two steaks because he was drooling over them, and ingenuous enough to admit he had deceived prison authorities because he wanted to attend his son's wedding, was naive enough to admit that the Mafia really existed. And in the same breath, he confirmed that in Montreal, that organization was built around a core of some twenty "men of honour" who came from the same small town, Cattolica Eraclea, as well as other nearby towns in the Sicilian province of Agrigento, like Siculiana.

Other Sicilians were part of the Montreal Mafia, as well as Calabrians such as Francesco Arcadi, but the hard core was indeed made up of *paesani* from Cattolica Eraclea and Siculiana. Outside that extremely rarefied inner circle were some four to five hundred associates, most of whom were of Italian origin.

The overwhelming majority of Montrealers, Torontonians and New Yorkers of Italian heritage have nothing to do with the Mafia, and they quite rightly bristle whenever their fellow citizens automatically associate the words "Italian" and "Mafia." At the same time, those who truly are Mafia members tend to play the racism card to their advantage: "See!" they declaim when they make headlines: "They call us Mafiosi simply because we're Italian!"

Ragusa took exactly that tack with the parole board commissioners. "Anyway, it doesn't matter: wherever you are, in Montreal or elsewhere, whether you're Sicilian or Italian, in people's minds, you're in the Mafia," he told them. Then, in a bewildering ballet, alternating between admission and denial, he added: "From now on, the Mafia, it's over. My crimes, over. I want to live with my wife and my grandchildren."

Very well, the commissioners replied, but what of your relations with Vito Rizzuto? Ragusa said that he had never met him before their children Eleonora and Nicolò had started seeing each other. The statement was difficult for anyone to believe, to say the least. "I know that he comes from Cattolica Eraclea also, but I've never met him in thirty years," Ragusa insisted. "Now I know him: he's the father of my son-in-law Nicky Rizzuto."

Noting the commissioners' doubtful stares, Ragusa qualified his statement: "I moved in the circles associated with the Rizzuto clan," he admitted. "But I've never had any dealings with him. The Mafia, it's clans."

"Vito Rizzuto is indeed the godfather of the Mafia in Canada, is he not?" one of the commissioners ventured.

Ragusa answered with the slightest of smiles.

"And what about your relations with your other son-in-law, Luigi Vella, who is also in prison for drug trafficking?" the commissioner asked.

"That's another group," the prisoner answered. "He's not with me."

"How do you explain the fact that you have not been extradited to Italy?" he was asked, even though the question would have been more appropriate if posed to senior Canadian government officials.

"These are crimes by association," Ragusa offered. "They are considered crimes in Italy but not here."

That much was true, but Ragusa was clearly being cagey. The parole board decided he should remain in prison. The most important question of all was never even asked, likely because the commissioners didn't know enough of the story to ask it: Was Emanuele Ragusa the same

"Emanuele" who had taken part in the massacre of the three Bonanno capos in 1981, along with Vito Rizzuto and the man referred to only as "the old-timer"?

A U.S. police report based on the confessions of Salvatore Vitale states that Ragusa was one of the triggermen. In the many accounts of the triple slaying, his presence in the social club is described in no uncertain terms, although his name is sometimes misspelled. In his book *Five Families: The Rise, Decline, and Resurgence of America's Most Powerful Mafia Empires*, *The New York Times* journalist Selwyn Raab states that "Emanuel Raguso" was there: "Four were assigned as shooters, armed with a sawed-off shotgun, pistols, and a submachine gun," he wrote. "Three were Canadian Zips: Vito Rizzuto, Emanuel Raguso and a gangster who Vitale and Massino knew only by his nickname, 'the old man' . . . The plan called for Rizzuto and Raguso to mow down the intended victims, if possible by lining them against a wall."

In his book *Iced: The Story of Organized Crime in Canada*, Stephen Schneider goes into similar detail, explaining that Joe Massino and Salvatore Vitale had used gunmen from Canada so that others present that night would not be able to identify them: "Among the imported hit men was Rizzuto, another suspected member of the Montreal mob named Emanuele Ragusa, and a silver-haired man simply referred to as the 'old timer' (whose identity was never revealed but who possibly was an associate of Nick Rizzuto's) . . . On Massino's orders, Rizzuto and Ragusa were the lead gunmen, while Vitale and the 'old timer' guarded the exits."

Ragusa was never charged or even investigated in connection with the murders. He was released in 2004 after serving two-thirds of his sentence for drug trafficking.

Vito Rizzuto's fate would be altogether different.

An oft-quoted tenet of chaos theory holds that the beating of a butterfly's wing can trigger a chain of events that ultimately leads to a tornado halfway around the world. The fall of Vito Rizzuto would be similarly set in motion by the work of two young forensic accountants thanklessly slaving away in the United States. Much like those that brought down the most well-known figure of Cosa Nostra, Al Capone, the Montreal godfather's troubles began with an income tax investigation. It was conducted some seven hundred kilometres away and, at first, had nothing to do with him. Yet the toppling of a single tax evader eventually led to the across-the-board collapse of the Bonanno crime family, and among the last victims of that vast network of falling dominoes was Vito Rizzuto.

In late 1998, FBI special agent Jeffrey Sallet, aged twenty-nine and blessed with an unusually accurate memory, enthusiastically joined a probe into Bonanno family boss Joe Massino. He was a member of the bureau's Squad C-10 in New York City and was joined the following year by twenty-six-year-old Kimberly McCaffrey, a former medal-winning gymnast and a workaholic investigator. The young woman was hard to miss; she stood barely over five feet tall and had jet-black hair. "The wise guys can lie and cheat but bank records don't change," their boss Jack Stubing, a veteran renowned for his single-mindedness, was fond of saying. Stubing assigned his two young charges the task of poring over the bank statements and income tax returns of Bonanno family higher-ups.

From 1996 to 2001, Joseph "Big Joey" Massino and his wife, Josephine (Josie), had declared gross annual income amounts varying between $373,000 and $590,000. Year after year, they claimed that large portions of those gains were lottery winnings. Such frequent luck seemed unlikely, to say the least. But proving that the claims were fraudulent would be a difficult task. In addition to the lottery earnings, the Massinos' tax returns, as well as those of Salvatore "Good-Looking Sal" Vitale and his wife, listed income from several parking lot businesses.

Sallet and McCaffrey discovered cheques signed by Massino's and Vitale's wives made out to one Barry Weinberg; the payments were for their stakes in the parking lot enterprise. The wife of a Bonanno captain, Richard Cantarella, was also a shareholder in companies that ran parking lots. The two forensic accountants scrutinized Weinberg's transactions. At their suggestion, meanwhile, other C-10 agents began tailing him. They soon reported that Weinberg was meeting frequently with Cantarella and his Mafiosi bodyguards.

At first glance, it seemed unnatural for these two individuals to be consorting with each other. One was a businessman looking for a little spice in his life; the other was a murderer whose nasty past deeds had included plotting the murder of his uncle for delaying his induction into the Mafia.

Raised in a Jewish family in Brooklyn, Barry Weinberg was a parking lot manager. He had earned good money in that trade by buying leases on lots, which he then sold to third parties at a profit. The business was lucrative enough, but it didn't make for a particularly sexy calling card. Weinberg was convinced that hanging around with the Mafia would make him more attractive to women. Since his youth, he had been fascinated by tales of gangsters and their exciting, dangerous lives. Now he was drawn to them like the proverbial moth to a flame. He had nothing of the stuff of a criminal and certainly didn't want to bear the risks of the trade—like being shot or ending up in jail—but he was convinced he could benefit from the heat of the underworld without getting his wings singed.

The opportunity presented itself in the form of Richard Cantarella.

Cantarella, while still in his teens, had been shown the ropes of the Mafia by his uncle and had proven to be an excellent learner. Barely into adulthood, he bribed a municipal bureaucrat to secure authorization to operate newsstands and snack bars at the Staten Island ferry terminals—and then used them as a cover for illegal betting. His uncle, Al Walker Embarrato, got him a no-show job as a distribution assistant with the tabloid *New York Post*. It was a union position that paid eight hundred dollars a week, but he gave three hundred of that to another man to do the work for him. Eventually, Cantarella's uncle Al took a dislike to him; he thought he was doing too much business with a soldier in the Gambino family, and opposed the young man being made a member of the Bonanno family.

Cantarella thought about killing his uncle, a solution he was comfortable with—he had been the driver for a hit squad that murdered his cousin Tony Mirra, a Bonanno family soldier who had committed the unpardonable sin of associating with FBI agent Joe Pistone, alias Donnie Brasco. And four years later, when he feared his newsstand racket would be exposed, he killed the city bureaucrat he had bribed to win the contract. Joe Massino resolved the conflict between uncle and nephew by inducting Cantarella.

Robert Perrino, superintendent of deliveries for the *New York Post,* was a Bonanno family associate. When police began investigating the paper's bogus employment racket, he anticipated becoming a suspect but made it known that he wasn't about to take the fall for others. Sal Vitale told Cantarella that Perrino was a liability and would have to be removed. A short time later, Perrino vanished. His body would not be found until eleven years later, beneath a concrete slab in a Staten Island repair garage.

Mafiosi love to saddle their peers with nicknames, most often derisory ones. Richard Cantarella's was Shellackhead, owing to his penchant for exceptionally greasy pomades. His meeting with Barry Weinberg was providential. Weinberg showed him how to get rich running parking lots: the secret was to charge customers sales tax but neglect to declare it. It was simple enough to implement, because motorists picking up their vehicles always paid cash. Armed with Weinberg's advice, Shellackhead went into business, adding a personal touch: he dispatched goons to persuade competing parking lot owners to pay a kickback, or they would be forced to close down. His wife and son invested in the business. Eager to please his superiors, Cantarella gave Joey Massino and Sal Vitale a piece of the action as well. This earned him a rapid rise through the Bonanno family ranks. He was made a captain, and he became one of Massino's close confidants. The boss let him in on plenty of family secrets—including the story of how he had ordered the massacre of the three renegade captains in 1981 and had the job done by Vito Rizzuto, Emanuele Ragusa and an "old-timer" who had also come from Canada.

At the same time, Weinberg was making the most of his association with this new gangster friend. His competitors began to fear him, which allowed him to broaden his business. He drove a Rolls-Royce, a Bentley or a Mercedes, whichever struck his fancy, and was in the habit of carrying up to sixty thousand dollars in cash. Cantarella noted that flashy excess and quite rightly believed he had a lot to do with it. He demanded tribute money. One day, he punched Weinberg in the face for complaining about him to other mobsters. "You owe me for everything," Cantarella hissed at him after throwing him to the sidewalk. Cantarella then milked more than $800,000 from his unfortunate partner. Another Bonanno captain, Frank Coppa, partnered with Weinberg in the parking lot racket and extorted more than $85,000 from him.

Agents Sallet and McCaffrey spent a year dissecting Weinberg's income tax returns, bank account statements and accounting paperwork. Their intuitions had served them well: they found he had neglected to report fourteen million dollars in income and defrauded the Internal Revenue Service (IRS) to the tune of one million dollars. On the morning of January 9, 2001, Weinberg was at the wheel of a brand new ninety-thousand-dollar Mercedes when a police officer pulled him over for a traffic violation. He was immediately led to an unmarked van; waiting inside were Sallet and McCaffrey. They gave him a choice: go directly to prison for tax fraud or wear a recording device that would surreptitiously capture his conversations with Cantarella. He had fifteen minutes to make up his mind.

Barry Weinberg's life as a Mafia groupie was over. It took him less than the allotted quarter-hour to agree to collaborate with the authorities. He was invited to make a full confession the same day—he was told, in fact, that he had to reveal everything, otherwise prosecutors would refuse to make a deal. Weinberg had a lot to say, not only about his own crimes, but about the actions of Shellackhead Cantarella and Frank Coppa, as well as secrets they had shared. He also told them about another Mafia hanger-on, Augustino Scozzari. Before long, Sallet and McCaffrey recruited Scozzari as an informer as well.

Weinberg and Scozzari went on to record more than a hundred incriminating conversations they had with Cantarella and his crew. Finally, in October 2002, Sallet and McCaffrey knocked on the door of Shellackhead's house, a cozy little mansion worth more than two million dollars. He was arrested and indicted on racketeering and murder charges. By compiling and comparing information, the two young FBI agents had amassed enough evidence to charge Cantarella with conspiracy in the murder of Robert Perrino, the Bonanno family's inside man at the *New York Post,* committed a decade earlier. They also arrested Cantarella's wife and son for aiding and abetting in instances of fraud, breaking and entering, and kidnapping.

Twenty other Bonanno family members and associates were also indicted. Among them was Frank Coppa. The captain, who had previously counted Cantarella among his crew, had already been in jail for the past four months, serving a five-year term for securities fraud. He had begun this second stint behind bars by bursting into tears in front of fellow inmates. It was a sign of psychological fragility that had made him a laughing stock among his entourage—and which the FBI hoped to exploit. The sixty-one-year-old Coppa knew what this third series of criminal charges meant: if found guilty, he would end his days in prison. A month later, he did what no Bonanno member had dared do since the founding of the family some seventy years earlier: he agreed to turn state's evidence. "I didn't want to do no more time," he told the police and prosecutors. In exchange for a reduced sentence, he provided investigators with the initial ammunition they would need to bust Massino, Vitale, Cantarella and several other mobsters whose crimes he had been privy to.

Coppa had been present at the murder of Dominick "Sonny Black" Napolitano in 1981. Napolitano was the capo who had unwittingly allowed FBI undercover agent Joe Pistone, alias Donnie Brasco, to infiltrate his crew and spy on the Bonanno family for years. When Joe Massino learned that Brasco was FBI, he ordered Sonny Black killed. Coppa was there in the house on Staten Island when Frank "Curly" Lino pushed Sonny Black down the basement stairs, where he knelt and prepared to die *(see Chapter 1).* Massino had waited outside; Coppa had seen everything.

He revealed to police that Cantarella told him he had helped Salvatore Vitale do away with *New York Post* superintendent of deliveries Robert Perrino. Cantarella also admitted to having led his cousin Tony Mirra to the site of his execution. At that point, things began to move very quickly.

When Cantarella learned that Coppa had become a rat, he knew that his former captain's testimony likely meant supplementary murder charges would be brought against him. A month after Coppa's defection, Cantarella, his wife and his son also agreed to collaborate with authorities. Agents Kim McCaffrey and Jeff Sallet now had enough evidence to go after the biggest fish of all.

At six in the morning on January 9, 2003, the two FBI agents arrested Joseph Massino at his house in Howard Beach, which he had ringed with security cameras. He was already up and had slipped into comfortable, low-cost sweatpants and a black pullover. He had not bothered to put his watch on and was carrying no money. The boss of the Bonanno family knew he was going to be arrested and would have his valuables confiscated before being shown the way to his jail cell. Trading jokes with agents Sallet and McCaffrey, he held out his hands, ready to be cuffed.

Massino's brother-in-law Salvatore Vitale was arrested the same day and taken to the twenty-sixth floor of the FBI building in New York. McCaffrey and Sallet paid him a visit and told him the prosecution had evidence that Massino was ready to kill him because he thought he too had decided to talk to police. The news hit Sal like a roundhouse to the stomach. For months Vitale had been under the impression that Massino had sidelined him, and had often complained about his hostility toward him. He naturally assumed the agents were bluffing in the hopes of getting him to testify for the prosecution as well. But what if they were telling the truth? At any rate, they'd succeeded in instilling an oppressive doubt in his mind.

A month after their arrests on murder and racketeering charges, Massino and Vitale stood side by side in a courtroom for a preliminary hearing. The lead prosecutor, Greg Andres, explained to the judge that the two men were being held in separate prisons and there was a good reason for that: according to information Andres possessed, Massino had spoken of the possibility of "bothering" Vitale. Everyone present understood that the word was a euphemism for "killing." Andres did not mention that his information came from reliable sources, which included Coppa and Cantarella.

Two weeks after that hearing, Vitale agreed to turn state's evidence.

If the defection of Bonanno captain Frank Coppa was unusual, that of Sal Vitale, the boss's lieutenant, was devastating. Vitale would be the first underboss of a New York City Mafia family to testify against his boss since February 1992, when Salvatore "Sammy the Bull" Gravano had helped to bring down Gambino family head John "The Dapper Don" Gotti. But, as long-time mob watcher Jerry Capeci wrote in *The New York Sun*, Vitale's testimony would prove even more decisive than Gravano's, because Vitale was much closer to Massino than Gravano had been to Gotti.

Good-Looking Sal Vitale would henceforth be known by a new epithet: Good-Looking Rat. Like any state's witness bargaining for a lighter sentence, he had to confess everything. The list was long. He comprehensively recounted his own crimes as well as those committed by other members of the family that he knew of. Among other things, he admitted to having taken part in eleven murders.

Defence lawyers visited the Brooklyn prison where Joe Massino and Frank Lino were being held, and informed them of Vitale's defection. Massino remained impassive: he had long ago prepared himself for this eventuality. Lino was devastated. Up to that point, Frank Coppa had been the only man who could implicate him in the murder of Sonny Black Napolitano. A skilled lawyer might have been able to discredit Coppa's testimony in court and persuade a jury that he was ready to say anything to stay out of jail. But now Sal Vitale was prepared to corroborate Coppa's version of events. Lino betrayed no sign of weakness in front of Massino, but later, he too joined the ever-growing list of defectors.

Vitale's and Lino's defections would hasten the fall of yet another key Mafioso. Not only could both men attest to Rizzuto's presence at the three capos massacre in 1981, they could confirm that he had been the lead gunman. On the morning after the triple slaying, FBI cameramen had photographed Vito Rizzuto, Joe Massino, Gerlando Sciascia and a Sicilian heroin smuggler named Giovanni Ligammari (later to be found hanged in the basement of his home) leaving a motel in the Bronx. The photos had fuelled police's suspicions but were hardly evidence of Rizzuto's participation in the carnage the night before.

Now U.S. authorities had that evidence, in the form of sworn statements by Salvatore Vitale and Frank Lino. They began their preparations to extradite Vito Rizzuto under the RICO Act. Since that legislation did not provide for the death penalty, there would be no obstacle to securing the collaboration of the Canadian authorities.

From his cell in Brooklyn, Massino managed to get a message out to a man he trusted. He asked that man to travel to Canada and inform Vito of Vitale's treachery. In the end, however, the mission fell to a member of the Gambino family. The meeting was held in a restaurant in a shopping centre in Longueuil, on Montreal's South Shore. Fearing he could be arrested any day, Vito fled Canada two weeks later with his wife, Giovanna. They spent the months of March, April and May 2003 in Cuba and the Dominican Republic. Their son Leonardo had driven them to Dorval Airport. Commander Mario Plante, head of organized crime investigations with the Montreal police, was nervous: he worried that the godfather of the Canadian Mafia was about to drop off the face of the earth.

Vito came back to Montreal, however. He kept the lowest of profiles and avoided the Consenza Social Club, where in more carefree times, he could be counted on to join the four other leaders of his clan: his father, Paolo Renda, Rocco Sollecito and Francesco Arcadi.

In recent years, the Hells Angels and other biker gangs had gained a reputation as Canada's most dangerous criminal organizations. In 2003, however, "traditional (Italian-based) organized crime" reclaimed top spot on CISC's list of national intelligence priorities; CISC cited the Mafia's stability, discretion and connections with almost all the other organized crime groups in the country. CISC identified Vito as "the Godfather of the Italian Mafia in Montreal," a label already employed in a Revenue Canada document.

On December 8, 2003, the man himself uncharacteristically seized an opportunity to voice his own opinions on the subject during one of his appearances in Montreal Municipal Court to answer charges of impaired driving, in connection with his arrest while driving the Jeep registered to OMG in May 2002. Montreal *Gazette* reporter Paul Cherry approached him during a recess and asked for his comments. The godfather accusations were "nothing more than allegations," he said. "I deny everything they say."

Cherry then "asked how he would describe himself professionally." Rizzuto smiled and replied, "I'm the jack of all trades." And master of none, he was no doubt implying.

On that grey December day in 2003, Vito projected an air of insouciance, telling a crowd of reporters that he didn't understand why he attracted so many "spectators." Mugging for the cameras, he pulled his black coat up to hide his face and pretended to charge the journalists, joking that he felt "like a bullfighter."

In truth, he was more like the bull. Wounded, but making a last stand. Like so many picadors, the Bonanno family defectors had jabbed their lances into his spine, and it would not be long before the matador, in the guise of the U.S. government, pointed a long, sharp sword at the space between his eyes. Vito Rizzuto had barely a month of freedom left.

CHAPTER 14

JAILED

THE 2003 HOLIDAY SEASON was anything but relaxing for Commander Mario Plante of the Service de Police de la Ville de Montréal. The idea that Vito Rizzuto might slip through the net he and his men had worked so hard to cast gnawed at him the entire time. No sooner was he back at his desk in January 2004 than he decided to order permanent surveillance on Vito Rizzuto. Detective Sergeants Nicodemo Milano and Pietro Poletti were assigned to supervise three teams of operatives. The RCMP, SQ and Montreal police pooled resources over the next three weeks to ensure Rizzuto was tailed twenty-four hours a day, seven days a week.

Milano and Poletti secretly studied the extradition dossier submitted to them by Ginette Gobeil, a lawyer with Canada's Justice Department. These documents contained detailed descriptions of Rizzuto's role in the three capos massacre. Meanwhile, officers Yves Messier, of the SQ, and Patrick Franc Guimond, with the Montreal police, combed through archives with an eye to assembling a comprehensive dossier of their own on the godfather of the Canadian Mafia, in preparation for his arrest and prosecution.

Commander Plante had even more cause for worry on January 15, when mob watcher Jerry Capeci posted an article to ganglandnews.com, a website then run in association with *The New York Sun*. "Feds Eye 'John Gotti of Montreal,'" the headline blared. "Sources say [Vito] Rizzuto, now fifty-seven, was a member of the select hit team that blew away capos Alphonse (Sonny Red) Indelicato, Philip (Philly Lucky) Giaccone and Dominick (Big Trin) Trinchera in a Brooklyn social club," Capeci wrote, adding that Rizzuto's name had emerged as part of the testimony of a high-ranking mob turncoat—though he did not specify that the turncoat was Salvatore Vitale.

When asked about the allegations, Canadian law enforcement officials feigned ignorance. "I am not aware of the information, other than what I read in the [newspaper], but if it is true, it will be a blow to organized crime," declared RCMP Chief Superintendent Ben Soave, commander of the Toronto-based CFSEU, who in the 1990s had helmed Project Omertà, which dealt a severe blow to the Cuntrera-Caruana organization.

Rizzuto, meanwhile, was still feigning indifference. To Commander Plante's immense relief, he showed no signs of varying his daily routine. He stuck to his habit of taking lengthy evening meals with friends and associates at restaurants in Little Italy, heading to his home in the Saraguay district in the early morning hours. His wife, Giovanna, was now criticizing him regularly for his excessive drinking.

At 6:20 A.M. on January 20, Vito was fast asleep when Nicodemo Milano and Pietro Poletti knocked on his front door. With the detective sergeants were members of a special intervention team headed by Sergeant Gino Amorelli. The sun would not rise for another hour. A heavy-lidded Giovanna opened the door. Minutes later, Vito's tall, spectral silhouette appeared. He stood at the top of the marble staircase in a white bathrobe, blinking the sleep from his eyes. With the massive chandelier blocking his view of the entryway, he couldn't tell how many police officers were there. At length, he descended the stairs—his breath redolent with alcohol, the investigators noticed. Standing in the middle of Rizzuto's living room, Milano announced that he had come to arrest him.

"Is it for that thing in New York?" Rizzuto immediately wanted to know. Had he been waiting for this moment for the past quarter century? The investigators read him his rights—in Italian—and asked him to get dressed. They followed him to his walk-in closet, where he picked out a black turtleneck, then slid a few hangers back and forth before choosing a chic pair of slacks with a jacket in a matching fabric. Wrists cuffed, surrounded by police officers, he stepped out into the chilly January air as first light broke onto Antoine-Berthelet Avenue. At the bottom of the front steps, he lost his footing on a thin sheet of ice; one of the officers seized him by the arm to keep him from falling onto the walkway.

Giovanna watched him go as he climbed into the back of an unmarked police car. Then, perhaps gripped by an intuition that she would not see her husband again for a long time, she waited for the convoy to get underway and disappear around the corner before slowly closing the door. The police vehicles turned off Antoine-Berthelet and onto Gouin Boulevard, along the Rivière des Prairies. Vito, now very much awake and alert, began questioning the two officers who sat on either side of him. He wanted to know which part of Italy Milano and Poletti were originally from, and asked who was in charge of the police operation. He seemed calm, in perfect control of his actions and emotions.

After arriving at the North Region police station, Vito called his lawyer, Loris Cavaliere, who hurried over. Cavaliere didn't want to take instructions from his client over the phone; he wanted to see him in person. When he arrived at the station, officers handed him several documents. He studied them briefly, then conferred with Rizzuto in a small meeting room.

After that consultation, Vito spent the rest of the morning in a cell. Early in the afternoon, he was taken to the courthouse in Old Montreal. By then he looked drawn, tired and worried. He bowed his head as Quebec Superior Court Justice Réjean Paul, presiding over the hearing, summarized the serious charges pending against him in the United States. Vito Rizzuto's name appeared on an indictment alongside those of twenty-six other men with such off-putting nicknames as "Patty Muscles," "Mickey Bats" and "Joe Shakes"—all members of the Bonanno family facing a plethora of charges, from fixing baccarat games to murder.

After more than two decades, the secret of the three capos' massacre was finally out. And the Montreal godfather's role in the killings was spelled out in the twenty-one-page indictment: "Bonanno family soldier Vito Rizzuto has been charged with multiple murders . . . specifically the 1981 conspiracy to murder, and murders of Bonanno family captains Alphonse 'Sonny Red' Indelicato, Philip 'Phil Lucky' Giaccone and Dominick 'Big Trin' Trinchera."

The document described the Bonanno outfit as "the only La Cosa Nostra family with a significant presence in Canada," adding that Vito Rizzuto was its "most influential" Canadian representative. Unlike his last time in court, Vito was not answering charges for anything as ordinary as drunk driving. He was staring at a possible twenty-year prison term for murder and a $250,000 fine.

From the vast scope of the accusations, it was clear that the house of Bonanno was overflowing with traitors. A shuddering wave of panic now shook its walls. A few months earlier, an FBI surveillance detail had picked up a particularly worrisome conversation in New York City: Anthony Urso, then *consigliere* and acting boss of the family, had pushed for the murder of the defectors' children and other loved ones. He believed this was the best way to stem the tide of treason. Nicknamed "Tony Green," Urso had climbed every rung in the family hierarchy and won the trust of Joe Massino. He was the man Massino had sent to Montreal along with Salvatore Vitale following the murder of Gerlando "George from Canada" Sciascia, to gauge Vito Rizzuto's interest in replacing Sciascia as official captain in charge of the Canadian faction (see Chapter 8).

"You gotta throw somebody in the streets; this has gotta stop," Urso told other members of the Bonanno organization after Massino's arrest in 2003. "You turned . . . we wipe your family out . . . Why should the rats' kids be happy where my kids or your kids"—he was addressing James "Big Louie" Tartaglione—"should suffer because I'm away for life? If you take one kid, I hate to say it, and do what you gotta do, they'll fuckin' think twice." Urso didn't know his words were being recorded: Big Louie was among the defectors and had agreed to wear a wire. Urso was arrested the same day as Rizzuto, along with his lieutenant, Joseph "Joe Saunders" Cammarano, seven current and former captains, and several soldiers. A U.S. prosecutor said the sweep was the result of "the broadest and deepest penetration ever of a New York City–based organized crime family."

Those winds of panic began to blow over Montreal as well. On Antoine-Berthelet Avenue, Giovanna and other members of the family huddled in the Rizzuto home, holding meeting after meeting to prepare the don's defence—and to set in motion the post-Vito succession. Frank Campoli, one of Rizzuto's key Ontario associates, who had been an employee of OMG and was a cousin of Giovanna's, travelled from Toronto on several occasions to take part in the discussions.

Vito had once boasted to Michel Auger—the veteran *Journal de Montréal* crime chronicler and intended victim of a Hells Angels' assassination attempt—that he was a man out to make peace, not trouble. "I'm a mediator," he said. "People come to me to solve disputes because they believe in me. They have respect in me." He believed he wielded enough power to keep rivals on the sidelines and dissuade criminal elements from perpetrating excessive acts of violence on the streets of Montreal.

He wasn't entirely wrong, judging by the chaotic events that swept the city's underworld in the months after his arrest. Independent drug traffickers began dealing their wares to whoever would buy, wherever they pleased—flouting the agreements that had prescribed distribution territories for specific criminal organizations, including the Mafia and the Hells Angels. One such maverick was Essy Navad Noroozi, alias Javad Mohammed Nozarian. The Iranian-born criminal's specialty was importing relatively cheap brown heroin from his native country or from Afghanistan, and it had already earned him several trips behind bars. On the night of April 18, 2004, mobster Lorenzo "Skunk" Giordano ran into Nozarian at the Globe, a chic restaurant on lower Saint-Laurent Boulevard. He decided it would be a good idea to deal with him right there and then, but the Iranian drew a gun. While Giordano stabbed repeatedly at Nozarian's head with a knife, with an associate trying to hold the Iranian trafficker down, a gun went off, the shot hitting Nozarian in the groin. Two police investigators, one from the RCMP and one from the Montreal police, visited the injured man in hospital, but he refused to identify his assailant. Alarmed at the surge in violence, police also met with Loris Cavaliere: Vito's lawyer assured them that he would relay their concerns to the parties concerned and said that those responsible for the attack on Nozarian would "stop drinking and making trouble." A conversation captured by police microphones hidden in the walls of the Consenza Social Club suggested that the message had been transmitted: Paolo Renda, Vito's brother-in-law, was heard warning Giordano to go easy on the drinking and, more important, to refrain from gunplay, which was likely to "attract attention."

Giordano, aged forty-two, and thirty-six-year-old Francesco Del Balso, another irascible antagonizer, often met with Francesco Arcadi at the Bar Laennec in Laval, a hangout for Montreal's younger generation of Sicilian Mafiosi. Police had placed microphones and cameras in this establishment as well. Arcadi's crew answered to the Rizzuto clan, but most of its young members lacked the judgment of old-school mobsters like Vito's father, Nicolò, and Paolo Renda. Aggressive, impulsive, they seemed not to care about the consequences of their actions. Arcadi associated with members of a street gang called the Syndicate, who were subordinates of the Rockers, a Hells Angels puppet club—and indeed he shared the hotheaded disposition of many a criminal biker. He was a hardened criminal but had nothing of the charisma, finesse and leadership qualities that Vito displayed. Those shortcomings would soon provoke plenty of hostilities both inside and outside the Rizzuto clan.

Star witnesses had been lined up for the trial of Joe Massino during the summer of 2004. The Bonanno family boss faced a slew of racketeering charges, ranging from loansharking to money laundering, illegal betting, arson and murder.

One of the witnesses for the prosecution was a Bonanno associate who stood out because he wasn't Italian. Duane "Goldie" Leisenheimer, of German and Irish stock, had thick blond hair spilling over his ears and forehead, giving him the look of an early British Invasion rocker. Massino, who was fourteen years his senior, had picked him out from among the on-the-skids teens in Maspeth, a neighbourhood in Queens, and taken him under his wing. He hired Duane to ride shotgun with him in his catering truck. Massino sold more than just coffee to neighbourhood workers: his truck was a front for trafficking of all sorts. The young Goldie's job was to look out for "bad cars"—that is, police cruisers. The two gradually bonded, to the point that Massino trusted his protegé enough to enlist him in a precarious enterprise: Goldie would help Massino commit his first Mafia murder. Massino was eager to get in the good graces of the Gambino family boss, Paul Castellano, and to kill for him would be his ticket. The opportunity arose in 1975. Castellano, nicknamed "The Pope," had flown into a rage when he learned that a wet-behind-the-ears kid who was dating his daughter had said he looked like chicken magnate Frank Perdue. In the world where pride rules, the cavalier young man had signed his death warrant. Massino delivered his dead body to Castellano as a token of his loyalty.

Despite the decades of camaraderie, Goldie knew that, without a drop of Italian blood in him, he could never aspire to become a made member of a family. He was doomed to a bit part. By the time he was indicted on racketeering charges along with other Bonanno associates, he had already partially detached himself from the crime family's orbit. When authorities suggested he could avoid a lengthy prison term by testifying against his former mentor, he didn't exactly stew over the decision. He accepted immediately.

At Massino's trial, Goldie revealed all he knew about the three capos massacre. He testified that, at the time, he thought Gerlando Sciascia, one of Massino's closest associates and the official captain of the Bonannos' Montreal crew, didn't trust him. He was right. George from Canada was on tenterhooks: he was nervous about letting the blond-haired, blue-eyed Leisenheimer play an important role in such a crucial crime. Still, Massino managed to convince him that his apprentice could be trusted, and Sciascia agreed that Goldie would be the one to drive him, Vito Rizzuto and another Montrealer to the social club on Brooklyn's Thirteenth Avenue, where the triple hit would take place. While the bullets flew inside, Leisenheimer kept watch outside, sitting in his car a few doors down from the club, ready to signal Massino's team by two-way radio if the police arrived. Years had passed, but it seemed Goldie's job was still, in part, to look out for "bad cars."

A helpless Josephine Massino attended her husband's trial. The most she could do for the defendant was bring him food, freshly dry-cleaned suits and news about his granddaughter's latest softball game. She brought him takeout meals, or fixed them herself—after all, she had worked in the restaurant business with Big Joey for over forty years. The couple owned the CasaBlanca, a family restaurant on Sixtieth Avenue in Maspeth with signs in block letters advertising its specialties: pasta and brick-oven-baked pizza. Inside, subdued lighting was reflected in mirrors tinted with a thin coating of bronze, and waitresses laid out placemats on tables decorated with bouquets of plastic flowers. Customers had a hard time choosing from among the delicacies on offer, from antipasti to oregano shrimp, veal scaloppini, linguine with roasted peppers, and desserts like *sfogliatelle*, a classic seashell-shaped pastry. The menus announced "CasaBlanca . . . where you're treated like family!" The walls were plastered with photos of actors who had played mobsters in films and dined there, including Hugh Grant (*Mickey Blue Eyes*), James Caan (*The Godfather*) and, ironically, Johnny Depp (who played the title role in *Donnie Brasco*). If the house pianist wasn't around to play everyone's favourite Sinatra ditties, the hosts would pop a CD in the player and ensure the right ambiance with some choice cuts from the *Godfather* soundtrack.

Joe Massino was himself an excellent chef who liked to taste his cuisine as much as he enjoyed cooking it. In custody he had lost a lot of weight but still hovered around three hundred pounds, and food was for him an inexhaustible source of pleasure. Josie made sure to always have a snack at the ready for recesses during the trial. The Bonanno boss was facing the possibility of spending the rest of his life in prison. Worse, he had another trial pending, for the murder of Gerlando Sciascia, the end result of which might well be a lethal injection coursing through his veins. If ever there was a guy in need of comfort food, it was Big Joey.

Josephine knew that her husband felt each successive testimony from a former associate like a knife in his heart. Frank "Curly" Lino was another who took the stand, explaining to the court the rules of membership in the American Mafia. "Well, once you're a made member, you are not allowed to disrespect a member's wife or daughter, you can't cooperate with the government, and if you are called to a meeting, you can't carry a gun."

"If you are called to a meeting and you choose not to go?" prosecutor Greg Andres inquired.

"You'll be gone," Lino answered.

"When you say, 'You'll be gone' . . ."

"You're dead."

If the trial was already an ordeal for Josephine, it took an even more unpleasant turn when Salvatore Vitale began his testimony, recounting everything he knew about her husband. The two men had been friends since boyhood, when Massino had taught Vitale how to swim. Years later, Joey presided over Sal's Mafia induction ceremony, and was best man at his wedding. Most painful of all, Sal was Josie's younger brother.

Josephine refused to stand in court when the judge and Good-Looking Sal walked in. She remained seated in the front row with her two daughters, her face inscrutable, and steeled herself for what was to follow. Earlier, she had confided to Kati Cornell Smith, of the *New York Post,* that she felt simultaneously bitter and incredulous. "He wanted to hurt Joe because he's looking to save himself," she said to the reporter, explaining that Vitale had plea-bargained with the prosecution after confessing to eleven murders. She added that she couldn't understand how her brother could have sunk so low: "It's still too painful," she said. "It's really taken a toll on my family."

His sister may have been devastated, but Good-Looking Sal didn't appear the least bit troubled when he took his seat in the witness box. True to form, he had carefully combed his salt-and-pepper hair and put on a freshly pressed suit. Journalists were seated too far away to tell whether he had splashed on his favourite cologne, Boss, but he clearly cared about how he looked. An Associated Press scribe opined that he resembled a "paler version of the actor George Hamilton" (who, as it happened, had played an adviser to the Corleone family in *The Godfather Part III*). Anti-Mafia investigators had joked in the past that Vitale looked like a wedding cake figurine.

Sal pulled no punches in exposing the family's secrets. "I was the official underboss of the Bonanno crime family," he proclaimed, with a certain grandiloquence, in response to Greg Andres's initial questioning. Andres, who was famed for his to-the-point style of questioning, got right down to business and asked Vitale if he had ever committed crimes for Joseph Massino. "I killed for him," Vitale replied, without so much as a glance in the direction of his imposing brother-in-law. "Did many murders for Mr. Massino . . . Every dollar I made, I would split with [him]. I didn't look at it like an obligation. He made me what I am. He made me a goodfella."

Vitale told the court that, in addition to murders, he had been personally involved in "arson, hijacking, breaking and entering, extortion, shylocking." A reporter for *The New York Times* wrote that he "described killings, schemes and plots the way an accountant might list profits and losses." The witness floundered somewhat, though, as he tried to recall the names of the murder victims. It wasn't that he was trying to hide the truth. The reason was chillingly banal: the list was simply too long.

He was far more composed when asked why he had decided to stool on his brother-in-law and erstwhile best friend. He claimed it was Massino who had broken his trust first, ostracizing him even though he had the title of underboss. When Massino was jailed at one point, Vitale had enjoyed a brief spell at the top. But after his release, Massino had modified the outfit's organizational structure such that none of the captains was required to report to Vitale. Good-Looking Sal in effect no longer had any power within the family. He said he knew he had fallen hard when Massino forbade him from accepting the traditional Christmas presents from Bonanno captains. "I was more or less being shelved—you have the title, but you're not doing anything." He said he felt that if he were imprisoned, his "wife and kids would be just left in the street."

"That's why I decided to do what I'm doing today," he concluded.

His sister's and nieces' gasps were audible at the mention of family members. The witness continued to touch on the filial theme, declaring that he had done what his brother-in-law couldn't: he had looked out for his sister Josephine while Big Joey was doing time. Massino remained impassive in the defendant's dock. It was too much, however, for his thirty-seven-year-old daughter, Joanne: she leapt up and strode purposefully from the courtroom.

Mere months earlier, the disclosure of such stories would have been unthinkable. But on this day, there was nothing holding Vitale back. He unveiled secrets that other goodfellas had kept hidden until then, many about their victims' last moments on earth. Besides admitting his own crimes, he described in detail those committed by other associates of Big Joey, men with ludicrous mob nicknames like "Dirty Danny," "Louie Bagel" and "Monkey Man." Life was cheap in the Bonanno family: someone could be killed for reasons as superficial as selling a counterfeit Rolex to a captain of the clan. The motive could also be far more serious: Sal Vitale revealed that the execution of the three renegade capos in 1981 had indeed been a bid to consolidate power in the hands of Joe Massino. The death sentence on Dominick "Sonny Black" Napolitano, meanwhile, had been issued for the unforgivable sin of having introduced Joe Pistone, in the guise of Donnie Brasco, into the family ranks.

Massino, who was diabetic, sucked on lollipops in court to quench the rage boiling up inside him. Steered by Greg Andres's precise questioning, Good-Looking Sal outlined a raft of Bonanno family crimes, from minor to major. He explained how Persian carpets were smuggled into Canada and how money was loaned on the streets of New York at a yearly interest rate of 75 percent. He even became a reluctant linguistics teacher, explaining to the court the meanings of the many macabre yet colourful euphemisms of Cosa Nostra culture. Victims weren't killed; they were "packaged." And how was this "packaging" conducted? Andres wondered. Vitale recalled having murdered two individuals by shooting them in the back of the head, but he couldn't remember having shot another victim between the eyes nor having gunned him down from the front.

Massino's defence lawyer, David Breitbart, accused Salvatore Vitale of lying to escape the death penalty, and of using Andres and his fellow prosecutors to bring down Massino. Breitbart added that Vitale had even planned to kill his client with help from John Gotti, Massino's neighbour and so-called friend.

Not troubled in the slightest, Vitale delved into highly personal topics: he spoke of issues his son had, and recounted family counselling sessions they had attended together. One day, he said, his son had come home with slash marks on his face, claiming he had been attacked by a homeless man. An enraged Vitale enlisted two associates to track down the guilty party. The hunt lasted for two months. At one point they thought they had their man and decided to kill him with an ice pick. The unfortunate vagrant escaped with his life when the pick got stuck in his tattered clothing. The truth emerged later: "My son slashed his own face," Vitale explained. "During a therapy session he admitted it to me."

It hardly took a degree in psychology to guess at the deep-seated reasons for Vitale's son's erratic behaviour. In the early 1990s, when the boy was given a no-show job in the distribution department of the *New York Post* by a low-level Bonanno soldier who thought he was doing the right thing, Vitale responded with one of the fits of rage that he had a knack for displaying. There was no way his son was going to be paid for sitting and doing nothing; he wanted him to go back to college. "I flew over the coffee table and was strangling him," he told the court. "I said, 'Don't go back to the *New York Post*.'"

For Josephine Massino, listening to her brother on the stand had brought nothing but pain for three straight days. On the fourth day of his testimony, however, her disgust for him reached its zenith. Good-Looking Sal made it known that Joe Massino had transgressed the Mafia code by making him a Bonanno member on the basis of their friendship and family relationship. The established rules of Cosa Nostra stated that no one who had been employed in state correctional services could be inducted into a family. Salvatore Vitale had worked for a year as a guard in a Queens prison.

"Mr. Massino knew you were a correction officer?" Greg Andres asked.

"He knew," Vitale replied.

After court recessed for the day, Josie unburdened herself in the presence of John Marzulli, a reporter for the New York *Daily News*. "I don't ever want to see him again," she said. "He's my flesh and blood, but how could you forgive what he has done, not only to me but to my husband and the father of my children?" She had noticed that her brother hadn't dared look in her direction the entire day, as she once again sat in the front row. After the hearing had resumed following a recess, she must have had the feeling her brother was purposely twisting the knife in the wound: Vitale told of how he had felt nothing but contempt for his brother-in-law on the day the two were arrested: "He don't deserve the respect and honour for me to sit next to him," he said. "I feel that Mr. Massino segregated my sister and her children from me."

Breitbart was curious to know how it was that Vitale remembered the precise date of the three capos massacre, more than two decades after the fact. "My sons are born May 3 and May 6, so I can never forget May 5," Good-Looking Rat said. He then reiterated that Vito Rizzuto had been the lead gunman that night, and explained how the signal for the killers to emerge from the closet had been given by Gerlando Sciascia running his hand through his hair.

The jurors needed only four days to return a verdict. On July 30, 2004, the jury forewoman read out each of the accusations against Joseph Massino; it took her ten minutes. As she came to the end of each count, she looked up and pronounced the fateful word: "guilty." Big Joey was convicted of racketeering; extortionate extension and collection of credit (i.e., loansharking); arson conspiracy; the murders of Philip Giaccone, Dominick Trinchera, Alphonse Indelicato, Dominick Napolitano, Anthony Mirra, Cesare Bonventre and Gabriel Infanti; the attempted murder of Anthony Giliberti, a union official; extortion conspiracy; money-laundering conspiracy; illegal gambling and other crimes. There was not a single acquittal. Massino looked at his wife and shrugged his shoulders. Josephine remained stoic. As the jury's findings were read out, she stared at the floor, every so often glancing at Adeline, the couple's forty-three-year-old daughter, who sat beside her. "Not one we got," Adeline murmured.

The federal government also sought to recover some ten million dollars in criminally acquired assets, which meant the Massino family risked losing their house as well as the CasaBlanca restaurant. On her way out of the courtroom, Josephine's only comment to questioning reporters was a curt "I don't have anything to say." Her daughter Joanne, who had decided to stay home on the day the verdict was pronounced, was more forthcoming. "I don't understand," she told a reporter from *Newsday*. "All of the inconsistencies with these rats. It really is disgusting. I hope my uncle drops dead, I really do."

Not so long before he faced justice, Joe Massino had made much of the fact that no member of the Bonanno family had ever co-operated with the authorities. At his trial, he had seen seven turncoats take the stand. Seven men he had trusted, and because of whose treachery he could very well be sentenced to life. And an even worse fate loomed. He still had to stand trial for the murder of Sciascia. Murder in aid of racketeering carried the death penalty. Big Joey might yet achieve the distinction of being the first U.S. Mafia boss in decades to be executed—for having spoken four words to his brother-in-law, Sal Vitale: "George has to go."

In prison since his arrest in January, Vito Rizzuto had been making desperate attempts to win bail. The Quebec Superior Court had rejected his first request so he'd tried the Quebec Court of Appeal. Justice François Doyon issued his ruling in August 2004, a week after Joe Massino's initial conviction in New York. He refused the bail request and decreed that Rizzuto remain imprisoned pending a court decision on his extradition to the United States.

Legal observers questioned the strategy adopted by Rizzuto's lawyers. They had urged their client to admit a number of things in a written declaration, which was then appended to the bail request. They

believed that the tactic would keep the bail hearing process from dragging on and, more important, curtail further police investigations,
which would likely spell trouble for other members of the clan. Despite
the concessions, the report submitted by police to Justice Doyon was
very incriminating indeed.

In his bail request, Vito admitted to having remained a member of the
Mafia since 1981, the year the three rebel capos were murdered. He also
acknowledged that he had been offered a promotion within the Bonanno
ranks in 1999. He said he had had "constant contact with persons having
extensive criminal records or working in higher levels of organized crime,
including drug trafficking and money laundering." Some described him
as "the chief, the boss, or the one who puts people in their positions." He
did not refute those characterizations. Lastly, he admitted that he had
behaved as "a man of influence within organized crime."

The avowals were of no use to him. Justice Doyon dwelled on details
that the accused had glossed over, which were contained in the police
report prepared by Detective Sergeant Nicodemo Milano. In the
Montreal godfather's statement of income and expenses, something
didn't add up. Rizzuto had no known employment aside from the position he claimed to hold with Renda Construction. The company had
declared income of $8,031 in 2002 and $34,032 in 2003—hardly amounts
that could justify his lifestyle.

Rizzuto styled himself a businessman, but curiously he had no credit
cards or bank accounts in his name (except a joint account with his
wife). From 1980 to 1985, however, he had held power of attorney over
a number of Swiss bank accounts for members of his family. Since 2001,
Rizzuto had travelled to eight countries, including Mexico, Cuba, St. Kitts,
the Bahamas and the Dominican Republic. He had no vehicles registered
in his name. Yet, Milano's report stated, he had often been seen driving
an SUV and any number of luxury sports cars.

Rizzuto had neglected to mention another fact, namely that he had
accumulated wealth by illicit means including loansharking. Posing as a
high-stakes gambler, Sergeant Detective Nicodemo Milano had met a
man named Giuseppe Triassi at the Le Cheval bar, part of the Casino de

Montréal. The Sicilian-born Triassi confided to Milano that he had been working for Vito for more than twenty years. He also told him that he lent money at 10 percent interest—for a three-day term. On multiple occasions, police observed Triassi delivering the profits from those loans to the Consenza Social Club.

Vito had been seen in the company of known criminals in hotels and restaurants, on golf courses and at boxing matches in Montreal, Quebec, and Cornwall, Ontario. Milano's report listed some fifty Mafiosi with whom Vito had been observed on various occasions in Montreal, Toronto, New York City and elsewhere, often at social events, weddings, birthdays and funerals.

"This report—indeed, the evidence as a whole—demonstrates that the appellant has spent the last twenty-five years and more in a highly criminalized environment," Justice Doyon concluded. "In fact, for the purposes of this bail hearing, the parties admit that he has been a member of the Mafia since 1981. The defendant's participation in criminal activities of the Bonanno family and more generally in the Mafia for a number of years, plus the importance of his role and the respect accorded him within the organization, provide him with access to diverse resources." In short, the judge believed that, given the means at his disposal, Vito Rizzuto was a flight risk if he were to be released on bail.

That same month, Frank Cotroni succumbed to cancer, aged seventy-two. Assuming eternal life exists, he was off to join, in heaven or hell, old Joseph Bonanno, who had died two years previously, having reached the venerable age of ninety-seven. A page had been turned in the history of the North American and Montreal Mafia. As the founder of the eponymous crime family, Bonanno had rubbed shoulders with such legendary figures of organized crime in the United States as Lucky Luciano and Al Capone. He had dispatched Carmine Galante to Montreal, assigning him the task of modernizing the city's underworld. With his cousin Stefano Magaddino, who ruled over Ontario from Buffalo, Joe Bonanno could be considered a godfather of the Canadian Mafia. In a world where men are often cut down in the prime of life, most often by gunfire, Cotroni and Bonanno shared the distinction of having lived long lives, ended in the usual manner, by illness or old age. Joe Bonanno expired on May 10, 2002, in his Arizona retreat. Since disclosing certain secrets in his autobiography, he had been viewed by his successors as a pariah. No soldier of the Bonanno family—which its most recent boss had seen fit to rename the Massino family—attended his funeral.

Vito Rizzuto's father, Nicolò, did, however, pay his respects to Frank Cotroni, at the Loreto funeral home as well as at the Church of the Madonna della Difesa, on Dante Street in Saint-Léonard. Very few others in Montreal's Sicilian Mafia were at the funeral ceremony, though, to see the deceased's loved ones release seventy-two white doves into the sky over Little Italy—one for each year of his life, despite the fact that they had not been especially peaceful.

By October 2004, nine months after he had been incarcerated, Vito Rizzuto must have been wondering just how many rats there were in the house of Bonanno. News travels fast in mobland, and prison walls are no obstacle to its propagation. The latest information coming through from New York was not at all reassuring.

Aided by a backhoe operator, a dozen shovel-wielding FBI agents and other police officers had sifted through the muck in a vacant lot at the southern end of Ozone Park, on the border between Queens and Brooklyn, not far from the spot where, twenty-three years earlier, a group of children had stumbled upon the hand of Sonny Red Indelicato sticking out of the ground. Shifting aside concrete slabs, this was when the searchers had found what was left of Dominick "Big Trin" Trinchera and Philip "Philly Lucky" Giaccone. The marshy lot was well known as a clandestine cemetery for the Gambino family, New York's most powerful mob outfit; the Gambinos had graciously allowed the Bonannos' undertakers the use of a few plots. While they were at it, the FBI agents hoped to turn up other remains. With a bit of luck, they reckoned, they might uncover the body of John Favara, a former neighbour of Gambino boss John Gotti.

In March 1980, Gotti's second-oldest son, twelve-year-old Frank, was riding a minibike in the street when Favara, driving home from work, struck and fatally injured him. Police ruled the death an accident. Favara knew the boy well; his own children often played with him. When he stopped by the bereaved family's house to apologize and offer his condolences, Gotti's wife attacked him with a baseball bat. Death threats were dropped off in his mailbox, and someone spray-painted the word "murderer" on his car.

Favara decided to move out of the neighbourhood. Four months after the accident, he was walking through the parking lot of the furniture store where he worked when, according to witnesses, a man beat him with a baseball bat and, aided by several others, forced him into a van. He was never seen again.

The federal agents also believed they might find the remains of Tommy DeSimone, who had been executed shortly after Christmas in 1978 for having killed two of Gotti's men. DeSimone had achieved immortality, in a way, inspiring the character of Tommy DeVito in the Martin Scorsese film *Goodfellas,* played by Joe Pesci. As it turned out, police hopes of finding either Favara or DeSimone were dashed. Clearly, however, the FBI had known exactly where to look for the bodies of Trinchera and Giaccone—a mob informant had told them. But who was it?

Rumour had it that the latest stool pigeon was a most improbable one: Joseph Massino himself.

Confirmation came in January 2005 via New York's tabloids and their inimitable headline style. "Mob Boss a Rat," the *Daily News* announced in its usual oversize type. "Canary on Top Perch—Godfather Turncoat" was the *Post*'s take.

No one was more stupefied by the news than Josephine Massino. Born in Sicily, raised in Queens, New York, she had been close to Joe since first meeting him at age thirteen. They were both seventeen when they married. Josie had steadfastly supported Big Joey through all of his recent hardships, in court as well as in prison. Earlier in their marriage, even as she watched her husband's waistline grow more expansive, her love for him had remained unchanged. She had even stayed loyal after learning that he had taken a mistress while on the run from police, hiding out in the Poconos, in northeast Pennsylvania. Josie had resigned herself to giving up their sprawling home in Howard Beach, evicting her mother-in-law from her house in Maspeth (also purchased using proceeds of crime), abandoning the CasaBlanca and selling off all of the family's property to pay the ten-million-dollar fine that was part of the verdict against her husband. But nothing had prepared her for the shock of seeing those tabloid headlines. Big Joey was now guilty of something even more reprehensible than infidelity or murder.

The articles explained that Joe Massino had decided to co-operate with federal authorities immediately after his conviction for racketeering, the previous August. The man who had forbidden members of the Bonanno family from uttering his name had been working with the FBI for six months. He had agreed to wear a wire and record conversations with Bonanno members incarcerated in the same prison as him, but who had not betrayed the organization. Vincent "Vinny Gorgeous" Basciano was one of them. Massino had made him acting boss, responsible for street operations, but by November, Basciano had become a fellow inmate of Big Joey's at the Metropolitan Detention Center in Brooklyn. Unaware he was being recorded, he let Massino in on a plan of his to kill Greg Andres, the crusading federal prosecutor. Big Joey knew that, with this particular recording, he now had a powerful card to play: by relaying the information about the murder plot to the FBI, he would save Andres's life. In return, he wanted his own life saved. He offered to become a co-operating witness for the prosecution against Basciano.

The government agreed to waive the death penalty for Big Joey's part in the murder of Gerlando Sciascia, and also offered to forgo the ten-million-dollar fine. Massino's wife and mother could keep their houses. Despite that, Josephine must have felt as if the Rock of Gibraltar had collapsed beneath her. Only weeks before, the New York papers had called her husband "the last of the godfathers," since the bosses of the other four families were all behind bars. Now she was doomed to a decidedly inglorious role in Mafia history: the wife of the first New York Cosa Nostra boss to co-operate with police. Josie and her family had enjoyed membership in the Mafia aristocracy. Now they were ostracized. Lepers.

Joseph Massino's treasonous behaviour was a bombshell, roiling not only the Bonannos but the Gambino family as well. Big Joey's friendship with Gambino boss John Gotti meant that he knew plenty of secrets about the largest of the Five Families. Now the Genovese, Colombo and Lucchese outfits had reason to worry as well. In the ensuing months, several high-ranking Bonanno members pleaded guilty to racketeering and murder charges, among them Anthony "Tony Green" Urso, the former *consigliere* and acting boss; Joseph Cammarano, a past underboss; and Louis Restivo, a soldier. Their families were thus spared the potentially prohibitive cost of legal proceedings and confiscation of their assets. Besides, with their boss now playing for the opposing team, they knew there would be no chance of acquittal.

So heinous was the crime of betrayal in mob culture that even the wife of one of Big Joey's victims heaped scorn on Massino. "In my eyes, the guy is a sissy," Donna Trinchera, the widow of Dominick "Big Trin" Trinchera, told John Marzulli of the *Daily News*. Nor could Massino's daughters, who had loyally stuck by him during his trial, hide the disgust they now felt toward their dad. "I am done with him. I'm ashamed that he's my father," said Joanne. Her older sister, Adeline, said she couldn't understand how her father could do such a thing: "We supported my dad through the trial but now feel it impossible to support or condone his actions any further," she wrote in an email to a reporter.

Josephine refused to go to court for the sentencing. At that hearing, Massino made this confession: "As boss of the Bonanno family, I gave the order . . . to kill George from Canada." Minutes later, he was handed his sentence: life imprisonment.

News of his superior's defection could not have come at a more critical juncture for Vito Rizzuto, who by then was fighting extradition to the United States with the desperation of a drowning man.

CHAPTER 15

ILLUSTRIOUS RELATIONS

V ITO RIZZUTO WASN'T THE only man worried about the cascading
revelations out of New York. They were extremely disquieting to
a Canadian with a public profile of considerably more esteem: Alfonso
Gagliano, member of Parliament for the riding of Saint-Léonard from
1984 to 2002, the Liberal Party of Canada's chief organizer in Quebec,
minister of labour and subsequently minister of public works and government services in the Jean Chrétien government, and Canada's ambassador to Denmark until his forced repatriation in February 2004 in the
wake of the so-called sponsorship scandal.

Rumours had swirled around Parliament Hill in Ottawa for some
time about Gagliano's alleged Mafia links. A web of suspicion had
descended upon the powerful minister, from which he had tried to extricate himself more than once. The explanations were occasionally
laboured. One opposition MP had even hummed the theme from *The
Godfather* in the House of Commons at the mention of Gagliano's name.

Up to November 17, 2004, Gagliano had answered a number of questions about certain people he knew and the reasons why he had provided
services to individuals with somewhat tarnished reputations. But on that

day, allegations of a far more serious association appeared in the pages of the New York *Daily News*. Frank "Curly" Lino, the Bonanno family captain–turned FBI informant, claimed that Alfonso Gagliano was a made member of the Mafia. Lino was the capo who had reluctantly witnessed the three captains massacre and who had pushed Sonny Black Napolitano down the basement stairs of the house in Staten Island where he was executed. He had also been a co-operating witness for the prosecution in the spring 2004 trial of Joe Massino.

In a deposition to the FBI, Lino stated that he had met Gagliano in a Saint-Léonard banquet hall in the early 1990s. Lino was part of a Bonanno delegation that had travelled north in the wake of boss Philip "Rusty" Rastelli's death from liver cancer to inform the Montreal faction that Joe Massino was taking over as leader. FBI agents Christine Grubert and Jay Kramer noted in their report that, on the same occasion, Anthony Spero was introduced to the Montrealers as the new Bonanno *consigliere*. Accompanying Spero were Lino, Frank "Big Frank" Porco, Anthony Canale, Anthony Basile and Gerlando "George from Canada" Sciascia. Only made members of the family were authorized to attend the banquet; mere associates were *personae non gratae*.

According to the FBI summary of Lino's deposition, Giuseppe (Joe) LoPresti introduced Alfonso Gagliano to the Americans. Like any secret society, the Mafia operated under strict rules of security. One of the most important of these rules is that a made member must never divulge the fact that he belongs to the organization. When one made member is introduced to another, the presentation must be made by another made member who is acquainted with both men, using the expression "this is a friend of ours." LoPresti, born in Cattolica Eraclea like Vito Rizzuto, was the Montreal crew's ambassador to the Bonanno family. Curly Lino told the FBI that he "socialized with Gagliano when he was hanging out with Vito Rizzutto [*sic*]" (the misspelling of Rizzuto's surname is apparently an FBI transcription error). Lino identified Gagliano in a photograph shown to him by investigators during his questioning. He added that he had also seen the Canadian politician on other occasions.

While in Montreal, the Bonanno family envoys took the opportunity to attend a baseball game between the Expos and the New York Mets. The tickets had been supplied by Mets relief pitcher John Franco. The left-handed bullpen ace was a good friend of Frank Lino. His brother, James Franco, worked at Shea Stadium, the Mets' home field in Queens, and was known to associate with Mafia members. He had given tickets to Lino and other Bonanno members on several occasions, and often invited mobsters to hang out with members of the team after games.

Following the game at Montreal's Olympic Stadium, the Bonanno group got a tour of the Mets' dressing room and spent the rest of the evening with some of the players, making the rounds of some Montreal nightclubs with Vito Rizzuto and Joe LoPresti.

The story of the mobsters' visit with the ballplayers began to filter out in New York newspapers in October 2004. Franco was the first player forced to defend himself: Mets management and Major League Baseball officials demanded an explanation. The league regularly warned players against contact with disreputable individuals likely to tarnish their reputation and that of the sport, and they were obviously displeased to see reports in the sports pages of an athlete keeping such doubtful company. Franco, who had grown up in Brooklyn's Italian community, issued a brief statement through his agent, in which he made no denials: "I am proud to be an Italian-American and have lived my life in a respectable fashion," he said. Then aged forty-four, the reliever was in the twilight of his playing days; the Mets did not renew his contract, and he pitched for only part of the 2005 season, with the Houston Astros, before retiring. Franco's socializing with mobsters may end up as a minor footnote to his career. But the scandal that was soon to erupt north of the forty-fifth parallel was something else entirely: it damaged the reputation of one of the most influential politicians in Canada.

Frank Lino said he could not recall the date of the trip to Montreal. It can be inferred from his statements, however, that it happened between June 24, 1991, the date of Philip Rastelli's death, and April 29, 1992, that of Joe LoPresti's murder. During that time, the New York Mets were the visiting team at Olympic Stadium twice: there was a four-game series on

July 1 to 4, 1991, and a three-game stand from April 17 to 19, 1992. Joe Massino would not have waited almost a year after Rastelli's death to tell the Montreal faction that he was the new boss, so it is likely that the trip occurred in July 1991.

The November 17, 2004, article alleging that Alfonso Gagliano was an inducted member of the Mafia caused consternation in Ottawa. In Parliament the next day, Stephen Harper, the future prime minister of Canada and the opposition leader at the time, demanded an explanation from Liberal prime minister Paul Martin. "The allegations are in the New York *Daily News*," Harper said. "According to FBI documents, they link former Liberal cabinet minister and ambassador Alfonso Gagliano to organized crime. The report claims that in the 1990s he was a 'made' member of the Brooklyn-based Bonanno crime family. My question is simple. Since Mr. Gagliano was in cabinet and ambassador during this period, was the government aware of this information and when did it become aware of these allegations?"

Martin's predecessor as prime minister, Jean Chrétien, was very close to Gagliano; the latter had helped him win the leadership of the Liberal Party of Canada. Martin opted for a prudent reply, even though he had few affinities with the former minister. "I have not seen the report and was not aware of the allegations until this morning, in fact," he said. "Let me simply say that these are very serious allegations and everyone should be very careful about accepting or repeating such allegations."

Verifying the credibility of the man with whom those allegations originated was indeed a tall order. Sixty-six-year-old Frank "Curly" Lino wasn't exactly a choirboy. While Canada's political leaders were debating in the House of Commons, Lino was preparing to testify in court, including at one trial involving the three captains massacre. In return for his co-operation with authorities, he was being granted lenient punishment for his role in six murders, including that of Sonny Black Napolitano. Lino had been a chief orchestrator of the Bonannos' incursion into Wall Street trading, a venture that led to his being convicted for a three-million-dollar securities fraud. The transcription of his statement to the FBI ran to two hundred pages; only a summary had leaked to the media. In it, Lino had shown few scruples in ratting out his own son Joseph as well as several cousins and dozens of friends.

One may well wonder why it would have been in his interest to make up such a story about a Canadian politician. Mentioning Gagliano as part of his confession would have been of no benefit to him. In all likelihood, the FBI investigators asked him who had been in attendance at the banquet in Montreal, and he simply answered the question. That being said, it remains possible, of course, that this part of his account was the fruit of an overactive imagination.

That, at any rate, was how the man at the centre of the controversy saw it, and he said so repeatedly. Alfonso Gagliano categorically denied the accusation that he was a Mafioso. "That is utterly false!" he told *La Presse.* "I have no connection to any [Mafia] family. I don't know anyone mentioned in the article [in the New York *Daily News*]. I don't even know who those people are. I have never seen them. Just because it comes from the FBI doesn't mean it's the truth. It's not the first time they've been wrong, and it's not the last."

"I'll tell you one thing, I'm not a member of a Mafia," he told the Montreal *Gazette.* "I never met these people. I never went to this so-called meeting. I really don't know what it's talking about . . . I've been fighting other things in the past, and one day, when you tell the truth, the truth will always win out in the end."

In an interview with the CBC, he said, "This is . . . shocking to me and my family. It's absurd. Everything. I never heard, met anybody. I read the article. I don't know all the names mentioned in the article. I have no idea what they're talking about."

A statement issued by Gagliano's lawyer, Pierre Fournier, read: "If Frank Lino identified [Mr. Gagliano], it can only be by error, as he has certainly never participated in such a meal, neither in Montreal nor anywhere else. He is now trying to find out more than what is contained in the New York *Daily News* article in order to rebut this information; without a precise date for this alleged dinner, it is extremely difficult for him to state precisely what he was doing at that time. As soon as he has more information, he intends to present as many of the facts as he will be able to. But he repeats, he has never attended a Bonanno family dinner, he has never been involved with this family, about which all he knows is what every one [*sic*] can read from time to time in the newspapers."

Jean Chrétien flew to the rescue of his former cabinet minister. Speaking in Little Rock, Arkansas, where he was attending the inauguration of former U.S. president Bill Clinton's library, he laconically declared, "I don't believe any of it." He then added that all members of Parliament had to pass background checks before being appointed to cabinet and that, at the time of his appointment, Gagliano's file was spotless (which wasn't entirely true). Those in charge of the background check "never mentioned to me that he had any problems of that nature," the former prime minister told the CBC's French-language all-news network, RDI. "If there had been any, he would not have been appointed a minister."

In New York, Joseph Massino's lawyer, David Breitbart, seized on the affair to vilify Frank Lino. Curly's devastating testimony at his client's trial, six months earlier, was still fresh in his mind. In November 2004, Breitbart was unaware that Massino had confessed to all his crimes and decided to co-operate with the FBI to avoid facing the death penalty for the murder of Gerlando Sciascia; the news of the Bonanno boss's defection would not emerge for another two months. Breitbart, well known for his colourful oratorical style, spewed his venom all over Lino, saying in no uncertain terms that no one should believe a word of what he said. The informant, he declared, was a mass murderer, a sad case who hadn't made it past the sixth grade, a dope dealer, an addict, an extortionist, a compulsive gambler, and nothing less—or, rather, nothing more—than "one of the lowest pieces of garbage that ever walked the earth."

A few days after his initial denials, Alfonso Gagliano qualified his remarks. It was possible, he said, that he had crossed paths with Mafia members during his lengthy political career. His activities as a member of Parliament, cabinet minister and prominent member of Montreal's Italian community brought him into contact with all kinds of people from all walks of life. He continued, however, to refute allegations that he had ever had personal ties to organized crime. It was impossible, he added, that he could have met Frank Lino and the rest of the Bonanno delegation in Montreal: I wasn't even in Montreal, so how could I even be at that meeting?" he said to *The Globe and Mail*, explaining that he had been in an apartment in Daytona Beach, Florida, at the time of the Bonanno gathering in Montreal. Apparently, then, he did know the date of that meeting—or had learned of it since the allegations were made.

Alfonso Gagliano was born in 1942 in Siculiana, the cradle of the Cuntrera-Caruana clan, in the province of Agrigento. Half of the town's residents emigrated to North America after the Second World War; indeed, some say there are more Siculianesi in Montreal than in Siculiana. Young Alfonso arrived in Quebec in 1958, the same year as the Renda family, which included Calogero and his son Paolo, who would later become *consigliere* to the Rizzuto clan. It seemed inevitable indeed that he should sometimes run into Mafiosi, and from his home province to boot.

After completing studies in accounting, Gagliano was elected chairman of the Jérôme Le Royer School Board in east-end Montreal in the early 1980s, then in 1984 won election to Canada's House of Commons as the Liberal member for Saint-Léonard–Anjou (now Saint-Léonard–Saint-Michel). His victory was notable in that Saint-Léonard was one of the few seats that the Liberals held on to in that election, which was a landslide victory for the Progressive Conservative Party under Brian Mulroney. Fellow Liberal Jean Chrétien retired from active politics that year but began a long battle to win the leadership of his party (a battle that began with a loss to John Turner leading up to the 1984 election). Chrétien was strongly supported by Gagliano as well as Senator Pietro Rizzuto, founder of the public works contractor Inter-State Paving, and another native of the Sicilian province of Agrigento—more specifically, the town of Cattolica Eraclea, also the birthplace of Nicolò and Vito Rizzuto, to whom he was distantly related.

The tandem of Gagliano and Rizzuto played a vital role in financing and organizing Chrétien's campaign. Members of Montreal's Italian community were delighted to see two of their most illustrious representatives play such an active role on the country's political scene. The team held several strategy sessions at Pietro Rizzuto's luxurious home in Puerto Vallarta, Mexico. After a second Liberal defeat in the 1988 federal election, the senator and the MP for Saint-Léonard orchestrated a rebellion against Turner. They were tremendously efficient and succeeded in undermining rank-and-file party members' confidence in their leader, which forced his resignation in 1990. Further mobilizing their network in the run-up to the leadership convention in Calgary, Alberta, in June of that year, Gagliano and Rizzuto marshalled a majority of Quebec delegates in support of Chrétien's bid. He crushed his rival, Paul Martin, on the first ballot.

The Liberals swept to power in the October 1993 election, and Chrétien realized his dream: he became Canada's twentieth prime minister and went on to lead the country for ten years. He owed part of his success to Senator Pietro Rizzuto and to MP Alfonso Gagliano, whom he regularly described as "great friends." Political observers were surprised when the member for Saint-Léonard was not appointed a cabinet minister. Chrétien simply named him chief whip, a job that entails ensuring that the majority party has enough members present in the House of Commons (or at a committee meeting) to win important votes.

There was a reason for Gagliano's appointment, but Canadians knew nothing of it at the time. They learned about it the following year, following the work of investigative reporters at La Presse. "The Chief Whip for the federal Liberal government and MP for Saint-Léonard, Alfonso Gagliano, has done business for a number of years with at least one prominent member of Montreal's Sicilian Mafia, Agostino Cuntrera," the Montreal newspaper revealed in April 1994. "The Royal Canadian Mounted Police informed the office of Prime Minister Jean Chrétien of this as he was preparing to form his cabinet, in November [1993]. Following standard procedure, the RCMP conducts checks, at the Prime Minister's request, of MPs likely to receive cabinet appointments. The RCMP red-flagged Mr. Gagliano's candidacy . . . The Mounties indicate that Mr. Gagliano is not a suspect in any crime. But they mentioned certain relations that they find disconcerting, to say the least."

Back in the spring of 1985, the RCMP investigated, jointly with British police, a heroin smuggling plot orchestrated by the Cuntrera-Caruana clan. The drugs, concealed in teak tables, left Thailand and transited through Great Britain on their way to the Port of Montreal (*see Chapter 6*). A thorough search of the furniture on the docks at Felixstowe and Southampton, England, turned up hidden packages of the narcotic. The tables were destined for a Montreal import-export firm headed by Antonio Zambito and that had been founded by Pasquale Caruana and his brothers.

On the morning of June 4, an RCMP surveillance detail was following a suspect in the plot, Filippo Vaccarello, and an unidentified companion. To the officers' surprise, the suspects' car stopped in front of the home of Alfonso Gagliano, who had been elected to Parliament the year before. Vaccarello got out of the vehicle and headed for the basement office of the accounting firm owned in equal parts by Gagliano and his wife, Ersilia. The drug trafficker re-emerged some twenty minutes later. He was arrested the following month along with Luciano Zambito and Pasquale Caruana, and eventually convicted and sentenced to twenty years in prison.

Toward the end of the 1980s, Dima Messina, a financial adviser to Vito Rizzuto, was also seen at the Gagliano family accounting firm, which by then occupied offices at Place Saint-Zotique in Saint-Léonard. Messina was involved in a scheme to launder some $24 million. Police were unaware of the reasons for Vaccarello's and Messina's visits to Gagliano's accounting firm (*see Chapter 6*).

The firm kept the books for two companies that belonged to Agostino Cuntrera: a food wholesaler called Distribution John & Dino, and the numbered company 115685 Canada Inc. Gagliano's office was also the mailing address for the numbered company, which managed a Mikes restaurant franchise on Pie-IX Boulevard in Saint-Léonard. The company had been set up by Cuntrera and his brother-in-law Giovanni DiMora soon after both were released from prison. (Four years previously, in 1978, the pair had pleaded guilty along with accomplice Domenico Manno—Nicolò Rizzuto's brother-in-law—to charges of conspiring to murder Paolo Violi.)

In 1990 and 1991, Montreal police were busy probing several cases of arson and a bombing at the newly opened Pizza Hut franchise on

Jean-Talon Street, just a few hundred metres from the Mikes restaurant. The investigators suspected that Cuntrera sought to discourage the competition. On November 19, 1990, they obtained a warrant to place listening devices on the phone lines at Mikes. The Pizza Hut was bombed on February 12, 1991; two weeks later, police heard Cuntrera's daughter tell her mother about the Pizza Hut owner "not wanting to understand" (*see Chapter 12*). Acting on that information, police searched the Mikes restaurant, looking for the owners' financial statements. Cuntrera's wife informed them that the documents they were seeking could be found at the office of their accountant, Alfonso Gagliano.

On the morning of May 3, 1991, police went to Gagliano's office. They were greeted by his son, Vincenzo, who telephoned his father in Florida. The elder Gagliano told him to surrender the documents. The officers left with account statements, two financial statements of 115685 Canada Inc., and weekly sales reports from the Mikes franchise. No charges were laid. These events took place two months before the Montreal Expos' four-game homestand against the New York Mets, which has been established as the time of the Bonanno family delegation's visit and Gagliano's alleged meeting with them.

Alfonso Gagliano and Agostino Cuntrera are both past presidents of the Associazione Siciliana di Montreal, a non-profit organization whose membership has at various times included up to three hundred Montrealers originally from Siciliana, Sicily. Its offices were located on Chamilly Street in Saint-Léonard, in a building that belonged to Gagliano and his brother-in-law Mario Gidaro. Gagliano founded the association in 1979 and was its first president, holding the position for a few years. Cuntrera was elected its president in 1990.

During his interview with *La Presse,* the member of Parliament admitted that he knew the mobster. "Mr. Cuntrera is an acquaintance," he said. "We both come from Siciliana, which has a population of five thousand. He arrived in Montreal after I did. I met him during a premarital class in church. He came back to see me in the 1970s when he wanted me to do the accounting for his restaurant. We have since seen each other from time to time, at weddings and at Associazione Siciliana functions."

Cuntrera's businesses, Gagliano added, were "legitimate companies." "Now, if there are issues to be raised," he went on, "I am neither a judge nor a policeman." When asked whether he was bothered by the fact that he had a client involved in the killing of Paolo Violi, he responded that yes, Cuntrera had been a client before the murder, and added: "Afterward, we wondered about it . . . In reality, Mr. Cuntrera was never found guilty. He made an arrangement with the justice minister to stop the trial. He ended up with a few years [in prison]. We said to each other: 'we're going to limit ourselves to commercial activity, completely legitimate'."

Throughout his career and even after his retirement, Gagliano has maintained that such meetings with Mafia members were chance encounters. But there were many such events. Italian police found the telephone number of Gagliano's riding office in the pocket of one Antonio Enzio Salvo after he was killed by a *lupara* blast in Cattolica Eraclea on December 14, 1991. Aged thirty-four, Salvo had lived for a number of years in Laval and Saint-Léonard. While in Quebec, he had worked in construction. Before being deported to Sicily, he had asked his member of Parliament to put in a good word for him with Immigration Canada authorities.

So, upon his election as prime minister in 1993, Jean Chrétien wanted to name his loyal supporter to a cabinet position, and the RCMP conducted its standard background check. Some officers, well aware of the member for Saint-Léonard's unconventional fraternizations, believed it would be appropriate to ask him a number of questions. Senior RCMP officials were against the idea of an interview, but the ranking officer in charge of investigations in Montreal, Rowland Sugrue, green-lighted it. The interrogation was conducted by officers Yvon Thibault, of the RCMP, and Michel Gagné, with Montreal police. Neither police officials nor Canada's Privy Council have disclosed the post-interview report.

La Presse reporters asked Gagliano why, in his opinion, he had not received a ministerial portfolio. "Well, let's say, there were certain things," he said. "Mr. Chrétien told me that there were doubts. But all that was cleared up. The cabinet appointments are done very quickly, and there wasn't time to clarify everything before the swearing-in. I said to Mr.

Chrétien: 'In the meantime, it's better if I remain whip.' Since the Prime Minister appointed me whip, that means he had confidence in me. In late January [1994], I was informed by the Chief of Staff, Jean Pelletier, that the Prime Minister had received a new report and there was no longer anything preventing me from eventually becoming a minister."

In February 1994, police in the United States examined notes and documents that had been abandoned in a San Diego, California, hotel room by a suspect under investigation. The young man, a resident of Saint-Léonard, Quebec, had left behind records of securities and real estate transactions worth $342 million, as well as documents concerning the Vatican Bank. Gagliano's name appeared on a handwritten note, next to those of four known organized crime bosses. "Alfonso Gagliano, friend. Whip and Minister of Finance of Canada," it read. The U.S. investigators conveyed the information to their Canadian counterparts. The young man later resurfaced in Montreal. Police would not reveal his name, and it has proven impossible to learn anything more about the mysterious hotel room find.

Gagliano was never in fact made minister of finance, but after a two-year purgatory as chief whip, he was appointed to a cabinet post by Chrétien as minister of labour. He was also given responsibility for the Canada Lands Company and Communication Canada, and was eventually named minister of public works and government services. The successive promotions did not spell an end to the controversy surrounding him, however.

In February 2001, La Presse broke the story that Gagliano's riding office in Saint-Léonard had sent a letter to Citizenship and Immigration Canada inquiring about the status of a request for permanent residency filed by the wife of Gaetano Amodeo, a Sicilian contract killer.

Despite being on Interpol's five hundred most wanted list, Amodeo had been able to settle in Canada with his wife and children several years earlier, and was living a tranquil life in Saint-Léonard, where he had bought a jewellery store. A notorious member of the Mafia in Cattolica Eraclea, he was wanted for two murders, one in Italy and the other in Germany. He was also suspected of having taken part in the assassination of *carabinieri* marshal Giuliano Guazzelli, who headed an anti-Mafia squad and had been shot dead on the outskirts of Agrigento by killers wielding machine guns. The RCMP and Immigration Canada finally bowed to pressure from the Italian government, arrested Amodeo in east-end Montreal and began extradition procedures. The matter soon wound up on the floor of the House of Commons: opposition members wanted to know why it had taken so long for Canadian police to collar a mobster wanted on murder charges in his home country.

Days later, *La Presse* revealed the contents of the May 2000 letter sent from Gagliano's riding office to Immigration Canada's client services department. The writer inquired about "the status of the residence file" of Maria Sicurella di Amodeo, the killer's wife. "I know that the Government of Quebec selection certificate is valid until June 2000, and the visitor visa is valid until 2001," added the author of the missive, which bore the MP's letterhead. "Have the audits come in? And what about the medical results? Do you think the visas will be issued shortly? Thank you for your kind co-operation."

It is not known whether that request for information was followed up in any way. Even so, Maria Sicurella di Amodeo and her two children were granted permanent residency in July 2000. The publication of the excerpts from the letter led to further commotion in the House of Commons. It was on this occasion that an opposition MP began humming the *Godfather* theme. When Gagliano heard about this, he was livid. He said he "was the victim of false and vicious attacks" by *La Presse* and opposition MPS because of his Sicilian roots. "If my name were Lapierre or Arcand, this sort of thing would not happen," he added. In his opinion, there was nothing at all wrong with the approach taken by his office with Immigration Canada.

Amodeo was extradited to Italy, where he was tried, convicted and sentenced to life in prison. He died some years later. In spite of all the secrets kept from Immigration Canada, his wife was allowed to remain in Montreal.

The "false and vicious" insinuations did not cease, however. Drug trafficker Oreste Pagano, who had been indicted at the same time as

Alfonso Caruana, made a number of unsettling revelations after agreeing to submit to questioning by RCMP investigators. When he explained how, in Italy, the Mafia have close links to powerful politicians that, among other things, allow them to secure lucrative public works contracts, an RCMP officer asked if to his knowledge the Mafia had any similar relationships in Canada. Had Alfonso Caruana ever mentioned any such cases to him? "We once spoke about it," Pagano replied. "There was a person who was going into the [Canadian] government and was from the same village as Alfonso [Caruana] . . . I don't know this person."

Later, Gagliano's name was closely linked to Canada's so-called sponsorship scandal (known in some quarters as "AdScam"). In the mid-1990s, after the narrow defeat of the "yes" side in the second referendum on Quebec sovereignty, the government of Canada devised a sponsorship program designed to counter the Quebec independence movement via subtle propaganda in favour of the federalist option. Gagliano was the senior member of government in charge of the program, as minister responsible for Quebec and minister of public works and government services. Before long, the federal government was subsidizing a wealth of cultural, economic and social initiatives that aimed to carpet Quebec with Canadian flags and convince the province's residents of the benefits of remaining in the Canadian Confederation. More than $300 million was showered on advertising agencies whose managers, conveniently, made hefty contributions to the Liberal Party of Canada's electoral war chest. The Auditor General of Canada, Sheila Fraser, found that approximately $100 million had been granted for services that involved little or no actual work. In one case, the government had paid an ad agency three times for identical studies.

The scandal led to Gagliano losing his ministerial post. He then reportedly angled for the position of ambassador to the Vatican but was eventually named ambassador to Denmark, where daily newspapers delighted in informing their readers about the new appointee's woes. Jean Chrétien's successor as prime minister, Paul Martin, appointed Justice John Gomery to lead a commission of inquiry into the sponsorship scandal and recalled Gagliano from his Denmark post.

The RCMP launched new investigations. The scandal played a large part in the Liberals' defeat in a November 2005 confidence vote, and in the January 2006 election of a minority Conservative government with Stephen Harper as prime minister. Gagliano filed a civil suit against the government and retired to Dunham, in Quebec's Eastern Townships, where he bought a winery. *La Presse* readers offered several sarcastic ideas for the name of his wine: *Le Puy sans Fonds* (roughly, "Bottomless Pit," although *fonds*, "bottom," also means "funds"), *Les Raisins de la Colère* ("Grapes of Wrath"), *Le Clos du Scandale* ("Scandal Vineyard"), *Cuvée Commandito* and *Pot-de-vin* (literally, "jug of wine," but also the French slang for "bribe"). The vintner of Dunham, evidently not fond of any of these suggestions, simply called it Gagliano.

There is no hard evidence that Alfonso Gagliano ever collaborated with the Sicilian Mafia, much less that he was a made member of the Bonanno family. There is a lesson to be learned, however, from the many incidents that punctuated his long political career: in Canada, and elsewhere, the Mafia seeks to broaden its influence among politicians and business-people. It may succeed or fail in such efforts, but one thing is certain: it does not give up. Often, honest but naive politicians are taken in, believing there is no risk of dirtying their hands by shaking those of mobsters. In Gagliano's opinion, Agostino Cuntrera had paid his debt to society following the murder of Paolo Violi, and was therefore a businessman like any other. So there was no sin in rendering a professional service to him—in this case, keeping his books. Such reasoning is unsound. Except in the rarest of cases, there are only two ways to leave the Mafia: by lying down in a coffin or by co-operating with police. Did Gagliano really believe Cuntrera had repented after his years in prison and quit the *onorata società*? Perhaps, but such naïveté suggests very mediocre knowledge of Mafia culture.

Inquisitive minds have only to look to Italy to understand the workings of that culture. If there ever was a country where the Mafia wields true political influence, it is the motherland. For decades it has maintained a web of "illustrious relations" with Italian politicians, bureaucrats, judges and police officers, sometimes through intermediaries and sometimes not. There, more than anywhere, the Mafia is at war with the state and siphons its resources with formidable efficiency. Like an army, it uses espionage and counter-espionage to gather intelligence on the enemy's movements. The assassinations of judges Giovanni Falcone and Paolo Borsellino provided harsh proof of its familiarity with its adversaries' habits. The beast knew where and when to strike.

It also knows where to feed. And no larder is better stocked than the public procurements market. Whether it be the Neapolitan Camorra, the Calabrian 'Ndrangheta, or the Sicilian Cosa Nostra, the Mafia in Italy has highly imaginative ways of tapping this inexhaustible source of revenue—which, moreover, offers them a royal road for the laundering of their mountains of dirty money. One government plan in particular has made their mouth water in recent decades: the building of a bridge from Italy's mainland to Sicily, across the Strait of Messina. The pharaonic project has also whetted the appetite of an Italian-Canadian: Vito Rizzuto. In 2005, by a cruel reversal of fortune, it came back to haunt him in prison.

Mariners of antiquity who crossed the Strait of Messina believed they had to steer between a rock called Scylla and a whirlpool called Charybdis—in trying to avoid one danger, they could well fall prey to a greater one. In the *Odyssey*, six of Odysseus's sailors are devoured by Scylla, whom Homer represented as a nymph who had metamorphosed into a monster. On the other side of the strait from Scylla lived Charybdis, the beautiful daughter of Poseidon and Gaia, whom Zeus changed into a sea monster that swallowed and then regurgitated vessels and sea life.

Two thousand years ago, Roman engineers came up with a plan for a bridge across the strait made up of boats lashed together, but the force of its currents soon dissuaded them from implementing that daring design. Before the Second World War, Benito Mussolini dangled a bridge project like a carrot before Sicilians, all the while brandishing a stick to repress anyone who challenged his regime. Once the war was over and Il Duce was strung up by his feet, the project became little more than an electoral pipe dream.

It would take no less a personage than Silvio Berlusconi to revive the idea. The maverick prime minister has insisted on the need to open up Sicily, made up mostly of agricultural provinces and handicapped by poor infrastructures. His government has pointed out, with good reason, that slow ferry service across the strait is a hindrance to both trade and tourism. In summer, thousands of passengers must wait on the docks, sometimes as long as ten hours, to make the short crossing. The minister of transport, Pietro Lunardi, unveiled the plans in June 2002. The structure would be the world's longest suspension bridge, with a central span 3,360 metres in length, 64 metres above the water level, and a total length of 3,690 metres. There would be four traffic lanes and two railway tracks, with rail, route and port infrastructures upgraded on both the Sicilian and Calabrian sides. The traffic forecasts were staggering: 100,000 vehicles and 200 trains would cross the bridge each day. Studies conducted in 2001 had pegged the cost of the project at €5.6 billion, more than Can$7 million at the time. That preliminary figure was later eclipsed by a €6.5 billion estimate. The government would contribute two-thirds of the cost, with the remaining third put up by Italian and European firms according to a public-private partnership model. The private-sector contractors were to recoup their investment through a share of toll revenues. The prime contractor was supposed to be named by spring 2005, with work to begin at the end of that year, for completion in 2011.

Hoping to circumvent controversy, Minister of Transport Lunardi acknowledged that it would probably be impossible to prevent Mafia involvement in such a huge project: "In southern Italy there is the Mafia, and we need to come to terms with it," he said. The bridge has yet to be built, but the minister's prediction certainly proved correct.

On February 11, 2005, Italian police arrested Giuseppe Zappia, an eighty-year-old engineer, at his luxe villa in Rome. He was charged with attempting to win the bridge construction contract on behalf of Vito Rizzuto. The Direzione Investigativa Antimafia (DIA) announced it had issued four other arrest warrants. The first targeted Rizzuto, but he was already in prison in Laval, Quebec, awaiting the decision on his extradition to the United States. The other warrants targeted three middlemen: Filippo Ranieri, sixty-eight, described as a manager of buildings in downtown Montreal; Hakim Hammoudi, forty-two, a resident of Paris, accused of having been a liaison between Zappia and Rizzuto; and Sivalingam Sivabavanandan, fifty-two, a Sri Lankan businessman living in London.

At a press conference in Rome, Colonel Paolo La Forgia announced that the group had planned to launder billions of dollars. A few months earlier, the conspirators had participated in a preliminary bid on the bridge contract through Zappia International. This front company had submitted an expression of interest to Stretto di Messina S.p.A., the public company created to oversee the project. According to La Forgia, the group had already sunk some $6.4 million into the venture. "The anti-Mafia police investigation confirms what we have been saying for a long time: the Strait of Messina bridge is a magnet for the Mafia and organized crime," commented Alfonso Pecoraro Scanio, president of Italy's green party, which opposed the bridge project on environmental grounds. "Going from drug smuggling to the bridge is only a small step for the Mafia," added Claudio Fava, a member of the European Parliament with the Democrats of the Left party.

Canadians were getting to know Vito Rizzuto, whose name had been in the headlines for months. But they could have been forgiven for not recalling the name of Giuseppe (Joseph) Zappia. It may have stirred vague recollections for those old enough to remember the 1976 Summer Olympics in Montreal and the scandalous budget overruns that crippled Quebec's provincial finances for years afterward. Zappia was born in 1925 in Marseilles to Calabrian parents and immigrated to Canada. He sweet-talked Montreal's mayor, Jean Drapeau, providing assurances that the Olympic village required to house the Games' 9,500 athletes, coaches and delegates could be built in no time and at a rock-bottom price. His sketches of the project, inspired by an advertising flyer for the Marina Baie des Anges near Nice, France, called to mind Egyptian pyramids. The mayor was delighted. He ignored the advice of municipal bureaucrats, who were concerned about the lack of discussions on how the project would be financed, and awarded the construction contract to Zappia's company, Les Terrasses Zarolega. No call for tenders was issued.

In November 1974, less than two years before the scheduled date of the Games' opening ceremonies, work had still not begun. Along with the Olympic Stadium, the Olympic Village construction project was mired in delays. Fearing disaster, in late 1975, the provincial government took over responsibility for organizing the Games from the City of Montreal. In the end, the Village's twin pyramids cost close to $100 million—three times the original estimate.

Zappia quietly left Canada. A police investigation led to him being charged on twenty-six counts of fraud, extortion and payment of secret commissions, to the detriment of the Olympic Games Organizing Committee and several contractors. An international warrant was issued for his arrest. The globe-trotting engineer was finally nabbed in Switzerland in 1985 and spent two months in prison before an SQ officer was dispatched to bring him back to Montreal. Two key witnesses died before his trial could enter its final phase. Zappia was acquitted in 1988, capping a legal saga that had lasted twelve years.

In the meantime, Zappia had acquired film rights to a play by one Karol Wojtyla, *The Jeweler's Shop*—a work that had gone totally unnoticed until its author became better known as John Paul II, the first non-Italian pope since Adrian VI in 1522 to 1523. For reasons lost to history, though, the engineer's foray into film production never bore fruit. Zappia subsequently refocused his energies on a trade with which he was slightly more familiar: construction. He did business in the Middle East, but it seemed that he had a knack for attracting trouble. The government of Abu Dhabi seized his passport—an original but effective method of forcing him to finish a project in the oil-rich emirate, from which he stood to earn an estimated one billion dollars. The engineer-turned-real-estate-developer also boasted of having built residential complexes in Saudi Arabia, Libya and Kuwait.

In 2001, Alexander Norris, a reporter for the Montreal *Gazette*, managed to track down Zappia in Rome and phoned him. Zappia told him that he had recently made a new acquaintance: Silvio Berlusconi, the

Italian press magnate and prime minister—a politician who had himself been investigated for tax evasion, money laundering and corruption. The reporter prodded him to confirm: "You know Mr. Berlusconi?"

"Mm-hmm."

"Really?" a skeptical Norris asked. "Are you good friends, or . . . ?"

"No."

"What's your relationship with him?"

"Well, I know him."

"You know him?"

"Yeah."

"How long have you known him?"

"For some time."

"Mm-hmm . . . Have you had a business relationship or is it more just friends?"

"No, no, no, no, no, no. It's nothing that way. It is a situation whereby I met him and we discuss matters together," Zappia replied, still enigmatic. "We formed a certain friendship."

The developer, it seemed, was well connected with the prime minister. Though he was unaware of it at the time, he was also well known in the offices of the DIA. The department had heeded the transport minister's warning and was convinced that gangsters were aiming to get their dirty hands all over the bridge project. They bugged Zappia's phone. On June 13, 2003, he was heard conversing with a lawyer, explaining how he dreamed of becoming the man who would finally succeed in building the world's longest suspension bridge. He would realize his dream, he said, not simply because he was a brilliant engineer, but because he had access to huge sums of money. "You know that I want to do the bridge of Messina, and if I do that bridge of Messina, I won't do it because of politicians," he said. "I'll do it because I have €5 billion."

On August 1, 2003, police listened in as he spoke with Filippo Ranieri, later to be named by the DIA as a Montreal middleman for Vito Rizzuto. "We can do this bridge," Zappia reiterated. "I'll do the bridge and you know that I can do it."

In Italian organized crime circles, plenty of mouths salivated at the potentially colossal profits in the offing. There would be enough money to satisfy hungry maws on both sides of the strait. Like Scylla and Charybdis, the Calabrian 'Ndrangheta and the Sicilian Cosa Nostra waited eagerly. Both criminal organizations had proven themselves to be masters at infiltrating the construction industry, corrupting bureaucrats, threatening competitors, terrorizing work sites, muscling in on contracts, inflating costs and pocketing the profits. That a Canadian, Vito Rizzuto, was the chief architect of this massive campaign to plunder Italian government funds and European Community subsidies spoke volumes about his reach and influence. This was power that not even the bosses of New York's Five Families had ever dreamed of possessing. In 2003, as his Rome-based proxy Giuseppe Zappia wove the threads of the scheme, Rizzuto could sit back and dream of a triumphant return to his native Sicily. The wealthy baron of Antoine-Berthelet Avenue might soon be able to flee Montreal's frigid winters—and stop worrying about the growing defections within the Bonanno family ranks. Through an intermediary, Zappia promised him the opportunity to retire peacefully to a Mediterranean climate and rounds of golf all year long.

"If everything goes well," Zappia told Ranieri, in the same conversation, "I will build the bridge and when everything is finished, the friend can return to Italy . . . On one side, there is the Mafia, on the other side is the 'Ndrangheta. We will make both of them happy and we will do the bridge."

Four days later, police picked up another overseas phone call. Ranieri was filling Zappia in on a meeting that had taken place in a Montreal restaurant. He told Zappia that Vito Rizzuto was worried about the health of Sheikh Zayed bin Sultan Al Nahyan, ruler of Abu Dhabi and the founder of the United Arab Emirates. His concern had nothing to do with some improbable friendship with the sheikh; it was financial in nature. Sheikh Zayed owed Zappia a lot of money—money that Rizzuto was counting on to invest in the bridge construction project. Vito, Ranieri told Zappia, had said, "If he dies, we will have a problem. We hope that the old man doesn't die." Zappia agreed: "Yes, we're fucked because if the son replaces him, he doesn't want to pay."

On September 19, 2003, Zappia and Ranieri were heard wondering how they might go about persuading the sheikh to pay up. Rizzuto could always dispatch a biker squad, Zappia ventured. "What about our friend? I think our friend should send someone to get this money. He should send those people on motorcycles," he said, referring to the Hells Angels. "He has to send the French people, with the bikes."

The DIA managed to intercept two brief conversations between Zappia and Rizzuto. In the first recording, Zappia says he is sure he will win the bridge contract. In the other, Rizzuto advises his agent in Rome to persuade their Arab partners to cough up further millions.

Zappia: "I'm waiting for their phone call."

Rizzuto: "They're going to give us something, but it's not enough. I think we can ask for more."

Zappia: "I agree."

Nevertheless, Zappia was worried. He feared that the authorities might somehow connect him to Rizzuto.

"We have to understand one thing," he told Ranieri one day. "I cannot be seen with him. Nobody can see me with him. You understand?"

"But he sent me," Ranieri countered.

"I can come to Montreal, but I can't see him," Zappia went on. "If they see him—if they see me with him, my reputation is over. You understand?"

"You know what you have to do, Mr. Zappia," Ranieri replied.

"Yes. I have to do the bridge of Messina," Zappia said, as if reciting a mantra.

On January 19, 2004, Ranieri had some news for Zappia that set the engineer on edge.

"Have you spoken with the friend?" Zappia asked.

"I couldn't do that because in the local paper was news about an investigation in the United States for some murders that took place fifteen years before," Ranieri answered (he had the date wrong; the three capos' massacre had taken place twenty-three years earlier).

"You've got to understand, if something happens, I'm finished," Zappia gulped.

Two days later, Ranieri called Zappia. Rizzuto had been apprehended the day before. "You know, our friend was arrested. It's because of the murders in 1981. Three people were shot to death in 1981."

"I know," Zappia replied. "I'm aware of the story."

"A crazy guy started to talk with the FBI."

"Yes, some crazy people."

Shortly thereafter, police intercepted a conversation between Zappia and an unidentified woman.

"The story is over, they arrested all of them," the woman said.

"Yes, there are twenty-seven," Zappia said. "Don't forget, he's [Vito Rizzuto's] like Saddam Hussein. When the police arrested him, that's the end of the world."

"But if he went to Italy, do you think they would have arrested him?" the woman asked.

"Yes, they would have arrested him."

"This story makes me nervous," she said.

Nine days later, on January 30, 2004, Zappia and Ranieri spoke again, trying to gauge the impact of the arrests on their bridge plan.

"What's going on?" Zappia asked.

"What they're trying to do is avoid extradition," Ranieri explained. "If they send him [to the United States], we won't see him any more."

Despite the setback, the two men did not abandon hope. On October 26, 2004, Zappia was heard telling Ranieri not to worry: he would not say anything incriminating at a meeting that he had scheduled a few days later with some Italian government officials. "I'm not so stupid as to tell them where my money comes from," he said. However, money did become cause for worry one week later: Sheikh Zayed died on November 2, 2004. Apparently, his heir was much more interested in camel racing than in paying back a debt to the Mafia or entering into a joint venture with them.

Anti-Mafia prosecutor Adriano Iasillo and DIA investigator Silvia Franzè gave a few interviews after the arrest of Zappia and the issuing of warrants against Rizzuto and his co-conspirators in February 2005. They could not hide their surprise at the scale of the Rizzuto clan's network. "His organization relies on contacts in the political realm as well as the criminal realm," Iasillo told Isabelle Richer of Radio Canada television, who had travelled to Rome to interview him. "Without Rizzuto," he continued, "it would have been impossible for a criminal organization from outside to invest in one of the biggest projects of the century. And it was here [in Italy] that this project of the century was supposed to see the light of day." Franzè said she thought Rizzuto showed considerable skill in using an old man like Zappia to place his pawns: "He [Zappia] didn't arouse suspicion because he is an eighty-year-old man and seemingly had no contact with organized crime. He has dual citizenship, Italian and Canadian. That made him the perfect intermediary for the organization."

The Italian investigators said they were surprised at Canadians' naïveté. "Canadians are again asking us what is so illegal about this investment in the Messina bridge," Iasillo sighed. "Well, if organized crime injects billions of dollars into the economy, we can say that there is an impact, no? Especially when it gets the approval of politicians."

Sivabavanandan, the Sri Lankan partner, was arrested in France, then extradited to Italy. He pleaded guilty to charges of Mafia associations and served half of a two-year term. Hammoudi, the Algerian-born associate who had once lived in Montreal, turned himself in to Italian authorities and was given a two-year suspended sentence. Ranieri remained in the city of his birth, Montreal. Zappia's trial became bogged down in legal wrangling. As for Vito Rizzuto, having to answer charges from the Italian authorities was the least of his worries. He had more immediate concerns; namely, fighting his extradition to the United States.

In July 2005, Italian judges decreed that a senior adviser to Prime Minister Berlusconi, Senator Marcello Dell'Utri, had provided "a concrete, voluntary, conscious, specific and precious contribution to the illicit goals of Cosa Nostra, both economically and politically." Dell'Utri was sentenced to nine years in prison for Mafia associations. The following year, Berlusconi was toppled by a centre-left coalition, and the plans for the Strait of Messina bridge were shelved. Berlusconi's centre-right coalition retook power after a snap election in 2008, however, and revived the project.

CHAPTER 16

OPERATION COLISÉE

GIULIANO ZACCARDELLI WAS a controversial cop. The first Italian immigrant to be appointed commissioner of the RCMP, he was also the only head of Canada's national police corps ever forced to resign. Zaccardelli was born in Prezza, a mountain village in the Abruzzo region, just after the end of the Second World War. During the final phases of the conflict, artillery and arms fire often echoed through this sparsely populated, mountainous region in Italy, between Rome and the Adriatic. From their strongholds deep in the forests, well-organized resistance fighters led successful attacks against Mussolini's Fascist troops and their German allies. The villages of Abruzzo emerged from the war battered; their inhabitants eked out a living with half the average income of residents of Northern Italy. The Zaccardellis immigrated to Canada when young Giuliano was just seven, in the mid-1950s—around the same time as Vito Rizzuto's family.

Vito and Giuliano, who were about the same age, both grew up in Saint-Léonard, in east Montreal. But they would follow diametrically opposite paths. The former became the head of his adopted country's most influential criminal organization; the latter, head of its largest police force, and one of organized crime's most formidable adversaries.

Zaccardelli's career with the RCMP ended in such a barrage of criticism that it's easy to forget that he did more than many people to expose the extent of organized criminal activities in Canada, as well as their ramifications in business and political circles.

When Zaccardelli joined the RCMP in 1970, he was one of a handful of officers with university degrees (a bachelor of commerce in business administration from Montreal's Loyola College, which would later merge with Sir George Williams University to become Concordia University). Over thirty years, Zaccardelli rose through the RCMP ranks: from recruit in Alberta to investigator in the force's Commercial Crime Branch, first in Toronto and then in Calgary; officer in charge, Immigration and Passport Branch, at Ottawa headquarters and several other increasingly senior postings before becoming deputy commissioner, Organized Crime and Operational Policy and, finally, commissioner.

"I . . . bring an insatiable appetite to succeed, to do well," Zaccardelli told *Concordia University Magazine*. His old friend Roy Berlinquette, himself a former deputy commissioner, remarked that "Zack" had "started at the bottom of the latter and proudly made his way to the top as an immigrant." He added, "He's the perfect example of integrity, no doubt about it," noting that his friend had an interesting hobby: studying the history of the Mounties. In Berlinquette's opinion, Zaccardelli was a Type A personality: nervous, highly competitive, ambitious, incapable of taking things easy. The commissioner agreed with that assessment of his character. "I accept that by most definitions I may be a bit of a dysfunctional person and a bit of a workaholic," he said. "But if that's what it takes to provide better quality public service to Canadians, I'm willing to be a little dysfunctional."

The word "dysfunctional" almost certainly would have sounded like an understatement in the poorest of taste to the ears of another immigrant, Maher Arar, who had been handed the rawest of deals by his adopted country. From his perspective, the term "iniquitous" was surely a more adequate characterization of the behaviour of Canada's top cop. Arar, who lived in Ottawa, had the misfortune of knowing a man who, like him, was an engineer and had been born in Syria, but who had also had a business relationship with an Egyptian-born Canadian labelled an associate of Osama bin Laden. After the terror attacks of September 11, 2001, it was inevitable that someone who knew someone who knew someone who knew the sworn enemy of all Western democracies should be suspect. The RCMP placed Arar under surveillance, and informed U.S. law enforcement about him. In September 2002, on his return from a vacation in Tunisia with his wife, Arar made a stopover in New York. U.S. authorities arrested him there and, despite the fact that he was a Canadian citizen, deported him to Syria, a country known to practise torture. American and Canadian intelligence agencies doubtless hoped that the Syrians' use of "coercive interrogation techniques" would force the engineer to spill secrets about al-Qaeda. He had none to give. Arar's expulsion from the United States and the conditions of his incarceration in Syria outraged Canadians. Bowing to public opinion, Ottawa repatriated him. Zaccardelli was summoned to explain the RCMP's role in the affair before a parliamentary committee. He evaded questions, got bogged down in his answers, gave contradictory testimony, lost credibility and had no choice but to tender his resignation, which Prime Minister Stephen Harper, only too happy to put an end to the saga, duly accepted.

The dethroned commissioner then had to face a further parliamentary committee to explain another thorny issue: RCMP officers alleged there had been misappropriation of the force's pension and insurance plans, and suspected senior management of turning a blind eye to widespread fraud. Zaccardelli vehemently rejected the accusations, but by then it was clear that his famous reputation for integrity was fast ebbing.

Such is the sombre side of the man's legacy. It would be a shame if its brighter facets do not prove as enduring. All too familiar with the Mafia's pernicious influence in his homeland, Giuliano Zaccardelli wanted to keep his adopted country from being similarly poisoned, and he threw himself heart and soul into that mission.

Zaccardelli was given senior responsibility for criminal investigations in Quebec just as the massive Operation Compote probe was wrapping up, with the arrests of nearly four dozen drug traffickers and money movers associated with the Rizzuto clan, stung by the RCMP's covert currency exchange. Later, after his transfer to headquarters in Ottawa, Zaccardelli studied all of the pertinent analysis reports. Their conclusions were worrisome. In 1998, CISC had once again sounded alarm bells about the Sicilian Mafia's expansion. CISC maintained that it was the most influential criminal organization in Canada, by reason of its "ties to other Sicilian clans within the country, as well as throughout the world, particularly in Venezuela, the United States and Italy" and alliances with outlaw motorcycle gangs as well as South American, Eastern European, Asian and Aboriginal gangs. "There is less violence within the Sicilian clan, in sharp contrast to groups like the outlaw motorcycle gangs," the report went on. "This shows that this criminal organization has total control over its jurisdiction and its criminal activities. It is fully mature and is able to use the accumulated wealth from proceeds of crime to invest in legitimate enterprises and to engage in corruption."

In 1999, Zaccardelli was named deputy commissioner, Organized Crime and Operational Policy; it was a newly created position. With the appointment came an invitation to Prime Minister Jean Chrétien's office. The policeman looked forward to the meeting with a Boy Scout's enthusiasm, confident that a pat on the back and assurances of the prime minister's steadfast support would be forthcoming. The encounter lasted barely longer than a handshake. Chrétien congratulated the new deputy commissioner on his appointment and, with his characteristic loose informality, asked, "Organized crime, does that exist for real?"

"I left his office flabbergasted," Zaccardelli recalled in a conversation with one of the authors of this book. "Talk about a fine way to start my new assignment."

Chrétien, it seemed, cared more about defying Quebec separatists than organized crime. His government had certainly needed a lot of persuading before it finally enacted anti-gang legislation. It was also his government that had amended the law to permit early release for non-violent offenders after one-sixth of their prison terms. The drug traffickers who had been netted thanks to Operation Compote ended up being the first prisoners to benefit from that measure. Zaccardelli, however, could count on plenty of public support for his cause, especially in Quebec, where the biker war was raging. In 1997, hundreds of ordinary citizens, fed up with living in fear of car bombings, had demonstrated outside the Hells Angels' fortified clubhouse in Saint-Nicolas, south of Quebec City. For hours, they marched back and forth in front of the grim, fenced-in blockhouse bristling with surveillance cameras, chanting slogans demanding it be shut down. The mayor of Saint-Nicolas, who wasn't known for his finesse, evicted the bikers thanks to anti-gang legislation and sent in the bulldozers. The City of Montreal also banned the Hells Angels from clubhouses on its territory. Lawyers for the bikers denounced these presumed infringements on freedom of assembly, and instituted legal proceedings.

The municipalities countered by joining a nationwide movement calling for tougher anti-gang provisions in the Criminal Code. In April 2000, the Federation of Canadian Municipalities held a conference on the topic in Montreal and invited Zaccardelli to speak. "Criminal groups are more powerful and sophisticated than ever before," he said. "They constitute a true threat to democracy. Like the criminals, who are taking advantage of market globalization, we must, now more than ever, work hand in hand. Just as they do, we must maximize the exchange of information and better target our investigations." In that regard, he added, Quebec was blazing trails: regional joint forces squads (*escouades régionales mixtes*, or ERMS), comprising officers from the RCMP, the SQ, Montreal police and other municipal forces, had recently been developed to go after the outlaw biker gangs. Anti-Mafia operations in the province, meanwhile, were now being spearheaded by the CFSEU, overseen by the RCMP.

On September 2 of that year, Zaccardelli became RCMP commissioner. A week later, he laid out his concerns before journalists at a press conference. "For the first time in this country, we are seeing signs of criminal organizations that are so sophisticated that they actually are focussing on destabilizing certain aspects of our society," he said. Right across Canada—except, notably, in Quebec—editorialists took him to task for being alarmist, and demanded that he provide evidence to bolster his assertions.

Events quickly proved that he wouldn't have to.

On September 13, veteran *Journal de Montréal* crime reporter Michel Auger had just parked his car in the lot of the newspaper building on Frontenac Street when, as he bent to retrieve his laptop from the trunk, a hired killer shot him several times in the back. The man fled in a car, which was then abandoned and set fire to a few streets away. His modus operandi strongly suggested that criminal bikers were behind the hit. As he lay on the ground, Auger kept a cool head. He reached for his cellphone and called 911. In wheezing tones, he explained what had just happened and gave precise instructions as to his whereabouts. Police and paramedics arrived quickly. Miraculously, the journalist survived and would recover almost completely from his wounds.

The attempted murder of a newspaperman, along with the killing of prison guards and the placing of explosives under police cars, certainly qualified as attempts by organized crime to "destabilize aspects of society." Hundreds of people took to the streets of Montreal to express their outrage. Amendments were made to the anti-gang legislation to make the work of prosecutors easier: from now on, they could charge an individual for associating with a criminal organization even if that person claimed not to know the names of any other members. Operation Springtime, on March 28, 2001, saw police arrest 128 Hells Angels members and associates. Maurice "Mom" Boucher, leader of the Angels' elite Nomads chapter, faced more first-degree murder charges, including for the killings of prison guards Diane Lavigne and Pierre Rondeau. He had been acquitted of those murders at an earlier trial in 1998, but this time he would be found guilty and sentenced to a lengthy prison term.

With that crippling blow struck against the bikers, police could direct their heavy artillery at Canada's other criminal organizations. Zaccardelli asked the RCMP's Montreal, Toronto and Vancouver divisions to map out a plan of attack. In Montreal, home base of the Canadian Sicilian clan, police identified the Mafia as their priority target. Following an established bureaucratic convention whereby RCMP operations in Quebec are given code names beginning with the letter *C* (the Mounties' Montreal detachment is "C" Division), this latest initiative was dubbed Project

Cicéron, after the French name of the famous Roman orator Cicero. Over the past thirty years, a dozen or so investigations had specifically targeted the Italian Mafia, but they had all come up empty: none had succeeded in incriminating the godfather, Vito Rizzuto. This time, Zaccardelli hoped the RCMP would prevail where other probes had failed.

His hopes were soon dashed. For months, a surveillance detail of about a dozen officers was assigned to watch Vito. They tailed him whenever he left his home on Antoine-Berthelet Avenue, and tried to listen in on as many of his conversations as possible. But the don was crafty. He was a man of very few words on the telephone. He delegated a great deal. If he had to give his assent, for example in settling a conflict or approving a drug shipment, he did so on the sly, far from prying electronic eyes and ears. He might hold meetings during the daytime, in the evening or at night, in all manner of locales: in restaurants, at nightclubs, on the golf course or in the street. The police had neither the time nor the technical resources to eavesdrop on every single occasion.

Undaunted, Zaccardelli succeeded in marshalling a budget for an even more extensive operation. Using intelligence gleaned from Cicéron and investigations conducted in Ontario, officers drafted a new affidavit and obtained authorization from a judge to order surveillance on dozens of mobsters and their associates. The fox was too elusive; they had no choice but to lay traps throughout the entire forest. Projet Cicéron was supplanted by Operation Colisée, named this time for the Colosseum in Rome. It eventually mobilized about a hundred officers, along with dozens of translators, analysts and civil employees, lasted four years and cost nearly $35 million—making it the most expensive investigation in RCMP history. The Mounties' law enforcement partners in the CFSEU, the SQ and Montreal police, along with other organizations such as Revenue Canada, also took part.

On September 23, 2002, a team set up a camera across from the Consenza Social Club (which would change its name three years later to the Associazione Cattolica Eraclea), the café that served as the Rizzutos' headquarters on Jarry Street in Saint-Léonard. On June 18, 2003, police installed hidden microphones inside the café, followed on January 19,

2004, by tiny cameras. That was the day before Vito Rizzuto was arrested at his home for "that thing in New York": the murder of the three Bonanno capos. The Mounties had high hopes that he would be handed over to the FBI, but that wasn't enough for them: they wanted to decapitate the organization, by amassing sufficient evidence to imprison Vito's father, Nicolò, and every other senior member of the clan.

In the space of four years, Old Nick went to "The Cos" 860 times—an average of once every two days. Now balding and rotund, but always impeccably dressed, Nicolò Rizzuto had celebrated his eightieth birthday in 2004. His name had first appeared on the public radar thirty years earlier, during Quebec's organized crime commission hearings. Despite the position of ultimate power he had held within the Mafia since then, he had never been convicted of a crime in Canada. In his younger days in Sicily, he had earned a reputation as a calm, polite man. But with advancing age had come increasing bitterness: more than once, the police heard him tell associates to respond with violence in trifling matters. He haggled over sums of money, even small amounts. And every once in a while, he had a bit too much to drink. He was arrested in the Montreal borough of Ahuntsic-Cartierville on New Year's Eve, 2005, on charges of driving while impaired: he had driven his Mercedes into a fire truck.

In view of his reputation and his "record of service," every member and associate of the Mafia treated the patriarch with the utmost deference, affectionately calling him Zio Colà ("Uncle Nick"). More than once, the hidden cameras at the Consenza captured scenes of his men kissing him on both cheeks—the sign of respect due to Sicilian "men of honour."

Paolo Renda, Nick Rizzuto's son-in-law, was recorded entering the café on 667 occasions during the police probe. Despite his deep involvement in the clan's activities, the *consigliere* was the most discreet of the four members of the "executive committee" that took over for Vito Rizzuto after his arrest in early 2004. Then in his sixties, Renda had never been convicted of any crime, save setting fire to his Boucherville barbershop in 1972, apparently to collect the insurance. He owned a company, Renda Construction, and co-owned another, the Loreto funeral home. He was by turns an arbitrator and a prefect, weighing members' grievances and sanctioning cases of misconduct: the Consenza, he joked, was "the house of problems." Up until Vito's departure, he had spent far more time in business circles than at the café.

Rocco Sollecito was seen 561 times in the Jarry Street establishment, which he had managed for many years. He had been mixed up in the Penway stock swindling affair. Sollecito was an old friend of Nicolò Rizzuto's who was often involved in settling issues with the up-and-coming generation of Mafiosi. In the mid-1980s, he had spent a few years in prison for an affair involving illegal immigration. His name appeared often in investigators' reports, and he was a frequent sight alongside Vito Rizzuto in police photo albums, including that of the wedding of Alfonso Caruana's daughter in Toronto. Like the Rizzutos and Paolo Renda, he came from Cattolica Eraclea.

Francesco Arcadi stopped by "The Cos" 616 times. This former Cotroni crony was Calabrian, but that hadn't stopped him from becoming a very active member of the Sicilian Mafia; after Vito's arrest, police had pegged Arcadi as a possible successor. He was the clan's street boss, liaising with the outlaw bikers and Montreal's street gangs. Reporting to him were two younger men, Lorenzo Giordano and his associate Francesco Del Balso.

Like Arcadi, this extremely aggressive pair of mobsters ran networks of drug traffickers, bookmakers and enforcers. They made regular reports to Arcadi at the Consenza but maintained their own headquarters at the Bar Laennec in Laval. On November 2, 2004, the RCMP installed a camera outside that establishment, located in a strip mall near the Cité de la Santé hospital complex. They set up another camera inside, on the night of February 14, 2005. Over a two-year period, Giordano entered the Bar Laennec 221 times, and Del Balso went on 541 occasions—almost every day.

Police deployed cameras and listening devices in several locations, but installing them was problematic. A man hired by the clan kept watch over the Consenza until early in the morning, seven days a week. The Mounties' technicians had a window of just a few hours in which to set up their surveillance gear. Once it was installed, problems could still crop up. Cameras and microphones regularly broke down. Camera angles had to be tweaked. Major renovations were planned in at least one location, meaning the gadgetry had to be removed, then reinstalled after work was complete. Crews had to return to the Consenza under cover of darkness no less than thirty-four times. Each installation or repair cost an average of eighty thousand dollars. The technical teams were supported by a small armada of plainclothes officers. Staying out of sight or riding in unmarked cars, police patrolled the environs of "The Cos," on the lookout for any suspicious activity near 4891 Jarry Street East, and gave the alert at the slightest sign of danger. As needed, other teams watched suspects' residences, notifying colleagues whenever they came or went.

Day after day, translators transcribed hours upon hours of electronic surveillance; analysts watched videotapes; and liaison officers exchanged information with their counterparts in Italy and the United States. When necessary, investigators tracked their targets in bars, restaurants and even the Casino de Montréal, favoured by younger Mafiosi looking to launder their money. Operation Colisée aimed to crack down on all of their criminal activities: drug imports; illegal sports betting; marijuana sales in the United States, New Brunswick and Ontario; loansharking; corruption; muscling in on public works contracts; money laundering; extortion; assault; kidnapping and murder.

During the investigation, 80 percent of the 125 people seen at the Consenza and who could be identified by officers were either in police files or had criminal records.

It was in this unsavoury café, which for decades had been the de facto headquarters of the Sicilian clan, that the organization's profits wound up. Week after week, Rizzuto family soldiers arrived there to collect money to deposit. Businessmen, Mafia victims and accomplices alike, came bearing protection money and commissions. Between February 2, 2004, and August 31, 2006, a camera recorded 192 such transactions in the backroom of the social club. In a style devoid of literary embellishments, a police analyst wrote the following account, among thousands of others: "The leaders of the organization, the recipients of this money, were present for the majority of transactions . . . On April 1, 2004, Rocco Sollecito and Nicolò Rizzuto are observed counting money in the small office at the rear of the Consenza. A few moments later, Rizzuto is seen taking this money and putting it in his right sock as well as his jacket pockets."

Men brought wads of banknotes in plastic bags or boxes. The bills were dumped onto a round table in the middle of the "office" and sorted into stacks.

"*Sette, otto . . . venticinque,*" Rizzuto counted.

"*Uno, due, tre, quattro, cinque, sei, sette,*" a visitor said. "*Otto, duecento . . .*"

"Twelve and twelve, that's twenty-four? No?" Rizzuto asked.

"Yes," the visitor replied, and resumed counting: "*Dieci, undici, dodici, tredici . . . trentaquattro,* that's thirty-four for you."

"Three thousand dollars," Rizzuto concluded.

Just before ten o'clock in the evening on May 23, 2005, Rocco Sollecito welcomed Beniamino Zappia to the backroom; he was an old friend of the family who lived in Milan. A few years later, Zappia (not to be confused with engineer Giuseppe Zappia, of the Messina bridge project) would be arrested in Italy for his role in a money laundering operation that involved high-ranking members of the Rizzuto clan. Sollecito explained to his visitor how things worked: each time a member of the organization earned any money, he had to turn over part of it to the "executive."

"Whenever they do something . . . they always bring something and we split it amongst us, all five: me, Vito, Nicolò and Paolo [Renda]," he said (neglecting to include Francesco Arcadi on the list). "Seeing that when they do something big . . . we participate."

"How do you see this; what do you think?" asked a keenly interested Zappia.

"Tito, I told you," Sollecito answered. "You have to look at it from the right side, because we are splitting it in five, and it is right that we split."

Zappia told him he understood.

Sometimes, part of the proceeds went to lieutenants like Lorenzo Giordano and Francesco Del Balso. Around two-thirty in the afternoon of April 12, 2006, Francesco Arcadi was observed with Paolo Renda separating cash into stacks for this purpose. "Arcadi takes one of the three stacks and Renda takes the other two, which he wraps in an elastic band," the police summary reads. "While this is going on, Arcadi says, as he counts: 'This is *compare* Rocco's [Sollecito's] and Lorenzo's [Giordano's].' Later, Arcadi tells Renda that today Moreno [Gallo] gave him this money and they agreed never to tell anyone else about it." (Moreno Gallo, on lifetime parole after spending several years in prison for a murder, regularly visited his cronies at the Consenza, in so doing violating the conditions of his release.)

These fortunes—the sums merited that description—were cheerfully thrown away by Lorenzo Giordano, Francesco Del Balso and the other nouveaux riches of Laval. Several of them were incorrigibly compulsive gamblers.

Giordano and Del Balso ran a sports betting website, worldsport-center.com. Gamblers made their wagers online or via a toll-free telephone line to an employee in a call centre. Each was given an account number and password allowing them to place bets. The outfit, initially located in Montreal, then in Laval, employed between thirty-four and fifty-eight agents. At first, the website was hosted on servers in Belize, until it could be transferred to the Kahnawake Mohawk Reserve, on Montreal's South Shore, once a gambling licence was secured by the Kahnawake Gaming Commission. The RCMP asked a bookmaking expert to study the operation's revenues over an eighteen-month span. In a year and a half, 1,609 gamblers had made more than 820,000 bets, enabling the clan to pocket gross profits of $26.8 million. "And that was in spite of the National Hockey League players' strike," one police spokesperson joked. The group also operated in Ottawa and Toronto.

Francesco Del Balso got rich very quickly indeed. He was the sort who liked to gamble in person, at the Casino de Montréal, instead of, say, in front of a computer monitor on his own website. He was enrolled as a lifetime member, No. 71351, of the government-run casino. It wasn't unusual for him to put down five thousand dollars in chips on the gaming tables, and he often blew tens of thousands of dollars in a single evening.

Like all high-stakes players, of course, Del Balso lost far more than he won. Between 2001 and 2003, he bet $7.6 million and won back only $2.5 million. A normal player would have sunk into depression, or worse, after losing $5.1 million. But Del Balso's priority was not winning; it was washing his dirty money. Should the taxman grow suspicious and ask him to justify his income, he could simply claim that lady luck happened to smile on him often, and offer cheques for $100,000; $150,000 and even $200,000, bearing the casino stamp, as proof.

Besides Giordano, born in 1963, and Del Balso, born in 1970, the Rizzuto clan's youth wing included another big-time habitué of the Casino de Montréal. Giuseppe Torre, who was thirty-three in 2005, variously nicknamed "Pep" and "Joe," had made his money moving mass quantities of cocaine through Montreal–Pierre Elliott Trudeau International Airport, where he had once worked. He didn't throw down gaming chips as recklessly as Del Balso, but he loved a good game of poker and also wagered impressive sums on NFL games. A typical week might see him win ten thousand dollars and lose fifteen thousand.

Torre's wife, Polisena, a former Air Canada flight attendant, was less than pleased with the amount of time he spent away from home. Police heard her complain about his habits to a girlfriend: "He's never at home," sighed Polisena, mother of their two young children. "He's an animal. I'm going to get myself a divorce lawyer for my next birthday present."

Despite those regular frustrations, there were benefits to Polisena's conjugal status. She told her friend about her $60,000 gold ring set with a diamond, a diamond-studded bracelet worth $56,000, and two other diamonds worth $12,000. At age eight, the couple's daughter had taken some fifty trips with the family. She and her younger siblings wore the latest designer fashions and were cared for by a live-in Filipino nanny who earned a pittance, three hundred dollars a week. Mrs. Torre, meanwhile, thought nothing of spending three thousand dollars on a pair of boots. Giuseppe, who was prematurely balding, spent the same sum in a bid to stay young-looking: he endured 1,050 painful hair transplant grafts.

In keeping with their jet-setting lifestyle, the couple paid five thousand dollars for second-row seats at a World Cup soccer match in

Hamburg, Germany. In a span of less than ten years, the young couple had owned some twenty status-symbol vehicles, including a Ferrari, a Land Rover, a Mercedes, an Infiniti, a Jeep Grand Cherokee, two Jeep Sport TJs, a Harley-Davidson motorcycle and a Vespa scooter. On May 29, 2006, Torre added a Hummer to his collection of toys and presented Polisena with a BMW M3. She was upset because she had wanted a Porsche 911, in her opinion a sportier ride. Unable to sulk in silence, she picked up the phone and unloaded to her friend again: "He gave me an M3. It's not what I wanted; I wanted a 911. I gave him shit! I wanted a red interior; this one's grey."

Giuseppe Torre was no better than his wife at suffering the miseries of the rich. He called his Land Rover dealership to complain: "Listen to me, Ben. Your $100,000 lemon doesn't run right." Then he explained that it was embarrassing to "have a useless Land Rover in front of a million-dollar house."

Lorenzo Giordano and his wife also lived in a home valued at more than one million dollars, in the Vimont neighbourhood of Laval. Giordano drove a Porsche Cayenne SUV and also owned a BMW Z8 Roadster worth $190,000, along with a Ferrari 550 Maranello, which he showed off every year in downtown Montreal on Formula 1 Grand Prix weekend. His wife settled for a Mercedes-Benz convertible. The couple owned a sizable piece of land in the Laurentians, north of the city, and had hundreds of thousands of dollars invested here and there, or sitting in a variety of bank accounts.

Giordano's black hair was streaked with white, which had earned him the nickname "Skunk." He certainly lacked the tiny mammal's generally peaceful disposition, however. His lapses in judgment had brought remonstrations from the *consigliere,* Paolo Renda—most notably after the violent scuffle with Iranian heroin dealer Javad Mohammed Nozarian at the Globe restaurant on Saint-Laurent Boulevard. Giordano was up to his old tricks one August evening in 2006, this time on Peel Street in downtown Montreal, outside Cavalli, another trendy Italian eatery.

Giordano was having a drink with Francesco Del Balso when they got into an argument with Charles Huneault, a Hells Angels supporter.

During the altercation, Huneault briefly grabbed Del Balso by the throat. An enraged Giordano later walked out into the street, where he spotted Huneault sitting in his Porsche not far away. Skunk pulled out a gun and fired several shots into the rear of the car as stunned bystanders watched. Police were on the scene within minutes. While officers busied themselves collecting shell casings from the street and questioning witnesses, Del Balso called his good friend Domenico Macri. "So why does this guy have the honours of grabbing my throat?" he roared, then issued contradictory orders. He instructed Macri to come and help him out, saying, "Bring your toy [handgun]," then changed his mind, saying he would settle the issue himself. "You want me to show you what the fuck I'm able to do in front of these fuckin' cops?!" he spat into his cellphone. "I'll shoot them all." Giordano was arrested and charged with possession of a weapon for a dangerous purpose.

Far more serious accusations awaited him.

Gambling breeds debts and violence as surely as night follows day. The officers assigned to Operation Colisée had a front-row seat as events attesting to the truth of that aphorism unfolded. In November 2004, they had started tracking the movements of Frank Faustini, a compulsive gambler, former Air Canada baggage handler, and sometime drug smuggler. The thirty-seven-year-old had run up a tab of $823,000 in lost wagers made via the Rizzuto clan's worldsportcenter.com gambling site. After issuing several warnings, Del Balso gave Faustini one month to settle his debt. When that deadline ran out on December 8, he called the website agent who had recruited Faustini and told him to warn the foolhardy gambler that he had "a fucking serious beating coming to him if he doesn't pay."

A week later, Faustini was summoned to the Bar Laennec. Police caught sight of him on their video screen. The view from their camera, concealed outside, was through the window of the establishment, and they could see Faustini, hands to his forehead, grimacing in pain. With him were Del Balso, Giordano and the latter's right-hand man, a thirty-six-year-old bald-headed behemoth named Mike Lapolla. The officers could also make out blood on Giordano's shirt. Faustini, severely beaten, could barely stand; his aggressors had to help him to his car. Shortly thereafter, Del Balso contacted him: "Please go get some money," he told him. Faustini promised to bring $200,000 the next day. "He [Giordano] didn't have to do that, man," he added, referring to the beating he had just received. "Now my face is fucked up. Broke my fuckin' nose, my teeth are gone . . . Now I have to get my face to the hospital."

The dispute was serious, and complicated, and settling it would take skill and time. Faustini was also in hock for a significant amount to another creditor, Richard Griffin, aged thirty-nine, an associate of Montreal's West End Gang.

Griffin had plotted with members of the Sicilian Mafia to import 1,300 kilos of cocaine from Venezuela, but the scheme had gone awry. In the fall of 2005, an initial shipment of three hundred kilos was on its way, hidden amidst barrels of motor oil in the hold of a freighter. The coke was unloaded in the port of Newark, New Jersey, where a cousin of Francesco Del Balso lived, and loaded onto a truck bound for Quebec. Griffin had protested: because of the stepped-up surveillance by U.S. customs agents after September 11, 2001, he thought the itinerary was unnecessarily risky. His partners at the Consenza brushed off his objections. In the end, the RCMP seized the drugs in a Boucherville warehouse. Griffin was furious: he'd invested $1.5 million in the purchase and transportation of the coke, and now, because of these incompetent Italians, he'd lost it all. He demanded that Faustini, whom he viewed as a Rizzuto underling, pay him the $350,000 that he owed him, and he threw all his energies into making him cough it up.

Faustini was now pinned between the proverbial rock and hard place, feeling the heat from both the Rizzuto clan and Griffin. He told both parties that a lawyer had deposited $1.2 million on his behalf in an account in the Bahamas, but that he couldn't touch the money until the investment matured. After months of wrangling and shouting matches with Del Balso, Griffin finally met with Nicolò Rizzuto at the Consenza. Both wanted to be paid first.

Griffin ordered Faustini to threaten the lawyer who had invested his money in the tax shelter. "I'm not gonna tell you to kill him. But get the money back," he said. The lawyer authorized the withdrawal of $350,000 from the Bahamian account; it was handed over to Griffin. On June 27, 2006, Del Balso telephoned him and told him to bring the money immediately. Griffin told Del Balso he would do no such thing, claiming he had an agreement with Old Nick. Del Balso didn't buy it and said he wanted the money, right away. Griffin again refused. Early in the morning of July 12, he was fatally struck by several bullets outside his home on Terrebonne Street in the Montreal neighbourhood of Notre-Dame-de-Grâce. An automatic weapon was found near his body, and a handgun turned up on the lawn of a nearby church. There were no arrests in the case.

The killing of Griffin apparently put an end to the dispute. "After July 20, 2006, surveillance revealed nothing more about Faustini's gambling debt to Del Balso and his organization," an RCMP officer later testified in court.

Frank Faustini wasn't the only one in the Rizzuto clan's orbit with a knack for getting himself into sticky situations.

Several years earlier, the Mafia had infiltrated Montreal-Trudeau Airport. A dozen customs agents, baggage handlers, employees and former employees of companies on the airport site, including Air Canada, Globe Ground North America, and Cara Operations (a food services company), were part of a network headed by Francesco Arcadi that brought large quantities of drugs into Canada.

Giuseppe Torre was one of those able to use the precious "doorway," a code word for the network of accomplices at the airport. But he had to pay the Rizzuto family kingpins a commission equivalent to 3 percent of the wholesale price of each kilo of cocaine delivered. In January 2005, in a bid to dodge the "tax" payment, Torre's associates lied to the clan about the quantity of coke that was in a shipment they were preparing to bring in by air via Haiti. They said they were expecting 120 kilos but had in fact purchased nearly twice that amount.

The RCMP uncovered the plot as part of the Colisée probe. When the plane landed, police and customs agents thoroughly searched it but turned up no contraband—even after removing wall panels inside the cabin. The drugs were already on the tarmac, inside concealed compartments in two baggage containers. One of the smugglers' inside men nervously watched the investigators and decided to pile up large mounds of snow around the containers to keep them out of sight. The worried conspirators conferred several times on their cellphones, mentioning a container number. The police were listening in. Fearing the evidence might slip through his fingers, RCMP Sergeant Mike Roussy spent a sleepless night, studying the manifests of all baggage containers that had recently been unloaded. He climbed into the vehicle of an RCMP colleague assigned to the airport beat and scoured the cargo areas, checking the numbers of each container. None of them matched the number the smugglers had mentioned. Suddenly, he spied the two containers peeking out from behind a snowbank near a loading dock. As he cleared away the snow, a broad smile spread across his face.

Shortly thereafter, the Canada Border Services Agency issued a news release announcing it had seized 218 kilos of cocaine at Montreal-Trudeau Airport. Giuseppe Torre feared his life would be in danger if the Rizzuto clan put two and two together and realized he had lied about the size of the shipment. He asked his father, Gaetano, an old hand in the Montreal mob, to intercede on his behalf with Francesco Arcadi and the other clan bosses. Gaetano Torre spun a story about his son not knowing that the amount of cocaine was almost twice as much as planned, because his associates had ordered more without telling him.

Arcadi was skeptical and asked some trusted associates to investigate. One night, Frank Faustini, his lips loosened by alcohol, let slip that he and accomplices Ray Kanho and Chadi Amja had brought drugs in without telling the "executive." Arcadi ruled that the three had to pay the clan a fine of $100,000 each. As for Torre, he was barred from earning a commission on his next cocaine delivery and warned that from then on he had to follow the rules to the letter if he wanted to keep using the "doorway."

Torre, Kanho and the rest of the gang switched strategies immediately after the seizure of the 218 kilos, and began importing their coke from Jamaica. Their couriers had no shortage of either resources or imagination when it came to moving the drugs and took to stuffing cocaine in food and drink containers destined for aircraft passengers. Accomplices then recovered them at Montreal-Trudeau Airport and handed them over to the backers. At the same time, baggage handlers intercepted suitcases that had been identified for them before they reached the carousels and held on to them for a later handover.

The smugglers also used every technique possible and imaginable to corrupt airport employees and civil servants. If the latter were women, they advised their associates to turn on the charm.

Marilyn Béliveau, who was twenty-five years old in 2004, worked at the head office of the Canada Border Services Agency on Place d'Youville in Old Montreal. She was in a position to clear containers holding drugs through customs, bypassing inspections. She had access to the agency's information systems, and could log in from her computer to track the location of any container and find out where it was being stored. A gang member with whom she had become romantically involved introduced her to others in the trafficking network, and she agreed to work with them. The sideline paid well, there was the thrill factor, and she thought it wasn't especially risky. "If it doesn't work out, I won't start crying," she said on the phone one day, unaware the line was tapped. "I have a degree, I could find work somewhere else. If it works, well, so much the better." Instead of pocketing $100,000, as she'd hoped, she lost her job and wound up in court.

Nancy Cedeno, a thirty-year-old mother of two from Laval, was also a customs agent but worked at the airport. In the summer of 2004, she met twenty-nine-year-old Omar Riahi, who had worked as a trainee customs officer. The two became friends. Riahi left Montreal for Halifax, Nova Scotia, hoping to reorient his career by becoming a military police officer. Several months later, the two met by chance as they stepped outside to take a cigarette break at Montreal-Trudeau Airport. Cedeno's marriage was on the skids; her husband was neglecting her. As a result, she was receptive to Riahi's advances. He flattered her, cheered her up, told her she was pretty. "He told me all the things I wanted to hear," she said later at her trial.

"Things that your husband wouldn't do?" her lawyer asked.

"Exactly."

By the end of the summer of 2005, Riahi had convinced Cedeno to supply him with pre-stamped customs cards; more specifically, the E311 Customs Declaration Cards that flight attendants hand out to Canada-bound passengers before landing. Travellers enter the quantity and nature of goods they are bringing in from abroad on the card, and hand them in at an initial customs control point, at the same time as they show their passports. The customs agent may then stamp the card or direct the traveller to a second control point where his bags are searched. At her trial, Cedeno testified that she had asked Riahi why he needed pre-stamped cards. "You don't need to know, baby," he said. "The less you know, the better." She told the court she thought he might be helping someone import contraband goods—like Gucci handbags, for example.

In fact, Riahi was working for Giuseppe Torre and Ray Kanho. Upon arrival at Montreal-Trudeau, their couriers simply had to show their pre-stamped E311 cards, and they knew their bags wouldn't be searched. On September 27, 2005, one mule was arrested as he boarded a plane in Haiti carrying nine kilos of drugs in his luggage. When they searched him, customs agents found one of the cards pre-stamped by Cedeno. She heard about it, and when Riahi next asked her for cards, she told him she was worried and asked him straight out if he was using them to smuggle drugs. "Come on, baby!" Riahi said. "Where are you getting this from? You know me; I'd never put you on the hook." Cedeno told the court that Riahi had seemed annoyed by her questions. She was paid a mere five thousand dollars for her services.

The network was bringing in huge amounts of money, with the lion's share going to Torre and Kanho. The former had the keys to the airport "doorway," while the latter handled the supply of cocaine. A thirty-year-old Canadian born in Lebanon, Kanho spoke English, French, Italian, Arabic and Creole. He was in tight with Montreal street gangs and had connections in Haiti, Jamaica, the Dominican Republic, Mexico and South America. In one phone conversation recorded by police, he told of how he had paid the Rizzuto clan three million dollars in "taxes" in a single year. "I make a lot of money too, but I end up blowing it," he said one day.

Kanho was in the habit of hiding the cash from his dealings under the stairs in the basement of his parents' home on Pie-IX Boulevard in Laval. He reckoned it was safe, but he hadn't counted on the cleverness of certain burglars. Worse, those burglars happened to be cops.

As Operation Colisée moved into its home stretch, investigators began worrying that some evidence, notably the proceeds of their suspects' crimes, might vanish before they had time to proceed with arrests. They had been tailing Ray Kanho and his accomplices for two years. On the night of September 14 to 15, 2006, they knew the house in Laval would be empty: Kanho's parents were holidaying in Las Vegas with his sister, his wife and their young children. The thieves could expect no surprises as they went about their work. The police had secured special authorization from a judge to commit a perfectly legal break-and-enter.

The team neutralized the home's alarm system and made their way to the basement. Under a plastic sheet beneath the stairs they found a sports bag along with a metal aircraft food container that had been stolen from Air Canada. They contained 28,794 hundred-dollar bills, neatly rolled and secured with elastic bands. The police grabbed the booty, re-armed the alarm system, purposely damaged the back door to make it look as though a real burglary had taken place, and left. At 4:41 A.M., an employee of Sentinel Alarm called Kanho, who lived close by. Kanho rushed to his parents' house, saw that the money was missing, and, to the delight of the police listening in, started making frantic phone calls. He called his wife first: "There's been a robbery at my parents'! The money's gone, they took the two million!" (In fact, there had been almost three million dollars under the stairs.) Most of the money belonged to Giuseppe Torre and Francesco Del Balso. Kanho resigned himself to calling Torre before sunrise. When he did, Torre listened, stunned.

"There was nobody home, the thieves came in and took everything," Kanho bleated. "Don't tell me this, man," a furious Torre answered, wanting to know how Kanho could have been so stupid as to leave the house unattended.

Kanho suspected Alfred, his sister's husband. He called Las Vegas again. "They knew what they were looking for," he told his sister. "They were looking for the money. That means it's someone who knew there was money here. They went downstairs and went through everything. They took all the money, but they didn't touch the gold or the Rolex in Mom's room." He asked whether Alfred had the alarm system code, and where he had been during the night.

"I'm gonna fuckin' choke the guy," he later told Torre when he arrived at Kanho's parents' house. "I'm gonna kill him!" The phone was ringing constantly. Kanho's mother theorized that perhaps his "black friends" or his "Italian friends" were responsible. "Nobody knew there was money downstairs," an infuriated Kanho retorted. Kanho's wife then called Torre, asking him to move a large sum of money that she and her husband had hidden in their bathroom. She was already considering putting her and her in-laws' houses up for sale. "It's all worth at least two million. We'll go live in an apartment," she sighed.

Kanho, armed with a handgun, set out to scour the streets of Montreal in search of his brother-in-law. Up to that point, RCMP officers had found the unfolding story quite entertaining as they listened to the wiretapped conversations. But now the tale had taken a grim turn, and it might well end with a murder. They asked Montreal police for reinforcements, and at approximately a quarter to nine in the morning, officers in a patrol car stopped Kanho's car at the corner of Dorchester Boulevard and Greene Avenue in Westmount. He was with Woodley Zéphir, age thirty, a known member of a street gang aligned with the Crips. The handgun was fully loaded. Kanho was escorted to the nearest police station, where federal agents were waiting to let him in on their secret: "It's the RCMP that has your money." The stunned trafficker stared at the business card that one officer held out to him. "The RCMP?" he repeated.

———

There was nothing incongruous about the fact that Woodley Zéphir was in Ray Kanho's car. Made up mostly of young men of Haitian origin, Montreal's street gangs were an increasingly active component of the city's underworld. They had become more prominent since the spring 2001 crackdown on the Hells Angels Nomads and the Rockers, the Angels' puppet club, and were vying for the attention of the Sicilian Mafia and their associates. The emergence of these new players, who were only loosely organized, who were extremely combative and who thought nothing of flaunting the established rules of the street, inevitably sparked tension. Some Mafiosi admired the street gangs' pugnacity and were delighted that there was now a seemingly inexhaustible supply of drugs from Haiti. Others voiced unabashedly racist sentiments to associates: they called the street gang members wild animals, ruthless and disrespectful.

Many among the younger contingent of the Mafia hung out in the same bars and nightclubs as the gangs. One such establishment was the Moomba Supperclub, a trendy night spot that was part of Centropolis, an upscale "lifestyle centre" in Laval that included restaurants and stores for all tastes. The sixty-hectare "village" was promoted as a fine place to "walk, talk, shop and dance"—in a safe and secure atmosphere. Wednesday was Latin Music Night at the Moomba, and it attracted a well-heeled young clientele in their late twenties and early thirties. Their Jaguars, Porsches and Ferraris filled the huge parking lot.

Early in the morning of Thursday, March 9, 2005, Thierry Beaubrun, a twenty-eight-year-old goateed Haitian, elbowed his way onto the Moomba's crowded dance floor, where about 250 people were gyrating to the throb of salsa music. Beaubrun's bellicose stare met that of Mike Lapolla, age thirty-six. Harsh words were exchanged, soon followed by flying fists. Then Beaubrun pulled out a handgun, shot Lapolla at point-blank range and ran out toward his car. Friends of Lapolla followed and took Beaubrun down with several bullets to the body and head. Police and ambulance technicians arrived to find both men mortally wounded. They were taken to nearby Sacré-Cœur Hospital, where they died a short time later.

Both men were known to police. Beaubrun was a member of the 67s and the Crack Down Posse (CDP), extremely aggressive gangs who claimed allegiance to the Crips, or "Blues"; their sworn enemies were the Bo-Gars and other outfits aligned with the Bloods, or "Reds" from northeast Montreal. At the time of the Moomba shooting, Beaubrun was facing armed robbery charges. The 67s had provided him with a Hummer and a Jaguar, which said a lot about his rank. This particular gang was fearless: its members sold drugs in Italian cafés, knowingly and defiantly infringing on Mafia turf. There were even rumours that they'd stolen drugs from Mafiosi, or sold them powdered soap passed off as cocaine.

"Big Mike" Lapolla had been Mafia muscle. He owned a small transport company and was a close associate of Lorenzo Giordano. Lapolla also had a prior drug conviction. Five years earlier, he had barely escaped an ambush in the offices of a construction firm in southwest Montreal. His associate Francesco Veltri, Agostino Cuntrera's brother-in-law, had not been as fast, or as lucky, and had not survived.

A member of the Sicilian clan immediately notified Francesco Arcadi that Lapolla had been murdered. It was a little after four in the morning. "Our Mike?" an incredulous Arcadi asked. That afternoon, Giordano, who had seen it all go down at the Moomba, went to the Consenza to give an account of the events to the "executive."

The shooting was on everyone's mind for several days. There was no consensus among the clan's caretaker leadership as to how to proceed. It was at times like these that Vito Rizzuto was sorely missed: Arcadi and the others lacked his faculty for conflict resolution. Arcadi thought that there was no sense playing cowboy; that they should wait and see how things played out—a strategy that surprised even the police investigators who were listening in. Rocco Sollecito's son Giuseppe, on the other hand, said they should "send a message" to the 67s to keep them away from the Italian cafés. "There will be blood," he predicted (it was in fact an accurate forewarning). He said the "blacks" were "not people you can sit down and reason with. They're not like us. They are animals."

Blue, the colour of the 67s, dominated at Beaubrun's funeral, with blue-ribboned floral arrangements and even blue-dyed water in the vases. The Lapolla family, meanwhile, urged the friends of the deceased to donate to the Montreal Children's Hospital, "as a token to Mike's unfulfilled desire to have children of his own one day." The obituary notice described him as a "man who was a loyal son, the forever baby brother and pillar to his sister, a true friend to all that he befriended," and would "be remembered for his *joie de vivre* but most of all his unrelenting desire to make everyone around him happy and safe. In his short life he had many accomplishments, whether in his business life or the sports he chose to participate in. We ask ourselves, why did he have to be at the wrong place at the wrong time and why did he have to be involved at all. But that was Mike; if danger was imminent then he had to help in taking care of the problem."

Management at Correctional Services of Canada feared the deadly duel at the Moomba might spill over into the Regional Reception Centre in Sainte-Anne-des-Plaines, present home to Vito Rizzuto. The federal detention centre also housed a number of street-gang members, who might seek to avenge the death of Beaubrun by going after the Mafia godfather. Guards moved Vito to an isolated cell for a few days, hoping the storm would blow over.

The street gangs were not the only source of danger, however. Francesco Arcadi found that out one day at the Consenza when he was visited by some disagreeable customers. One Luigi D'Amico, accompanied by one of his sons, Tiziano, had come to complain about the outcome of a job that involved smuggling marijuana into the United States, overseen by the Hells Angels chapter in Sherbrooke, Quebec. The D'Amicos claimed the Rizzuto clan owed them $900,000. The dispute would soon degenerate into violence.

Luigi D'Amico, an old Mafia hand, did his business in the Eastern Townships. He used to run a sheep, goat and chicken farm with one-time Calabrian clan chieftain Vic Cotroni, and later opened a restaurant in Granby, an hour's drive east of Montreal.

Arcadi rebuffed the D'Amicos' demand of payment and was later heard complaining that they had threatened to cut off his head. The Consenza crew then decided to do a little intimidating of their own. They chartered a helicopter and flew over the D'Amicos' houses. One of their cars was set on fire as well.

The counterpunch was not long in coming. On Halloween night in 2005, four costumed men rang the front doorbell at the north Montreal home of a close associate of Arcadi's, Nicolò Varacalli. The quartet weren't trick-or-treaters. They were armed, and they had come to take Varacalli away. His wife found one of her husband's slippers among the decorative pumpkins in front of the house and realized he'd been abducted. The kidnappers explained to the Rizzuto clan that they had nothing against Varacalli in particular, but demanded payment of the drug debt. Arcadi, whose underlings associated the D'Amicos with the "Frenchmen"—meaning, in this case, the Sherbrooke Hells Angels—was despairing and admitted he was afraid. The police microphones at "The Cos" recorded him saying, "There's no more money now. Just leftovers."

The D'Amicos videotaped their hostage and circulated the cassette. "A mistake has been made; we have to find a way to fix it," Varacalli said to the camera, addressing the Rizzuto clan leadership. "You need to talk to them [the D'Amicos]. Don't think you're untouchable. You might be surprised. Don't think they're farmers. There are lots of them and they can get you."

Soon afterwards, Luca D'Amico, Luigi's nephew, dropped off a letter at the Consenza. Apparently written by his uncle in Italian, it was addressed to Nicolò Rizzuto. Arcadi read it out loud in the backroom of the social club: "Dear Zio Nicolà, I am still against forgiving those who have done this [to] me. [We] have to reach a friendly agreement." The D'Amicos mistrusted Arcadi and asked that his boss intercede. As a gesture of good faith, they freed Varacalli. Interrogated by police, he said he had been treated well by his abductors and declined to press charges.

When old Nick procrastinated with the money, the D'Amicos' next tactic was a show of force. Nephew Luca, accompanied by Patricio D'Amico, another of Luigi's sons, and a colleague walked into the

Consenza, casting hostile glances at the customers at the counter, who included Paolo Renda and Rocco Sollecito. One of the visitors was armed. The trio departed within minutes, flashing signals as they reached the sidewalk. A motorcade of suvs and Mercedes sedans—eight vehicles in all—rolled up to the café door to pick them up, then cruised slowly out of the strip mall parking lot. Two hours later, Arcadi was heard ordering clan members to round up a few soldiers and watch out for trouble, because the "crazy guy," Patricio D'Amico, was still roaming the neighbourhood.

Soon, Arcadi wasn't leaving home without a handgun at his hip, and men were constantly guarding the interior and exterior of the Consenza. The "executive" were now escorted round-the-clock by young armed soldiers. Nicolò Rizzuto reportedly sent for a quartet of seasoned hit men from Venezuela.

Police worriedly observed all these signs that seemed to suggest there was a violent rift within the local Mafia—or rather, that it might fracture into several rival factions. Far from placating internecine tensions, as Vito Rizzuto had so often done in earlier years, Francesco Arcadi was only worsening them.

On August 11, 2005, Giovanni "Johnny" Bertolo, aged forty-six, was leaving the Metropolis gym, in the east-end Montreal neighbourhood of Rivière-des-Prairies, and about to step into a BMW SUV when he was cut down by a burst of automatic weapons fire. Bertolo had two careers; he was a representative for a painters' union as well as a loan shark. He was a good friend of both Jocelyn Dupuis, director general of QFL-Construction, the powerful construction wing of the Quebec Federation of Labour, and gangster Raynald Desjardins, Vito Rizzuto's long-time drug-trafficking partner. Bertolo had been arrested and jailed as part of a cocaine importing scheme with three accomplices, one of whom was Desjardins's brother. Released after four years, he decided to go back to dealing drugs as soon as his parole period ended. In the interim, a member of Arcadi's crew had taken over. Bertolo was warned that his old turf was now controlled by someone else, but he started dealing there regardless, believing he had protection in high places. When he ignored the warning, he was eliminated.

Bertolo's protector was convinced he had been killed on orders from Arcadi. He let his desire for vengeance ripen on the vine for a year, until a hit team murdered Arcadi's nephew Domenico Macri. A frequent sight in Rivière-des-Prairies cafés that were fronts for drug dealing, Macri had been convicted of heroin trafficking. Police theorized that whoever ordered the hit might in fact have asked the killers to go after Arcadi and that Macri was taken out by mistake.

At around three in the afternoon on August 30, 2006, Macri was riding in a Cadillac driven by Mario Iannitto in the Rivière-des-Prairies neighbourhood. As Iannitto waited at a red light at the intersection of Henri-Bourassa Boulevard and Rodolphe-Forget Boulevard, two men on a Japanese motorcycle rode up at high speed and braked sharply, pulling even with the Cadillac. The passenger, clad in black, his face hidden by a helmet and visor, jumped to the ground and unloaded his weapon at the occupants of the car. The bullets shattered the Cadillac's passenger side window, mortally wounding Macri. It was over in seconds. The killer jumped back on the rear of the bike, the driver opened up the throttle, and they were gone in a deafening roar. Though hit by gunfire as well, Iannitto managed to keep driving and made it about a kilometre farther. They were now near Arcadi's house.

The 911 call was recorded at 3:19 P.M. The two victims were transported to hospital. Iannitto had a neck injury, but it was not life-threatening. In Macri's case, however, the doctors could do little more than pronounce him dead. He was thirty-five years old. At 3:36, Francesco Del Balso's BlackBerry chimed. He was talking to Giuseppe Torre in front of a hair salon next to the Bar Laennec. The hidden police camera recorded his image as he raised the BlackBerry to his ear. The caller, an associate named Salvatore Scali, told him to be careful, and that something serious had just happened.

"Who?" Del Balso asked.

"Domenic."

"Where?"

"Near the *compare*'s (Arcadi's) house. Domenic and Mario are in the hospital."

Del Balso, who thought of Macri as a brother, hurled the BlackBerry and a chair at the bar window in a rage. Then he ran to Torre's Land Rover. The two men sped toward the scene of the murder. On the way, Del Balso called his superior, Lorenzo Giordano.

"Yeah, bro, they shot DM, man," he cried. "He's dead! He's dead in front of the *compare*'s house! What are we going to do now?"

"I want to see you in person," Giordano answered.

Torre reckoned the killers were street gang members. "But that doesn't mean anything," he told Ray Kanho. "Everybody's using those guys for hits now."

The next morning, the Consenza and the Bar Laennec were the scenes of frantic activity. The members of the Mafia braintrust, who had so dismally failed as Vito Rizzuto's successors, were upset, talking about the need for a quick counterattack, then realizing they didn't know who the target should be and changing their minds. Police noted the presence of Nicolò Rizzuto, Rocco Sollecito, Paolo Renda, Francesco Arcadi, Lorenzo Giordano, Francesco Del Balso, Moreno Gallo and Tony Mucci. The conversations were rambling.

"I really don't know what happened," Giordano said in a low voice, punctuating his admission with an Italian curse. True to his hard-case reputation, he favoured quick action to deal with the aggressors. "They got one of ours this time," he added. "We can't let this pass." He insisted that Arcadi's crew and the members of the "family" needed to mobilize, and he even mentioned a rival faction in Montreal North. "How many are they, twelve, thirteen, fifteen?" he asked.

"When the order comes to play with the band, they're gonna have the instrument in their hands but not know how to play," Sollecito pontificated, imploring Giordano and Del Balso not to act in haste. "*Compare*, we are already starting to study the situation," he added. "As far as I'm concerned, it's a big fucking problem."

"Me, I agree. Here we are, Father, Son and Holy Spirit," Arcadi declaimed, as if begging for divine intervention. "I agree that it's things that we have to reason out; things have to be measured, things have to be evaluated. But when it gets to a certain point and we are touched by some stupidities, the discussions have to be short."

If Arcadi seemed to be stumbling over his own thoughts, it was doubtless because he knew he had probably been the intended target of the killers on the motorbike. He often rode with Mario Iannitto in the Cadillac that had just become his protegé's hearse. And just moments before the hit, he had been in a car ahead of Iannitto and Macri, his brother Stefano by his side. They had beaten the red light and crossed the intersection. They'd even driven past the two hit men, he said. His brother had looked right at them.

"Can you imagine in what position I find myself? In front of the door of my house?" he said. "Domenic dead. Dead in the car . . . My brother, nephew, my daughter-in-law, my wife and everything . . . Immediately I loaded everything in the truck and headed to the airport."

Renda agreed that the situation was becoming dangerous for all of them. "See, what you gotta do now, find an island. Take your wife and leave," he told Arcadi.

"Yes, even your wife. Come on, come on, they're getting worried, *compare*, you know what I mean?" Giordano added.

"The others will be all right, *compare*," Renda said.

Arcadi didn't have to be told twice. He flew to Europe with his wife, where they spent several months, staying in Italy at first, then taking a cruise with stops in Malta, Tunisia, Spain, the Balearic Islands and the Canary Islands.

The top brass of the Montreal Mafia treated the late Domenico Macri with the deference due a "man of honour." For two days, they paid their respects to the family of the deceased at the Loreto funeral home, owned by the Renda and Rizzuto families, on Des Grandes-Prairies Boulevard. On September 5, 2006, they prayed for his soul at Marie-Auxiliatrice Church on Maurice-Duplessis Boulevard—barely two kilometres from where he had been killed. A dozen armed guards, including Charles-Édouard Battista and Giuseppe Fetta, kept watch outside. As usual, the funeral was an occasion for mob members to socialize. Police noted the presence of Francesco Cotroni Jr., son of Frank, who had died two years earlier. Not far away were Agostino Cuntrera, who had taken part in the killing of Paolo Violi in 1978, and Vito Rizzuto's two sons, Nick Jr. and Leonardo, the lawyer. Nick Sr. did not attend; and of course Francesco Arcadi was gone (word was going round among police that he was hiding out somewhere or had already fled to another country). The other habitués of the Consenza and the Bar Laennec were all there at church, with their fathers or sons—Paolo Renda, Rocco Sollecito, Lorenzo Giordano, Francesco Del Balso and Giuseppe Torre among them.

A few days after the funeral, Girolamo Del Balso, Francesco's father, expressed his sadness at seeing young people drawn into such deadly enterprises by the thirst for material gain: "It's true they have a lot of money. They don't know what to do with it, and you see what happens today. It's the price to pay for making money like that." Then, more philosophically, he wondered: "How can they live with serenity when they need $100,000 a day to survive? It's a huge problem . . ."

His son had more pragmatic preoccupations. "Today it was him [Macri]. Tomorrow, it could be me," Francesco was heard saying. He ordered two armoured vehicles from a Toronto manufacturer that he located on the Web. He told the sales rep he wanted the most secure vehicles available and that he needed them immediately; they had to be able to stop AK-47 rounds and have bombproof flooring to boot. The salesman ran off a list of what he had in stock. Del Balso chose two armoured SUVs: a Nissan Pathfinder Armada and a Toyota 4Runner. When told the cost for both would be $160,000, he said, "Doesn't matter. What matters is that I get them right away."

Now, Del Balso and his cronies never went out in the streets without a handgun tucked into their belts or shoulder holsters. A five-man squad was put together to escort bosses Nick Rizzuto, Paolo Renda and Rocco Sollecito. Hidden cameras filmed them on the eve of Macri's funeral, in a warehouse garage belonging to Del Balso on Saint-Laurent Boulevard. Charles-Édouard Battista was seen handing a machine gun to Giuseppe Fetta, then assembling another automatic weapon, then testing a silencer-equipped pistol by firing a shot into the floor. A later search by police turned up a bona fide arsenal in the garage, including a sawed-off shotgun, body armour and ammunition.

Police were on the qui-vive, fearing a bloodbath. With Francesco Arcadi having fled the country, investigators worried that other suspects might drop out of sight as well. Operation Colisée had been ongoing for the past four years. Vito Rizzuto had been extradited to the United States on August 17, two weeks before Domenico Macri's murder. Anything could happen now. It was time to strike.

On November 22, 2006, hardly any of the seven hundred police officers ordered to be ready early the next morning knew exactly why they were being asked to rise at such an ungodly hour. But orders were orders. For security reasons, only the Operation Colisée senior investigators knew what was going on. It was only when they arrived at their respective stations that the others learned that they were about to be part of the biggest roundup of Mafia members in Canadian history. They donned their bulletproof vests, secured their holsters and set out in hundreds of vehicles. Their mission: arrest ninety people in all, and search dozens of homes, stores and offices.

At precisely 6 A.M., eight unmarked police cars, followed by two vans, all with headlights off, turned from Gouin Boulevard West onto Antoine-Berthelet Avenue. The drivers switched off the ignition. Officers stepped out and quickly circled the stately homes of Nicolò Rizzuto and Paolo Renda. Investigators rang the front doorbells. Renda's wife, Maria, Nicolò Rizzuto's daughter, opened the door. Paolo Renda was already waiting on the mezzanine above. He wore work pants. One of the officers said, in a loud voice, "You are under arrest," then climbed the stairs to where he was. After Paolo had been escorted to a vehicle for the ride to the police station, Maria offered the remaining officers coffee. She offered no protest when they proceeded to search the house and the two Mercedes in the garage. They seized more than ten thousand dollars in cash, two rifles, a vintage revolver, ammunition and hundreds of photos (several of which, according to the search and seizure report, depicted "known subjects" in the company of a businessman who was just as well known).

Officers had to wait a bit longer on the doorstep of the Rizzuto mansion. They rang three times at the door flanked by tall white columns, but no one answered. Officer Tonino Bianco called the couple's number on his mobile phone. Libertina Rizzuto answered. Bianco asked her, in Italian, to let them in. Libertina slowly opened the door. Sergeant Michel Picard told her they were there to see her husband. Nicolò Rizzuto emerged from the bedroom in his underwear.

Mrs. Rizzuto, who was seventy-nine years old, suddenly became short of breath. A female officer tried to calm her down. Old Nick, three years his wife's senior, said that Libertina occasionally had anxiety attacks, and that they should give her a pill to relax her. Not wanting to take any chances, the police decided to call an ambulance. Officers then asked Nicolò to get dressed so that he could accompany them down to the station. They showed him their search and arrest warrants, and began reading him his rights, in English. "Never mind that," Rizzuto said. "A lawyer will take care of that." Unlike his wife, he seemed unperturbed by the officers' early-morning visit.

The Sicilian Mafia's éminence grise sauntered over to his huge, methodically ordered closet, where he chose a brown jacket, matching trousers and a spotless white waistcoat. Told that her mother was feeling unwell, Maria Renda rushed over from next door. The matriarch was seated on a stretcher, surrounded by ambulance workers, but defiantly refused to leave her home.

Now dressed, Nicolò Rizzuto sank into a couch on the ground floor. He had changed his mind and wanted to read the search and arrest warrants in detail, himself. As he perused the papers, the investigators began their search of his home. It would take eleven hours. Officers noted the obsessive care with which the owners had arranged every last one of their possessions. Nothing, absolutely nothing, was lying about. Clothes and shoes were neatly aligned in racks and on shelves, carefully folded and stored, as if on display in a luxury boutique. The knobs on the closet doors had been freshly painted and, in the drawers, socks were stacked according to colour. It was as if the owners were expecting a visit from inspectors. Some psychologists theorize that a chaotic arrangement of one's possessions represents life, while rigorous order symbolizes death. If there is any truth to that school of thought, then the Rizzutos' home was a crypt.

There was life on display, however, in the many family photographs adorning the walls and the Italian-style furniture. Officers' eyes were especially drawn to those showing their beloved son, Vito, in happier times. They also found three video cassettes of Nicolò and Libertina's fiftieth wedding anniversary, eleven years earlier. The guests smiling and carefree, the theme from *The Godfather* playing repeatedly in the sumptuous banquet hall of the Sheraton Montreal Centre-Ville: yes, there had been far happier times in the couple's life.

Before facing the television and newspaper cameras, Old Nick slipped into a grey overcoat and set a chestnut-brown fedora on his bald head, tilting it to just the right rakish angle. He was the picture of a 1940s Hollywood gangster. Officers put the finishing touch on that likeness: a pair of handcuffs. Then, escorting their prize catch, they stepped outside. Nicolò Rizzuto grinned broadly for the assembled photographers and video camera operators. One of the photos was seen around the world, widely published in newspapers and on websites in the United States, Germany and China, among other countries.

At RCMP regional headquarters in Westmount, Rizzuto was escorted into a gymnasium, laid out for the occasion into several cubicles for the purpose of interrogating the Mafia members and collaborators who would be arrested and brought in throughout the day. Like the other top clan leaders, Rizzuto was treated to a short film screening: the surveillance video showing him dividing up stacks of cash with Renda, Sollecito and Arcadi, then stuffing his share of the loot into his socks. After ten minutes or so, he stood and asked to be taken to his cell. "Nice work," he said to one investigator. "We'll see each other in court with my lawyer."

Francesco Arcadi, who had by then returned from his self-imposed exile in Europe, was arrested that same morning outside his country home near Hemmingford, sixty kilometres due south of Montreal, minutes from the U.S. border. He was wearing a camouflage jacket and was about to go hunting with a friend. As he saw the police vehicles racing up the narrow road leading to his luxury cottage, he lost control of his vehicle, which slid into a ditch. The hulking Arcadi's wrists were so thick that officers were unable to get their steel handcuffs around them and had to use plastic restraints. No doubt still fearing reprisals from the D'Amico gang of Sherbrooke, Arcadi had an arsenal of weaponry in the cottage.

That day, police netted seventy-three of the ninety suspects on their list, including big fish like Rocco Sollecito and Francesco Del Balso, as well as co-conspirators like Nancy Cedeno, the corrupted customs agent. Seventeen others were still at large. Marilyn Béliveau, the other customs agent involved in the Montreal-Trudeau Airport cocaine network, was in the United States. A few days later, on the advice of her lawyer, Gary Martin, she turned herself in to Canada Border Services agents at the Saint-Bernard-de-Lacolle–Champlain border crossing. It took a bit longer to reel in Lorenzo "Skunk" Giordano, who was arrested six months later in Toronto, where he was hiding out. He had dyed his hair black to hide the characteristic white streaks that had earned him his nickname, and had grown a chinstrap beard. He had kept constantly on the move, but eventually gave himself away when he made a phone call to Montreal.

Giordano and a few cronies had expected to be arrested long before the massive sweep on November 22, and had made plans to leave town by the fifteenth of the month. That was the date that the officers in charge of Operation Colisée had originally set for the arrests, but they had to postpone the raid by a week because of an unexpected constraint: there would not have been enough judges at Montreal's Palais de Justice that day, because they were in a meeting.

The authorities levelled 1,179 charges at the suspects for crimes committed between 2003 and 2006, including gangsterism, conspiracy to import drugs, drug trafficking, illegal gambling, extortion, corruption of civil servants and tax evasion. Almost all of the accused pleaded guilty or were found guilty by the courts, and were sentenced to prison terms of varying length.

Libertina Rizzuto complained to friends that her family was the victim of discrimination. Her son was in prison in the United States; now her husband and son-in-law had been arrested. It was all too much for her. "More than fifty years we've been here," she groaned, in Italian. "We've always been good to everyone. We never refused anyone's cry for help, and they put my husband and my son in prison. It is damnation."

The RCMP's chief superintendent for Quebec, Richard Guay, congratulated his officers. "Thanks to our investigators, we penetrated the heart of this criminal organization," he said. "We were able to observe the activities of members of this group and obtain evidence in places where the organization felt it was safe. We were able to expose this criminal group where they thought they were out of sight. Project Colisée has exceeded all our expectations."

"We think it is a very serious blow to Italian organized crime," added Corporal Luc Bessette.

Commissioner Giuliano Zaccardelli's RCMP commented simply that the raids were the culmination of "one of the most important police operations in the history of Canada." It was true, but hardly anyone was listening to the commissioner himself anymore, given that he was by this point deeply mired in the Maher Arar and RCMP pension-fund scandals. Three weeks later, he would hand in his resignation.

CHAPTER 17

TENTACLES

I N SEPTEMBER 2008, the leaders of the Rizzuto clan arrested nearly two years earlier pleaded guilty, and so the prosecutors' massive document summarizing the evidence gathered by Operation Colisée finally became public. At a hefty four hundred pages, it was teeming with previously unknown, and often surprising, information.

In one sample of electronic surveillance, Francesco Del Balso is heard calling a building contractor in the Quebec City region. Del Balso had heard that the contractor had been hired to lay ceramic tile in a large building under construction in the Greater Montreal Area.

"You've been doing some ceramic work in Montreal?" Del Balso asked in the same cavernous voice that he used to threaten hapless gamblers who failed to pay amounts owed to his online sports betting outfit.

"Yeah," the contractor replied.

"We'd like for you not to come here any more to do work."

"Who is this?"

"Enough already with the 'who is this,' okay!" hissed Del Balso, his tone more threatening. "Because the next time, you won't leave here, okay? You've been warned. It's over. Okay?"

It was just one example among many.

When they had installed their hidden microphones and cameras in the Consenza Social Club and the Bar Laennec, and tapped the phone lines of the Rizzuto clan's top men, the RCMP investigators expected to hear talk of drug transactions, bookmaking, loansharking and money laundering. There must have been a few raised eyebrows, however, as they began to grasp the scale of the Montreal Mafia's involvement in another traditional activity of organized crime groups. Not only were members of the Sicilian clan running a profitable extortion racket, but they were also seeking to influence businessmen who were above suspicion. This was doubtless the investigators' most worrisome discovery. It told them that the "octopus" believed it was unassailable, so much so that it could spread its tentacles beyond its usual waters: it boldly threatened people who had nothing to do with organized crime and was attempting to infiltrate their businesses.

No fewer than six hundred businesses in Saint-Léonard and the other boroughs in east-end Montreal, the vast majority of them run by Italians, paid a *pizzo* to the Montreal Mafia. During testimony given in Italy in 2010, recorded by a Télévision de Radio-Canada news crew, Sergeant Lorie McDougall of the RCMP stated that the Mafia controlled a significant portion of the construction industry in southern Quebec. He added that several building contractors had to pay their own *pizzo* as well, in the form of a commission equivalent to 5 percent of the contract value.

If Francesco Del Balso had taken an interest in ceramics, his boss Francesco Arcadi—increasingly seen as the heir apparent to the clan leadership since the arrest of Vito Rizzuto—turned out to have a penchant for coffee. He was heard telling his cronies that "the coffee problem was settled" with a particular restaurant on Saint-Laurent Boulevard, but that others had to be brought into line: they were stubbornly buying the wrong brand of ground coffee.

"We'll send a message from Jarry," Arcadi announced (meaning the Consenza, which was located at 4891 Jarry Street East).

"Yeah, I'll go see the guy; he'll get the message quick," another Mafioso, Antonio (Tony) Vanelli, agreed.

The boss told him to be clear: "You tell him you do this and that . . . And after, you tell him that you can be in his bar for twenty-four hours a day. As soon as you see a different package of coffee, you tell them I'll break down the whole place."

Clearly, the Consenza gang was promoting an Italian coffee brand. Lorenzo Giordano got involved and forced somebody named Rick to buy that brand and no other. These mobsters proffered no idle threats; they acted on them. Three goons strolled into a restaurant in South Shore Boucherville, took seats at the counter, lit cigarettes, and each ordered a coffee. After barely sipping at the brew, they called the barista over and asked to speak to the manager. The manager appeared. "Your coffee's disgusting," one of the tasters said, rolling his shoulders threateningly. "Like juice from a dirty sock. You don't feel like selling good stuff?"

"I don't choose the brand," the manager ventured. "The owner does."

"You call him. You tell him to come here right away. We have some coffee to sell him."

Reached by telephone, the owner said he wasn't going anywhere. The visitors upset their cups, trashed the restaurant and beat up the manager. RCMP officers learned of the incident as they listened in on a phone call made to the Consenza three hours later. An acquaintance of Arcadi's, apparently acting as an intermediary for the Boucherville restaurant owner, wanted to know if the Calabrian mobster knew the three men who had just wrecked his establishment, as well as the brand of coffee they were "promoting," Moka d'Oro.

"They're friends of ours," Arcadi explained, and asked that a clear message be sent to the restaurateur: he had to switch brands and buy nothing but Moka d'Oro. On its website, the coffee roaster described itself as "a leader in the coffee industry for over forty years" and advertised Moka d'Oro as *"Il Caffè dell'Amore"*—the coffee of love.

Police officers recovered the cups and cigarette butts left in the restaurant by the trio of enforcers, and took saliva samples for analysis. One DNA sample came back from the lab with a match for Leonardo Vanelli, son of Tony Vanelli. According to the prosecution's court document, the company that distributed Moka d'Oro at the time was linked to Vanelli and Nicodemo Cotroni, son of the late Frank Cotroni. The distributor was located in a building in Montreal North that belonged to Vanelli and Cotroni. Vanelli was an influential member of the Cotroni clan; years earlier, he had been convicted of murdering a drug dealer who had been operating without the Mafia's say-so.

The relevant section of the court document summarizing the evidence gathered during Operation Colisée reads like a treatise on extortion. In January 2004, Francesco Arcadi called Francesco Del Balso to a meeting at the Consenza. He told him Zio Colà (Nicolò Rizzuto) wanted him to call the owner of a small machinery company in Rivière-des-Prairies that owed six thousand dollars to a firm specialized in precision machining. Hundreds of similar disputes flared up every day in various industries, but in this case, the supplier thought he could settle the matter faster by asking his friends at the Consenza to help out, rather than entrusting the task to lawyers. Among the senior members of the clan, Del Balso was the man who normally inherited such jobs: over the years, he had perfected the art of "talking" to debtors. He picked up the phone and called the contractor in question, in east-end Montreal:

"You ordered some stuff, some precision hardware?"

"Yeah?"

"Any idea when you plan to pay the bill?"

"Who is this?"

"The guy that's going to make you eat out of a straw for six months if you don't go pay him."

"I beg your pardon?"

"You hear me? I know you have on tape, don't worry about it. Just go pay the bill, okay? And I'm not going to come and tell you again. The next time I break your head. Okay?"

"Is this a joke or what?" the contractor asked with a laugh.

"You fucking clown, don't laugh at me," Del Balso said, losing his temper. "You understand? Go pay the bill!"

Del Balso hung up the phone. Two hours later, he called back.

"So, the bill, you gonna pay?"

"I don't want anything to do with you guys," the contractor replied curtly, in a brazen, and obviously unwise, display of impatience.

A goon was then dispatched to the company to meet the owner in person. He was ordered to "go in and beat the guy," but got lost while searching for the company warehouse in the Rivière-des-Prairies industrial park. The dispute later came up in a discussion at the Consenza between Nicolò Rizzuto, Francesco Arcadi, Paolo Renda and Lorenzo Giordano. They concluded that it might be better to negotiate further: "We'll see how he'll fix it up; if he accepts it, the deal which he wants to make," Giordano was heard saying.

All manner of corrupt contractors went to the clan to force debtors to pay, or to avoid having to pay their own debts. Del Balso would take down details about his victims and then send enforcers to deliver his messages. One friend asked him for help in erasing a $148,000 debt from his line of credit. "The guy wears braces!" Del Balso said gleefully, referring to the president of the indebted company. "We're gonna send two guys; make them break his face!" Upon further investigation, the RCMP confirmed that the company president indeed wore braces on his teeth. The court document does not specify how this particular dispute was settled.

It does, however, go into substantial detail regarding the unfortunate Mafia dealings of Montreal businessman John Xanthoudakis. The founder of Norshield Financial Group, a hedge-fund company involved in a major scandal, Xanthoudakis had transferred several investors' funds into tax havens. When some of them wanted to recover their money, they ran into all sorts of difficulties. The financier made repeated promises that the funds would be accessible soon, but the investors soon grew restless and impatient. One of them was the animated film production company Cinar (which was embroiled in problems of its own, including accusations of fraudulent use of federal tax credits, and would eventually be found guilty of copyright violation for having plagiarized scripts and character designs by a creator/writer named Claude Robinson). Cinar took Norshield to court in a bid to recover approximately $120 million. Norshield went into receivership, and the investors were out $472 million: their money had vanished. A report filed in Ontario Superior Court stated there was little chance they would ever see it again.

Among the alarmed investors were members and associates of the Rizzuto clan, who had entrusted Xanthoudakis with at least five million dollars.

Just before noon on November 25, 2005, Francesco Del Balso picked up the phone. It was his friend Cosimo Chimienti, owner of Intermarché Lagoria, which operated three grocery stores in northeast Montreal. Chimienti himself claimed to have invested $300,000 with Norshield, and he wanted his money back. He gave the Rizzutos' "head bailiff," Del Balso, the phone number of Xanthoudakis's former partner Vincent Casola. Del Balso arranged for an appointment that very afternoon at a law firm at Place Ville Marie, an office building in the heart of downtown Montreal.

Del Balso took an elevator to the law offices with Lorenzo Giordano and a henchman—a hulking, iron-fisted fellow by the name of Carlos Narvaez Orellana. When they arrived, they were ushered into a conference room normally used for board meetings. Xanthoudakis explained to the trio that he would gladly refund their money if he could, but the Norshield funds were unfortunately frozen in overseas accounts. He apologized. His visitors were unmoved. A signal was given, and Orellana administered a severe beating to the financier as a satisfied Giordano and Del Balso looked on.

The three men left the law offices and got back in the elevator. Del Balso filed his report with Chimienti: "The guy was pissing blood over there," he said, adding that if Xanthoudakis hadn't got the message, he didn't know what else he could do. Then he called Casola, who was elsewhere in Place Ville Marie, and asked him to meet him in the lobby. Casola called back three minutes later.

"Don't come," he said. "We're gonna bring Xanthoudakis down to see a doctor and have him patched up. He's gonna need ten or twelve stitches. What the hell did your guy hit him with?"

"With his fist," Del Balso said drily.

"He's fucking bleeding all kinds over there on the boardroom floor. The lawyers are gonna send you a bill. Xanthoudakis can't leave the way he is. He's gonna wait until 5 P.M. to go to the hospital. For now we're putting compresses on his face," Casola explained.

"When's he gonna bring the money?" Del Balso asked.

"He told me to tell you to call him when he gets out of the hospital."

"Tell him to bring me that cheque," Del Balso insisted.

"He says he doesn't have any money left. People aren't giving him time to finish liquidating," Casola said.

Several more of the clan's associates wanted their due as well and were counting on Del Balso to get Xanthoudakis to pay up. To prove he was telling the truth about the money, Xanthoudakis invited Del Balso to come and watch him submit to a polygraph test. Del Balso went, and left the session angrier than ever. "The Greek was hooked up to a lie detector," he told Rocco Sollecito during a conversation at the Consenza. "He said he didn't steal the money and he's gonna pay eventually. I told him to go get the fucking money. I should've told him to unhook the wires otherwise I'm gonna strangle him with 'em."

Xanthoudakis pressed charges. Del Balso, Giordano and Orellana were arrested on March 8, 2006, and released on promises to appear in court to face assault charges. A week later, Del Balso was at the Consenza. Francesco Arcadi, Paolo Renda and Nick Rizzuto wanted to know where things stood with Xanthoudakis. Del Balso was hesitant now, because of the charges pending against him.

"I wanna take care of it, but it's just—"

"Yes, but not this way," Renda said, cutting him off. "I'm sorry, you have to tell me 'yes' or 'no.'"

Fearing for his safety, Xanthoudakis withdrew the charges. An investigative report by *La Presse*'s Francis Vailles revealed that the financier had previously managed investments for Vito Rizzuto's wife and son-in-law, through another firm, Mount Real, which Xanthoudakis had founded with a long-time business associate, Lino Matteo. Domenico Arcuri, son of a veteran mobster in the Sicilian faction, had also entrusted assets to Mount Real. The firm's operations were halted by Quebec's securities regulator (the Autorité des marchés financiers), and it declared bankruptcy a few months later, in December 2005. As a result, the vast majority of the 1,600 investors lost the bulk of their money—$130 million in all. Police believe, however, that the Mafiosi among them succeeded in recovering a sizable portion of their investments through intimidation.

In the fall of 2005, Del Balso and his crew employed the same brutal tactics to recover monies invested through Magdi Garas Samaan, a Rivière-des-Prairies businessman. About four hundred members of Montreal's Italian community, including a number of Mafia members, had entrusted their savings to Samaan's firm, Services Financiers Rdp. Samaan had promised them a 30 percent return in just six months on speculative investments in commodities including sugar, gold and diamonds. The promised yields, however, were not materializing.

Del Balso was out to recover $2.5 million and took the usual threatening approach. Samaan's nerves were obviously none too solid: on November 29, he tried to drown himself. "He was floating on the water," a neighbour told Del Balso, which only ramped the mobster's unease up a notch. Samaan had been supposed to pay him an initial instalment of fifty thousand dollars. On December 19, Del Balso considered forcing Samaan to go before a notary and mortgage his four-million-dollar home on the shore of the Rivière des Prairies. The next day, Samaan took a room at the Motel Florence, in South Shore Brossard. Five days later, on Christmas Day, he had not left the room. The motel owner knocked on the door. There was no answer. He called the Longueuil police. When officers arrived, they found Samaan lying on the floor dead, flasks of liquor and empty pill bottles at his side. The coroner ruled his death a suicide. Samaan hadn't left a note, but his wife said he had taken his own life because of the mounting pressure from the Mafia.

The day Samaan dropped out of sight, one of Del Balso's men had made the rounds of local hotels trying to locate him, to no avail. At that point, Del Balso began pressuring Samaan's wife—who had power of attorney—to get his hands on Samaan's properties. He succeeded: "The house is done," he told Francesco Arcadi and Paolo Renda in a conversation at the Consenza on December 22. Del Balso then asked Malts Financing, a firm based in Laval, to do the paperwork. The next day— two days before Longueuil police found his body—Malts registered a mortgage on Samaan's main residence. In early January, two other buildings owned by the financier were mortgaged, one by Malts and the other by Domenico Arcuri.

The RCMP already had Malts in its sights, believing it to be a front company for money laundering, achieved through several kinds of transactions, including mortgage loans. In 2004 and 2005, drug trafficker Giuseppe Torre had been one of its directors. His cousin Carlo Sciaraffa, who had no criminal record but was known to be connected with the Mafia, was one of the firm's three owners. Malts operated an office in Laval and specialized in property seizures, loans bearing as much as 46.9 percent interest, and large cash transactions. It had previously handled the acquisition of a luxury villa in Acapulco in the name of Torre's and Del Balso's spouses. The property had cost Can$352,000, and payment was made in cash. The three-bedroom villa was perched on a mountainside and featured a patio and pool, as well as an apartment for the housekeepers.

Malts Financing was closely connected to a pair of grocery stores, Intermarché Bellerose, in Laval, and Intermarché Saint-Michel, in Montreal North. Malts and the two grocery stores were held by the same group of shareholders. Del Balso was among the administrators of Intermarché Bellerose. Between November 2005 and August 2006, $2.1 million in cash was withdrawn from a Malts account at Scotiabank for transfer to the grocery store, which seemed to have an insatiable need for hundred-dollar banknotes. According to the RCMP, five hundred of them wound up at the Bar Laennec, but police were unable to determine the purpose of the money transfers.

Del Balso, who in his true line of business as a mob enforcer used the Bar Laennec as his headquarters, used a third store, Intermarché Lagoria, as the source of his income in tax returns. In February 2006, he asked Cosimo Chimienti, president of the chain of grocery stores, to fill out a Record of Employment form for him so that he could apply for employment insurance benefits for one year. Chimienti seemed quite amused by the request. "I'm serious," said Del Balso. "I want the forms."

Twenty minutes later, Carlo Sciaraffa, the owner of Intermarché Bellerose, called Del Balso to tell him he would be receiving his weekly paycheque a bit late, and apologized. "It's going to be next week," he said. Del Balso told him he would be bringing him six times $1,200: in other words, he was paying Intermarché cash in return for official paycheques proving that he worked for the grocery store. Three days later, Sciaraffa told him his cheque was ready, along with his T4 slip (an employee's annual income statement used for tax purposes). Del Balso then told him he would stop by to pick them up and then go see Chimienti. The dealings resulted in some friendly conversations picked up on tape:

"They [Intermarché] will pay you for one year, minimum," Sciaraffa told Del Balso. "Because it's more than a year that you have been with us."

"Four years, my friend," Del Balso corrected him.

"Oh, yeah?"

"Time flies."

"Okay, no problem."

Del Balso made a lot of money in cash, and that was a problem. A problem that he solved in part by washing the money through people who weren't involved in organized crime. His drug trafficking, illegal online gambling and extortion rackets were bringing in thousands of twenty- and hundred-dollar bills all the time. He could funnel some of them back into the licit economy by gambling at the Casino de Montréal, but he knew he couldn't spend more than ten thousand dollars cash per day there without his name being communicated to the Financial Transactions and Reports Analysis Centre of Canada, an agency that reports to the federal finance minister on suspicious transactions linked to money laundering, funding of terrorist groups and other security threats.

Del Balso busted that ten-thousand-dollar limit one night in December 2005. He was photographed by security cameras at the casino in the company of three high-rolling businessmen: George Dayan, David Bitton and Ariel Hassan, all well known in Montreal fashion and real estate circles. Del Balso passed rolls of cash to the trio, who then bought chips. Del Balso would then play some of the chips on the tables himself and give the rest to the others, who placed bets for him. Del Balso repeated the ruse several times before casino security officials approached him and informed him he was done betting for the night.

The three entrepreneurs accompanying Del Balso that night weren't just anybody. Dayan was the driving force behind the revitalization of Chabanel Street, in Montreal's north end, having enlisted the backing of the City of Montreal to redevelop the industrial area, historically home to the city's garment trade, and rebrand it as an "international fashion district." His company, Dayan Group, partnered with PSP Investments, an agency with an "arms-length" relationship to the federal government that manages the pension plans of Canadian public sector employees, to buy and renovate the medium-rise buildings on Chabanel Street west of Saint-Laurent Boulevard. Fashion designer Bitton was the president of Buffalo International, which sold clothing under the popular Buffalo Jeans brand (he would sell the company a year later to a Los Angeles–based company for an estimated $120 million). Hassan was an administrator and shareholder of Importations Rallye. Located in the Dayan Group building on Chabanel Street, it specialized in importing and selling fashion accessories such as sunglasses, socks and handbags under the Private Member label.

Flouting the thou-shalt-not-bet ban he had just been issued, Del Balso promptly flipped Dayan $1,500 in twenty-dollar bills. Dayan bought chips and split them with Hassan and Bitton. Del Balso, a roulette fiend, told them how to bet. He gave another wad of cash to Dayan, which the latter passed to Hassan. Hassan put the bills into his jacket pocket and soon went to buy several thousand-dollar chips. Later in the evening, Del Balso discreetly slipped a five-thousand-dollar chip to Bitton, who laid it on the table for him. On ten or so occasions, Del Balso also gave chips to a woman so she could place bets too.

All of those surreptitious exchanges were captured by the dozens of cameras at the casino. Each day, after reviewing their tapes, the casino's investigative team prepared a report of suspicious transactions (a *déclaration d'opérations douteuses*). The RCMP used warrants to obtain copies of the reports concerning Del Balso's group and summarized their evidence in another document introduced at trial. When reporters for *La Presse* attempted to gather the three businessmen's versions of the story for an article, they were unable to reach Bitton and Hassan, but obtained an interview with Dayan in his Chabanel Street office.

"Bitton and Hassan, they're friends who I may have gone to the casino with—absolutely, clearly. I have nothing to hide about that," he said angrily. "I don't know Del Balso. Whether he may have been at the casino, sure, that's also clear. Well . . . I know him in the sense that he's an acquaintance; we would say hello to each other . . . But this is nothing more than people chatting around a gaming table and giving each other chips."

Del Balso obviously didn't shout his Mafia associations from the rooftops, and the casino patrons he'd met that night were unaware of them. At the same time, Del Balso did nothing to hide his true nature. Members of the clan described themselves as "Italian" or members of "the family," but rarely, if ever, as members of "the Mafia." Still, it was a designation, a trademark that they sought to protect and that no one was allowed to use without authorization.

On November 22, 2005, Paolo Renda was caught on tape asking Del Balso to "talk to" a real estate agent by the name of Félix Plyas. Renda apparently had a copy of a letter, addressed to a well-known businessman, that denounced Plyas for having referred to the businessman in question by name and asserting that he was linked to the Mafia. The author of the letter also said Plyas himself had claimed to have friends in "the family."

After trying for two days, Del Balso finally reached Plyas by phone. From the sound of his voice on the police recordings, he had clearly been instructed to tone down his normally brutal manner.

"I need to see you fast; it's important," he said, without introducing himself.

"What about?" Plyas wanted to know.

"You said [businessman's name] was part connected to the Mafia. You can't do that. We don't even know him."

"Who is this?"

"We have to meet. Then you'll know who I am. I'm going to show you a letter. It says you're using our name too. We don't want that."

"I'm using your name?"

"Yeah. You said you have Italian friends in the Mafia."

"Are you part of the family?" Plyas asked.

"Yes, of course I am. What, you think I'm gonna call you for a joke?" Del Balso replied, and again asked the real estate agent if he had used "their name." Plyas said no, that wasn't the case, but that it was true he had friends in "the family."

"Did somebody authorize you to use our name?" Del Balso asked.

"Well . . . I sold two properties belonging to family members," Plyas ventured.

Del Balso then repeated his question, asking if one of those particular "family members" had consented to Plyas using the "family name." The summary of the electronic surveillance does not include Plyas's reply, stating only that the two men then agreed to meet that evening. Del Balso then called the nephews of the "family member" in question to tell them the meeting would be at a pizzeria on Décarie Boulevard. "Don't worry," he told one of them. "I won't get violent with the guy, I just wanna talk to him."

The next morning, Del Balso was at the Consenza, reporting to Renda. He told the *consigliere* that it wasn't the first time a letter had been sent to the Consenza by the same whistle-blower. Renda lost his temper: in his opinion, the "family member's" nephew should have asked the letter-writer, "Why the fuck are you writing these letters to my uncle?!"

Paolo Renda was well acquainted with another businessman, Joe Sciascia, the owner of Centre de jardin Brossard, a gardening and land-scaping supply retailer on Montreal's South Shore. Joe was the nephew of the late Gerlando "George from Canada" Sciascia. In the early 1990s, Gerlando had been planning to build a house on Antoine-Berthelet Avenue, not far from where Renda, as well as Nicolò and Vito Rizzuto, lived, when he was ordered by Immigration Canada to remain in the United States.

Joe Sciascia was involved in a business dispute with cousins of his, members of the Piazza family. His mother was the sister of Giuseppe Piazza, who lived in New York. Sciascia wanted to buy cedar shrubs and other evergreens from his cousins, but the two families were haggling over prices. During the fall of 2005, Paolo Renda intervened in the conflict. He called Nick Piazza, one of Joe's cousins, and asked him to come see him with his father, Giuseppe (the latter, as it happened, was due to travel to Montreal soon for a wedding). Renda suggested that they all meet at the Loreto funeral home, which he owned, then contacted Sciascia to set up the "peace talks" between the two families.

A month later, Paolo Renda was heard asking one of Giuseppe Piazza's sons whether the dispute over the shrubs had been settled. Piazza said yes, it had, except for the evergreens: half of them couldn't be sold. "We're here to settle this business," Renda told him. "But tell your father not to open his mouth too much. I don't like the lack of respect. This problem has to be fixed today." The following week, Nick Piazza informed Renda that Joe Sciascia had been to see him, and everything was settled. Sciascia later called Renda himself, telling him he had sent a gift to his house as a token of thanks for his mediation efforts.

"You people, Piazzas and Sciascias, you should try to get along," Renda advised Sciascia. "You're from the same family. You can keep your distance when it comes to business, but you have to keep the family ties. You should tell your parents to do the same and make peace, even with the family [the Piazzas] that's in the States."

Members of the Italian community were not the only beneficiaries of the Rizzuto clan's services. Six months before his arrest, Vito Rizzuto had taken pains to help one Terry Pomerantz, president and CEO of TRAMS Property Management, recover his stolen SUV, in which he had left a briefcase with valuable contents. Pomerantz was a high-profile Montreal real estate developer. He had helped build the Tropiques Nord condominium complex, next to the iconic Habitat '67 building in the Cité du Havre waterfront district, and a twelve-storey building near the

Hippodrome de Montréal, formerly the Blue Bonnets Raceway. He had also partnered with Antonio (Tony) Magi, another Montreal business-man, for the 1 Avenue du Port project, which involved the residential repurposing of a huge cold-storage facility just east of Old Montreal.

In the spring of 2003, Pomerantz bought a pearl-white Cadillac Escalade suv from John Scotti Automotive, a deluxe car dealership in Saint-Léonard. On May 28, he parked the vehicle in front of Il Grappa restaurant in Dorval. Upon leaving the restaurant, around ten o'clock that evening, he found that the Cadillac had vanished, and went to the nearest police sta-tion to report it stolen. He apparently didn't have much faith in the ability of Montreal's finest to recover his vehicle: at about twenty to one in the morning, he filed a similar report, this time to Vito Rizzuto.

"Listen, somebody's stolen my Escalade; I just bought it from Scotti," he said. "Can you help me get it back? There's a briefcase inside, and it's very important that I get it back."

"Your truck, did it have a boomerang [GPS locator] on it?" Vito asked.

"Yeah, but I hadn't activated it yet."

"All right, I'll see what I can do."

Twenty minutes later, Vito called his lieutenant, Francesco Arcadi, and told him that one of his "Jewish friends" had had his brand-new white Cadillac suv stolen in the city's west end. He mentioned the valu-able briefcase and asked Arcadi to try to find the vehicle, suggesting that he enlist the "young ones" in his crew. At 1:27 A.M., Arcadi contacted one of those young ones: Francesco Del Balso. He said he already knew about the theft.

Del Balso started searching. It wasn't long before he hit pay dirt. Shortly before noon, he got word from André Laporte, a used car dealer, that the thief was prepared to sell him the Cadillac for $3,500. Del Balso told him to proceed. Fifteen minutes later, Vito informed Tony Magi, Pomerantz's business partner, that the suv had been found, but that he didn't yet know where it had been left.

Another series of phone calls ensued. Del Balso learned that the Cadillac had been dropped off at the corner of Saint-Jacques and Montfort Streets, near the Montréal Planetarium, and relayed the information to

Vito through a third individual. Pomerantz got his luxury suv back but not the cryptic briefcase. Magi told Vito, who told Del Balso that the brief-case had to be located at all costs. Del Balso called Laporte.

"The briefcase isn't there," he said.

"Another guy has it," Laporte told him. "I'll have it tomorrow."

"Make sure you do. The Tall Guy [Vito] is freaking out," Del Balso said.

Finally, on June 1, Vito called Pomerantz and told him he would be leaving the briefcase for him at Il Grappa. Pomerantz thanked him, reiter-ating to the godfather that the briefcase was very important indeed. The summary of the electronic surveillance does not specify what made its contents so valuable. It was curious, to say the least, that a businessman should go through the head of the Mafia to recover a stolen vehicle. When reporters asked about the matter, Pomerantz refused to comment.

Three months later, Operation Colisée investigators heard the name John Scotti again. On September 24, Francesco Del Balso and Carmelo Cannistraro, who managed Del Balso's bookmaking network, gave a blue-grey Ferrari 550 Maranello to Lorenzo Giordano as a gift. Giordano took his new toy out for a spin that very evening, although he had yet to file the registration papers under his name. He stopped at a bar, downed a bottle of grappa, then got behind the wheel again and headed along Highway 440 in Laval. As he took the exit for the Des Laurentides Boulevard, he failed to notice a small car that had stopped on the shoul-der. His Ferrari collided violently with the second car, and Giordano left the scene without leaving a note. There was considerable damage.

The next morning, barely sobered up, Giordano called a trusted asso-ciate, Mike Lapolla (who would be shot dead three years later inside the Moomba Supperclub). "My wife is gonna kill me," Giordano told him sheepishly. "Can you help me out?" Lapolla told him to relax; if there was any problem, he was prepared to take the fall and say he was respon-sible for the accident.

Del Balso suggested that Giordano take the Ferrari in to John Scotti, whom he described as "a master at disguising cars." Giordano was afraid he'd be picked up if he drove the car himself. Del Balso called Scotti, told him what was going on and asked if he could repair his friend's Ferrari.

Scotti warned him that it would be best if nobody knew about the repair job, and that they should bring the car in at night.

The owner of the small car damaged at the highway intersection had called 911 after the accident. An SQ officer examined the scene and collected parts, including a bumper fragment, which he determined came from a Ferrari. He later visited Ferrari Québec, where an employee provided the details he was missing: the bumper was from a blue-grey Ferrari Maranello, and an identical model had been delivered to a leasing company the previous week.

The owner of the leasing company refused to co-operate with investigators. The SQ officer went back to Ferrari Québec and found out the number of the licence plate previously issued for the Ferrari, which in turn allowed him to trace the vehicle identification number and the name of the former owner, a numbered company belonging to Richard Krolik, another of Giordano and Del Balso's partners in the Rizzuto clan's bookmaking rackets. The officer went to the numbered company's head office, where he was received by Carmelo Cannistraro, who said he had no information about the Ferrari.

Del Balso happened to arrive a few moments later. Lying through his teeth as well, he told the investigating officer that he knew nothing about the accident but added that he would "fix things." He advised Cannistraro to call a lawyer. The next morning, a lawyer showed up at the police station—with Mike Lapolla.

Lapolla made good on his promise to Giordano. He gave a statement taking responsibility for the hit-and-run, saying he had been at the wheel of the Ferrari on the night of the accident. Intrigued, the SQ officer asked a few questions. It quickly became clear that Lapolla knew no details of the accident—not even what time it had occurred. Regardless, Lapolla was ordered to pay a fine and earned nine demerit points on his driving record.

Reached at his office by *La Presse*, John Scotti claimed to know nothing about the matter and categorically denied having ever spoken to Francesco Del Balso or his friends. "I don't know these people," he said. "I've never spoken to them."

———

Members of the Rizzuto clan also had connections to Frank Catania, another businessman above suspicion, which can be described only as curious. He ran Construction Frank Catania et Associés, one of the biggest building contractor firms in the Montreal area. Year in year out, following above-board tendering processes, the company was awarded public works contracts worth several million dollars from the City of Montreal and several South Shore municipalities.

That Frank Catania should be seen at the Consenza café with Nick Rizzuto was cause for surprise. After viewing one particular sequence from their hidden camera videos, RCMP investigators noted the following: "At approximately 2:02 P.M. on June 15, 2004, Nicolò Rizzuto is seen entering the middle room at the Consenza. He counts a stack of money, lifts his pant leg and places the stack in one of his socks. Rizzuto does this in the presence of Francesco Catania, seated at the table having a conversation on his cellular phone. A few minutes later, Catania and Rizzuto leave."

On November 24 of the following year, Paolo Renda called Pasquale Sciascia. Before dealing with the topic at hand—how to settle the dispute between Pasquale's son Joe, the Brossard tree-nursery man, and the Piazza family of New York—Pasquale asked Renda if he wanted to contribute to a gift to be bought for Frank Catania. Renda answered yes, and added that not only he but all of the Consenza brain trust would be chipping in: Rocco Sollecito, Francesco Arcadi, Nick Rizzuto and his son, Vito, despite the fact that the latter was in prison waiting for word on whether he would be extradited to the United States.

Paolo Catania, who had since taken over management of the construction company from his father, Frank, explained to reporters when asked that the gift in question was given on the occasion of his father's retirement. A party was held at the Hotel Omni in downtown Montreal, attended by at least 250 people, including "a large number of friends, *paesani* from the same village as my father," he said, adding that none of the Mafia leaders had been among the guests.

With the exception of the Calabrian Francesco Arcadi, all of these men—Renda, Sollecito, the Rizzutos and Catania—were natives of Cattolica Eraclea.

The Consenza was a meeting place for immigrants to Canada who came from that Sicilian town, just as the Associazione Siciliana di Montreal had been for mobster Agostino Cuntrera and MP Alfonso Gagliano, natives of nearby Siculiana. At any rate, Frank Catania seemed to find nothing morally suspect in sitting down in a private room with a leader of the Mafia, or in receiving a retirement present from his clan.

Catania was engaged in no criminal activity, unlike some others, who were simultaneously public works contractors and drug traffickers. They included Nello Di Rienzo, an equal shareholder with Tony Tallarita in the company Pavage Tallarita Asphalte, a start-up company based in Saint-Léonard that successfully won a number of public paving contracts. The two partners also ran Construction Rockburn, which had offices in the same building, on Du Creusot Street.

Following Operation Colisée, Di Rienzo and Tallarita were described in court as the bosses of a cell of the Rizzuto clan specializing in mass marijuana exports to the United States. The evidence stated that their crew regularly sent amounts of anywhere between eleven and twenty-seven kilograms of marijuana to Florida and Maryland. They planned to ship a hundred kilos a month, bringing in U.S.$8.2 million per year. The drugs were moved through the Akwesasne Mohawk reserve, which straddles the Quebec, Ontario and New York State borders.

Following negotiations with lawyers for several accused, the Crown agreed to withdraw charges against Tallarita. Faring less well was Nello Di Rienzo, who had taken over the drug smuggling racket previously managed by his brother Giovanni, extradited to the United States for having helped Colombian traffickers launder more than $100 million in drug money in the early 2000s. Nello pleaded guilty to charges of gangsterism and conspiracy to traffic marijuana, and received a three-year prison sentence. In June 2005, police had found a hydroponic grow-op in a commercial building adjacent to the former offices of Pavage Tallarita Asphalte, on J.-B.-Martineau Street in Saint-Léonard.

Before going into business with Tallarita in the early 2000s, Di Rienzo had co-founded Construction Ulisse, a building contractor. He testified at his bail hearing that Ulisse's sales had jumped from $80,000 to $2.5 million within a few years. He also admitted having done work at the home of Francesco Del Balso. Di Rienzo's wife, a hair stylist who drove a Porsche, said she was prepared to post $100,000 bail for her husband. If need be, she said, she would borrow part of the sum from her father, Nicola Speranza. Speranza was one of the owners of the Bar Laennec, the main hangout for the "young ones" in the Rizzuto clan. That wasn't necessary: the judge refused bail for Di Rienzo.

The criminal charges didn't stop Pavage Tallarita Asphalte from successfully bidding on major infrastructure contracts from the City of Montreal and neighbouring municipalities. The biggest of these contracts were awarded as part of a major road improvements program in 2008. The firm also did work in other municipalities on and around the Island of Montreal, including Westmount, Terrebonne, Longueuil, Town of Mount Royal, La Prairie and Salaberry-de-Valleyfield. In Salaberry-de-Valleyfield, the contract was for paving three streets and the parking lot of the local police station.

The director of public works for the City of Montreal, Robert Marcil, was in charge of all road construction projects. He declared in a December 2008 interview that there was no requirement in the Quebec Cities and Towns Act for municipalities to screen companies bidding on public contracts: "Whether owners have a criminal background or not—these are not aspects that we check," he said. "We aren't required to check, and we probably can't." Marcil was forced to resign six months later when it emerged that he had taken a trip to Italy with the owner of one of several firms that, according to the city's auditor general, snapped up the lion's share of public works contracts year after year.

If a senior bureaucrat at Montreal's city hall didn't seem particularly worried about Mafia infiltration of the licit economy, specifically the construction industry, senior police officials were openly concerned. When he was appointed RCMP commissioner in 2000, Giuliano Zaccardelli had spoken about the risk of organized crime groups "destabilizing certain aspects of . . . society," and uttered the taboo word "corruption." In the wake of Operation Colisée, investigative journalists brought to light several cases of collusion and undue influence. These involved, notably, municipal contracts and QFL-Construction, the construction wing of Quebec's largest trade union. Those revelations set off a new round of police investigations.

In 2009, SQ Director General Richard Deschesnes said that as far as he could remember, he had never seen so many simultaneous investigations into allegations of corruption in Montreal. The SQ had already launched four. A fifth, then a sixth, followed. One of them was probing attempted extortion and corruption by Nicolò Rizzuto Jr., related to a $10.6 million contract to restore the roof of Montreal City Hall. The successful tenderer, Paul Sauvé, alleged that Nick Jr. had asked him for forty thousand dollars, an amount destined, according to Rizzuto, for two city councillors elected under the banner Union Montréal, the party of Mayor Gérald Tremblay. Sauvé's understanding was that, in return for the bribe, he would receive assurances that his masonry company, L.M. Sauvé Construction, could continue to work on the site and be paid by the city every month, per the contract, despite the fact that L.M. Sauvé was under bankruptcy protection.

Sauvé claimed that he had refused to pay and that, as a result, no elected officials had been bribed. The two city councillors said they had never been mixed up in the incident. Sauvé had met Nicolò Rizzuto Jr. on several occasions in the company of other building contractors. Two of them are mentioned in the Operation Colisée investigative report: the electronic surveillance summary shows that they dealt directly with Vito Rizzuto when they had "problems."

Sauvé had gone to the other contractors because, although his firm had been awarded the City Hall roof restoration contract, a variety of obstacles was keeping his company from starting work. "Everyone was in cahoots to keep me from getting up and running on the work site," he said. At that point, he decided to ask another contractor to join him. He said he knew that particular company had all sorts of connections, in the construction industry, with politicians and with organized crime.

The second contractor agreed to help, provided that Sauvé get rid of one subcontractor and hire another. "Lo and behold, everything started running smoothly," Sauvé said. "I was able to start work. I said to myself, 'Damn, these guys are powerful.' I couldn't believe it. But at the same time, I was thinking: 'You know what? There's going to be a price to pay. Wake up; you know you're going to get shaken down.' I rationalized my decision by saying that's the way things work in construction. I convinced myself that it was okay to make a deal with the devil.'"

Mayor Tremblay's office filed a complaint with the Quebec Press Council against *La Presse,* which had reported on the new police investigation and quoted Paul Sauvé. The mayor's office stated that the report contained nothing more than a mishmash of unproven insinuations and allegations (in the end, the complaint was dismissed). The mayor did admit, however, that there was "a problem." "There's a problem in Montreal, there's a problem in Quebec . . . There's corruption in the construction industry. It is a fact," he said.

Around the same time, François Beaudry, a retired civil servant who had worked for the Quebec Ministry of Transport, told a crew from the investigative journalism program *Enquête,* broadcast on Télévision de Radio-Canada, that the Italian Mafia played an "arbiter role" in the distribution of major road infrastructure contracts in the province. Beaudry claimed that a select club of contractors shared a major portion of the ministry's contracts. Outwardly, it appeared the firms belonging to the club, known as the "Fabulous Fourteen," were awarded the contracts because they were the lowest bidders, but in fact they had agreements to rig bids at prices far higher than the true costs, and made it clear to competitors outside their clique that they would face serious problems if they dared submit bids lower than theirs (i.e., at market rates). "The Mafia's in control," Beaudry said. "The Italian Montreal Mafia." Police theorized that contractors who wanted to be in the club had to pay a commission to the Rizzuto clan. If the information was correct, they were at once victims of extortion and complicit in a system of collusion. Contractors who were not among the Fabulous Fourteen said on camera that they had indeed received threats when they had tried to submit bids.

This Mafia system may well explain why road work seems to cost more in Quebec than elsewhere in the country. A comparative study conducted by Canada's Ministry of Transport found that in 2008, it cost 37 percent more to lay a kilometre of roadway in Quebec than in the rest of Canada; the cost was 46 percent higher in urban areas and 26 percent higher in rural regions (the Quebec government has challenged these figures). Billions of dollars are at stake. In 2010, the Quebec Ministry of Transport alone was slated to award 1,800 contracts worth a total of between $2 billion and $2.5 billion.

While still in the employ of the government, Beaudry had developed contacts with a contractor who kept him regularly informed of the schemes used by the Fabulous Fourteen to circumvent sealed-bid systems, not only for Ministry of Transport contracts, but also for municipal public works. In 2003, that informer had told him in advance which companies would submit the lowest bids for ten road improvement contracts in Laval, the island suburb north of Montreal. In eight of those ten cases, his predictions proved correct.

Journalists Alain Gravel and Marie-Maude Denis of Télévision de Radio-Canada also uncovered the disturbing relations of some key senior directors of QFL-Construction, which plays a front-line role in the hiring of workers for construction sites throughout the province. Its director general, Jocelyn Dupuis, had friends in organized crime, specifically Normand Marvin "Casper" Ouimet, a full-patch member of the Hells Angels; Giovanni "Johnny" Bertolo, the painters' union representative and drug trafficker murdered in 2005; and Raynald Desjardins, who had long been one of Vito Rizzuto's right-hand men and, during that time, was easily the highest-profile French-speaking Quebecer in the inner circle of the Montreal Mafia. Dupuis once tried, but failed, to secure funding from the Quebec Federation of Labour's (QFL's) investment fund (Fonds de solidarité FTQ) for a soil-decontamination company run by Desjardins. According to Télévision de Radio-Canada, after leaving QFL-Construction, Dupuis went to work for that company.

Desjardins was out on parole by then, having done time from 1993 to 2004 for his role in a plot to import 740 kilos of cocaine in association with the Quebec City Hells Angels. When interviewed, he denied he was a business partner of his "good friend" Jocelyn Dupuis but said he hoped to become one. He added that he had turned his life around and begun a career in real estate and construction after his release from prison.

Like many other drug traffickers of his calibre, Raynald Desjardins was a multi-millionaire. He had started his own construction business. He headed the companies Desjardins & Cie, Desjardins & Company, and Investissements Lasister et Kane, which held stakes in Samara Group, a real estate developer active in east-end Montreal. Among other transactions, it had purchased plots of land from the City of Montreal for a fraction of their market value.

"For the past five years, all the money's been in construction," Desjardins told the newspaper. "I started out with small jobs, rebuilding damaged commercial and industrial buildings. Now I'm buying up land and hiring subcontractors to do the building." He added that Jocelyn Dupuis had guided him through the intricacies of the construction industry: "He gave me advice on how things work. He told me how to go about getting work permits and cards; he introduced me to the APCHQ [the provincial association of residential builders]. That's normal; he was a QFL boss, a union man, and it's also in those guys' interest for things to go smoothly in construction. He became a personal friend. We took vacations together with our wives on the Lower North Shore. He'll still be my friend, no matter what."

Desjardins acknowledged that on two occasions—at a party organized by the QFL and while at a restaurant—he had met another QFL-Construction executive, Jean Lavallée. At the height of his powers in mobland, when he was a player at the highest level of the Montreal Mafia's international narcotrafficking networks, Vito's right-hand man had been very rich indeed. He had made huge stock-exchange and real-estate investments. In court testimony, he once said he was the representative of Amusement Deluxe, a company based in Saint-Léonard that distributed pinball machines, coin-operated video games and billiard tables to taverns, bars and convenience stores. The police believed

Amusement Deluxe to be a front company that chiefly served to disguise Desjardins's ill-gotten gains.

It wasn't the first time that QFL-affiliated construction unions had been mixed up with underworld figures. Many Quebecers remembered André "Dédé" Desjardins (no relation to Raynald), the former director general of the Quebec Building Trades Council and vice-president of the QFL. He was killed by a professional hit man on April 27, 2000, after having breakfast at Shawn's restaurant in Saint-Léonard. As he left the restaurant and headed for his SUV, he was cut down by rounds from a silencer-equipped semi-automatic rifle. The weapon was found next to his body. The day before, he had been seen having lunch with Maurice "Mom" Boucher.

For most of his adult life, Desjardins, Quebec's "King of Construction," had also been closely linked to the Italian Mafia and their cronies.

In 1974, he had been charged with incitement to violence after the clash between members of the QFL and those of Quebec's other major labour federation, the Confederation of National Trade Unions (known by its French abbreviation, CSN), at the mammoth LG-2 hydro dam construction site in James Bay. The related vandalism caused thirty million dollars in damages. A commission of inquiry into the construction industry was set up, headed by Quebec Provincial Court Justice Robert Cliche. Desjardins was forced to resign his union position when the commission established proof of his close ties to organized crime figures, including an associate of then Mafia chieftain Vic Cotroni; the Building Trades Council was put under trusteeship.

Even as he pursued criminal activities, including loansharking, Desjardins succeeded in maintaining a degree of influence with construction unions. In 1983, the U.S. government requested his extradition to Florida for allegedly trafficking in Quaaludes, the prescription medication popular as a recreational drug in the 1970s and 1980s. One of the orchestrators of that ring was William Obront, a former money man in the Cotroni clan who, some years earlier, had been mixed up in the Expo 67 tainted meat scandal. The Canadian government did not follow up on the extradition request.

———

In 2006, Operation Colisée blew huge holes in the Mafia's new power structure. The investigations by journalists and police forces in its wake stirred up plenty of old ghosts for Quebecers who remembered the Quebec Police Commission hearings into organized crime and the Cliche Commission of the 1970s. SQ director general Richard Deschesnes said he was so concerned by organized crime groups' infiltration of the licit economy that he requested extra funding from the government of Quebec to create a special unit to look into collusion and corruption. Rather than bow to mounting public pressure to institute a new commission of inquiry, the provincial government under Premier Jean Charest accepted Deschesnes's request, and the *Escouade Marteau* ("Hammer Squad") was set up in June 2009.

Tax inspectors also redoubled their efforts, going after the company BT Céramique, among others. Located in a commercial building on Henri-Bourassa Boulevard East, valued at $1.5 million by the City of Montreal and belonging to a company controlled by Vito Rizzuto and Paolo Renda, the company specialized in the sale and installation of ceramic tile. It had been awarded several major public works contracts and had done work in a federal Justice Ministry building, at the U.S. Embassy in Ottawa, and at the Casino de Montréal. BT Céramique belonged to businessman Francesco Bruno and two members of his family.

The tax investigation stemmed from evidence gathered during Operation Colisée. In court documents, the Canada Revenue Agency alleged that BT Céramique received false invoices so as to avoid paying hundreds of thousands of dollars in taxes. The documents also stated that Bruno and his partners had received advice from and benefited from lenient audits by at least two Canada Revenue Agency auditors. Bruno and the tax agency employees controlled secret Bahamian and Swiss accounts, through which more than $1.7 million had transited in less than two years.

The Swiss account had been opened following the arrest of Quebec financier Martin Tremblay, with whom the three men did business in the

Bahamas. When Canada's minister of revenue, Jean-Pierre Blackburn, disclosed details of the matter at a press conference, Tremblay was already in jail in the United States on money laundering charges. During their probe into BT Céramique's fraudulent dealings, Canada Revenue Agency investigators also focused their attention on three large public works contractors owned by one of the most prominent construction magnates in Quebec, Antonio (Tony) Accurso. The Canada Revenue Agency alleged that Accurso paid $4.5 million to two shell companies controlled by Francesco Bruno in return for false invoices. Accurso's three companies used the bogus bills to fraudulently reduce their revenues, the tax collections agency said in a press release.

In the spring of 2010, Francesco Bruno was charged with committing criminal acts in helping these companies evade tax payments to the tune of several hundred thousand dollars. As of the writing of this book, Accurso himself had not been charged with any crime. The Canada Revenue Agency fired the two auditors who had conspired with Bruno, and took them to court.

The investigation by the Canada Revenue Agency, assisted by the RCMP, opened up a veritable Pandora's box that hinted at a massive network of tax fraud with any number of ramifications. Search warrants were issued and executed. One, during the summer of 2010, targeted the LaSalle offices of a consulting firm specialized in tax-credit applications, Groupe Conseil Delvex. The firm belonged to Marcello Furgiuele, brother of Adriano Furgiuele, an audit team leader in the Canada Revenue Agency's Tax Services Office.

Adriano Furgiuele had been relieved of his duties a year earlier. The Agency suspected him of having helped falsify a tax audit on behalf of BT Céramique. The Furgiuele brothers were cousins of BT Céramique's owner, Francesco Bruno.

Groupe Conseil Delvex had helped three of Tony Accurso's companies—Construction Louisbourg ltée, Simard-Beaudry Construction and Hyprescon—secure sizable tax credits for research-and-development expenses. According to the search warrants, however, in many instances the expenses were fake. An email message intercepted by the RCMP, sent to Marco Accurso, Tony Accurso's son, by Delvex owner Marcello Furgiuele, read: "I have those [development] costs and we modified them by boosting the hours to include more time for the conception phase." That was just one example. Another email message, written by Lisa Accurso, Tony Accurso's daughter, urged Furgiuele to request tax credits for nonexistent R&D work.

The RCMP investigation focused on other Canada Revenue Agency employees, including Antonio Girardi, another team leader, and Americo Comparelli, a financial reviewer with the Agency's R&D tax incentive program. A search warrant alleged that Francesco Bruno, Antonio Girardi, Americo Comparelli, Adriano Furgiuele and Marcello Furgiuele were all business partners of Delvex. It went on to state that fifteen thousand dollars had been withdrawn on their behalf from one of the company's accounts, and the five men had used part of that amount to donate two thousand dollars each to a Liberal Party of Canada fundraising campaign.

Tony Accurso sold Hyprescon. Constructions Louisbourg ltée and Simard-Beaudry Construction, two other companies that he controlled, pleaded guilty to tax evasion in December 2010. Renovations worth $1.7 million to Accurso's luxury yacht *Touch* were among the expenses fraudulently claimed in order to lower the amount of tax payable by Louisbourg. Accurso had invited several prominent figures on board the thirty-six-metre vessel, described in one boating magazine as a "floating palace."

The Chairman of the City of Montreal Executive Committee, Frank Zampino, was among those who had enjoyed the amenities of the *Touch*, on not one but two cruises, while negotiating a $365-million contract with a consortium co-managed by Accurso. That contract, for the installation of thousands of water meters in Montreal buildings, came under fire from the city's auditor general and was cancelled—leading the SQ to open yet another inquiry into the City of Montreal administration.

Meanwhile, the probe into the Canada Revenue Agency employees suspected of being mixed up in the tax fraud scheme encountered some difficulties. One of the investigators, André Saint-Arnaud, the Agency's Assistant Director of Audit, was brutally assaulted on his way out of a banquet hall in Montreal's Little Italy a week before Christmas. As he walked toward his car with a group of colleagues after an office party, an unknown assailant beat him repeatedly and caused lacerations to his face. The reasons for the attack were never determined.

Francesco Bruno and BT Céramique pleaded guilty in turn to tax fraud. But two other co-shareholders in that company, Rodolpho Palmerino and Alfredo Magalhaes, were acquitted after the government lawyer, seeking to protect the identity of an RCMP informant, decided not to introduce any further evidence against them.

Another businessman, Guy Marc-Aurèle, who was a friend of Vito Rizzuto, also faced criminal charges of tax fraud. Marc-Aurèle had owned Place Vincent Massey in Gatineau, Quebec, which houses offices of Environment Canada, but sold the twenty-one-storey building to associates just a week before the anti-Mafia sweep of November 2006. The Canada Revenue Agency accused him of fraudulently claiming maintenance expenses of $408,788. A search warrant included transcripts of business conversations between Marc-Aurèle and Rizzuto, a year before the latter's arrest. The two also stayed in touch after Vito's arrest and imprisonment.

During another conversation captured in an electronic surveillance operation, Marc-Aurèle was heard telling someone that he had bought a Mercedes from Vito Rizzuto. "She's silver with black interior, a 2004 S500, fully loaded," he was heard saying. "Every available option. Heated seats in the front, rear, you name it." The businessman had also supplied a BMW to Nick Rizzuto Jr. The latter had lent Marc-Aurèle a sizable sum of money, and the luxury car was a form of repayment.

Interviewed by La Presse, Marc-Aurèle implied that the tax agency was making life difficult for him because of his friendship with Vito Rizzuto. "I don't know why Revenue Canada got a search warrant for my home," he said. "The only reason I can think of is that Vito is an old friend. I can't go back on that friendship."

Operation Colisée dealt a severe blow to organized crime, not only because it led to the arrests of senior members of the Rizzuto organization, but because it exposed the clan's ties to several outside individuals and revealed the scale of its influence on government and its infiltration of the legitimate economy. After ruling over Montreal for thirty years, the Sicilian Mafia was in disarray.

CHAPTER 18

COLLAPSE

Nicolò Rizzuto, in prison since the November 22, 2006, culmination of Operation Colisée, had to be hospitalized for respiratory and urinary problems in April of the following year. Fourteen years earlier, he had claimed a prostate condition as an excuse to secure his release from prison in Venezuela. Rather conveniently, he had ailments that seemed to flare up whenever he was incarcerated. Prison authorities took the Mafia patriarch under heavy escort to Montreal's Jewish General Hospital, where doctors put him through a battery of tests. He spent two weeks in a private room on the third floor of the hospital on Côte-Sainte-Catherine Road, in the city's Côte-des-Neiges district. SQ officers stood guard round the clock for the duration of his stay.

Rizzuto was then returned to the Centre de détention de Montréal, formerly known as Bordeaux Prison. The aging facility, built before the First World War, had not welcomed such a notorious Mafia figurehead since Joe Bonanno's 1964 visit, when he'd attempted to immigrate to Canada. Bordeaux's inmates had given "Joe Bananas" a hero's welcome, and old Nick, too, was treated with all the respect due his underworld rank. "On the first day, when he arrived in the wing, there were convicts who just froze," one guard recalled. "You could tell he wasn't like the other inmates, that he had the respect of the prison population." Like a bar patron paying for a round for everybody, Nick bought several items from the canteen and distributed them among his companions.

He may not have felt all that disoriented in his new surroundings. The huge prison, with its six spoke-like wings radiating outward from a central block topped by a dome, was on the shore of the Rivière des Prairies in the borough of Ahuntsic-Cartierville, barely five kilometres from Rizzuto's home on Antoine-Berthelet Avenue. And his cell was in the same wing as that of Paolo Renda and several other organized crime figures, mostly outlaw bikers and street gang members, all awaiting trial too. Mario Brouillette, a member of the Trois-Rivières Hells Angels, watched out for Old Nick at Bordeaux. The two enjoyed conversing in Spanish, a language the biker had learned on his many trips to the Dominican Republic, and that the Mafioso had assimilated during his extended stays in Venezuela. Both men shared an interest in criminal activity, naturally, and business. Brouillette exemplified the new generation of criminal bikers who fancied themselves captains of industry. He had gone into business with one Marc Saulnier, a man without a criminal record who ran a lucrative concrete formwork company in Lavaltrie, about fifty kilometres northeast of Montreal.

Rizzuto's Consenza cronies Rocco Sollecito and Francesco Arcadi were also at Bordeaux but in another wing. Old Nick slowly got used to the tedium of life inside: eating, sleeping, watching TV. There were limited opportunities for leisure pursuits, but he did find a few fellow prisoners to play cards with. At night, he sometimes had trouble finding his way back to his cell, stopping in front of the wrong one every now and then—until another inmate fashioned a handmade Italian flag and facetiously stuck it above Rizzuto's door.

The old don was fairly confident he would win early release. The Colisée investigators had accumulated damning proof against the Sicilian clan's other dominant figures, most notably Arcadi and his enforcers Francesco Del Balso and Lorenzo Giordano, but discussions with his lawyers had convinced Rizzuto that the evidence against him was more tenuous.

On September 18, 2008, guards escorted him down the tunnel linking the prison to the Gouin Judicial Services Centre, a courthouse that had been built especially for the so-called megatrial of several of the more than one hundred bikers arrested in the Operation Springtime 2001 crackdown. Clad in a light-coloured cardigan that accentuated his age, Rizzuto simply nodded when Justice Jean-Pierre Bonin of the Court of Québec asked if he wished to plead guilty to two charges: possession of the proceeds of crime and concealment of the proceeds of crime for the benefit of a criminal organization.

Four weeks later, he was sentenced to four years in prison. Since he was entitled to double credit for time spent in custody pending trial, however—and that time happened to be two years—he was released the same day. Still, the conviction was hailed as a victory for anti-Mafia investigators: for the first time in his life, Nicolò Rizzuto had admitted in a court of law that he belonged to a criminal organization. The aging patriarch—he was then eighty-four—soon let it be known to his entourage that he no longer wished to occupy a leadership position in the Mafia. His sentence included a three-year probation; the slightest misstep would likely land him back in jail. Paolo Renda, then aged sixty-nine, entered a plea of guilty to the same charges, as well as another related to a handgun and one of two hunting rifles found at his home on Antoine-Berthelet at the time of his arrest. He would be paroled in February 2010. Rocco Sollecito, age sixty, was sentenced to eight years. Arcadi, fifty-four, Giordano, forty-five, and Del Balso, thirty-eight, were handed much stiffer sentences of fifteen years each. The "young ones" were understandably embittered to see the three senior members of the Consenza "board of directors" get off far more lightly.

Hours after the sentences were pronounced, the clan's senior lawyer, Loris Cavaliere, arrived at the Montreal headquarters of the RCMP on Dorchester Boulevard in Westmount, carrying a briefcase containing approximately two million dollars cash in various denominations to pay the fines that the court had levied. Later, at Bordeaux, old Nick retrieved his personal effects and put them in a green plastic garbage bag, bid his fellow inmates and the guards goodbye, and headed for the prison exit where he was met by Cavaliere. The lawyer took the garbage bag and drove the old man home.

In the event that Rizzuto and the others accused had decided not to plead guilty, the prosecution had made arrangements to hear expert testimony from an Italian brigadier-general, Angelilo Pellegrini, who had studied the evidence gathered during Operation Colisée and would have attested to the similarities between the Rizzuto organization's modus operandi and that of traditional Mafia clans in Sicily. Pellegrini was "prepared to describe those criminal organizations in Italy, define what a man of honour is to these organizations, describe the activities of a Mafia family, the role of a boss, and to testify about a certain type of vocabulary they use. The same terms were used by the organization in Montreal," explained Alexandre Dalmau, one of the Crown prosecutors.

At Nicolò Rizzuto's bail hearing back in August 2007, another expert witness, Michel Fortin, an RCMP officer and member of the CFSEU, had explained that the Sicilian clan ran the same kinds of rackets as the Cotroni outfit of the 1950s, 1960s and 1970s. For example, both outfits earned considerable sums by deploying coercive debt-collection tactics—sometimes on behalf of legitimate businesses. Along with the other members of the CFSEU, Fortin was loath to engage in any grandstanding: Operation Colisée had inflicted grave wounds to the Montreal Mafia, he said, but the beast wouldn't die that easily.

While his father had been whiling away the time at Bordeaux playing cards, Vito Rizzuto waited, despondent, at the Metropolitan Detention Center in Brooklyn. On May 4, 2007, he was led, under heavy guard, into a newly renovated wood-panelled hearing room of the nearby U.S. District Court building. Of the twenty-seven Bonanno family members arrested in 2003 and 2004, he was the last to appear in court. All the others had already pleaded guilty or been found guilty. Vito was the only Canadian citizen among the defendants.

Vito walked into the hearing wearing his prison-issue attire: a blue cotton T-shirt, khaki pants and canvas sneakers. The baggy clothing emphasized the fact that he had lost weight and muscle tone during his three years behind bars. Gone was the slicked-back look: Vito's salt-and-pepper hair was now cut short. The deposed don appeared pale and shuffled like a beaten man. It had been a long time since his feet had trod the manicured grass of a golf course. He sat down in the defendant's box, beside his principal defence lawyer, John W. Mitchell, and looked up with dark eyes at the presiding judge, Nicholas Garaufis. Two federal marshals stood close by.

Like so many other Bonanno members brought to trial, Vito had agreed to admit his guilt in exchange for a lighter sentence. And as often happens when a plea deal is reached between parties, the hearing that Friday morning began with a boring litany of legalese. The judge and lawyers wanted to be sure the accused properly understood what was at stake. They went over the indictment in detail. Under amendments that had been made to the RICO Act, Rizzuto could have faced life imprisonment. Judge Garaufis, however, reminded the court that since the murder of three renegade Bonanno capos had taken place in 1981, he had no choice but to sentence the accused according to the provisions that had been in force at the time. The maximum sentence was therefore twenty years in prison, plus a $250,000 fine.

Rizzuto kept his head lowered, looking up only when he had to answer Garaufis's questions. During occasional short, hushed exchanges with his attorney, his expression grew livelier but only hinted at his former characteristic bravado.

"Mr. Rizzuto, how old are you?" Judge Garaufis asked.

"Sixty-one, Your Honour."

"How long did you go to school?"

"Until ninth grade."

Garaufis asked other questions about Rizzuto's level of education and marital status.

"Your principal language is English?" he wanted to know.

"I would say yes," Vito replied. "But I also speak Italian, French and Spanish."

The judge then addressed defence attorney Mitchell. "Mr. Mitchell, have you had any difficulty communicating with your client in English?" he asked.

"No."

"Very well . . . Mr. Rizzuto, whatever decision you make today, I must have assurances that it is being made knowingly . . . Do you have any health problems?"

"Yes," Vito said. "I had an X-ray and the doctors told me I have a spot on one lung. I'm supposed to go for a scan, but it hasn't been done yet."

"When was the diagnosis made?"

"Two months ago."

"The delay seems normal. Is your mind clear?"

"Yes, Your Honour," Vito said.

Garaufis pressed his point. He wanted to be certain Rizzuto understood the consequences of pleading guilty to the racketeering charge of conspiracy to commit murder for a criminal organization, stemming from the triple slaying that had taken place twenty-six years earlier almost to the day. Under the terms of the plea deal, he would be sentenced to ten years in prison and fined $250,000. The prison term would be followed by three years' probation. Once satisfied, the judge asked, "Okay, Mr. Rizzuto. How do you plead to the charge?"

"Guilty," Vito replied. Then he put on glasses and, in a hoarse voice, read aloud his allocution, a brief statement in which he admitted, in vague terms, having taken part in the three murders. Then he formally filed the five-page document with the court.

"Between February 1, 1981, and May 5, 1981," it reads, "I conspired with others to conduct the affairs of an association, in fact, enterprise through a pattern of racketeering." It continued, "Specifically, on May 5, 1981, acting with others in Brooklyn, New York, I committed the racketeering acts of conspiracy to murder and the murder of Alphonse Indelicato, Philip Giaccone and Dominick Trinchera."

While Rizzuto read his statement, district attorney Greg Andres studied Garaufis's face. He immediately understood that the judge was not happy. Andres had pleaded more than a hundred cases involving members of the Bonanno organization (and others in that family had even put out a contract on him). Several of those trials had been presided by Garaufis. The prosecutor had learned to interpret the judge's slightest facial expressions. He rose and explained the legal foundations of the agreement that had been reached between the prosecution and the defence.

"The association [in which Rizzuto was a member], in fact, was the Bonanno/Massino organized crime family of La Cosa Nostra," Andres said. Had there been a trial, the district attorney went on, he would have entered evidence to support his assertion in the form of surveillance reports and all manner of expert scientific testimony, including forensic examination of the remains of the three victims. He would have called police investigators as well as mob informants to the stand. Joe Massino, the turncoat Bonanno family boss, and his brother-in-law Salvatore Vitale would have been the star witnesses.

"Your Honour, I understand that you wish to know the evidence surrounding the murders, but I would say once again that it is the same evidence introduced at the trial of Joseph Massino," Andres emphasized. "More than that, Your Honour, we are in a position to prove that Mr. Rizzuto has maintained links with the Bonanno family all this time and, moreover, that he is an active member of that family."

"You're asking me to hand the defendant a sentence ten years less than the maximum, but you are telling me nothing about what Vito Rizzuto did," Garaufis intoned. "At this point, all I know is that he's admitted to doing something!" he said, glaring at both lawyers.

"There are several defendants in this case who have admitted their guilt or been found guilty," the judge went on. "But they weren't content to simply tell me they were involved in the crimes they were accused of. Why should I accept a specific sentence when I don't know what he did? Frankly, it's not enough. So tell me what he did. Do you know what he did? I want to know his exact role."

Mitchell rose and said, "Your Honour, the accused admits in his allocution to have committed a crime of racketeering. In fact, he participated in the murder conspiracy. More precisely, he participated in the murders of the three individuals."

"I'm being asked to sanction an agreement that I am not obligated to sign, is that right?" the judge said, growing more irritated.

"I understand . . . ," Vito's lawyer began, then faltered.

"In that case, I want to know what he did. This is not some game; I'm the judge and it's unacceptable. Was he the driver? Was he one of the shooters? I've spent weeks listening to people explain what happened in this murder case. But I still don't know what the defendant who is here today did. Why should I accept his plea and accept a ten-year sentence when he could be sentenced to twenty years? People have gone to jail for the rest of their lives . . . because of their involvement in these murders. If he's got something more to tell me, I'd like to hear it before I accept this plea."

Caught unawares, Mitchell asked for a short recess to speak with his client, who was clearly alarmed by the turn of events. Seated in the area normally reserved for the jury, a half-dozen Canadian and U.S. journalists watched as Mitchell and Andres conferred in low tones. Then the defence attorney and Vito retired to a small room adjacent to the courtroom.

An irate Garaufis left the room as well. He returned ten minutes later, as did the defendant and his attorney.

"So, where are we now?" he asked curtly.

"Well . . . I was one of the guys who was to participate in this," Rizzuto said. "My job was to say, 'It's a holdup,' . . . so everybody [including the three rebel captains] would stand still. This moment the other people [those waiting in the closet with him] came in and they started shooting."

"You were armed?" the judge inquired.

"I was armed."

Rizzuto said nothing more. He did not say whether he himself had fired his weapon and, oddly, Garaufis never asked him. At an earlier trial in 2004, Salvatore Vitale had testified that Rizzuto was the lead gunman, also mentioning that he was with two other hit men brought in from

Montreal. Neither of them had ever been formally identified (other than as "Emanuele" and "the old-timer"), much less charged. "I seen Vito shoot. I don't know who he hit," Good-Looking Sal had said. Garaufis did not ask Rizzuto to comment on that earlier testimony.

He then asked Rizzuto whether he was a member of a criminal organization; the defendant admitted that he was.

The hearing was adjourned. Rizzuto was escorted back to his cell, secure in the knowledge that he would only have to serve out half of the ten-year sentence. U.S. prison authorities had decided that the incarceration clock had started running on January 20, 2004, the date of Vito's arrest in Montreal. On top of that, under U.S. law, the time he had spent in prison awaiting trial had earned him a reduction of nearly 15 percent of the overall prison term. Depending on whether he is also awarded credit for good behaviour, Inmate No. 04307748 could therefore be freed in the spring of 2012, at age sixty-six.

In Italy, an accused who wishes to reach a deal with the prosecution must agree to become a *pentito*. This rule serves two purposes: the police gather valuable information, and the defendant's underworld reputation is sullied forever. Vito Rizzuto and his associates did not have to suffer that ignominy (unless they voluntarily turned state's evidence) because no such provision exists in Canada or the United States.

Rizzuto was back in the Brooklyn hearing room three weeks later, on May 25, for his final sentencing. Judge Garaufis said that he was unenthusiastically assenting to the jail term of only ten years as recommended by the prosecuting and defence attorneys.

"Today marks the final chapter in the sad story of the execution of three people some twenty-six years ago in the pursuit of power and money," he said. "It has been the subject of books, multiple prosecutions and at least one motion picture. Despite such efforts to glamorize these incidents . . . it is apparent to the court that such a sordid and cynical act deserves only our scorn and condemnation. It is with reluctance that I am pronouncing this prison sentence. Participation in a triple murder is punishable by a minimum twenty years in prison. But the justice system has its advantages . . ."

The matter of the fine remained. Rizzuto and his lawyers presented financial statements that claimed he was in the red, but the judge was skeptical. According to his lawyers, Vito had assets worth $471,000 but debts of $475,300. He held one-third of the shares in Renda Construction, worth $468,000, but did not own much more than that, they asserted. He had supposedly contracted debts with family members to defray his legal expenses. According to the statements, he owed $103,000 to his youngest son, Leonardo; $92,000 to his daughter, Libertina (sometimes called Bettina); and $280,000 to his mother, Libertina.

His net worth was therefore "close to zero," said John Mitchell, who was accompanied that day by a second attorney representing Vito, David Schoen.

Greg Andres's reaction was withering: "His net worth is absurdly and conveniently equal to his liabilities," he noted. "Like everyone in the mob, his relatives hold all the assets."

If Rizzuto's assets had been in the United States, they could have been audited and accounted for, Andres added. The U.S. government believed Rizzuto had "substantial assets in Canada," he said, while acknowledging the evidence was in part anecdotal.

"He lives in a house worth a lot of money," the district attorney ventured, adding that the accused had previously evaded payment of income tax and been forced to pay $400,000 to the Canada Revenue Agency, which was proof of his wealth.

The judge in turn derided Vito's pretensions to poverty and once again displayed his irritation at having agreed to a jail term that, in his opinion, was far too short. As a result, he decided to impose the maximum fine permitted under the law, U.S.$250,000, and gave Vito three months in which to pay it.

"The court is not convinced that the information provided regarding his liabilities can be considered reliable," he declared. "We have a businessman from Canada here who doesn't own his own home? His only asset is a share of this company [Renda Construction]? It's not much to show for thirty years in business, and I'm not convinced that the representations are complete or accurate."

Rizzuto's lawyers then attempted to persuade the judge to allow their client to pay the fine in instalments, over several years, protesting Andres's suggestion that Rizzuto's shares in Renda Construction serve to guarantee payment of the fine. This was too much for Garaufis, who unloaded on the defence lawyers.

"I want those shares, otherwise I'm going to review the case! I'm not going to play this game with you. He has shares worth a substantial amount. But apparently all his other assets are secret."

After the hearing, Schoen, the second defence attorney, complained to reporters that his client was the only one of the twenty-seven co-accused ordered to pay a fine. Vito's youngest son, thirty-seven-year-old Leonardo Rizzuto, said he was relieved, however, and pleased that the judge had recommended that his father serve his time at the Ray Brook medium-security correctional facility in northern New York State, just a two-hour drive from Montreal. It meant Leonardo and other family members would be able to visit him easily.

"It's very important to him," said Leonardo, himself a lawyer, during a brief interview with a reporter. "He has five grandchildren and it's very important for him to be able to see them often."

Vito got off very lightly. Especially given the fact—which emerged later—that he had admitted his crime in full during a trip to the Dominican Republic in 2003, a year before his arrest. The confession was surreptitiously recorded by Dominican police. They provided the tape to Canadian investigators, but in the end, it wound up gathering dust on a shelf. That recording would have made an extremely persuasive trial exhibit, but to this day it has never been used.

By January 2003, the Canadian godfather had been making an annual golf pilgrimage to the Dominican Republic for at least ten years. That month, he flew to the tiny Caribbean country with several cronies, including Francesco Arcadi and Joe Di Maulo, the influential Calabrian Mafioso.

The small group settled in at Casa de Campo, the famous seaside resort that includes three outstanding golf courses, including Diente de Perro (Teeth of the Dog), long rated as one of the world's best. Vito and Arcadi shared a room overlooking one of the courses. At the request of the RCMP, Dominican police planted bugs in their room as well as in Di Maulo's.

Vito had no inkling that he might be under surveillance while so far from Canada. When investigators listened to the recordings, they were stunned to hear him confide in Arcadi regarding his role in the three captains massacre twenty-two years earlier. He told him how he had burst from the closet, gun in hand, and started shooting. "There was blood all over the place," he said.

Rizzuto spoke in Italian. The recording was hard to understand, so much so that RCMP investigators thought it might not be usable. They did not have it translated until after Vito's Brooklyn guilty plea. Besides Arcadi and Di Maulo, the other men accompanying Vito on the golf trip included Paolo Renda, Domenico Chimienti, Giuseppe Triassi and Vincenzo Spagnolo. The Mounties had all of them in their sights. Renda, as the Rizzuto clan's *consigliere,* was a prime target of Operation Colisée. Chimienti was suspected of laundering money for the organization but was never charged.

The Sicilian-born Triassi was Vito's representative at the Casino de Montréal. He specialized in loansharking, charging 10 percent interest for three days to gamblers who contracted debts with him.

Vincenzo Spagnolo was another of Vito's friends. Back in 1988, he had offered to post one million dollars bail for Vito after the seizure of thirty-two tonnes of hashish in Sept-Îles. The judge had refused. Spagnolo spent his days at Buffet Roma, a banquet hall in Saint-Léonard that was sometimes used for political party fundraisers. It was also a hangout for Mafia higher-ups. After he left the Consenza for the day, old Nicolò Rizzuto often stopped by the Roma before going home. When he spoke to Spagnolo on the phone, he would almost always ask him how business was going, as if the banquet hall belonged to him.

Judge Nicholas Garaufis's gracious recommendation notwithstanding, Vito was not sent to the Ray Brook facility in Upstate New York, but to a federal penitentiary in Florence, Colorado, more than three thousand kilometres from Montreal. Before long, he sank into depression. As soon as he could, he telephoned his wife. Giovanna was finding their separation progressively more difficult to bear; she told him she was having trouble sleeping and was taking barbiturates and sedatives. Vito advised her to be wary of abusing them. He also regularly phoned his mother, Libertina, and his sister, Maria, to keep up with family news as well as what was going on in Montreal.

For an inmate in a U.S. prison, life is about as Spartan as it gets. Vito had little choice but to get used to it, after living much of his adult existence in the lap of luxury, golfing on the finest courses, dining in chic restaurants and enjoying VIP treatment everywhere he went. He could do little more than reminisce about the small pleasures of life as a free man: relaxing under a masseuse's nimble fingers, or receiving manicures and skin care sessions at a spa boutique in the Galeries d'Anjou shopping centre in east-end Montreal. Thursday dinners at home with his wife, children and grandchildren, a sacred family ritual, were now no more than distant memories.

Six months after he was interned, Rizzuto penned a pathetic plea to Judge Garaufis, begging for early release, in 2010 rather than 2012.

"May all be well for you at this time," the letter began. "As Your Honor is aware, my name is Vito Rizzuto, the defendant." In his opinion, he had been the victim of an error. The U.S. Federal Bureau of Prisons had abolished parole in 1987, replacing it with a rule whereby the best an inmate can hope for is a shorter term in exchange for good behaviour. Vito claimed that since he had committed his crime in 1981, when the old parole regulations were still in effect, he should be eligible for early release. "Should I be contacting the wrong office in an effort to have this error correct [sic], I apologize," he continued. "However, I am not from the U.S. and am only made aware of this incorrect calculation recently."

Judge Garaufis replied. In similarly cordial terms, he rebuffed Inmate No. 04307748's request: "I suggest that you consult with your attorney regarding this case and that you follow the appropriate administrative and judicial procedures."

Vito had sent his letter to the judge on October 25, 2007. That was two days after Italian authorities announced the issue of a second wave of arrest warrants targeting him and his accomplices. In 2005, the DIA had already issued warrants against Vito—then imprisoned in Quebec pending his extradition to the United States—and a number of his cronies in Montreal, Italy and other locales, alleging their attempts to muscle in on the massive Strait of Messina bridge construction contract. According to the Italian police, the Mafiosi planned to finance the work as part of a public-private consortium using dirty money. After the bridge project was shelved, the DIA's ongoing probe had uncovered another plot.

On October 23, 2007, a series of raids and arrests took place in Italy, France and Switzerland. Bank accounts containing a total of €500 million (nearly Can$700 million at the time) were frozen, and twenty-two companies along with property and assets worth a total of US$212 million were seized. Seventeen men faced charges of being part of a mammoth money laundering operation under Vito Rizzuto's direction.

Those arrested that day in Europe included bankers, businessmen, stockbrokers and even a man with links to Italy's royal family. Besides Vito, the Italian warrants targeted his father, Nicolò, and the three other members of the Consenza inner circle: Paolo Renda, Rocco Sollecito and Francesco Arcadi. All were in prison in Montreal awaiting trial in the wake of the Colisée investigation.

"We believe that even from jail they are able to control the organization," Silvia Franzè, an investigator with the DIA, said. "We blocked a lot of bank accounts and money," she explained in an interview with Canada's *National Post*. "We have seized many companies and hundreds of millions of euros all around the world because we believe that behind these companies is Vito Rizzuto."

"From prison, they pulled the strings of their Italian colonies," added Colonel Paolo La Forgia of the DIA.

One of Vito's contacts was a businessman named Mariano Turrisi, founding president of a company called Made in Italy Group, which promoted Italian products worldwide. Police said that wiretaps had picked him up in conversation with Vito, and an Italian court document claimed

Turrisi and an associate had travelled to Montreal in September 2005 and met with Nicolò Rizzuto Jr., Frank Campoli (Vito's cousin by marriage) and Antonio Papalia, a co-owner of Vancouver-based Metals Research.

Turrisi was also the vice-chairman of a nascent political party founded by Prince Emanuele Filiberto, heir apparent to the House of Savoy, Italy's former royal family. Barely a year after the end of the Second World War, Italians voted in a referendum to replace the monarchy with a republic, and the royals were expelled from the country for having colluded with Benito Mussolini's Fascist regime; male descendants were only authorized to re-enter Italy in 2002. After returning from exile, Prince Emanuele Filiberto, grandson of Italy's last king, Umberto II, launched a political movement called Valori e Futuro (Values and Future), which Turrisi joined.

Mariano Turrisi had privileged access to Italian government officials. The head office of Made in Italy in Rome was across from the Palazzo Chigi, which housed the offices of the president, Romano Prodi, and his cabinet. When police arrested Turrisi in Rome, a search turned up a bond certificate in the amount of one billion dollars, though they suspected it was a forgery. Fake or not, the document served as surety for lines of credit that Turrisi had with Swiss and Italian banks. On December 19, 2008, a judge sentenced him to a six-year prison term.

Through Turrisi and others, Vito Rizzuto maintained "illustrious connections" in Italy and other countries. The Italian court documents alleged that he and his father wielded significant influence in his homeland and elsewhere. After moving to Canada, the Rizzutos "gave birth to a transnational society" designed to unify Italian Mafia clans and created "overseas cells," according to a document from the anti-Mafia prosecution office in Rome. The DIA investigation also uncovered suspected dealings as far away as the United States and Singapore.

The organization led by Vito, the document added, aimed to "manage and control the economic activities connected to the acquisition of contracts in public works" and "commit a series of crimes—killings, international drug trafficking, extortion, frauds, smuggling, stock-market manipulation, insider trading and criminal transfer of securities."

The Italian authorities accused the cartel of using companies listed on stock markets in Europe and North America, including one based in Vancouver, to help mount ventures connected with gold mines in Canada and Chile. Two bank employees were arrested in Switzerland.

The men arrested in Italy included two individuals with Canadian citizenship. The first, Roberto Papalia, was picked up in Milan. He was a businessman who had been expelled from the Vancouver Stock Exchange for suspicious transactions. He had been seen with Vito Rizzuto in Zurich, Switzerland, in the mid-1990s *(see Chapter 10)*. Roberto Papalia and his twin brother, Antonio, co-owner of Metals Research, owned a small gold mine on Texada Island, in British Columbia. In their teens, both Papalias had gone to St. Pius X Secondary School in Montreal with Vito.

The second Canadian was Felice Italiano, a resident of the Montreal borough of LaSalle. Police arrested him in Rome as he was preparing to fly back to Montreal with his wife. He was in Italy on a business trip, representing his company Ital-Peaux, an animal-hide export firm based in Sainte-Julie, a suburban town on Montreal's South Shore. Italiano had previously been linked to one of the biggest drug busts in Canada. He was arrested in 1994 along with brothers Gerald and Richard Matticks, of Montreal's West End Gang, following the discovery of twenty-six tonnes of hashish in the Port of Montreal. Charges against Italiano and his alleged accomplices were later withdrawn after the presiding trial judge ruled that the SQ had fabricated part of the evidence.

Businessman Beniamino Zappia, born in Cattolica Eraclea and described by the DIA as "the right arm of the Rizzutos in Italy," was also arrested in Milan, where he had been living for several years. Along with many others, he had opened several Swiss bank accounts on behalf of the Rizzuto clan. This was the same Zappia whom hidden RCMP cameras and microphones had filmed and recorded on multiple occasions at the Consenza, including in May 2005, when Rocco Sollecito explained to him how the five leaders divided up the proceeds of the clan's criminal operations.

The investigation that led to this wave of arrests and searches was an outgrowth of the probe into the Strait of Messina bridge funding plot, which had been launched on the basis of information transmitted to Italian police by the RCMP. A partial transcription of electronic surveillance conducted during operations Cicéron and Colisée had been handed over to DIA officers, who then mounted their own operation. The surveillance included long-distance phone conversations between Vito and money launderers in Europe and Asia.

Investigations begat other investigations. The Italian anti-Mafia sleuths must have felt like cats rolling a giant ball of yarn around, unravelling strands of evidence bit by bit. Several of them eventually led to Cattolica Eraclea, the Rizzutos' hometown, where in November 2008, police seized properties belonging to Beniamino Zappia. They also confiscated the house, car, bank accounts and stock portfolio of a local wine merchant suspected of being in league with the Rizzuto family, and who had previously sought election to the legislature of Agrigento province.

Then, before dawn on November 27, 2009, some eighty police officers massed in the rocky hills near Cattolica Eraclea. They covered their faces with hoods, put on vests bearing the DIA insignia, then surrounded the village and marched in silence through its narrow streets, on their way to nab their suspects while they slept. The arrests, dubbed Operation Minoa, sought to wipe out the Rizzuto clan's ongoing influence in the town and, by extension, throughout Sicily and the rest of Italy.

Antonio Calderella, a DIA captain, explained in an interview with the *National Post* several months later that "Operation Minoa originated from the prosecutor's office of Palermo, which requested investigations into Vito Rizzuto, and was designed to shed light on the possible involvement of the Italian-Canadian Mafia in illegal activities in the province of Agrigento." Those activities included money laundering as well as other crimes. "The investigation also highlighted the close proximity of leading members of the Canadian criminal clique, who originally come from this town," Calderella said.

The clan's man in Cattolica Eraclea was Domenico Terrasi, who kept in regular contact with his compatriot Beniamino Zappia in Milan. Terrasi owned a construction company and held sway over business and economic activity in the surrounding area. One day, angry that he had not been awarded a contract to repair local streets and roads, Terrasi summoned the father-in-law of the municipal bureaucrat who oversaw public works in the town and commune.

"Fuck!" he erupted, unaware he was being recorded. "I will show you how I will kick him . . . You know how I will crush him? Like this!"

"I am telling you, if anything can be done, do it and I will support you," the father-in-law promised slavishly. "I am very sorry, truly. You know I am sorry."

Though Terrasi's firms did not win that particular roadwork job, they did secure the contract to build part of an extensive aqueduct across western Sicily. According to Italian police, the entire structure, which cost seventy million dollars, was built by Mafia-controlled companies who shared the contracts among themselves.

"The investigation also dealt with the subject of the municipal elections of 2007 in Cattolica," the *National Post* quoted authorities as saying. "It has been verified that the Mafia group headed by Domenico Terrasi acted effectively for the election of the current mayor, Cosimo Piro, and of a municipal councillor. The investigation also pointed out the illegal activity of the above-mentioned group in controlling the election."

Things had come full circle. In 1955, Vito Rizzuto's father-in-law-to-be and other clan members had murdered Giuseppe Spagnolo, the staunch Mafia opponent and first elected mayor of Cattolica Eraclea. Half a century later, the same clan had manoeuvred to put their man in the town mayor's chair.

In other ways, though, times had changed. After the Second World War, political authorities had left the way clear for the Mafia. By the early twenty-first century, courageous police officers, prosecutors and judges in both Italy and North America were determined to fight it.

Nicolò Rizzuto and his son, Vito, could only watch as their empire began to crumble under killing blows dealt by police and judicial authorities. For years already, members of rival clans in Montreal had been circling, like so many sharks sensing blood in the water. As the organization foundered, the predators had greedily torn off strips. Now they relished a final feeding frenzy.

———

In the months and years following Vito Rizzuto's arrest in January 2004, some forty individuals in and around Montreal were murdered, were abducted, or disappeared under mysterious circumstances. Several of them had ties to the city's Mafia. Unpaid debts often constituted the motives for the crimes, but sometimes other factors could be inferred. Investigators were nonetheless at a loss for leads in many cases.

On January 19, 2004, one Carmelo Tommassino called his wife to say he wouldn't be able to pick up their young daughter at school. When his wife asked him why, he couldn't give her an explanation. He hung up and was never seen or heard from again. Paolo Gervasi, the former owner of the Castel Tina strip club who had fallen out with the Sicilian clan, was murdered the same day, killed by gunfire as he got behind the wheel of his Jeep after leaving a pastry shop on Jean-Talon Street *(see Chapter 11)*.

In February 2005, Calabrian mobster Domenico Cordeleone was kidnapped, by all accounts because of a drug debt, but was released in short order. Years earlier, he had been tight with Colombian *narcotraficante* Jairo Garcia, who'd become a powerful member of the Cali cartel after returning to his native country. The two had been neighbours in La Plaine, a semi-rural suburb north of Montreal, where they each owned huge estates.

Real estate developer Antonio (Tony) Magi, who was often seen with Rizzuto family members, was abducted the following April. Two strangers stopped him on Saint-Jacques Street in LaSalle, handcuffed him and took him to a house in Laval. The businessman was slightly injured. In his version of the story, he managed to break free of his restraints and flee. Rather than file a police report, he called Vito Rizzuto's son Nick Jr. and arranged to meet him at the Bar Laennec, in Laval, with Francesco Del Balso and Antonio (Tony) Volpato. The latter was another of Vito's former classmates at St. Pius X Secondary School (and would make headlines three years later, when it was revealed that he was a former lover of model Julie Couillard, who in 2008 would find herself infamously at the centre of a scandal involving Canada's foreign minister). All wondered who might have planned the kidnapping and why.

Leonardo D'Angelo was abducted a few days later, on May 1. He was the nephew of Vincenzo Spagnolo, the former Buffet Roma owner who had been one of the men accompanying Vito on his Dominican Republic golf trip. D'Angelo had built up a debt of $400,000. Nicolò Rizzuto Sr. and Paolo Renda had been trying to help him out for two months, but it wasn't enough. Money was raised among his relatives and friends, and he was freed.

Three weeks later, on May 25, 2005, it was the turn of Frank Martorana, a close associate of Francesco Arcadi, to be snatched. He was talking with someone in the backroom of Paduano, a barbershop on Jean-Talon Street in Saint-Léonard, when four men burst in. When he tried to resist, blows from the butt of a revolver rained down on his head, and he was subdued.

Police believed his abduction was related to various long-standing debts, which exceeded a million dollars. He returned to his home in Lorraine, north of Montreal, a week later, his face still bearing the traces of the aggression. He refused to press charges. Drug trafficker Christian Deschênes had previously planned to kidnap Martorana, along with Francesco Arcadi, in July 2001 (see Chapter 13).

Martorana had also been mixed up in a convoluted case of extortion. He owed $500,000 to John Scotti, the Saint-Léonard luxury car dealer, and Scotti was eager to be paid. A garage owner in Toronto happened to owe Martorana the same amount. Vito Rizzuto and his cronies had leaned on the garage owner to force him to pay Martorana so that Martorana could refund Scotti. The garage owner went to the police. The ensuing investigation then had a significant influence on the unfolding of Operation Colisée, leading police to focus on crimes of extortion.

The same day, May 25, Domenico Dettori was assaulted by several men in the Rivière-des-Prairies district of east-end Montreal. They threw him in a van, gave him a severe beating, ensured that he properly understood the message they were relaying, and let him go. Dettori refused to tell police anything about his aggressors and would only admit that the incident had been sparked by a drug debt.

Mike Lapolla and Giovanni "Johnny" Bertolo were murdered in 2005, and Richard Griffin and Domenico Macri met the same fate in 2006, as detailed elsewhere in these pages. There were more killings in 2007. On March 9, thirty-two-year-old Carmine Guarino, a small-time drug dealer with ties to the Sicilian clan, was shot dead at Café Albano on Jarry Street. On April 26, the charred body of Ezechielle De Bellis, thirty-seven, was found next to Highway 125 near Rawdon, northeast of Montreal. De Bellis, who had attended Macri's funeral, was an enforcer for the Montreal Mafia and had a drug trafficking charge pending against him.

On the morning of July 5, a panic-stricken resident of Pointe-Claire, a community on Montreal's West Island, called 911 to report that she had seen a body lying in the backyard of a house. Hasan Eroglu, a thirty-nine-year-old heroin dealer and close friend of Lorenzo Giordano, had been shot three times. A handgun equipped with a silencer was found nearby.

On September 12, Calabrian-born Francesco Velenosi, age fifty-six, who was involved in loansharking and illegal gambling, left his home in LaSalle, saying he was going out to meet friends. He was murdered later the same day or the next day. Five days later, a family member called police to inform them that they had found Velenosi's grey Volvo, with his body stuffed in the trunk. He had been horribly beaten, probably with one or more golf clubs.

On December 21, Tony Mucci, the man who shot journalist Jean-Pierre Charbonneau in the newsroom of Le Devoir in 1973, was himself the target of a murder attempt. Unknown assailants fired at him as he sat in the Café Maida—Francesco Arcadi's headquarters, on Lacordaire Boulevard in Saint-Léonard—but missed. Mucci was the lieutenant of Moreno Gallo, a well-respected underworld boss.

Gallo, then aged sixty-one, was widely believed to be in line to take over the leadership of the Montreal Mafia. He had immigrated to Canada at age nine with his mother and sister, two years after his father. He had obtained permanent residency but had never become a Canadian citizen. In 1974, he had been convicted of murder in the shooting death in Old Montreal of Angelo Facchino, a drug dealer who worked for the Dubois brothers' gang. He had been paroled nine years later.

Operation Colisée investigators had observed Gallo in the company of the Rizzuto clan leaders on several occasions. Along with many others, he had been a featured player in the RCMP's hidden-camera videos, bringing tribute money to the Consenza. Police had compiled a report on his Mafia relations—one persuasive enough for his parole to be revoked. Gallo was sent back to prison but, even so, maintained close ties to members of criminal organizations. "Recent information . . . reveals that you stayed in direct contact with people connected with biker gangs, street gangs and Italian organized crime," noted a report by the Canada Border Services Agency, which was seeking to deport him to Italy.

During this turbulent period, a bona fide declaration of war against the Rizzuto clan was issued by one Sergio Piccirilli, a protegé of the Ontario Calabrian clans and a staunch ally of the D'Amico crime family of Granby, Quebec. Though it was only with hindsight that investigators would grasp the full import of these events, the attack was direct and unambiguous. It was the first formal offensive against the Sicilian clan that had exterminated the Calabrian Paolo Violi in 1978 and ruled the Montreal Mafia in the intervening three decades.

Born in Calabria on New Year's Day, 1960, Sergio Piccirilli, variously nicknamed "Big Guy" and "Grizzly," was a prolific drug merchant in the Montreal region, dealing in marijuana, cocaine and various so-called designer drugs. He and his accomplices manufactured ecstasy out of a garage on Leman Street in the Saint-Vincent-de-Paul industrial park of Laval. Piccirilli peddled his wares in Montreal and New York. Business really started booming when he hooked up with Sharon Simon, a trafficker nicknamed the "Kanehsatake drug queen" by the media. She owned a huge estate at the end of a private road in the Mohawk community of Kanehsatake, near Oka, off the northwest tip of the Island of Montreal. She and Piccirilli were romantically involved for a time, which provided Grizzly with new connections for marijuana and contraband cigarettes.

For twenty years, Piccirilli had paid the Rizzuto clan—more precisely, Francesco Arcadi—a commission on the proceeds of his drug sales. The more he dealt, the more he had to cough up in "taxes." Eventually he got fed up and vowed to stop paying. He told associates that if Arcadi wanted to make money, all he had to do was work as hard as he did. Such effrontery, of course, was the sort of thing that could cost him dearly. Piccirilli's Calabrian boss in Toronto, Franco Mattoso, learned that there was a contract out on him and told him about it.

On February 4, 2005, Piccirilli went to Toronto with Domenico D'Agostino, his right-hand man. He sought advice from Mattoso, then went to Hamilton for a meeting with the brothers Giuseppe and Domenico Violi. When their father, Paolo, had been killed by the Rizzuto clan, Giuseppe and Domenico were eight and twelve years old, respectively. They were now aged thirty-five and thirty-nine, and intensely involved in the activities of the Ontario Mafia, specifically in the Hamilton underworld, where their grandfather on their mother's side, Giacomo Luppino, had long held sway. RCMP investigators who tracked their movements are unaware of the precise nature of the Violis' conversation with Piccirilli, but it can safely be surmised that they did not prevail upon him to make peace with the clan that had executed their father.

On police surveillance recordings, Piccirilli's mother is heard expressing worry for her son's safety. He tried to reassure her by insisting he was well shielded. "I still have my friends supporting me," he told her. "I even called some friends from Toronto and the U.S. They're all coming." He added that he was sick and tired of being under the Rizzuto clan's thumb: "Those bastards, they're jealous because I don't wanna work for them."

Piccirilli was armed almost everywhere he went. As an additional precaution, he often slept away from his home in the northeastern Montreal suburb of Terrebonne. For a while, he holed up at a hotel in Saint-André-Avellin, a small town partway between Montreal and Ottawa. True to his boasting, he did have powerful allies, including Salvatore Cazzetta, the paroled former leader of the Rock Machine biker gang, who were about to patch over to the Hells Angels. But those Piccirilli could most count on were the D'Amicos of Granby. The marijuana-smuggling family worked closely with the powerful Hells Angels chapter in nearby Sherbrooke and had their own bone to pick with Francesco Arcadi and his Consenza cronies, over a murky matter of drug money (*see Chapter 16*).

Police had pegged Piccirilli as one of the quartet of costumed, armed men who kidnapped Arcadi associate Nicolò Varacalli on Halloween night in 2005. Two days before Christmas, he joined the D'Amico delegation that showed up to intimidate the regulars at the Consenza, leading investigators to fear a bloodbath. Police knew there was a contract out on Piccirilli, and they knew Piccirilli planned to murder old Nick, whom he blamed for all his troubles with Arcadi. "We're fed up with living like this," he had warned. "Enough is enough, it's time to make a move."

For several days, Piccirilli posted men near the Consenza to discreetly watch Rizzuto and his cronies come and go.

"I'm looking at him right through the café window!" one of them reported to his boss by cellphone as old Nick came into view. "I can see him perfectly; I could do it easy!"

"Do nothing tonight," Piccirilli answered. "I have to go to Toronto first."

On February 16, 2006, police officers paid Piccirilli a visit to warn him that he was playing a dangerous, and possibly fatal, game. "I'm not afraid to die," he retorted. "I know how to watch out for myself; I don't need anybody's help." A few hours later, he was on the phone to one of them, Sergeant Jos Tomeo of the RCMP.

"Is it illegal to wear a bulletproof vest?" he asked ingenuously.

"No, no, you can if you want to," the Mountie assured him.

That same evening, through an intermediary, Piccirilli asked to acquire weapons from Sharon Simon. The next day, at the request of the RCMP investigators, SQ officers stopped a Volkswagen Touareg on Highway 640, not far from Oka. Simon was seated in the vehicle with a man. She was on her way to deliver an AK-47 to Laval. The automatic weapon was of the same type that Mohawk warriors had favoured during the Oka Crisis of 1990, the infamous seventy-eight-day standoff sparked by a land dispute and pitting First Nations activists against the SQ, the RCMP and eventually the Canadian army. The officers also found a black case containing a .380 calibre pistol, a magazine and ammunition. They seized the weapons, then sent Simon and her companion on their way so as not to jeopardize the ongoing investigation.

Police never ascertained how the conflict between Piccirilli and the Rizzuto clan leadership was settled. The latter were arrested and jailed later that year on November 22, as Operation Colisée drew to a close. By that time, Piccirilli, the Kanehsatake drug queen and several accomplices had themselves been nabbed, and faced gangsterism, drug trafficking and money laundering charges. A Court of Québec judge threw out the charges against Piccirilli, but Canada's Ministry of Justice appealed.

Around six-thirty in the morning of August 11, 2008, an unknown assailant tried to kill Antonio Magi (who had been kidnapped three years earlier but managed to escape his captors). The forty-nine-year-old Montreal real estate developer was at the wheel of his Range Rover, waiting for a red light at the intersection of Cavendish Boulevard and Monkland Avenue in the Notre-Dame-de-Grâce neighbourhood, when the killer fired several bullets into him and then fled on foot. As the critically wounded Magi slumped in his seat, his foot came off the brake pedal of his suv, which rolled slowly along Cavendish, ran into several parked cars and came to rest against a tree. He was rushed to hospital, where he fell into a coma. He eventually recovered but remained hospitalized for six months, during which time he had ample opportunity to reflect on the reasons for the attempt on his life and who might have ordered it.

Police, meanwhile, tried to piece together their own theory. They knew that Magi had benefited from the Rizzuto clan's protection for years. But that umbrella now seemed to be in tatters in the wake of Vito's arrest and extradition to the United States, one investigator noted. Magi had been doing business with Nick Rizzuto Jr. They had bought a piece of land together, in Montreal's west end, and planned to build a residential complex on it. They often met at the second-floor offices of FTM Construction, the company Magi ran with his younger brother, Alberino (Rino) Magi, on Upper Lachine Road in Notre-Dame-de-Grâce.

Magi was a prominent figure in Montreal real estate. His wife ran a private daycare that received subsidies from the Quebec government. In 1999, he had partnered with an acquaintance of Vito Rizzuto, condo developer Terry Pomerantz—he of the stolen Cadillac suv recovered by Vito's men—on the project to convert the former cold-storage warehouse in Old Montreal. The project, 1 Avenue du Port, had been announced with pomp and ceremony at a press conference held on a cruise ship moored in the harbour basin between the warehouse and the clock tower in Montreal's Old Port. Acting as spokesperson for his company of the time, Harbourteam, Magi had posed for photographers with the heritage building in the background. Before long, though, problems cropped up, partners abandoned him, and buyers who had left large deposits began wondering whether they would ever be able to move into their promised condos in one of the city's most prestigious harbourfront addresses. The project was eventually taken over by another developer but not completed until several years later. Tony and Rino Magi also held a significant stake in a high-rise construction project in Montreal's downtown core, at the corner of De la Montagne Street and De Maisonneuve Boulevard. As debts continued to pile up, in 2005, Tony sought bankruptcy protection for Harbourteam and another firm of his, Gescor. His brother wouldn't fare much better and was involved in dodgy relations as well. In 2008, Rino and several other Montreal businessmen faced charges from U.S. authorities for having backed a telemarketing scam that preyed on senior citizens in California and other states.

A police search warrant filed at the Montreal courthouse stated that Tony Magi "had close ties to Montreal's Italian Mafia"—a charge that he has always denied. He was also known to be acquainted with street gang members. Upon his discharge from hospital, he hired bodyguards. That precaution couldn't prevent one of his enemies from firing shots at his wife, Rita Biasini, in February 2011, as she drove away from the family home on a quiet street in Notre-Dame-de-Grâce in her suv. She escaped unharmed, managing to drive to a nearby police station.

The next kidnapping victim was Mario Marabella. On December 4, 2008, as he stopped to buy gas at a service station in Laval, he was waylaid by three or four men. Later that evening, his car was found torched and abandoned in east-end Montreal. Marabella had a prior conviction for loansharking and was involved in several other illicit pursuits, including trafficking in marijuana. Police reckoned he was abducted because he owed a significant amount to creditors and, moreover, had adopted an excessively high profile on the street. Marabella answered to Agostino Cuntrera, still one of the most influential members of the Sicilian clan. With Moreno Gallo behind bars and under threat of deportation to Italy, it was Cuntrera who was now tapped as a potential successor to the Rizzutos as leader of the Montreal Mafia. In that light, the kidnapping of Marabella, his right-hand man, took on even greater importance.

Many more blows—some of them far more devastating—awaited the clan.

On January 16, 2009, in the early afternoon, Sam Fasulo, age thirty-seven, was in his Jeep Cherokee waiting for a red light to change at the intersection of Henri-Bourassa and Langelier Boulevards in Montreal North when a light-coloured suv pulled up beside him. One of its two occupants sprayed Fasulo with a volley of bullets, almost two dozen in all, hitting him several times in the head and body. One round pierced a wad of bills in his jacket pocket. Fasulo found the strength to make a call on his cellphone. When police and ambulance workers arrived, he was slumped against the steering wheel. He was taken to hospital, where he succumbed to his injuries two days later.

Fasulo was very well known to police. He had close ties to Francesco Arcadi, Vito Rizzuto's lieutenant, who by then was incarcerated as well. Around one in the morning on December 8, 2002, an Operation Colisée wiretap had picked up Arcadi ordering Fasulo to settle a problem. A mob-linked drug trafficker was being hassled in a bar on Fleury Street in Montreal; Arcadi told Fasulo to head straight there but to use verbal threats, not violence, on the troublemaker: "I don't want you to go there and start hitting right away. When you get there you grab this piece of shit . . . You tell him: 'Don't you touch this fellow or I will slit your throat like a goat.'" Another recording from three-quarters of an hour later suggests that Fasulo settled the problem in short order but that he did use his fists, not just his mouth.

The elimination of Fasulo was significant in more than one respect. Whoever ordered the hit had succeeded in taking out not just the right-hand man of a key Rizzuto clan leader, but a drug dealer who controlled the market in several Italian cafés in Saint-Michel and other northeast Montreal neighbourhoods.

Fasulo had been arrested in February 2003 with seventeen others, accused of running a ring that dealt up to $100,000 in heroin and crack cocaine every week. The network operated out of cafés with decidedly unsubtle mob-inspired names like "Scarface" and "Goodfellas." Neighbourhood residents complained that the drug dealing led to a host of other problems including fights, prostitution, and syringes littering the streets. After a year-long investigation, Montreal police had asked for the support of the RCMP and the SQ; some 185 officers were marshalled to arrest the members of the network in multiple raids. They seized hashish, marijuana, crack, heroin, Viagra tablets, luxury cars, automatic weapons, handguns and a silencer, as well as sticks of dynamite, detonators and other bomb-making materials. Many of the cafés were dirty and poorly maintained, obviously serving only as fronts for drug dealing. "During our search and seizure operations, we had to look pretty hard before finding any coffee machines," said one officer who had been part of the investigation, appropriately dubbed "Operation Espresso." They did, however, discover more than a hundred thousand dollars' worth of sophisticated video surveillance gear.

Fasulo had been sentenced to four years in prison but won early release in 2005, after which he discreetly resumed his former line of work. His murder was a prelude to several more significant ones. And, coincidence or not, it also occurred at the same time as the first in a wave of firebombing attacks on Italian cafés. Molotov cocktails were lobbed at around twenty of them in northeast Montreal during 2009 and 2010. With some rare exceptions, the perpetrators followed the same modus operandi, striking at night or in the very early morning, when the establishments were unoccupied. They would smash the café window, light the rag "fuse" stuffed into the neck of a gasoline-filled bottle and throw the projectile onto the floor inside. In some cases, fairly serious blazes ensued, causing considerable damage, but often the flames died out quickly or were extinguished by firefighters. There were no deaths. Police eventually made an initial arrest: nineteen-year-old Mickendy Démosthène, who had links to Montreal's street gangs. Arrests of other street gang members followed, and investigators put forward various theories on motives for the attacks.

One was that since the arrests of the Rizzuto clan leadership, the street gangs had decided they could directly confront Sicilian operatives on their turf in the city's northeast neighbourhoods. Other investigators, however, thought it far more likely that rival Italian clans were using street gang members to send a message. One person who thought so was Jacques Robinette, deputy chief with the Montreal police force and the man in charge of special investigations. He believed it was quite possible that the young criminals had been hired by Ontario's Calabrian clans looking to take advantage of the weakened Sicilian organization and gain a foothold in Montreal.

It was a scenario that fit with what investigators had learned about Sergio Piccirilli and his February 2005 meetings with his Calabrian boss in Toronto and with Paolo Violi's two sons in Hamilton, prior to his declaring war on the Rizzuto clan.

Late in the morning on August 21, 2009, long-time Rizzuto family associate Federico del Peschio was shot and killed behind La Cantina restaurant, on Saint-Laurent Boulevard near Legendre Street in the north-end neighbourhood of Ahuntsic. The fifty-nine-year-old, who lived in Laval, was starting his business day. He locked the door of his silver Mercedes and headed across the parking lot toward the restaurant, which he co-owned. A hired killer, obviously well acquainted with del Peschio's daily routine, was lying in wait. Just after the fatal shots rang out, a witness saw a dark-skinned man flee down the alley behind the restaurant and into a waiting van driven by an accomplice. The driver pulled away immediately, before anyone could note the licence plate number. "I walked over to the victim and saw the pool of his own blood," the same witness recounted. "The restaurant staff were hysterical. They were going round in circles, completely hysterical." Investigating officers found a firearm and spent cartridges in the parking lot. They strongly suspected that the killer was a street gang member.

At a trial in 2002, the restaurant had been described as a meeting place for drug traffickers. One of those accused, lawyer José Guede, had been ordered not to visit the establishment because he would likely run into Vito Rizzuto and other mobsters there (Guede was cleared of the charges against him and that decision was later upheld on appeal). Vito was a regular at La Cantina; it was there that del Peschio introduced him to *La Presse* sports columnist Réjean Tremblay one evening in the winter of 2003, when Vito complained about journalists looking into his links to OMG Media, the company that installed public garbage and recycling bins emblazoned with advertising.

In 1979, del Peschio had been convicted of trafficking in hashish along with Sidney Lallouz, a drug dealer who also made headlines when, after his release from prison, he was involved in land deals with the Société de développement industriel de Montréal (SODIM), a paramunicipal agency responsible for industrial development in the city.

In February 1988, del Peschio had been arrested in Caracas, Venezuela, with Nicolò Rizzuto and two other accomplices, when police found cocaine in Rizzuto's home. Del Peschio spent a few months in a Venezuelan prison with old Nick. Their two other cellmates were Antonino Mongiovì, Paolo Cuntrera's son-in-law, and Gennaro Scaletta. Not long before del Peschio was killed behind La Cantina, Scaletta, who had since become an informant, had testified at a trial in Italy pursuant to an investigation dubbed Operazione Orso Bruno (Operation Brown Bear) that exposed money laundering operations involving Rizzuto family members.

Del Peschio had become co-owner of La Cantina after his return from Venezuela. He was not content merely to play the host when patrons came to dine in his restaurant, however. In his entourage, there were whispers that he had a discreet hand in several illegal pursuits, including loansharking and hashish trafficking. Some said he had been exterminated because he had interceded in a dispute over a debt. Others believed he had been called to the rescue by the Rizzuto clan after Operation Colisée, and had agreed to act as a "compromise candidate" as boss, pending the release of the clan leaders from jail.

There was little doubt that rivals were out to widen the vacuum around the old-guard Sicilian family and their associates. Ironically, del Peschio was killed just a block north of the spot where Pietro Sciara had been shot dead as he left the Riviera cinema on Valentine's Day 1976. The slaying of Sciara, *consigliere* to Vic Cotroni and Paolo Violi, was the event that hastened the end of the Calabrian clan's reign and the start of the Rizzuto family's ascendancy. The Riviera cinema, long since closed, was now the Solid Gold, a bar that attracted members of organized crime groups. Its manager was Moreno Gallo.

The viewing for del Peschio took place at the Loreto funeral home, which belonged to the Rizzuto and Renda families. Some three hundred people attended the funeral at the Church of the Madonna della Difesa, the same place of worship where Paolo Violi's funeral had taken place in 1978.

Huge floral arrangements hung from the rears of two limousines parked in front of the church, in the heart of Montreal's Little Italy. One had been sent by mobster Tony Mucci, who had survived a murder attempt himself a year and a half earlier; the other was from Lorenzo LoPresti, age thirty-eight, the son of Giuseppe (Joe) LoPresti, murdered in April 1992. Several familiar faces from the Montreal Mafia lingered on the forecourt after the casket was borne from the church. Libertina Rizzuto, Vito's mother, was seen weeping in the arms of a man; she had been very fond of del Peschio. Her daughter, Maria Renda, also quite upset, was by her side.

The tall figure of Nicolò Rizzuto Jr., Vito's eldest son, stood out from the crowd of mourners. Curious onlookers could not help but remark on how much he looked like his father, with his hair carefully combed backward, his brooding gaze and his stocky build. With him were his mother, Giovanna, as well as his brother, Leonardo, and sister, Bettina. Five months later, Nick Jr.'s life came to a violent end as well.

Rizzuto, forty-two, was hit by four bullets shortly after noon on December 28, on Upper Lachine Road in Notre-Dame-de-Grâce. Area residents told reporters they heard at least six gunshots. "It sounded just like someone setting off firecrackers," one neighbour said. Witnesses described a dark-skinned man wearing jeans and a dark coat, his head partly covered by a hood, who ran from the scene after the shots rang out and disappeared down Melrose Avenue.

When first responders reached the scene, a crowd had already gathered. In Montreal, a killing at midday in a fairly busy area is anything but an everyday occurrence. Vito's son lay in the parking lot of a residential building, next to his black Mercedes coupe. Firefighters and ambulance workers tried in vain to resuscitate him. Police quickly cordoned off a security perimeter. Investigators climbed the stairs to the second floor of a building right next door, site of the office of FTM Construction, real estate developer Tony Magi's firm. Rizzuto and Magi had partnered on real estate projects in the Montreal suburbs of Lachine and LaSalle, and Rizzuto had often been to the office over the past three years. Four months earlier, in September, he had been there with Magi when police investigating various mobland murder attempts went to question the developer.

Police had been back to FTM Construction in November, armed this time with a search warrant. They were looking into incidents of assault and attempted extortion involving members of a street gang. A week later, in connection with that investigation, they arrested Lamartine Sévère Paul, a member of a gang aligned with the Crips, and a cousin of alleged street gang kingpin Ducarme Joseph. Police alleged Magi lent money to a wide variety of clients and hired Joseph to intimidate those who refused to pay.

Magi, however, had no criminal record, and neither did Nicolò Rizzuto Jr., apart from three impaired driving convictions. But police knew that Vito had naturally chosen his eldest son to take over, at least in part, the reins of the family business if need be. After returning from Cuba, not long before his January 2004 arrest, Vito had introduced Nick Jr. to several of his underworld contacts as well as businessmen in the clan's orbit. Nick's principal task had been laundering money for the family. He had also thought he had the necessary clout to put a stop to the wave of Italian café firebombings. According to police, Nick had at least one "face to face" meeting with street gang members and was heard saying, "The blacks aren't laughing any more," a week before his death.

These attempts at conflict resolution had been welcomed with shrugged shoulders, if not outright contempt. Nicolò Jr. may have resembled his father physically, but the comparisons ended there. He had inherited none of Vito's charisma, possessed none of his experience and failed to impose respect in the milieu. He seemed not to understand that the street gang members were in all likelihood being manipulated by a rival Italian Mafia faction looking to topple the Rizzuto clan. A faction very probably aligned with the Ontario Calabrian clan but also comprising younger Sicilian mobsters rebelling against the old guard represented by Nick Sr., Paolo Renda and Rocco Sollecito. "The Calabrians have started taxing the base again, starting with the bars run by the Sicilians, and they're using the street gangs," one investigator contended.

On the evening of December 28, a few hours after the murder, the clan huddled urgently at the home of Nicolò Rizzuto Sr., who had been released from Bordeaux prison the year before. The family, understandably, was shattered. Reached by phone at the penitentiary in Florence, Colorado, a distraught Vito said he thought he could convince prison authorities to grant him a furlough so he could attend the funeral, but his relatives persuaded him not to. His wife, Giovanna, and their two surviving children, already torn by grief, feared Vito's presence would attract even more media coverage of the ceremony. And they didn't relish the thought of him making only a brief visit to Montreal, showing up at the church in handcuffs and escorted by police.

Nick Jr.'s gold casket was carried into the Church of the Madonna della Difesa, where the clan had bid *addio* to Federico del Peschio five months earlier. Old Nick now said goodbye to his grandson, accompanied by his wife, Libertina, his daughter-in-law, Giovanna, and numerous other family members. The deceased's widow, Eleonora, sat with her two children nearby. Her son was named Vito, like his grandfather and his great-great-grandfather, murdered in a quarry in Patterson, New

York, in 1933. "Forgive us our sins and lead us to eternal salvation," intoned Father Jacques du Plouy, addressing the faithful in Italian. "Nicolò was promised eternal joy at his baptism . . . Now, he is in good hands with God."

After the ceremony, eight pallbearers lifted the casket and placed it in the hearse. The cortège of ten limousines got underway, headed for a cemetery in east-end Montreal. Press photographers had set up on some balconies on the other side of the street that provided the best vantage point from which to record the scene. Plainclothes police officers trained their camera lenses on the forecourt as well; later, analysts would determine who exactly had attended but also who was absent. A few friends of the family spoke to journalists. "It's a monstrous way to end your life. It's a sad, sad day for me," said Ricardo Padulo, the owner of the restaurant Buffet Da Enrico, located on Saint-Zotique Street in the same neighbourhood as the church; his wife had gone to high school with Nick Jr. Padulo said the Rizzutos "help poor people, and people in trouble with their businesses. We can criticize, but they did a lot of good."

The murder of Vito's son was by far the most severe blow ever struck against the family to that point. The various arrests, Vito's extradition, Nick Sr.'s jail sentence and the murder of close associates like Federico del Peschio seemed almost trivial events next to this shocking tragedy. "To have a son murdered is the worst thing that can happen to a Mafia boss," said Pierre de Champlain, former Criminal Intelligence Directorate analyst with the RCMP in Ottawa. There were rumblings in the underworld that Old Nick was prepared to pay his family's enemies two million dollars to be at peace.

Bullets flew in broad daylight in a busy neighbourhood once again, on March 18, 2010. This time, the target was forty-one-year-old Ducarme Joseph. Early in the afternoon, two masked hit men burst into his clothing store, FlawNego, on Saint-Jacques Street in Old Montreal, firing dozens of times. Joseph managed to flee by the rear exit, but the others present in the store were not as lucky. Peter Christopoulos, Joseph's bodyguard and drug-trafficking partner, and Jean Gaston, the store manager, were killed. Frédéric Louis, another of Joseph's bodyguards, was injured. Alain

Gagnon, an electrician who happened to be working in the store and had no links to organized crime, was shot in the face but survived.

Joseph, the alleged street gang leader, lived in a downtown apartment, above an Eggspectation restaurant franchise at the corner of De Maisonneuve Boulevard and De la Montagne Street. The building had been put up by Tony Magi and his partners. A search warrant states that the promoter had given Joseph the apartment in lieu of payment after he hired him to shake down debtors. The day after the shooting, police caught up with and arrested Joseph as he was leaving Magi's office, FTM Construction, not far from the parking lot where Nicolò Rizzuto Jr. had been shot dead.

The close ties between Joseph and Magi, and the fact that Magi was known to consort with Mafiosi, led investigators and crime watchers alike to believe that the FlawNego shooting was connected to the conflicts that were destabilizing the Italian Mafia in the city, but the precise motive for the attempt on Joseph's life remained murky. Three members of rival street gangs were arrested and charged with murder and attempted murder. A persistent rumour had it that the Sicilian clan had offered a bounty of $200,000 to whoever could rub out Ducarme Joseph.

Five months after the murder of Nick Jr., a second enemy thrust cut deep and close to the heart of the Rizzuto family. Seventy-year-old Paolo Renda vanished—from all appearances, he was the victim of a kidnapping. Until recently, such a move would have been unthinkable. No one would have dared attempt such a brazen, direct attack on someone so high up in the clan—the *consigliere* was the number-three man after Vito Rizzuto and his father. Renda, of course, was not merely an associate of the Rizzutos: he was tied to them by blood. He was Old Nick's cousin: the latter's mother was the sister of Renda's father, Calogero Renda, who had murdered a Mafia boss in Siculiana before moving to Montreal—and, in 1978, was suspected of having planned the killing of Paolo Violi. Paolo Renda had then married Vito's only sister, who became Maria Renda. Moreover, he was godfather to Nick Jr.

Thursday, May 20, 2010, was shaping up to be a fine spring day. Paolo Renda was continuing to enjoy the sweet taste of freedom, having been released from prison just three months earlier—but these would be his last moments of liberty. He made himself a cup of coffee—he liked powdered decaf, which his acquaintances must have viewed as heretical behaviour for an Italian, and one who grew grapes to make his own wine, to boot—then left his home on Antoine-Berthelet Avenue to go play a round of golf.

Arrested with the rest of the Consenza clique in 2006 at the close of Operation Colisée and sentenced to six years in prison for gangsterism and possession of the proceeds of crime, Renda had won release in February 2010 after serving two-thirds of his sentence. Correctional Service of Canada, however, was worried that he might seek revenge for the murder of Nick Jr., and the National Parole Board had subjected him to stricter conditions: he had to present a monthly statement of income and expenses, and refrain from associating with other dangerous offenders. Items he was forbidden from carrying included a pager, a cellphone and, of course, a firearm. "Unfortunate events took place on December 28, 2009, during which your godson was killed," the parole board commissioners remarked on the day of Renda's release. "The Correctional Service of Canada fears reprisals on the part of Italian organized crime. A tighter framework is recommended to assure public security."

After his golf game, Renda went to the Loreto funeral home, which his family owned, to pay his respects to a recently deceased friend. He then left Rivière-des-Prairies and headed for home. On the way, he stopped at a Saint-Léonard butcher shop, where he bought four steaks for a planned supper with his wife, Maria, his daughter, Domenica, and her husband, Antonio Cammisano. He had said he would be home by 4 P.M. His son, forty-three-year-old Calogero, knew his father's habits well and began to worry when he didn't return at the promised hour. Maria hoped her husband had simply been stopped by police for some violation of his parole conditions. She called the Correctional Service; an officer then contacted Montreal police.

Calogero went out to look for his father and quickly spotted his car. The light-grey Infiniti sedan was sitting not far from the family home, in front of a house on Gouin Boulevard near Albert-Prévost Avenue. The driver's side window was open, and the key was still in the ignition. Renda always drove with the windows up and the air conditioning on—details that were noted by investigators when they later tried to reconstitute the sequence of events. Apparently, the individuals who pulled Renda over to the side of the road had been wearing police uniforms, which might explain why he had willingly lowered the window. All the available evidence suggested he would have had no reason to be suspicious. But the key in the ignition meant he had probably left the vehicle in a hurry, perhaps under threat from someone with a gun in his hand.

A woman who lived in the home opposite the spot where the abandoned Infiniti was found said a man—probably Calogero—had come to her house around six o'clock. "This man knocked on the door and asked me if I'd seen the driver of the car," she told a reporter. "I said no and he left in a panic."

Police officers went to the Renda residence to complete the missing person report. When they arrived, the house was full of visitors. Besides Maria Renda, they noted the presence of Calogero, his sister, Domenica, and her husband, Antonio Cammisano, as well as Paolo Renda's in-laws and neighbours: Nicolò and Libertina Rizzuto. All appeared to be in a state of shock. Seated at the kitchen table with her daughter, Maria told the officers what she could about her husband's abduction. Libertina hovered nearby. The three men remained in the living room. When they wanted to converse, they got up and went outside, making sure to slide the patio door shut behind them. A pensive Nicolò, still shaken by the murder of his grandson, narrowed his small, dark eyes. Once or twice, Calogero Renda tried to insert himself into the conversation with the police officers, nervously trying to taunt them, but his efforts fell flat. The officers closed their notebooks and left a phone number with Mrs. Renda. Police asked for the public's help in finding Paolo Renda and issued a description: white male, age seventy, grey hair, brown eyes, height five feet eight inches, weight 170 pounds, last seen wearing a striped polo shirt and navy blue pants. In the ensuing weeks, neither Maria Renda nor any other family member ever contacted police to ask how the investigation was progressing.

Paolo Renda had long suspected that something like this could happen to him and had made arrangements accordingly. In late 2005, there had been the threats from drug trafficker Sergio Piccirilli and the members of the D'Amico family of Granby. In the waning weeks of Operation Colisée, Renda had had surveillance cameras installed around his home. Like the other clan leaders, he travelled with bodyguards. On the day of his arrest, November 22, 2006, police had searched his house for more than twelve hours and discovered a vintage .32 calibre pistol, loaded, in a secret compartment built into a piece of furniture. They had also seized two illegally stored rifles.

The day after his son-in-law cousin disappeared, Nicolò Rizzuto was due in Montreal municipal court to answer charges of impaired driving. The trial was put off—not for the first time. The Crown prosecutor, Jean-Christofe Ardeneus, explained to Judge Robert Diamond that a court appearance might be a risky move for the accused, given the events of the day before. "A detective sergeant [with the Montreal police] said it could cause certain problems with his security," the prosecutor said.

The judge was reluctant to grant a further delay, noting that the charges stemmed from the incident four years previously when Rizzuto had driven his Mercedes into a fire truck that was responding to an emergency on December 31, 2005. Police arriving on that scene had noticed that he appeared confused and had trouble standing up; and now, Rizzuto family lawyer Loris Cavaliere told Judge Diamond that the news of Renda's disappearance was stressful for Old Nick, who had a respiratory illness to boot.

"This happened yesterday and his health is already at risk," Cavaliere said. On his way out of court, the lawyer told reporters that he could not find the words to describe his feelings in the wake of Renda's disappearance. A month earlier, he had represented Renda before Quebec's construction regulation agency, the Régie du bâtiment, which was considering revoking the licence of Renda Construction because of Paolo's conviction on gangsterism charges. Renda had written to the agency that he preferred to withdraw his renewal request rather than see the licence revoked.

Cavaliere said he was dismayed by the "bizarre" circumstances of Renda's disappearance. "That's the hardest thing to comprehend," the lawyer said. "He's a good, quiet man. Since his release he's been following his conditions by the book."

Investigators, once again, could only speculate for the most part. Both the criminal world and the Italian community were rife with all manner of fanciful rumours. Some said Renda had been abducted at the behest of senior Mafia leaders in Sicily bent on forcing the Rizzutos to hand over money they had hoarded over several years. Others said the orders had come from New York City. Still others claimed that Renda hadn't been abducted at all, but had vanished of his own volition and was hiding out in Venezuela. Police, meanwhile, had every reason to believe that he had been first tortured, then killed by his abductors, who were out to learn the Rizzuto organization's secrets. Whichever theory was correct, it was clear that a rival clan was intent on removing the Rizzuto clan and taking over the Montreal underworld. There was no "war" per se, for the simple reason that the Rizzutos, no doubt too severely weakened, weren't striking back after any of the attacks. Thirty years previously, the Rizzutos had eliminated the Violi brothers in succession to usurp their throne. Now they were tasting their own proverbial medicine.

Whoever the enemy was, he continued sending messages written in blood. On June 29, Agostino Cuntrera, aged sixty-six, one of the Sicilians who had taken the rap for Paolo Violi's slaying in 1978, one of the senior Montreal representatives of the tentacular Cuntrera-Caruana-Rizzuto alliance and one of the men thought to be in line to succeed Vito, was murdered. Once again, the slaying took place in broad daylight. The hit squad also killed Cuntrera's driver and bodyguard, forty-year-old Liborio Sciascia.

The two men were outside Cuntrera's wholesale food distribution company, John & Dino, on Magloire Street in the Saint-Léonard industrial park. Cuntrera was seated at a picnic table normally used by employees on cigarette breaks, not far from his armoured vehicle. Though he may well have suspected that it was only a matter of time before killers had him in their sights as well, the old mobster hadn't changed his routine, stopping by his food warehouse daily. Around four in the afternoon, a black Chevrolet Impala turned onto Magloire Street, discharging a masked man who raised a hunting rifle and fired. A single bullet struck Cuntrera in the head, sending him sprawling to the ground and killing him instantly. Sciascia, who was standing beside the picnic table, was hit in the chest and abdomen. He died soon afterward at Santa Cabrini Hospital. The Chevy was gone as quickly as it had appeared. A nearly identical car was later stopped by police, who held its occupants for questioning but later released them after determining they had nothing to do with the shooting.

The twin killings created a commotion in the surrounding area. Dozens of workers poured out of nearby workshops and warehouses and rushed to the crime scene, massing up against the police barriers. Cuntrera's body lay under a yellow sheet, with one foot protruding, for several hours while investigators combed the scene. "My boss called me and told me to watch it on the news. He said, 'It's him! It's Cuntrera!'" one woman said. "He was well known in the community," a bystander added. Several men banded together, leaning on the hood of a car, speaking in hushed tones and casting annoyed glances at journalists. One of them approached photographers, saying, "You can take as many pictures as you want. Just make sure none of us is in any of them." As afternoon turned to evening, limousines and luxury cars including Jaguars and Mercedes cruised past the food warehouse repeatedly.

After the convictions of Nicolò Rizzuto and the clan's inner circle in the fall of 2008, Cuntrera had agreed—though not particularly enthusiastically—to come to the aid of the now rudderless leadership. Under the yoke of three years' probation, Old Nick was rebuffing all requests for help: when a mobster or businessman came to him with a problem, he replied that he could do nothing and suggested that they go see Cuntrera.

Nicknamed *"le seigneur de Saint-Léonard,"* Cuntrera had sent out a message that all those who owed money to the clan had to pay up immediately. That entreaty had led to a wave of conflicts, reprisals, kidnappings and attempted murders, and generally provoked much grumbling against the Sicilian Mafia bosses, who no longer had the respect of the "young ones." In the United States, most of the Cosa Nostra families had seen a shift in authority toward fourth-generation mobsters, but in Montreal, the old-timers were stubbornly clinging to power.

Well aware of the threats against him, Cuntrera had left the funeral of Nicolò Rizzuto Jr. in Tony Mucci's armoured vehicle. A few months later, he bought his own. Police had met with him shortly before his death and warned him that he might be gunned down. He had confirmed to them in veiled terms that he was filling the role of acting family boss "a bit," but added that he was getting old and was not at all happy to be doing so. Nevertheless, he'd thanked the officers for their warning and said he would take it under advisement.

Liborio Sciascia, who had done time in the United States on a cocaine trafficking conviction, had agreed to become Cuntrera's driver and bodyguard despite attempts to dissuade him by family members, who feared for his safety. The assignment paid well—$1,500 a week—and it was a way of paying tribute to Cuntrera, who had helped him after his release from prison. Sciascia's wake was held at the Loreto funeral home. The Cuntrera family paid all expenses.

The viewing for Agostino Cuntrera was at the Loreto as well. Henchmen stood guard outside, and Nicolò Rizzuto arrived discreetly through a side entrance. The room was awash in white flowers. A photograph of the deceased, adorned with a rosary, sat on the closed casket. Above it was the word *nonno*—"grandpa" in Italian. The coffin was then placed in a hearse for the trip to Notre-Dame-du-Mont-Carmel Church in Saint-Léonard, followed by three limousines blanketed in floral arrangements. Some six hundred mourners packed the church, almost all of them clad in black. They included Leonardo Rizzuto, Vito's second son. Bells pealed, and the casket was borne into the church and under the nave. As it passed through the front door, bodyguards made the sign of the cross.

It was, apparently, the only remaining gesture that the members and associates of the Sicilian clan could muster. They had towered over the landscape of organized crime in Montreal, Quebec and a good part of Canada for decades, but now a page of history was being turned.

EPILOGUE

T HE SUN HAD ALREADY SET ON WEDNESDAY, November 10, 2010, when a man armed with a high-powered rifle slipped into the protective cover of the woodland behind Nicolò Rizzuto's home on Antoine-Berthelet Avenue. A thin, waxing crescent moon hung above the horizon. The temperature had risen steadily throughout the day, from the freezing point at dawn to nearly eight degrees Celsius by dusk—well above normal for that time of year.

The intruder chose a spot some fifteen metres from the house, near the edge of the woods. He settled behind a hedge, adjusted his rifle's telescopic sight and waited. A wind had blown up, reaching twenty-six kilometres an hour. But at that distance, it would have no impact on the trajectory of the bullet.

Since his release from prison, old Nick had spent most of his time at home. The eighty-six-year-old patriarch's health was faltering. Moreover, police had warned him that his life was in danger. He had taken the threat seriously and installed surveillance cameras around the property. The mid-November evening was dark, though, and the cameras picked up no suspicious movements.

At around twenty minutes to six, Rizzuto entered the solarium at the rear of the house and prepared to sit down for dinner with his wife, Libertina, and his daughter, Maria—whose husband, Paolo Renda, had disappeared several months earlier, presumably kidnapped and murdered.

The killer sighted the old don's head in the rifle scope and pulled the trigger.

The .300 calibre bullet—a heavy projectile, typically used for hunting big game like bear or moose—flew from the mouth of the weapon at some one thousand metres per second. As it punched through the double glass of the window, its copper jacket tore away, leaving the lead core to pursue a straight trajectory, barely missing Libertina and striking the old man in the jaw. The slug did not penetrate as far as the brain, and did relatively minor—at least, not lethal—damage. A fragment of the jacket, however, took a slightly different path, severing his aorta and proving instantaneously fatal. Nicolò Rizzuto collapsed to the floor.

After an initial moment of shock, one of the two women called 911. Ambulance technicians and police arrived within minutes. Rizzuto was taken to hospital, where a physician pronounced him dead; the body was sent on to the Laboratoire de sciences judiciaires et de médecine légale, part of SQ headquarters in the former Parthenais Detention Centre in east-end Montreal, for an autopsy. Ballistics testing on the fatal bullet and its fragments was conducted in the same lab. Every projectile bears the markings of the gun barrel from which it is fired, much as a child's DNA corresponds to that of his or her parents. When viewed under a microscope, these impressions are irrefutable proof of the "paternity" of a bullet—as long as the matching firearm can be found. With luck—a lot of it—a search may one day locate the weapon that was used to kill Nicolò Rizzuto. In the meantime, all that ballistics experts can do is theorize. It is possible that the hit man used a sniper rifle, but more likely that he was armed with a simple hunting rifle, perhaps a Remington, a Winchester or a Savage.

Police cordoned off Antoine-Berthelet Avenue, unrolling a length of orange tape to prevent curious onlookers from approaching the house, and set about taking photographs. The single bullet had left a neat hole in the windowpane. Investigators seized and viewed the surveillance video recordings, but they would reveal no clues as to the assassin's identity. A search of the area around the house, to see whether the man had left any incriminating items or marks, was no more fruitful.

News of the patriarch's demise spread swiftly. Reporters descended on Mafia Row in time to see a woman leaving the home of Vito Rizzuto, right next door to his parents'; another woman helped her walk to a third nearby house, the Renda residence. Family lawyer Loris Cavaliere, who had accompanied Nicolò Rizzuto on his release from Bordeaux Prison, joined them there.

Commander Denis Mainville, the head of the Montreal police force's anti-gang squad, explained to reporters that officers had previously warned other individuals that their lives were also at risk. "We have to advise them. So it was not only [Mr. Rizzuto] who was advised. Other people were, too," Mainville said. "It's a regular part of our work."

Mainville went on to say that police had taken individuals with known links to the Rizzutos into custody, along with their bodyguards, and seized armoured vehicles as well as bulletproof vests. He also mentioned that they had recently arrested Tony Mucci as well as Tony Magi, the construction contractor who had been a business partner of Nick Rizzuto Jr., Vito's murdered son.

"Our organized crime division has been very active in recent months," he added. "There have been several multidisciplinary teams on the ground in different locations. Our best investigators have been working to clarify the latest events . . . [Rizzuto] was an important member of the Mafia; everyone knew it. Several theories are being looked at right now. Is this something on the inside [of the Mafia]? Are there factions or different clans? Organized crime is in the midst of change, and I can honestly say that we are looking at all theories."

The major blows struck by police, starting with Operation Colisée, had severely weakened organized criminal groups' foundations, Mainville concluded. "The field is wide open, and everybody wants to claim their turf . . . The Bonannos are major players, but there are others."

There were striking parallels between the murder of Nicolò Rizzuto and the execution of Paolo Violi's brother Rocco thirty years earlier, on

October 17, 1980. Violi had been sitting at the kitchen table, in his home on Saint-Léonard. On that evening as well, the killer had hidden behind the residence, waited until he could see his victim through the window, then fired a single shot, killing him outright in front of his wife. Rocco was the last of the three Violi brothers eliminated by the Rizzuto clan. These facts were not reason enough to conclude that a vendetta had been carried out, three decades later. Nonetheless, the two killings shared a troublingly similar modus operandi.

After the autopsy, the Loreto funeral home held a weekend-long visitation. Outside, officers with Montreal police, the RCMP and the SQ videotaped and photographed each visitor and took down the licence numbers of the vehicles arriving in the parking lot. Inside, through the three rooms of the lavish complex, the line stretched to a hundred people long for two whole days.

Close relatives spoke in hushed tones in the foyer, under the watchful eyes of the family's earpiece-wearing bodyguards. No fewer than two hundred floral sprays covered the walls, from floor to ceiling, each adorned with the name of an individual or family who had expressed their sympathies: Arcadi, Renda, Cammalleri, Giordano, Morello, Caruana, Vanelli . . .

Nicolò Rizzuto lay in an open casket, his hallmark fedora at his side. His widow, Libertina, aged eighty-three, and daughter, Maria, sixty-three, stood by him one last time, receiving the condolences of hundreds of well-wishers. Also present were two of the deceased's grandchildren, lawyers Leonardo and Libertina Rizzuto, as well as great-grandchildren.

When he had learned of his eldest son's murder almost a year earlier, speaking to family members by phone from prison in Florence, Colorado, Vito Rizzuto had been devastated. Apparently, he was not quite as overwhelmed at the news of his father's demise. He was angry, however, that his family's enemies had gone after an old man. During one of his phone conversations—almost all of them were monitored by U.S. prison authorities—he implied that it would have been more understandable to target him rather than his elderly father. He suggested that the family hold a modest funeral, but one worthy of Nicolò's stature. His daughter,

Libertina, to whom he often spoke on the phone, seemed to be the tower of strength in the Rizzuto family as they faced this latest in a succession of ordeals.

On the morning of the funeral, Monday, November 15, five private security guards fanned out in Dante Street in front of the Church of the Madonna della Difesa. An hour and a half before the ceremony was due to start, someone spotted a small black box on the steps of the church and alerted police. Two lengths of white tape had been stuck to the lid of the box in the shape of a cross. Police moved people out of the area and waited for the tactical squad to arrive. When they did, they opened the box with the greatest of care. A visibly nervous Loris Cavaliere was anxious to find out what its contents were: he wondered whether officers had found "a finger or an ear" severed from Paolo Renda, the family *consigliere*. As it turned out, the package held neither human remains nor an explosive device. Inside was a simple note written in Italian: "Down with the Mafia! Down with the collaborationist Church!" At first, police wondered whether the message was meant for the Rizzutos: was this an admonition from rivals to concede defeat permanently, pending the emergence of a "new regime"? Eventually, though, they floated a less spectacular but more plausible theory: the box had probably been left by an ordinary citizen with no ties to organized crime.

There were growing numbers of ordinary people paying attention to the Mafia, and many of them were enraged to learn just how far its influence extended.

The original French edition of this book had been published just two weeks before Nicolò Rizzuto's murder and was having quite an impact. The authors had emphasized the large scale of the Montreal mob's *pizzo* racket, notably within the city's Italian community. A year earlier, *La Presse* had broken the story of the "Fabulous Fourteen," the select club of contractors who split the lion's share of Quebec public works contracts amongst themselves, under the protective umbrella of the Mafia. Other media reports had helped focus public opinion. And on the morning of

November 10, just hours before Nicolò Rizzuto's murder, corruption in the construction industry and the role of the Mafia had fuelled intense debate in Quebec's national assembly. The day before, Radio-Canada's *Le Téléjournal* TV newscast ran an interview with an honest contractor who complained of having received threats from the Mafia after he responded to a public call for tenders. A petition demanding a public inquiry into construction industry practices had been tabled in the Quebec parliament. The leader of the opposition Parti Québécois (PQ), Pauline Marois, stood in the national assembly and challenged Premier Jean Charest:

> For the past seven years, the highest authorities have been aware of the existence of widespread collusion, but the Liberal government has turned a blind eye to it. More seriously, we learned that this closed system of collusion operated thanks to the Mafia in exchange for a *pizzo* of $500,000 a month—$6 million a year—using intimidation to stop honest contractors from bidding. Everyone who watched *Le Téléjournal* yesterday heard that threatening phone call, which sent shivers down the spine. Mr. Speaker, this is happening in Quebec, under a Liberal government that is tolerant of it. There are brave people risking a great deal to denounce the system, because the government refuses to cut out the cancer and shed the full light on the corruption that is rampant in Quebec. We have to break the silence, break this regime of terror. What does the premier have to gain from protecting *omertà*?

"When facing allegations of that nature, it's really a matter for police forces at all levels to investigate, so that evidence can be assembled, and people can be charged and prosecuted in court," Charest replied cautiously.

"The Colisée investigation was in 2006; that's four years ago," Marois retorted:

> We now know that, just for fourteen contractors, there is a minimum surcharge of $500,000 a month. How many of those

$500,000-a-month surcharges are there? For how many contractors in Quebec? How many government contracts are we going to pay too much for? And who are we paying too much to? Organized crime, that's who. How much longer are our taxes going to support the Mafia?

"When the subject is collusion, corruption, the Mafia, it really is a matter for the police, for all police forces," the premier reiterated. "These allegations, these situations must be firmly attacked. That is what the government is doing."

Stéphane Bergeron, PQ member of the national assembly for Verchères, pressed the point, citing a statement by the head of the SQ's recently formed Hammer Squad, who had acknowledged that ties existed between the Mafia and construction contractors. Bergeron then asserted that such police investigations would not suffice: only a public inquiry could shed the proper light on the workings of the Mafia system, he insisted. While the police investigate, he said, "the mob keeps on getting rich at our expense."

Hundreds of citizens gathered in the street in front of the Madonna della Difesa church for the funeral, but very few were allowed inside. The clan's private security detail closely guarded both entrances, deterring curious ordinary folk and potential enemies alike. Mobile news trucks thrust their satellite masts skyward, transmitting live coverage of the event. As at the funeral of Nicolò's namesake grandson in 2009, plainclothes police made sure they had the best views of the arriving guests. One such group of officers sat in a nondescript van, behind tinted windows and away from prying eyes. A colleague stood outside, waving away bystanders who stopped in front of the vehicle.

Few well-known figures stepped through the church doors. Conspicuously absent were members of the Bonanno family. But the attendees did include an influential construction company manager, one of the Fabulous Fourteen, as well as Giuseppe Borsellino, a founding member of the Italian-Canadian Community Foundation and president of Groupe Petra, a firm that co-owned two of Montreal's tallest sky-scrapers, the Stock Exchange Tower and the CIBC Tower. What was such an esteemed real estate promoter doing at the funeral of a mob boss? He was born in Cattolica Eraclea, like Nicolò Rizzuto, and had come to Canada the same year as him, in 1954. Had he simply felt compelled to pay his respects to another native of his hometown? The answers never came, as Borsellino refused a reporter's request for an interview.

The church, which can seat eight hundred faithful, was not quite full. A few empty places remained at the ends of several pews. Many Mafiosi and associates had obviously preferred to stay at home, no doubt having anticipated the strong turnout by police wielding cameras and video-tape recorders. Media representatives, meanwhile, were decidedly un-welcome inside the church. One journalist who did manage to make it inside was quickly ordered out. Four hulking security guards patrolled the pews, looking for trespassers.

The funeral mass was sober, lasted an hour and was conducted entirely in Italian. Four sprays of white roses had been placed before the altar, and a small bouquet sat atop the closed casket. A choir sang several hymns in Latin, capped off with a stirring rendition of "Ave Maria."

No family member spoke during the ceremony. The celebrant, Monsignor Igino Incantalupo, delivered no personalized message and offered no testimonials about the deceased. After giving Communion, he announced that the family wished to thank all those who had expressed their condolences, and that they would be laying Nicolò to rest at a private burial in Saint-François-d'Assise Cemetery.

A few days later, during a phone conversation with her brother, Vito, Maria Renda said she felt insulted that "hardly anybody" had come to the funeral. If the rest of what they said during that call is true, the family was firmly set against leaving Montreal, in spite of the accumu-lating tragedies. As a precaution, Maria's nephew, Leonardo Rizzuto, laid low for a while in Florida, making occasional trips to the Bahamas and to Colorado, where he visited his father in prison. Her son, Calogero (Charlie), was told to keep quiet.

The killing of the patriarch had come six weeks after that of yet another Rizzuto clan member. On September 29, 2010, Ennio Bruni was shot dead in front of Café Bellerose, in Laval, where he hung out almost daily. The thirty-six-year-old had already survived an attempt on his life: a year earlier, he had been shot while walking to his car. With three bullet wounds in one shoulder and another in his back, he had managed to get in the car and drive to a convenience store, where he called police. He recovered quickly from those injuries. Police attempted to interrogate him, but he refused to file charges. In legal documents filed in connection with the Colisée investigation, Bruni is described as a "bill collector" for the Rizzuto family. He worked Laval gambling houses and was part of Francesco Arcadi's crew. According to police, he was eliminated "because he had infringed on another Mafioso's territory."

Later, another Arcadi associate, Antonio Di Salvo, aged forty-four, was murdered. Di Salvo, a drug dealer, was found dead in his luxury home in the Rivière-des-Prairies neighbourhood on January 31, 2011, felled by at least one bullet to the head.

Investigators racked their brains trying to find a common thread linking the many murders in the Italian organized crime milieu in Montreal over the past two years. Not all of them were necessarily connected. True, most stemmed from the power struggle to fill voids left in the Mafia hierarchy after the dragnet that capped 2006's Operation Colisée. But there were exceptions. Police were almost certain that the August 2009 slaying of Federico del Peschio, behind his restaurant, La Cantina, had nothing to do with that struggle. Perhaps most surprisingly, nor did the murder of Nick Rizzuto Jr., it seemed. All signs pointed to both killings having been prompted by a dispute over money: a businessman with close Mafia ties who felt threatened by both men had supposedly ordered them killed, contracting the hits out to members of a street gang.

The rash of Molotov cocktail attacks in east-end Montreal wasn't linked exclusively to internecine Mafia squabbling either: restaurant owners of Turkish origin engaged in a pizza price war were taking advantage of the incendiary backdrop to settle their own accounts. Meanwhile, owners of Italian food importing and distribution businesses were employing the same means to similar ends. They may have been confrontational, but they weren't stooping to murdering their business rivals, and they weren't necessarily connected to Italian organized crime.

On the other hand, it was clear that certain notorious criminal figures had it in for the Rizzuto clan, notably for interim leader Francesco Arcadi.

One such figure was Raynald Desjardins, Vito Rizzuto's partner in crime over many years. Convicted on cocaine importing charges in 1993, Desjardins had served out a lengthy prison sentence and, after his release in 2004, had gone into the residential construction business. Desjardins wasn't Italian, which prevented him, of course, from ever becoming a made member of the Mafia. But his wealth, charisma, extensive criminal experience and impressive network of contacts made him a very powerful figure. And he held a grudge, having never gotten over the 2005 murder of his protegé Giovanni Bertolo.

Police suspected Desjardins and his brother-in-law Joe Di Maulo were playing a discreet behind-the-scenes role in the parade of collusion, rivalries, partnerships and betrayals that followed the killing of Nick Rizzuto Jr. Far from being shut out of the proceedings, the pair were plotting actively to install a new regime.

Born in 1943 in Calabria, Joe Di Maulo remained a pillar of the Montreal Mafia. He had accompanied Vic Cotroni to Paolo Violi's wedding in Hamilton, in 1965. At age twenty-eight, he was charged in connection with a triple murder that took place March 12, 1971, inside a disco that he managed, the Casa Loma. He was initially found guilty, but the conviction was overturned on appeal. On November 11, 1973, along with Violi and Desjardins, he went to New York City to represent the Montreal *decina* for the election of Phil Rastelli as head of the Bonanno family.

After Violi's murder in 1978, Di Maulo and other Cotroni clan members wisely fell into line with the Rizzuto camp. In the early 1990s, he helped Vito Rizzuto in his oddball quest to recover part of former Philippine dictator Ferdinand Marcos's purported hidden gold. In 2003, and on several other occasions, he accompanied Vito on his Dominican

Republic golfing trips. Then, the following year, Vito was arrested, followed not long afterward by his father. By that point, Di Maulo had already sensed the winds shifting. It was said that he owned a dozen or so perfectly above-board companies. He led an extremely discreet lifestyle, steering clear of bars and clubs. Like Desjardins, he was skilled at working both the underworld and the legitimate business world.

Di Maulo operated in the shadows, normally trusting only his old confederates from the Cotroni clan, among them Moreno Gallo, Tony Vanelli, Tony Mucci, Tony Volpato and the members of the Cordeleone family. He also had a wealth of contacts outside Quebec, especially in Ontario, and his ambassadorial acumen had long been recognized.

Desjardins, for his part, could count on solid relationships with the province's construction unions and contractors. He began working with a little-known businessman who was also Calabrian-born. This new henchman was extremely comfortable financially, and, like Desjardins, had extensive real estate investments.

Another mobster who bore a heavy grudge against the caretaker leaders of the Rizzuto clan was Giuseppe De Vito. Nicknamed "Ponytail," De Vito was determined to hold them accountable for all of his setbacks—of which there were plenty.

As a young man, he had cut his criminal teeth in Paolo Gervasi's crew, active in drug dealing, bookmaking and clandestine gambling. He was deeply upset by the 2004 killing of the sixtysomething Gervasi, who had close ties to the Rock Machine biker gang and had been digging for clues on the murder of his son, Salvatore.

Along with his loyal allies Andrew Scoppa and Alessandro Succapane, De Vito had privileged contacts both with criminal bikers and various Italian groups. His hangouts were Beaches Pub, on Langelier Boulevard, and Bar Route 66, on Jarry Street. He was considered a significant player in the Montreal Mafia and owned businesses in the city's east end. Most important, he was well versed in the art of importing cocaine through Montréal–Trudeau Airport.

Over the years, he developed a profound aversion to the Rizzuto clan leadership, to whom he had to pay a "tax" on drug imports. In his eyes, their lack of judgment and their arrogance were the chief reasons for all his troubles.

De Vito was one of the heavy hitters holding a "key" to the "doorway" at Montréal–Trudeau, which allowed traffickers to slip drug shipments past customs. It was expressly forbidden to use the system without De Vito's say-so and that of the Rizzuto clan. In 2005, according to the Colisée investigation, De Vito had put up some of the money in a plot to import 120 kilos of cocaine from Haiti. Everything had initially proceeded following the rules laid down by the Mafia: each investor stood to reap a hefty profit from the operation but had to pay a percentage of his earnings to the clan. Along the way, though, some opportunists ordered an additional 98 kilos of the drug, bundling it with the original 120-kilo consignment. The secret was uncovered in a most unpleasant manner. The RCMP found the dope on the airport tarmac and the Canada Border Services Agency issued a press release mentioning the size of the seizure: 218 kilos (*see Chapter 16*). This touched off a serious crisis among the traffickers. Who were the parasites that had dared take advantage of the "doorway" and tried to weasel out of paying the tax on 98 kilos? Along with the others who had put up the money for the original 120 kilos, De Vito set out to find the guilty party or parties.

De Vito went to the Consenza Social Club on a number of occasions, meeting and engaging in acerbic exchanges with Arcadi and his key lieutenants. He didn't know, of course, that his every move and word were being recorded by the RCMP's hidden cameras and microphones. He learned of the surveillance at the same time as everyone else, after the mass arrests at the close of Operation Colisée. De Vito was incensed: what kind of idiots would be so stupid as to allow the police to spy on Mafia headquarters so easily, and in so doing incriminate every person who went there on illegal business?

Yet another event deeply aggrieved De Vito: the July 2006 killing of Richard Griffin, a West End Gang member and one of his best drug-trafficking contacts. The two had grown to respect one another enormously. Police sources contend that De Vito disagreed strongly with the decision by old Nick and his cronies to eliminate Griffin. In his eyes, Griffin, despite his arrogance, had been right to complain and demand to be paid back after a failed plot to import cocaine from Venezuela (*see Chapter 16*).

De Vito was one of the ninety suspects arrested or still at large after the November 2006 police sweep. The specific charges against him were conspiracy to import cocaine over a two-year period through Montréal–Trudeau Airport. He was so furious at the Rizzuto clan that he had the fateful date, November 22, tattooed onto his arm.

To boost his chances of escaping police, he got a nose job and shed more than fifty pounds. He had changed so much that he managed to fool RCMP investigators who hoped to question him on his way out of a plastic surgery clinic in Laval in the spring of 2009. He said he wasn't the one they were looking for, brandished fake ID to prove it and then coolly left the premises, even wishing the officers luck with their investigation. The man they had come to interrogate looked nothing like the pudgy, scowling fellow in the wanted photo issued three years earlier.

De Vito's ire was to be further exacerbated by a horrendous tragedy. That same spring, his daughters, eight-year-old Sabrina and nine-year-old Amanda, were killed in the family's luxury home in Laval. Their mother, Adele Sorella, was arrested and charged with the murders. Already suffering from depression, she had sunk into even deeper despair once her husband, on the run, had left home. De Vito saw his murdered children as collateral victims of the Rizzuto clan's callous negligence.

Law enforcement finally caught up with Giuseppe De Vito on October 4, 2010. Members of the Montreal police anti-gang squad arrested him on De Capri Street in Saint-Léonard, at the home of a female friend whom he regularly visited. Police also seized weapons. In March 2011, while in prison, he was called to the Laval courthouse to testify at the preliminary hearing for his spouse, accused of murdering their children.

Like a photographic print slowly revealing itself in a tray of developer, the presence of one Salvatore Montagna, erstwhile acting capo of New York's Bonanno family, gradually began to be felt on Montreal's Mafia landscape.

Montagna had actually been born in Montreal in 1971 but was raised in Castellammare del Golfo, the small Sicilian town famed as the birthplace of key U.S. Mafia figures, including Joseph Bonanno, Salvatore Maranzano and Joseph Barbara. He moved with his family to New York, more specifically the Bronx, when he was around fifteen. By early adulthood he had founded a small business, Matrix Steel, in the Brooklyn neighbourhood of Bushwick—which would inspire his nickname, "Sal the Iron Worker." He got married, had children, bought a house on Long Island. Outwardly, he led a life no better or worse than those of thousands of immigrants like him, proud to have earned their green cards. In reality, he was moving up quickly through the ranks of the Mafia.

In 2002, Montagna was arrested with other members of Patrick "Patty from the Bronx" DeFilippo's crew and indicted on illegal gambling and loansharking charges (DeFilippo was the man who had killed Gerlando "George from Canada" Sciascia in March 1999). Apparently suffering from "selective amnesia," Montagna gave very evasive answers under questioning from grand jury prosecutors, and was charged with criminal contempt of court. He pleaded guilty to that charge and was sentenced to five years' probation.

In 2006, at age thirty-six, Montagna was made acting capo of the Bonanno crime family after Joseph Massino decided to co-operate with the government, and his successor, Vincent "Vinny Gorgeous" Basciano, was jailed for murder. Police sources explained to New York *Daily News* reporter John Marzulli that the remaining senior Bonanno members had wanted a true "man of honour" with Sicilian roots to lead the family. Montagna filled the bill. Because of his relatively young age, he was quickly dubbed the "Bambino Boss."

Three years later, Montagna got some bad news: U.S. authorities decided that his contempt-of-court conviction was reason enough to strip him of his green card and deport him. On April 6, 2009, FBI and ICE

(Immigration and Customs Enforcement) officers arrested him as he left Matrix Steel. Asked by Marzulli whether the federal government had tried to persuade Montagna to turn state's evidence, Montagna's lawyer said, "I think it is clear to the government if they would ask him to co-operate he would take that as a personal affront." Immigration officials gave Montagna a rather unique choice: deportation to either of the countries of which he is a citizen—Italy, where his parents were born, or Canada, where he was born. He chose to settle in Montreal, where he could hope to continue fulfilling his duties as boss.

Montagna moved into the home of a cousin in South Shore Saint-Hubert. In the months following his arrival, Federico del Peschio was mur-dered behind his restaurant, and Nick Rizzuto Jr. was gunned down near his office. Montagna had nothing to do with either killing but, like many others, he could clearly see that the Rizzutos had lost the confidence of the city's underworld, especially its younger generation. In the words of a police report, "Calabrian Mafiosi from outside Montreal" were eager to see a changing of the guard. Paolo Violi's two sons, who lived in Ontario, had been spotted in Montreal just a week before old Nick was gunned down, which plenty of observers found intriguing, to say the least.

Montagna made several trips to Toronto and Hamilton. With founda-tions laid in those Ontario cities, he then made the rounds of the restau-rants and cafés in the Greater Montreal Area that Mafia members traditionally frequent. He was received with respect. As 2010 drew to a close, he also began visiting influential businessmen in Montreal's Italian community, in the company of Domenico Arcuri Jr. The latter's father was dubbed the city's "king of Italian ice cream," having inherited the Ital Gelati company from Paolo Violi.

The Arcuris were not strangers to Montagna: a cousin of theirs lived in his former fiefdom in Brooklyn. The elder Domenico, also Sicilian-born, had helped the Rizzutos rise to power in Montreal thirty years earlier. Domenico Jr. and his brother, Antonino, now owned Carboneutre, a firm specializing in soil decontamination that had offices in a building owned by Raynald Desjardins. Before long, Desjardins was introduced to Salvatore Montagna, and the two men decided to work together.

All this meant that Montagna now had a firmer power base than the Rizzutos, not only in Quebec but in Ontario and New York City as well. No longer reluctant to overtly wield his power, he sought out Nicolò Rizzuto and tried to reason with him, telling the patriarch that his reign was over. Old Nick coldly rebuffed Montagna. He had lost all esteem for the Bonanno family, who in his eyes had committed far too many sins of betrayal. Yet he failed to realize that he himself no longer commanded respect. And that in his milieu, more than in any other, the end of respect heralds the end of everything.

CHRONOLOGY

OCTOBER 16, 1828: The chief prosecutor in the province of Agrigento, Sicily, files a report with the Ministry of Justice describing the illicit activities of approximately one hundred criminals. All are related in some way, making the group a forerunner of the modern Sicilian Mafia.

OCTOBER 20, 1925: The Fascist dictator Benito Mussolini, in a bid to rid Italy of the Mafia, appoints Cesare Mori Prefect of Palermo.

1931: Commission established in New York City; Five Families begin to develop.

1945: Nicolò Rizzuto marries into the mob by wedding Libertina Manno, daughter of the local Mafia boss in the town of Cattolica Eraclea, Sicily.

FEBRUARY 21, 1946: Vito Rizzuto is born in Cattolica Eraclea.

1953: The Bonanno crime family of New York City delegates Carmine Galante to Montreal with the mission of organizing the city's Mafia.

DECEMBER 19, 1953: Leonardo Caruana and Pasquale Cuntrera are charged with a double murder and theft of cattle in Trapani, Sicily. They are freed a month later for lack of evidence. Around the same time, Giuseppe Cuffaro of Montallegro, Sicily, and members of the Cuntrera family from Siculiana, Sicily, immigrate to Montreal.

FEBRUARY 21, 1954: Vito Rizzuto arrives in Canada on his eighth birthday along with his father, Nicolò, aged twenty-nine, his mother Libertina, twenty-seven, and his sister Maria, seven.

OCTOBER 12–16, 1957: Senior members of the Sicilian Mafia meet at the so-called Palermo Summit and restructure their organization. After the fashion of the American Cosa Nostra, they decide to create provincial and regional commissions. The era of large-scale narcotics trafficking and moneylaundering begins.

NOVEMBER 14, 1957: The "Apalachin Summit," in Upstate New York, is broken up by police. Working closely with their Old World counterparts, North American mafiosi map out new drug trafficking routes. Although no official documents exist to prove it, some have claimed that Montreal was represented at the meeting by Giuseppe Cotroni and Luigi Greco.

1959: Nicolò Rizzuto becomes a Canadian citizen.

JUNE 30, 1963: Seven *carabinieri* are killed when a car bomb explodes in Ciaculli, Sicily. The Italian government strikes back. Many mafiosi flee, settling in Brazil and Canada, among other countries.

1964: Nicolò Rizzuto's father-in-law, Antonino Manno, leaves Sicily. The clan chief's immigration to Montreal is facilitated through a political contact.

SEPTEMBER 27, 1966: Vito Rizzuto becomes a Canadian citizen.

DECEMBER 1969: Influential Sicilian godfather Tommaso Buscetta, exiled in Brazil, makes a brief visit to Montreal.

1971: From their principal base in Venezuela, the Caruana, Cuntrera and Rizzuto families, closely knit by blood and marital ties, set up the organization that, over the next thirty years, will flood North America and Europe with heroin, cocaine and hashish, as well as launder colossal amounts of money. Montreal is their second most important base of operations. Today, the group boasts dozens of partners in North and South America, Sicily, Europe, Canada and even Africa and the Middle East.

JANUARY 29, 1972: Along with his brother-in-law, Paolo Renda, Vito Rizzuto is convicted of setting a fire in a strip mall on Montreal's

South Shore four years earlier. He is sentenced to two years in prison.

MAY 1972: Tension begins to mount between the Calabrian and Sicilian factions of the Montreal Mafia. Mindful of maintaining authority, Calabrian mob boss Paolo Violi criticizes Nicolò Rizzuto for his "lone wolf" behaviour. Mafia leaders in Sicily dispatch Giuseppe Settecasi to Montreal to mediate the conflict.

FALL 1976: After two years of hearings, the Quebec Police Commission on organized crime (known by the French acronym CECO), which investigated the Cotroni clan's activities, issues its report. Vincenzo "Vic" Cotroni and Paolo Violi are identified as the godfathers of the Montreal Mafia. Nicolò Rizzuto's name barely rates a mention, much less Vito's.

JANUARY 21, 1978: Paolo Violi is murdered in the bar that he used to own on Jean-Talon St. in Montreal.

JULY 12, 1979: Carmine Galante is executed in Brooklyn, New York.

NOVEMBER 16, 1980: Vito Rizzuto attends the New York City wedding of powerful Sicilian Mafia leader Giuseppe Bono.

MAY 5, 1981: Deemed by superiors to be plotting rebellion, three captains in the Bonanno Family, Alphonse Indelicato, Dominick Trinchera and Philip Giaccone, are lured to a meeting at a hangout in Brooklyn and murdered.

FEBRUARY 4, 1984: Vito Rizzuto is named in RCMP drug squad investigative files for the first time.

DECEMBER 10, 1986: Vito Rizzuto is acquitted on charges of having driven a vehicle while impaired in Saint-Laurent, Quebec.

DECEMBER 18, 1989: Vito Rizzuto is acquitted of charges of importing thirty-two tonnes of hashish in Sept-Îles, Quebec.

NOVEMBER 8, 1990: In St. John's, Newfoundland, further drug charges against Vito Rizzuto are dismissed; the case involved a load of sixteen tonnes of hashish.

AUGUST 30, 1994: Operation Compote, a four-year investigation during which the RCMP operated a covert currency exchange in downtown Montreal, wraps up. Vito Rizzuto narrowly avoids arrest in the largest ever police sweep of drug traffickers in Canada.

SEPTEMBER 1, 1994: Two days after the police operation, Vito Rizzuto's mother is arrested in Switzerland, where she has gone to empty several bank accounts. She remains in custody for six months before returning to Montreal.

JULY 15, 1998: Project Omertà culminates with the arrest of the Caruana brothers, Alfonso, Gerlando and Pasquale, on cocaine trafficking charges. Nicolò Rizzuto's name is mentioned during the investigation, but he is never charged. An informant, Oreste Pagano, later tells police that Vito Rizzuto earned commissions on cocaine imported from South America by the Caruana–Cuntrera clan.

AUGUST 2001: Vito Rizzuto settles out of court with Revenue Canada; he stood accused of failing to report income of $1.5 million. The terms of the settlement are never made public.

MAY 30, 2002: In Montreal, Vito Rizzuto is again arrested for impaired driving. He is at the wheel of a Jeep Grand Cherokee registered to the company OMG Media Inc., a supplier of advertising-sponsored garbage and recycling bins to the cities of Montreal and Toronto.

SEPTEMBER 24, 2002: Vito Rizzuto is again named in a police investigation, this time as part of a plot to import cocaine, but is not charged with any crime.

JANUARY 20, 2004: At the request of U.S. authorities, Vito Rizzuto is arrested for his role in the 1981 murders of three Bonanno Family captains in Brooklyn, New York. Despite hiring the best lawyers he can afford, he remains in prison pending extradition

JUNE 2004: Returning to Canada under an assumed name after having been deported to his native Spain, Ramón Fernández is arrested, convicted and sentenced to twelve years in prison on charges of conspiracy to commit murder and drug trafficking. A former Montrealer, he was Vito Rizzuto's representative in Toronto, Ontario.

AUGUST 17, 2006: The Supreme Court of Canada rejects Vito Rizzuto's final request for an appeal, and he is extradited to the United States.

NOVEMBER 22, 2006: Another key blow is struck against Montreal's Sicilian clan: Nicolò Rizzuto, the family patriarch, and his principal associates are arrested as part of a sweep capping Operation Colisée, an anti-Mafia probe of unprecedented scope in Canada.

MAY 4, 2007: In a Brooklyn courtroom, Vito Rizzuto admits he "participated" in the 1981 triple slaying ordered by Bonanno Family leaders. In return, he receives a reduced sentence. Allowing for the three years he has spent in preventive custody, he will be due for release in five-and-a-half years. He begins serving his sentence at the Florence Federal Correctional Complex in Colorado.

DECEMBER 28, 2009: Nicolò Rizzuto, Jr., Vito's son, is murdered in the Montreal neighbourhood of Notre-Dame-de-Grâce.

MAY 20, 2010: Paolo Renda, son-in-law of Nicolò Rizzuto, Sr., and the family's *consigliere*, disappears, and is presumed to have been kidnapped.

JUNE 29, 2010: Agostino Cuntrera, a key member of Montreal's Sicilian Mafia clan, and his bodyguard Liborio Sciascia are murdered in an industrial park in Saint-Léonard, on the Island of Montreal.

NOVEMBER 10, 2010: While dining with family members, eighty-six-year-old Nicolò Rizzuto, Sr., is killed by a single bullet fired by a sniper hidden in the woods behind his home.

GLOSSARY

ASSOCIATE: Someone who works for a Mafia family but is not a "made" member of it.

CAMORRA: The name given to the Mafia of Naples, Italy.

CAMPIERO (PLURAL CAMPIERI): An armed guard hired by a rich landowner in feudal Sicily. See *Gabelloto*.

CAPO: The head of a Mafia family; also "boss," "don," "godfather."

CAPODECINA (ALSO CAPOREGIME): The chief or captain of a group of soldiers in a Mafia family; also called a lieutenant.

CARABINIERE (PLURAL CARABINIERI): A member of Italy's Corps of Carabiniers, the national police force.

COMMISSION: The highest decision-making body of the American Cosa Nostra, encompassing the so-called Five Families of New York and Mafia families in other U.S. cities (compare *Cupola*).

CONSIGLIERE: The chief adviser to the head of a Mafia family.

COSA NOSTRA: Literally, "this thing of ours"; another name for the Mafia in Sicily and the United States.

CUPOLA: The highest decision-making body of the Sicilian Mafia.

DECINA: A team of ten or more soldiers in a Mafia family.

GABELLOTO (PLURAL GABELLOTI): The leaseholder of a large estate in feudal Sicily. See *Campiero.*

MAFIA: Another name for the Sicilian Cosa Nostra and, by extension, any Italian organized crime group. Without the capital M, the word has come to mean any similar criminal organization, regardless of its culture of origin.

MAFIOSO (PLURAL MAFIOSI; ALSO "MADE MAN," "GOODFELLA"): A formally inducted member of a Mafia family.

'NDRANGHETA: The name given to the Mafia of Calabria, a province in southern Italy.

OMERTÀ: A code of conduct imposed on Mafia members, which includes remaining silent about the organization's activities and never co-operating with police.

PENTITO (PLURAL *PENTITI*): Literally, "penitent." The name given to a Mafia informant in Italy.

PICCIOTTO (PLURAL *PICCIOTTI*): A soldier in a Mafia family.

PIZZO: Tribute or "protection" money paid to the Mafia by a business.

SOTTO CAPO (UNDERBOSS): The second-in-command of a Mafia family.

VENDETTA: Literally, "vengeance"; the word is also used to describe an extended conflict between two Mafia clans.

ZIO: "Uncle" in Italian. Used as a sign of respect toward senior mafiosi.

BIBLIOGRAPHY

BOOKS AND MONOGRAPHS

Arlacchi, Pino. *Men of Dishonor: Inside the Sicilian Mafia: An Account of Antonino Calderone* [trans. Marc Romano]. New York: William Morrow, 1993.

Benjamin, Sandra. *Sicily: Three Thousand Years of Human History.* Hanover, NH: Steerforth Press, 2006.

Blickman, Tom. "The Rothschilds of the Mafia on Aruba." *Transnational Organized Crime*, Vol. 3, No. 2, Summer 1997.

Blumenthal, Ralph. *Last Days of the Sicilians: At War with the Mafia: The FBI Assault on the Pizza Connection.* New York: Times Books / Random House, 1988.

Bonanno, Bill. *Bound by Honor: A Mafioso's Story.* New York: St. Martin's Press, 1999.

Bonanno, Joseph with Sergio Lalli. *A Man of Honor: The Autobiography of Joseph Bonanno.* New York: Simon and Schuster, 1983.

Bourassa, André-G. and Jean-Marc Larrue. *Les Nuits de la «Main». Cent ans de spectacles sur le boulevard Saint-Laurent (1891-1991).* Montreal: VLB Éditeur, 1993.

Campbell, Rodney. *The Luciano Project: The Secret Wartime Collaboration of the Mafia and the U.S. Navy.* New York: McGraw-Hill, 1977.

Catanzaro, Raimondo. *Men of Respect: A Social History of the Sicilian Mafia.* New York: Maxwell Macmillan International, 1988.

Champlain, Pierre de. *Le Crime organisé à Montréal, 1940/1980.* Hull: Asticou, 1986.

Champlain, Pierre de. *Mafia, bandes de motards et trafic de drogue: Le crime organisé au Québec dans les années 80.* Hull: Asticou, 1990.

Champlain, Pierre de. *Mobsters, Gangsters and Men of Honour: Cracking the Mafia Code.* Toronto: HarperCollins, 2005.

Charbonneau, Jean-Pierre. *The Canadian Connection* [trans. James Stewart]. Ottawa: Optimum Publishing, 1975.

Crittle, Simon. *The Last Godfather: The Rise and Fall of Joey Massino.* New York: Berkley Books, 2006.

DeStefano, Anthony M. *The Last Godfather: Joseph Massino and the Fall of the Bonanno Crime Family.* New York: Citadel Press, 2006.

DeVito, Carlo. *The Encyclopedia of International Organized Crime.* New York: Checkmark Books, 2005.

Dickie, John. *Cosa Nostra: A History of the Sicilian Mafia.* New York: Palgrave MacMillan, 2004.

Edwards, Peter. *Blood Brothers: How Canada's Most Powerful Mafia Family Runs Its Business.* Toronto: McClelland-Bantam, 1990.

Edwards, Peter and Antonio Nicaso. *Deadly Silence: Canadian Mafia Murders.* Toronto: MacMillan, 1993.

Edwards, Peter and Michel Auger. *The Encyclopedia of Canadian Organized Crime: From Captain Kidd to Mom Boucher.* Toronto: McClelland & Stewart, 2004.

Falcone, Giovanni with Marcelle Padovani. *Men of Honour: The Truth About the Mafia* [trans. Edward Farrelly]. London: Warner Books, 1992.

Fiévet, Marc with Olivier-Jourdan Roulot. *Dans la peau d'un narco, infiltré au cœur de la mafia.* Paris: Hugodoc, 2007.

Frattini, Eric. *Mafia, S.A.: 100 años de Cosa Nostra.* Pozuelo de Alarcón, Madrid, Spain: Espasa, 2002.

Giuffrida, Calogero. *Delitto di Prestigio: La storia di Giuseppe Spagnolo, dirigente politico ucciso dalla mafia*. Palermo: Instituto Gramsci Siciliano-onlus, 2005.

Humphreys, Adrian and Lee Lamothe. *The Sixth Family: The Collapse of the New York Mafia and the Rise of Vito Rizzuto*. Mississauga, ON: John Wiley & Sons, 2006.

Lamothe, Lee and Antonio Nicaso. *Bloodlines: The Rise and Fall of the Mafia's Royal Family*. Toronto: HarperCollins, 2001.

Lupo, Salvatore. *History of the Mafia* [trans. Antony Shugaar]. New York: Columbia University Press, 2009.

Maas, Peter. *Underboss: Sammy the Bull Gravano's Story of Life in the Mafia*. New York: HarperCollins, 1997.

Newark, Tim. *Mafia Allies: The True Story of America's Secret Alliance with the Mob in World War II*. St. Paul, MN: Zenith Press, 2007.

Oms, Georges. *La Mafia, hier et aujourd'hui*. Paris: Bordas, 1972.

Padovani, Marcelle. *Cosa Nostra: Le juge et les « hommes d'honneur »*. Paris: Austral, 1991.

Pistone, Joseph D. with Richard Woodley. *Donnie Brasco: My Undercover Life in the Mafia*. New York: New American Library, 1987.

Plante, Pacifique "Pax." *Montréal sous le règne de la pègre*. Montreal: Éditions de l'Action nationale, 1950.

Possamai, Mario. *Money on the Run: Canada and How the World's Dirty Profits Are Laundered*. Toronto: Viking, 1992.

Raab, Selwyn. *Five Families: The Rise, Decline, and Resurgence of America's Most Powerful Mafia Empires*. New York: Thomas Dunne Books, 2005.

Schneider, Stephen. *Iced: The Story of Organized Crime in Canada*. Mississauga, ON: John Wiley & Sons, 2009.

Shawcross, Tim, and Martin Young. *Men of Honour: The Confessions of Tommaso Buscetta*. London: Collins, 1987.

Stanké, Alain and Jean-Louis Morgan. *Pax: Lutte à finir avec la pègre; un portrait-robot du célèbre incorruptible Pacifique Plante*. Montreal: La Presse, 1972.

Sterling, Claire. *Octopus: The Long Reach of the International Sicilian Mafia*. New York: W.W. Norton & Company, 1990.

Sterling, Claire. *Thieves' World: The Threat of the New Global Network of Organized Crime.* New York: Simon & Shuster, 1994.

REPORTS

Bureau de recherche du Québec sur le crime organisé (BRQCO). *Rapport stratégique,* 1990.

Centro interprovinciale criminalpol, questura di Roma, squadra narcotici. *Rapporto giudiziario di denuncia a carico di Bono Giuseppe + 159 ritenuti,* volumes I and II, February 7, 1983.

Citizenship and Immigration Canada. *Chronologie des événements se rapportant à la mafia au Québec, 1878-1994,* 1995.

Commission d'enquête sur l'administration de la justice en matière criminelle et pénale au Québec. *La société face au crime.* Quebec City: Éditeur officiel du Québec, 1969–1971.

Commission de police du Québec. *The Fight Against Organized Crime in Quebec: Report of the Commission on Organized Crime and Recommendations.* Quebec City: Éditeur officiel du Québec, 1976.

Commission de police du Québec. *Rapport d'enquête sur l'étude de liens possibles entre Nicolas Di Iorio et Frank Dasti, membres du crime organisé, Pierre Laporte, ministre, René Gagnon, chef de cabinet, et Jean-Jacques Côté, organisateur politique.* Sainte-Foy, QC: Commission de police du Québec, 1975.

Criminal Intelligence Service Canada (CISC). Computer-searched document including report on the situation of traditional organized crime, Ottawa, 1997.

CISC. *Le Canada est-il à l'abri du crime organisé?,* 1994.

CISC. *Traditional Organized Crime,* 1995.

CISC. *Traditional (Italian-based) Organized Crime,* November 1995 (police document submitted to Justice Canada and the Solicitor General of Canada in February 1996).

Criminal Intelligence Service Ontario. Report on Traditional Italian Organized Crime, 1997. (Report drawn in large part from intelligence gathered during the RCMP's Project Pilgrim investigation, 1978–1984.)

Federal Bureau of Investigation (FBI) and United States Department of Justice. *La Cosa Nostra in Canada*, 1985.

FBI. Report on statement by informant Frank Lino on his meeting in Montreal with Alfonso Gagliano, March 29, 2004.

Projet Benoît: G-8. *Conversations à la Gelateria Violi*, 1974.

Royal Canadian Mounted Police (RCMP), C Division, Montreal. *Mémorandum Tommaso Buscetta, Rocky Graziano*, 1987.

RCMP. *Famille Siciliana: Organisation Rizzuto, synthèse des activités criminelles reliées à l'organisation Rizzuto*, 1995.

RCMP. *Importations majeures à participation canadienne sur la côte Est, de 1990 à 1994*.

RCMP. *La mafia au Québec*, 1991.

RCMP. *La mafia au Québec*, 1994.

RCMP. *Project Pilgrim: Gerlando Caruana et al., conspiracy to import & traffic, and possession of assets derived from the commission of crime from 1978 to 1988*.

Service de police de la Communauté urbaine de Montréal (SPCUM). *Dossier italien*.

Service de police de la Communauté urbaine de Montréal (SPCUM). *Principales organisations criminelles à Montréal*, 1990.

Toronto Police Service and Corpo dei Carabinieri, Naples. *Statements by informant Oreste Pagano, July 7 and September 21, 1999, Toronto, and November 17, 2004, Italy*.

COURT DOCUMENTS

Court of Appeal, District of Palermo. Republic of Italy v. Pasquale Caruana and Giuseppe Cuffaro, sentence, Angelo Passantino (presiding), Giancarlo Trizzino and Salvatore Di Vitale (counsel), 14-04-92 (Sent. N. 833, reg. gen. 810/91).

Court of Appeal of Québec. Admissions by Vito Rizzuto in his extradition file, August 3, 2004.

Court of Québec. The Queen v. Vito Rizzuto, Judge Bernard Lemieux, Bail hearing, November 23, 24 and 25, 1988, and Decision, November 30, 1988 (650-01-001221-886).

Court of Québec. The Queen v. Vito Rizzuto, Judge Louis Charles Fournier, Trial, October 3, 4, 5 and 23, 1989, and Decision, December 18, 1989 (650-01-001221-886).

Court of Québec. The Queen v. Normand Dupuis, Judge Louis Charles Fournier, Verdict and sentencing re. contempt of court, December 19, 1989 (650-01-001221-886).

Court of Appeal of Québec. Vito Rizzuto v. the United States of America, report by Montreal police filed June 29, 2004 (500-10-002800-041).

Court of Appeal of Québec. Vito Rizzuto v. the United States of America, Decision, Justice François Doyon, August 6, 2004.

Court of Appeal of Québec. Vito Rizzuto v. Solicitor General of Canada and Solicitor General of Québec, Argument of Me. Clemente Monterosso, September 12, 2005.

Court of Québec. Rogatory commission requested by the Republic of Italy re. the criminal prosecution of Gerlando Caruana et al. Master in Chambers André Chaloux and Examining Magistrate Gioacchino Natoli, Transcript of hearings, December 4 and 6, 1990.

Court of Québec. The Queen v. Cotroni et al., Bail hearing, Summary of facts, "Projets Caviar-Scoop-Overdate," Judge Jean-Pierre Bonin, June 1996.

Court of Québec. The Queen v. Glen Cameron, Trial, Judge Claude Millette, Transcripts of testimonies, hearings of April 6, 7, 8 and 9, 1998 (500-73-000368-979).

Court of Québec. The Queen v. Glen Cameron, Preliminary hearing before Judge Jean-Pierre Bonin, Transcript of testimony by Vito Rizzuto, June 25, 1998 (500-73-000475-976).

Court of Québec. Information to obtain a search warrant for the home of Gerlando Caruana, in Montreal, Project Omerta (Toronto), Judge Serge Boisvert, July 14, 1998.

Court of Québec. Application for a restraint and management order, Appendices C and 2-C. Project Colisée.

Court of Québec. The Queen v. Francesco Arcadi, Francesco Del Balso, Lorenzo Giordano, Paolo Renda, Nicolo Rizzuto, Rocco

Sollecito; Project Colisée, Summary of Evidence, Sentence (500-73-002671-069).

Court of Québec. The Queen v. Sergio Piccirilli, Bail hearing, July 6, August 18 and August 21, 2006, and Preliminary hearing, March 8 and 9 and April 4, 2007. Judges Paul Chevalier and Valmont Beaulieu (700-01-065331-061 and 540-01-030095-064).

Court of Québec. The Queen v. Arruda et al., Decision in bail hearing, Judge André Perreault, December 27, 2006. Appendix C, Project Colisée 2002-UMECO-3438.

Court of Québec. Bail hearing for Nicolò Rizzuto and Francesco Del Balso, September 2007, Project Colisée. Transcript of an audio recording of Nicola Varacalli dated November 5, 2005.

Court of Québec, The Queen v. Chadi Amja et al., Decision in preliminary hearing, Judge Hélène Morin, April 21, 2008.

Court of Québec. The Queen v. Rocco Carruso (72-03-09); The Queen v. Nello Di Rienzo (69-07-18); The Queen v. Georges Lappas (75-01-30), Indictment and Agreed Statement of Facts, Submissions on sentencing (540-73-000285-066).

Court of Québec. Reports of the Combined Forces Special Enforcement Unit (CFSEU): Appendix C, Project Colisée; Summary of the Colisée investigation into various instances of cocaine importing using "the doorway," i.e., Montréal–Pierre Elliott Trudeau International Airport. Dossier of excerpts from electronic surveillance.

Federal Court of Canada. Vito Rizzuto v. Revenue Canada. Notice of Appeal, September 14, 1998 (docket: 98-2497 (IT) G).

Federal Court of Canada. Alain Charron v. the Attorney General of Canada. Statement by Charron and complementary information. Me. Josée Ferrari, February 18, 2004 (T-255-04).

Immigration Tribunal. Canadian Immigration Cards Nos. 632-633-634-635, Nicolò, Libertina, Vito and Maria Rizzuto, February 21, 1954, Halifax.

Information to obtain a search warrant, Appendix F regarding conspiracy to kidnap, forcibly confine and extort as well as conspiracy to murder Frank Martonara by Christian Deschênes and Denis Girouard (500-26-021093-012), Quebec Court.

Information to obtain a search warrant, Vincent Massey Building, Revenue Canada, November 20, 2006 (500-26-042012-066), Federal Court.

Municipal Court of Montréal. The Queen v. Victor Rizzuto, Promise to Appear, July 22, 2002.

Ontario Court, Newmarket. Agreed Statement of Facts: The Queen v. Ramon Fernandez, June 2004.

Request for judicial assistance by Canada to Switzerland. Project Pilgrim: Gerlando Caruana et al., January 28, 1987.

Request for judicial assistance by Canada to Switzerland. Project Pilgrim: Gerlando Caruana et al., Assistant Deputy Attorney General of Canada, W.J.A. Hobson, February 26, 1987.

Request for urgent judicial assistance by Switzerland to Canada. Case of Rizzuto-Manno Libertina et al., Public Prosecutor for the Canton of Ticino, Fabrizio Eggenschwiler, December 16, 1994.

Request for judicial assistance in a penal matter by the Public Prosecutor for the Canton of Ticino, Switzerland, December 16, 1994. History of Project Contrat and origin of funds brought to the Centre monétaire international de Montréal (CIMM).

Royal Canadian Mounted Police (RCMP). Affidavit of electronic surveillance: Appendix B "Proceeds of Crime" and Appendix E "Project Compote," 1990–1994.

State of New York, Department of Agriculture and Markets. In the Matter of Application of Utica Cheese Inc., Base Road, Oriskany, New York, for a Milk Dealer's License, Pursuant to Agriculture and Markets Law, Article 21. Hearing Memorandum, July 1980.

Superior Court of Justice of Ontario. The Queen v. Alfonso Caruana, Gerlando Caruana, Pasquale Caruana and Giuseppe Caruana, Summary of evidence regarding guilty plea, as well as a document entitled "Omerta-noms," March 1 and 12, 2000 (F0383).

Superior Court of Québec. Gilles Mathieu et al. v. Her Majesty The Queen and Jean-Guy Bourgouin et al. Electronic surveillance affidavits, "Project Rush and Ocean," (500-01-003088-017).

Superior Court of Québec. Michael Divito v. the Attorney General of Canada et al., Habeas corpus proceedings, Me. Marie-Hélène Giroux and Me. Clemente Monterosso (500-36-001251-977).

Superior Court of Québec. The Queen v. Vincenzo Di Maulo and Valentino Morielli, Transcripts of testimony by Vito Rizzuto, November 21, 1996 (500-01-001861-951).

Superior Court of Québec. Motion to obtain an arrest warrant following a request from the United States of America for the extradition of Vito Rizzuto, Me. Ginette Gobeil, January 15, 2004.

Superior Court of Québec. United States of America v. Victor "Vito" Rizzuto, Judge Jean-Guy Boilard, April 5, 2004 (500-36-003292-045).

Supreme Court of Canada. Supreme Court of Canada Case Information, Summary 31259 and Summary 31260.

U.S. Department of Justice, Eastern District of New York. Record of the case following the police raids against members of the Bonanno Family of New York, January 20, 2004.

U.S. Eastern District Court of New York. United States v. Ronald Filicomo, Memorandum of Law in support of the government's motion for a permanent order of detention, U.S. Attorney Roslynn R. Mauskopf, May 2003.

U.S. Eastern District Court of New York. United States v. Joseph Massino, Robert Lino, Daniel Mongelli and Ronald Filocomo, Superseding Indictment, May 21, 2003 (2000R02722).

U.S. Eastern District Court of New York. United States v. John Joseph Spirito, Memorandum of Law in support of the government's motion for a permanent order of detention, U.S. Attorney Roslynn R. Mauskopf, August 2003 (2003R01783).

U.S. Eastern District Court of New York. United States v. Joseph Massino, Trial, transcripts of hearings of May 25, 28 and 29 and June 30, 2004.

U.S. Eastern District Court of New York. United States v. Vincent Basciano and Patrick DeFilippo, Trial, transcripts of hearings of May 1 and 2, 2006.

U.S. Eastern District Court of New York. United States v. Vito Rizzuto, Transcript of Judgement, Judge Nicholas Garaufis, May 4, 2007.

U.S. Western District Court of New York. United States v. Alain Charron, September 1995.

NEWSPAPERS AND MAGAZINES

The research documentation used in the writing of this book also included hundreds of articles from Canadian and international newspapers and magazines. Space constraints mean it is impossible to cite them in full. See the acknowledgements for the names of the main authors.

ACKNOWLEDGEMENTS

This book is the result of a collective effort. From the earliest stages of its creation we benefitted from the contributions of two Toronto-based journalists: Antonio Nicaso, who has written articles in several newspapers in Canada and abroad, and Peter Edwards, reporter with the *Toronto Star*. Both have authored numerous books about the Mafia and organized crime. They generously provided us with an impressive trove of information that would have been difficult for us to access from Montreal, and also gave us the written summation of their research. Without their help, many chapters of this book would have been impossible for us to write.

We also wish to thank Pierre de Champlain for his exceptionally generous assistance. Along with suggestions, advice and encouragement, he shared with us his phenomenal knowledge of the Mafia. Without his input, this book would still be nothing more than a project.

We take the liberty of paying special tribute to two law enforcement professionals, now deceased: Gilbert Côté, of the Montreal police, and Mark Bourque, of the RCMP. Both these men did their utmost for many years to persuade governments and police forces to equip themselves with the tools necessary to combat organized crime. They understood, better than most, the insidious threat represented by the wealth and corrupting power of mafiosi vis-à-vis the political and economic institutions of cities, provinces, even an entire country. We salute the many police officers, active and retired, who have provided such invaluable assistance to us over the years, most especially Yvon Gagnon, Jean-Pierre Lévesque, Gilles Veilleux, Denis Brouillette, René Charbonneau, Jacques Duchesneau, John Norris, Guy Ouellette, Pierre Primeau, Mike Roussy, Yves Roy, Yvon Thibault and Michel Vien.

We would be remiss in not acknowledging the friendly, patient registrars and exhibits clerks at the *Palais de Justice* in Montreal as well as at courthouses in other judicial districts. Special thanks are due to Marielle Gagnon, of Sept-Îles, Quebec, who sent us the complete documentation pertaining to the charges filed there against Vito Rizzuto in 1988.

Anne-Marie Campbell, an interpreter, and Paulette Arsenault were of great help in the writing of this book.

We are indebted to Selwyn Raab, author of the encyclopedic *Five Families: The Rise, Decline, and Resurgence of America's Most Powerful Mafia Empires,* and Stephen Schneider, author of the excellent anthology *Iced: The Story of Organized Crime in Canada;* both of these works provided information that was valuable at critical junctures in the writing of this book.

We made abundant use of newspaper articles penned over the years by our colleagues at *La Presse,* including Joël-Denis Bellavance, Lisa Binsse, Bruno Bisson, Yves Boisvert, Christiane Desjardins, Martha Gagnon, Richard Hétu, Judith Lachapelle, Marcel Laroche, Martin Pelchat, Caroline Touzin, Francis Vailles and many others. Some of them have since gone on to work elsewhere, taken on new duties, or retired. We trust that none of them will be too taken aback when they notice the many passages in this book that are directly inspired by their writings.

Our superiors at *La Presse,* Philippe Cantin and Éric Trottier, granted us many leaves of absence to work on this book. We are most grateful to them.

We were also fortunate to benefit from the assistance and expertise of many colleagues from other media outlets, and extend special thanks to Michel Auger of the *Journal de Montréal,* Jean-Pierre Rancourt, formerly of television network TQS, Paul Cherry of *The Gazette*, and Isabelle Richer of Télévision de Radio-Canada.

Lastly, more than anyone, the members of our families deserve our deepest, warmest gratitude for their unflagging encouragement throughout this adventure.

PHOTO PERMISSIONS

INDEX

Accurso, Antonio, 273, 433–434
Adams, George, 244
Agnello, Francesco, 54, 56
Agrigento (Sicily), 2, 6, 29, 35, 38, 51, 53, 57, 60, 85, 93, 94–95, 97, 113–114, 122, 183, 280, 312, 315, 353, 359, 453, 495
Akwesasne Mohawk reserve, 425
Al Capone, 42, 227, 318, 342
Al Pacino, 7, 22, 101, 194–195
Al-Qaeda, 373
Albany (New York), 43
Albino, Antonina, 111
Alevizos, Constantin ("Big Gus"), 296–298, 300, 309
Alfano, Nicolino, 93, 95
Allard, Robert ("Ti-Cul"), 213
Amato, Baldassare, 109–110
Amja, Chadi, 388
Amodeo, Gaetano, 358–359
Amodeo, Maria Sicurella di, 359
Amorelli, Gino, 328

Amuso, Vittorio, 195
Amyot, Michel, 241
Andres, Greg, 197, 323, 335–339, 345, 443–444, 446–447
Angelil, René, 305
Annick C II (ship), 170
Apalachin (New York), 49–50, 67, 109
Arar, Maher, 372–373, 406
Arcadi, Francesco, 250, 271–272, 277, 303–304, 312, 315, 325, 332, 379, 381, 382, 387–388, 394–402, 404–405, 408–411, 413–414, 421, 424–425, 438–439, 447–448, 450, 456–460, 463, 482, 487–488, 490
Archambault, Pierre, 246
Arcuri, Domenico (son), 493
Arcuri, Domenico (father), 95, 102, 112, 134
Arcuri, Giacinto, 31–32, 280–281, 413, 415
Ardeneus, Jean-Christophe, 474
Arlacchi, Pino, 94, 182

Armeni, Giuseppe, 140
Aruba, 139–140, 144, 243, 253
Associazione Cattolica Eraclea, 52, 377
Associazione Siculiana di Montréal,
    356, 425
Attanasio, Louis ("Louie HaHa"),
    18–19
Auger, Michel, 275, 331, 376
Aznavour, Charles, 61

BT Céramique, 432–433, 435
Badalamenti, Gaetano, 47, 114,
    119–120, 124
Bakker, Jim, 14
Balsamo, Giuseppe, 38
Banca Privata Edmond de Rothschild,
    228
Banco Ambrosiano, 146
Banderas, Antonio, 185
Bank of Commerce, 70
Bank of Canada, 203
Bar Jean-Talon (Saint-Léonard), 103–105,
385, 398–399, 401, 408, 415, 426, 455
Barbara, Joseph, ("Joe the Barber"),
    41, 48–50, 67, 492
Barillaro, Carmen, 280–284
Barrette-Joncas, Claire, 107
Barry, Leo, 161
Basciano, Vincent ("Vinny
    Gorgeous"), 75, 345, 492
Basile, Anthony, 348
Battista, Charles-Édouard, 400–401
Baulu, Roger, 61
Beaubrun, Thierry, 393–395
Beaudry, François, 428–429
Beaudry, Paul, 202
Bedia, Lucio, 150
Bélanger, Claude, 212, 216–217
Béliveau, Marilyn, 389, 405
Belize, 262, 382
Bellanca, Sebastiano ("Benny the
    Sicilian"), 64
Bellehumeur, Michel, 229–230

Bellemare, Claude, 209
Bentenuto, Luciano, 15
Bercowitz, Louis, 83
Berlinquette, Roy, 372
Berlusconi, Silvio, 363, 365–366, 370
Bernardelli, Vincenzo, 30
Bertolo, Giovanni ("Johnny"), 241,
    397–398, 429, 456, 488
Bertrand, Steven, 299
Bianco, Tonino, 403
Bilotti, Thomas, 190
Bin Laden, Osama, 373
Bitton, David, 416–418
Blackburn, Jean-Pierre, 433
Black Hand, 38
Blanchard, Claude, 125
Blanchette, Diane, 139
Blass, Richard, 213
Blue Bonnets Raceway, 66, 421
Bo-Gars, 394
Bolognetta, family, 90
Bonanno, Giuseppe ("Joe"), 39, 41,
    46–49, 66–68, 70–76, 79–80, 86, 91,
    95, 108–109, 131, 279, 342–343,
    437, 492
Bonanno, Salvatore ("Bill"), 73–75, 95
Bonfire, restaurant (Montreal), 66
Bonin, Jean-Pierre, 171, 216, 222, 439
Bono, Alfredo, 257
Bono, Giuseppe, 90, 111–112, 117,
    130, 136–137, 144, 150, 183
Bontade, Francesco Paolo, 46
Bontade, Stefano, 114, 119
Bonventre, Cesare ("Tall Guy"), 19,
    109–112, 189, 339
Bonventre, John, 47
Bordeleau, Luc, 170–171
Borsellino, Paolo, 182–183, 268, 362
Boucher, Francis, 168
Boucher, Maurice ("Mom"), 8,
    167–168, 270, 376, 431
Boulanger, Raymond, 164–167
Bourassa, Robert, 77–78, 143

Bourque, Mark, 143–144, 149, 250
Bourque, Pierre, 308–309
Breitbart, David, 20, 338–339, 352
Bresciano, Maria, 61
Brigante, Natale, 79
Brisebois, Normand, 179–180
Bronfman, Sam, 40
Brouillette, Mario, 438
Bruneau, Serge, 274
Brunet, Hélène, 274
Bruno, Francesco, 432–435
Brusca, Bernardo, 137, 183
Brusca, Giovanni, 183
Bureau, Marcel, 259–260
Burrows, Susan, 193
Buscetta, Antonio, 120
Buscetta, Benedetto, 120
Buscetta, Tommaso, 47, 86, 89–92,
    119–124, 136, 182, 189
Buttafuoco, Nicolò, 56, 95

Caan, James, 334
Cabaret Au Faisan Doré (Montreal),
    61, 64
Cadieux, Pierre, 315
Café Albano (Montreal), 457
Café de la Paix (Montreal), 64
Café Maida (Montreal), 457
Caisse populaire Notre-Dame-de-la-
    Merci, 156
Calabro, Antonio, 160
Calderella, Antonio, 453
Calderone, Antonino, 94
Calò, Guiseppe ("Pippo"), 146
Calvi, Carlo, 146
Calvi, Roberto, 146
Cameron, Glen, 269–271, 291
Cammalleri-Rizzuto, Giovanna (wife of
    Vito Rizzuto), 9, 15, 32, 58, 111, 128,
    138, 246, 280, 302, 310, 325,
    328–329, 331, 449, 467, 469
Cammalleri, Leonardo, 28, 31–32, 55,
    77, 90, 280

Cammarano, Joseph ("Joe Saunders"),
    331, 346
Cammisano, Antonio, 472–473
Cammisano, Vincenzo, 130
Campbell, Robert, 243, 244
Campins, Luis Herrera, 177
Campo, Carlo, 58
Campoli, Frank, 297, 307, 310, 312,
    331, 451
Canale, Anthony, 348
Cannistraro, Carmelo, 422–423
Cantarella, Richard ("Shellackhead"),
    318–323
Cantieri, Jorge Luis, 141–142, 207,
    209–211, 218
Capeci, Jerry, 302, 324, 328
Carcajou, police unit, 274
Carneglia, John, 191
Caron, François, 62–63
Carpinelli, Lina, 219
Cartel de Cali, 164, 174, 218–221,
    234–236, 455
Caruana, Alfonso, 8, 88–89, 92,
    143–147, 150, 185–186, 249–255,
    258–268, 285, 312, 360, 379
Caruana, Francesca, 250–251, 267, 379
Caruana, Gerlando, 8, 88, 93, 149–150,
    251, 259, 261–262, 264, 266
Caruana, Giovanni, 97–98, 261
Caruana, Giuseppina, 88, 150,
    251–252, 254
Caruana, Leonardo, 1, 93, 102, 113
Caruana, Pasquale, 8, 88, 90, 143,
    145–146, 148–150, 251, 266, 355
Caruso, Rento Martino, 88
Casa Loma (Montreal), 116, 135, 488
Casablanca, night club (Montreal), 188
CasaBlanca, restaurant (New York),
    334, 340, 345
Casey (Quebec), 165–167, 175
Casino de Montréal, 380, 382–383,
    416, 432, 448
Casola, Vincent, 412–413

Cassarà, Antonino, 150

Casso, Anthony, 195

Castel Tina, bar (Saint-Léonard), 154, 155, 172, 218, 271–272, 455

Castellammarese War, 41, 68, 73

Castellano, Paul, 109, 115, 187, 189–190, 333

Catalano, Salvatore ("Totò"), 89, 111, 116, 136, 189

Catalanotto, Anthony, 250

Catania, Frank, 424–425

Cavaliere, Loris, 247, 260, 278, 280, 369, 399–400

Cavallero, Roberto, 89

Cazzetta, Salvatore, 8, 274, 459

Cedeno, Nancy, 389–390, 405

Centre International Monétaire de Montréal (CIMM), 201, 203–209, 211–212, 215, 218, 220, 233, 240

Chagnon, Jocelyn, 215

Chaput, Réjean, 133

Charbonneau, Jean-Pierre, 83, 273, 457

Charest, Jean, 432, 484

Charlotte-Louise (ship), 158–159, 161

Chavez, Francisco, 239

Cheetah Club (Montreal), 58–59

Cherry, Paul, 325–326

Chez Parée, bar (Montreal), 154

Chiara, Vincent, 252, 254, 264

Chicago (Illinois), 42, 69

Chimienti, Cosimo, 412, 415–416

Chimienti, Domenico, 448

Chopin, Frederic, 125

Chouinard, André, 273

Chrétien, Jean, 149, 223, 229, 347, 350, 352–354, 357–358, 360, 374

Christian Democrats (Italy), 29, 45

Christopoulos, Peter, 470

Churchill, Winston, 44, 170

Ciancimino, Giovanni, 118

Ciancimino, Sergio, 118

Ciancimino, Vito, 117–119, 123–124

Cicéron, 377, 453

Cilienti, Andrew, 6

Cinar, 411

Civic Action League, 67

Cliche, Robert, 431

Clinton, Bill, 352

Colombo, Joseph, 69, 101

Commission d'enquête sur le crime organisé (CECO), 7, 78, 81–83, 92, 98–99, 101–103, 116, 131, 136, 173

Commission (of Mafia Families in New York), 13, 41–43, 47, 67, 69, 73, 75–76, 84, 95–96, 106, 109, 115–116, 186–187, 279, 302

Commission d'enquête sur le jeu et le vice commercialisé, 62, 67

Commisso, Antonio, 285

Comtois, Chantal, 252–255

Connery, Sean, 185

Consenza Social Club (Saint-Léonard), 18, 179, 244, 250, 272, 277, 302–304, 325, 332, 342, 377–382, 386, 394–397, 399, 401, 408–411, 413–414, 419, 424–425, 438–439, 448, 450, 452, 458–460, 490

Contact Club (Montreal), 64

Coppa, Frank, 321–324

Coppola, Francis Ford, 101

Coppola, Leonardo, 110

Cordeleone, Domenico, 455

Corneau, Jean, 214

Cornell Smith, Kati, 335

Corriere Italiano, 125

Costa, Gaetano, 113, 121

Costello, Frank, 40–41, 63

Côté, Danielle, 211

Côté, Gilbert, 11

Cotroni, Francesco, 17, 135, 205, 401

Cotroni, Frank, 2, 17, 64, 79, 89, 117–118, 131, 134–135, 157, 212, 278, 288, 342–343, 410

Cotroni, Giuseppe ("Pep"), 49, 66–67

Cotroni, Nicodemo, 410

Cotroni, Vincenzo ("Vic"), 1, 2, 49, 59–64, 66, 74, 76–80, 84–85, 90, 92–93, 95–96, 98–99, 101–102, 106, 108, 116–117, 125, 311, 395, 431, 467, 488

Couillard, Julie, 455

Court, Richard, 259–260

Courville, Armand, 59, 61, 99, 117

Couture, Bernard, 74

Crack Down Posse (CDP), 394

Crédit Suisse, 129, 225–228

Crémerie Ital Gelati (Saint-Léonard), 134

Croswell, Edgar D., 48–49

CSN, 431

Cuffaro, Giuseppe, 31, 32, 56, 93, 95, 97, 98, 122, 143–144, 149, 252, 312

Cuntrera, Agostino, 104, 106–107, 131, 178, 191, 250, 289, 311–312, 354–357, 361, 394, 401, 425, 463, 475–477

Cuntrera, Gaspare, 91, 100, 177, 183–184, 249, 251, 264–265, 286

Cuntrera, Giuseppe, 251, 261

Cuntrera, Liborio, 85, 90, 100, 106, 145–146, 261

Cuntrera, Maria, 178

Cuntrera, Paolo, 92, 177–178, 183–184, 249, 251, 253, 264–265, 286, 466

Cuntrera, Pasquale, 56, 85, 89–91, 106, 113, 117, 139, 177, 183–185, 189, 249, 251–253, 264–265, 267, 286

Cusson, Mario, 131

Cutolo, Raffaele, 257

Cutolo, Rosetta, 257

D'Agostino, Antoine, 63–65

D'Agostino, Domenico, 459

D'Amico, family, 395–396, 405, 458–460, 474

D'Amico, Luca, 396

D'Amico, Luigi, 395–396

D'Amico, Patricio, 396–397

D'Amico, Tiziano, 395

D'Angelo, Leonardo, 456

D'Asti, Frank, 77–78

Dalla Chiesa, Carlo Alberto, 147

Dalmau, Alexandre, 440

Dansereau, Pierre, 127

Daoust, Raymond, 84

David, Shimon Ben, 209

Davis, Harry, 63, 83

Dayan, George, 416–418

De Ballivian, Gloria Mercado, 140

De Balzac, Honoré, 128

De Bellis, Ezechielle, 457

De Champlain, Pierre, 125, 470

De Filippo, Patrick, 74

De Filippo, Vito, 74

De Francesco, Fernand, 214–215

De Niro, Robert, 101

DeFilippo, Patrick, 196–197, 492

Del Balso, Francesco, 332, 379, 381–387, 391, 398–399, 401, 405, 407–408, 410–419, 421–423, 426, 438–439, 455

Del Balso, Girolamo, 401

Del Peschio, Federico, 178, 301, 308, 465–467, 469, 470, 487, 493

Dell'Utri, Marcello, 370

DeMaria, Vincenzo ("Jimmy"), 286

Démosthène, Mickendy, 465

Denis, Marie-Maude, 429

Depp, Johnny, 7, 195, 334

Dershowitz, Alan, 14

Deschênes, Christian, 153–157, 166–167, 303–304, 456

Deschesnes, Richard, 427, 432

DeSimone, Tommy, 344

Desjardins, André ("Dédé"), 431

Desjardins, Jacques, 290

Desjardins, Raynald, 17, 135–136, 140, 157, 159–161, 167, 169–173, 246, 290–291, 397, 429–431, 488–489, 493

Desrochers, Daniel, 274

Dettori, Domenico, 456

Dewey, Thomas E., 44

Di Carlo, Francesco, 146–148, 150

Di Iorio, Nicola, 77, 79, 96
Di Massimo, Ricardo, 215
Di Maulo, Joe, 96, 99, 116, 134–135,
    199, 212–215, 240, 447–448, 488–489
Di Maulo, Mylena, 135
Di Maulo, Vincenzo ("Jimmy"), 212,
    215–217, 219, 233
Di Rienzo, Giovanni, 425
Di Rienzo, Nello, 425–426
Diamond, Robert, 474
DiBella, John, 69, 73
DiGregorio, Gaspare, 73–75
DiMora, Giovanni, 107, 131, 355
Dion, Céline, 305
Distributions John & Dino, 355, 475
Divito, Mike, 175
Divito, Pierino, 173–175
Donnie Brasco (film), 7, 22, 194, 334
Doyon, François, 340–342
Drapeau, Jean, 62, 67, 364
Du Plouy, Jacques, 470
Dubois, Adrien, 214
Dubois, famille, 136, 214, 457
Duguid, Brad, 309
Dumas, Denis, 171
Dupuis, Jocelyn, 397, 429–430
Dupuis, Normand, 161–163
Dutil, Renaud, 315

Eggenschwiler, Fabrizio, 228–229
Ellmenrich, Frederic, 134
Embarrato, Al Walker, 319
Erb, Brian, 158–159
Eroglu, Hasan, 457
Escobar, Pablo, 237
Escouade Marteau, 432
Eve Pacific (ship), 174–175
Evola, Natale ("Joe Diamond"), 75,
    95–96

Faber, Claude, 131
Facchino, Angelo, 457
Falcone, Francesca, 124, 180

Falcone, Giovanni, 87, 89, 121–124,
    137, 177, 180–183, 249, 312, 362
Fasulo, Sam, 463–464
Faucher, Fred, 275–276
Faustini, Francesco, 385–388
Fava, Claudio, 364
Favara, John, 343–344
Fernandez, Eduardo, 178
Fernandez, Juan Ramon, 270–271,
    288–300, 307, 309–310
Fiévet, Marc, 175
Filiatrault, Denise, 62
Filiberto, Emanuel, 451
Financial Transactions and Reports
    Analysis Centre of Canada, 416
FlawNego, store (Montreal), 470–471
FLQ, 78
Fontaine, Paul, 214
Forces armées révolutionnaires de
    Colombie (FARC), 156
Fortier, Jean, 308
Fortin, Michel, 440
Fortune Endeavor (ship), 17, 169–170, 173
Fournier, Louis-Charles, 163
Fournier, Pierre, 351
Franc Guimond, Patrick, 15–17, 327
Franco, James, 349
Franco, John, 349
Franjieh, Suleiman, 157
Franklin, Benjamin, 249
Franzè, Silvia, 369–370, 450
Fraser, Sheila, 360
French Connection, 47–48, 64, 67, 79,
    137, 281, 312

Gagliano, Alfonso, 149, 347–348,
    350–361, 425
Gagliano, Ersilia, 355
Gagliardi, Alfredo, 125
Gagné, Michel, 244, 357
Gagnière, René, 249
Gagnon, Alain, 470–471
Gagnon, Patrick, 229

Gagnon, Yvon, 204, 212

Galante, Carmine, 2, 46, 48–49, 64–67, 75–76, 86, 100, 108–112, 115, 131–132, 186, 189, 281, 342

Galeries d'Anjou (Montreal), 149, 449

Gallo, Moreno, 382, 399, 457–458, 463, 467, 489

Gambino, Carlo, 69, 73, 91, 107, 109, 186

Ganci, Giuseppe, 111

West End Gang, 10, 136, 164, 206, 214, 288, 290, 386, 452, 490

Garaufis, Nicholas G., 18–20, 23, 25, 441–445, 447–449

Garcia, Jairo, 202, 445

Garibaldi, Giuseppe, 37, 69

Garneau, Raymond, 143

Gaspésienne VI and VII (ships), 216

Gaston, Jean, 470

Gaudreau, Guy, 28

Geagea, Samir, 154

Gelateria Violi (Saint-Léonard), 80, 85, 98

Gelli, Licio, 146

Genovese, Vito, 49–50, 65, 186

Gervasi, Paolo, 154, 179, 271–273, 455, 489

Gervasi, Salvatore, 271–272

Gestapo, 63

Giaccone, Philip ("Philly Lucky"), 12–13, 18, 20–22, 115, 328, 330, 339, 343–344, 442

Giammarella, Luca, 225–229, 233

Gibbs, William, 223

Gidaro, Mario, 356

Gigante, Vincent ("the Chin"), 23, 42, 187, 191, 195

Gignac, Fernand, 62

Giliberti, Anthony, 339

Giordano, Lorenzo ("Skunk"), 331–332, 379, 381–386, 394, 399, 401, 405, 409, 411–413, 422–423, 438–439, 457, 482

Giordano, Tony, 22

Girouard, Denis Rolland, 303–304

Giuffrida, Calogero, 28

Gobeil, Ginette, 327

Gomery, John, 360

Gonzáles, José Manzo, 178

Goodfellas, (film), 344

Gotti, Frank, 343

Gotti, Gene, 188, 190–191

Gotti, John ("the Dapper Don"), 6, 14, 16, 20, 22–23, 187, 189–191, 193, 195, 324, 328, 338, 343, 346

Grande Albergo e delle Palme (Grande Albergo), 46, 48, 50, 67, 86, 89, 109

Grant, Hugh, 334

Gravano, Salvatore ("Sammy the Bull"), 191, 193, 324

Gravel, Alain, 429

Gravel, Ginette, 315

Graziano, Antony ("T. G."), 195–196

Greco, Luigi, 49, 63, 66–67, 74–76, 79, 84–85, 93, 96, 116, 131, 281

Greco, Michele, 114

Greco, Salvatore ("Ciaschiteddu"), 47, 86–88, 91, 114

Gretzky, Wayne, 264

Griffin, Richard, 386–387, 457, 490–491

Grubert, Christine, 348

Guarino, Carmine, 457

Guazzelli, Giuliano, 359

Guay, Richard, 406

Guede, José, 293–294, 298–299, 466

Guernier, Patrick ("Frenchy"), 289–290

Guimond, Patrick Franc, 15–17, 327

Gurreri, Rosario, 27–28, 30–33, 280

Guthrie, Derek, 252–255

Guthrie, Woody, 6

Hamilton, George, 336

Hammoudi, Hakim, 364, 370

Handelsbank, 129

Hassan, Ariel, 416–418
Harper, Stephen, 350, 361, 373
Hart, John, 260
Hellenic Canadian Trust, 144
Herrera-Lizcano, Luis Carlos, 164
Hervieux, Serge, 274
Hill, John Curtis, 259–260
Hilton, Dave, 131
Hiscock, Gerald Harvey, 158–161
Hitler, Adolph, 44
HMCS Cormorant (ship), 171
Hoover, J. Edgar, 70
Hudon, Richard, 169
Huneault, Charles, 384–385
Hussein, Saddam, 369

Iacono, Carmine, 291
Iannitto, Mario, 398, 400
Iasillo, Adriano, 369–370
Imbeault, André, 169
Indelicato, Alphonse ("Sonny Red"), 6,
    12–13, 18, 20–21, 24, 111, 115, 328,
    330, 339, 343, 442
Indelicato, Anthony ("Bruno"), 24,
    111
Infanti, Gabriel, 339
International Ladies' Garment
    Workers' Union, 116
Inzerillo, Giuseppe, 114
Inzerillo, Pietro, 114
Inzerillo, Salvatore ("Totuccio"),
    113–114, 119, 121
Italiano, Felice, 452

Jacques, Carole, 291
Jadran Express (ship), 174
Jeanne-D'Arc (ship), 162
Jeannotte, Pierre, 209
Johnson, Thomas Malcolm, 154
Johnston, Robert Steve, 206
José, Rico, 239
Joseph, Ducarme, 468, 470–471
Judd, Richard, 203, 209–210, 222

Jumblatt, Walid, 154

Kanho, Ray, 388–393, 399
Kane, Dany, 274
Kefauver, Estes, 66
Kemp, Micheline, 215
Kenkel, Joseph, 300
Kennedy, John F., 70
Kennedy, Robert, 70
Kerouac, Jack, 6
Kibble, C. E., 260
Kirchhoff, Jurgen, 174
Kopp, Elisabeth, 227
Kramer, Jay, 348
Krolik, Richard, 423

La Cantina, restaurant (Montreal),
    178, 301, 308, 465–466, 487
La Forgia, Paolo, 364, 450
Lady Teri-Anne (ship), 174
Laforest, Francis, 276
Lagana, Giuseppe ("Joseph"), 201–203,
    205–206, 208–211, 219, 222–223,
    225, 228, 234, 239–240
Lallouz, Sidney, 466
Lamarche, Jean, 142
Lansky, Meyer, 40–41, 43, 59, 63,
    83–84, 91, 227
LaPolla, Mike, 386, 393–395, 422–423,
    456
Laporte, André, 421–422
Laporte, Pierre, 77–78
LaRosa, Nunzio, 259–260
Lascala, Michelangelo, 130
Lastman, Mel, 295–296
Lavallée, Jean, 430
Lavigne, Diane, 274, 276, 376
Lavoie, Marc, 207
Le Baron Complex (Saint-Léonard), 108
Leblanc, Jean-Pierre, 217–218
Leblanc, Raymond, 174–175
Ledesma, Lise, 243
Leggio, Luciano, 114, 120

Leisenheimer, Duane ("Goldie"), 22, 333–334

Leithman, Sydney, 202

Lemieux, Denis, 141–142

Lemieux, Mario, 275–276

Lepage, Pierre-Louis, 163

Le Privé, bar, (Montreal), 141

Lévesque, Denis, 166

Lévesque, Jean-Pierre, 275

Lévesque, Raymond, 62

Leyrac, Monique, 62

Liberal Party of Canada, 61, 347, 350, 360, 434

Liberal Party of Quebec, 77

Ligammari, Giovanni, 324

Lindsay, Steven ("Tiger"), 295–296

Lino, Eddie, 189–191

Lino, Frank ("Curly"), 25, 322, 324, 335, 348–352

Lino, Joseph, 351

Lobos, 276

Locatelli, Pasquale Claudio, 174–175

Lockaby, Jim, 138

Lopes, Luis, 270

LoPresti, Enzo, 192, 467

LoPresti, Giuseppe ("Joe"), 52, 106, 112, 117, 125, 130, 188–193, 196, 216, 228, 348–349

Lord, Jean, 170–171

Loreto, funeral home (Saint-Léonard), 343, 378, 400, 420, 467, 472, 477, 482

Lorraine (Quebec), 303–304, 456

Louis, Frédéric, 470

Lucchese, family, 42, 195, 346

Lucchese, Tommy, 69, 73

Luciano, Salvatore Charles ("Lucky"), 40–47, 63–67, 84, 86, 342

Lumia, Rosa, 130, 188

Lunardi, Pietro, 363

Luppino, Domenico, 95

Luppino, Giacomo, 79–80, 95, 106, 108, 279–282, 459

Luppino, Grazia, 79

Luppino, Natale, 284

Luppino, Vincenzo, 284

Lusinchi, Jaime, 139

Lussier, Jean-Michel, 220

Macri, Domenico, 385, 398–402, 457

Macri, Jos, 82

Made in Italy, 450–451

Magaddino, Gaspare, 47

Magaddino, Peter, 39, 74

Magaddino, Stefano, 42, 49, 69, 72–74, 79–80, 279, 342

Magharian, Barkev, 227

Magharian, Jean, 227

Magi, Alberino ("Rino"), 461–462

Magi, Antonio ("Tony"), 421–422, 455, 461–462, 468, 471, 481

Magliocco, Joseph, 69

Manno Rizzuto, Libertina, (mother of Vito Rizzuto), 54–58, 129, 179, 225–229, 232–233, 244, 246, 403–405, 446, 449, 467, 469, 473, 480, 482

Manno, Antonino ("Don Manno"), 31–32, 55–57, 89, 102

Manno, Domenico, 1, 58, 104–107, 131, 312, 355

Manno, Pasquale, 55

Marabella, Mario, 462–463

Maranzano, Salvatore, 41–42, 492

Marchettini, Mauro, 82

Marcil, Robert, 426

Marcinkus, Paul, 146

Marcos, Ferdinand, 226, 238–242, 488

Marcos, Imelda, 226, 238–242

Mariano, Luis, 61–62

Marino, Salvatore, 30

Marra, Giovanni, 205

Marro, Sylvio, 138

Martin, Edmond, 61

Martin, Gary, 405

Martin, Marius, 61

Martin, Paul, 350, 354, 360

Martorana, Frank, 303–304, 456

Marzulli, John, 339, 346, 492–493

Masseria, Giuseppe, 41

Massino, Adeline, 339, 346

Massino, Joanne, 337, 340, 346

Massino, Joseph ("Big Joey"), 12–13, 19–25, 75, 109, 115, 187–188, 193–198, 302, 315, 317–318, 320, 322–325, 330, 332–340, 344–346, 348, 350, 352, 443, 492

Massino, Josephine, 318, 334–335, 337–340, 344–346

Matteo, Lino, 413

Matthew D. (ship), 170

Matticks, Donald, 9

Matticks, Gerald, 10, 452

Matticks, Richard, 452

Mayers, Morris, 209–210, 215

McAllister, William, 290

McCaffrey, Kimberly, 318, 321, 323

McClellan, John L., 70

McDougall, Lorie, 408

McSorley, Marty, 275

Melo, Eddie, 278

Ménard, Robert alias Bob Wilson, 80–81, 97, 105, 122

Messier, Yves, 327

Messina, Dima, 149, 156, 160, 205, 244, 355

Messina, Sebastiano, 103

Milano, Nicodemo, 15–17, 327–329, 341–342

Milioto, Francesco, 53

Milioto, Liborio, 53, 56

Minelli, Alberto, 260

Miraglia, Vincenzo, 134

Mirra, Tony, 319, 322

Mitchell, John W., 14, 441–442, 444, 446

Mongiovì, Antonino, 178, 466

Montagna, Salvatore ("Sal the Iron Worker"), 75, 492–494

Montreal City and District Savings Bank, 143

Montreal Expos, 57, 349, 356

Montréal-Trudeau Airport, 15, 387–390, 405, 489–491

Moomba Supperclub (Laval), 393–395, 422

Moon, Peter, 236–237

Mora, Enio, 280–281, 283, 307

Morais, Pierre, 206–207, 213, 240

Moreau, Guy, 161

Morello, Antonio, 172

Morello, Nicolò, 58, 154

Morgan, James, 154

Mori, Cesare, 39, 44, 68

Morielli, Valentino, 163, 216–217

Morneau, Pierre, 160–161

Mount Real, 413

MS Vulcania (ship), 57

Mucci, Antonio ("Tony"), 83, 273, 399, 457, 467, 477, 481, 489

Murdock, Kenneth James, 282–284

Musitano, Angelo, 280, 283

Musitano, Pat Anthony, 279, 282–284

Mussolini, Benito ("Il Duce"), 29, 39–40, 57, 65, 362, 371, 451

Napoli, Antonio, 91

Napoli, Domenic, 284–285

Napolitano, Dominick ("Sonny Black"), 24–25, 322, 324, 337, 339, 348, 350

Nardo, Giuseppe Antonio, 32

Nasser, Abraham ("The Turk"), 293–294

National Bank of Canada, 144, 203

National Parole Board, 222–223, 286, 300, 303, 311, 313–314, 472

Natoli, Gioacchino, 143

Navarro, Héctor Hurtado, 179

Naviglia, Umberto, 267

'Ndrangheta, 78–79, 94, 284, 286, 362, 367

Newfoundland, 148–149

Newman's, restaurant (St. John's, Newfoundland), 160

New Miss Mont-Royal, restaurant
   (Montreal), 27–28
Nicastro, Filippo, 122
Nicolucci, Sabatino ("Sammy"), 132,
   137–141, 218–222, 228, 237
Nomads, 270–271, 293, 295, 376, 393
Noriega, Manuel, 184
Normand, Jacques, 61
Noroozi, Essy Navad, alias Javad
   Mohammed Nozarian, 331–332,
   384
Norris, Alexander, 365–366
Norris, John, 137–140
Norshield Financial Group, 411–412
Notaro, Peter, 74

Obront, William, 431
Oliveti, Salvatore, 306–310
OMG Media Group, 306–310, 312,
   325, 331, 466
Operation Colisée, 377, 380, 385, 388,
   391, 402, 405–407, 410, 422, 425,
   427, 432, 436–438, 440, 448, 450,
   453, 456, 458, 461, 463, 467, 472,
   474, 481, 484, 487, 490
Operation Compote, 8, 204, 211–213,
   216–217, 238, 312, 373–374
Operation Espresso, 464
Operation Minoa, 453
Operazione Orso Bruno, 466
Oppedisano, Antonio, 284–285
Orena, Victor, 195
Orellana, Carlos Narvaez, 412–413
Ouellette, Guy, 275
Ouimet, Normand Marvin ("Casper"),
   429

Pagano, Oreste, 254, 255–269, 312,
   359, 360, 498, 507
Palazzo, Paolo, 251
Palazzolo, Vito, 129
Panepinto, Anita, 286
Panepinto, Gaetano ("Guy"), 277–278,

   284–286, 288, 291, 296, 298, 300,
Pantaleone, Michele, 45
Pantaloni, Jean-Yves, 291
Papadakis, Costa, 243, 244–245
Papalia, Antonio, 203, 235, 239, 242,
   379–380, 281, 451
Papalia, John, 83, 131, 279
Papalia, Johnny ("Pops"), 83, 279–282,
   283, 284
Papalia, Roberto, 241–242, 452
Papier, William, 137–138, 140,
Pappalardo, Salvatore, 182–183,
Para-Dice Riders, 276–277
Patton, George S., 44
Paul, Lamartine Sévère, 468
Paul, Réjean, 329
Pavo, Juan Carlos, 255
Pecoraro Scanio, Alfonso, 364
Pellegrini, Angelilo, 440
Pelletier, Jean, 358
Penway Explorers, 242, 242–246, 307,
   379,
Perrino, Robert, 320, 322
Persico, Carmine, 115, 195
Pesci, Joe, 344
Petrosino, Joseph, 38
Petros Z (ship), 154–156
Petrula, Frank, 63, 66–67
Petruzziello, Cesare, 255, 267
Piazza, Giuseppe, 420
Picard, Michel, 403
Piccirilli, Sergio ("Big Guy" or
   "Grizzly"), 458–461, 465, 474
Pierre Hotel (Manhattan), 111–112,
   117, 134, 136, 183, 188
Pietrantonio, Antonio ("Tony
   Suzuki"), 294, 299
Piro, Cosimo, 454
Pisces IV (ship), 171
Pistone, Joseph alias Donnie Brasco,
   24–25, 186–187, 195, 320, 322, 337
Pizza Connection, 67, 90, 112, 124,
   189–190, 227

Pizza Hut, restaurant (Saint-Léonard), 289–290, 355–356
Plante, Mario, 325, 327
Plante, Pacifique ("Pax"), 62, 67
Plescio, Tony, 271
Ploianu, Lori, 292
Plyas, Félix, 418–419
Pogharian, Varoug, 220–221, 236–238
Polakoff, Moses, 84
Poletti, Pietro, 327–329
Polifroni, Sylvestro, 112, 138–139
Pomerantz, Terry, 420–422, 462
Pope Jean-Paul II (Karol Wojtyla), 365
Pope Pie IX, 74, 107, 355, 391
Porco, Frank, 348
Poulin, Yvan, 233
Pozza, Franca, 124
Pozza, Michel, 112, 116–119
Priziola, John, 47
Prodi, Romano, 185, 451
Project Cicéron, 376–377, 453
Project Jaggy, 17
Project Omertà, 254–255, 259–260, 264, 328
Propaganda Due (P2), Masonic lodge, 146
Puliafito, Palmina, 101

QFL-Construction, 397, 427, 429–430
Quebec Building Trades Council, 431
Quebec Federation of Labour (QFL), 397, 429–431

Raab, Selwyn, 107, 197, 317
Rabbat, Samir George, 156
Rachelli, ice cream factory (Saint-Laurent), 133
Rachelli, Roberto, 133–134
Rachelli, Sergio, 133–134
Ragusa, Antonia, 312
Ragusa, Emanuele, 95, 173, 210, 219, 311–317, 320
Ragusa, Pat, 311, 314

Randisi, Giuseppe, 103,
Randisi, Vincenzo, 104, 106
Ranieri, Filippo, 364, 366–370
Rastelli, Philip ("Rusty"), 13, 75, 96, 99–100, 102, 108–109, 115, 186, 348–350, 488
Reggio Bar (Saint-Léonard), 80–81, 83, 85, 101, 103–104, 106, 122
Reid, Emily, 137
Renault, Jean-Pierre, 210
Renda, Calogero (father of Paolo Renda), 53–54, 93, 471, 473
Renda Construction, 341, 378, 446–447, 474
Renda, Domenica, 472–473
Renda, Francesco, 29, 32, 55,
Renda, Joe, 286–287
Renda, Maria (grandmother of Vito Rizzuto), 53–54,
Renda, Maria (sister of Vito Rizzuto), 403, 467, 471, 473, 486
Renda, Paolo, 58, 106, 129, 277, 303, 311, 325, 332, 378–379, 381, 384, 397, 399, 401–402, 411, 413–414, 418–420, 424, 432, 438–439, 448, 450, 456, 469, 471, 473–474, 480, 483, 497, 499
Renoir, Pierre-Auguste, 46
Restivo, Louis, 346
Riahi, Omar, 389–390
Richer, Isabelle, 370
Riina, Salvatore ("Totò"), 114, 120, 147, 150, 183
Rivard, Lucien, 64, 66
Riviera, cinema (Montreal), 101–102, 467
Rizzoto, Giuseppe, 35
Rizzuto, Giovanna, 9, 15, 32, 58, 111, 128, 138, 246, 280, 302, 310, 325, 328–329, 331, 449, 467, 469
Rizzuto, Leonardo, 447, 477, 486
Rizzuto, Libertina ("Bettina") (daughter of Vito Rizzuto), 226–229, 233,

403, 405, 467, 473, 482
Rizzuto, Nicolo junior (son of Vito),
   1–2, 31, 53–54, 56, 58–60, 64, 68, 76,
   78–79, 83–85, 87–88, 91–96, 100,
   102–103, 105–106, 108, 113–114,
   129–130, 134,136, 139, 177–180, 207,
   233, 243, 249, 312, 355, 378–379, 381,
   386, 396–397, 399, 402–404, 410–411,
   424, 427, 437, 439–440, 448, 451, 454,
   456, 466–469, 471, 474, 476–477,
   479–484, 486, 494–495, 499
Rizzuto, Pietro, 52–53, 102, 147, 302,
   353–354
Rizzuto, Vito (grandfather of Vito),
   3–4, 6–8, 12–14, 16, 18–20, 23, 27,
   32, 42, 53–54, 56, 59, 77–78, 90, 106,
   111–112, 115, 117–118, 125, 128,
   131–132, 134–135, 137–141, 145, 149,
   151, 153–157, 159, 162–163, 166–168,
   171, 175, 179, 183, 187–188, 192,
   194–195, 198–199, 202, 205–206,
   210–211, 214, 216, 218, 222, 233–234,
   239–241, 243–247, 250, 255, 265,
   267–272, 274–281, 284–286, 290,
   293–296, 299–300, 302, 304–305,
   307–312, 316–318, 320, 324–330, 334,
   339–340, 342–343, 346, 347–349, 353,
   355, 362–364, 366–367, 369–371,
   377–379, 394–395, 397, 399, 401–402,
   408, 413, 419–421, 427, 429, 432,
   435, 440, 443, 445, 449–456, 461,
   463, 466, 471, 481–482, 488, 495–499
Robinette, Jacques, 465
Robinson, Claude, 411
Robitaille, Normand, 271, 273–274
Rock Machine, 8, 270–271, 274–276,
   291, 295, 459, 489
Rock, Allan, 223, 230
Rockers, 293, 295, 332, 393
Rodrigue, Pierre, 210
Rojas, Rodolfo, 293–294
Rondeau, Pierre, 274, 276
Ronderos, Juan Gabriel, 237–238,

Roosevelt, Franklin Delano, 44
Rose, Michel, 273
Rosenblum, Norman, 142, 207–210, 218
Rossi, Tino, 62
Rothstein, Marshall, 194
Rouleau, David, 210
Roussy, Mike, 388, 514
Routhier, Michel, 159–161
Rowdy Crew, 276
Roy, Yves, 233, 514
Ruggiero, Angelo ("Couac Couac"),
   188–191
Ruggiero, Benjamin ("Lefty Guns"),
   22, 195
Russo, Giuseppe Genco, 46–47
Ryan, Paul, 246

Salamone, Antonio, 145
Salemi, Carmelo, 97–98
Sallet, Jeffrey, 318, 321, 323
Salois, Jean, 112, 160, 162–163, 229, 269
Salvo, Ezio Antonio, 457
Salvo, Leonardo, 28, 31–33
Samaan, Magdi Garas, 414–415
Sanchez-Paz, Alexis, 184
Sandra & Diane II (ship), 155
Sangollo, Pierre, 175
Saputo, Giuseppe, 69–71, 73–75
Saulnier, Marc, 438
Sauvé, Paul, 158, 214–215, 427–428
Scaletta, Gennaro, 178, 244, 466
Scali, Salvatore, 398
Scarcella, Pietro, 131, 296
Schneider, Stephen, 317
Schoen, David, 446–447
Sciammarella, Bill, 250–251
Sciara, Pietro ("Zio Petrino"), 1, 83,
   93, 95, 97–99, 101–103, 113,
   415–416, 467
Sciascia, Gerlando ("George from
   Canada"), 21–23, 32, 112, 115, 117,
   130, 137, 188–191, 193–198, 324,
   330, 333, 335, 339–340, 345, 348,

352, 419, 492
Sciascia, Joe, 419–420
Sciascia, Joseph Mark, 191
Sciascia, Liborio, 475, 477, 499
Sciascia, Mary, 193
Sciascia, Pasquale, 424
Scotiabank, 415
Scott, Terry, 160
Scotti, John, 421–423, 456
Scotto, Salvatore, 268
Scozzari, Augustino, 321
Serpe, Giancarlo, 307
Settecasi, Giuseppe, 94–95, 113, 497
Sévère Paul, Lamartine, 468
Sforza, Antonio, 166
Shaddock, James Gordon, 292
Shemilt, John, 243
Sherman, Arthur F., 242–243, 245
Schifani, Rosaria, 181
Ship, Harry, 62–63, 66
Shoofey, Frank, 202
Shumai, Hummy, 239
Sicilian Association of Montreal, 58
Siegel, Bugsy, 84
Simaglia, Lino, 82
Simaglia, Quintino, 82
Simard, Réal, 117–118
Simari, Carlo, 74
Simon, Sharon ("Kanehsatake drug
    queen"), 458, 460
Simpson, O. J., 14
Sinatra, Frank, 185, 334
Sivabavanandan, Sivalingam, 364, 370
Sizler, Larry, 138–139
Soave, Ben, 261, 264, 328
Société de Banque Suisse, 228
Société de financement Malts, 414–415
Solid Gold, bar (Montreal), 467
Sollecito, Giuseppe, 394,
Sollecito, Rocco, 244, 246, 250, 277,
    286, 325, 379, 381–382, 394, 397,
    399, 401, 404–405, 413, 424–425,
    438–439, 450, 452, 469

Sollecito, Stefano, 286
Sorel, Paul, 298
Sorrentino, Salvatore, 98–99
Spagnolo, Giuseppe, 28, 30, 32, 56, 58,
    77, 280, 454
Spagnolo, Maria, 33
Spagnolo, Vincenzo, 10, 448, 456
Sperenza, Nicola, 426
Spero, Anthony, 348
Spirito, John, 196–197
St. Pius X Secondary School, 58, 452,
    455
Sterling, Claire, 114, 253
Strizzi, Michael, 307–309
Stubing, Jack, 318
Suchowlinsky, Majer, 83
Sultan Al Nahyan, Zayed bin, 367
Sypniewski, Kazimir, 203–205, 210

Tallarita, Tony, 425–426
Tartaglione, ("Big Louie"), 330
Terrasi, Domenico, 453–454
The Godfather (film), 101, 232, 334,
    336, 347, 404
Thibault, Robert, 287
Thibault, Yvon, 130, 136, 190, 357
Tommassino, Carmelo, 455
Torre, Gaetano, 388
Torre, Giuseppe, 383–384, 387–388,
    390–391, 398, 401, 415
Torre, Polisena, 383–384
Torres, Miguel, 274
Tortorici, Elena, 311–312
Tozzi, Domenico, 179, 206–207, 210,
    213–216, 219, 222–223
Tremblay, Gérald, 309, 427–428
Tremblay, Martin, 432
Tremblay, Réjean, 308, 466
Trenet, Charles, 62
Trépanier, Robert, 161
Trépanier, Robert junior, 161
Tresca, Carlo, 65
Triassi, Giuseppe, 341–342, 448

Trinchera, Dominick ("Big Trinny"), 12–13, 18, 20–22, 115, 328, 330, 339, 343–344, 346, 442, 497
Trinchera, Donna, 346
Tromso (ship), 213–214, 216–217
Trudeau, Yves ("Apache"), 167–168
Tucci, Aldo, 143
Tupper, Brian, 15, 18
Turano, Giuseppe, 110
Turner, John, 353
Turrisi, Mariano, 450–451
Tutino, Frank, 83

Union Bank of Switzerland, 228, 240
Union nationale, 61
Urso, Anthony ("Tony Green"), 198, 330–331, 346

Vaccarello, Filippo, 149–150, 355
Vailles, Francis, 413, 514
Valachi, Joseph, 70
Valenti, Salvatore, 6
Vallée, Richard, 15
Van Schaack, Willis Marie, alias Lili St-Cyr, 60
Vanelli, Leonardo, 409
Vanelli, Tony, 409–410, 489
Varacalli, Nicolò, 396, 460
Vasisko, Vincent, 49
Vecchio, Vincenzo, 203, 209–210, 222
Velenosi, Francesco, 457
Vella, Luigi, 312, 316
Vella, Salvatore, 92, 149
Veltri, Francesco, 394
Victoria Sporting Club, 77
Vinci da, Leonardo, 16
Violi, Domenic (son of Paolo Violi), 284
Violi, Domenico (father of Paolo Violi), 79, 106, 108, 459

Violi, Francesco, 82, 91–92, 94–95
Violi, Giuseppe (son of Paolo Violi), 108, 284, 459
Violi, Paolo, 1–2, 59, 74, 77–85, 87, 90, 92–108, 112–113, 116, 122, 129, 131, 134, 153, 173, 188, 191, 250, 279, 284, 289, 311–312, 355, 357, 361, 401, 458, 465, 467, 471, 475, 481
Violi, Rocco, 107–108, 481–482, 488, 493, 497
Vitale, Salvatore ("Good-Looking Sal"), 13, 19–25, 115, 187–188, 193–199, 317–318, 320, 322–325, 328, 330, 335–340, 443, 444
Vizzini, Calogero, 45, 47
Volpato, Antonio, 58, 163–164, 465, 489
Volpe, Paul, 131

Wagner, Richard, 46
Warriors, 460
Weinberg, Barry, 318–321
Wiazer, Ivan Israël, 139

Xanthoudakis, John, 411–413

Yamashita, Tomoyuki, 239

Zaccardelli, Giuliano, 371–377, 406, 426
Zaffarano, Michael, 95
Zambito, Antonio, 148, 355
Zambito, Luciano, 149–150, 355
Zappia, Beniamino, 228, 381, 452–453
Zappia, Giuseppe ("Joseph"), 363, 367, 381
Zaza, Michele, 112, 137
Zbikowski, Steve, 313
Zéphir, Woodley, 392–393
Ziegler, Jean, 226

ANDRÉ CÉDILOT was a justice reporter at Montréal's *La Presse* for thirty-five years, with a special interest in Italian Mafia and organized crime. Often interviewed as an authority on these subjects, he regularly acts as a consultant for documentaries and television series.

ANDRÉ NOËL has been an investigative reporter at *La Presse* for over twenty years. His work has won him several prestigious awards in Québec and across Canada. He often writes with André Cédilot about the Mafia. In the course of his career, he has published six books on a wide range of subjects.

MICHAEL GILSON has over fifteen years experience as a Montreal-based translator and editor. He works with a variety of subjects, particularly art essays for film, photography and art gallery catalogues, although his preference is translating non-fiction books.